SECRETARIAL PROCEDURES and ADMINISTRATION

Eighth Edition

Estelle L. Popham, Ph.D.

Professor of Business Education Emerita
Hunter College of the City University of New York

Rita Sloan Tilton, Ph.D.

Consultant, Business and Office Education

J. Howard Jackson, Ph.D., CPS

Professor and Chairman of the Department of Business Education and
Office Administration
Virginia Commonwealth University

J Marshall Hanna, Ed.D.

Professor of Business Education Emeritus
The Ohio State University

Published by

SOUTH-WESTERN PUBLISHING CO.

K78   CINCINNATI   WEST CHICAGO, ILL.   DALLAS   PELHAM MANOR, N.Y.   PALO ALTO, CALIF.

Preface

To achieve higher productivity at lower costs, business is adopting new organizational patterns and investing millions of dollars in sophisticated equipment such as intelligent typewriters, text editors, high volume copiers, microcomputers, and electronic mail systems. But of what value are new organizational patterns and new technology if there is an inadequate office force to fill the jobs available? One of the greatest needs of business is an adequate supply of secretaries to fill the over three million jobs in this category.

The Eighth Edition of *Secretarial Procedures and Administration* provides the capstone for the college-trained secretary preparing to meet the increasingly exacting requirements of a secretarial position. You are acquiring marketable skills so that you can perform the operational functions required of the secretary. Basic typing and transcription abilities are assumed; operational functions affected by changes in technology are presented as if they were new to you. You will perform some of these new functions. Others will be handled by specialists, but you will need to understand how these functions relate to your work. Even if you work in an office with limited new technology, your daily activities will relate to the new technology to such an extent that you need to understand it.

You will also develop the know-how to perform an assistant's functions as you develop an understanding of the organizational patterns in an office and the people who work there. A top-level secretary makes many decisions, both about how to handle work assignments and how to deal with colleagues at all levels—executives, subordinates, and co-workers. Throughout this course emphasis is placed on the development of decision-making ability and the exercise of that most needed skill—good human relations. Without good human relations, it will be difficult for you, no matter how technically qualified, to be successful in business.

As you examine this book, you will see that it consists of 27 chapters organized in nine parts and a Reference Guide. It is possible to omit any part with which you are familiar without seriously affecting your understanding of the other sections. When you complete this textbook, you will understand why it is more than just a textbook. You will want to take it with you to the office and use as an on-the-job reference.

When you read this book, you will notice that Part 1 discusses the changing organizational pattern of secretarial work and the secretary's role in the total office environment. Parts 2, 3, and 4 deal with information processing, the transformation of ideas into typewritten or printed form. These parts cover such topics as typewriting, reprographics, word and data processing, dictation/transcription, composition, incoming/outgoing mail, postal and shipping services, and telecommunications. Parts 5, 6, 7, and 8 are devoted to administrative support services. Part 5 is concerned with records control and micrographics. Alphabetic filing rules are also covered. Part 6 enables the secretary to expedite travel arrangements and plan and facilitate meetings. Part 7 explains how to research business data and organize it into usable management information. Part 8 encompasses the financial and legal support that the secretary is expected to give to management. In Part 9, you have an opportunity to look at your professional future; that is, how to select and obtain a position and how to enter secretarial employment and advance in it.

At the end of each chapter is a list of carefully selected suggested readings. You will find many uses for this list, especially when you are writing a term paper for this or another course, when you are asked to speak on a secretarial subject, or when you want to delve more deeply into a topic of special interest. The end of each chapter also has discussion questions and special problems. These questions and problems allow you to apply to office related situations material that you read in the text.

At the end of each part are case problems that are close adaptations of actual office situations. These cases bring realism to this course. As you solve them, try to develop a set of principles you can use in coping with similar situations that you may encounter on the job.

The Reference Guide at the end of the book (Part 10) can be of enormous value if you will let it help you become the "word specialist" that a competent secretary must be. It identifies accepted practices for abbreviating and capitalizing words, writing and using numbers, spelling, using plurals and possessives, punctuating, and using grammar correctly. Following these sections are a communications guide and a brief review of business math.

We hope that this textbook will help you adopt high standards of performance consistent with your abilities. We hope, too, that you will experience some of the excitement that can be found in the business office by those who are prepared to perform competently and who bring with them a zest for learning new things as the office environment changes. Whether you are preparing for your first secretarial position or are updating your skills, you will find your secretarial education invaluable in equipping you for a successful career path. If you are flexible and adapt to the changing office environment, you can eventually reach your ultimate goal, whether it is a higher level secretarial position or a changeover to supervision or management.

Estelle L. Popham
Rita Sloan Tilton
J. Howard Jackson
J Marshall Hanna

Contents

v

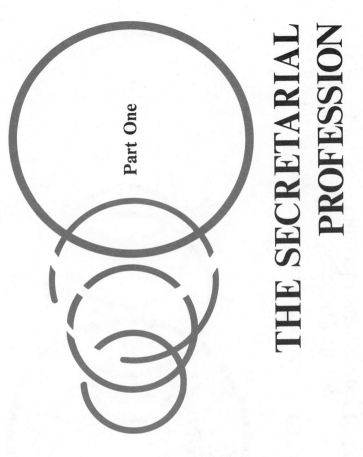

Part One

THE SECRETARIAL PROFESSION

At a time when challenging jobs are hard to obtain, secretarial openings are at an all-time high. Advancements in technology have eliminated many of the routine, repetitive tasks formerly associated with secretarial work. Career paths have opened with countless opportunities for decision making in the performance of office tasks. When you join the ranks of secretaries, you will want to benefit from the privileges and responsibilities of membership in the secretarial profession.

Part I discusses the many dimensions of the secretarial position and the basic contributions a college-trained secretary can make to the managerial functions of the office.

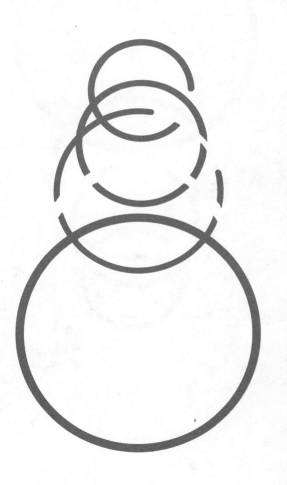

Chapter 1

The Role of the Secretary

Slightly more than ten years ago the United States Department of Labor estimated that a mere 2.5 million secretaries were employed in the work force. At that time women occupied approximately 99 percent of the secretarial positions. There are several reasons why the secretarial profession has been so attractive for female workers. For the career-minded secretary, the profession has been and continues to be a stepping-stone to higher administrative posts. For the reentry secretary, the secretary who has been away from the office for several years, the profession has offered employment after only a minimal period of retraining.

Twenty years ago automation entered the secretarial work place in the form of the Magnetic Tape Selectric Typewriter. This machine was supposed to revolutionize the office and the secretarial position so crucial to the operation of an office; but it proved only an aid to the secretary, not a substitute. In the past decade technology has made inroads in the office; yet the secretarial position is still very much alive and strong and continues to provide employment opportunities for the entry level and experienced secretary.

In addition, automation in the office has not reduced the need for secretaries. In 1980 the Department of Labor estimated a 3.9 million secretarial work force, a tremendous increase in the past ten years. Women have continued to dominate this area of office employment (still approximately 99 percent female),[1] and the reasons that attracted them to become secretaries are still the same as in the past. Yet secretarial duties are not exclusively women's work. Rather vigorous attempts are being made to eliminate the sexist role associated with this job category. A number of large companies are making conscious efforts to add male secretaries. Over 34,000 men are employed in secretarial positions and undoubtedly have found opportunities in the field.

The demand for secretaries exceeds supply in every geographical area and in every type of business, government, or philanthropic organization. Secretarial openings are available in all cities—certainly an important factor to an individual who prefers a certain location or an individual who plans to augment the family income. Even in times of economic recession, such as a period with 6 percent unemployment, secretarial positions are available and go begging. In addition, this decade has brought high salaries to the entry level

[1]Bureau of Labor Statistics Update "Secretarial Jobs, Salaries," *The Secretary* (March, 1981), p. 8.

and experienced secretary. All these facts lead to the conclusion that the secretarial field continues to be a most stable and lucrative source of employment for women and men, for the experienced, for the inexperienced, for career-minded employees, and for those with relatively short-term career aspirations.

In the 1980's and beyond, office technology will be expanding at a mind-boggling pace. Secretaries who enter the office now and in the near future must understand that change is inevitable. The career-oriented secretary will be in an excellent position to suggest and direct any changes in procedures relating to the secretarial position. The secretary taking that leadership position will require a kit of basic intelligence, the background of a college education, the will to work, and, to some extent, the spirit of adventure.

This first chapter presents an overview of the secretarial field today and discusses the personal qualities so extremely important in the successful pursuit and fulfillment of the secretarial role.

DEFINITION OF A SECRETARY

The job classification *secretary* is probably the least understood and most misused of all office occupations. For instance, to attract applicants, a company may advertise for a secretary, when actually the position is stenographic in nature. A stenographer primarily types and transcribes from either shorthand or machine dictation.

Recently the United States Department of Commerce revised its Standard Occupations Classification (SOC), a system that other federal agencies must follow, to include the position of secretary in the category of "Administrative Support Occupations" rather than in the previous classification of "Clerical." This change is considered a major advance for the secretarial profession, since this new classification recognizes that secretarial work is not clerical.

One common definition of *secretary* is that adopted by Professional Secretaries International (PSI), an organization representing more than 43,000 secretaries in the United States and other countries:

A *secretary* shall be defined as an executive assistant who possesses a mastery of office skills, demonstrates the ability to assume responsibility without direction or supervision, exercises initiative and judgment, and makes decisions within the scope of assigned authority.

Within this concept a secretary is a highly qualified person who possesses not only "mastery of office skills" but also personality requisites of the highest order. A secretary must know the scope of authority given and must discharge the responsibilities that are within that sphere. The secretary must judge correctly when to follow through alone and when to consult the employer about how to handle a job. Here is a person capable of making many decisions, of composing routine correspondence independently, perhaps of supervising other office workers and of keeping their personnel records.

The person who fits the PSI definition is frequently secretary to the chief executive, acting many times as the *alter ego* (second self) to a busy employer. This secretary is often referred to as an *executive secretary* or *secretary to an executive.* A secretary to a president or to a managing official in a large organization is sometimes given the title and salary of *administrative assistant.* In other organizations a secretary may perform these functions without being given this title. The executive secretary often enjoys informal rank within the company according to the formal rank of the executive. The executive secretary has access to privileged information and knowledge of official power in that organization, and thus occupies a unique position of influence and power in the office.

The Administrative Management Society classifies secretaries into four categories (Secretary B, Secretary A, Executive Secretary/Administrative Assistant, and Legal Secretary). The first three descriptions that pertain to general secretarial positions are given here. (Legal secretarial work is discussed in Chapter 24.)

Secretary—Level B

Performs a limited range of secretarial duties in a small company or for a supervisor in a large firm. May take dictation and transcribe from notes and Dictaphone with speed and accuracy. Screens calls, makes appointments, handles travel arrangements, answers routine correspondence, and maintains filing systems.

Secretary—Level A

Performs an unlimited range of secretarial duties for middle management personnel or more than one individual. Composes and/or takes and transcribes correspondence of a complex and confidential nature. Position requires a knowledge of company policy, procedures, and above average secretarial and administrative skills.

Executive Secretary/Administrative Assistant

Performs a full range of secretarial and administrative duties for a high-level member of executive staff. Handles project oriented duties and may be held accountable for the timely completion of these tasks. Relieves executive of routine administrative detail. Position requires an in-depth knowledge of company practice, structure, and a high degree of technical skills.[2]

These groupings are of special interest because they were adopted by the people who usually administer salaries and supervise job evaluations. Obviously they are advantageous to secretaries in clarifying job functions.

---

[2]Administrative Management Society Salary Survey (1981) as published in the AMS *Office Salaries Directory for the United States and Canada.*

Illus. 1-1
An executive secretary performs duties of a highly confidential nature requiring initiative, judgment, and knowledge of company practice.

It is likely that in a first secretarial position the beginner will be classified as Secretary B (or even Stenographer). With experience and increased knowledge, the beginner will eventually rise to the Secretary A level and ultimately to Executive Secretary/Administrative Assistant. It is also possible that as the employee gains more experience, a shift may be made to a supervisory level.

THE SCOPE OF SECRETARIAL WORK

The secretary operating in the established role performs a variety of office tasks—sometimes all at once! The job variety leads to job satisfaction for many secretaries. In fact, a national survey of office environments by Steelcase[3] indicates that 84 percent of secretaries have a positive attitude toward their positions, and a job satisfaction level surpassed only by management. To be sure, frustrations and stressful situations occur, and anxious moments are not uncommon. Secretaries in such positions must keep calm while performing their work with dispatch and efficiency.

Perhaps the best analysis of the scope of secretarial work comes from secretaries themselves. PSI defines the position on page 4.

PROTOTYPE SECRETARIAL JOB DESCRIPTION

A secretary relieves executive of various administrative details; coordinates and maintains effective office procedures and efficient work flows; implements policies and procedures set by employer; establishes and maintains harmonious working relationships with superiors, co-workers, subordinates, customers or clients, and suppliers.

Schedules appointments and maintains calendar. Receives and assists visitors and telephone callers and refers them to executive or other appropriate person as circumstances warrant. Arranges business itineraries and coordinates executive's travel requirements.

Takes action authorized during executive's absence and uses initiative and judgment to see that matters requiring attention are referred to delegated authority or handled in a manner so as to minimize effect of employer's absence.

Takes manual shorthand and transcribes from it or transcribes from machine dictation. Types material from longhand or rough copy.

Sorts, reads, and annotates incoming mail and documents and attaches appropriate file to facilitate necessary action; determines routing, signatures required, and maintains follow-up. Composes correspondence and reports for own or executive's signature. Prepares communication outlined by executive in oral or written directions.

Researches and abstracts information and supporting data in preparation for meetings, work projects, and reports. Correlates and edits materials submitted by others. Organizes material which may be presented to executive in draft format.

Maintains filing and records management systems and other office flow procedures.

Makes arrangements for and coordinates conferences and meetings. May serve as recorder of minutes with responsibility for transcription and distribution to participants.

May supervise or hire other employees; select and/or make recommendations for purchase of supplies and equipment; maintain budget and expense account records, financial records, and confidential files.

Maintains up-to-date procedures manual for the specific duties handled on the job.

Performs other duties as assigned or as judgment or necessity dictates.[4]

[4]Reprinted with permission of Professional Secretaries International, *The Secretary* (April, 1981).

The analysis encompasses four areas: technical skills, an understanding of business functions and interlocking functions, skill in human relations, and facility in oral and written communication. A check of this list against the table of contents of this textbook shows coverage of each of these divisions.

The secretary performing all these functions operates in the established or traditional role and will be referred to henceforth as a *multifunctional secretary*. The multifunctional secretary may work in any of a number of environments. A physician or owner of a small business may have only one secretary on the staff. The office may be a small one, and the secretary may have access to limited equipment. Or the secretary may hold a position in a large corporation with a variety of electronic equipment and sophisticated organizational patterns. In this situation, the higher the secretarial level, the greater the number of functions to be performed.

The secretary in the smallest office in a remote area will increasingly find it necessary to use services performed by automated equipment situated in another location. Every secretary, then, needs to be familiar with the equipment and concepts of the modern office.

SECRETARIAL OPTIONS

In addition to the multifunctional secretary, two new classifications of secretary have evolved as office technology has advanced. The secretary entering the labor force today has the option between choosing the traditional role or becoming either a *correspondence secretary* or an *administrative support secretary*. These divisions of the secretarial function encompass new procedures and equipment designed to achieve higher productivity at a lower cost to the business organization.

Word Processing

Although words have been processed ever since man put chisel to stone, the term *word processing* has been adopted to describe a new method of improving the efficiency of business communications. Early in the 70's automated word processing equipment became available. This breakthrough made possible the mechanization of much of the secretary's production of typed material. Since this new equipment was too expensive to place at every secretary's desk, a new approach was introduced to maximize the use of the equipment. Secretarial functions were reorganized and were divided into two parts —typing activities and nontyping activities (see Illus. 1-2).

One group of employees, identified as *correspondence secretaries, word processing specialists,* or *word processing operators*, was trained to operate the expensive equipment located in a central *word processing center*. The center was responsible for most, if not all, the typing activities formerly accomplished

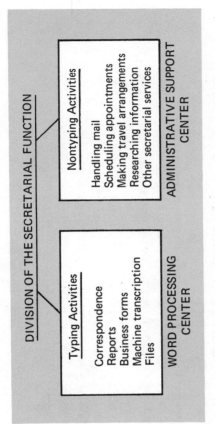

DIVISION OF THE SECRETARIAL FUNCTION

Typing Activities

Correspondence
Reports
Business forms
Machine transcription
Files

WORD PROCESSING CENTER

Nontyping Activities

Handling mail
Scheduling appointments
Making travel arrangements
Researching information
Other secretarial services

ADMINISTRATIVE SUPPORT CENTER

Illus. 1-2
Summary of secretarial functions

by individual secretaries. Dictation was transmitted to the center over the telephone or by machine. Rough draft or *hard copy* (paper material) was sent to the center by messenger. The nontyping activities of the secretarial position were performed by *administrative support secretaries*, and these secretaries were in a central location and served several employers.

In theory these secretarial options are specialized in nature. Secretaries who enjoy mechanical activities are directed toward a career in the word processing center. Those whose interests are in the other areas of secretarial work are encouraged to select the administrative support activities.

Instead of the centralized word processing center concept, many firms are now using a decentralized approach. *Satellite* (or *departmental*) centers and clusters of administrative support secretaries dispersed throughout the organization have proved more advantageous to both company and personnel. The advantages of departmental centers are that (1) operators can master the specialized vocabularies of the departments involved; (2) there is better communication between the originator of a document and the transcriber; and (3) the operator has a stronger sense of identity with the originator and, as a result, a more personal relationship.

Word processing equipment today is much more sophisticated than the equipment introduced in the early 60's. The capabilities of today's equipment are amazing. It is possible to show both copy being typed and stored copy on the screen (often called a *video display*) in front of the operator. Then the operator can correct it and can verify the corrected copy as it appears on the screen. It is possible to merge materials from several sources to produce one document. For instance, one source produces customer addresses, another produces numerical data, and another produces selected paragraphs. The result might be a letter using Paragraph 7 and Paragraph 234 of sample form letters to delinquent customers and a summary of the customer's overdue bill covering two invoices. Sending material from the word processing center to a distant company location over telephone lines is also possible. This procedure saves time in delivery. This material may be read from a screen or printed out (printout) as hard copy.

The Word Processing Center/Administrative Support System

Word processing centers are organized according to a company's needs —one large center serving all departments, a center for each heavy volume department, or a center for several related departments. The flowchart in Illus. 1-3 shows one possible organizational pattern. It shows the interrelationships of the word processing center and the secretary in an administrative support center.

In this plan the administrative secretary gets materials ready for dictation and the principal (originator) dictates (or perhaps the administrative secretary dictates if the material is routine). In this word processing unit there are four components:

1. The receiving station, which logs in the received dictation
2. The word processing supervisor, who decides the order in which work is to be done and assigns the work to individual operators
3. The word processing operator, who operates the automatic equipment
4. The center proofreader, who proofreads the transcripts

The approved transcripts are then sent back to the administrative secretary, who attaches the necessary enclosures and approves the document for signing. The principal signs and the administrative secretary distributes the output.

Group needs determine the number of administrative secretaries in a center; for example, six administrative secretaries may serve as many as twenty principals. Administrative secretaries may have general functions for all other-than-typewriting tasks, or they may be assigned special functions in which they excel. For instance, an administrative secretary may handle all records management or travel arrangements or library research for all the principals served by a unit.

The correspondence secretary keyboards (types) dictation from voice-writing equipment. Typing as rapidly as possible, the secretary corrects errors by using the typewriter's automatic erasing features. Sometimes the dictator wants only a rough draft so that corrections and changes can be made before a final copy is prepared. Most of the time, though, a final, usable document is produced from the keyboarded material.

The correspondence secretary is responsible, too, for playing out stored magnetic tapes or disks when the same material is needed again. The whole document may be reproduced or portions of different stored transcripts may be merged into new output.

English skills are the most important qualification of the correspondence secretary, who must be able to spell and punctuate correctly. The correspondence secretary must have to an exceptional degree the same first qualification required of a traditional secretary: to understand words and their correct use in business communication. Since dictation is from a remote (distant) station, there is no opportunity to ask about terms. But the transcriber cannot make

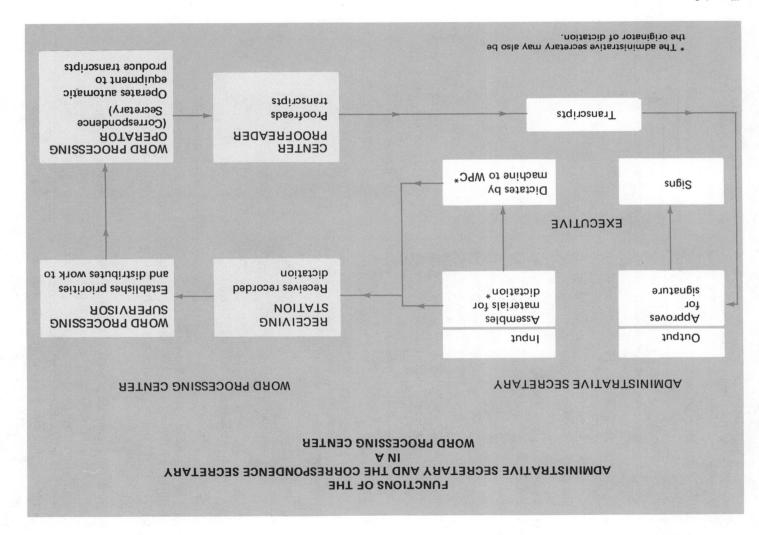

**FUNCTIONS OF THE
ADMINISTRATIVE SECRETARY AND THE CORRESPONDENCE SECRETARY
IN A
WORD PROCESSING CENTER**

WORD PROCESSING CENTER

ADMINISTRATIVE SECRETARY

**WORD PROCESSING
SUPERVISOR**
Establishes priorities
and distributes work to

**RECEIVING
STATION**
Receives recorded
dictation

Input
Assembles
materials for
dictation*

Output
Approves
for
signature

**WORD PROCESSING
OPERATOR**
(Correspondence
Secretary)
Operates automatic
equipment to
produce transcripts

**CENTER
PROOFREADER**
Proofreads
transcripts

Dictates by
machine to WPC*

EXECUTIVE

Signs

Transcripts

* The administrative secretary may also be
the originator of dictation.

Illus. 1-3
Interrelationships of the word processing center and the secretary in an administrative support center

sensible transcripts without an understanding of the nature of the business referred to in the dictation. Therefore, a top-notch correspondence secretary must be a highly intelligent person who knows a great deal about the organization's operations. Typewriting speed is not very important; accuracy is. Finally, a correspondence secretary must be interested in mechanical equipment and understand its capabilities.

Word Processing/Administrative Support Job Titles. From the inception of the word processing/administrative support centers, a number of job titles have emerged, particularly in the word processing center category. Illus. 1-4 summarizes and describes these titles.

WORD PROCESSING/ADMINISTRATIVE SUPPORT JOB DESCRIPTIONS[5]

Title	

Word Processing

Manager	Overall responsibility for word processing center, budgets, reporting, forecasts
Supervisor	Schedules and coordinates work, institutes work measurements, analyzes production
Proofreader	Proofreads all work; may be responsible for training programs
Trainer	Responsible for training operators
Specialist II	Acts as assistant word processing supervisor; knowledgeable in all equipment
Specialist I	Experienced operator and capable of revising and formatting complicated documents; lengthy, technical, and statistical work.
Operator	An experienced operator capable of meeting deadlines and quality standards
Trainee	Entry level position.

Administrative Support

Manager	Responsible for all services under the administrative support area.
Supervisor	Schedules and administers work flow, responsible for staffing requirements, budgets, etc.
Senior Adm. Secretary .	Acts as assistant to supervisor, composes documents for principals (employers), researches information, and other semiprofessional duties.
Administrative Secretary .	Works for a number of principals under the direction of a supervisor. Duties are varied.

---

[5]Adapted from the International Information/Word Processing Association's Word Processing Administrative Support Salary Survey, 1981. Reprinted with permission of International Information/Word Processing Association, Willow Grove, Pennsylvania.

Illus. 1-4
Typical job titles and brief job descriptions for word processing and administrative support personnel

AUTOMATION A MISNOMER

The term *automated office* is a misnomer and has negative connotations when used to describe the Office of the Future, according to John J. Connell, executive director of Office Technology Research Group.

"The office, by definition, is a place where information is processed and communicated," states Connell. "The myriad of developing office technologies are not aimed at automating the office, but rather at facilitating the communication of information."

Administrative Management (April, 1979).

As Illus. 1-4 indicates, there is a career ladder for word processing and administrative support personnel. The various positions represent promotions and salary increases for those persons working in a word processing center environment. Also, opportunities for promotion may be enhanced since the administrative secretary works with several principals and can demonstrate special capabilities that attract more management attention than a secretary to only one person can hope for.

Impact of Word Processing Equipment on the Traditional Secretary. Many secretaries work in small organizations where the volume of work may never justify the purchase of expensive word processing equipment. Secretaries in these offices will at best enjoy typewriters with self-correcting ribbons, which are helpful in producing neat, original copies. Many equipment manufacturers are offering at a nominal price word processing typewriters that have limited capacity to store and retrieve typewritten copy. As prices decrease, many traditional secretaries will have automatic typewriters at their desks.

In large companies even the secretary who works with one executive will be able to enjoy the advantages of processing many documents by automation. He or she will become a modified administrative secretary, freed from routine tasks for more challenging ones. Material can be dictated to a center by either the executive or the secretary. In some situations part of the dictation and transcription can be completed at the location of the executive's office and part can be sent to the center. The secretary who formerly had an assistant, or even more than one, may now be able to handle all the executive's work alone.

Management's Reactions to Word Processing. A management consulting company has estimated that word processing techniques can usually result in a decrease of 15 to 30 percent[6] in clerical payroll and overhead for every 100

[6]Walter Kleinschrod, Leonard B. Kruk, and Hilda Turner, *Word Processing: Operations, Applications, and Administration* (Indianapolis: The Bobbs-Merrill Co., Inc., 1980), p. 9.

work stations placed under the program. (This is another indication that word processing systems are feasible only in large companies.) One company executive says that production has doubled with word processing—from 250-300 lines a day previously produced by typists at individual work stations to 500-800 lines a day by correspondence secretaries. In another company 10 employees now handle the work previously done by 42. Naturally management is sold on the concept for its cost-cutting features.

Management likes word processing too because secretarial output can be measured. Under the traditional system the only supervisor of output was the executive for whom the secretary worked. Such a person was neither trained in nor especially interested in work measurement. Now management is trying to staff the administrative support center and the word processing center with supervisors who know how to apply standards of both quality and quantity.

Some executives, who regard their secretaries as status symbols, resist the reorganization of the secretarial function. They dislike dictating to a machine, and they believe that the whole concept of word processing is dehumanizing.

Many offices are not organized for word processing. For these companies outside word processing centers are available to do repetitive jobs. However, rapid progress is being made toward automating the offices of large organizations.

THE SECRETARIAL SHORTAGE

Government sources cite a shortage of 305,000 secretaries each year from 1978 through 1990.7 These vacancies exist even in times of high unemployment. Incredible? Perhaps. Yet there are sociological and psychological forces that have been and are contributing to this nationwide shortage of entry-level and experienced secretaries.

Two important influences in this shortage are the women's movement and government affirmative action programs. The women's movement has created a negative attitude toward secretarial work, suggesting that it is demeaning with little chance for advancement. On the other hand, women's rights efforts have undoubtedly improved the lot of working women at every level, secretaries included. In their drive for equal opportunities, women have been a major factor in securing affirmative action legislation that prohibits discrimination in hiring and promoting. Some of the largest corporations in the country have been ordered to pay women employees millions of dollars in back pay for discriminatory promotion practices. Women have opened the doors, although on an admittedly limited basis, into new professions, new management training programs, and new attitudes.

7Kay Fusselman, "U.S. Bureau of Labor Statistics Occupational Outlook for Secretaries," The Secretary (February, 1981), p. 18.

The secretarial shortage is compounded by the fact that fewer women and men are training to be secretaries, and many who are taking such positions are ill equipped to become secretaries. Poor skills in shorthand, typing, and language arts have been mentioned as deficiencies.

In this age of mechanization it may come as a surprise to hear that personnel managers continue to value shorthand skill. In fact, most companies want applicants with typing skills of 50 to 60 words a minute and 80 to 100 words a minute in shorthand.

According to Harvey Rubenstein, president of the Los Angeles VIP Corporation, a personnel recruitment agency, shorthand skill is worth an additional $100 to $200 a month or an extra $1,800 a year. Further, as reported by the editor of the magazine *Infosystems* in April, 1979, "dictation directly to a secretary's shorthand remains the dominant mode. Sophisticated, automated dictating systems have so far had little impact."

As a result of the shortage of applicants for secretarial positions, secretaries who have good typing and stenographic skills are demanding and receiving high salaries. A survey conducted by PSI in 1979 revealed that over 70 percent earned a salary of over $12,000 a year and over 80 percent indicated they had not reached a salary ceiling. Top-notch secretaries easily earn $15,000 to $20,000 a year, and within a few years these figures should reach $24,000 to $30,000. Mr. Rubenstein continues, "It is virtually impossible to hire a qualified secretary with shorthand skills for under $10,000 a year, and really top executive secretaries can command salaries of $18,000 to $20,000 a year or more."[8] Overall it is estimated that secretarial salaries are rising at more than 10 percent a year, which eventually will be a factor in making the field attractive to men and women.[9] "Secretarial work can be a stimulating, well-paid career in itself; or it can be an effective stepping-stone to a higher level position in the field of your choice."[10]

PERSONAL SECRETARIAL REQUISITES

A good secretary is a staff assistant and the executive's office memory. As a public relations expert, the secretary must represent the company and the employer effectively to the public. Of equal importance is the ability to work cooperatively with all employees inside the organization: with executives on a high level, with co-workers on the same level, and with those to be supervised. Strangely enough, research tells us that human relations problems rise infrequently with those at high and low levels and that most personality

Cooperation is doing with a smile what you have to do anyway.

[8]Anne Mayer, "Wanted: 250,000 Good Secretaries," *The Secretary* (February, 1980), pp. 6–9.

[9]"The Secretary Is Becoming an Endangered Species," *Forbes* (December 11, 1978).
[10]Sally P. Koslow, "Secretarial Jobs: Great Career or Great Career Stepping-Stone," *Family Circle* (June 14, 1978), p. 34.

problems occur in contacts with employees at the same level, in this case with other secretaries. Working in harmony with others requires diligent application of the three *C*'s of effective human relations: courtesy, cooperation, and cheerfulness.

Illus. 1-5
Working in harmony with others requires diligent application of the three *C*'s of effective human relations: courtesy, cooperation, and cheerfulness.

The enormous problem of ethics in business is attracting a great deal of attention, so much so that the **PSI** has adopted a secretary's code of ethics described in Chapter 26 and available for class use in solving some of the problems the secretary encounters in relations with employers and peers. A secretary's code of ethics can serve as a guide to behavior on the job. In addition a person's good judgment should suggest the importance of loyalty to the employer, respect for the employer's materials and property, and adherence to company policies and rules.

Because secretaries are close to management, they should look and act like management. Most college students try to conform to the standards of dress and hair styling that will win the acceptance of their peers. When they move into a new environment, that of the office, they must try equally hard to meet new standards—those of business.

Some employees, especially at the entry level, do not realize that good grooming and appropriate business dress are even more important to their business success than are their skills. Observing the appearance of secretaries to executives in the office will provide insights on what is considered proper business attire for that office. In general, dresses, suits, and blouse and skirt combinations are considered acceptable for women, while pantsuits may not be. For men the traditional business suit is recommended, and in some offices sport coat and slack combinations are appropriate.

Good grooming requires efficient scheduling of grooming activities and having each garment clean and pressed. If you are overweight, you may have to consider body training exercises, jogging, tennis, and/or calorie counting. Equally important are good posture and good health habits. The secretary to an executive must be in top physical condition. As pressures on the executive increase, so do they upon the secretary. To meet capably all the demands of the day, the secretary must begin the day well rested and well nourished.

College students usually take a speech course—but not very seriously! Yet the personnel officer in charge of work assignments for 20 college students who were on an internship program between their junior and senior years reported that the one universal complaint of the executives with whom the students worked was, of all things, *speech.* Students should analyze their speech patterns and, with faculty help, embark on a speech improvement campaign.

QUALITIES OF AN IDEAL SECRETARY

Accurate, alert
Neat, nicely groomed

Industrious, intelligent, interested
    in job
Dependable, diligent
Efficient, exercises poise
Ambitious, agreeable
Loyal, logical

Sincere, systematic
Enthusiastic
Cheerful, courteous, cooperative, confident
Reliable, resourceful
Eager to please, exercises good judgment
Tactful, thorough, trustworthy, truthful
Attentive, adaptable
Responsible, refined
Your attitude (thoughtfulness and helpful-
    ness toward others)

Anonymous

ADVANTAGES OF THE COLLEGE-TRAINED SECRETARY

Most of you reading this chapter have made the secretarial profession your vocational choice, and wisely so. You are obtaining your secretarial training at the college level and are about to embark on your business career. You will bring to your new employer the background of business knowledge studied in your college program. You are well grounded in the functional areas of business—accounting, marketing, management, and so forth. At the end of your college study, you will be well qualified to act as a partner in the employer/secretary team. In this position you are considered a multifunctional secretary, because of your general rather than specialized duties, such as those found in the word processing center environment. As a multifunctional secretary, you are part of the management team and will associate with executives at the exciting core of the company's activities. Often you may find yourself as a decision maker, perhaps in a position to recommend change in procedures and/or equipment.

A Manager of Change

You undoubtedly have heard the adage, Nothing is more certain than change. You can be assured that this observation aptly describes the procedures and equipment in the office in this decade. The Steelcase[11] survey cited early in this chapter reports that 59 percent of the secretaries questioned have within the past five years experienced changes in their jobs that required learning new skills, 66 percent experienced changes in tasks or duties performed, and 50 percent have learned to use electronic or data processing equipment. Because of the rapid expansion of computer technology, secretaries can expect to work in an automated office. Many offices will operate through shared technology and technical service centers. In later chapters of this book you will see interrelationships among office activities, such as data processing, word processing, reprographics (reproduction of copies), telecommunications (electronic communicating), and records storage and retrieval.

How changes will affect the office you join is difficult to say. Changes do not happen overnight. Generally, when changes in the office are implemented, office employees do not meet them gracefully. You, as a college-educated secretary, have the advantage of a strong background in office technology, and thus you have the flexibility to assume different office functions.[12] In addition, you should be in a position to make recommendations whereby you and your office will *work smarter, not harder.* You certainly must welcome the challenges that will increase office efficiency.

Promotion Possibilities

For the qualified, ambitious secretary, a secretarial position is not a dead-end job, as some would have us believe. It can be a stepping-stone to

11 *The Steelcase National Study of Office Environments: Do They Work?* Louis Harris & Associates, Inc., 1978.

12 In a survey conducted by Manpower, Inc., over 53 percent of the secretaries questioned indicated that flexibility and adapting to changing situations are the keys to their success.

THE PROFESSIONAL SECRETARY

A Self-Evaluation

The secretary's behavior in an office setting sets the stage for the employer-secretary relationship.

	Yes	No
When I work, I work.		
I dress appropriately for the office.		
I address my employer or employers in a formal manner.		
I leave my personal life at home.		
I respect my employer.		
I am punctual.		
I mind my own business.		
I execute my duties with dispatch and with accuracy.		
I keep confidential work confidential.		
I do not contribute or listen to office gossip about my employer.		
I owe allegiance to the company first, then to my immediate employer (if in controversy).		
I recognize that materials and equipment with which I work belong to my employer.		
I will criticize in private and compliment publicly.		
I continue to educate myself to enhance my value to my employer.		
I am committed to create and encourage a pleasant working atmosphere.		
I recognize that my position is a supportive one.		
I attempt to maintain good health to better execute my duties.		
I am dependable.		
I adhere to company policy.		

Illus. 1-6
Can you answer yes to each of these statements?

another career. Further, if the secretarial shortage continues, those who do enter the field will have a decided advantage in moving into management positions. Since the implementation of affirmative action programs, secretaries probably more than any other group have benefited. Many an executive has looked within the firm for possible candidates for promotion. Often the executive's choice has been a secretary whose quality of performance is known, who perhaps has a college background or is the holder of the coveted Certified Professional Secretary designation or both.

A sampling of former secretaries promoted to management level attests to the possibilities for advancement. Luanna Vaughn, construction real estate loan officer for a branch of the Bank of America in California, began her banking career as a secretary. Joan Manley, chairperson of the board of Time-Life Books, started her climb upward as a secretary at Doubleday & Company, Inc. At Philip Morris, Mary W. Covington rose from a secretarial position to that of vice-president. The vice-president in charge of special programming at American Broadcasting Company is Barbara Gallagher. Herbert Nelson, a secretary for twenty-five years, is secretary to the chairman of New Jersey's *Bergen Record*, a position that pays him well over $30,000 a year.

Asked what advice they would give to young secretaries entering the office today, most of these men and women agreed that working hard, assuming responsibility, continuing their education, and learning every aspect of every job held lead to promotion into management.

What about promotional opportunities for the word processing operator and the administrative support secretary? The word processing operator was probably attracted to word processing because of the ability to produce larger volumes of higher quality documents than the multifunctional secretary in a given period. The word processing operator who has demonstrated competency in English and in decision making related to equipment capabilities will probably advance through the job titles within the word processing center as illustrated on page 12.

Administrative secretaries realize that they may have to adjust to the whims of several principals rather than just one. Still, they see their opportunities for promotion increasing in direct proportion to the number of principals served.

THE REENTRY SECRETARY

One of the attractive features of the secretarial profession is the relative ease with which one can become employed after years away from the field. For example, recruitment of former secretaries (now homemakers) has become a necessity in some areas of the country. One of the advantages of a corporation move to the suburbs is the attraction of qualified secretaries. Employers usually are willing to adjust workday hours to accommodate secretaries with small children in school. Some companies have adopted a flexitime work schedule, i.e., a schedule requiring employees to be on the job during specified "core hours" but providing flexibility in their arrival and departure times. The time schedule is approved by the employer and must total the number of hours in the company workweek.

Some former secretaries anticipating reentry into business enroll in a college course to revitalize their knowledge and skills. Those of you in this situation will find this text valuable in bringing you up to date on office technology and procedures.

A SELF-CHECK ON YOUR SECRETARIAL PERSONALITY

Performance Components	Human Relations Components
Accuracy	**Consideration**
How good am I at finding and correcting errors?	Do I often do kind things without being asked?
Good Judgment	**Tact**
Are my decisions usually thoughtful rather than impulsive?	Do I avoid ruffling the feelings of others?
Follow Through	**Discretion**
Do I see a job through—doing implied and specific assignments?	Do I refrain from divulging business and personal information?
Resourcefulness	**Loyalty**
Do I usually try various possibilities until I solve a problem?	Do I stand by my family and my friends through thick and thin?
Initiative	**Objectivity**
Do I often initiate action in my group?	Can I—and do I—look at personal situations impersonally?
Organization	**Respect**
Can I develop a work plan that, when necessary, can be flexible in its execution?	Do I recognize the need for lines of authority as part of a team effort?
Efficiency	**Forbearance**
Am I aware of the importance of time and the economy of motion in the completion of assignments?	Can I hold my tongue and refrain from petty remarks to a co-worker who is being difficult?
Skill Development	**Attitude**
Do I make a definite effort to improve my weakest skills?	Do I accept work assignments cheerfully?

SUMMARY

This chapter has indicated some of the changes that are occurring in the secretarial field. These changes logically lead to the following conclusions.

Although many offices are reorganizing for word processing, many are not and never will. The multifunctional secretary in offices large enough to organize word processing centers need not feel threatened. Rather, the multifunctional secretary should welcome the equipment as a way of obtaining freedom from much of the routine typing, so that more challenging work can be accomplished. The secretary of tomorrow must be flexible. Technological advancements in the areas of communication (telephone, telegraph, computer, for example) are having their effect on the ways secretaries perform their duties. Anyone now in secretarial work or preparing for it must accept change and adjust to it. In fact, the areas in which change is occurring may be the areas of greatest opportunity.

Secretarial work provides a satisfying life career. It also offers demonstrated possibilities for promotion into management. Labor shortages continue in this field even in a time of high unemployment.

Various parts of the text may be of special interest to the multifunctional secretary, to the administrative secretary, or to the word processing operator. However, all sections of the book should be studied carefully for the development of a strong foundation in secretarial knowledge and skill.

SUGGESTED READINGS

Casady, Mona. *Word Processing Concepts.* Cincinnati: South-Western Publishing Co., 1980.

Dowling, Ralph A. "Men Are Secretaries, Too!" *The Balance Sheet,* September, 1980, pp. 9–10, 48.

Levitt, Mortimer. *The Executive Look and How to Get It.* New York: AMACON, 1979.

Molloy, John T. *The Woman's Dress for Success Book.* New York: Warner Books, 1978.

Professional Secretaries International. *Code of Ethics for the Professional Secretary.* Booklet. Abbreviated version appeared in *The Secretary,* April, 1981, p. 20.

PERIODICALS AND SUBSCRIPTION SERVICES

Administrative Management. A monthly magazine available by subscription from Geyer-McAllister Publications, Inc., 51 Madison Avenue, New York, NY 10010.

From Nine to Five. Twice monthly pamphlets on specialized topics, available by subscription from Dartnell Corporation, 4660 Ravenswood Avenue, Chicago, IL 60640.

Information and Word Processing Report. A semimonthly technical/management newsletter published by Geyer-McAllister Publications, Inc., 51 Madison Avenue, New York, NY 10010.

Management World. A monthly magazine published by the Administrative Management Society, AMS Building, Maryland Road, Willow Grove, PA 19090.

Modern Office Procedures. A monthly magazine available from the Industrial Publishing Co., Division of Pittway Corporation, 614 Superior Avenue West, Cleveland, OH 44113.

Office Guide for the Working Woman. A twice-monthly bulletin from the Bureau of Business Practice, Inc., Division of Prentice-Hall, Inc., 24 Rope Ferry Road, Waterford, CT 06386.

Personal Report for the Professional Secretary. Twice-monthly high-level report on research of value to the secretary. By subscription from Research Institute, 589 Fifth Avenue, New York, NY 10017.

The Office. A monthly magazine available by subscription from Office Publications, Inc., 1200 Summer Street, Stamford, CT 06904.

The Secretary. The official monthly publication of Professional Secretaries International, 2440 Pershing Road, Crown Center, Suite G-10, Kansas City, MO 64108.

The Secretary's Improvement Program including *P.S. for Professional Secretaries, Secretary's Memory Jogger, The Secretary's Complete Portfolio of Letters,* and *The Executive Secretary's Word & Phrase Finder* published by Bureau of Business Practice, Inc., Division of Prentice-Hall, Inc., 24 Rope Ferry Road, Waterford, CT 06386.

The Secretary's Workshop. Monthly bulletins covering all problem areas such as math and spelling, as well as office skills, published by Bureau of Business Practice, Inc., Division of Prentice-Hall, Inc., 24 Rope Ferry Road, Waterford, CT 06386.

Word Processing and Information Systems. Monthly magazine published by Geyer-McAllister Publications, Inc., 51 Madison Avenue, New York, NY 10010.

Words. Bimonthly magazine of the International Information/Word Processing Association, 1015 N. York Road, Willow Grove, PA 19090.

Working Woman Magazine. Published monthly by HAL Publications Inc., 600 Madison Avenue, New York, NY 10022.

QUESTIONS FOR DISCUSSION

1. In what ways has this chapter changed your concept of the secretary's role?
2. Do you think that PSI's definition of a secretary is valid? Why or why not?
3. What effect do you think the rapid development of word processing will have on future secretarial opportunities?
4. Have affirmative action programs been beneficial or detrimental to the secretary?
5. Do you think the secretarial field will become more attractive to men as a career?
6. In this chapter the comment is made that a secretarial position may be a stepping-stone to another career. In what ways do you think this is true? How do you plan to use your secretarial career?
7. In the light of your own capabilities and interests, which type of secretary would you prefer to become: a multifunctional secretary, a correspon-

dence secretary, an administrative secretary, or a supervisor in a word processing center?

8. Why would the PSI decide to adopt a code of ethics?

9. What are the advantages of secretarial programs over such programs as economics, business administration, or liberal arts for the college student in today's job market? the disadvantages?

10. What advice would you give a reentry secretary to update business knowledge and skills after being out of the office for the past ten years?

11. In the following sentences select the correct verb to agree with the subject. Check the Reference Guide at the end of the book to correct your work.

(a) Each of the members (has, have) one vote.

(b) Neither the chairman nor the committee members (is, are) present.

(c) The number of votes (was, were) insufficient to elect a president.

(d) Your pair of scissors (is, are) being sharpened; my scissors (needs, need) sharpening, too.

(e) Not only the speaker but also the members of the panel (were, was) late.

(f) No prices or delivery date (was, were) quoted.

(g) Ten pieces of fine jewelry, as well as the ancient bronze statue, (was, were) sold.

PROBLEMS

1. Visit a word processing center or talk with either an administrative support secretary or a correspondence secretary to determine whether the conclusions in this chapter coincide with those of someone working in one of these jobs.

2. One way to develop a secretarial personality that will later enable you to get a high score on the chart on page 21 is to evaluate yourself today and acquire as yet undeveloped desirable traits. Rate yourself excellent, so-so, or needs improvement on each question. Then, to determine whether you perceive yourself as others see you, ask a classmate, a friend, or a family member to check your characteristics on the same scale. Next, set up a specific program for improvement, pinpointed to your low ratings. Concentrate on one or two traits at a time until the desirable behavior seems to be instinctively yours. Then work on two or three more traits until they are habitual. Repeat the process until you have an attractive, pleasant-to-work-with personality that will earn a high score on this chart.

Chapter 2

The Secretary in the Office Environment

In selecting a suitable position a secretary has choices that go far beyond the fundamental decision about the type of secretarial work preferred—namely, a traditional secretarial, an administrative secretarial, or a correspondence secretarial (word processing) position. A secretary must make a decision about a specific area of interest to pursue: law, medicine, banking, industry, or government. In addition a secretary may prefer a specific geographic area. To an extent, too, a secretary may have a choice concerning salary and/or promotional possibilities. A secretary may also have the opportunity to make a decision regarding the size of the organization he or she wishes to join. A company's organization chart, financial strength, reputation, and buildings and grounds may well be factors in the decision-making process. Environment and office arrangement also may influence a secretary's decision.

After careful consideration of these factors, a decision is made and a secretarial career—let's say your secretarial career—is launched. This chapter classifies your duties and discusses the organization of your work and the management of your time. It provides guidelines in the event you are assigned to more than one principal. It concludes with suggestions for securing outside assistance for overloads and for supervising other office employees.

UNDERSTANDING THE ORGANIZATIONAL STRUCTURE

As a newly hired secretary, one of the first things you will do is acquaint yourself with the organizational structure of the office. You need to know where your employer fits into the management team. If you join a one-secretary office or a small company, the hierarchy is readily apparent. If you are in a large company, however, the situation is quite different. There you must learn the names of persons to whom your employer reports. You must also know the names of those who report to your employer and of those of equal status with your employer. An organization chart can give you this information. If one is not available, ask questions of your employer and research the files. In general, keep your eyes open! The discussion that follows describes the line organization, where authority flows vertically from the top executive down, of a large manufacturing firm.

Company Officers

The administration of a company usually consists of a president, an executive vice-president, one or more vice-presidents, a secretary, and a treasurer. Each of these officers will have a staff to provide assistance.

President. In most corporations the president is the chief executive officer who is responsible to the board of directors for the profitable operation of the business. This position is one of liaison between the board of directors, on which the president usually serves, and management personnel. Thus, the president interprets the board's actions to management and management's plans to the board. The office of the president puts board resolutions into effect.

The duties of the president are as varied as the activities of the firm. To many people, the president is a company symbol. What this executive does has a bearing on the reputation of the firm and possibly on the community in general. The leadership ability of the holder of this office often determines the type and caliber of management personnel in the organization.

Executive Vice-Presidents, Vice-Presidents, Secretary, and Treasurer. The executive vice-president (or senior vice-president) is second in command in the organization. This officer serves in place of the president and may be selected to succeed a president. Generally it is the responsibility of the executive vice-president to suggest changes in policy and to coordinate the efforts of the other vice-presidents in carrying out their specific programs and functions. This executive also coordinates the work of various departments.

Often there are two, three, or more vice-presidents. Each is a general officer of the company and, with the president and executive vice-president, is involved in achieving the goals of the firm. Each vice-president is responsible for a special phase of administration, such as production or marketing, and strives to reach the objectives set for that division.

The secretary of the company, often an attorney, is responsible for the legal actions of the business. Typical activities of this office include scheduling stockholders' meetings, drafting resolutions, recording the proceedings of meetings, executing proxies or powers of attorney, and preparing contracts. The treasurer, who is the financial officer of the firm, directs all monetary, budget, and accounting activities.

Divisions of a Company

A large company is usually organized into departments or divisions. The functions and titles of these divisions vary depending on the type of business in which the company is engaged. For example, a manufacturing firm may have such operational divisions as production, purchasing, marketing, finance, research and development, and administrative services. A retail chain may have the same divisions with the exception of a production, or manufacturing, department.

Production. The executive in charge of the production division is the vice-president, production. In some companies this executive's title may be director of manufacturing, director of engineering, or factory manager.

The production division controls and is responsible for all matters pertaining to the manufacture of the company's products. The objective of this division is to manufacture the product to its specifications (quality), in the proper quantity, and at the lowest possible cost. This division must cooperate closely with other company divisions, such as marketing and finance.

Purchasing. The purchasing division is responsible for procuring materials, machinery, and supplies for the company. The complexity of the division will, of course, depend on the size of the company. In a small company, one person (with perhaps some clerical help) can accomplish all purchasing functions. In a very large corporation, the head of the division may be at the vice-presidential level. Purchasing functions are specialized according to the needs of the organization. One buyer, for example, may be in charge of purchasing all raw materials for production. Another may be responsible for the packaging requirements for the corporation's various products. Further divisions in the purchasing procedure occur as necessary.

In general, the procedure is this: A department initiates a purchase requisition, providing as many specifications as necessary. The appropriate buyer locates a source of supply; considers quality, quantity, price, and service; and negotiates the purchase.

Marketing. Because a business survives only if it sells its products, there must be an effective marketing/sales organization. The marketing division may be separated into two or more departments, the heads of which report to the vice-president of marketing. *Synonim - selling*

Sales Department. The sales director (or sales manager) usually directs a staff of salespeople. The department may employ the members of the sales staff, give them special training, and assign them to territories. It may supply samples and literature, introduce new products, and perform myriad other activities through the sales staff. In addition to managing the sales department, the sales director may be responsible for developing product policy, approving credit extensions, and preparing a sales budget.

The selling function, of course, is one of the most important activities of the company. How well this function is performed often determines the company's profit.

Advertising Department. The advertising department also is concerned with selling. It is responsible for devising a broad advertising plan appropriate to

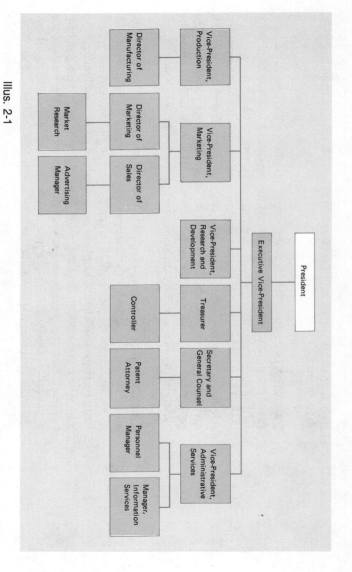

Illus. 2-1
The organization chart for the company described on these pages might look like this. Positions will, of course, vary among companies. This chart clearly identifies the levels of administrative authority in a line structure.

the overall marketing program of the company. This department coordinates its advertising with the selling effort. In some instances it turns over the advertising entirely or partly to an outside advertising agency which, in turn, plans and executes the program. In this event the advertising department acts as a liaison. It supplies information to the agency about the company's products and marketing goals and approves the agency's proposals.

Market Research Department. The work of a market research department is statistical and interpretive in nature. This department gathers useful data to guide the business in marketing current products or in launching new ones. Its scope is extensive. It continuously reexamines and estimates the market for the company's products. Market research also evaluates new products of other manufacturers and provides management with the information necessary for sound decisions.

Finance Division. The finance division handles the monies and accounting procedures, recording, analyzing, summarizing, and interpreting the financial affairs of the company. Thus, the financial division provides a continuous record of company financial transactions. It is also responsible for devising systems, forms, and procedures to summarize company financial activities. This division is involved in formulating company policy.

Often the financial vice-president is in charge of the finance division. This officer directs the work of the treasurer and the controller. The controller (sometimes spelled *comptroller* but always pronounced *controller*) usually directs all phases of accounting. These phases include the general accounting department; cost accounting department; and the combined tax, internal auditing, and procedures department.

Research and Development Division. Recognizing that their survival depends upon success in developing better products, large companies are increasing their budget allotments for research. Scientists and engineers work to develop new and improved products or production methods. These specialists occupy a position of high status in the company.

Administrative Services Division. Departments that serve all other departments are presented here as administrative services departments. These departments generally report to the vice-president, administrative services.

Personnel Department. The personnel director or manager directs the work of the personnel department. One function of this department is the interviewing and hiring of employees. This responsibility involves exploring labor sources, processing and filing application forms, organizing and conducting interviews, administering tests, and adhering to government standards in fair employment practices. Some personnel departments also conduct training programs for new employees (usually excluding sales trainees) and in-service training for present employees. It is the function of the personnel department to administer employee services and fringe benefits; establish health and safety programs; and accomplish the work involved in transferring, promoting, and discharging employees. The department also develops job descriptions and job analyses. An increasing number of corporations are renaming this department the Human Resources Department.

Information Services. Some companies centralize certain office functions, such as records management, reprographic services, mailing, and word processing, by maintaining a specialized staff to perform these activities. The offices of this staff are located where the services provided are as accessible as individual office designs permit. The company with specialized services relieves the individual office force of some routine office jobs. For example, a company using word processing centers can group all secretaries serving one division into a unified location in the division. This type of organization is called the satellite concept.

In a company without centralized office services, each functional division or department operates as a complete, self-sufficient unit. It handles all office duties that would otherwise be turned over to a centralized department.

OFFICE LAYOUT

The first observation of change in today's modern office is in its appearance, its floor plan, and its furniture. Because of the increase in all office activity, the avalanche of paperwork, and the need for more communication at every level of the office hierarchy, there has been a tremendous strain on office budgets. One means of economizing has been in the design of the office. The *open plan* office design with its *furniture systems concept* is fast replacing the conventional office and its traditional furniture. The location of the secretary's work area in both types of offices is included in this section.

The Conventional Office Layout

The traditional office is recognized by its floor-to-ceiling walls, its solid doors, its ceiling light fixtures, and heavy wood or metal office furniture. The secretary's work station in this office is referred to as the secretary's desk. A wood or metal desk, chair, and credenza are standard equipment. Lighting, file storage, and shelving are separate components and sometimes not easily accessible to the secretary.

In a conventional office the secretary's desk usually is located in any one of four places. Probably rare in these times of cost consciousness, in terms of space and energy conservation, is the secretary who has the luxury of a private office. Still, the secretary to an executive may enjoy this privilege. The secretary's desk also may be immediately inside the employer's office or outside the employer's office, or in a nearby location with several other secretaries. Whatever the arrangement, an important consideration is that the employer and secretary be able to see each other.

The Open Plan Design

The modern approach to office design is popularly known as the *open plan* or *open landscape*. Instead of floor-to-ceiling walls, the open office has movable partitions and acoustical screens as dividers. Rather than standard office furniture, colorful systems furniture having panels and panel related components is used extensively. Individual work stations are self-contained, movable units, which are far less expensive than traditional office furniture. Each station is adaptable to the particular needs of the employee and is furnished with necessary lighting, tools, and equipment. In addition, paintings, thick carpets, live or artificial plants, plenty of sunlight and windows typify the new office. Because of its flexibility in changing the location of personnel and furniture, the reduction in square footage required by each employee, and its lower original cost outlay, substantial savings are possible.

Besides visible changes in the office, the open plan facilitates work flow and communication. Employees are positioned according to the flow of work and are readily visible to their supervisor. This office planning system emphasizes the fact that employees are a part of the total process and thus an integral part of the company team. Advocates of this approach say that it increases worker productivity and job satisfaction. In addition, the colorful surroundings have a positive effect on the company's customers.

Ergonomics, the science of work and work place design, is the technical term used to describe this total office planning system. Ergonomics integrates both the physiological and psychological factors involved in creating an effective work area. Thus, it is concerned with the tools and equipment, furniture, acoustics, color, spatial layout, methods of work, and organization of work within an office.

One problem of the open plan is the loss of visual and audio privacy. Scientific aids are effective in reducing the noise level and congestion produced by many workers and visitors in a given area. The fact remains, however, that in the open office the square footage available to each worker is reduced considerably. Thus, distractions are greatly increased. A secretary placed in this situation must develop the ability to concentrate and must show consideration toward co-workers at all times.

Another disadvantage of the open office is the need for increased personal and equipment security. The greater accessibility of open space may force an office to maintain a staff of security personnel 24 hours a day.

In an open plan the executive's office generally has two sections: a large area for individual work and a meeting room for group interactions. In the future it is likely that this conference area may become an information center complete with data input and output devices, visual display boards, and audio-

"The same technologies that are reshaping office systems, procedures, and organizational structures are also reshaping office layouts. Planning work spaces demands knowledge of interrelationships. In a word: ergonomics."

John B. Dykeman
Executive Editor
Modern Office Procedures

Panel Concepts, Inc.

Illus. 2-2
Open plan office
design

visual aids in communication. Secretaries will work with input, output, and retrieval equipment. Their work area will become a multifunction work station in which to process and communicate information in a variety of modes and media. Secretaries may also be responsible for projecting the data visually. Even more than now, the secretary will be the facilitator of communications between the employer and other staff members.

OFFICE SAFETY PROCEDURES

Most offices today make every effort to ensure the safety of their employees. It makes good sense. It is good business practice. Yet accidents can and do happen. Accidents can be due to employee carelessness, or the company can be at fault. In fact, the Occupational Safety and Health Act of 1970 (OSHA) established safety and health standards for businesses dealing in interstate commerce.

Large organizations have established written procedures to follow in case of accidents or emergencies. Bulletins outlining these procedures are posted on every floor or where employees have access to them. Every employee should be aware of these procedures and, if necessary, follow them explicitly.

Office Mishaps

Most office accidents are falls, and most can be avoided. Falls can occur when

1. A desk or file drawer is left open.
2. A tear in a carpet goes unnoticed.
3. An employee walks or runs on a highly waxed floor.
4. Obstructions, such as extension cords or wastebaskets, are left in the aisle.
5. Equipment is not in its regular place.
6. Hallways and stairways are poorly lighted.
7. Insecure filing ladders are used.
8. An employee rushes through a swinging door, and someone is on the other side.

Accidents involving fire can result from careless smoking habits: leaving a burning cigarette unattended or emptying an ashtray containing smoldering ashes into a paper-filled wastebasket. Every employee should know where the fire extinguisher is located and how to use it.

Office Security

It is not uncommon for some employees to arrive at the office very early or to stay late in order to finish a rush job, to work without interruption, or to adhere to a commuter train or car pool schedule. Working overtime (hours in addition to the regular 35- or 40- hour schedule) is standard in many offices. An hourly wage employee who is willing to work overtime is rewarded with increased income and the appreciation of management, which frequently leads to promotion to a better position.

Security guards who monitor the entrances and exits of a building are quite common in metropolitan areas and in businesses whose operation is of a classified nature. They control visitors by issuing passes and sometimes by conducting office visitors to their destinations. Security guards are on duty longer than other employees in the building to ensure the safety of the employees and property. Although the building may be monitored either by a television screen or by security guards, employees should not take a lax attitude about their personal property. Valuables should be kept out of sight in a safe place. Furthermore, any stranger to the office should be intercepted, or at least questioned.

If you are accustomed to arriving very early or expect to work late, you should inquire as to the security measures the company follows. If there are no obvious procedures, you should set your own and then abide by them. Secretaries who often work after hours recommend these practices:

1. Notify the guard or personnel department that you are working late and when you expect to leave.
2. Situate yourself near others who are working late.
3. Work next to a telephone and have emergency numbers handy.
4. Lock all doors leading to your work area.
5. Know when to expect custodial help and establish a cordial relationship with them.
6. Call the self-service elevator before locking your office door. Enter the elevator only after you are sure it is unoccupied. Stand next to the panel buttons.
7. Travel home in a group or have the guard escort you to your car or transportation.

If the office or building is small, it is not likely to have a security force. If you work in such an office, avoid being the only person in the office before and after working hours and during the lunch period. If you must work in an unprotected office alone, particularly after hours, notify someone at your home that you are working late and call again just as you are leaving for home. While working, have all doors locked and admit no one to your office. If you are typing, be aware that the sound carries throughout the floor and perhaps to other floors, and that it is obvious someone is in the office. If you hear any strange noises, call for help. Do not investigate on your own. Another suggestion is to avoid using the restroom if it is located off a hallway or thoroughfare. It is not safe to enter even a locked restroom if you are the only person working late.

As you leave the building look around the parking lot before locking the door. Be sure you have your keys ready to unlock your car. As a reminder, it is always a safe practice to lock your car when entering or leaving it.

Office Emergencies

Office emergencies are sudden and unexpected; they require immediate attention. Delays in responding can result in chaos, destruction of property, and/or loss of life. Offices should have plans for such emergencies posted at conspicuous spots.

In case of a fire or bomb scare, employees must evacuate the building using stairways, not elevators. If you are at your desk when the alarm sounds, take your valuables with you. If you are away from your desk, do not add to the congestion by returning to your desk. Go to the nearest exit.

If you are in charge of valuable company records, put them in a safe place as quickly as possible. Supervisors leave the office last, and then only after they are sure all employees have vacated.

For illnesses or severe accidents, such as heart attacks, burns, or choking, the office should have established procedures which include a list of employees who can administer first aid, phone numbers of the emergency squad, ambulance, physicians or nearest hospital, and similar information. Equipment such as an oxygen kit and first aid kit are standard in most offices.

If there is no established procedure, take it upon yourself to (1) post emergency numbers at your desk, (2) suggest purchasing a first aid kit, and (3) take a first aid course.

AREAS OF SECRETARIAL RESPONSIBILITY

Secretarial work can be divided into three areas: (1) routine duties, (2) assigned tasks, and (3) original work. These areas apply to the multifunctional secretary, the administrative secretary, and the correspondence secretary.

Routine Duties

All secretarial jobs involve some routine tasks, although automation has reduced the amount of routine work required. The multifunctional secretary and the administrative secretary perform such routine duties as opening the mail, filing, replenishing supplies, answering the telephone, and locking up confidential materials at the end of the day. The correspondence secretary locates already transcribed materials and reproduces additional copies.

Assigned Tasks

Assigned tasks are those that are given to the secretary by the employer. The task can be simple, complex, or a mixture of both. In any event, it is work that must be done, usually in a limited amount of time. Tasks assigned to either the multifunctional secretary or the administrative secretary may include making travel reservations, making a bank deposit, or getting technical material from the library. In completing these assignments the secretary may have to make adjustments in the work schedule to accommodate emergencies. The correspondence secretary performs such assigned tasks as transcribing a letter or report, inserting changes in a report, or merging addresses and content so that identical letters can be sent to several correspondents.

Original Work

Original work is defined here as that area of responsibility in which the secretary displays initiative and creativity in assisting the employer. Work that demonstrates thinking ahead or following through on the part of the secretary is typical of this category.

The secretary's contribution in the area of original work is especially appreciated by the employer. At the same time it is most gratifying to the secretary. The more efficiently the secretary handles the work in the assigned and routine areas, the more time remains for service of an original nature. Such service earns the attention that may lead to promotion for the secretary.

The opportunities for creative work on the part of the secretary depend largely on the executive's willingness to delegate responsibility. Such action is an indication of progressive leadership. The secretary can, however, increase the scope of responsibility by demonstrating competence in initiating supportive activities. For example, a multifunctional or administrative secretary who wants to perform work of an original nature will anticipate a request for data supporting a business report and supply it before the employer requests it. Or perhaps the secretary will initiate an instant reference system to increase the employer's effectiveness. In addition, the creative secretary may notice an important article in a magazine and call it to the employer's attention.

Creativity is not a trait one inherits. Creativity can be nurtured, and there are several ways this can be done. First, gather ideas from everywhere, developing an "idea bank" for yourself and then brainstorm with these ideas. Second, learn to be independent in your thinking and in your impressions about office problems. Third, continue to expand your thinking by reading about secretarial work, office technology, and office environment. Always be curious about new developments.

Although the multifunctional secretary and the administrative secretary may have more opportunities to be creative, it is possible for the correspondence secretary to show originality and creativity as well. For instance, since margins, headings, or spacing can be changed without difficulty, a correspondence secretary may experiment with various formats to improve the appearance of a document. Or perhaps the correspondence secretary may redesign the arrangement of the work station to make materials more accessible. Although these suggestions apply more to improving methods of handling assigned duties, they do demonstrate that the job of the correspondence secretary is not so limiting as to exclude opportunities for creativity.

ORGANIZATION OF TIME AND WORK

> Time is the scarcest resource and unless it is managed nothing else can be managed.
>
> Peter Drucker

Time theft, the deliberate waste and misuse of on-the-job time, costs American business at least $80 billion a year, which translates into 3 hours and 50 minutes per employee per week. A cost-conscious and work-conscious secretary, therefore, will make every minute in the workday count. Punctuality is expected in reporting for work, in completing material for the employer, in submitting periodic reports, in relaying messages, and so on. A lackadaisical attitude about time can be a source of irritation to the employer. It can also directly affect other office workers in their attitude toward time. An effective secretary also maintains an efficient work area and has supplies, tools, and equipment well arranged and within easy reach. As in most office behavior situations, the secretary is a role model and thus sets the standard in time and work organization.

The Working Day

Secretaries may work from 8 to 5, from 9 to 5, or any other variation of employer specified workday. They may follow a flexitime schedule or work part-time, perhaps 15 to 20 hours a week. Flexitime divides the day into two parts, a core time during which all employees are working and discretionary hours which fall on both sides of the core. With their supervisor's approval, employees set their arrival and departure times at the office so that they complete the total number of hours to be worked each week. This plan is especially attractive to employees with home responsibilities. The person holding a multifunctional secretarial position may also have a time schedule different from that of other employees in the same office. The secretary's working time, scheduled to suit the employer's convenience, must at the same time cover a full workweek in terms of hours. Any comments of co-workers are irrelevant, since this secretary is accountable only to the employer. Vacations, too, may be more irregular for this secretary than for other office employees. A secretary must defer to the employer's schedule by remaining on the job when the work load is the heaviest. The administrative support secretary, though, must be available at regular hours to all principals.

The Secretary's Work Station

To work efficiently with the least amount of time, effort, and frustration, a well-organized and well-equipped work station is necessary. The objective is to have all that is needed to accomplish daily tasks either on the desk, in the desk, or within easy reach.

A flat, uncluttered surface is needed as a work area. A right-handed secretary should find the following recommendations helpful (reverse if the secretary is left-handed).

1. An in/out basket for mail is placed on the right-hand corner of the desk.
2. A message pad and pencil are beside the telephone that is within reach on the left side of the desk. The telephone is answered with the left hand, thus the right hand is free to take messages.
3. Desk references are placed at the front of the desk.
4. A stapler and scotch tape dispenser are next to the reference books.
5. A desk calendar is at the front of the desk.
6. The typewriter is placed on a separate table, an extension of the desk, or, if systems furniture, on the work surface.

Drawer space is also organized. Pencils, pens, and paper clips are kept in special compartments in the top center drawer. Stationery is kept in a deep drawer in an organizer that has slats for each type of paper used. For instance, company letterhead stationery might be in the first bin, carbons in the second, second sheets or lightweight paper in the third, memorandum paper in the fourth, and so on. A place for envelopes is often provided in front of the stationery organizer. Position the envelopes with the flaps down and facing the front of the drawer so that they are in the proper position for placement in the typewriter. A deeper desk drawer is used for files that are used daily. These include certain instructions, mailing lists, work in process, and other types of reference files. Before leaving for the day, you should remove all papers from your desk. A clean drawer at the bottom of the desk is a good place to put unfinished work at the end of the day. In addition, during lunch hours, coffee breaks, and at the end of the day, the secretary should lock the desk to safeguard any material of a confidential nature from curious employees.

The Secretary's Work Plan

Planning each workday is a necessity for any secretary. Work does not come in an even flow. There are periods when the employer, and accordingly the secretary, must turn out important work in a limited time. The secretary's own analysis of the time and motion spent on routine tasks may free additional time in anticipation of high priority work. A thorough analysis of all the activities performed by the secretary may provide clues to where time can be conserved. If the secretary anticipates periodic jams and distributes part of the rush period work to slack days, it may be possible to reduce, but still not eliminate, the pressures of peak loads.

Work Analysis. Every secretary should strive to perform repetitive tasks such as typing and filing as efficiently as possible by working with a minimum of

A place for everything and everything in its place.

motion, effort, time, and fatigue. As an interested secretary, you may wish to analyze the factors involved in completing each task so as to reduce motion, effort, time, fatigue, or any combination of these.

The first step in organizing time and work is to make an analysis of your duties. An example of a work analysis sheet is given below. For at least two weeks keep a record of each duty and the proportion of time given to each activity. Or you may record only those duties at predetermined time intervals. For easy implementation, you can establish a coding system, such as *IM* for incoming mail, *D* for dictation, and so forth. A careful study of this chart will show where time is not being used to best advantage. For instance, you may see that you spend too much time on tasks that someone else can do, such as searching for a file, typing a mailing list, or other routine activities.

WORK ANALYSIS SHEET

Date _October 15_   Position _Secretary to V-P_

TIME		TASK	CLASSIFICATION					TOTAL TIME	Evaluation
Start	Complete		Outside Contact	Intraoc. Contact	Subor-dinates	Adm. Matters	Routine		
8:00	8:10	Housekeeping duties					✓	10	Total time necessary to maintain standards
8:10	8:15	Telephone confirmation of meeting	✓				✓	5	Train Susan to distribute standards
8:15	9:05	Open, sort, distribute mail		✓	✓			50	Train Susan to distribute
9:05	9:52	Dictation		✓	✓	✓		47	Suggest holding telephone calls
9:53	11:30	Transcription of memo, letters						97	
12:30	1:00	Explanation of monthly report preparation				✓		30	No reco to replicate

Illus. 2-3
A work analysis that incorporates time involved and classification of each task. The amount of time and the type of work involved can suggest to the secretary which tasks can be delegated to others in the office.

Time Wasters. The work analysis log will identify weaknesses in the use of your time and indicate changes that can be made. You may find that one of the biggest robbers of time is the telephone. The trend today is for employers to answer the phone directly. Interruptions, generally between the employer and the secretary, are time wasters. These can be reduced by the employer-secretary team communicating with each other by written memorandums and then consulting orally at convenient times during the day. Another time thief is socializing with co-workers. Certainly some employee socialization is acceptable and even encouraged in offices, but never at the expense of getting the work done. In open plan offices this problem is more acute than in traditional design offices. Other wasters of your time are lack of complete information, failure to delegate, lack of a daily plan, and procrastination.

Be mindful, too, of subtle time wasters, such as filing papers that could be thrown away, duplicating information on several company forms, or recording information that is no longer valid or necessary. Concentrate your energy and your time on those activities that lead to increased efficiency and work productivity. Such activities are most valuable to your employer and to yourself.

Certainly the secretary alone can implement timesaving practices. Certain changes, though, require the cooperation and approval of the employer or even the purchase of new equipment. For instance, if you answer all phone calls, you may wish to discuss with your employer the possibility of changing the procedure.

Daily Work Plan. The key to the wise use of time lies in making and following a daily work plan. This plan is prepared the night before or the first thing in the morning. A daily work plan requires setting objectives for the day, recording the work to be done, and assigning priorities to the work. You judge priorities of work by your employer's requests or by a built-in schedule, such as a weekly report due every Friday. An example of a daily work plan appears on page 40.

In preparing your daily work plan, you should follow these principles on the use of time:

1. Do the most complex tasks at your best working time.
2. Do routine work when your momentum is not as great.
3. Do the hardest tasks in uninterrupted blocks of time, if possible.
4. Group similar tasks such as making copies or telephone calls.
5. Stay with a task until it is completed.
6. Pick up a paper only once and finish the task now. (Time managers estimate that over 50 percent of the daily paperwork can be disposed of in the first handling.)
7. If you have a tremendously long task, divide it into manageable parts and complete one part at a time.
8. Do tasks right the first time.
9. Put spare moments to work for you.
10. Rate each task by priority:

> A or 1—work to be done immediately
> B or 2—work to be done today
> C or 3—work to be done when convenient

11. Coordinate your daily plan with your employer's work plan.

Illus. 2-4
A daily work plan incorporating a listing of objectives for the day, a time analysis, and the priority of work

---

DAILY WORK PLAN

Date _October 16_

Goals: 1. _Complete research for report_
2. _Select meeting time/place_
3. _Compose notification letters_
4. _____

Priority Code
1 – Urgent
2 – Do today
3 – Do when convenient
4 – Do when all other duties
are accomplished

Time	Task	Priority	Evaluation
8:00	Open, sort, distribute mail	2	delegate to Susan
8:30	Library research	1	
9:00	"	1	
9:30	Compiling data	1	

Both secretary and employer complete a daily work plan, and if the plans do not agree, the employer's plan is followed. You may possibly have to organize your employer. With a great deal of tact and perseverance, this can be done. In fact, you can do it by example. For instance, the first thing in the morning you can submit your plan to your employer and by give-and-take discussion and your example, a daily plan for the employer/secretary team is made. Then follow this practice on a daily basis.

If you work for more than one individual, it may be difficult to decide which job to do first, second, and so forth. There are some guidelines, however. If one employer holds a higher position than another, generally the higher ranked employer's work takes precedence, unless a matter is of such urgency that it must take priority. If your employers are at the same management level or if you are in doubt about which work takes precedence, ask your employers to assign work priorities as a matter of routine. Some secretaries have devised a system whereby employers complete a priority slip when assigning work, so that there is no question about the order in which work must be completed. If there appears to be a conflict, you may have to rely on your own judgment to make priority determinations. Often, if you work swiftly, you may be able to do all the work within reasonable time limits so that the question of priorities is academic.

Some office forms, such as the work analysis log and the daily work plan, are handwritten and must be legible. To assure legible handwriting, place both elbows on the desk surface and use proper writing tools: a sharp pencil or ball-point pen. In order to write uniformly, allow proper spacing between letters and words, make lowercase letters one third the height of capital letters, and cross the t's and dot the i's. When writing numbers be sure to distinguish between 1's and 7's and 3's, 5's, and 8's.

In an automated office some entry data are handwritten; therefore, you should begin a program now to develop handwriting skill. You can be a good judge of your penmanship. If you cannot read your own handwriting when it is cold (24 hours old), you can be sure that others will have a difficult time.

Periodic Peak Loads. A study of a month's flow of work over the secretary's desk may indicate patterns of fluctuation. For instance, Mondays traditionally bring heavier mail and subsequently heavier dictation. Thus, other Monday plans should be light. A secretary who must issue first-of-the-month statements of account could spread their preparation throughout the month in an organized pattern. Slack periods are ideal for transferring files, typing new record cards, bringing address files up to date, and duplicating sets of frequently requested materials. At all times, then, the secretary should be on the lookout for ways to simplify work.

To help meet the demands of periodic peak loads, a secretary thinks ahead and makes preliminary preparations, such as addressing envelopes, partially completing forms, preparing enclosures, and purchasing or requisitioning all necessary supplies. In this way the office will run smoothly even during the busiest times.

Real Emergencies. Even with the best planning, unavoidable emergencies will occur. An unexpected illness or tragedy may upset the normal functioning of the office force. All at once you may be faced with a difficult job and insufficient time in which to perform it.

With experience you will know which jobs are critical and how and when each is to be accomplished. If subordinates are available, some of the work may be delegated to them. If not, other secretaries in the office should be approached to assist you. You will find that office employees usually will cooperate with each other to accomplish what must be done. If the work load is far more than the present office force can handle, you may want to suggest employing temporary help.

Office Memory Devices

A secretary needs a good memory to maintain office efficiency. The daily work plan is a reminder to the secretary to complete pending assignments or to follow through on assignments having specific due dates. Several other types of memory aids are described here.

Secretarial Desk Manual. Every secretary should compile and keep up to date a loose-leaf desk manual. It should cover each duty, responsibility, and procedure of that desk. It may also provide a useful place in which to keep often-needed company information. Chapter 26 of this book explains the contents and organization of such a manual.

Secretarial Desk Calendar. Employer and secretary should have individual desk calendars for notes and reminders, business as well as personal. To supplement the employer's calendar, a secretary usually maintains an appointment book for recording the employer's appointments. This book is consulted daily; future appointments should also be reviewed regularly in the event advance preparation is necessary for an appointment—travel arrangements, for example.

At the end of the year prepare next year's desk calendar. Using your present calendar as a guide, mark important dates, meeting times, and other regular dates on the calendar. If deadlines for projects are known or vacations set, note these on the calendar as well. Keep your employer's calendar for several months at least or until you are sure its notations are of no further use.

The Tickler. The most widely used reminder system, filed according to dates, is the tickler. This efficient office aid, the tickler, derives its name from the accounting term *tick*, meaning to *check off*. A tickler is an accumulating record, by days, of items of work to be done on future days. The items are then ticked off when completed.

The daily calendar also can be used as a tickler for recording items to be handled on specific dates. Calendar page space is limited, however, so a separate tickler is usually set up and maintained. The most flexible tickler is a file box with 5- by 3-inch colored guide cards. There are cards for each month, one to three sets of date guides numbered from 1 to 31, and one card labeled "Future Years." The guide for the current month is placed in the front of the file. A set of day guides is placed behind the guide for the current month. Additional guides may be placed behind the next one or two months. An item of future concern is written on an individual card, and the card is filed behind the guide for the proper month and date. If the item is to be followed up several months later, it is dropped behind the month guide. It will be filed according to date when that month comes to the front.

Since an item is often forwarded and reforwarded, the follow-up date is written in pencil so that it can be erased and changed when necessary. In fact, since this is a memorandum type of record, the entire item is usually written in pencil. Annual events, such as due dates of taxes, insurance premiums due, and wedding anniversaries, are refiled for next year's reminders as soon as they are ticked off.

It is the secretary's responsibility to remind the employer of tickler items. An oversight can be very embarrassing and costly to the firm. You will, therefore, want to use the tickler device as a memory aid in these ways:

Sooner or later a busy person learns to write things down. It's the best way to capture things we are apt to forget. "The strongest memory," says an old proverb, "is weaker than the palest ink."

Bits and Pieces
June, 1976

1. To remind yourself of work to be done
2. To tick off items accomplished
3. To record work for a future date

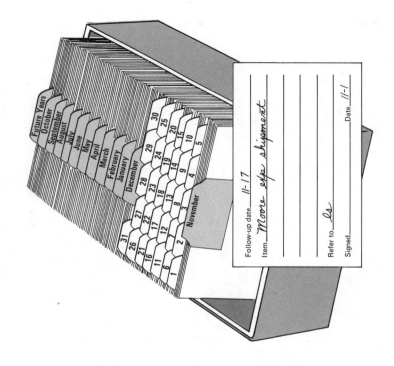

Illus. 2-5
The secretary
enters a tickler
item concerning
an express
shipment due
before the end of
the week. Notice
the abbreviated
form of writing
memorandums.

As a matter of routine, the secretary checks the tickler file when making the next day's work plan. After this check, the secretary places that day's guide in the file at the end of the numbered guides, thus leaving the following day's numbered guide at the front of the file. Near the end of the month arrange the reminders for the next month behind the appropriate numbered guides.

Pending File. The pending file is also a memory aid. It is a file folder in which the secretary temporarily holds mail concerning matters that are pending. It is kept in the secretary's desk, in the employer's desk, or in some other place near at hand. If the secretary's desk has a deep file drawer, the pending file can be kept conveniently there. It is not too satisfactory to keep the folder in a flat position because the folder and its contents often become dog-eared. The secretary must be careful not to isolate in the pending file letters that should be available in the regular files. This can be avoided by making extra copies of incoming and outgoing letters and filing the originals in their respective files. If a letter is not involved, type a special note about the item and place it in the pending file. A regular check of the pending file should be made to determine which matters need to be called to the employer's attention. A notation should be made on the daily work plan. Any letters that have been answered should be released to the regular files and extra copies should be discarded.

Desk Reference Files. The secretary can organize the office work more efficiently by keeping desk reference files. Such files should include the names of important clients, telephone numbers frequently called, addresses of regular correspondents, items that must be followed through before they are placed in the central files, stock identifications and descriptions, and work in process. These reference files are kept in a deep drawer in the secretary's desk. They save much time that would otherwise be lost in hunting for necessary information. Desk reference files are frequently needed files; they can be planned only after the secretary is thoroughly familiar with the job.

The Chronological File. Some secretaries make an extra copy of everything they type in order to maintain a complete chronological file. This file is kept in the secretary's desk. A different colored paper is sometimes used for this file. Many a day has been saved by this ready reference file. If the secretary is also in charge of the employer's files, it is a good practice to note the location of the file copy on the chronological copy.

How long you keep the chronological copies is a matter of preference. Some secretaries keep them for the past three months in the desk drawer; copies of older correspondence are kept in a file drawer. (Also see page 331 for additional information.)

Outside Assistance

It is good judgment for the secretary to request assistance if the situation warrants such action. When there is not sufficient time to complete a sizable office job, the secretary should ask for additional workers. If a word processing center is not available, this assistance can be secured through the office manager. If those avenues fail, a secretary may obtain the employer's permission to contact an agency that supplies experienced temporary help. Among such agencies are Manpower, Kelly Services, Inc., Olsten Temporary Services, and others. A secretary who supervises temporary help should acquaint them with the company hours, facilities, office procedures and, most important, introduce them to other office employees. Give them a copy of the procedures manual or forms guide. Have the work for the temporary person well organized so that time won't be wasted on waiting for information.

Sometimes the work requires professional skills or abilities beyond those of the secretary. Or perhaps the job is of such size that it can be done more quickly and less expensively outside. In such cases, with the employer's permission, the multifunctional secretary often turns to a special service agency.

These agencies prepare multiple copies of original letters and mail them, obtain hotel and travel reservations, take full recordings of meetings and prepare transcripts, handle any or all the operations of reproducing materials, furnish and maintain mailing lists, or provide competent help for other jobs of a specialized or technical nature.

On completion of the work, the secretary writes a note in the desk manual identifying the agency or the individuals employed. Also, a record of the total cost and a brief evaluation of the service should be kept for future guidance.

Supervision of Subordinates

The secretary may be assigned one or more full-time assistants or temporary helpers. With relatively inexperienced assistants, the supervisor assumes the role of *teacher*. In this capacity, the secretary provides the assistant with opportunities for the development of efficient work habits. In addition, the secretary teaches the proper use of equipment and physical facilities.

When assigning work, the secretary gives thorough directions to subordinates. There should be no doubt as to what is to be done. If the work is complicated, written instructions should supplement the oral directions. Periodically the secretary checks on the progress of the work, so that any misunderstandings can be avoided. Assignments of varying difficulty should be given to subordinates to give them the opportunity to display exactly what they can do.

In addition to being a teacher, the secretary is also a *student*—a student of human behavior. The secretary studies the abilities of the office assistants. Also, it may be useful to read literature concerning supervision. It is the secretary's responsibility to motivate subordinates so that they work to their full potential and take pride in their work. A supervisor gives credit and praise when due. If criticism becomes necessary, however, a supervisor discusses the *work* and not the *worker*.

At specified intervals the secretary formally evaluates the subordinate's performance, perhaps by using an evaluation instrument similar to that given on page 46. Note that such an instrument lets the evaluator comment on each factor being rated. This is an advantage both to the evaluator and to the employee. Remember that the responsibility for objective evaluation is implied.

In more and more offices a supplementary evaluation form, such as that shown on page 47, is being used along with the standard evaluation form. The supplementary form encourages understanding and receptiveness by identifying future action needed by the employee. The completed form provides a basis for discussion during the supervisor-employee conference.

An additional discussion on the elements of supervision is given in Chapter 27.

EMPLOYEE EVALUATION

Name of Employee _Joe A. Morgan_   Department _Word Processing_

Directions: Read over each section carefully. Appraise employee performance by placing a check mark in the box below the comment that applies to the employee. Check only one box in each section. Appraisers are encouraged to use the remarks section for additional comments pertinent to the employee's evaluation.

KNOWLEDGE OF THE JOB — Technical job information and practical know-how	Proficient on job; makes the most of experiences--a "self-starter" ☑	Rarely needs assistance but asks for it to save time ☐	Knows job fairly well; regularly requires super-vision and instruction ☐	Job knowledge limited; shows little desire or ability to improve ☐

Remarks: _has thorough understanding of machines_

QUALITY OF WORK	Doesn't care; work is inferior in many respects ☐	Work is usually passable; regularly requires reminder to do a better job ☐	Usually does a good job; seldom makes errors ☑	Consistently does an excellent job; errors very rare ☐

Remarks:

QUANTITY OF WORK	Slow; output below minimum requirements ☐	Turns out the required amount of work--seldom more ☐	Fast; usually does more than is expected ☑	Exceptionally fast; efficiency unusually high ☐

Remarks: _line count is above average_

ADAPTABILITY — Mental alertness; ability to meet changed conditions	Learns new duties easily; meets changed conditions quickly ☑	Grasps new ideas if given a little time; adjusts to new conditions ☐	Routine worker; requires detailed instructions on new duties and procedures ☐	Slow to learn; requires repeated instructions; unable to adjust to changes ☐

Remarks:

RELIABILITY — Confidence in employee to carry out all instructions conscientiously and completely	Requires frequent follow-up, even on routine duties; apt to put things off ☐	Generally follows directions, but needs occasional follow-up ☐	Conscientious; follows instructions with little need for follow-up ☑	Dependable; on time, does what you want, when you want it ☐

Remarks: _capable of formatting documents without instructions_

Summary Statement: _Mr. Morgan is highly productive and extremely creative in his work_

Signature and Position of Evaluator _P. B. Schultz, Supervisor_

SUPPLEMENTARY EVALUATION FORM

EMPLOYEE _Wilson_   _Jane_   _E._
    (last)   (first)   (initial)

This form is not intended to be used for scoring past performance. It is "supplementary to" standard evaluation forms, and should be used to identify characteristics where changes in employee behavior are needed.

Column headers: CONTINUE AS NORMAL / TAKE NORMAL / TAKE NEW DIRECTION

QUANTITY

EFFICIENCY: proper use of resources; no wasted time or effort; energy used versus product produced.

SPEED: length of time required to complete tasks.
needs to put tasks in order of priority

QUALITY

ACCURACY: amount of mistakes in work performance.

DECISION-MAKING ABILITY: conclusions and actions are timely and accurate; reaching the right answer after proper analysis.

WORK HABITS

ACCEPTANCE OF RESPONSIBILITY: willing to be the person in charge of a task's success or failure.

CREATIVE ABILITY: finding new ideas and new and better ways of doing things.

DEPENDABILITY: can be counted on to do what is needed when it is needed.

OBSERVATION OF WORKING HOURS: works within the proper time frames.

OPENMINDEDNESS: ability to examine and consider new thoughts and ideas; consider things without a preconceived notion.

PERSONAL RELATIONS

APPEARANCE: personal impression, clothing, cleanliness, etc.

COOPERATIVENESS: willingness and ability to work with others.
always willing to assist colleagues

ADAPTABILITY

ALERTNESS: the ability to grasp instructions; able to meet changing conditions, and to "catch on" quickly.

FLEXIBILITY: ability to meet changing or new situations.
learns new applications quickly

INNOVATIVENESS: coming up with something new; making needed changes.

SUPERVISION   _not applicable_

DELEGATION OF PROPER RESPONSIBILITY: allows employees to have the opportunity to succeed or fail on their own and use the power that gets things done.

FAIRNESS: applies the rules in a consistent manner toward all employees equally.

GENERAL

AMBITION: desire to reach a goal or objective; projecting one's self into a new role.
attend company seminars

ENTHUSIASM: active desire and interest in the work.

HONESTY: truthfulness; not given to fraud or deception.

LOYALTY: maintains allegiance to the work group; does not tell others all the bad stories of the work group.

Source: Water H. Smith, Jr., "An Evaluation Form That Improves Employee Relations," *Management World*, Vol. 4, No. 11 (November, 1975), p. 27.

SUGGESTED READINGS

Clark, Freda. *Secretary's Desk Book of Shortcuts and Timesavers.* West Nyack, N.J.: Parker Publishing Company, 1978.

Douglass, Merrill E., and Donna N. Douglass. *Manage Your Time, Manage Your Work, Manage Yourself.* New York: AMACOM, 1980.

Keeling, B. Lewis, Norman F. Kallaus, and John J. W. Neuner. *Administrative Office Management,* 8th ed. Cincinnati: South-Western Publishing Co., 1983.

Kristt, Carolyn. *The Successful Creative Secretary.* West Nyack, N.J.: Parker Publishing Company, 1979.

Mackenzie, R. Alec, and Billie Sorensen. "It's About Time . . ." *The Secretary,* January, 1980.

Sapier, Michael. *Planning the New Office.* New York: McGraw-Hill Book Company, 1978.

Winston, Stephanie. *Getting Organized.* New York: W. W. Norton & Company, 1978.

QUESTIONS FOR DISCUSSION

1. Considering your interests, abilities, and aptitudes, in which department of a business organization (purchasing, personnel, research, sales, advertising, accounting) would you prefer to work? Give reasons for your choice.

2. You work in an open plan office. What is your responsibility concerning the workers in your immediate area? concerning the security of equipment and confidential files?

3. At work where would you recommend keeping your wallet and other personal valuables?

4. As a secretary what efforts would you make to guard against accidents in your work area?

5. Determine whether each of the office duties given below is a routine, an assigned, or an original task. Describe the working situation in each case (working with an employer, other company employees, things, or outsiders).

   (a) Filing a piece of correspondence
   (b) Answering the telephone
   (c) Looking up a word in the dictionary
   (d) Answering employer's buzz
   (e) Typing a letter from dictation
   (f) Setting up your own chronological file
   (g) Proofreading a document with another person
   (h) Compiling information from periodic reports

6. What are some of the advantages of the flexitime office schedule?

7. Since typewriters are a standard piece of office equipment, why should a secretary be concerned about the quality of handwriting?

8. Your employer frequently calls you for rush dictation late in the afternoon. This calls for much overtime work on your part. What steps would you follow in suggesting the reorganization of your employer's work, so that efficiency could be increased and overtime reduced?

9. What is the weakness of using a pending file? How can this danger be averted?

10. What would you do first if all the following happened at the same time: you were composing an urgent communication; your employer, who was talking on a long-distance call, buzzed you to enter the office; the secretary to the company president walked by your desk into your employer's office; and your subordinate was at your desk wanting to borrow a file from your desk drawer? Explain your reasoning.

11. In your opinion which factors should be considered in the employee evaluation process of an organization? Which person in the organization should be responsible for an employee's evaluation?

12. Capitalize the appropriate words in the following sentences. Refer to the Reference Guide to correct your sentences.
(a) The pilot was awed by the view of the north star and the big dipper; the moon cast a silver shadow over the earth below.
(b) The contents of hague towers will be auctioned at the hanover courthouse.
(c) All students must take american history.
(d) Prices are slightly higher west of the mississippi river; customers on the east coast should take advantage of this sale.
(e) A special session of congress will be called because the senate was late in completing the bill.
(f) When spring comes to georgia, all the sights and sounds of nature delight the tourists.

PROBLEMS

1. The following items are on your desk on March 2 to be marked for the tickler file. Before filing these items in the regular files, you type a card for each one for the tickler file. Indicate on each card the date under which the card would be filed. Note on the card where the original material is filed.
(a) Notes for an article to be written for the September *Journal of Accountancy.* The deadline for the article is April 1.
(b) A note about setting up a conference with a bank official about a short-term loan to pay an invoice due April 1.
(c) A letter accepting an invitation to speak at a meeting of the School of Business seniors on May 8.
(d) The program of the annual convention of the International Controllers Institute to be held on April 6 in Brussels. Your employer plans to attend.
(e) A notice of a meeting on March 8 of the Administrative Committee. Your employer is a member.

2. It is 11:30 a.m. and you are busy completing the last-minute details for a 2:00 p.m. conference your employer has called. Ev-

erything is going according to your schedule until your employer calls you into the office to tell you the following:

(a) An additional ten people will attend the meeting. It will be necessary to change the meeting room and to obtain more copies of the brochures and other papers to be discussed at the meeting.

(b) Set up a short meeting with the chief accountant at 1:30.

(c) Arrange for an overhead projector and screen for the meeting.

(d) Bring the Smith contract file into the office immediately.

(e) Call Henry Carter and request a postponement of the appointment scheduled for 1:30 today. On a sheet of paper, type the order in which you would handle these matters. Explain the rationale behind your decisions.

3. It is late Friday afternoon and you are 15 minutes away from your two-week vacation. Your employer is out of town until Monday. You have a number of pending matters on your desk. Decide which of the following tasks you should handle yourself in the time remaining, which to leave locked in your employer's desk, and which to leave for your replacement to handle. On a sheet of paper, type your decisions and give the rationale behind them.

(a) Payment of your employer's insurance premium due the following Wednesday. You are authorized to make payment. *Do NOW*

(b) Notification of meeting scheduled for Thursday of the following week. *Replacement*

(c) Shorthand notes of a letter dictated by one of the staff members. *Do NOW*

(d) Confidential promotion papers concerning a staff member. *Lock in desk*

(e) Interoffice memorandum requesting technical data to be provided by your employer. *Replacement*

(f) A letter from your employer's daughter at college. *Lock in desk*

Chapter 3

The Secretary's Public Relations Duties

A very interesting and oftentimes challenging responsibility of the multifunctional or administrative support secretary is the public relations aspect of the position. Greeting visitors, maintaining a businesslike office atmosphere, and making appropriate introductions are examples of this very important function. The secretary is often the first contact a visitor has with the company or with the employer. In this instance the secretary creates an impression of the company, and, needless to say, the impression must be a good one. Creating and maintaining a favorable company image requires courtesy, patience, persistence, sensitivity, tact, and the ability to get along with others.

Skill in dealing with people *inside* and *outside* the company can be worth uncountable dollars in goodwill. Some of that skill is innate to certain individuals, but for most people it comes with on-the-job experience.

In addition to the other aspects of public relations, the secretary must consider the personal preference of the employer in receiving callers. In the case of an administrative secretary who reports to several principals the personal preference of each employer must be known and must be followed.

This chapter discusses the public relations duties involved in receiving office visitors. Appropriate behavior in meeting the public is described. Also, the efficient handling of appointments is presented. The use of the telephone, which is another important public relations function, is covered in Chapter 12.

OFFICE ORGANIZATION FOR RECEIVING VISITORS

Methods of receiving visitors vary among companies. Large organizations generally have a reception area near the main entrance. Here a trained receptionist assists callers in determining which department or person to see, and then calls the appropriate secretary for instructions as to the availability of the employer. Or, if the visitor is known, the receptionist telephones the secretary without delay. If the caller has an appointment, the receptionist gives the visitor directions to the office. In some offices, such as the open plan, the receptionist requests the visitor to wait until the secretary can personally escort the caller to the correct location. When a secretary shows a visitor the way to

51

the office, he or she walks slightly ahead, opens any doors, pushes elevator buttons, and talks about generalities.

In small companies a telephone in the lobby or entrance may be used by visitors to announce their arrival. Assuming the caller has an appointment, the secretary may give directions or personally escort the visitor to the office.

Secretaries in very small offices are a visitor's initial contact with the company. Callers may or may not have appointments. These secretaries must decide immediately whether the visitor is at the right place, whether to admit the visitor, whether to schedule an appointment at a later time, or whether to refuse an appointment.

Whatever the office organization, the secretary has a twofold obligation: first, to adhere to the employer's preferences in admitting visitors, and, second, to be courteous to all who come in.

The Employer's Preferences

Office visitors can be from outside the company, with or without appointments; they can be employees of the company, personal friends, or members of the employer's family who usually arrive without appointments. As a new secretary or a secretary who has a new employer, you will want guidelines for handling office visitors. Your predecessor, if available, can give you this information. If the former secretary is not there or if your employer is new, you can ask general questions or you can learn through experience. If you report to several employers, you will need to determine each one's preferences.

Here are some questions about employer preferences and comments regarding them:

Questions

1. Does your employer want to see everyone who calls?

2. Does your employer prefer to see certain callers (salespersons, for instance) at specified times only?

3. Which personal friends and relatives are likely to call? Which of these should be sent in without announcement? Who else should be admitted without appointments?

Comments

Many employers pride themselves on their open-door policy, meaning they will see any caller during office hours. You should ask this question.

Some employers find this policy useful in making the best use of their time. Learn the answer to this question.

Do not ask these questions directly. You will soon sense the answer. Certain persons can always enter the employer's office without first obtaining your permission: top executives to whom your employer is responsible; their secretaries; co-executives and their secretaries; and the employer's immediate staff. Special privilege callers come in with confidence. They know they will be welcome, and usually they will introduce themselves to the new secretary.

4. How should callers be announced?

You may use the telephone or go directly into the office to announce a caller. Procedure may differ depending on the caller or the work the employer is presently doing. You may have to learn from experience. Watch your employer's reactions to your way of approaching different circumstances.

5. When should you attempt to terminate visits?

For some appointments, your employer will instruct you when and how to initiate a termination. When an appointment is running overtime and another caller is waiting, you should inform your employer that the next appointment is waiting. You can do so by a note or by using the telephone.

6. Are there callers that your employer prefers to avoid?

Feel free to ask this question. Often an employer is plagued with overzealous salespersons.

Welcoming the Visitor

Some secretaries are quite adept at welcoming visitors. They are comfortable at meeting strangers; they have a knack for recognizing visitors who have been in the office previously; and, in general, they have a courteous manner that makes the office visitor feel welcome. Experience has taught them this very important public relations function. As a new secretary, you can learn to be gracious in this area.

To be successful, you must adopt the attitude that office visitors are not *interruptions*; they are *office guests*. When a visitor comes to your desk, look directly at the person, smile, or speak immediately. Your greeting should be friendly and cheerful. A simple pleasant "Good morning" or "Good afternoon" sets the stage for effective communication. To finish typing a line, to file another three letters, or to continue chatting with another employee is rude. If you are on the telephone, acknowledge the caller with a nod or a smile indicating that you will be free momentarily.

If the caller has a scheduled appointment, greeting the person by name adds a personal touch to the welcome. After the usual pleasantries, the secretary escorts the visitor to the executive's office and makes any necessary introductions in a courteous manner.

If an *unscheduled caller* wishes to see your employer, you should identify yourself and ask the caller's name, the company the caller represents, and the purpose of the visit. A greeting such as the following is appropriate: "Good morning. May I help you? I am Alice Brown, Mrs. Alexander's secretary. May I tell her who is calling?" The caller's business card provides some of this information and may give a clue to the reason for the visit. However, actually questioning the caller about the purpose of the visit may be necessary. In this case, tact and patience often are important. An experienced secretary handles the situation graciously and obtains the information for the employer.

The visitor on legitimate business is accustomed to making office calls and will approach you, provide identification, state the purpose of the visit, and ask to see your employer. Occasionally, however, it may be necessary for you to ask: "May I tell Mrs. Alexander what you wish to see her about?" or "I am Alice Brown, Mrs. Alexander's secretary. May I help you?" If you need clarification from the visitor, ask questions. The easiest way to be sure that you have the information correct is to repeat what has been said. State it as you understand it.

In conversations with visitors, always refer to your employer by his or her last name—for instance, Mrs. Alexander. The same is true when addressing your employer in the presence of guests.

Clients and customers are always given cordial and gracious treatment by the secretary. Marketing representatives from businesses that supply materials and services related to the employer's work are treated with courtesy and attentiveness.

Deciding Whom to Admit

Scheduled appointments generally do not pose a problem. These visitors are admitted readily. For unscheduled appointments or in making appointments, some secretaries are inclined to become too protective of their employer's time. Often they turn away visitors the employer should see. Engage in a conversation with the caller long enough to determine if he or she should be admitted. When in doubt, ask if your employer wants to see the visitor.

A caller's business may involve a matter *outside the scope of your employer's duties*. You will save everyone's time by determining the nature of the visit first and, if necessary, referring the caller to the proper person. If you do not know the department or person the visitor should see, make every effort to find out before dismissing the visitor. The transfer should be made immediately by telephoning the proper office and explaining the situation. If an appointment is made at once, the secretary directs the caller to the correct office. If an appointment must be made for another day, the secretary confers with the visitor and then sets a mutually convenient time. In most cases the secretary's helpfulness in arranging this appointment will more than offset any inconvenience which the visitor may experience.

If your desk is placed inside the executive's office, callers will be inclined to bypass you and go directly to your employer. But if your desk is just outside the office, you will probably be fully responsible for determining who may enter. Although certain co-workers, friends, and family may enter your employer's office without your permission, they usually ask courteously if it is convenient to go in. When a visit is concluded, the secretary may usher an infrequent caller to the exit, particularly in the open plan office design where traffic patterns may not be obvious.

Remembering Names and Faces

One extremely valuable secretarial technique is remembering names and faces so that you may greet callers in a sincere and natural manner. To remember names requires the following:

1. *Listening skill* The key to good listening is paying attention to the speaker. Listen carefully without interruption when the name is pronounced. If in doubt, ask the person how to pronounce it or spell it. Writing the name phonetically in shorthand or in longhand will prevent mispronunciation. Being called by name is pleasant, but having one's name mispronounced is very annoying.

2. *A forceful effort to remember the name.* You can train yourself to remember a person's name by repeating it when you first hear it; using it when addressing the person; recording it, perhaps in a reference notebook or card file; and associating the person's name and face with the business represented or with sound alike words or phrases.

The ability to remember faces is another attribute of the superior secretary. Several devices similar to those used in remembering names may be used to develop this skill. The secretary may keep a card file of frequent callers, or may file a business card and associate the name on the card with the face of the caller. To recognize the employer's colleagues, the secretary should watch

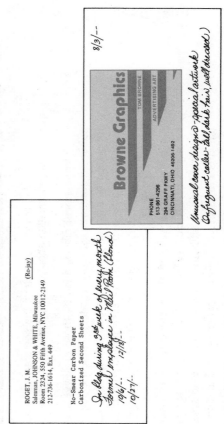

Illus. 3-1
These cards are examples of efficient memory aids. Prepare a card for each caller, recording the name, affiliation, purpose and date of visit, subsequent visits, etc. Or make notations directly on the caller's business card.

carefully for their pictures in company publications, newspapers, or magazines. While recording a committee meeting, the secretary might draw a seating chart and list some outstanding features about any unfamiliar faces. This will assist in remembering their names later.

Several companies whose success depends on effective public relations have developed techniques for improving internal relations. To help personnel recognize other members of the organization, one advertising agency publishes in its company induction manual an organization chart with the picture, title, and name of each executive.

Keeping a Record of Visitors

A record of visitors which includes names, dates of calls, business affiliations, purposes of calls, and other pertinent information is helpful (see Illus. 3-2). Often the secretary uses this record to locate needed facts.

To keep a record of visitors some offices use a printed registration form which the caller is asked to complete. In some cases the secretary may secure the information from the caller and add it to the register at a later time.

REGISTER OF OFFICE VISITORS

Date	Time	Name and Affiliation	Person Asked For	Person Seen	Purpose of Call
6/8/--	9:30	H. Norton, Core Lighting Fix.	S.G.	✓	Sales rep.
"	10:30	L Alton, Standard Printing	R.B.	✓	service rep.
"	11:45	R. Krause, Luncheon appt.	R.B.	✓	"
"	1:40	G. Fuller, Personnel consultant	S.G.	✓	"
"	3:50	Peerwood Delivery Driver	--	--	Brought samp.

Illus. 3-2

With this ruled register of visitors, the secretary can easily keep a daily record of helpful information about callers, including the purpose of the visit.

Professional offices, such as those of lawyers, doctors, engineers, and public accountants, use daily registers. These are helpful in preparing periodic time reports used in computing costs of services rendered to clients. The register serves as a checklist for each period so that the time spent with each client, as recorded, is also correctly entered and charged for on the proper time report.

Some offices keep an alphabetic card file of visitors, recording all visits as they occur. A card is filed by the caller's name and is cross-referenced to show the business affiliation. Doctors use the card system as a basis for billing patients and as a record of each patient's medical data. Purchasing agents can more easily remember the correct names of products and sales representatives by using such a file.

If the flow of visitors is small, the efficient secretary can keep a simple record of visitors conveniently and permanently on the desk calendar.

THE SECRETARY'S CONTRIBUTIONS

The individual secretary's personality, maturity, and knowledge of business etiquette set the stage for the employer to develop a positive rapport with the office visitor. A receptive climate includes making the visitor comfortable, making introductions, if necessary, and using good judgment in interrupting the visitor's conference with the employer.

Pleasant Waiting

The secretary, acting in the role of public relations representative, provides the means for a comfortable and pleasant waiting period for the visitor. In order to accomplish this, the secretary may attend to the visitor's hat and coat, offer a cup of coffee or an ashtray, provide current magazines, or the morning newspaper.

If a visitor is early for an appointment, check with your employer for instructions. Perhaps the appointment time can be changed. If it is not convenient, and the visitor must wait, give some indication of how long the waiting period will be.

After an unduly long wait, you may remind the executive that the caller is still waiting. If the executive indicates that it will be only a few more minutes, you may report this to the caller.

You are not expected to entertain office visitors. After exchanging pleasantries, such as talking about the weather, travel time, and so forth, return to your duties. If the visitor persists in talking, avoid any discussion about company business or your employer.

If several visitors are waiting, admit each in proper turn. You are under no obligation to introduce them to each other unless all are waiting to meet in the same conference.

Admitting the Visitor

If this is the visitor's first call, you should lead the way to the employer's office. Before leaving your desk, cover your work or unobtrusively slip it into a folder. If the executive's door is closed, knock, and after a slight pause, enter the office with the visitor. When the proper introductions have been made, leave and close the door quietly.

In some instances you will not be able to leave your desk to escort the visitor to your employer's office. In this case, a simple suggestion will indicate that the visitor may enter.

Sometimes the executive walks out to greet the caller. Should there be two callers waiting, indicate who is first.

Introductions

When the secretary is responsible for making introductions, the person given the greater courtesy is named first. In business introductions, this means that the name of the person of higher position is given first. Titles such as Doctor, Captain, or Sergeant are included if known.

When the employer introduces the secretary to a client, business position takes precedence. Therefore, the client is addressed first. The secretary responds to introductions in a natural way. A simple hello is sufficient, never "How do you do?"

As office receptionist, the secretary should be aware of the following situations where sex, age, and sometimes rank, rather than strict business position, apply:

Introduction	Factor in Presentation	First Named
1. Woman and man	Sex (usually)	Woman
2. Dignitary (head of state, church dignitary, politician) and employer	Rank	Person with higher position
3. Young person and mature person	Age	Mature Person
4. Member of armed forces or college faculty and employer	Rank	Person with higher rank
5. Distinguished visitor and employer	Rank	Visitor
6. Individual to a group	Convenience	The individual, then each person in the group

Handshaking

The practice of shaking hands reduces barriers between people. It is said that the way a person shakes hands, like other forms of body language, reveals a great deal about that person. An enthusiastic handshake, for example, is interpreted as pleasant since it signifies that the person is sincere in offering the greeting.

Handshaking is customary and almost automatic between men. However, when a man and a woman shake hands, usually the woman must make the first move by offering her hand. In a business office the position of the other person may preclude the secretary from taking the initiative. It is well to remember that one always accepts an extended hand. To do otherwise is a slight to the other person and probably will cause embarrassment.

The Difficult Visitor

Being courteous to certain visitors may require considerable discipline and restraint. Some callers are gruff; some are condescending; some are self-important or aggressive; some are even rude. To be gracious to these persons requires strong willpower.

A nuisance visitor can resort to all sorts of ruses to get past the secretary's desk. In such cases the secretary must exercise tact and firmness. Be wary of a person who, without giving a name, says, "I'm a personal friend" or "I have a personal matter to discuss with Miss Jones." The caller with important business has everything to gain by providing a name and stating the purpose of the visit. You may explain to the caller that you are not permitted to admit visitors unannounced. If the caller still refuses to give you this information, offer a piece of paper and request that a short note be written. Then enclose this note in an envelope and take it to the executive, who can then decide whether to admit the caller.

Some callers try to obtain information from the secretary either about the executive or about the company. Be wary of such questions. Do not answer them, except in generalities. A remark such as "I really don't know" will ordinarily stop such inquiries.

Interrupting a Conference

Most employers do not like to be interrupted during a conference. Interruptions are distracting and waste the time of all participants. For certain conferences you will be told that there are to be absolutely no interruptions. Most of the time, however, employers realize that an interruption is sometimes necessary. You and your employer should come to an understanding as to what matters warrant an interruption and also the best method to use—a written note or a telephone call.

An unobtrusive way to handle an interruption is to type the message on a slip of paper and take it into the office, usually without knocking. Give the message directly to your employer, and if it requires a reply wait for the answer.

As a general rule, however, keep interruptions to a minimum. Try to handle matters that arise yourself.

When there is a telephone call for the visitor, ask if you can take the message. If so, type it along with the caller's name, the date, and the time of the call. Then the message can be given to the visitor after the conference. If the one calling insists on speaking to the visitor, go into the conference room and say something like this: "Mr. Lawrence, Mrs. Rowett is on the telephone and wants to speak with you. Would you like to take the call here (*indicating which telephone he is to use*) or would you prefer using the telephone on my desk?" If the latter is chosen, the secretary takes care of other business away from the desk to afford the visitor privacy.

Some inconsiderate visitors do not know when to leave. Usually the employer rises as an indication that the conference is over; but occasionally a caller will not take the hint. You may help by taking a note in to the executive. This provides an opportunity to announce apologetically that it is time for another meeting. In order to free your employer, you may telephone from another person's desk to ask if an interruption is required. Often the mere

Mrs. Judkins

Your secretary just called and asked that
you call back within 20 minutes for a very
important message. There is a telephone
which you can use just outside the conference room. (Dial 9 for an outside line.)

A. A.

Mr. Zants

The secretary of Dr. Joseph Chou is on the
line at my desk and asks that you come to
the telephone for an important message from
the doctor. I'll wait outside my office while
you talk. Will you please let me know when
you are ready to leave my office?

A. A.

Illus. 3-3
Shown here are
two acceptable
ways in which to
handle typical
interruptions of
business
conferences.
Before acting, the
secretary decides
which procedure
will make the
interruption as
unobtrusive as
possible.

THE EMPLOYER'S APPOINTMENT RECORDS

A busy employer may see a number of visitors in the course of each day.
Therefore, in order to keep the work of the office running smoothly, you must
keep a record of the daily appointments. It is also a good practice to keep the
appointment records from year to year as a general reference source. The
effective secretary follows the employer's personal preferences in scheduling
appointments, keeps a close watch on the employer's time, and uses good
judgment in maintaining the appointment schedule.

Scheduling Appointments

Appointments are arranged in different ways. For example:

1. Using the appointment calendar from the previous year, the secretary
   schedules appointments for all recurring meetings at which the employer's

answering of the telephone affords a sufficient break in the conversation to
make the caller realize that the visit is over. Finally, you can reduce overlong
visits by informing the visitor upon entering of another scheduled appointment
in ten minutes.

presence is necessary (i.e., regularly scheduled conferences of boards or corporation committees) on the calendar at the beginning of the year. Additional recurring appointments are scheduled as new commitments are made.

2. The employer or the secretary may schedule an appointment over the telephone.

3. The executive or the secretary may schedule an appointment by mail.

4. The executive may ask the secretary to schedule an additional conference with someone who is in the office at that time.

5. The secretary may schedule a definite appointment with a caller who happened to come in when the employer was out.

6. The secretary may arrange for an appointment for the executive with individuals outside the company.

The secretary uses an appointment book to record the employer's appointments (see Illus. 3-4). Note that appointments are for half hour intervals. Calendars are also available in fifteen-minute segments.

In maintaining this book, the secretary follows the four *W*'s of scheduling appointments:

WHO the person is—the name, business affiliation, and telephone number
WHAT the person wants—an interview for a position, an opportunity to sell a product, or a business discussion (Indicate any materials that will be needed for the appointment.)
WHEN the person wants an appointment and how much time it will take
WHERE an appointment is to be held, if other than in the executive's office (Be sure to include the address and room number.)

Illus. 3-4
Appointment book illustrating memorandum column

APPOINTMENTS
FRIDAY, APRIL 9, 19--

Time	Engagements	Memorandums
9:00	Mr. Smith	HR—Call DC Mfrs re contract
9:30		
10:00	Meeting with Sales	
10:30	Personnel	See Jane Kumar for annual sales graph
11:00		
11:30	Mrs. Alice Carter	
12:00	Dr. Pardi	

If the individual making the appointment is in the office at the time of scheduling, the secretary furnishes a written reminder to that person.

In addition to the official appointment book, the executive generally keeps a pocket diary or calendar as a convenient reference when attending meetings or visiting outside offices. If this is the situation, you should check daily with the executive for possible conflicting dates and times.

The secretary's first duty each morning is to remind the employer of the appointment commitments for the day. Pertinent information and files are placed on his or her desk. Some employers prefer a typed list of the day's appointments along with other matters that must receive attention. This list can be placed on the employer's desk the day before or the first thing in the morning. The list may be on 8½- by 11-inch paper or even on a 5- by 3-inch card (see Illus. 3-5). Some employers prefer a separate list of matters to be handled that day. The appropriate files are then attached to this list. Any matters not completed that day will be carried over to the next day's list.

APPOINTMENTS AND REMINDERS FOR

Monday, April 7, 19--

```
10:00   Staff Meeting

11:00   James F. Syzek, Chamber of Commerce, 829-2300,
        Ext. 509, concerning the center development

11:30   Sally Bennington, Mutual Life, 829-4502,
        renewal of policy

12:00   Luncheon Meeting with Frank Snyder, University Club

2:00    Budget Meeting


Today's Reminders:

        Call Frances Prouloz, 425-0034
        Follow up on Emerson contract
        License No. 533-429-3001 expires end of month
        Review Inundo's proposal
```

Illus. 3-5
The secretary types the employer's appointments in appropriate format and places the list on the employer's desk the day before or the first thing in the morning.

Another successful practice is to include in the list any questions you may have. The executive can write the answers directly on the sheet and then leave the paper on the desk. In this way you can get the answers without disturbing your employer.

In addition to the official appointment book you maintain and the pocket calendar retained by the executive, your employer also may have an informal calendar on the desk. To avoid conflicts in scheduling appointments, you must check all calendars on a daily basis.

The administrative secretary who works for several executives maintains a separate appointment listing for each. The procedure for scheduling appointments is the same as that described in the foregoing paragraph (see Illus. 3-6).

JANUARY 14

	Altman	Cross	McNutt	Haynes	Froehlich
8:00		In Miami 305 989-1011			Courthouse 9-5
8:30					
9:00	R. Bunker 821-4211		L. Timmons 356-8254	C. Basil 789-9339	
9:30					
10:00			V. Stern 215-6139	Mrs. Kodtu 981-7991	
10:30	L. Samuels 203 420-1481				
11:00				T. Benjamin 201-621-0319	
11:30					
12:00	T. Bandino Lunch 973-1891		Lunch	Lunch	
12:30				R. Braun 239-7969	
1:00			F. Perry 888-6239	S. Solomon 914-6199	
1:30					
2:00	D. Amos 739-4989		S. Silver 219-4569	Leave for Chicago 3 p.m. flight	
2:30					
3:00			J. Taylor 819-1699		
3:30					
4:00	Out from here		B. Matthews 819-9393		
4:30					
5:00			L. Nelson 766-7916		
5:30					
6:00					
6:30					

Illus. 3-6
Appointment book kept by an administrative secretary for five principals

Keep appointment books and calendars for at least one year; they provide an excellent record of names, dates, and activities.

Date and Time Preferences. In selecting the date and time for an appointment, consider the personal preferences of the employer. Some guidelines to be considered are:

1. Schedule few, if any, appointments on Monday mornings, because the weekend accumulation of mail requires attention.
2. Provide unscheduled time between appointments so that they will not overlap.

3. On any day allow ample time in the schedule to take care of the mail.
4. Avoid late afternoon appointments so that the employer can complete the work of the day.
5. Avoid appointments just before a trip because of the last minute rush of work.
6. Avoid appointments on the first day after the executive's absence of several days, because of the accumulation of work.
7. Suggest two alternate times for the appointment rather than ask the caller when it would be convenient for an appointment.
8. Make appointments outside the office at convenient times for your employer; for example, the first thing in the morning on the way to the office, before or after lunch, or just before the end of the day.

Unless advised to the contrary, you must seek the approval of the employer in granting appointments. The appointment is tentatively recorded in the appointment book to be explained later and approved.

Avoiding Unkept Appointments. Nothing destroys good relations faster than an appointment not kept. Preventing conflicting appointments is one of the secretary's most difficult problems. Sometimes the executive forgets to tell the secretary about appointments made outside the office. Three suggestions from experienced secretaries may prove helpful:

1. Each morning try setting aside some time to review the day's appointment schedule with the employer. This may bring to mind an unrecorded appointment.
2. Provide the executive with a pocket diary to carry at all times. You may ask to see this book until the employer becomes accustomed to giving it to you for checking.
3. At the end of the day, remind the executive of any unusual appointments. These may include a very early morning appointment or a night meeting.

Sometimes an employer may be unavoidably detained in keeping an appointment. If so, you should, if possible, notify the next visitor by telephone and, after checking both calendars, suggest a later meeting time. Occasionally your employer may forget an appointment. You can be helpful by quickly locating him or her and seeing that the appointment is kept as scheduled. Sometimes the employer may be called out of town, necessitating the cancellation of appointments or arranging for another person to see the visitor. You should contact the visitor and tell of the cancellation without going into great detail. In all these situations the secretary should be discreet and noncommittal. Comments such as "Mr. Sloan has been unavoidably detained" or "Something unexpected has come up requiring a cancellation" are all that are required.

Saying No Tactfully. Obviously appointments should be refused as tactfully as possible. Refusals should be prefaced by a sincere "I'm very sorry, but . . . ." A logical reason for the refusal should always be given. Remember to use your employer's name rather than the impersonal pronoun when explaining the situation to the caller. Other tactful ways to refuse appointments are to explain that the executive is in conference, must attend a meeting on that day, has a heavy schedule for the next two weeks, or is preparing to leave town. If a caller seems very disappointed over a refusal, you might offer to talk with the caller yourself. From this conversation you can relay a message to the executive or take other appropriate, helpful action.

The Actual Appointment

From the appointment book, the secretary knows when to expect a person's arrival. If an individual within the company is late, it is entirely proper for you to telephone that person's office to see if there has been a delay.

Often more than one person is involved in an appointment or meeting. If possible, check the office before the meeting and see that there are enough chairs, pencils, note pads, and ashtrays. When the first conferee arrives, a problem is posed: Shall you tell the executive of the arrival or wait until the entire group has assembled? There is no hard and fast rule. The decision depends on the visitor's status, the employer's activity at the time, and individual preference. If the first visitor is very important, you may not only inform the employer of the arrival but may also notify the other conferees to assemble now. Otherwise, it is appropriate to wait until the whole group is assembled before informing the executive.

Before a meeting, you should provide any correspondence or material that will be helpful during the conference. Also, you should remain near the office during the conference in the event that additional information is needed. This is not the time to run office errands or take a coffee break.

When your employer is going to another office for a meeting, anticipate the papers and files that will be required and place them in the briefcase.

Scheduling Appointments by Letter

Appointments with persons out of the city are frequently made by letter. A request for an appointment should be answered promptly and completely. A typical letter granting an appointment follows:

```
Dear Mr. Graham

Mrs. Andrews will be pleased to interview you
on Friday, April 3, at 11 a.m. If you can't
be here at that time, please let me know. I
shall be glad to reschedule the appointment.

                        Sincerely yours
```

When refusing a request for an appointment, include a tactfully phrased explanation. Note the following example:

> Mrs. Andrews will be out of town the week of May 8. Therefore, she will not be able to meet with you on that date.
>
> She has asked me to express her regrets and has suggested that you contact her during the third week in May.

Canceling Appointments

If an appointment must be canceled, the secretary usually writes the out-of-town visitors concerned and telephones the local visitors. In the latter case, the executive often asks the secretary to write a letter confirming the cancellation to prevent embarrassment in case the telephone message was not received. If possible, the secretary schedules a new appointment immediately to take the place of the canceled one. The following is a typical letter of cancellation:

> Because Mrs. Andrews has been called out of town unexpectedly, she is disappointed that she cannot keep her appointment with you at 3 p.m. on July 19. When she returns I shall let you know so that we can arrange another appointment at a mutually convenient time.

SUGGESTED READINGS

The Amy Vanderbilt Complete Book of Etiquette, revised and expanded by Letitia Baldridge. New York: Doubleday & Company, Inc., 1978.

Doris, Lillian, and Besse M. Miller. *Complete Secretary's Handbook*, 4th ed., revised by Mary A. DeVries. Englewood Cliffs, N. J.: Prentice Hall Inc., 1977.

QUESTIONS FOR DISCUSSION

1. Why is the secretary often considered a public relations representative of a company?
2. Describe the uses of a card file for frequent callers, the register of visitors, and the appointment book. Which of these three office tools would you

regard as most important, and why? Do most offices need all three of these kinds of records? Explain your answer fully.

3. Contrast the problems of the administrative secretary with those of the multifunctional secretary in handling visitors.

4. When greeting office visitors, how can a secretary show *active* listening?

5. In the following situations you are asked to introduce the two persons specified. Which person would you afford the greater courtesy by naming first?
   (a) Your employer's 14-year-old daughter and a secretary in the office
   (b) A well-known politician and your employer, president of the company
   (c) Your elderly mother and your employer, Carl Samson
   (d) Miss Alvarez, a business product sales representative, and your employer, Ralph Hazelton
   (e) Rabbi Harold Silverman and your employer, Mr. Fishburg
   (f) Professor James Ford and Alfred Bostick, Dean, College of Business, both visitors in your office

6. In discussing an employer's absence from the office or in canceling an appointment, why should a secretary guard against giving specific reasons to a person outside the organization?

7. Generally employers do not like to be interrupted during a conference. Yet, as a secretary, you may have to talk with your employer. How would you proceed to do this?

8. Circle the proper word in parentheses. Then refer to the Reference Guide to correct your answers.
   (a) There were (less, fewer) people at the concert this year.
   (b) Linda can (cite, sight, site) the regulations from memory.
   (c) The (eminent, imminent) author has written so many best sellers that the literary prize seemed (eminent, imminent).
   (d) Because I will be moving (farther, further) away from the city, I have no (farther, further) interest in the position.
   (e) As a member of the (consul, council, counsel) on banking, he is in a position to give the president wise financial (consul, council, counsel).
   (f) The legislative committee will meet in the east wing of the (capital, capitol).

PROBLEMS

1. Analyze the following situations. How would you handle each of them? If the solution requires a conversation or note, indicate exactly what you would say. On a piece of paper, type your answer to each situation.
   (a) A visitor, while waiting for a scheduled appointment, makes the following statement: "I understand your employer was in New York last week."
   (b) Your employer's daughter has called the office three times within the last hour. Your employer is in a meeting with other officers of the company.
   (c) Your employer has called an important meeting in the office for 10:30 a.m. The company's most important customer arrives fifteen minutes early.

(d) A visitor whose appointment you forgot to cancel arrives as scheduled. Your employer is working under pressure to complete an important contract.

(e) An unscheduled visitor comes into the office to talk with your employer.

(f) Two important visitors are in the office with your employer. It is time for your coffee break.

(g) A caller who failed to keep the last two appointments telephones for a third one.

2. As secretary to Russell Sabin, of Universal Interiors, one of your responsibilities is to maintain his appointment book. The following appointments and activities have been scheduled for October 30. Type a list in attractive style to give to Mr. Sabin before the office closes the day before. Note any reminders at the bottom of the page.

(a) Mr. Sabin has an appointment with the president of Universal Interiors, Charles Mackey, at 9 a.m., in Mr. Mackey's office.

(b) A letter from S. T. White, of San Francisco, requested a 10 a.m. appointment which was granted by return mail.

(c) Mr. Sabin is to attend an Administrative Management Society meeting at 7:30 p.m. at the Hyde Hotel.

(d) Mrs. Unger, a marketing representative with Universal, has an appointment at 2 p.m. to show samples of home show decorations.

(e) Mr. Sabin must appoint a committee by November 1 to handle an outing for the Advertisers' Club.

(f) Luncheon at 12:30 with Carl Miller, controller of Universal, at Sullivan's on 10th Street. Mr. Sabin is to meet Mr. Miller downstairs at 12:15 for the short walk to the restaurant.

(g) Mr. White wrote that he is unable to keep the scheduled appointment for 10 a.m.

(h) Mr. Sabin is to interview an applicant, Miss Ellen Crane, at 11 a.m.

(i) Mr. Thornton, office manager, has requested Mr. Sabin to sit in on a meeting concerning office security at 3 p.m. in Thornton's office.

(j) Mr. Sabin requested that you make an appointment with Mr. Andrews at the bank sometime in the morning. You made the appointment for 10 a.m.

Part One

Case Problems

Case 1-1
WINNING
PROFESSIONAL
STATUS[1]

Ruth Freed was in her first week as secretary to Howard Gerard, sales manager for Consumer Products. She had been selected from a dozen applicants and was enthusiastic about her new position until she heard Mr. Gerard on the telephone: "Yes, I will get the figures to you immediately. In fact, I'll have my girl hand deliver them to you within fifteen minutes."

Ruth was annoyed by her designation as "my girl" and by the tactless "I'll have her. . . ." She immediately decided that she had made the wrong decision and would not work for such a sex biased person.

She delivered the figures, however, and said nothing. After thinking over the situation she realized that she liked everything about the new position except Mr. Gerard's attitude. She decided to plan a course of action that would change his feelings about secretarial employees and came to you for advice.

What would you tell her? Why?

Case 1-2
WHO'S THE
BOSS?

Sarah Gelazny was an administrative secretary assigned to four principals in the executive offices of NJL Company. She reported to Luis Carullo, the manager of the administrative support unit. One of Sarah's principals was Jo Peretta, who had been in her present position for 15 years and had had her own secretary until the introduction of a word processing center ten months ago.

Sarah soon found that of all her principals Miss Peretta was her favorite. She seemed more appreciative of the work Sarah did for her, brought her little gifts occasionally, and, as she said, "treated her like a lady." She realized that Miss Peretta sought her out for doing work. Because Sarah sensed that Miss Peretta disliked the new structure, she sympathized with her and whenever possible gave her time for the extras that were formerly handled by Miss Peretta's secretary. One morning Miss Peretta asked Sarah to type a confidential memorandum, saying, "I don't want to dictate to that infernal telephone, since just anybody could get hold of the information if it gets out of my office."

[1]Adapted from Ann Machele's interview by a panel of specialists charged with selecting the Secretary of the Year and used in an article in *Mademoiselle* (January, 1980), p. 132.

As Sarah was typing the memorandum on the only typewriter allowed in the unit, she was interrupted by Luis, who said, "Sarah, you must be working for Miss Peretta again. You know that your responsibilities do not include taking dictation. You know, too, that your work is to be assigned by me and that you are responsible only to me. You've got to learn who is in charge around here."

What should Sarah do in regard to both Luis and Miss Peretta? Is the new organization pattern dehumanizing the office? What argument can be made that could cause Miss Peretta to accept the change? How can Sarah retain good relations with her favorite principal?

Case 1-3
ENFORCING
SAFETY
REGULATIONS

Janet Simms works as a secretary in the Research and Development Department, an area that is vulnerable to accidents. She is a member of the Safety Committee, which has just issued a safety manual for all corporate employees. As a member of the committee, she is safety inspector for her division.

Dr. Fred Larrimore, a research chemist, is one of the worst violators of the safety measures. As Janet walked into his office to pick up a report for her employer on her way to lunch, he was reading a statistical report while smoking and leaning back in his chair with his feet on his desk. She stumbled over his briefcase, which he had left on the floor beside his desk when he came to work. Exasperated as well as frightened, Janet exclaimed, "Dr. Larrimore, haven't you read our safety manual? I could have injured myself by your carelessness. Why do you suppose we have a safety committee if the executives themselves are going to ignore the regulations?"

Dr. Larrimore apologized, but failed to remove the briefcase to safe quarters, gave her the report, and returned to his former position. Janet, too, apologized for speaking to a superior rudely, and left.

What management principle should Janet follow to secure compliance with regulations?

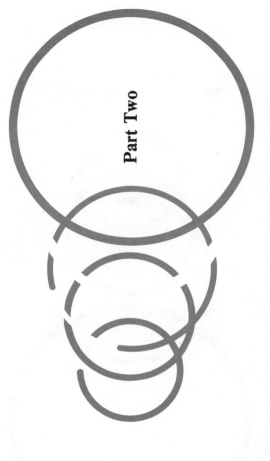

Part Two

INFORMATION PROCESSING: EQUIPMENT AND ITS UTILIZATION

The impact of new office technology has influenced both the organizational structure and working procedures in the modern office. Text editors, computer access terminals, and high-speed copiers are only a few of the electronically controlled devices designed to take the drudgery out of routine office tasks. As a college-trained secretary, you will be at the center of the changes taking place in information processing.

To cope with these technological advances, you must learn the new equipment and procedures discussed in the following chapters. Keep in mind that your ability to master new equipment and methods of performing secretarial tasks will increase your value to your employer and put you ahead of your competition for a job.

Chapter 4

Secretarial Typing and Supplies

The ability to produce error free, attractive typewritten copy is still a basic requirement of the secretarial position. This is true whether you see yourself as an administrative support secretary or correspondence secretary to a number of executives, or a multifunctional secretary working on a one-to-one basis with your employer.

This chapter focuses on the various kinds of typewriters, the supplies associated with the typing tasks, and the most effective procedures for producing superior work. Familiarity with different kinds of typewriters, supplies, and procedures will help make your job easier and your output more attractive.

TYPEWRITERS

The secretary may have to operate one or more of these basic types of electric typewriters: standard type bar, single element, and electronic. This section will discuss the features of these typewriters and their variables.

Standard Type Bar Electric Typewriters

The standard type bar electric typewriter is marketed by a number of manufacturers, but it is gradually being replaced in the office by the single element machine. Although designed primarily for correspondence and general office work, the type bar electric can be equipped for such special purposes as billing, preparing material for the bulletin board, typing name tags for conventions, typing statistical tables, and preparing oversized letters for TV and movie prompting materials.

Single Element Typewriters

The single element typewriter eliminates the type bars and movable carriage, and replaces them with a sphere the size of a golf ball that moves on its own carrier from left to right across the paper. Alphabetic and special symbols are embossed on the surface of the sphere. Striking a key positions

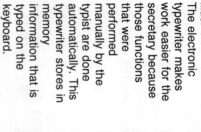

the element to type that letter or symbol. There is no problem with jamming the keys, and there is less vibration when the single element typewriter is used.

The first single element typewriter to receive wide acceptance was the IBM Selectric. Many other manufacturers, such as Adler, Cimatron, Facit, Olympia, Royal, and Sperry Remington have single element machines on the market today.

A distinctive feature of the single element machine, which the type bar machine cannot match, is that it permits the use of a wide variety of type styles and special symbols. Over 75 interchangeable elements are available, each with a different type style or with different symbols. To change the type style, the operator removes the element and, in a few seconds, inserts one with the desired type style. Furthermore, some single element machines enable the typist to switch from pica type (ten characters per inch) to elite type (twelve characters per inch) simply by releasing a lever and changing the element.

One single element machine that has gained wide acceptance among secretaries is the self-correcting typewriter introduced by IBM. Through the use of lift off tape and a single button on the keyboard, errors are lifted off the page. The correction key makes it unnecessary to erase on the original; therefore, typing is faster, neater, and easier.

Electronic Typewriters

The electronic typewriter is a relative newcomer to the office. Unlike an electric typewriter with roughly 1,000 levers, springs, gears, and screws inside the case, the electronic typewriter has almost no works. Only a printing

The typist can change the pitch on the IBM Selectric II from 10 to 12 characters per inch merely by moving a lever.

Illus. 4-1
The electronic typewriter makes work easier for the secretary because those functions that were performed manually by the typist are done automatically. This typewriter stores information that is typed on the keyboard.

A. B. Dick Company

FEATURES OF ELECTRONIC TYPEWRITERS

Automatic Centering and Underscoring	Copy can automatically be centered between margins or between tab settings.
Electronic Margins and Tabs	Frequently used margins and tabs can be stored and recalled when needed.
Error Correction	The operator can correct errors by backspacing and striking over. A word or full line can be erased with one key stroke.
Decimal Tab	Statistical columns are automatically aligned at the decimal point. This feature is especially useful in typing financial and other statistical reports.
Automatic Carriage Return	A hot zone is established consisting of five to seven characters before the right margin. The carrier automatically returns when the word ending the line comes within the hot zone. Some systems perform no hyphenations but automatically wrap any word that will not fit entirely on the line being typed to the next line. Generally it is possible for the typist to bypass the automatic carrier return and make manual word divisions to maintain a more even right margin.
	Some systems provide a feature called Scan which permits the operator to examine the material. The system will stop at any place where a hyphenation decision is required.
	The automatic carrier return has the advantage of allowing the operator to type text at a uniform pace without having to pause at the end of each line to return the carrier.
Dual Pitch	Most electronic typewriters provide ten and twelve characters to the inch and a wide variety of type styles.
Proportional Spacing	Models containing this feature permit the operator to justify (even up) right margins.
Automatic Indentation	By depressing the carrier return key, the operator returns the carrier automatically to the desired place in the copy. In other words, the typewriter remembers where to indent once the operator has decided where indentations are needed.
Automatic Relocate	When it is necessary for a typist to go into the body of a document to make a correction, the relocate key will return the carrier to the point where typing is to be resumed after the correction has been made.
Phrase Dictionary Storage	Some electronic typewriters provide a self-contained dictionary that will store 7,000 to 8,000 characters on an electronic chip. This is the equivalent of storing five one-page letters of average length. Frequently used words, phrases, sentences, and paragraphs can also be stored and played back without retyping.

element glides across the paper. When the keys are depressed, a handful of tiny silicon chips about one-fourth inch square tell the machine what to do. The distinguishing feature of this typewriter is its memory. Material once keyboarded is often stored internally and retrieved automatically.

Most major typewriter manufacturers have introduced electronic typewriters with a wide range of special features.

RIBBONS, STATIONERY, AND CARBON PAPER

Most supplies with which a secretary works are available in a wide range of quality. Many factors, particularly the use and quality, must be considered in the selection of supplies.

Typewriter Ribbons

Typewriter ribbons are of three types: one-time film, multiuse film, and fabric. Each type has certain properties to recommend it for the specific kind or quality of work desired.

The sharpness of typewritten work will depend upon the thinness of the ribbon used: the thinner the ribbon, the sharper the imprint; also, the thinner the ribbon, the more yardage on a spool. This means less frequent ribbon changes. Ribbons range from cotton (the thickest) to nylon, to coated Mylar, to polyethylene film (the thinnest).

One-Use Film Ribbon: Also called carbon ribbon. Continuous, narrow, coated strip that advances at the rate of one stroke per space on the ribbon. Used once and discarded. Produces uniformly even type on page. Preferred for high quality work.

Multiuse Film Ribbon: Similar to one-use film ribbon, except that the same spot can be struck from six to nine times. No variation in print density. Designed to travel very slowly from spool to spool. Does not reverse and is discarded when it comes to the end. Provides security of information, since the imprinted ribbon on the spent spool cannot be read as it can on the one-use film ribbon. Has longer life than one-use film ribbon.

Fabric Ribbons: Because they print very sharply, do not fill the letters, are clean to handle, and erase easily, film base ribbons are preferred for high quality work.

Nylon longest wearing and thinnest. Fabric ribbon economical and appropriate for most in-house communications. Available in several colors and concentrations of ink.

Special Purpose Ribbons: Offset ribbon for typing offset masters, photostat ribbon for preparing copy for photostating, and opaque ribbons for photocopy work.

Colored
Ribbons: Available in various colors to complement company letter-heads and add distinction to correspondence. Available with lift off tape for the IBM Correcting Selectric typewriter.

Bond Paper

Bond paper is so called because originally it was used for printing bonds, which had to have long lasting qualities. It can be made from all cotton fiber (sometimes called *rag*), from all sulfite (a wood pulp), or from any proportion of the two. High cotton fiber bond suggests quality and prestige, and it ages without deterioration or chemical breakdown. It has a good, crisp crackle. It is hard to the pencil touch and is difficult to tear. High sulfite bond is limp, soft to the pencil touch, and easy to tear.

There are excellent all sulfite papers in crepelike, ripple, or pebble finishes that many companies use exclusively. Letterhead paper is usually made of 25 percent, or more, cotton fiber bond. Forms for business records usually are made of all sulfite or high sulfite bond.

Watermarks. Hold a piece of paper up to the light. See the design or words? That is the *watermark*. It can be the name or trademark of the company using the paper or the brand name of the paper. Since only better bond paper is watermarked, the mark is a hallmark of quality.

There is a right side and a top edge to the plain watermarked sheets. Always have the watermark read across the sheet in the same direction as the typing. Put watermarked sheets in your stationery drawer in such a manner that they will be in the right position automatically when they are inserted in the typewriter.

Substance. The weight of paper is described by a substance number. The number is based on the weight of a ream consisting of 500 sheets of 17- by 22-inch paper. If the ream weighs 20 pounds, the paper is said to be of substance 20, or 20-pound weight. Two thousand sheets of 8½- by 11-inch paper can be cut from one ream. Paper is produced in a wide range of weights. Regular letterhead paper and envelopes are usually of substance 16, 20, or 24. Airmail stationery, now used primarily for overseas correspondence, is usually of substance 9 or 11.

Erasability. You can erase typing from some bond papers very easily. This feature is usually indicated in the brand name of the paper, such as *Ezerase* or *Corrasable*. Ribbon ink or carbon rests lightly on the surface of the paper at first, until it is gradually absorbed into the paper. Thus, you can quickly and neatly remove fresh typing with a pencil eraser. But you can also easily smear or smudge the surrounding typing.

The most difficult papers on which to make neat erasures and corrections are the inexpensive all sulfite ones like those you probably used in your typing course. A neat erasure can be made without too much difficulty on a 16-pound high cotton fiber bond.

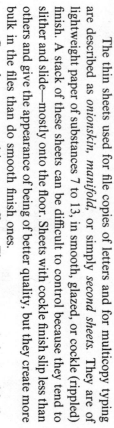

Second Sheets

The thin sheets used for file copies of letters and for multicopy typing are described as *onionskin, manifold,* or simply *second sheets.* They are of lightweight paper of substances 7 to 13, in smooth, glazed, or cockle (rippled) finish. A stack of these sheets can be difficult to control because they tend to slither and slide—mostly onto the floor. Sheets with cockle finish slip less than others and give the appearance of being of better quality, but they create more bulk in the files than do smooth finish ones.

Copy sheets are used in many offices. They are second sheets with the word COPY printed on them and are used for copies of material that should be so identified. When necessary, indicate that a plain sheet is a copy by typing the word COPY conspicuously in all capital letters, letterspaced, and centered from seven to nine line spaces from the top of the sheet.

Letterheads

Letterheads vary widely and depend on individual taste and the nature of the company's business. Most large companies have a standard company letterhead that includes the company's name, address, telephone number (including area code), and sometimes the name and title of an individual. The letterhead may contain information about the company's product or display the company's trademark. All letterheads may be ordered with matching envelopes and blank sheets for two-page letters.

Top management usually has prestige letterheads that differ from the standard company letterhead in style, printing process, weight, and cotton fiber content.

The letterhead of top management usually shows only the company name, address (no phone number), and the executive's name and title. In addition, the executive may have a personal letterhead that is used mainly for outside work with foundations or charity organizations. Personal letterheads may show only the executive's name and address, or the name only. In general, as an individual is elevated in the company, his or her letterhead acquires simplicity and the dignity befitting the position. The trend in all letterheads is toward simplicity.

Carbon Paper

Traditional typewriter carbon paper is thin, dark-colored tissue, coated on one side with carbon. It is available in a great variety of sizes, colors, weights, finishes, and qualities. It can be obtained in special purpose packs as well as in single sheets. Following is a brief description of the various kinds of carbon paper.

Topcoated: Top side coated with finish that prevents curling. Reduces wrinkling which causes "trees" or "veins" on the copy. A good grade is usually smudge free and long lasting.

Conventional: Basically the same as topcoated but comes in different finishes, such as soft and hard. The finish preferred depends on the typewriter (manual or electric), size of typeface, hardness of cylinder, and number of copies to be made.

Plastic Base: Similar in appearance to carbon paper but more accurately described as a copying film. It employs ink, not carbon. Made of film, not paper. Curl free, easily handled, and difficult to tear. Smudge free. Long wearing. Used for high quality work.

Special Features: *Extended uncoated side or bottom edge* that permits easy, smudge free handling. *Micrometric edge* that contains a numbered guide on an extended right edge which shows unused lines on the page. *Carbon sets* which are preassembled and convenient to use; can be used only once.

GUIDE TO SELECTION OF CARBON PAPER FINISH AND WEIGHT

Finish

Soft	USE IF—typewriter has a soft cylinder
	USE IF—copies are grayer than desired when using other finishes.
	DO NOT USE IF—typewriter has elite or smaller typeface.
Hard	USE IF—typewriter has a hard cylinder.
	USE IF—typewriter has elite or smaller typeface.
	USE IF—gray copy is acceptable.
Medium	USE—for all typing situations not covered above.

Weight

FOR MAKING ORIGINAL PLUS:

Light	9 or more copies
Medium	5 to 8 copies*
Medium Standard	2 to 7 copies
Standard	1 to 4 copies

*Consider weight of copy paper used and adjust weight of carbon.

LETTERHEADS AND ENVELOPES

Letterheads	Matching Envelopes

Letterheads

Standard Company Use
Business size: 8½" × 11"

Usually of 16 or 20 # bond, 25% cotton fiber (rag) | No. 10 (4⅛" × 9½")

Top Executive Use

Standard and Monarch size (Monarch size: 7¼" × 10") | No. 10 and No. 7 (3⅞" × 7½")

Usually 24 # bond, 100% cotton fiber content | Same weight and fiber content as letterhead

Color

Usually white; however, tinted pastel shades are increasing in popularity.

Plain Sheets to Match Letterheads

Same weight, cotton fiber content, and size as letterhead (*Never use a letterhead for the second or subsequent pages of a letter.*)

Letterheads and Envelopes for Overseas Correspondence

Letterheads: lightweight, 9 to 11 # maximum
Envelopes: Bordered for AIRMAIL, weight to match letterheads

Interoffice Letterheads

Business size or half size (8½" × 5½"); usually of 16 or 18 # sulphite

Interoffice Envelopes

Oversize, strong, perforated, reusable envelopes with many ruled lines for the names of successive addressees

Oversize Envelopes

Strong white or manila envelopes that allow letters and reports to be mailed unfolded; 9" × 12", 10" × 13"; gummed flaps with or without metal clasps.

OTHER PAPER SUPPLIES

Carbon Copy Paper

Thin sheets, usually 8# to 13#, in various sizes, colors, and finishes; called second sheets, onionskin, or manifold paper.

Carbon Paper

For description and use, see page 78.

Duplicator Paper

Business[1] and legal[2] sizes, white and colors, various substances; often called by the process the paper is made for, such as mimeograph paper, offset paper. *Duplicating* paper usually refers to paper designed for use with the direct process duplicator. Many modern duplicators do not require special paper.

Forms

Usually in pads to prevent waste. Multicopy forms may be continuous, accordion folded, and perforated. After the "chain" is inserted in the typewriter to type the first set, the rest feed through automatically. Accordion folded forms often have spot carbon coating on the back of each copy exactly where the typing is to appear on the copy underneath. This eliminates handling interleaved carbon.

Labels, Return Address

Small slips of paper showing company's return address; are usually gummed on the back.

Legal Paper

Top quality legal size bond; plain or with ruled margins

Second Sheets

Thin sheets for typing rough drafts or carbons; legal size or business size

Plain Sheets

Paper 8½" × 11", usually 13# to 16#, most often used for reports and for general typing; may or may not be of easy-to-erase bond

Writing Pads

Ruled Paper: Legal size or business size, usually yellow
Scratch: Assorted sizes; usually sold by the pound

---

[1]*Business size: 8½" × 11"*
[2]*Legal size: 8½" × 13 or 14"*

OFFICE FORMS

American business *runs* on paper forms. In fact, every business function involves some type of business form at some point in its operation. A function is either initiated by a form, authorized by one, recorded on one, or summarized on one. Thus, everyone in a business organization is involved with paper work, and the secretary is no exception. A significant portion of the secretary's time is spent in completing forms, copying information on forms, reading forms, interpreting forms, routing forms, filing forms, using forms for reference, and handling and transmitting forms. Furthermore, the secretary is not only a user of forms but may be a designer of them.

Types of Forms

Modern technology and business ingenuity have provided multiple copy business forms in different configurations that encompass many timesaving features.

Unit Set and Snap-out Forms:	Also called carbon sets or carbon packs. Preassembled with interleaved one-time carbons. Each unit is self-contained. Permits easy removal of carbons; timesaving; convenient, since they allow one-motion removal of the carbons.
Carbonless Forms:	Permits impressions from copy to copy through dyes and chemicals built into the paper. Timesaving. Smudge free. Less bulk increases the number of copies that can be made.
Continuous Forms:	Forms joined together in a series of accordion-pleated folds. Timesaving. Used for quantity work, such as processing invoices, statements, purchase orders, payroll checks, and the like.
Spot Carbon Coated Forms:	Carbon applied at designated spots on back of each form in pack. Permits production of a number of different forms at one writing: packing slip, shipping order, address label, inventory withdrawal slip, and invoice—each containing only the appropriate data.

Forms Control and Design

As a business expands, the number of forms that it needs seems to multiply at an astonishing rate. Consequently, most large business and government organizations have established systems for forms control. Such systems provide for a periodic review and the discontinuance of any forms that have become useless or obsolete. Provision is also made for the establishment of definite procedures for the preparation and approval of new forms.

The secretary may be expected to exercise a similar control over the forms originating in the executive's office. This would include a systematic review of all forms for their possible improvement, the elimination of unneeded forms, and the designing of new forms that will expedite the work of the office. In designing new forms, consider the following factors:

Necessity. Is a separate form really needed? Could it be combined with an existing form? In what ways will a new form save time?

Wording. Does the title clearly indicate the purpose of the form? Does it contain a code number for filing reference? Does the form contain all necessary information? Does it provide *only* necessary information? (Example: The company name is not needed on intra-company forms.) Does the form mechanize the writing of repetitive data? Are code numbers and check boxes used to eliminate unnecessary typing?

Disposition. Does each copy of the form clearly indicate its disposition? Is color coding or other appropriate means used to facilitate distribution?

Arrangement. Is the form compatible with the equipment on which it is to be used? (Example: If it is to be filled in on a typewriter, do the type lines conform to typewriter vertical line spacing and require a minimum of tabulator stops?) Does the sequence in which the data are to be inserted on the form follow the sequence of the information on the data source? Is there the right amount of fill-in space? Will the arrangement of the form speed operations?

Retention. If the form is to be retained, how and where? Does the form size fit the filing system?

BEFORE DESIGNING A FORM—Answer these questions:

What is the purpose of the form?

How does it affect other procedures? other forms?

Can it be combined with another form?

Where does the information originate? Where does it go?

Where do parts go?

How is the form filed?

Will additional copies ever be needed?

What types of data will appear on the form? Words? Figures? Checkmark responses?

Does the form present information in a logical sequence?

Can the form be easily identified by title, number, or color?

Is the form a standard size that can be processed on existing equipment?

OFFICE SUPPLIES

The executive usually delegates to the secretary the responsibility of procuring the proper office supplies. Unless the executive has a special need or high cost factors are involved, the secretary uses personal judgment in making selections. The procedures for obtaining office supplies differ for the secretary in a large office and the secretary in a small office. However, both must have a knowledge of supplies in order to choose those that best fill particular executive and secretarial needs.

The secretary in a small office is a direct buyer. In a large office, however, the secretary may request forms and supplies from a central stock or requisition them from the purchasing department. The secretary who has supervisory responsibilities may select and purchase for a department or company. In this case the sources of product information must be used to learn the comparative factors and to find dependable sources. Businesslike purchasing procedures, of course, must be followed.

Quality of Supplies

Some business people believe it important to use only the highest quality stationery, forms, and office supplies; others find medium quality adequate. Every office uses a pride factor and an economic factor to determine the level of quality it pursues. You will not find this quality level precisely stated or written out for you. Nor is it a question you can tactfully ask. You can deduce it, though, by observation of the present supplies and cost records.

Local Sources of Supply

Local office supply stores cannot carry all varieties of all brands of all office supplies. Each store carries one or two brands of an item (perhaps not your favorite) in the varieties most commonly sold, none of which may exactly fill your needs. Therefore, your selection is limited and often you cannot buy as discriminatingly as you would like.

Sales Representatives. Representatives of office supply agencies may call on you with samples or price catalogs. They, too, limit themselves in brands and varieties; so choice is again restricted. The secretary orders over the telephone from the sales office. Since you cannot possibly know everything about all supplies, it is helpful to have a dependable sales representative of whom you can ask advice. When you are in the market for an item, explain your exact needs. Sales representatives are trained to help you make a wise selection.

Brand Name Supplies. Sometimes you want a *specific variety of a specific brand*. If the variety is not sold locally, you can order it from the manufacturer or ask your local office supply store to order it for you.

Some pieces of equipment, you may decide, produce better results if you use the supplies that are sold by the manufacturer. These might include using A. B. Dick ink for the mimeograph, or Gestetner correction fluid for Gestetner stencils. If no local source is listed in the telephone book, you can request the manufacturer to send your dealer information on the availability of their products.

Collecting Information

Collect specific information about each kind of office supply you use. Suppliers furnish helpful literature. Descriptive, informative folders are often furnished by sales representatives or are given away at exhibits of office equipment and supplies. Collect and file such information by subject. It will help you to be a better buyer.

Choosing Supplies

Choose supplies that are in the quality range of your office. There is no economy in cheap supplies. Unknown brands may contain inferior materials or may be off-sized. Consequently, they may be more expensive in the long run than the better grades. *Usually you get just about what you pay for.* A carbon paper of good quality gives many more writings.

There is no reason for shifting from one brand of supply to another as long as the one in use is satisfactory and fair in price. On the other hand, supplies are constantly being changed. A product may now be made of entirely different materials and hence may be greatly improved since the last time you examined or tested it.

When contemplating a change in brand, get samples of competing products and test them all under the same circumstances. Compare net prices and quality. Analyze the extra service or added efficiency claimed. If the price is higher, you should decide whether the difference is justified.

Overbuying

Some office supplies deteriorate when they are held in stock too long. For example, carbon paper dries and hardens, typewriter ribbons dry out, some paper becomes yellow, liquids evaporate, and erasers harden. New products may be preferable to those you have stocked. It is better, then, to err on the side of underbuying than of overbuying. Repeat orders can always be placed shortly before supplies are needed.

You may tend to overbuy because of quantity prices. An item that costs 50 cents a unit in small quantities usually costs appreciably less when bought in large quantities. Consequently, it may seem to be economical to order in large amounts. The monetary saving is not always the prime consideration, however.

Some suppliers of paper have arrangements whereby a year's supply may be purchased at one time. Thus you obtain the price advantage of a bulk purchase. The paper is delivered in specific lots at designated intervals through the year. Such a plan provides a price advantage without the problem of storing the paper before it is needed.

Requisitions and Invoices

In a large company, most of the supplies are kept in stock and are obtained by submitting a supply requisition or a written request. Items not carried in stock must be requested by submitting a purchase requisition to the purchasing department. This form should provide as detailed a description of the needed item as the secretary can provide.

A secretary or supervisor who has the authority to purchase supplies has added responsibilities. These include making a careful record of each item purchased or ordered, checking out the delivery of the items, and verifying the accuracy of the items and extensions of the invoice or bill that accompanies or follows delivery.

When an item is invoiced (included and charged on an invoice) but is omitted, substituted, or defective, the secretary notes that fact on the invoice and requests an adjustment.

Storage of Supplies

If you wish to determine how neat and orderly a secretary really is, examine the supply storage cabinet. Certainly a storage cabinet that presents an array of boxes, packages, and articles in complete disorder is no recommendation for efficiency.

The well-arranged storage cabinet has several characteristics. Similar materials are placed together. Materials used most frequently are placed to the front at the most convenient level for reaching. Small items are placed at eye level; bulk supplies and reserve stock are placed on the lower shelves. Shelf depths should be adjustable to fit the items and thus to conserve space.

All packages are identified by oversize lettering made with a marking pen, or by a sample of the contents affixed to the front. Unpadded stationery items are kept in flip-up, open-end boxes. (There are no carelessly torn-open, paper-wrapped packages.) Loose supplies, such as paper clips, are kept separately in marked open boxes. A list of all supplies by shelves is often posted on the inside of the door.

YOU AND YOUR TYPEWRITER

Typing competence is more than speed with accuracy. It is economy in using time and supplies and knowing how to organize your work. It is also discovering ways to increase your output and efficiency. These competencies come only with experience. Become at ease with your typewriter quickly by exploring its features and learning its capabilities. Then give it the care it requires.

Instruction Booklets

Every typewriter has a helpful, reassuring booklet of instructions on its use. The booklet accompanies the machine on delivery but often disappears before the machine does. If your predecessor has not left the instruction booklet for you, request one from the manufacturer. It will save you time and give you confident know-how. There is nothing worse than struggling with a strange typewriter.

Learn the capacities of your typewriter. It may have features of which you are not aware, such as aids to accurate realignment of typing, scales to determine center positions, fractional spacing devices, and tabulation time-savers. The special features of your typewriter are illustrated and explained in the instruction booklet.

Typewriter Care

Even though a typewriter is sturdy and almost self-sufficient, it does require attention from you. Read the machine care section of your instruction booklet. No amount of skill is going to produce good copy if the typewriter is not kept in excellent working condition.

CARBON COPIES

The number of carbon copies being prepared in the office has been decreasing because of the accessibility of the copying machine. Making corrections on multiple carbons is a slow, costly, and boring process. Consequently, secretaries have a love affair with the copying machine, and in all too many cases the copier is overused to produce a very costly substitute for the carbon copy. The high cost of operating and maintaining the copying machine and the cost of time lost going to and from the copier results in a very high per copy cost. Consequently, management consultants are emphasizing that the carbon copy is the least expensive method of producing the necessary copies of outgoing correspondence and short reports.

Obviously, then, the copying machine is not a replacement for the carbon copy in all situations. There is a continuing need for the secretary to be skilled in handling carbon paper and in producing carbon copies. The secretary also needs to be able to make the decision when to use carbons and when to use the copier.

Time-Savers

Keep a tab stop permanently set for the center of your stationery. You can then center by the backspace method. When typing columns of figures with varying digits, set two tab stops for each column: one for 100,000 and one for 100. Keep a desk copy of frequently typed reports. Indicate on each the tab stop numbers and centering positions for all significant lines.

Time-Saver

To bring an address book up to date, type the new address on a gummed label and paste the label over the old address.

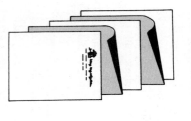

The typing techniques concerning carbon copies given here may seem commonplace; but the procedures are those used by master typists. They will allow you to produce quality typing and to save motion, time, and material.

Carbon Sheets—Copying Film

You will find the following practices in using carbon film sheets to be paper savers and time-savers:

1. Keep your desk supply of carbon film sheets flat with the carbon ink side down to prevent curling. Keep the sheets away from heat or dampness, and inside a folder or box.

2. Reverse carbon film sheets end-for-end each time you use them, because the carbon quickly wears off on spots where the dateline and other letter-part positions fall.

3. Discard a sheet at once if it becomes wrinkled or treed.

4. Do not discard a sheet just because it looks worn or because the shine is off the carbon side. Instead check the clarity of the last copy typed. Discard the carbon film sheet only when the copy is faint.

5. Use extended bottom edge carbon paper with cut off corners for the most efficient removal and reuse. If the carbon film sheets are square cornered, lay them carbon ink side down and cut off one-inch triangles from the top left and bottom right corners. This space provides room to hold the set of typed sheets and to remove the set of carbons intact in one quick, clean pull. See Illus. 4-3B.

6. Use carbon film sheets with cut off corners as a visual check for the proper insertion of carbons into the carbon pack. With the carbon pack in typing position, the cutoff should be visible in the top left corner. If the cutoff shows at the right, you have inserted the carbon ink side up (which happens occasionally to the most careful of secretaries).

Making Up a Carbon Pack

Two methods of making up and inserting a carbon pack are the *desk method* and the *machine method.*

Desk Method. Using the following procedure, assemble the carbon pack and insert it directly into the typewriter.

1. Place a sheet of paper on the desk; on top of that sheet, place a sheet of carbon film paper, *glossy side down.* Add one set (a second sheet and a carbon) for each extra copy desired. Place a letterhead or a plain sheet of heavier paper on top of the pack for the original copy.

2. Turn the pack around so that the glossy sides of the carbon sheets face you.

3. To keep the sheets straight when feeding, use a *leader*—place the pack in the fold of an envelope or in the fold of a narrow folded piece of paper.

4. Straighten the pack by tapping the sheets on the desk.

5. Insert the leadered pack with a quick turn of the cylinder; roll it up, and remove the leader.

Machine Method. Using the following procedure, build the carbon pack right in the machine.

1. Arrange the required number and kinds of sheets for insertion in the typewriter.
2. Insert the sheets normally, turning the cylinder until the sheets are gripped slightly by the feed rolls; then bring all but the last sheet forward over the cylinder.
3. Place the carbon film sheets between the sheets of paper, with the carbonized surface (glossy side) toward you. Flip each sheet back as you add each carbon.
4. Roll the pack into typing position.
5. When the typing is completed, roll the pack nearly to the bottom of the sheets. Operate the paper release lever and remove the copy sheets by pulling them out with one hand. The paper fingers will automatically hold the carbon film sheets in the machine. Remove these sheets with the other hand.

Illus. 4-3A
An efficient typist folds an envelope or a slip of paper over a carbon pack as a leader for inserting the pack in the typewriter rapidly and evenly.

Illus. 4-3B
Correct positioning of the cutoffs at the upper left and lower right corners of the carbon paper permits easy removal of the carbons from the pack.

Adjusting the Impression Regulator

Most electric typewriters are equipped with an impression regulator to adjust the pressure with which the key strikes the paper. This regulator should

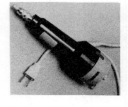

CORRECTIONS

be adjusted to the thickness of the carbon pack. In general, it should be set at the lowest pressure that will produce the required number of copies. Pressure set too high will emboss the letterhead or front sheet, and the carbon impressions will be heavy and lack sharpness.

Avoiding Bottom Line Slippage

To control bottom line slippage, roll the pack back to about mid-page. From the back, drop a sheet of paper between the original and the first carbon. Roll the pack forward. As you type near the bottom, the extra sheet will hold the pack securely in place. Steady the top sheet with one forefinger if necessary.

Typewriter corrections that defy detection are evidence of the master typist. They are an absolute necessity for quality typing. In fact, if any correction is evident in an otherwise excellent piece of typing, the typescript drops from quality level. The three techniques for making nonevident corrections are (1) careful removal of the error, (2) perfect positioning, and (3) matched typing.

Careful Erasing

A neat erasure results from the skillful use of erasing tools. The erasing tools are easily obtained, but erasing skill is acquired by patience and practice.

Erasers and Shields. Erasers and shields are available in a variety of sizes, forms, textures, and materials. For corrections you will need two kinds of erasers—a soft eraser to remove surface ink and carbon smears, and a more abrasive eraser to remove imbedded ink. Try various brands and shapes of erasers until you find those that you can use most effectively.

Unless you use an electric eraser, use a flat metal or plastic shield with letter height open spaces to confine the erasing. Such a shield can be used for erasures on papers in or out of the typewriter. The shield permits erasing to the extreme edge of the error without eradicating correctly typed adjacent letters.

A pressure proof shield of metal or card stock is used to protect the carbon copies under the page being erased. A curved metal shield that hugs the cylinder gives the best protection and is easiest to find among the papers on the desk.

Cover-Ups. To fade out an erasure, rub a whitening agent into the paper before typing the correction. A piece of chalk, an aspirin, or a commercial cover-up stick can be used.

Instead of erasing, a white correction fluid marketed under such trade names as Snopake and Liquid Paper may be painted over the error.[1] If this is done carefully and if the fluid matches the paper in whiteness, acceptable results can be achieved.

Another cover-up method is to put a chalk or chemically coated strip of paper, coated side down, over the error and retype the *error* so that some of the chalk transfers and covers it. Then go back and type the correction. A special type of cover-up paper is available for use on carbon copies.

White, self-adhesive correction tape is available in one-line, two-line, and three-line widths. The required length of tape is torn off and placed over the error. Corrections are then typed on top of the tape. Since the correction is obvious, restrict this method to use on copy where appearance may not be important, such as interoffice communications, dummy layouts, and material that is to be duplicated by photographic or offset process.

Lift Offs. Self-correcting devices consist of a separate correction ribbon attached to the typewriter or provided in a separate ribbon cartridge. When an error is made, the typist shifts to the correction mode. Errors are removed by typing over the error with the second ribbon. This ribbon contains a chemical that interacts with the ink on the paper and literally fades or lifts off the error. On some machines this is done by depressing a special key; on others, it involves shifting the ribbon control or inserting a special correction cartridge. The typist then backspaces, strikes over the error, and types the correction. On SCM machines the operator ejects the ribbon cartridge, inserts the correction cartridge, makes the correction, removes the correction cartridge, reinserts the ribbon cartridge, and resumes typing.

Perfect Positioning for Corrections

It is easy to reposition the carriage or element for an immediate correction, unless the error occurs at the very bottom of the page. In that case, do not try to correct it at once, for the sheets almost always slip out of line during erasing and repositioning. Instead finish typing the page, remove the pack from the typewriter, and then make the correction on each copy separately.

To save time in repositioning, learn the exact relationship of your typing line to your aligning scale. To acquire speed in realigning, watch intently as you type a line of words and notice the exact distance *at the typing point* between the bottom of the typed line and the aligning scale. It is the barest fraction of an inch, but memorizing it visually helps you to realign more quickly and accurately.

You can find the approximate letter position more quickly by keeping the paper guide set at one spot and using it squarely each time you insert sheets

Tips to the Typist

Proofread before copy is removed from the typewriter. This makes corrections easier.

---

[1] Send a sample of your office stationery to the manufacturer of the correction fluid, and the manufacturer will prepare fluid that matches your letterhead.

in the typewriter. On a reinserted sheet move the carriage or element to the first letter of the correction. The typing point will be in almost exact position. A quick position test can be made by shifting the ribbon mode to stencil and striking the correct letter.

Tests for Exact Positioning

To position a reinserted page for a correction, use the paper release lever to move the page sideways and the variable line spacer to roll it up or down. Test the exactness of position by the following procedure:

1. Cover the page of typing with a transparent second sheet. Roll the two sheets into the typewriter to the correction line.

2. Test for exactness of position by typing over a letter near the erased error. Adjust the sheets and type over another letter until the copy is in exact position.

3. Roll the sheets forward a couple of inches. Fold back the thin covering sheet, crease it all the way across, and tear it off. Roll the page into line position, set the carriage or element at the typing point, and type the correction.

This method wastes paper but assures exact positioning of corrections and is the cleanest way of correcting reinserted carbon copies. Proofreading the copy before it is removed from the typewriter, however, usually makes repositioning unnecessary.

Squeezing and Spreading. To insert a word containing one letter more than the error on a typewriter with a movable carriage, proceed as follows after the erasure has been made:

1 Move the carriage pointer to the space preceding the position of the first letter in the word.

2. Depress and hold down the half space bar or key, type the first letter of the correction, and release the bar or key.

3. Repeat the process for each letter of the correction.

This procedure will leave one-half space before and after the corrected word.

To insert a word containing one letter fewer than the error:

1. Move the carriage pointer to the space occupied (before erasure) by the first letter of the error.

2. Depress and hold down the half space bar or key, strike the first letter of the correction, and release the bar or key.

3. Repeat the process for each letter of the correction.

This procedure will leave one and one-half spaces before and after the corrected word.

Tips to the Typist

Date and write DRAFT across the top of every rough draft to avoid mistaking it for final copy.

On machines not equipped with a half space bar or key, depress the carriage release lever, move and firmly hold the carriage manually in the half space position, and strike the key.

Inserting a Space or Hyphen. To insert a space or a hyphen between two words, erase the two letters that must be separated. Retype the first letter one-half space to the left of its original position. Retype the second letter by spacing forward a half space. Center a hyphen in the space available by using the backspace key. In this manner, you can make a near perfect correction.

Inserting a Thin Letter in a Word. In some cases you can insert an *l*, an *i*, or a *t* within a typed word by fractional spacing. Experiment with your typewriter to determine in what instances you can use this method of correcting. Keep in mind that the correction will be discernible.

Making an Insertion between Lines. When time is of the essence, you may have to make a neat insertion between lines. Use the underline and diagonal keys to indicate the point of insertion. Find the midpoint between the lines for the line of typing. In single-spaced copy type the correction to the right of the diagonal; in double-spaced copy center it over the upper end of the diagonal.

Applying Printed Letters over Errors

Sheets of letters are available in pica, elite, and letter gothic styles that can be positioned over an error after the page has been removed from the

```
Xear Sir:

Xy the time you receive this memo . . . .

Xoncerning your memo of . . . .

COURIER   A B C D a b c l l 3 4
ELITE   A B C D a b c d l 2 3 4
LETTER GOTHIC   A B C a
```

CORRECTION SHEETS

```
A A A A A A A B B B B B C C C C C C
D D D D D D E E E E E E F F F F F F
F F G G G G G H H H H H I I I I I I
I I I J J J K K K K K L L L L L L l
M M M M N N N N N O O O O O O O O O (
O P P P P Q Q Q R R R R R S S S S S
_ m n u u u u U U U U U
```

```
askyou
ask  you
stilllife
still-life
```

```
alignment
insertion
letter
```

```
Time must be of the
essence/permit inter-
linear corrections.
```

```
Time must be of the
to
essence/permit inter-
```

Illus. 4-4
Correction sheets are available in pica, elite, and letter gothic styles to match your typewriter type.

typewriter. To correct an error, place the sheet of letters over the typed page, aligning the desired or correct letter over the error. Press the sheet with a pencil or pen so that the correct letter covers the error without retyping. Sheets should be ordered in a type style matching that of your typewriter. They are available three sheets to the package (5 ½ " × 8 ") for office use.

Correcting a Topbound Typescript

Typed pages that are bound at the top can be corrected without unbinding. Feed a blank sheet of paper into the machine in the usual way until the paper shows about a two-inch top margin. Insert the bottom of the sheet to be corrected between the top edge of the blank paper and the cylinder. Roll the cylinder back to the line to be corrected, position the carriage or element for the correction, and type the correction.

Matched Typing

To make a correction in carbon on a reinserted page of carbon copy typing, staple together several slips of paper and a small piece of carbon paper, carbon side out. A good size is 1 by 2½ inches. After positioning the carriage or element for the first letter of the correction, put this pad behind the ribbon with the carbon side against the paper. Type in the correction lightly.

Certain strikeovers are likely to be almost imperceptible in the specific type style on your typewriter. Experiment in order to learn those that match and blend into the typing. They may include: *d* over *c*; *h* over *n*; *o* over *c*; *E* over *F*; and, ; : or ? over the period.

TYPING SPECIALTIES

Typing specialties that expedite, control, and add visual appeal—in short, those that earn praise—are described here.

Display Typing

Very often a secretary must design a typing layout for reproduction (see illustration on page 95). It may be a notice, an invitation, a program, or the like. The finished piece requires that the units of copy, the decorations, and the white space be in pleasing arrangement and that the headings stand out. To achieve this effect, the secretary types blocks of copy and headings in various line lengths, spacings, and styles, and then experiments with their placement on a dummy layout.

A Suggestion

To reinforce paper to go into a loose-leaf notebook, attach a strip of tape along the back edge of the paper where the holes will be. Punch holes through both tape and paper.

(NONPRINTABLE MARGIN)

(PAGE 1)

YOU HAVE A
DATE
WITH PSI

(PAGE 2)

TO ATTEND a demonstration
of the newest
word processing equipment

EIGHT manufacturers will
show and explain
their newest products

(MARGINS AT CENTER FOLD)

(PAGE 3)

A Program
Sponsored by Your Local
PSI CHAPTER

COME and bring another
secretary

NO advance reservation
necessary

(PAGE 4)

WHERE
City Exhibition Center
Room 10A

WHEN
Saturday, April 4
9 to 12 a.m.

WHY
To make you the best
informed secretary
in your block

(NONPRINTABLE MARGIN)

Illus. 4-5

This is a dummy for an invitation to be duplicated on one side of an 8½- by 11-inch paper and then to be French-folded: first across and then up and down with the final fold at the left. The broken lines show the fold lines; the solid margin lines show the limit of the typing area. The copy in the upper half of the layout must be upside down to be in reading position when the sheet is folded. The typing is done on separate sheets and pasted on the full page dummy layout.

Sample Blocks of Copy. To find the most pleasing size and shape for the blocks of copy, type one paragraph or short unit of copy in different spacings and line lengths. Experiment with this set of samples on the dummy layout. You can vary sizes and shapes by:

1. Single line spacing or double line spacing
2. Different line lengths: full width, three-fourths width, etc.
3. Copy typed in columnar arrangement
4. Copy or columns typed with even right margins

Sample Headings. To make sample headings with which to experiment, take the longest heading and type it in different styles by:

1. Using uppercase and/or lowercase letters
2. Using different spacings between letters; using conventional spacing between letters
3. Varying the styles of underlining: continuous or broken underlining; single or double underlines; use of the underline, the hyphen, or the period key
4. Framing the headings: use of periods, small *o*'s, or asterisks; use of underlines with diagonals; use of hyphens and apostrophes

Justified Typing. Unless you have an electronic typewriter that automatically justifies the right margin, you will need to use the following technique. Even-right-margin or *justified* typing is illustrated below. To justify copy on a typewriter with standard spacing:

1. Set the margins for the exact column width desired. Type each line of copy in double-spaced form the full column width, filling in each unused space at the end with a diagonal.
2. Pencil in a check mark to indicate where you will insert each extra space within the line. Try not to use an extra space after the first word in a line or to isolate a short word with an extra space on each side.
3. Retype the copy, inserting the extra spaces.

```
First, set up the column width;///
then type each line of copy the///
full width of the column filling//
in each unused space at the end///
with a diagonal.
```

```
First, set   up the  column  width;
then type   each line  of copy  the
full width  of the  column  filling
in each  unused  space  at  the  end
with a diagonal.
```

Typing Labels. Most labels are packaged in sheets or strips. To prevent slippage, they should be typed before they are separated from these sheets or slips. When it is necessary to type a single label, make a carrier by folding a sheet of paper in the middle; then fold it again to make a pleat. Make the pleat so that enough of the label appears above the pleat to expose all but a slight bottom margin. Insert the label in the pleat and position it for typing.

If you use the same mailing list frequently, perforated carbon sets of labels are available that contain 33 labels per sheet. By using these carbon sets, you can type four sets of labels at once—a big time-saver in mailing such items as monthly statements and recurring announcements.

Decorative Typing. Distinctively typed words, designs, and patterns may be used occasionally as eye-catchers on the cover page of a notice, the announcement of a meeting, or an item to be posted on the office bulletin board. The illustrations at the left are a few that can be done by straight typing and spacing. Such decorative typing is rarely used in business work. It requires more time than the results justify, and frequently it is out of place on a formal business document.

Special Characters

A number of special characters can be constructed on the typewriter. Illus. 4-6 shows a partial list.

Brackets		*Left Bracket.* Type underline, backspace, backspace, strike diagonal, turn platen back one line space, and type underline. *Right Bracket.* Type underline, diagonal, backspace, turn platen back one line space, and type underline.
Degree sign	12°	Turn platen back slightly; strike lowercase *o*.
Ditto mark	"	Turn platen forward slightly; strike the quotation mark.
Division sign	÷	Type hyphen, backspace, and strike the colon.
Equal sign	=	Type hyphen, backspace, turn platen forward a bit, strike the hyphen.
Paragraph mark	¶	Type capital *P*, backspace, and strike 1.
Plus sign	+	Type hyphen, backspace, and strike diagonal.
Pound sterling	£	Type *f*, backspace, strike *t*.

Illus. 4-6
Special typewriter keys

High-Speed Envelope and Card Routines

You will occasionally have small typing production jobs to do or to supervise. These jobs might include addressing a hundred or so envelopes or

making up a 5- by 3-inch card index. Master the following high-speed routines used in specialized typing assignments.

Back Feeding Envelopes. When you have a number of envelopes to address, you can save time by back feeding them.

1. Stack the plain envelopes at the left of the typewriter, flap down and bottom edge of the envelopes toward you.
2. Feed the first envelope into the typewriter until only about one half of the bottom of the envelope is free.
3. Place the top of the second envelope between the platen and the bottom of the first envelope. Turn the platen to address position for the first envelope and type the address.
4. With the left hand pick up the next envelope and drop it into feed position as you turn the platen with the right hand to remove the addressed envelope.
5. With the left hand remove the addressed envelope and stack it face down at the left of your machine.

Front Feeding Envelopes. To front feed envelopes, roll a just addressed envelope *back* until about one inch of the top edge is free. Have a stack of envelopes at the side of the typewriter flap up with the flap edge toward you. Drop one of these face up between the cylinder and the top edge of the addressed envelope. Roll the cylinder back until the blank envelope is in typing position, then address it. The addressed envelopes stack themselves in sequence against the paper table on the typewriter and can be removed occasionally.

Front Feeding Small Cards. To front feed small cards, make a pleat a half inch or less deep straight across the middle of a sheet of paper to form a pocket. The depth of the pleat controls how far down you can type on the cards. Paste or tape the pleat down at the sides to hold it in place. Roll the pleated sheet into the typewriter and align the fold of the pleat with the alignment scale. Place the first card in the pleat and position it for typing. Draw a line on the paper along the left edge of the card to serve as a continuing guide for consistent margins. Specially designed platens are available for typing cards.

Government Postal Cards. Government postal cards can be purchased in sheets four cards wide and ten cards long. These sheets can be cut into strips and addressed. Postal cards are 5½" × 3¼" and should be typed lengthwise using a 4½" writing line.

Fill-Ins

The term *fill-in* refers to the insertion of some typed material in a space provided on duplicated or printed letters, bulletins, or business papers. The fill-in may be an address, a salutation, a word, a phrase, or some figures. On interoffice correspondence no attempt is made to disguise fill-ins, but on outgoing mail fill-ins should match the body of the message. The procedure is as follows:

1. Use a ribbon that matches the body of the message in darkness of color.
2. Set the carriage in position to insert the fill-in. Test the position by typing over a period or comma in the text.
3. When the position has been determined, set the paper guide and margins for use in succeeding fill-ins.
4. Salutations and addresses are placed more accurately if the lines are typed from bottom to top, unless a pinpoint placement dot from the master shows where to begin the first line.

Tips to the Typist

When typing on ruled lines, adjust the typing line so the bases of *y, g,* and *p* just touch the ruled line.

SUGGESTED READINGS

House, C. R., and K. Sigler. *Reference Manual for Office Personnel,* 6th ed. Cincinnati: South-Western Publishing Co., 1981.

Lovely, Yvonne. *Practical Secretarial Manual and Guide.* Englewood Cliffs, N. J.: Parker Publishing Company, 1978.

Wanous, S. J., *et al. College Typewriting,* 10th ed. Cincinnati: South-Western Publishing Co., 1980.

QUESTIONS FOR DISCUSSION

1. If your employer offered to let you select your own typewriter, what are some of the features you would want on a machine and how would you determine this?

2. You are employed as secretary to the manager of the R & D (Research and Development) Division. This is a highly sensitive area and thus under strict control for security leaks. A major security leak was traced to your wastebasket and to the snap-out forms you have been using.
   (a) Explain how this could happen.
   (b) Is there any solution other than discontinuing the use of these forms?

3. Office costs used to be 20 to 30 percent of the total cost in a company; now they have grown to 40 to 90 percent (e.g., in service-oriented businesses, such as insurance companies) of all costs. The cost of producing a business letter is 40 percent more than it was five years ago. List the things a secretary can do to help curb the spiraling costs of a business letter.

4. Faulty handling of carbon copies can mar superior workmanship. What precautions should you observe in handling carbon copies?

5. Rewrite the following sentences correcting those that have numbers expressed incorrectly. Then refer to the Reference Guide to check your answers.

(a) 14 men worked on the project.
(b) Enclose 5 20-cent stamps.
(c) Joe is nearly 18.
(d) Margaret is 19 today.
(e) He ran the thirty-five mile marathon.
(f) The temple was built in 13 b.c. and was uncovered by the British in 1848 a.d.
(g) He has a 2-year-old daughter.

PROBLEMS

1. The electronic typewriter is growing in popularity with secretaries because it provides many automatic features at an affordable price. There are several brands on the market but IBM, Olympia, Olivetti, and QYX were among the first to market this machine.

    Assume that your employer is interested in purchasing an electronic typewriter for your use. Prepare a report comparing two of these brands and indicate those features available on the basic model at no extra cost.

2. A secretary must know how to change a typewriter ribbon. As a supervisor, the secretary may need to demonstrate the ribbon-changing process for both film and fabric ribbons. Practice changing the ribbon on your typewriter and also on typewriters of other makes until you believe you are qualified to demonstrate the technique.

3. A study shows that it takes the following time to correct one typing error:

    Time per Error

    Original only   8 sec.
    Original and 1 carbon   17 sec.
    Original and 2 carbons   25 sec.
    Original and 3 carbons   35 sec.

    For the following questions assume an average of five correctable errors per letter. Also assume that the total cost for the secretary is $12.05 an hour. (This includes hourly rate, fringe benefits, employer payroll taxes, supplies, equipment costs, and overhead.).

    (a) What is the cost per letter for correcting errors on the original only? original and 1 carbon? original and 2 carbons? original and 3 carbons?
    (b) If an original and 2 carbons are made of each letter, how much would be saved per letter if the policy were to correct errors on originals only and not on the carbons? Do you see any disadvantage to this?
    (c) One business has a policy that no errors are to be erased. Errors are corrected by striking over or "x-ing" out and retyping. Can you present any good arguments against this policy?

4. You are employed as the secretary to an architect whose office is located in a small community. Because of the location, all office supplies are ordered via a letter from the Mid-West Office Supply, 23 East Town Street, St. Louis, Missouri 63130-1235. Prepare a letter ordering the following supplies. Design the letterhead (create the name and location), and use the current date.

    2,000 letterheads. These are for general use and should be of good quality, but not the very highest grade.
    2,000 envelopes to match the letterheads ordered above.
    1 dozen typewriter ribbons for your IBM Correcting Selectric typewriter.
    2 boxes of carbon paper.

Chapter **5**

Data and Word Processing

The explosive growth of data and word processing technology has dramatically changed the structure of the office and the role of the secretary. Sharp increases in office productivity have occurred through the application of data and word processing to office tasks. This chapter will define data and word processing and describe the equipment used in this rapidly expanding phase of office technology.

DATA PROCESSING DEFINED

Data processing is a series of operations that convert raw alphabetical and numerical data into useful information. For example, figures on costs, purchases, sales, inventories, and production can quickly be made available to management in summary form for effective decision making. Data processing today is characterized by computers that provide collection, fast processing, transmittal, storage, and retrieval of large quantities of data.

ELECTRONIC DATA PROCESSING

An electronic data processing (EDP) system consists of input equipment, a central processing unit (the computer), and output equipment. The processing of data is a continuous chain of operations performed within the system rather than by separately operated machines. Information can be stored for immediate or future use on magnetic tape or disks.

Operations are performed by entering a program of instructions into the computer system, and decisions and alternate courses of action are presented through the functioning of the arithmetic/logic unit of the computer.

The computer and its peripheral equipment are referred to as the *hardware* of the system. *Software* is the term used to indicate machine instructions, programs, procedures, rules, operator instructions, and other documentation concerned with the operation of the system.

This section discusses the basic components of the electronic data processing system—the input media and devices, the central processing unit, output media and equipment, and various computer applications.

101

Input Media

The term *input* describes the act of introducing data into an electronic data processing system. An input medium is the form or material on which data are recorded for processing. *Input media* range from magnetic tape to voice recognition. An *input device*, considered peripheral equipment to the computer, is used to read the input medium into the system. Input devices vary with the types of input media used.

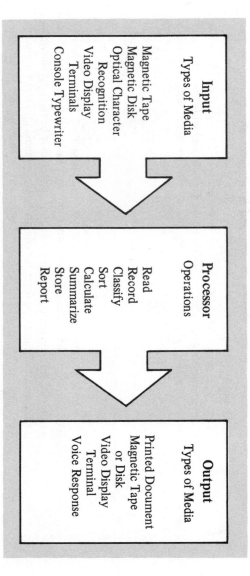

Input Types of Media	Processor Operations	Output Types of Media

Magnetic Tape
Magnetic Disk
Optical Character
  Recognition
Video Display
Terminals
Console Typewriter
	Read
	Record
	Classify
	Sort
	Calculate
	Summarize
	Store
	Report
		Printed Document
		Magnetic Tape
		  or Disk
		Video Display
		Terminal
		Voice Response

Illus. 5-1
The three components in a data processing system, their media, and operations

Magnetic Tape. Magnetic tape is plastic, coated with a metallic oxide, and comes in widths of ½ to 1 inch and lengths of 2,400 to 3,600 feet per reel. Data are recorded on the tape as invisible magnetized spots that, when read into the system, create electrical impulses. A tape drive unit is used to read the magnetized spots into the computer.

Magnetic tape is considered a *sequential access* medium; that is, what is first on the reel is read first, what is second is read second, and so forth. In other words, in order to locate information halfway through the tape, all the preceding material must be read first. For some business operations, such as periodic updating of customer accounts, the magnetic tape is ideal; but where information is scattered throughout a tape, the computer access time necessary to reach the desired data can delay the processing.

Data can be keyed directly to magnetic tape for reading to the computer using a keyboard similar to that of an electric typewriter. Furthermore, the operator can key data on miniature magnetic tapes in tape cassettes, which the computer can then convert to run size tape for processing.

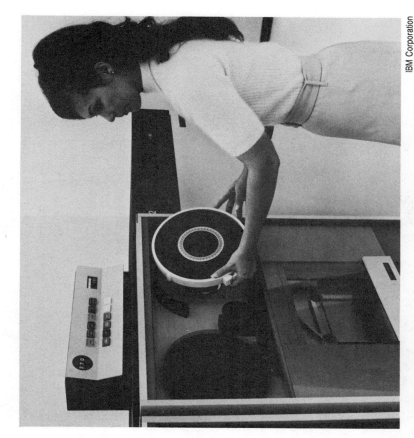

IBM Corporation

Illus. 5-2
The computer operator mounts a reel of magnetic tape on a magnetic tape drive.

Magnetic Disks. Magnetic disks are thin, circular, metal plates, coated on both sides with ferrous oxide. In appearance a file of magnetic disks resembles a stack of phonograph records. Information is recorded and stored as magnetic spots on both sides of a disk, using various key-to-disk devices. Data can be transferred from the disk to a tape for processing by the computer.

Like magnetic tape, disks are durable and erasable. Depending on the nature of the information recorded on the magnetic disk or tape, a second copy may be made to ensure the information against accidental erasure or destruction. Disks are available over a broad range of speed and storage capacities. Most computer systems today use disks rather than tape.

Whereas magnetic tape is a sequential access medium (the computer must search from the beginning of the tape for desired data), magnetic disks are a *random access* medium (the computer can go directly to any record on the disk and retrieve desired data). Thus access time to retrieve information is shorter with magnetic disks than with magnetic tape. Magnetic disks are used in computer installations for large volume storage capacity.

Optical Character Recognition (OCR). Optical scanners read and translate printed or handwritten characters into machine language and transfer the data directly into the computer. Optical character recognition devices are gaining favor as input devices of raw data. There are three basic methods for recording data on a document to be read by optical scanners: (1) optically readable marks; (2) bar codes; (3) optically readable characters, including handwritten characters.

The optical mark page reader is a device that can sense marks made by a pencil or pen on specially designed forms. It is used mainly for test scoring, inventory control, and data collection.

Bar codes are optically read by scanners that sense marks or bars that are prerecorded on tags or merchandise. The Universal Product Code (UPC) is a bar code that is placed on products to expedite checkout at some grocery stores.

Some optical scanners read only data recorded in a special type face. OCR-A is the most commonly used font that can be read by scanners. On some devices, handwritten data can be read. Machines that read handwriting are extremely versatile in their recognition capability. They can read handwritten numbers, machine printed numbers, imprinted numbers and marks, and a limited amount of alphanumeric data consisting of letters of the alphabet with any combinations of spaces, numbers, or special characters.

Video Display Terminals (VDT). A video display terminal has a cathode-ray tube (CRT), or televisionlike screen, and a keyboard linked to a computer. It

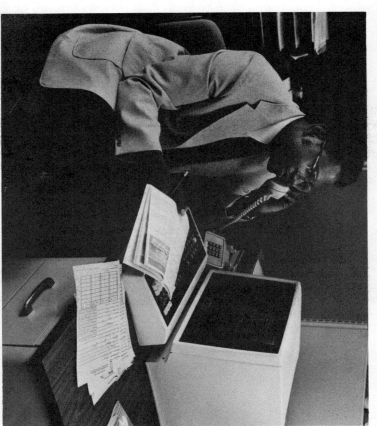

Illus. 5-3
The operator verifies data visually on a CRT.

is part of an input/output system. The user inputs data through the keyboard of the terminal. There are "dumb" and "intelligent" terminals.

Some terminals do not have the capacity to process data in any way; that is, the terminal transmits data directly to the central computer for processing. These terminals are sometimes referred to as dumb terminals.

Intelligent terminals are normally found at remote sites within the various departments of an organization. Preliminary processing can take place at the remote site. Errors can be corrected before data are transmitted to a central computer. Intelligent terminals increase the processing efficiency of the central computer by reducing the total time for results to reach the data users.

Recent innovations have increased the intelligence and versatility of these terminals. One example is the *portable intelligent terminal* that can be interfaced with a telephone line. Such terminals, which may or may not have a televisionlike screen, use a bubble memory. A magnetic bubble stores data on thin film and memory is retained even in a power failure. A sales representative calling on customers can enter order data (quantities, prices, colors, and sizes) on the portable terminal for storage in memory. Later the data can be printed out automatically as hard copy before being transmitted to the computer in the home office. The data can be sent rapidly over telephone lines permitting the customer's orders to be filled almost immediately.

Console Typewriter. Although a console typewriter keyboard can introduce data directly into the system, it is too slow for volume input and is used primarily for direct communication with the computer, such as in asking questions. For example, the operator may use the keyboard to ask the balance of an account. The typewriter then receives and types the computer's response.

Central Processing Unit

The heart of the electronic data processing system is the CPU. It consists of (1) an internal storage or memory file, (2) an arithmetic/logic component, and (3) a control unit. The central processing unit accepts data from any of the various input devices, processes the data according to the programmer's instructions, and sends results to storage or to the output device.

Illus. 5-4
The basic computer system consists of input and output units as well as a CPU. The CPU contains memory, arithmetic/logic, and control units.

Storage or Memory File. *Storage* (frequently called memory, or memory file) is the place where computer data and programs are stored magnetically.

Storage is organized into thousands of individual locations, each with a unique address by which it can be located in the same manner that a house can be located by a street address. The speed with which the processing unit can locate an address in the storage or memory file and transfer the amount in the computer's address to the arithmetic/logic component is referred to as *access time*. Since large processors can perform several hundred operations per second, the access time to stored data is critical; that is, slow access time uses up valuable computer time.

Most computers have two types of storage, internal and external. The internal storage is quick access storage. The quick access storage holds the program and the data that are being used at a given time. External storage consists of devices such as magnetic tape and magnetic disks where data are held until needed.

Arithmetic/Logic Component. The arithmetic/logic section of the computer is like an electronic calculator that performs addition, subtraction, multiplication, and division. It can also logically compare and select among alternate courses of action.

Arithmetic Ability. The arithmetic component has two sections, the adder circuits and the accumulator registers. The calculations are performed in the *adder* section at lightning speed measured in *microseconds* (millionths of a second) and sometimes in *nanoseconds* (billionths of a second) of time. Naturally this time varies with the size and complexity of the unit. A small computer might require .001 second (a thousand microseconds) to multiply a four-digit number by a five-digit number.

The *accumulator* is that portion of the arithmetic unit where results (answers) of the arithmetic operation are temporarily stored until the calculation is complete. The instructions may direct the equipment to do the following:

1. Copy a number from a storage location into the accumulator.
2. Get a second number from a storage location and add it to the number in the accumulator.
3. Multiply the sum of the two numbers (in the accumulator) by 25 and return the answer to storage.

Logic Component. One of the distinctive qualities of the computer is its ability to compare and select among alternate courses of action. The computer can be programmed to examine a figure and determine if it is above or below a certain amount. If it is above, the computer will follow one set of instructions. If it is below, the computer will follow another set. This logic component makes it possible, once data and a program have been fed into the system, for the computer to complete a sequence of operations automatically. For instance, it can process a payroll without any further human intervention after data on the individual time cards are fed into the computer. It calculates the wage for each employee; searches out the payroll information, obtains the number of withholding tax exemptions, and then determines the withholding tax and social security tax; makes other approved deductions; determines the net pay; and prints the paycheck. In addition, it stores the payroll information, produces complete payroll information on each employee and prints the W-2 forms (Withholding Tax Statements). A payroll for several thousand employees can be completed within a few hours.

Control Unit. The control unit directs the many functions of the computer system. It seeks instructions from the storage files, interprets, and executes them. It internally controls operations of the input devices, the storage unit, the arithmetic/logic unit, and the output devices.

Output Media

Output is defined as the information processed by the computer. The *output medium* is the form in which the processed information appears. The *output device* is the equipment connected to the system that records or displays the processed data. The output information can be in the form of magnetic tape or magnetic disks for use in further data processing, or in the form of records, reports, visual displays, or voice responses for immediate use. By far the most common output medium is the printed document.

Records and Reports. Processed data in the form of records and reports are printed on high-speed printing equipment that usually prints a whole line of characters at one time. Printers are of two types, *impact* and *nonimpact.* Impact printers are equipped with wheels, chains, or cylinders that press against a ribbon and paper to print letters, digits, and special characters. Nonimpact printers print information by the transfer of electrostatic charges directly onto paper. A new method uses a laser beam—a source of pinpoint accurate light. In terms of speed, impact printers can print at 400 to 2,400 lines a minute while nonimpact printers can produce up to 18,000 lines a minute.

Magnetic Tape or Disk. Data can be stored on magnetic tape and disks. On magnetic tape the data recorded are stored on one-inch magnetic tapes (similar to audio cassette tapes). With a magnetic disk, data are recorded and stored on an oxide coated disk as a series of electronic spots.

Video-Display Terminals (VDT). The user inputs data and control signals through the VDT keyboard. The computer responds and outputs data on the VDT.

Voice Response. For businesses like airlines, transportation companies, and banks, the most convenient means of data retrieval is a voice response terminal. For example, to check the credit reference of a customer, a bank representative can dial into the computer and a voice will respond with the requested information. The words in a voice response come from a vocabulary stored in the system and are generally restricted to the basic type of information requested.

Computer Services

In response to the growing need for computer access by business organizations that cannot afford computer services, computer service centers and computer usage arrangements have developed. Examples of these services are discussed in this section.

Leasing. Computer equipment can be leased from the manufacturer or an agency and installed on the user's premises. Under this arrangement, the leasing agent buys the data processing equipment specified by the user and then leases it to the user.

Data Processing Service Centers. Commercial data processing service centers provide computer service to small businesses and handle overflow loads for larger companies that have their own computer installations.

Considerable diversity exists among data processing services. Well-established centers may provide a complete data processing service: analyze customer requirements, offer consulting services, prepare computer programs, and implement the programs on their own equipment. Some centers have developed an area of expertise and industry specialization, such as processing pension plans, direct mail, or income tax forms.

Most service centers offer *batch* processing (periodic processing of data that have accumulated over a period of time, such as a monthly accounts receivable or a weekly payroll). The work is done on a fixed schedule.

Information Retrieval and Exchange. Information service centers have evolved to provide subscribers with business, scientific, and technical information by direct connection with computers through telephone lines.

For example, a business can subscribe to a local credit rating service. One strategically located center can store the credit ratings of most businesses and millions of individuals in its area.

MINICOMPUTERS AND MICROCOMPUTERS

A *minicomputer* is a small, inexpensive computer containing a CPU with one or more input/output devices. It is usually equipped with a CRT and can be used in business to process accounts receivable and accounts payable, enter orders, calculate payrolls, analyze sales, and record inventory. The minicomputer also has some scientific applications.

A minicomputer can serve as a company's complete computer system or as a supplement to a larger installation. In *distributed data processing,* minicomputers located in areas where processing is required are linked to a large centralized computer. Distributed data processing involves the distribution of computing power to the divisions or locations where that power is needed. The system also gives remote sites access to the data base of the large central computer.

NCR Corporation

Illus. 5-5
A minicomputer has a CPU and one or more input/output devices.

A major development that will impact significantly on the office in this decade is the microcomputer. A *microcomputer* consists of a **VDT**, a keyboard, and CPU functions based on a *microprocessor,* a silicon chip smaller than a fingernail. This desktop "computer on a chip" is revolutionizing the modern office. Although extremely tiny, the microprocessor has a control unit and an arithmetic/logic unit. The microprocessor chip is used alone in sewing machines, microwave ovens, automobiles, and many other devices to automate one or more functions. Illus. 5-6 shows an enlargement of a microprocessor held between two fingertips.

Illus. 5-6
A microprocessor chip, held between two fingertips, is an integrated circuit containing the components of an entire central processing unit.

IBM Corporation

The microcomputer is generally used in one of three ways. As a stand alone computer, the microcomputer is capable of performing information-processing functions without a communication link to any other equipment. Linked to a large computer through an intelligent terminal, the microcomputer will eliminate the need for much rekeyboarding and manipulating of data because its intelligence will permit processing of information before it is communicated to the CPU. As a terminal in a network of small machines, the microcomputer can link together former standalone systems, thereby making them more efficient and less costly to operate.

WORD PROCESSING DEFINED

Word processing is a system for processing written communications through a configuration of specialized personnel, automated equipment, and procedures. Although all three elements are important to the system, equipment will be emphasized in this chapter. Much has already been said about the impact of word processing on secretarial personnel in Chapter 1.

There are two types of equipment vital to word processing—dictation equipment and typewriting equipment. Dictation equipment provides the input, or the means by which the spoken word is recorded. Dictation equipment is discussed in Chapter 8. Automated typewriting equipment produces the output, or the printed word, from the recorded word.

Word processing emerged in 1964 when IBM introduced a new typewriter. The typewriter was the Magnetic Tape Selectric Typewriter (MTST). Automated typewriters, such as the MTST, were often placed in a central location and operated by specialists. Correspondence was dictated to dictation equipment in a word processing center. This new system was designed to save time and money; office efficiency was enhanced by eliminating the need for retyping. Automated typewriters permitted the typist to change original text by adding or deleting words without altering the entire document.

Since 1964, many modifications in procedures and a host of new machines and supplies have simplified the typing task. Word processing equipment has frequently replaced the secretary's standard typewriter. Many secretaries have found word processing a challenging opportunity for specialization.

WORD PROCESSING EQUIPMENT AND SYSTEMS

Automatic typewriters are manufactured by several companies, each producing models with different capabilities. In addition to automatic typewriters, devices that increase the efficiency of word processing equipment are available from a variety of manufacturers. For those users needing high-speed processing and increased storage capacity, shared logic and time-shared services are utilized for word processing.

Standalone Text Editors

Standalone text editors give an operator the capability of manipulating, editing, and altering copy. Since standalone text editors operate independently and do not need to be connected to other machines, they are described as standalone or all-in-one machines. The term *text editor* refers to the capability the machine has for making type corrections and editorial changes during and after the initial keyboarding of the copy.

Nondisplay Text Editors.   The nondisplay text editor is most commonly used for correspondence and short documents requiring limited revisions and for small quantities of personalized form letters. It consists of a high-speed typewriter console equipped with some form of magnetic medium recording-playback attachment. As the operator types each character or space on the keyboard, a hard copy is produced by the text editor while a unit records the character or space on the mag (magnetic) medium. When a typing mistake is made, the operator simply backspaces and strikes over the incorrect letter, word, or phrase. The process of backspacing and retyping automatically erases the error on the mag medium and replaces it with the corrected copy. This feature permits the operator to type at a rough draft rate. After the text has been recorded on the mag medium, additional copy can be inserted or unwanted copy can be deleted.

When the rough draft typing has been completed and the copy has been edited, the operator inserts a letterhead or a regular sheet of paper and any desired carbons in the typewriter console. Then the machine is changed to the playback mode by pressing a button on the typewriter console. The machine retypes automatically and completely error free. While retyping, the machine may be programmed to automatically respace and reposition words and sentences, control end-of-line hyphens, determine line and page endings, provide numeric column alignment, make high-speed forward and reverse underlining, and stop for the manual keyboarding of varying information in a form letter.

The mag medium used depends on the make and model of the machine. The most commonly used media are mag tape, card, and diskette (floppy disk).

Verbatim Information
Terminals Corporation

Illus. 5-7
Floppy disk

The tape may be packaged as a roll, cassette, or cartridge. Each medium offers advantages and disadvantages in its ease of handling, storage capacity, and access time. Access time refers to the length of time required to locate a specific point on the medium for editing or replay. The diskette provides the fastest access time, and for that reason it is becoming increasingly popular as a mag medium.

The machine may be a single or dual medium. The single medium machine facilitates minor editing, such as corrections of typing errors, making short insertions or deletions, and other small changes in copy. Wholesale modifications of copy that may be required in preparing reports, news releases, and manuscripts, however, are difficult to accomplish. To facilitate such extensive editorial changes, some manufacturers produce dual-medium machines. These machines are equipped with two recording-playback units. This feature permits the operator to transfer "good" copy from the original keyboarded rough draft medium onto the second mag tape, card, or disk. New material is keyboarded in and unwanted material is bypassed as the good copy is transferred to the second medium. This dual medium process is known as *transfer updating.*

Some machines have the added feature of being able to hold keyboarded text in *"flux"* (also called *"float"*) before it is committed to the mag medium. This permits corrections, deletions, additions, and restructuring of copy to be completed before the copy goes on the medium. Thus, the text is recorded on the medium only once, not twice as is necessary on the dual medium machine.

Courtesy Raytheon Data Systems

Illus. 5-8
This word processing unit has a full-page screen to show exactly what will be printed out.

Visual Display Text Editors. The visual display standalone text editor is growing in popularity because its capabilities exceed those of nondisplay or mechanical text editors. The visual text editor incorporates a display terminal that permits the operator to see the copy on a screen as it is keyboarded. Sometimes referred to as visual memory, this terminal provides a partial or full page display of keyboarded copy before it is committed to the magnetic medium. Most machines use a CRT (cathode ray tube) for video display. The memory capacity of the display terminal used for altering text and temporarily storing words is called the *buffer* or *buffer storage.*

Typing errors are corrected by typing directly over the error. Words, lines, or paragraphs may be added at any point in the copy by moving a cursor, or movable pointer, to the desired position and striking the appropriate keys. Once the copy has been fully edited, it can be scrolled off (transferred) from the memory to the magnetic medium for printout, storage, or both.

The visual display editors have separate units for keyboarding and printout, each operating independently of the other. These units free the keyboard console and display screen to produce new input while copy already stored on the mag medium is being played out on the printer. The visual display editor incorporates several useful features:

1. *Spelling Verification*—permits storage of words that are peculiar to a particular business—engineering terms, for example. This feature detects misspellings and typographical errors by matching the keyboarded word with the stored word. Unmatched words are highlighted on the screen.

2. *Global Search and Replace*—enables the operator to search for and replace information in the text. Words are changed in the text in every place where the word (or phrase) occurs. For example, if you typed CPA instead of CPS, the global search feature will locate, without your assistance, every CPA in the text and automatically change it to CPS.

3. *Wraparound or Word Wrap*—moves a word down to the next line when that word is too long to fit within the limits of the right margin.

4. *Word Division*—hyphenates words according to preprogrammed rules. The system is only about 85 percent accurate.

5. *Selective Search and Replace*—permits the operator to locate the position on the screen at which the editing process is to begin. The cursor (movable pointer that shows the position of text on the screen) indicates the first place that a word or phrase occurs, thus enabling the operator to replace the word or phrase.

6. *Justification*—automatically adjusts the right margin during playback so that the right margin is even as in printed copy.

7. *Pagination*—places page numbers sequentially on each page of the text.

8. *Decimal Alignment*—aligns numbers with correct decimal placement when statistical data are typed.

Programmed Software

Some text-editing machines are software programmable. In other words, special programmed packages instruct the text editor to perform a variety of functions. Most of these programs are stored on floppy disks that can be inserted in the machine to instruct the equipment to perform specific tasks. For example, software programs are available that can compute invoice extensions and totals as the invoice is being typed.

Communicating Text Editors

As a special feature some models of standalone text editors are designed to communicate via telephone lines with compatible equipment in near or remote locations. The word processing equipment is used to send processed text from one location to another, thus serving as a communication terminal. Communicating text editors can be interfaced with various message-sending equipment.

Optical Character Reader (OCR)

Optical character readers can recognize and interpret alphanumeric characters based upon their shape. These readers are able to recognize many different type fonts and can accept documents of various sizes up to letter size. Documents prepared on standard office typewriters can be read by some OCR page readers. Documents read may be entered into the memory of word processing equipment for immediate processing, or the documents may be stored on magnetic media (disks or tape) for future processing.

There are several advantages in using OCR as an input medium. Two major ones are reduced input time and increased accuracy. The entire page of a document is read and displayed on a display terminal for editing. The operator keys only changes to be made on the document. The corrected document is then typed out at a printer or stored on magnetic disks or tapes.

IBM Corporation

Illus. 5-9
The OCR page reader scans large volumes of pages.

Voice Recognition Units

A voice recognition unit is capable of converting spoken words into suitable input for a computer. Simply stated, the voice recognition unit enables the executive to dictate to a computer that prints out the message.

One type stores a dictionary of several hundred words. The user of the unit practices dictating to the unit until it will accept dictation by matching the sound of each word dictated to the prestored dictionary. Upon hearing a word, the unit searches the dictionary for the word that most closely matches the one dictated. It is limited in its application because of its inability to distinguish between words that sound alike, such as *then, than; bear, bare; for, far.* Other limitations stem from incorrect grammar used by the dictator, dialects, and foreign accents. Since the voice recognition unit must recognize the voice of a dictator who has been trained to use it, it cannot be used for taking telephone orders, reservations, and the like.

Another type of voice recognition input has the capability of asking the dictator for a definition or the clarification of a word it does not understand. This unit can take dictation and produce sentences, but is extremely expensive and will respond to a limited number of people.

High-Speed Print Devices

The Selectric typewriter has been commonly used as text-editing equipment for keyboarding and correcting copy on the mag medium. Usually the

DSG, Inc.

Xerox Corporation

same Selectric machine also has been used to print out the edited or final copy. The Selectric with its "golf ball" printing element has a maximum operating speed of approximately 180 words a minute or 15 characters per second (cps). To obtain a higher printout speed, other printer units that can obtain much higher rates of speed than the Selectric typewriter are available.

One type of printer uses the daisy wheel mechanism. This printer operates at speeds of up to 660 words per minute or 55 cps. Some printers of this type are bidirectional—printing from left to right and right to left alternately —at speeds up to 900 words a minute or 75 cps. Multiple type faces are available for the daisy wheel printer. A thimble printing device similar to the print wheel but shaped differently can print 128 different characters at speeds comparable to the daisy mechanism.

One of the fastest printout methods is the "jet ink" process. It is a nonimpact printer, capable of extremely high speeds, which utilizes tiny drops of ink to form copy images. As the print mechanism moves across the paper, it deposits electrostatically charged ink where type is desired on the page.

The laser printer can print multiple sets of documents at a rate of 36 pages a minute. The laser printer is a nonimpact printer.

Although these nonimpact printers provide high speed production of long documents, the quality is somewhat lower than that of impact printers —ball shaped elements, print wheels, and thimble elements. Because the characters are typed one at a time and at a lower rate, the quality of the print produced is more attractive than that of the nonimpact printers.

Computerized Text-Editing Systems

Text editors that interact with other text editors or computers offer many capabilities over standalone equipment. The two main categories of computer linked text editors are shared logic text-editing systems and time-shared services.

Shared Logic Text-Editing Systems. A number of text editors use the logic component and storage capabilities of a minicomputer or a microcomputer to produce either hard copy (a printed document) or screen displayed text. A shared logic system greatly increases the capabilities of single station equipment because it has more processing power, greater storage capacity, and the ability to handle the work of several stations.

In many large companies, shared logic systems allow word processing stations to be placed throughout the company. In some instances, the terminals can be used for word processing part of the time and for data processing the remainder of the time. A typical example is a manufacturing firm that uses word processing to prepare a personalized sales letter to a long list of customers and the same system to compute commissions. Thus, the terminal becomes an information-processing unit rather than a separate unit dedicated to word processing or data processing.

Time-Shared Services. Time-shared services link the text editor with a more powerful source—a remote CPU. Such an arrangement represents an expansion of the shared logic concept to permit several users in a variety of locations to share the costs of a large computer. When this is done, the text editor becomes primarily a computer input terminal and text-altering station. The computer records the input from the text editor, performs text manipulations as directed, and provides the full output through the computer's high-speed printer.

A GUIDE TO DATA AND WORD PROCESSING TERMS

ElectRonic

Automatic Typewriter—A typewriter that records or stores words as they are typed on a special medium (punched tape, magnetic tape or disks). Once the copy is recorded, it can be played back automatically for final copy.

Boilerplate—Stored letters or paragraphs used in multiple mailings. The paragraphs or letters permit the use of variables to give the impression of personalized, individually typed letters. Sometimes they are referred to as "canned" or prerecorded paragraphs or letters.

Computer—An automatic electronic machine capable of performing mathematical, logical, and control functions. There are several types of computers—digital computers that count numbers and handle numerical data in billionths of a second (called nanoseconds); analog computers that are used in scientific research for measuring speed of sound, air resistance, voltage, etc.

Compatible Equipment—Ability of one brand of information-processing equipment to send or receive information from another brand.

Cursor—A movable pointer on the screen of a computer or text editor that indicates the position of displayed copy.

Floppy Disks/Diskettes—Magnetic media similar in size and appearance to 45 rpm phonograph records. Floppy disks, also called diskettes, are used to store information from a computer or a text editor.

Form Letter—A basic letter sent to a variety of recipients. In word processing, variables can be inserted to personalize or tailor the letter to the reader's interests.

Hardware—The components or configuration of machines (such as input, output, or power units) that make up a system of equipment.

Interface—The point at which two machines or systems contact each other. For example, text editors can be interfaced with computers.

Magnetic Media—Cassettes, belts, tapes, or disks used to record and store data.

Merging—The assembly of two or more documents to create a new document. The most common application of merging in word processing occurs when one file contains the body of a letter, and this is merged with a list of names and addresses.

Microprocessor—The electronic components of an entire central processing unit contained on a very small single silicon chip.

Scrolling—The movement of text on a visual display screen either up or down or horizontally.

Software—A set of instructions (programs) that cause hardware to function.

Variables—Information to be inserted into prerecorded documents that gives correspondence the appearance of being individually typed. For example, in a form letter, each person's name may be inserted in the body to give the letter a personal touch.

Several text editors may interact simultaneously with one computer through time-sharing. The linkup with the more powerful computer enables the word processing operator to tap a vast amount of computer-stored information and have it automatically incorporated as a part of the printout.

The text-editing terminal may be connected to the computer by placing the telephone in a coupler (a device that connects a keyboard terminal to a telephone line) and by dialing the computer's number. The terminal operator must give proper identification before the computer will react. This procedure is followed to ensure confidentiality and security.

Time-shared services are most often used for processing long documents that require extensive text editing and format change. Users of these systems pay for computer time, telephone use, printouts, storage at the computer center, and the terminal connection.

INFORMATION PROCESSING AND THE SECRETARY

Word processing equipment manufacturers are introducing new equipment and software packages that give their equipment computer capabilities. On the other hand, producers of data processing equipment are enhancing computers so that they will perform word processing functions. As your office changes to accommodate the blending of word and data processing functions, you will find your work station becoming an automated information center.

In this information center, you will transmit data to other people through equipment that permits quick access to and retrieval of all kinds of information. There will be no limit to the opportunities for change and growth in the secretarial profession. One thing is certain. You will find yourself at the heart of a growing, constantly changing profession with fascinating possibilities for advancement. A broad understanding of economics, data and word processing, accounting, law, business organization and management, English, and human relations will provide a solid background for success in handling new responsibilities associated with the automated office.

SUGGESTED READINGS

Casady, Mona. *Word Processing Concepts.* Cincinnati: South-Western Publishing Co., 1980.

Gore, Marvin R., and John W. Stubbe. *Computers and Data Processors.* Hightstown, N. J.: McGraw-Hill Book Company, 1979.

Keeling, B. Lewis, and Norman F. Kallaus, *Administrative Office Management,* 8th ed. Cincinnati: South-Western Publishing Co., 1983.

Kleinschrod, Walter, Leonard B. Kruk, and Hilda Turner. *Word Processing: Operations, Applications, and Administration.* Indianapolis: The Bobbs-Merrill Co., Inc., 1980.

QUESTIONS FOR DISCUSSION

1. Since the time spent in keyboarding is greatly reduced with the addition of new automated equipment, do you think this will improve job satisfaction for the secretary?

2. Why is the manufacture of software one of the fastest growing technological industries?

3. Secretaries often say rather defensively, "I don't know anything about word processing or data processing, since we don't have either in my office." Discuss this attitude.

4. Surveys show that stenographers and typists average less than *15 words a minute* when transcribing from shorthand notes or dictation media. An average of 38 percent of their typing work is retyping. Manufacturers of text editors claim that using their equipment increases the typist's productivity over 100 percent. In your judgment is this claim exaggerated? Explain your answer.

5. Why is accuracy so important in feeding input data into a computer system?

6. The statement has been made that businesses could not return to manual processing of data even if they wanted to. Why would this be true?

7. Why should a secretary entering the office force today have a background in data processing?

8. For many years OCR was used to process checks, utility bills, and the like. Now OCR is finding its way into word processing. What are the advantages of using OCR as a word processing tool?

9. Select the correct word from the parentheses in each of the following sentences. Then refer to the Reference Guide to check your answers.

   (a) Every department was (effected, affected) by the budget cuts. The final (effect, affect) of this action will be the elimination of several jobs.

   (b) The captain will divide the prize money (among, between) the nine players.

   (c) All members (accept, except) John were present to (accept, except) the award.

   (d) She was (eager, anxious) to change jobs, but the interview left her (anxious, eager) about the added responsibility.

   (e) We have (adopted, adapted) the constitution of the national office, and we will (adopt, adapt) it to the objectives of our local chapter.

   (f) The students will (canvas, canvass) the dorms for donations to the fund.

   (g) The shoes and bag (complimented, complemented) her new dress so well that she received many (compliments, complements).

PROBLEMS

1. A number of companies manufacture equipment with text-editing capabilities. Each model has certain advantages as well as limitations. Assume that you have the responsibility of submitting specifications for a text editor to be installed in a newly organized word processing center for your office. Initially the center will be a one-person operation. The correspondence of the four executives in the office will be processed by one correspondence secretary.

   (a) Set up the criteria you will use for selecting the text editor. Gather data on two different makes and select the one you recommend for purchase. Support your selection with reasons for the decision.

   (b) What qualifications will you suggest for the correspondence secretary who will staff the newly formed word processing center?

2. Visit a computer installation in your community and prepare a report showing how the use of the equipment has reduced the amount of repetitive labor involved office work.

3. In the following bookkeeping applications, what are the step-by-step procedures in maintaining records, recording information, analyzing the data, and making decisions?

   Accounts Receivable

   Accounts Payable

   Payroll

   What types of input media for a computer will be appropriate?

Chapter 6

Reprographics

The demand for more and better copies has brought about some dramatic changes in the office. Thanks to continuous technological improvements, the production of multiple copies has become an easier, faster, cleaner, and, in some cases, a less expensive process. These advances have created a new classification of office work called *reprographics*.

Reprographics is the multiple reproduction of recorded images. Applied to the office, it involves the use of two primary kinds of equipment: copiers and duplicators.

Copiers use an image-forming process, similar to a camera, to create copies exactly and directly from existing originals. *Duplicators*, however, make copies from a stencil or master that must be prepared before the duplicated copies can be produced. Technological advancements in copying and duplicating processes have so greatly improved the speed and ease of machine operation, the quality of reproduction, and the per copy cost factor that some type of copier or duplicator is found in almost every office. In fact, the copying machine has become so commonplace and useful as to cause one enthusiastic secretary to comment: "The copier is the greatest boon to the business world since the telephone and electric lights."

Secretaries need to know how to prepare originals for copying, how to paste up camera ready copy, and how to type masters for duplication. It is also essential to know which reprographic process will provide the highest quality of copy at the lowest cost in the shortest time.

In many offices the secretary will determine the type of reprographic equipment to purchase and also assume the responsibility for its control. A thorough knowledge of reprographic equipment and supplies can reduce the expense and delays often associated with producing multiple copies. It is vital, then, that you understand those processes available to you and how to use them efficiently.

COPYING MACHINES

Copying machines, sometimes called *copiers* and other times called *photocopiers*, are used to reproduce quickly an exact copy of an original. Originals may include typewritten pages, pages from magazines and books, financial reports, photographs, artwork, graphic illustrations, and other legally reproducible materials.

Copiers may be classified according to use. Low volume machines placed in readily accessible locations throughout an organization are called *convenience copiers*. Time spent traveling to and from the machines is greatly reduced because of their accessibility, and no special skill is required to operate these copiers.

Illus. 6-1
Copying machines in general office situations are often electrostatic copiers.

In some organizations high volume copier-duplicators are used. These machines are usually operated by trained employees and are equipped with such features as automatic document feed, sorter, collator, and stapler. They can also reduce the size of the copy and enlarge it by use of pushbuttons.

Electrostatic Copiers

Most copying machines in general offices use the electrostatic process. There are two types: plain paper copiers (PPCs), and coated paper copiers (CPCs).

The plain paper copier (PPC) uses a dry process. A camera throws an image of the document to be copied onto a positively charged selenium coated drum. When a sheet of plain (untreated) negatively charged paper is passed over the drum, the image adheres to the paper and is permanently affixed by means of heat. A Federal Trade Commission ruling in 1975 required that patents held by the Xerox Corporation on the plain paper copier process be made available to other manufacturers. Thus, the number of PPCs on the market has greatly increased and costs have been reduced. The plain paper copier is the fastest growing segment of the copying industry.

The coated paper copier (CPC) uses an electrostatic process that reproduces the image directly on coated (chemically treated or sensitized) paper. A toner is used to develop the image on the exposed paper. Some users believe the coated paper copier produces copies with a higher image contrast than those obtained from the plain paper copier.

If you share the responsibility for selecting copying equipment and supplies, you should be aware that confusion often results from claims of manufacturers that their machines use *plain* paper. As a secretary, you should ask, "Will the copier use *any* paper?"

Fiber Optic Copiers

One of the most recent additions to the highly competitive office copier market is fiber optic technology. In some of the latest copier systems, this array of tiny hairlike strands of glass are replacing the lenses and mirrors formerly used in most conventional convenience copiers. These tiny strands of glass transmit information in the form of pulsating laser light. This development will

Olivetti Corporation

Illus. 6-2
Fiber optic copiers have few parts; they are smaller, less expensive, and more reliable than competitive conventional copiers.

be instrumental in reducing the cost of convenience copiers by making them easier to maintain and more energy efficient than competitive machines.

Fiber optic copiers have few parts; they are smaller, less expensive, and more reliable than competitive conventional copiers. Specialists predict that new markets will open for these copiers in schools and churches that previously used mimeograph machines and fluid duplicators. Fiber optic copiers are slower than the conventional convenience copiers because the optics (light source) must remain fixed while the paper moves past the light source on a moving platen.

Intelligent Copiers

The intelligent copier represents one of the most exciting and most versatile advances in copying technology. An intelligent copier may be defined as a self-instructing copier that combines the capabilities of the computer and the phototypesetter (an electronic device that transforms typewritten words into professional looking type). Intelligent copiers accept both hard copy (printed documents) or input from an electronic signal and can also communicate with other intelligent copiers. Because the intelligent copier is a hybrid, combining copier and computer capabilities, it is relatively expensive and will find its major application in large company in-house print shops producing high volume jobs.

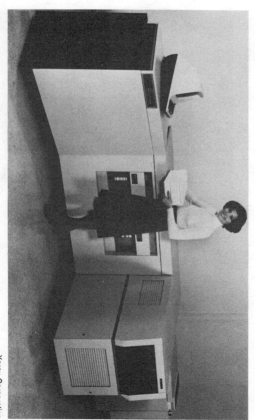

Xerox Corporation

Illus. 6-3
The trend is toward intelligent copiers, which will take on the new role of output device for a computer or text editor.

Intelligent copiers presently on the market can perform the following operations: reproduce hard copy at local or distant locations without operator intervention, communicate with other intelligent copier/printers, print up to 120 pages a minute, merge data from various electronic sources, depict graphic and alphabetic information, print high quality copy, and operate at a low noise level.

COLOR AND LARGE DOCUMENT REPRODUCTION

Several manufacturers produce reliable color copiers. However, because of high per copy cost, their use usually is limited to those situations where color is essential. An attachment to the Xerox color copier makes color prints or enlarges color slides on paper. Color prints can then be made and distributed to an audience after a management presentation using a transparency. (Transparencies are discussed in detail on page 139.)

Oversize originals are a source of frustration to the secretary. Not only is it difficult to fit these unwieldy documents on the platen of the copying machine but also documents such as computer printouts, large drawings, and oversize ledger sheets are too big to fit into the files. For easy handling and storage, a reduction feature has been added to many models of office copiers. Copiers capable of reducing oversize documents to 8½" × 11" or producing copies the same size as the oversize original are relative newcomers to the copying market.

COPY QUALITY

If any of the following questions is answered no, you are not obtaining the highest quality of reproduction from your copying machine.

1. Is the background as white as the original?
2. Is the copy free of specks or spots not on the original?
3. Is the copy free of streaks crossing the paper?
4. Is the intensity of the inklike impression similar to the original copy?
5. Does the copier compensate for less-than-perfect originals, such as those with dark backgrounds or light images?
6. Does the copier reproduce a pencil original into readable copy?
7. Does the copier adjust to the reproduction of originals on colored paper?
8. Do both black-and-white and colored photographs reproduce with strong images?
9. Can the copier produce good copies from such items as labels, card stock, transparencies, vellum, and specialty papers?

COPYING ABUSES

The ease with which copies can be made on reprographic equipment has led to the tendency to overcopy—that is, to make more copies than are needed. The urge seems to be almost irresistible. In addition to overcopying, there is also the cost of unauthorized personal copying—recipes, materials for clubs and other organizations, bowling scores, and personal letters. Although each copy costs only a few pennies, the cumulative total adds many dollars to the monthly copying bill.

To meet the problems of overcopying and unnecessary and unauthorized copying, some companies centralize all copiers in the word processing center and assign full-time operators to the machines. A reprographic requisition form must be submitted with each original. Assigning one operator has been known to decrease the volume of unnecessary copying by 20 percent.

Other companies, however, contend that centralizing the copiers increases the time it takes to get copies, takes the secretary away from the work station, and delays work. The cost of the time lost far exceeds the savings gained by eliminating unauthorized copying and overcopying.

Copiers can be equipped with a device, such as an *autotron*, that will ensure that only authorized personnel use the machine. Such devices also make it possible to charge copying costs to departments or individuals on a use basis. One such unit consists of counters installed in the copier. These counters cannot be reset by the user. The operator must have a key to activate the machine. When any one of the keys is inserted in the lock, the machine operates and the counter corresponding to that key records the number of copies made.

Another factor in the mounting cost of copying is the temptation, because of convenience, to use the copier rather than the duplicator to produce multiple copies of a page. Multiple copies of a page or several pages can usually be produced on a duplicator at a third or less of the cost of reproducing them on a copier.

Because of the ease of making photocopies and the availability of a copier in the office, there is a temptation to make copies of valuable personal papers and to use or carry the copies in place of the originals. There are rules against, and in some cases penalties for, copying certain papers. These papers include driver's licenses, automobile registrations, passports, citizenship papers, naturalization papers, immigration papers, postage stamps, copyrighted materials, and securities of the United States government.

DUPLICATING MACHINES

Unlike the copier which reproduces directly from the original, the duplicating machine produces copies from prepared masters and stencils. The three most commonly used types of duplicators are the fluid, stencil, and offset. Fluid and stencil duplicators, popular for so many years because of their simple operation and low initial cost, are rapidly being replaced by offset duplicators and the fiber optic copiers. Fluid and stencil duplicators are still used in some small offices and provide a means of quick and inexpensive reproduction.

Fluid (Direct Process) Duplication

The fluid process, also known as liquid, spirit, direct, and ditto process, is used for relatively short runs and is usually limited to the reproduction of materials to be used for interoffice or company distribution. The term *direct process* comes from the fact that copies are made directly from the master copy as it comes in contact with sheets of paper.

Copy to be reproduced is transferred in reverse image to the back of a master sheet from a direct process carbon sheet by one of several methods. The master is clamped to the cylinder of the duplicating machine carbon side up. The carbon deposit side of the master comes in contact with the chemically moistened sheets of paper as they pass through the machine. A minute portion of the dye from the master transfers to the paper, thus reproducing the copy. Up to 400 copies can be reproduced from one master.

Copies can be produced in purple, black, blue, green, or red. Using various colored carbons in producing the master allows several colors to be reproduced at the same time. Charts, pictures, and ruled forms can be traced onto the master. Also, a computer printout can go directly onto direct process masters and then multiple copies can be run.

Stencil Duplication (Mimeograph Process)

The stencil process involves a stencil and an inked drum or inked twin cylinders. The stencil is a thin tissue coated with a waxy substance which ink cannot penetrate. The copy to be duplicated is transferred to the stencil by one of several methods. The copy to be duplicated is transferred to the stencil by one of several methods. Each method results in pushing aside or removing the wax

Have you ever dashed to the duplicator to run off a few copies quickly, only to find that first you need to spend ten minutes cleaning up someone else's mess?
Suggestion: Initiate a sign-up sheet so that each person must register his or her use of the machine. It's amazing how tidy some people become when they know that the next user will definitely know who left the untidiness.

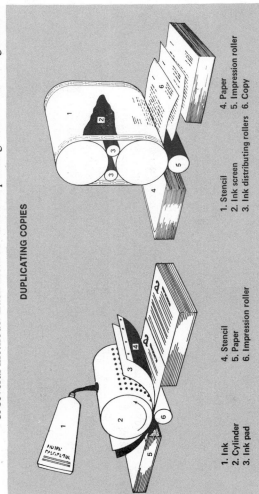

DUPLICATING COPIES

1. Ink
2. Cylinder
3. Ink pad

4. Stencil
5. Paper
6. Impression roller

1. Stencil
2. Ink screen
3. Ink distributing rollers

4. Paper
5. Impression roller
6. Copy

Illus. 6-4
Copies are produced by the stencil process through the meeting of the stencil, the ink, and the paper. The paper is fed, sheet by sheet, between the cylinder and the impression roller. As the paper passes through, the roller lifts, automatically pressing the paper against the stencil. Simultaneously, ink flows through the stencil openings, making a copy on the paper. At the left is a single drum duplicator, at the right, a twin cylinder.

coating, thus exposing the porous fibers. The stencil is placed around an inked drum or screen, and the ink flows through the exposed fibers to produce the copy as the paper passes through the machine.

The quality of reproduction in stencil duplication is superior to that of the fluid process. Several thousand highly readable copies can be reproduced from one stencil, thus making the process practical for both short runs and relatively long runs.

Fast drying emulsion inks make it possible to print on both sides of the paper without slip-sheeting (inserting a blotting paper between sheets). As many as five colors can be reproduced at the same time by using a special multicolor ink pad.

With the stencil process, near perfect registration (exact positioning on a page, column, and line) can be achieved, making it possible to duplicate fill-ins on printed or duplicated forms. Variable speed controls permit regulating the speed to lighten or darken the copy. Up to 200 copies a minute can be reproduced on the single drum machine, and 125 copies a minute can be reproduced on the twin drum machine. The machine may be set to shut off automatically upon completion of a preset number of copies.

Offset Duplication

In offset duplication (also known as photo-offset, lithography, photo-offset lithography, and offset lithography) an inked impression is first transferred to a rubber roller and then transferred from the roller to the paper. Offset duplication is based on the chemical principle that grease and water do not mix and on the lithographic principle of printing from a "flat" surface. The image area (outline) is receptive to ink; the nonimage area is receptive to water. Thus, this ink and water receptivity defines the image. The copy to be duplicated is reproduced by typing or other methods on the front side of an offset master. The master is placed on a cylinder and is inked as it rotates. The ink on the master deposits the copy in reverse image on a large drum of rubber called a blanket. The image is transferred from the blanket to the copy paper being fed through the machine when the impression roller presses the copy paper against the rubber blanket.

The offset process offers a wide range of possibilities for reproducing printed, handwritten, or typed copy as well as pictures and drawings. Various colors can be used, and several colors can be reproduced on the same page, but a separate master and a separate run are required for each color. As there is no offset on the back of the sheets, slip-sheeting is unnecessary. Copies can be run on both sides of a sheet to save both paper cost and bulkiness.

Offset duplicator manufacturers, such as A. B. Dick and Addressograph-Multigraph, market tabletop, office size machines designed to produce high quality work at a low per copy cost. Their objective is to provide a machine that is competitive for general office duplication. The operation of these machines has been so simplified that they may be operated satisfactorily by most members of the office staff.

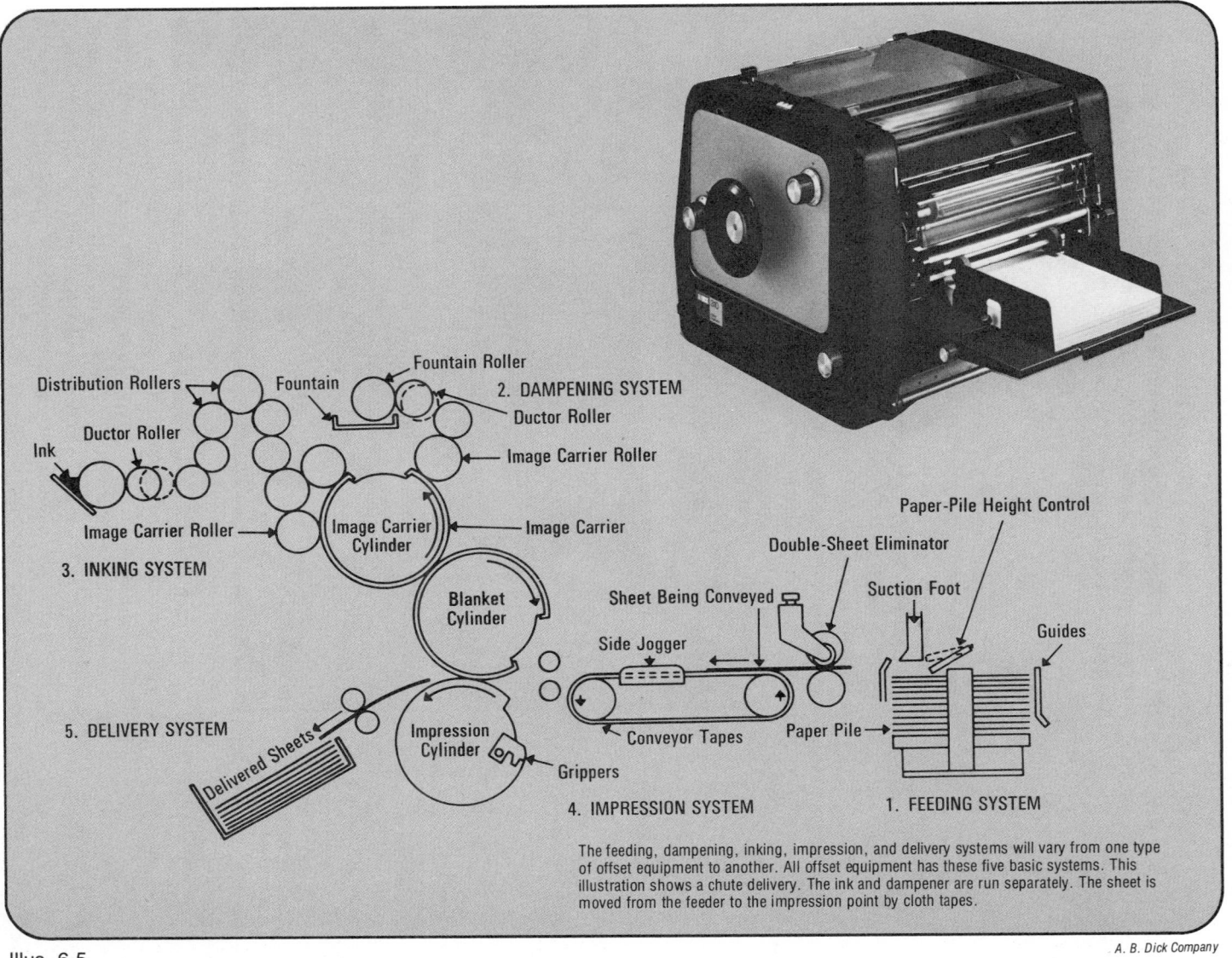

Distribution Rollers

Fountain

Fountain Roller

2. DAMPENING SYSTEM

Ductor Roller

Ductor Roller

Ink

Image Carrier Roller

Image Carrier Roller

Image Carrier Cylinder

Image Carrier

3. INKING SYSTEM

Blanket Cylinder

Paper-Pile Height Control

Double-Sheet Eliminator

Sheet Being Conveyed

Suction Foot

Side Jogger

Guides

5. DELIVERY SYSTEM

Delivered Sheets

Impression Cylinder

Conveyor Tapes

Paper Pile

Grippers

4. IMPRESSION SYSTEM

1. FEEDING SYSTEM

The feeding, dampening, inking, impression, and delivery systems will vary from one type of offset equipment to another. All offset equipment has these five basic systems. This illustration shows a chute delivery. The ink and dampener are run separately. The sheet is moved from the feeder to the impression point by cloth tapes.

A. B. Dick Company

Illus. 6-5
Table model offset duplicators are very easy to operate.

As many as 10,000 copies can be reproduced from one offset master and work of the highest quality can be obtained. The wide range of paper and variety of colors that can be used make the process especially appropriate where appearance is of major concern. This is most valuable for materials that are going outside the office to customers and to the public.

COPIER-DUPLICATORS

One of the most cost-effective developments in office reprographics is the copier-duplicator. This machine uses the copier principle of imaging but, unlike the convenience copier, is designed for high volume production, such as 100,000 to 500,000 impressions per month per machine. These machines operate at speeds of 4,500 or more copies per hour and compete favorably in per copy cost with offset duplicating. They offer the convenience of the copier, the speed and cost advantage of the duplicator, and certain automated features not available on duplicating machines.

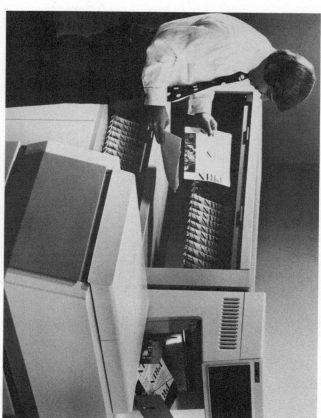

Xerox Corporation

Illus. 6-6
This Xerox 9200 copier has a collator that assembles pages into sequence, thus providing multiple sets of the copied material.

The sorter assembles duplicated pages in sequence to provide multiple sets of a duplicated document, such as a report. The automatic sorter unit is attached on-line to the copier-duplicator, meaning that the copies proceed directly from the copier-duplicator to the sorter without operator intervention. As the multiple copies of the first page of the original come off the copier-duplicator, they are automatically separated into a series of bins, one bin for each copy. The next page of the original is run and the copies are separated into the same bins. This process is repeated until all pages of the original have been copied. Each bin will then contain one complete copied set of the original. Similar sorter attachments for duplicators are also available.

In addition to assembling, some copier-duplicators carry the process one step further to include on-line *finishing.* The assembling unit receives the copies, jogs the set, staples one or two corners along one side, and deposits the set in a removable tray. Most copier-duplicators produce the number of desired copies of page one before proceeding to page two. Others, however, produce one copy of each page of the report, assemble and finish set one, then proceed to repeat the process and complete set two. This process is followed until the desired number of sets has been completed. The advantage of the latter system is that it is not necessary to wait until all the sets have been duplicated before getting the first finished set. The time involved here is called turnaround time —the lapsed time from submission of original to receipt of assembled copies.

AUTOMATED DUPLICATORS

The copier-duplicator offers the convenience of reproducing copy directly from an original without the intermediate step of preparing a master or

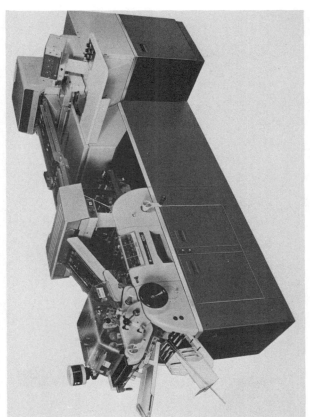

Addressograph Multigraph Corporation, Multigraphic Division

Illus. 6-7
In the continuous copy offset system, originals are fed into a copier at the right and an offset master is prepared. The master moves on a belt to a machine that processes the master without being touched by the operator. The master is then automatically attached to the cylinder of the offset duplicator, where many copies are duplicated very rapidly.

stencil. To compete, manufacturers of stencil and offset duplicators have produced highly automated machines for high volume users. Basically the automated duplicator combines three machines into an on-line assembly: (1) an automatic master or stencil making machine, (2) a high-speed duplicating machine, and (3) a sorter to provide assembled copies. The operator produces the master or stencil on the automatic plate or stencil maker and transfers the master or stencil to the duplicator. The duplicated copies feed automatically into a sorter and the operator receives assembled copies. The operation is even further automated by some manufacturers. The master or stencil moves via conveyor belt directly from the plate-stencil maker to the duplicator and attaches itself, and copies are run and assembled without operator intervention. The operator's function is to feed the original into the plate-stencil maker and to set the duplicator for the desired number of copies.

AUXILIARY REPROGRAPHIC EQUIPMENT

There are various types of equipment that supplement the work of copiers and duplicators. This equipment is usually located in a reprographic department or word processing center.

Headliners, Composers, and Phototypesetters

Equipment that can use a variety of type sizes and styles to produce copy resembling printing will improve the visual quality of the material to be duplicated or copied.

Headliners. Letter compositor machines are available for in-office use to create display type for headlines, subheads, and similar items for which large type is needed. The operator dials the letters in a heading one at a time. The heading is printed by the compositor on sensitized strips of tape. The tape is pasted on the original. The original is then converted to a master or stencil and duplicated.

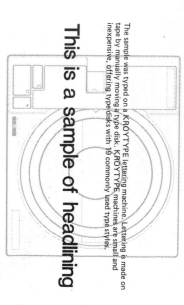

This is a sample of headlining

The sample was typed on a KROYTYPE lettering machine. Lettering is made on tape by manually moving a type disk. KROYTYPE machines are small and inexpensive, offering type disks with 19 commonly used type styles.

These machines are especially useful in preparing originals for *transparencies.* Because of their size, they enhance the readability from a distance.

Composers. Printed items requiring various type styles and sizes can be reproduced from typewritten copy to resemble the print found in magazines and advertising brochures. A VariTyper, IBM Composer, or text-editing machine can be used to prepare the copy. These machines have a regular typewriter keyboard and the capability to justify the right margin, permit the interchange of type style and size, and provide proportional letter spacing that resembles the printed page.

Phototypesetters. Phototypesetting is a process that electronically converts typewritten words into professional looking print. This process provides a variety of sizes and styles of type, justifies right margins, and spaces proportionally to create the appearance of print. Initial typing is usually done on text-editing equipment. Final copy is processed through an interface (black box) unit that permits the text editor to communicate with the phototypesetter. The interface translates the initial copy into simple commands that the phototypesetter can understand. No retyping is necessary, and the phototypeset pages contain about 40 percent more copy than a typewritten page.

The latest text editors eliminate the "black box" and combine the text-editing and phototypesetting processes into one operation. This makes the phototypesetting operation automated and requires no special operator. Illus. 6-9 shows one approach to phototypesetting.

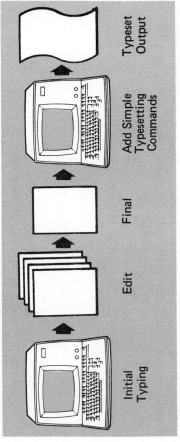

Initial Typing   Edit   Final   Add Simple Typesetting Commands   Typeset Output

Wang Laboratories

Illus. 6-9
Sample of phototypesetting

Finishing Equipment

Collating, stapling, binding, folding, addressing, and signing copies of duplicator output are time-consuming activities. There are machines that will perform these paper-pushing jobs quickly and accurately. They free the office staff for more productive work.

Collators. There are collators that operate independently of the copier or duplicator. The collator contains bins in which piles of papers are placed by the operator. Each bin will contain copies of the same sheet. When activated, the machine will automatically eject the top sheet from each bin and will assemble the sheets in a desired order. Fully automatic collators will stack the completed sets on a stacking bin. If the collator is semiautomatic, the operator is required to gather and stack the assembled sets.

Binders. Binding gives a professional appearance to copied or duplicated materials. Equipment consisting of a puncher and a binder is available for both softcover and hardcover binding. There are both manually and electrically operated punching, binding, and stapling machines.

Folding and Inserting Machines. Machines that fold duplicated sheets, such as letters and advertisements, and insert them in envelopes are significant energy savers and time-savers to businesses that have large mailings. For example, Insertamate Mailing System distributed by Pitney-Bowes is a fully integrated system that folds, inserts, seals, and meter stamps mail in one fast, accurate, and simultaneous operation.

Addresser-Printers. The addresser-printer is used to address envelopes to go to names on a mailing list. Each name and address on the mailing list is recorded on some form of plate or card called the data carrier. The data carrier may be a metal or plastic plate or a card with a small stencil or direct process master insert. A separate data carrier is used for each addressee. As the envelope or addressing tape passes through the addresser-printer, the plate or address card falls in place, one at a time. The address is then duplicated on the envelope or address tape. The addresser-printer may be manually fed or fully automatic. These machines are called addresser-printers because they may be used for other purposes than addressing, such as preparing inventory cards, monthly bills, and routing of multiple forms.

Signature Machines. When a large number of original signatures are regularly required, a signature machine can save the employer many tedious hours. Two types of signature machines are available: the template and the ribbon. The template machine traces the user's signature cut in a template (a thin plate used as a guide) as a mechanical pen writes the signature on the document. The ribbon machine impresses the signature on the document by means of pressure on a ribbon in much the same way a charge card is imprinted. This type of machine is often used for signing checks.

COMMERCIAL AND IN-HOUSE DUPLICATION

According to a national market research organization, the demand for duplicating increases at the rate of 150 billion copies every five years. Many companies are meeting this demand with their own in-plant reprographic shops. This is a growing trend and, of course, challenges the secretary to provide letter-perfect originals in acceptable format to the reprographic department. Some firms will continue to use commercial print shops for handling jobs that cannot be produced on copiers or duplicators and where the volume of work does not justify the purchase of reprographic equipment.

In every city there are commercial shops that make a specialty of reprographic work. These businesses are usually listed in the Yellow Pages under "Letter Shop Service," "Copying and Duplicating," or "Photocopying." Such shops will prepare stencils or masters, run the copies, address envelopes, and fold and insert the enclosures. They will do the entire job or any phase of it.

If the office does not have adequate reprographic equipment or if time is short, the secretary may need to turn to an outside shop. Factors that must be investigated and compared include (1) rates charged per copy, (2) quality of prepared copy, (3) cost for collating, (4) cost for binding copies, and (5) time needed for completion. The secretary should maintain a file of information about the shops available.

SELECTING THE REPROGRAPHIC PROCESS

The secretary usually makes the decision as to whether copies are to be produced on the copier, copier-duplicator, or duplicator, or by a commercial shop. Several factors enter into this decision: the number of copies required; the urgency; copying and duplicating facilities available in-company, and at outside agencies; the quality of reproduction desired; and the cost per copy.

If the number of copies required is ten or less, the use of the copying machine will probably be the least expensive, fastest, and most convenient. If the number required is 100 or more, the duplicator or copier-duplicator will be the fastest, will give the highest quality reproduction, and will result in the lowest per copy cost. However, when the number of copies required falls between ten and 100, the choice comes within what is known in the industry as the *gray zone*, meaning that the decision is not clearly weighted for copying or for duplicating. The copier-duplicator is economical in this range, but it is a high volume machine and usually is available only in large companies with a centralized reprographic department. The commercial shop may be the most economical in the 10-to-100-and-above copy range, but the inconvenience and the slow turnaround time of the shop may preclude its use. The convenience and quality of reproduction by duplicator will depend on whether equipment for stencil and master imaging is available, which duplicator process is used, and which automated features are on the equipment.

PREPARING MASTERS AND STENCILS

Copy to be duplicated may be transferred to an offset or direct process master or to a stencil in a number of ways. The traditional way is to image the copy on the master or stencil by typing. Technology, however, has provided new imaging devices that are more convenient, faster, and more versatile than typing. These new devices have been instrumental in keeping the duplicator in a competitive position relative to the copying machine. Imaging equipment is now used extensively in large offices, and the number of small offices purchasing this equipment is growing steadily.

Imaging techniques not only save the time of manually typing and correcting the master and stencil but offer many other advantages. For example, most of the time-consuming process of proofreading the stencil or master is eliminated. If the original is correct, the master or stencil will be correct. In addition, pasting up copy is practical. It provides the flexibility of including a printed graph or map, of preparing a four-page folded program, and of including photographs and other materials that would be impractical if not impossible to attempt to record manually on a stencil or master.

Thermal Imaging

The thermographic process is also known as the infrared or heat-transfer process. Material to be copied is placed beneath a heat-sensitive copy sheet. Infrared light is beamed through the sensitized copy onto the original as both sheets feed through the machine. The heat turns the sensitized paper dark in the same places as the original, thus producing the image.

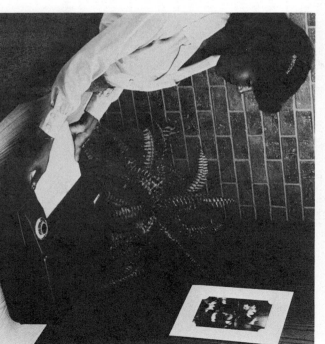

Illus. 6-10
The thermographic copier is excellent for the preparation of transparencies used on an overhead projector.

3M Audio Visual Division

Although copiers using the thermographic process were the first to be marketed for office use, today the process is used primarily to prepare overhead-projector transparencies and to laminate documents.

The thermographic (heat transfer) copier can be used to produce stencils and fluid masters. The original is prepared by typing, writing, or drawing on paper. Erasers, correction tape, or correction fluid may be used to make corrections. Copy can be cut and a paste-up original prepared. The original is then combined with a *thermal stencil* or *master* and passed through the copier. The heat causes a copy of the original to transfer to the stencil or master which may be placed immediately on the duplicator to reproduce copies.

One limitation of the thermal process is that certain colors will not transfer, but a copy of the original can be made on an electrostatic copier that will reproduce most inks and most colors. This copy can then be used in place of the original to produce the thermal stencil or master.

Photo Imaging

Small desktop offset platemakers transfer originals to offset masters (plates) within seconds. The original and the chemically sensitized offset master are placed on a flatbed window. When the printing button is pressed, a photographic-type lamp automatically exposes the master. A timer controls the exposure. No film or other intermediate step is required, and the process is almost error-proof.

Electrostatic Imaging

The process of producing an offset master on the copying machine is almost as simple and convenient as producing a copy of an original. The original is placed in the copier. A sensitized offset master is substituted for the copy paper. The image is transferred from the original to the offset master which may be immediately used to produce copies on the offset duplicator.

Facsimile Imaging

The facsimile process, sometimes referred to as the *electronic scanning method*, is used for preparing stencils and offset masters. The process is an adaptation of the principle of the photoelectric cell. Material to be reproduced is placed on the left drum of a two-drum machine. An electronic (plastic) stencil or offset plate is placed on the right drum. As the drums rotate slowly, a photoelectric eye scans each line. This activates a needle that moves across the second drum as the photoelectric eye moves across the first. The needle records the image on the stencil or offset master.

Drawings, forms, printed and typed copy, diagrams, and artwork (including photographs) can be transferred to a stencil or master with relatively

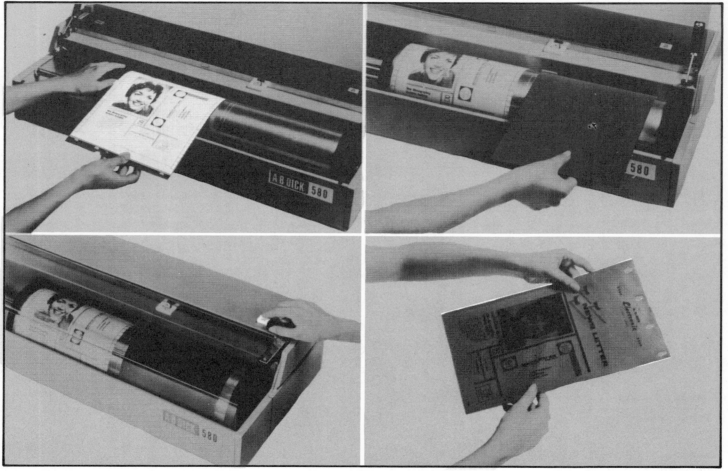

A. B. Dick Company

Illus. 6-11
The four steps in preparing a stencil by the facsimile process are: (1) the copy to be reproduced is placed on one drum; (2) an electronic stencil is placed on the second drum; (3) the operation switch is activated; and (4) the completed stencil is removed and is ready to be run on the duplicator.

high quality detail. A transparency may be prepared simultaneously with the production of the stencil or master. Thus, reproduced copies can be distributed to a group and the screen projected transparency can be used for an oral presentation.

PREPARING TRANSPARENCIES

Making a transparency is a quick process—as fast as producing paper copy. Before attempting to make a transparency, be sure you have the right film for the machine you are using. Damage to your copier can result if the film was designed for another type of machine. Special film has been produced for plain paper copiers that will enable you to make a transparency in much the same way you make a paper copy. Substitute the film for the paper in the copier's paper feed tray, place your original on the platen of the copier, and press the print button.

One type of transparency film is made for desk top convenience copiers and another type is manufactured for the high volume copier-duplicator systems. There are also many transparency films on the market capable of producing color transparencies in bright purple, red, blue, or green on clear film. Film is also available that will produce white frosted images that project black against clear or colored backgrounds. The following tips should help you get perfect transparencies on your first attempt:

1. If the transparency film becomes separated from the backing sheet, reassemble the sheets by matching the rounded corners.
2. To write or draw on an original, use a No. 2 pencil or black marking pen.
3. If the transparency is too light or too dark, adjust the exposure dial.
4. If the backing sheet does not peel away easily, the machine is too hot.
5. Some copiers, such as thermographic copiers, use a screen carrier to move the original and film through the machine. A screen carrier consists of two sheets of special paper fastened at the top. The original and the film are placed in the carrier before insertion into the copier. The screen carrier transports the packet through the machine.

PREPARING CAMERA READY COPY

Most in-house reprographic departments and commercial printers produce their most professional looking jobs from pasted up, camera ready copy (copy ready to be photographed for reproduction). Cutting and pasting copy affords the secretary an excellent opportunity to be creative and to improve the appearance of what would otherwise be an ordinary piece of duplicated correspondence. You can also type, write, or draw on the original; but you can avoid errors, delays, and frustrations by exercising care in preparing camera ready copy for reproduction. The printer with whom you will work will be able to help you until such time that you become proficient.

PAPER FOR COPIERS AND DUPLICATORS

The secretary may be assigned the responsibility for buying paper for the office copier and duplicator. The purchasing problem is complicated because several of the office copiers use sensitized papers, and each duplicating process requires its own type of paper.

Paper used in duplicating is usually wood sulfite. It comes in a wide variety of colors. The three standard weights for mimeo and duplicating paper are 16, 20, and 24 pounds. Offset paper may carry these same weight identifications or different weights such as 50, 60, or 70 pounds.

Offset paper comes in two general types—coated and uncoated. The coated paper is designed for high grade work, and offset enamel is the very highest quality. Uncoated paper is used for the majority of in-house work which does not require a high quality result from the reproduction process.

Paper for stencil duplicating, unlike that for spirit duplicating, is unglazed and absorbent. Since moisture affects the quality of reproduction and the ease with which the paper is handled by the machine, duplicating paper should be kept wrapped in the moisture proof covers in which it is received. It should be stored in a dry place and stacked flat.

Duplicator paper, like other paper, has a top and a bottom side. The best results are obtained by using the paper topside up. The printed label on the package usually indicates the correct printing side.

An important consideration in buying copier paper is to avoid overstocking. Most copier papers have a shelf life which should be checked before buying in quantity. Paper for copiers may be purchased in rolls (which use more storage space) and in a variety of sizes, such as executive, letter, and legal (precut).

SUGGESTED READINGS

Manson, Richard E. *The Manager's Guide to Copying and Duplicating.* New York: McGraw-Hill Book Company, 1980.

Pasewark, William R. *Duplicating Machine Processes: Stencil, Fluid, Offset, and Copier,* 2d ed. Cincinnati: South-Western Publishing Co., 1975.

QUESTIONS FOR DISCUSSION

1. What is meant by overcopying? Why is it a major problem in the office?
2. What factors and features should be considered in evaluating the quality of reproductions obtained from a specific copier?

3. Which reproduction process would you recommend for each of the following projects, assuming that all types were available to you?

(a) 5,000 copies of a form letter to be mailed to sales prospects

(b) 5 copies of an order to be distributed to department heads with the least possible delay

(c) 300 copies of a notice to be mailed to all sales representatives, announcing a new product

(d) 15 copies of a two-page report to be mailed to department heads

(e) 750 copies of a four-page house organ that is issued monthly and contains pictures and illustrations

(f) 45 copies of a one-page announcement showing directions to the recreational area for a company picnic (The notices are to be placed on bulletin boards throughout the plant.)

(g) 8 copies of the secretary's minutes of the directors' meeting

(h) 150 copies of a price list duplicated each week (The list covers 144 standard items arranged in alphabetical order. Since the prices fluctuate, a new price list is prepared, duplicated, and distributed weekly to all sales employees.)

(i) 500 preprinted time cards to be titled each week—one time card for each company employee (The title on the card shows the employee's number, name, address, social security number, and number of income tax exemptions.)

(j) 1,500 copies of a program cover for a secretarial seminar on which you would like to use the CPS key and the Professional Secretaries International emblem on the front and the state seal and motto of your home state on the back.

4. What finishing equipment may be purchased as auxiliaries to copiers and duplicators?

5. Which cost elements should be included in arriving at the duplicator or copier cost per copy?

6. Write the number of the response that best completes the sentence. Then use the Reference Guide to check your answers.

(a) Missing the reunion made her feel _____. (1) bad (2) badly

(b) The will contained a clause that was not understood by _____. (1) anyone (2) any one

(c) Once the documents have been shredded, they are tied in a _____. (1) bail (2) bale

(d) We test all applicants. If you apply, you will be screened on this _____. (1) basis (2) bases

(e) The order has been partially shipped. When can we expect the _____? (1) balance (2) remainder

(f) Carla is a graduate of Vassar and is considered their most outstanding _____. (1) alumna (2) alumnae (3) alumni (4) alumnus

(g) Flowers and candles decorated the _____. (1) altar (2) alter

PROBLEMS

1. There are many makes, models, and types of duplicators and copiers available. Furthermore, each duplicator and copier process offers certain advantages depending on the specific reproduction requirements of the office. Careful consideration is required to select the reprographic process and the make and model of machine that will best meet the needs of an insurance office. Prepare a list of the factors you would consider in selecting the process and the make and model of machine to be used in an insurance office.

2. To help the employees you are supervising, prepare an instruction sheet clearly explaining procedures for one of the following activities. Illustrate your explanation, if possible:

   (a) Placing the master copy on a direct process duplicator and running the copies

   (b) Placing the master on the offset duplicator and running the copies

   (c) Using a copying machine to make a transparency

   (d) Using a heat transfer copier to produce a direct process master, stencil, or transparency

   (e) Using a facsimile imaging machine to produce an offset master

3. Your company offices occupy six floors in an office building. One high-speed copier-duplicator is installed in a central location on each floor, and each staff person uses that machine for copying. You are aware of several problems:

   (a) The total cost for copying has been increasing at an alarming rate and you are suspicious that there is much overcopying and copying of personal material.

   (b) You have observed that staff members frequently lose considerable time waiting at the copier for the machine to become available.

   (c) The copying center has become a quasi-social center for office personnel.

   (d) Although the copier-duplicator is centrally located, it is a considerable distance from some of the offices. Secretaries frequently make the round trip to the machine to reproduce only two or three copies.

   (e) Senior staff members complain that secretaries are away from their desks too much of the time.

   Prepare a list of recommendations to improve the situation.

Part Two

Case Problems

Case 2-1
HELP YOURSELF TO COMPANY EQUIPMENT AND SUPPLIES

Hayes Malik was a recently hired secretary to the head of the Transportation Department. He was also secretary of the neighborhood association that was planning a block party. Mary Miller, secretary to the plant manager for the past ten years, was a friendly person who wanted to be helpful to new employees and had made a friend of Hayes.

When she went to the Reprographic Department with an order for photocopies of a report, she met Hayes, who said, "Want to see the posters we are distributing to every building on the block to advertise our block festival? I hope that you can come." A quick glance showed the job order for 50 posters. Mary replied, "They are very artistic and should attract a crowd. I hope that I can come. I think it is wonderful that you are so interested in community work."

When she got back to her office, she questioned whether she should have told Hayes that it is dishonest to use company equipment and materials for personal use. After all, he was involved in a commendable project. She realized, too, that "everybody does it." Did she have the authority to reprimand an employee at her own level anyway? She also wondered if she should report the violation of explicit company rules against using company equipment for personal use. If so, to whom?

Case 2-2
ADJUSTING TO NEW EQUIPMENT

When Ray Stamus came to work on Tuesday morning, he was amazed to find that a new electronic typewriter had replaced the familiar electric on his desk. He would have been delighted except for the fact that his employer, Ellen Farrell, had left a 30-page report on his desk with the request that he have it ready for her to present at a 2 p.m. meeting that afternoon when she returned from an out-of-town trip. He found that all the secretaries on the floor had received the same new equipment and that no instruction manuals had been left for the users.

Ray stormed into the office of the manager of administrative services and announced that he was taking the report to an outside agency for typing, would bring it back in time for Ms. Farrell's meeting, and meanwhile would attend a session given by the typewriter manufacturer.

What principle has been violated by the administrative services manager? by Ray? Do you approve of Ray's short-term solution? What long-range action do you recommend?

Case 2-3
PURCHASING EQUIPMENT—RESPONSIBILITY WITHOUT AUTHORITY

Myra Lancaster was secretary to William Noble, the purchasing agent. Mr. Noble told her, "Myra, I am so busy with procurement of raw materials for the factory that I wish you would take over the responsibility for learning about new office equipment and supplies. If you find something you think we should have, just call my attention to it."

Myra read all the office administration magazines, attended business shows, talked to sales representatives about office supplies and equipment, and informed herself in the field so that she became the company authority. She was justifiably proud of improvements made in office efficiency because of her choices.

Before she could buy anything, though, she had to get Mr. Noble's authorization. She believed strongly that she should have been given authority along with responsibility for the purchase of office supplies and equipment if she stayed within the budget and improved operations.

Do you agree that Myra should have this authority? If so, what steps would you suggest that she follow?

Case 2-4
CAUGHT IN THE MIDDLE—EMPLOYER'S REQUEST FOR PREFERENTIAL TREATMENT

Jean Smith, copywriter for an advertising agency, handed a 24-page market analysis to her secretary, Judy Dale, saying, "Take this down to Reprographics and tell them that this is a rush job. We have to have ten copies, collated and bound by four o'clock tomorrow, even if they have to let some of their other work go until later."

Aware that her employer had a reputation for making everything a rush job, Judy approached Joe Santini, supervisor of duplicating, with the written job order in hand and said cautiously, "Listen, Joe, Ms. Smith is really in a bind. She has to have ten copies of this market analysis by four o'clock tomorrow, and she knows that she can depend on you to get her out of this crisis."

Joe was unimpressed. "You tell that boss of yours that she has to learn that there are other people in this company who need duplicating. She just has to wait her turn. Look at that pile of work orders. Do you think that she has any right to ask to be put ahead of those requisitions? I've done my last rush job for Madam Smith."

Judy considered her alternatives. Should she try again by revealing confidential information that a million dollar contract was riding on that report? Should she accept Joe's refusal and, if so, what should she say to Ms. Smith? What else might she suggest to get the report finished by the deadline?

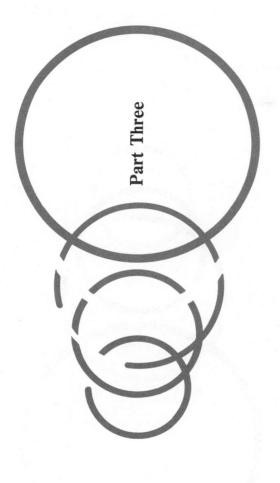

Part Three

INFORMATION PROCESSING: WRITTEN COMMUNICATIONS

"Put it in writing." Even with extensive oral communication, a large portion of business is conducted by written means—not only the communications to and from the outside world but also the many memorandums that circulate inside the organization and make operations possible. The costs of business communication are astronomical, so it is imperative that every business document pay its way. A communication must represent its writer so effectively that its purpose is accomplished and its expense justified.

One of the secretary's primary functions is handling the mail effectively—from recording its receipt so that nothing is lost, to organizing it, assembling data required for an answer, and finally processing the reply. Usually the executive dictates the communication, which is recorded either in shorthand or by machine. The secretary then becomes responsible for preparing the dictated material for signature, even to the extent of correcting obvious errors and sometimes improving the quality of the dictation. With experience the secretary can be given responsibility for originating some of the communications. The secretary is the *word specialist.*

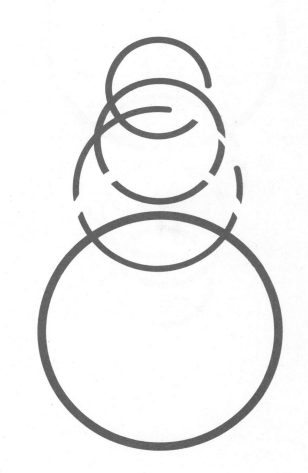

Mail Responsibilities

Preparing mail for effective handling is a primary secretarial responsibility. Handling incoming mail is a visible means of demonstrating efficiency and decision-making ability. The first and heaviest mail arrives from the mail room early in the morning, and many secretaries plan to *process* it (prepare it for executive attention) before the employer arrives so that action can be taken on it immediately. Throughout the day additional mail arrives and must be acted on in terms of its importance.

This chapter describes techniques for processing the mail: sorting it, opening it, recording it both upon receipt and when it is passed along to others for action, accumulating supporting information required for its handling, reading and annotating the contents, and arranging it for presentation for action. It also discusses disposition of mail when the executive is absent from the office and when the secretary works for several persons.

MAIL-PROCESSING PERSONNEL

The first step in the processing of mail is sorting the envelopes into groups for expeditious handling. The personnel involved differ according to the way the mail is addressed and, of course, according to the size of the company or firm.

The Mail Room

The mail room personnel receive mail from the post office, from a company mail service, or from a private mail service. It is not unusual for an organization to develop a mail service among its branches and most frequent correspondents. This can speed up delivery by at least a day. The secretary should become familiar with such services and their schedules.

If a letter is addressed to the company and not to an individual in the company, the envelope is opened in the mail room. The mail clerk follows established procedures for assigning the mail to appropriate departments for action. The clerk also makes a record of the receipt of the mail and the routing assigned to it. It is then usually delivered by messenger to the designated offices.

The mail room is prepared for quantity handling of mail and contains equipment more elaborate than that in individual offices. For instance, it may include a mail opener that feeds, transports, removes the envelope edges, disposes of waste, stacks and counts opened envelopes all in a single operation. Another letter opener automatically processes mail of mixed sizes. Still another opens envelopes on two sides, the long end and one side, so that the

Pitney Bowes, Inc.

interiors of the envelopes are completely exposed, making removal of their contents effortless and enclosures easily noticeable. Automated delivery systems may bring the mail to the secretary's desk. These self-powered unattended vehicles may either run on tracks or on an invisible guide path and are programmed to make designated stops for mail pickup and delivery.

The Secretary

If letters are addressed to specific employees or departments, the mail room delivers the envelopes unopened. The secretary usually gives the unopened envelopes to the addressees, with the exception of the employer's mail. That mail is sorted, opened, and processed in other ways that will expedite its handling when it is presented to the employer for action.

In a small office the secretary opens all mail that is not addressed to a specific employee, gives it to the appropriate person for answering, and prepares the employer's mail for action.

PROCEDURES FOR PROCESSING MAIL

The secretary's role in processing the mail is a very sensitive one. Offices are inundated with mail, and the desire to reduce unnecessary burdens on the employer may annoy the person who wants to see everything. On the other hand, the executive who wants to reduce the work load by giving attention to only the most important communications will appreciate the secretary who enables him or her to devote less time to mail that can be handled by someone else. Study your employer's preferences and work style. Then demonstrate that you can assume more and more responsibility for less than top-level mail but be careful not to assume unassigned authority.

Steps to follow in sorting, opening, reading, and expediting the handling of incoming mail are discussed here. The processing of outgoing mail is described in later chapters. Telecommunications are fully covered in Chapter 13 and special delivery, certified, and registered mail in Chapter 11.

Classifying and Sorting the Mail

The mail will fall into eight categories:

1. Telecommunications: telegrams, mailgrams, telex or TWX messages, and hard copy printouts of computer sent material (only in organizations with terminals)
2. Special delivery, certified mail, and registered letters and packages
3. Airmail and first-class letters, including bills and statements
4. Interoffice communications
5. Personal mail
6. Newspapers and periodicals
7. Booklets, catalogs, and advertising material
8. Packages

The first four groups, except mailgrams, will be received throughout the day and usually should receive first attention, although some first-class mail may be put aside until all other top priority communications have been processed. Telegrams will be delivered directly to you as soon as they are received. Your telex, TWX, or data processing operator will also deliver these messages as they are received. (You may be the receiver of computer messages as their use increases.) Someone, possibly you, has to sign for special delivery, certified, and registered mail, so that you will know when it arrives. Special delivery mail has additional postage attached to pay for delivery by a special letter carrier at an earlier time than the regular mail. Certified mail is so designated on the envelope and is signed for on a form that is returned to the sender as proof of delivery. Registered mail contains valuables, either papers or small articles, and involves special security measures to ensure safe delivery.

Mailgrams are sent by Western Union to your local post office and delivered with the regular mail the morning after they are filed. The word *mailgram* is printed on the envelope in large letters.

You can recognize first-class letters in regular envelopes by the amount of postage and the dated postmark. Oversize first-class mail is sent either in a large manila envelope with a distinctive border or the sender labels it *First Class* in a conspicuous way. By noting the sender's return address and postmark, you will learn to identify business and personal correspondents of high interest as you become familiar with the employer's business activities and personal associations.

Keep these points in mind when sorting the mail:

1. Bills can be identified by the window envelopes in which they are frequently sent; however, window envelopes are being used more and more for all mail, since they save addressing time and reduce the chance of error in addressing.

2. Be alert for first-class letters that are attached to packages or packages not marked *First-Class Mail Inside.*

3. Interoffice mail is always treated as important.

4. The mail may be sorted three times if it is received in considerable volume.

First Sorting. On the first sorting pull out all telecommunications, special class, important looking first-class and interoffice mail, and personal mail for immediate processing. Put a large X on the back of any incorrectly addressed or odd looking envelope for the executive's attention. Unless you are authorized to open personal mail, leave these letters unopened (even though they are not marked *Personal* or *Confidential*) and submit them with the processed mail. Distinguish between urgent and routine items, putting the important ones in the first group to be processed. These decisions are made after you have quickly scanned but not actually read the items.

After completing the first sorting, stop and process the important mail according to the steps on pages 151-156. Keep in mind that including something unimportant is preferable to missing something important.

Second and Third Sortings. Lay out the mail by kind in a second sorting. Process first routine first-class mail. Sort it into like kinds—envelopes from branch offices, from the home office, from customers or clients, from traveling associates, from suppliers, and so on. Group the first-class window envelopes that usually contain invoices or statements. If instructed to do so, the secretary accumulates bills and statements for a specific bill-paying day. Otherwise they are submitted each day.

The sorting of personal mail follows a pattern. If there is enough volume, sort it again according to the executive's outside activities and financial interests. You may want to maintain special files relating to these activities and interests. (This type of file is discussed in Chapter 22.) Separate the personal financial mail into like kinds—such as the bills, the bank letters, investment house letters, and stock ownership letters.

The third sorting involves advertising mail. *Advertising mail* comes in envelopes of all sizes, shapes, and colors—for attention value. You can easily spot it, although the advertisers try hard to mislead you. The envelopes rarely, if ever, carry first-class postage. They almost always have open ends with sealed flaps. They have precanceled stamps or printed permit numbers and are not postmarked. Open these when you have time, perhaps after the other mail has been processed and handed to the executive. Organize the contents of advertising mail (it is always full of floating, loose pieces, it seems) and give them to the executive at your convenience sometime during the day. Do not destroy them. The executive likes to keep up on *direct mail*—as it is called in the advertising profession—to know what is being advertised and whether to return the enclosed postcards. You can, though, reduce volume by consigning to the wastebasket duplicate copies of advertising that seem to keep coming in floods.

Because of their bulkiness, put aside publications; later on, open, scan, and perhaps stamp or initial them as your employer's copy.

Opening the Mail

You need special supplies for opening mail. Place them on your desk before you start to work, arranging them within convenient reach.

You need:
An envelope opener
A stapler or clips
Pencils (several colors)
The tickler
Mail expected list
A memo pad for *To-Do* items

You may also need:
A date or time stamp
A routing stamp or slips
An action stamp or slips
Transparent tape for mending

You can save two thirds of your envelope-opening time if you use a machine, either hand operated or electrically driven. You can also reduce the

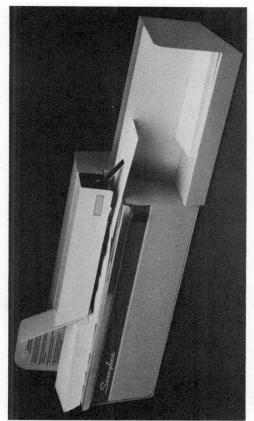

Swingline 6200 High-Speed Letter Opener

Illus. 7-2
An electrically driven mail opener for secretarial use. You can save two thirds of your envelope-opening time if you use a machine.

possibility of cutting the contents if you use a machine. In either case tap the lower edges of the envelopes on the desk before opening them so that the contents will fall to the bottom, and cut along the top edge. Keep the mail in the order into which it has been sorted for later efficient handling. Open all the envelopes before removing the contents.

Removing the Contents. Remove the contents, flatten them, and stack them *face down* at your right. If necessary, mend any cuts by attaching transparent tape to the back.

Hold the envelopes to the light to look for enclosures. Stack the opened envelopes to your left with open edges to the right and flap side up, in the same order as the contents to your right.

Use both hands to unfold and flatten the letter and attach enclosures. Scan the letter to see if it contains the sender's address; if not, retrieve the envelope and attach it to the letter. Scan also to see if the letter mentions enclosures and whether those you found agree with the letter. If not, after checking inside the envelope again, underline the reference notation of the enclosure or the mention of the enclosure in the letter and write *No* nearby. Attach any envelopes with missing enclosures to the letter to be given to the executive.

Specifically, save the envelopes for situations such as the following:

1. An envelope is incorrectly addressed. In this case, the executive may want to include the correct address in the return letter for the future guidance of the correspondent or as an explanation of why the letter was not answered more promptly.

2. A letter was missent by the post office and had to be forwarded. This information is needed to explain the reason for a delayed answer to the missent letter.

3. A letter does not contain a return address.

4. The return address in the letter differs from that on the envelope. Sometimes an individual uses business, hotel, or club stationery and does not indicate a return address. However, the reply should not be sent to the address given on the letterhead, and so the return address on the envelope is needed.

5. The date of the letter differs too much from the date of its receipt. A comparison of the letter date with the postmark date will reveal whether the fault lies with the sender or with the postal service.

6. Neither a handwritten nor a typewritten signature appears in the letter. The name of the sender may appear as a part of the return address on the envelope.

7. A letter specifies an enclosure that was not attached to the letter nor found in the envelope.

8. A letter contains a bid, an offer, or an acceptance of a contract. The postmark date may be needed as legal evidence.

Another envelope that is saved is the interoffice chain envelope. Draw a line through your principal's name on the envelope and reuse it. You will notice that these envelopes are usually perforated with holes so that all enclosures can be easily detected.

Registering, Dating, and Time-Stamping. It is often desirable for the secretary to keep a *mail register* of important mail for follow-up or tracing purposes. The mail register is used to record special incoming mail (such as registered, certified, special delivery, or insured mail), expected (separate cover) mail, and mail that is circulated to the executive's associates. For expected bulk mail it may be necessary to give the mail clerk or receiving clerk a memorandum that a package is coming. Telegrams and cables are also logged in on the mail register.

MAIL REGISTER

Name Arlene Dylan

Dates this page 3/14-

#	RECEIVED Date / Time	FROM Name/Address	DATED	ADDRESSED TO Dept.	Person	DESCRIPTION Kind of mail/enc/sep cov	SEP COV RECEIVED	REFERRED To / Date	WHERE FILED	FOLLOW UP
1	3/14 9:15 a.m.	F. Slyminsky, New York	3/12	Adv.		Ad. pamphlet - Layout	—	Adv. 3/14	Adv.	
2	3/18 9 a.m.	State Government Co., Chicago	3/11		MLA	Exquisitite catalog - file cabinets	3/21	RW 3/22	Pend.	
3	3/20 1 p.m.	L.H. Sumo, New York	3/19		MLA	ACA Banquet tickets				3/24
4	3/22 3 p.m.	F. Cort, Lima, Ohio	3/18	Adv.		Book - typeface	4/10	Adv. 4/11	Adv.	
5	3/23 2 p.m.	D. Schornett, Chicago	3/22		MLA	Special delivery - rush order	—	YP 3/23		
6	3/24 9 a.m.	IRS - local	3/23		E. Logan form enclosed	Quarterly taxes - form enclosed		LV 3/24		4/1
7	3/26 2 p.m.	Pomco, Inc., local	3/26 Avp			Registered Ck. #345	—	JP 3/26		
8	3/28 4:20 a.m.	R. Figgaggo, Detroit	3/26		C. Miller	Insured package	—	YP 3/28		

Illus. 7-3

Secretaries rely on the mail register as a protective record that verifies the receipt and disposition of mail.

Secretaries say that the mail register is worth its weight in gold as a protective record that verifies the receipt and disposition of mail. Only a few minutes are needed to record the entries since abbreviations are used freely. A ruled form similar to Illus. 7-3 may be used. The blank space in the "SEP. COV. RECEIVED" column, for example, indicates to the secretary that the executive's banquet tickets have not yet arrived. As an aid in tracing lost mail, the secretary usually indicates on the face of the item the number assigned to that item in the mail register.

For several reasons it is important to know the date on which each piece of mail is received:

1. It furnishes a record of the date of receipt.
2. It furnishes an impetus to answer the mail promptly. (Each reply should be regarded as a builder of goodwill, but no reply that is unduly delayed —no matter how courteous or affable it may be—will promote good public relations.)
3. A letter may have arrived too late to take care of the matter to which it refers. The date of receipt authenticates that inability.
4. The letter itself may be undated. The only clue to its date is the date of receipt. (You may find it hard to believe, but undated letters are frequently mailed—even letters typewritten by secretaries.)

If the mail has not been date- and time-stamped in the mail room, do this now, either by hand or with a stamp. Show both the date and time of day received if the hour is important. The date stamp is especially important if a letter is undated. It is also necessary because of the legal implications for some mail, such as a bid. Also, mail may be delayed in transit so long that the addressee needs the protection of the date to indicate where the time lag occurred. Stamping may also speed up action on correspondence, especially in organizations that target replies for a same day or 48-hour response. The stamp is placed in the upper left corner.

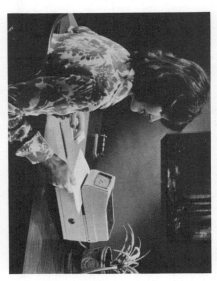

Illus. 7-4
The secretary uses a date-time recorder to indicate the time a letter is received. Time and date stamping may speed action on correspondence.

Reading, Underlining, and Annotating

After opening the envelopes and dating the contents, you begin the interesting part of handling mail as you follow these steps:

1. Read each letter through once, scanning for important facts. Make necessary calendar notations and notes to yourself about getting needed information.

2. Underline those words and phrases that tell the story as you read the letter again. Be thrifty with underlining. Call attention only to the necessary words and phrases.

3. Annotate (write in the margin) any necessary or helpful notes to the executive.

4. Color code (if your employer approves this procedure) those letters for employer handling, those you can answer, and those to be referred to someone else.

Illus. 7-5
The annotations and the date-time stamp indicate that this letter is ready for presentation to the executive.

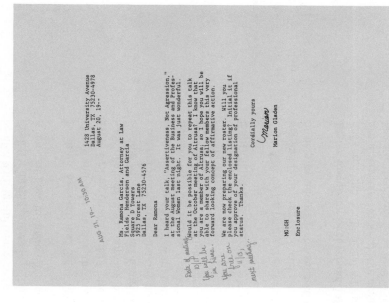

Marginal annotations come under two headings:

1. Suggested disposition of routine letters, such as *File, Ack.* (for acknowledge), and *Give to Sales Department.* (The secretary anticipates the executive's decision and makes a suggestion for handling, which may or may not be accepted.)

2. Special notes, such as "See our last letter attached" (The secretary will have removed this letter from the files and attached it to the annotated letter.); or "When Mr. B. was here, you agreed to give this talk." (Such notes are usually reminders, although some may be of a helpful identifying type—that is, a brief who's who of the writer or the company.)

You may be asking, "Shall I, as a new secretary, read, underline, and especially annotate, if my predecessor did not?" The answer is yes. Act as if it is a part of your understanding of a real secretary's service. If the employer questions the routine, abide by the decision. The employer is more likely to praise the practice, however, than to question it; if it is intelligently done, it saves time.

Notations for Filing. At this point save time by adding the filing notations on any letters that require no replies. For example, if a reply to your letter can be filed without further correspondence, the filing notation should be put on the letter during processing. (Methods of determining where to file letters and when and how to make filing notations are presented in Chapter 14.)

Limiting Annotations. Since original letters are sometimes copied on machines and sent outside the organization, an executive may request you to avoid writing on the face of letters and ask you to add annotations only on the back of them. Some copying processes will not, however, reproduce ink or colored pencil. If you are using a copying process that has this limitation, you need not worry about making notations on the face of the letter. On the other hand, many executives want notations copied to achieve compact yet comprehensive records. Removable adhesive paper slips are available in a variety of sizes and colors for annotating correspondence. These can be removed prior to copying.

Expediting the Executive's Handling of Mail

You can expedite the executive's handling of specific letters by anticipating and preparing for certain procedural steps that will be taken. You can be of help by adopting the suggestions described below.

Letter Requiring Background Information. In many cases a letter cannot be answered unless additional information is at hand. For instance, suppose you are a secretary to a sales manager who receives a letter canceling an order because the customer is tired of waiting for delivery. You would refer to your To-Do memo; then look up and attach all the pertinent information about the order, its date of receipt, its present whereabouts, and the cause for delay. You may have to judge how much background information you should supply. If the executive will ask you for it anyway, anticipate this request. If it only *might* prove useful, weigh the amount of time required to get it, the amount of time you have to give to it, and the executive's probable attitude concerning the information.

Letter Referring to Previous Correspondence. When there is need to refer to previous correspondence, get it and attach it to the current letter. Write, "See attached" in the margin. If the previous correspondence involves a bound file, put the letter on the file, and insert paper markers in the file at the pertinent points.

Letter Requiring Follow-Up. Often a letter may refer to mail that will follow or may contain a request that requires additional action besides the routine answer. Also, sometimes a letter must be answered within a certain time, or other time factors may be involved. In such cases, follow these steps:

1. Select the earliest date when the action should be taken.
2. Write that date on the face of the letter with a key (like *T* for *Tickler,* or *FD* for *Follow-Up Date*) in your mail register, so that the executive and you know that a reminder has been recorded.
3. Make a tickler entry under the selected date.
4. If material is expected in a separate mailing, write a note on your calendar page, or send a memo to the mail department describing the mail expected. Indicate such notifications in the margin of the letter. (See also mail register, page 153.)

Letter to Be Referred to an Associate. Often an executive passes along to an associate a piece of mail for either action or information. For instance, perhaps

---

DATE _____

TO _____

Refer to the attached material and

☐ Please note.
☐ Please note and file.
☐ Please note and return to me.
☐ Please mail to _____
☐ Please note and talk with me this a.m. _____; p.m. _____

☐ Please answer, sending me a copy.
☐ Please write a reply for my signature.
☐ Please handle.
☐ Please have _____ photocopies made for _____.
☐ Please sign.
☐ Please let me have your comments.
☐ Please RUSH — immediate action desired.
☐ Please make follow-up for _____

REMARKS:

Signed _____

Illus. 7-6
A secretary devised this check-off slip to save the executive's time in distributing information to and requesting action from assistants. There is room for a signature or initials at the bottom because an initialed or signed request is more personal than a printed name.

Please read the attached material and pass it on to the persons indicated.

Seq.	Refer to:	Date Received	Date Sent On
	Mr. Adams		
	Mr. Berger		
4	Miss Bessler		
	Mr. Caldwell		
	Ms. Carmen		
	Mr. Davis		
	Mrs. Goodman		
	Ms. Hessler		
	Mr. Holmes		
	Miss Kerr		
2	Mr. Perot		
	Mr. Robinson		
	Mrs. Rodriguez		
	Ms. Smith		
	Mr. Stretch		
1	Ms. Swillinger		
3	Mr. VanDerbeck		
	Ms. Zimmerman		

Return to: _____

Illus. 7-7
One of these duplicated slips is attached to mail to be distributed to others and indicates the order in which it is to be passed along. The secretary or executive checks in pencil or ink the names of those who should receive it. Since routing slips must conform with changes in personnel, they are often duplicated in the office rather than printed.

the communication is to be acknowledged, answered, or followed up by the associate. It may require the recipient to prepare a report, or it may provide information but not call for immediate action. In preparing this kind of mail for an employer whose action you can anticipate, you might fill out a routing slip or an action slip similar to those illustrated on page 157, lightly penciling in both the individual's name and the action needed. Give the letter and the slip to your employer. If the suggested action is approved, you may attach the slip to the letter. If there is any possibility that you may need later follow-up, photocopy the letter and indicate on the original the names of the persons to whom you sent the copies, the action to be taken, and your own follow-up date, if any. Photocopying is superseding the routing slip because it speeds up dissemination of information. If you send an original copy out of the office, *keep a record of where you sent it.*

Letter Misaddressed to the Executive. When a letter addressed to the executive actually should have been sent to another person, annotate the correct name in the top margin and put the letter with the employer's other mail. Although you will probably be asked to forward the letter to someone else, you should give the addressee the right to see the mail first.

Personal Letter Opened Inadvertently. If you should inadvertently open a personal letter addressed to your employer, stop reading the letter as soon as you discover that it is personal and not business. Refold the letter, replace it in its envelope, and attach a short note bearing your initials to the face of the envelope, ''Sorry, opened by mistake.''

Enclosed Bill or Invoice. When an envelope contains a bill or an invoice, if possible compare the prices and the terms with those quoted. Always check the mathematical accuracy of the extensions and the total. Then write *OK* on the face of the bill or the invoice if it is correct, or note any discrepancy. Any arithmetic computations in a letter should be checked for accuracy as well.

Enclosed Check or Money Order. Compare the amount of a check or money order enclosed in an envelope with the amount mentioned in the letter of transmittal or on the copy of the statement or invoice. If it has been mailed alone, check it with the file copy of the bill to verify the correctness of the amount. Handle the remittance according to the procedure of your office. If it is to be turned over immediately to a cashier, indicate the amount in the margin of the letter or invoice, or prepare a memorandum for the executive, reporting the amount and the date of receipt.

Packages Received. Packages should be processed before newspapers, periodicals, and advertisements, and certain packages should be opened before others. In some cases your mail register will have alerted you to watch for them. If you are handling a package marked *Letter Enclosed* or if a first-class letter is attached, check the package contents before separating the letter from the package. Always examine the contents of a package at the time it is opened. If the contents are bulky and represent a quantity of like items, put a sample on the employer's desk and store the rest.

Publications Received. Identify each publication permanently with the executive's name or initials printed on the cover. Scan the table of contents and indicate any item that might be of interest to the executive. If an article is of special interest, underline the salient points and paper clip all the preceding pages together so that the publication opens to the indicated material; or attach a note to the front cover calling attention to the article.

Final Arrangement of the Mail

Arrangement of processed and personal mail for presentation to the executive depends on preferences, daily schedule, or even mood. In general, though, the mail is separated into these five categories:

1. For immediate action—Possible order of precedence: telecommunications, important business letters, unopened personal letters, letters containing remittances, pleasant letters, unpleasant letters
2. To be answered—Routine letters having no great priority
3. To be answered by secretary—Letters that are usually turned over to you for handling. (Don't preempt the executive's right to make this decision.)
4. Letters to be answered by someone else
5. To read for information—Advertisements, publications, routine announcements

One successful secretary recommends the use of a four-pocket organizer for submitting mail, with each pocket clearly identified as to contents. This organizer keeps the mail confidential, even from those who seem able to read letters upside down. In any case, the mail should be covered if the executive is not at the desk when you present the processed mail. Another possibility is to separate the mail into color coded folders, a different colored folder for each of the above categories.

On a day when the employer has only limited time for the mail, you may wish to submit items from Category 1 only. On a day when working with the mail seems to have high priority, send in the first half as soon as it is ready, and take in the rest when it has been processed. If you know that a specific piece of mail is expected, take it in as soon as it arrives.

HANDLING MAIL DURING THE EMPLOYER'S ABSENCE

Some executives spend a great deal of their time in travel. When they are away from the office, crises occur in handling the mail. Simply forwarding personal mail or sending photocopies of incoming business mail will not always meet the situations that arise. The secretary is in a decision-making role and *must* evaluate each piece of mail before giving it routine treatment.

For instance, an employer may be out of the country when the quarterly income tax falls due. Before the due date, the secretary mailed the required checks and forms which had been signed before the executive's departure. If the trip is an extended one, the secretary may be asked to take care of rent, telephone, or utility bills and pay them with checks on which only the amounts are to be filled in. These bills should not be forwarded to a foreign country. Before the executive leaves, the secretary should get explicit instructions for such contingencies.

The same caution holds for business mail. The employer should not receive a photocopy, forwarded and reforwarded, of a letter about a major reorganization that may have personal ramifications. At times information should be transmitted by the most rapid service. The secretary must assume full responsibility for making the right decisions about handling mail in the employer's absence.

If the executive is traveling abroad, make copies of incoming mail and forward them overseas in packets. Number the packets. Overseas mail is not always dependable. If a packet goes astray, the numbering system helps the executive know whether all mail has been received. If 1 and 3 are the only ones received, 2 is obviously missing.

The Executive's Business Mail

In handling business mail, you will be expected to do the following:

1. Maintain the mail register meticulously.

2. Communicate with the executive immediately when mail of vital importance arrives that no one else can handle. Executives on business trips may telephone their secretaries regularly, but occasions arise when the secretary must initiate a call.

3. Set aside those letters that can await the executive's return, but acknowledge their receipt if the answer may be delayed for several days.

4. Give to associates or superiors those letters which must have immediate executive action. Make a photocopy or typewritten copy of each one for the executive's information, noting to whom you gave it and stating the action taken.

5. Send copies (not originals) of those letters that contain information of interest or importance or that require the executive's personal attention, if they will arrive in time.

6. Answer or take personal action on letters that fall within your province.

7. Prepare a digest of mail and either send it to the executive or keep it in the office, depending on circumstances (see Illus. 7-8).

8. Collect in a mail received folder (a) all the original letters awaiting attention, (b) copies of all letters given to others for action, (c) both the originals and answers of letters you have answered. Before giving the file to the

**Illus. 7-8
When handling mail during the employer's absence, prepare a digest of mail and either send it to the executive or keep it in the office.**

```
                DIGEST OF INCOMING MAIL

Date      From           Description

8/16      Clark Oil      Notice of Board of Directors
                         meeting 9/4 in Chicago at 9.

8/16      Syracuse U.    Request to give telephone
                         interview to School of Business
                         students on 11/3 at 10. Conflicts
                         with staff meeting.

8/16      J. K. Smith    Wants conference on proposed budget
                         cuts.

8/16      Forbes Mag.    Wants more info. on overseas operations.
                         Referred to MJB.

8/16      Mary Mason     Requests conference on patent application
                         for Project 117.

8/16      Helen Ball     Wants you to join husband and her for
                         dinner when in Chicago on 9/4.
```

executive, sort the letters into logical sequence, with the most important on top.

The Executive's Personal Mail

Before the executive leaves, ask what, if any, personal mail you are to open and attend to. Do not, however, open personal mail unless expressly asked to do so. Hold it in the mail received folder. If forwarded mail will have time to arrive before the executive leaves a destination, forward it. It is usually better to forward a letter in a fresh envelope with your business return address than to add the forwarding address on the original envelope. Keep in the mail received folder a running record of all letters mailed to the executive at an out-of-town address. Identify each forwarded letter by its postmark date and sender's name or by the postmark city if that is all that is shown.

The Executive's Advertising Mail

Hold the advertising mail in a separate large envelope. Sort it and give it to the executive when the press of accumulated work has lessened after the trip is over.

WORKING FOR MORE THAN ONE EXECUTIVE

When the secretary is working for more than one executive, the routine is basically the same. Probably a higher level of decision making is required because several employers' preferences and spheres of responsibility must be kept in mind and materials must be kept flowing to each one.

The secretary will, of course, keep the mail in separate piles for each executive. If one of them is obviously waiting, that principal gets the first delivery of processed mail.

The value of the mail register increases when the secretary is responsible for mail to several addressees, for it supplies proof of receipt for many different items of mail.

When one executive is more demanding than the others, the secretary must exercise tact to maintain a peaceful environment. Because several principals are sharing, many situations arise that require impartial decisions.

SUGGESTED READINGS

Periodicals and subscription services listed at the end of Chapter 1, pages 22-23. Especially recommended are current issues of *From Nine to Five*, *The Secretary's Workshop*, and *The Secretary's Improvement Program*.

Jennings, Lucy Mae. "Handling Incoming Mail," *Secretarial and Administrative Procedures*. Englewood Cliffs, N. J.: Prentice-Hall, Inc., 1978.

Winter, Elmer L. "How to Handle Your Mail," *The Successful Manager-Secretary Team*. West Nyack, N. J.: Parker Publishing Company, 1974.

QUESTIONS FOR DISCUSSION

1. If you were secretary to an executive who did not utilize your services in processing the mail as suggested in this chapter, what would you do?

2. In processing a morning's mail for the president of a corporation, decide what you would do if—

   (a) A letter refers to a letter the executive wrote nine months ago?

   (b) A customer's letter complains about the actions of a sales representative who was discourteous?

   (c) A letter asks that certain material be prepared and sent before the first of the month?

   (d) A letter requests a photograph, the responsibility for which is in the public relations department?

   (e) A letter contains important information for three department heads?

   (f) An envelope obviously contains a bill from an engraver who recently supplied personal stationery for the executive?

3. The executive, Miss Alva Miller, is away on a two-week trip. Decide what you would do with a letter that—

   (a) Asks her to give a talk five months from now?

   (b) Requires immediate management action?

   (c) Is from her mother, whose handwriting you recognize?

4. What steps could you take to obtain the address of a person who inquired about information and prices if the request was typed on a plain sheet of paper with no address given on either the letter or the envelope?

5. If the executive is out of town but expects to return tomorrow, what action should you take to record receipt of the following communications? How will you handle each situation?

   (a) A special delivery letter requesting an estimate on a large quantity of coated paper

   (b) A telex from one of your branch sales representatives sending in a rush order for a customer

   (c) A letter about a shipment of card stock complaining that one fourth of the blue is two shades lighter than the rest (Samples are enclosed as proof.)

   (d) A letter asking the length of time a Mr. Edwards was employed as a sales representative by your company, inquiring about his reason for leaving, and requesting a reference

6. Fill in the correct spelling in the following sentences. Then check your answers in the Reference Guide.

   (a) Our catalog gives ——— directions for ordering from your local supplier. (explicit, implicit)

   (b) He did a ——— job in publishing the school yearbook. (credible, creditable, credulous)

   (c) The ——— budget for 1984–85 will include additional funds for office salaries. (biannual, biennial, semiannual)

   (d) Please ——— your employees of the cost of this project. (appraise, apprise)

   (e) We have ——— assembled the booklets, and they are all ready to be shipped. (already, all ready)

PROBLEMS

1. Mari Rodriguez is a secretary with responsibility for processing incoming mail. Type your comments concerning the steps she follows in performing this task.

   (a) The secretary arranges all the mail in a stack and proceeds to open it and to remove the contents of each envelope in regular sequence.

   (b) She flattens out the letters and enclosures and discards the envelopes as useless items.

   (c) After all the letters have been removed, she checks the letters for stated enclosures. Pertinent enclosures she separates from the letters and sends to those concerned (such as orders for the order department). She discards the advertising.

   (d) She then time-stamps, reads, underlines, and annotates all letters. She

prepares a routing slip for letters requiring the attention of more than one person, and she fastens each routing slip to the proper letter with a paper clip.

   (e) She then places the letters, in the order in which they were processed, on the executive's desk face up for immediate attention.

2. Arrange the model desk in your secretarial practice room for sorting and opening incoming mail. Prepare a list of supplies needed. Have the instructor check the list and your demonstration of sorting and letter-opening techniques.

3. What action would you take to prepare the following four letters for your employer, Ms. Mary Jane Schmidt? Where would you locate the necessary information? Exactly what underlines and annotations would you make in each of the four cases?

W.W. KIM ENGINEER

Box 183 • Golden, Colorado • 80401-1029

March 15, 19--

M. J. Schmidt, Attorney
Anderson, Sakyo and Harmon
Bank of Utah Plaza
2651 Washington Boulevard
Ogden, UT 84401-4320

Dear Mr. Schmidt

At the suggestion of Alger Holmes, I am writing to inquire whether you would be willing to represent my nephew. The uranium mine near Provo that has now been closed and is being liquidated. I understand that a hearing is scheduled for May 4 and 5.

If you agree to accept this case, I will plan to come to Ogden on March 28 and would like an appointment with you then. What information would you like me to bring to such an appointment?

I will telephone you at ten o'clock on March 18 to discuss this letter.

Sincerely yours
W. W. Kim
W. W. Kim

---

340 Ocean Drive
Key Biscayne, FL 33149-1439
March 15, 19--

Ms. Mary Jane Schmidt
Anderson, Sakyo and Harmon, Attorneys
Bank of Utah Plaza
2651 Washington Boulevard
Ogden, UT 84401-4320

My dear Ms. Schmidt

We want to invite you to be the keynote speaker at this year's annual convention of the Professional Secretaries International at the Brown Palace Hotel on Thursday, May 4, at 10 a.m.

We understand that you began your business career as a secretary and that you have become one of our most distinguished women lawyers. It would be an inspiration to our members to hear from someone who has come up through the ranks.

Choice of topic is left to you. We know that you understand secretarial problems and will have something to say that will be helpful to us in raising our sights whether in our present jobs or in advancing to other levels.

Will you please indicate the fee you would expect in addition to travel expenses. Also please tell us by March 30 whether it will be possible for you to accept our invitation.

Cordially yours
Dolores Menotti
Dolores Menotti
Chairperson of the
Program Committee

Howard Enterprises

940 OAK BOULEVARD OGDEN, UT 84401-1150

August 15, 19--

Ms. Mary Jane Schmidt
Anderson, Sakyo and Harmon, Attorneys
Bank of Utah Plaza
2651 Washington Boulevard
Ogden, UT 84401-4320

Dear Ms. Schmidt

Will you please start collection proceedings against Jerry Youngman for $354.82. This amount represents two invoices, January 14 for $102.96 and February 8 for $231.86, copies of which are enclosed.

Mr. Youngman's last known address was 436 Maple Street, Ogden, but we have received no answers to our telephone calls to that address. Our letters, however, have been delivered.

Thank you for your very efficient handling of the overdue account of the Sports Shop. We received full payment of this account, which we did not expect to collect.

Sincerely yours
HOWARD ENTERPRISES
R. H. Howard
K. H. Howard Credit Department
KHH:AD
Enclosures (2)

---

711 State Street
Madison, WI 54303-2619
March 16, 19--

Ms. Mary Jane Schmidt
Anderson, Sakyo and Harmon, Attorneys
Bank of Utah Plaza
2651 Washington Boulevard
Ogden, UT 84401-4320

Dear Ms. Schmidt

In your talk before the Business and Professional Women's Club in Eau Claire recently, you mentioned a book about problems confronting men and women in management, especially women. All I can remember is that both the words men and women are in the title and that it is written by a woman. It may have the word corporation, company, or management in the title.

This book sounds most interesting, inasmuch as I have just been promoted to a position in middle management and need all the help that I can get. If you think that this book is something that would be beneficial, will you please tell me the correct title, the publisher, and the price?

Thank you again for bringing us not only facts but inspiration in your presentation.

Cordially yours
Regina Yoko
Regina Yoko

Chapter **8**

Taking and Giving Dictation

The secretary is involved in the processing of practically all written documents. Seventy-three percent of the members of the Professional Secretaries International reporting on their duties in 1980 indicated that they take shorthand dictation regularly. The administrative secretary will use shorthand to take notes while doing research or recording telephone conversations, informal meetings, or instructions. It is highly likely that the secretary will transcribe from either shorthand notes or voice-writing equipment.

This chapter discusses first the techniques required for taking symbol shorthand. Then it considers the responsibilities of the secretary when dictation is given to voice-writing dictation machines, which usually record in locations away from the dictator. Since secretaries as well as executives will probably dictate to these machines, instructions are included for giving easily transcribed dictation.

PREDICTATION RESPONSIBILITIES

Several of the secretary's predictation responsibilities apply regardless of how the dictation is given. Among them are preparing a list of items for today's attention, replenishing the executive's supplies, and assembling materials from the files that will be needed for the dictation.

Attention Today Items

The first preliminary to dictation is the collection of *attention today* items that the secretary prepares for the executive early each morning.

Some of the items will require dictation, while others may consume part of the executive's available dictation time. Overdue letters, reports, and shipments, or letters and reports that must meet deadlines—all will require dictating attention. The day's appointments, conferences, and meetings will also affect the time available for dictation.

Type in brief form, in duplicate, the attention today items, retaining a copy from which to take unfinished carry-over items each day. Clip the note (or separate notes for each item) to the edge of a portfolio or file folder. When an item has been attended to, the dictator can either tick it off the list or discard its note. Take the collection of items to the dictator's desk as early in the day as possible—definitely before dictation begins.

The Executive's Dictation Supplies

Another predication responsibility is the daily checking and replenishing of the executive's supplies to see that these items are provided in sufficient quantity:

Sharpened pencils—An executive often dictates with pencil in hand, jotting down self-reminders on the letter being answered or entering items on the calendar as certain dates are decided on.

A scratch pad—For auxiliary notes, general outlines, or reminders.

A filled stapler, paper clips, pins.

If the dictation will be given to a voice-writing machine, also include the following:

A supply of disks, belts, cassettes, or tapes, as appropriate

An empty file folder or portfolio in which the dictator can insert items related to the dictation

A wax pencil with which to date and identify the dictated units

A supply of printed forms for listing the material dictated on a unit, for special instructions regarding transcription, or for indicating any changes to be made

A supply of the special envelopes required for mailing dictation (This applies when the executive dictates while out of town.)

If the executive is dictating directly to the word processing center, always see that a supply of the usual pencils, paper, clips, and staplers is available at

Illus. 8-1
Folder containing carry-over correspondence and attached list of carry-over items in folder requiring attention

Pending

ITEMS CARRIED OVER FROM MARCH 7 AND FROM TICKLER

1. Answer letter from Bates on advertising schedule for next year (letter in folder)
2. Read my rough draft of report on yesterday's Finance Committee meeting (in folder.)
3. Shall I order flowers for your mother's birthday to arrive on the weekend?
4. Let RK know results of DP feasibility study

the desk. Also, provide a number of empty folders for the material related to the dictation. These folders of material do not go to the center. Retain them in your files for reference by you and the executive. Finally, provide the appropriate printed forms for listing special instructions to the center.

The Secretary's Dictation Supplies

If you take shorthand dictation, keep your supplies ready and waiting for instant availability. To avoid unnecessary clutter at the executive's desk, take adequate—but not excess—supplies.

A notebook—If you have a choice, use a notebook that has
a. Green pages ruled in green (easiest on the eyes, especially for transcription)
b. Spiral binding so that the pages lie flat
c. Stiff covers so that the book will stand alone for transcription (Take in only one book unless you are near the end of the current one.)

Several pens—Notes written in ink are easier on your eyes at transcription time.

Pointed pencils—Choose your favorite kind for size and shape, and for softness or hardness. Some secretaries prefer automatic thin lead pencils.

A colored pencil—The secretary most often uses red or blue.

Possibly an empty folder or portfolio with pockets on each side—Some secretaries clip notes to the portfolio as reminders to discuss the contents with the executive. If the executive wishes to put each answered letter in a file folder or portfolio, present it at each dictation session.

Answering the Call to Dictation

If the executive tries to dictate at approximately the same time each day, stay at your desk awaiting this call. If you must leave your desk, tell a co-worker or roll into your typewriter a note of your errand and the expected time of your return so that you can be located if necessary.

Before leaving your desk to take dictation—or for any extended time for that matter—cover, put away, or lock up all confidential papers and those of more than general interest. Ask someone nearby to take care of your telephone calls and visitors.

You may resent being called to dictation when you are engrossed in other work; but, when the call comes, do try not to act annoyed at being interrupted. Go to the executive's desk with an attitude of willingness and helpfulness.

PERSON-TO-PERSON DICTATION

The new secretary may hesitate to ask questions about vocabulary or to make a tactful suggestion, even if it would possibly improve the transcript.

Yet for best results dictation must be a cooperative effort. The secretary complements the dictator by catching omissions, errors, and ambiguities, and by either correcting them or pointing them out in a helpful way. Each person in the dictation situation has a role to play. The dictator's is the major, decisive role; the secretary's is a supporting but very important one.

At the Executive's Desk

During the actual dictation period the secretary should adopt certain accepted practices. Seemingly unimportant details that often affect the success of the session are the secretary's location and attitude.

In the give-and-take of dictation, the executive and the secretary work together at very close range. Your dictation chair should be placed conveniently for the executive; but, if you have a choice, sit where you have a generous-sized writing area.

As a thoughtful, considerate secretary, you need to be as unobtrusive as possible during the dictation. Only then can the dictator be most productive while concentrating on the content and searching for the most effective phrasing. Take the dictation without interrupting; manage your supplies and papers with few motions, refrain from unnecessary movements, such as tapping on the desk, and avoid any indication of a critical reaction to the dictation.

Enlarging Your Dictation Vocabulary

A secretary has to experience only once the embarrassment of using *iniquity* for *integrity, impetuous* for *impervious,* or *ambitious* for *ambiguous* to learn the meaning, spelling, and pronunciation of such pairs of words that sound somewhat alike in dictation and look somewhat alike in shorthand.

To learn the executive's vocabulary quickly, read file copies of recent letters and appropriate technical and trade publications. From them make a list of words new to you. Alongside each one write its shorthand equivalent. Learn the meanings of the words, their spellings, and their pronunciations. In other words, compile your own glossary.

The several secretarial handbooks in the special fields of law, accounting, medicine, real estate, and so on, have word lists that can hasten the enlarging of those vocabularies.

Types of Dictation

In addition to business communications, the secretary's dictation probably includes instructions, reminders, requests, and mail to answer. The dictation may include first a letter, then an interoffice communication, then a telegram, then a request to go to the bank to get a check cashed, then another letter, then instructions on a tabulation of sales costs, then a request to copy certain paragraphs from a magazine article, and then a memorandum to arrange an appointment for the employer with the mayor. One of the annoying faults of an inexperienced secretary is reluctance to take notes of anything except transcription items. Instead of recording the instructions in black and white, the secretary relies on memory to carry them out—and sooner or later gets into trouble.

Dictation falls into the two broad categories of communications and instructions.

Communications. The bulk of dictation is in the category of communications. It includes all the dictation to be transcribed—letters, memos, telecommunications, reports, outlines, drafts, and so on. Transcripts of telecommunications are first transcribed and then sent and received on automated equipment, which is fully discussed in Chapters 11 and 13.

Instructions. During the dictation period, numerous instructions are given to a secretary. *Take down all these in your notebook:*

Directions for Transcribing. Often at the end of an item the dictator gives a direction for transcribing the communication; however, you should place it at the beginning if it

Pinpoints the item for rush handling
Affects the kind of stationery to be used
Indicates the number of copies to be typed or filed
Refers you to another person from whom you must obtain information before transcribing the item

Use short abbreviations of your own devising and print them in oversized capitals, such as *RUF* for a rough draft request, *RU* for a letter that requires immediate handling, and *5CCs* to indicate that six copies must be typed. For the former you are usually handed at the secretary's desk. For fast finding at transcribing time, turn back corners of pages that contain rush items or mark them with paper clips.

Directions for Composing. The executive often delegates to the secretary the composing of a letter. It may be a letter answering one at hand or a letter to be originated at the secretary's desk. For the former you are usually handed the letter and told, "Respond thus and so. . . ." Take such directions in shorthand verbatim, either in the notebook or on the letter itself. For an originating letter, take down the directions verbatim in the notebook. It is imperative to have complete, exact directions for each letter or memo to be composed in order to cover the points that the executive requested. Often the secretary can use the dictator's language verbatim in composing a reply.

Specific Work Instructions. Take in shorthand in your notebook any specific instructions, such as canceling one of the executive's appointments, planning an itinerary, or writing and cashing a check. Conspicuously key such instructions for easy finding. One secretary draws a rough box around each work instruction; another writes each one in the right column, which is left blank for instructions and insertions.

General Work Instructions. Take in shorthand in your notebook all instructions or explanations of office routines and executive preferences concerning procedure. Transcribe them when there is time and insert them in your desk manual for reference use.

Good Dictation Practices

The overall most important practice in taking dictation is to *learn to listen.* The dictator's intonation will usually indicate the end of a sentence. A word emphasized may suggest underscoring. A comment from the employer will tell you which sources to consult before transcribing. A fuzzy instruction will force the alert secretary to ask for clarification before leaving the dictator.

Each of the dictation practices recommended below is a *good* one because it promotes efficiency. See how some of them are followed in Illus. 8-3.

1. Write the beginning date of use on the notebook cover—the month, the day, and the year. When the notebook is filled, add the final date and keep the notebook for six months.

2. Reserve one place in or on your desk for the notebook. For convenience, keep an extra notebook and pencils in the employer's office, too.

3. Keep a rubber band around transcribed pages to help you find the first blank page on which to write.

4. Keep a ball-point pen, sharpened pencils, and one colored pencil under the rubber band around the notebook ready for instant use. While transcribing, keep these items together *in one specific place* where they can be quickly reached when you are called for dictation.

5. Keep a few paper clips around the edges of the notebook cover for possible use during the dictation session.

6. When the executive receives a personal telephone call during dictation, leave the office quietly; stay nearby so that you can return as soon as the call is finished. When a visitor comes in who will undoubtedly stay for a while, take your materials to your desk and start transcribing. When dictation is resumed, read the last several sentences in your notes without being asked to help the dictator regain the thought.

7. During interruptions, write transcribing instructions in colored pencil and circle implied instructions, such as *attached* or *enclosed.* Use pauses and interruptions to read your notes, improve outlines, and insert punctuation.

8. Date each day's dictation on the first page with the month and day *in the lower right corner in red pencil.* Dictation notes are often the only source of valid reference. If the dictation load is heavy, add a.m. or p.m. to the bottom-of-page notation.

9. If you take dictation from more than one executive use a different notebook for each one.

10. Leave several lines between items of dictation or leave the right column blank to provide room for insertions, changes, and instructions. If the executive makes frequent or lengthy changes and insertions, leave six or eight lines or the full right column. If changes and insertions are rare, leave only three or four lines.

11. Should there be no lines available in which to write a transcribing instruction, print it in oversized capitals in abbreviated form diagonally across the beginning of the notes.

12. If there is the slightest possibility of inability to transcribe proper names, write them out during dictation.

13. Write uncertain words and unfamiliar terms in longhand if necessary to ensure correct transcription.

14. To remind yourself to clear up an error, a question, an omission, an ambiguity, a redundancy, or the repeated use of words that occurred during dictation, put down a conspicuous signal such as a very large X.

15. Indicate the end of each item of dictation, *be it a communication or an instruction*, in a conspicuous way, such as with a quick swing line across the column or with a cross. You need a visual aid to assure that you are transcribing the item completely or carrying out the instruction.

16. Put each letter that the dictator hands you face down on top of the last one to keep the letters in the same order as the dictation.

17. If the executive assigns a number to each letter being answered (so that it is not necessary to dictate the name and address of the recipient each time), write the number in the notebook. At transcription time, pair your numbered notes with the same numbered letter; and write the name of the addressee in your notebook *above the numbered item* for later identification if necessary.

18. Tape a small calendar on the back cover of your notebook for quick reference during dictation.

Making Changes

You will have to recognize changes of thought during dictation. An executive often starts to dictate a sentence and, after a pause, begins again. Watch carefully to determine whether it is a new thought or a rephrasing of a previous one. An executive who habitually rephrases can be a problem, but through some sixth sense the beginning secretary learns to recognize which phrase should be retained for clarity and which should be changed. When making a change, some dictators say, "Cross that out" and then begin to rephrase without mentioning what to cross out. They expect the secretary to know, and almost always their confidence is justified. When a long change is made far back in the notes, there is seldom enough time to go back, locate the notes to be deleted, and cross them out; nor is there likely to be enough room to write in the change. In such a case, treat the change as an insertion, taking down verbatim both the change and the instructions as to what is to be crossed

Editor Arthur Brisbane used to dictate his editorials. He spelled out everything, leaving nothing to his secretary's judgment. He even indicated punctuation by saying "Period" at the end of a sentence, "Quotation mark," etc. It was not an easy habit to shake. Once, at the University of Chicago, Brisbane delivered an address to the faculty. After some minutes, he could see that his listeners appeared puzzled. Later he asked one of the professors if something was wrong with his speech. "No, it was fine," the other assured him, "except that you used too many commas."

Reader's Digest
September, 1976

KEY TO THE PAGE OF DICTATION →

① A transcribing instruction is inserted as soon as possible in shorthand, in longhand abbreviations, or in king-sized capitals. Later, it is circled or underlined with a colored pencil for attention value.

② The swing line across the column indicates the end of an item.

③ All instructions for composition are written in full so that they can be followed carefully.

④ The personally devised abbreviation HW is used for Honeywell.

⑤ This instruction signals that a tickler notation must be made.

⑥ A transcribing instruction to make two carbon copies is inserted at the beginning of the item and later circled in color.

⑦ The circled X indicates a question: Should the regional sales manager also get a copy?

⑧ The corner is turned back to help locate quickly the page containing the rush item.

⑨ The right column is left available for work instructions and insertions.

⑩ A work instruction is always identified by a rough box.

⑪ The initials of the executive, JR, are used instead of his whole name.

⑫ The abbreviation *Ins C—3b* identifies the notes as Insert C to be used three pages back.

⑬ Lines are drawn through notes to be deleted.

⑭ *Hospitalization* was written in longhand because there was a mental block on the shorthand form. Rather than leave it out or waste time struggling to write it in shorthand, it was written in longhand.

⑮ Slash lines are used to segregate an insertion from the surrounding notes.

⑯ The date of dictation is always written at the *bottom* of the page.

Illus. 8-2
The practices followed by this secretary are numbered and explained in the key.

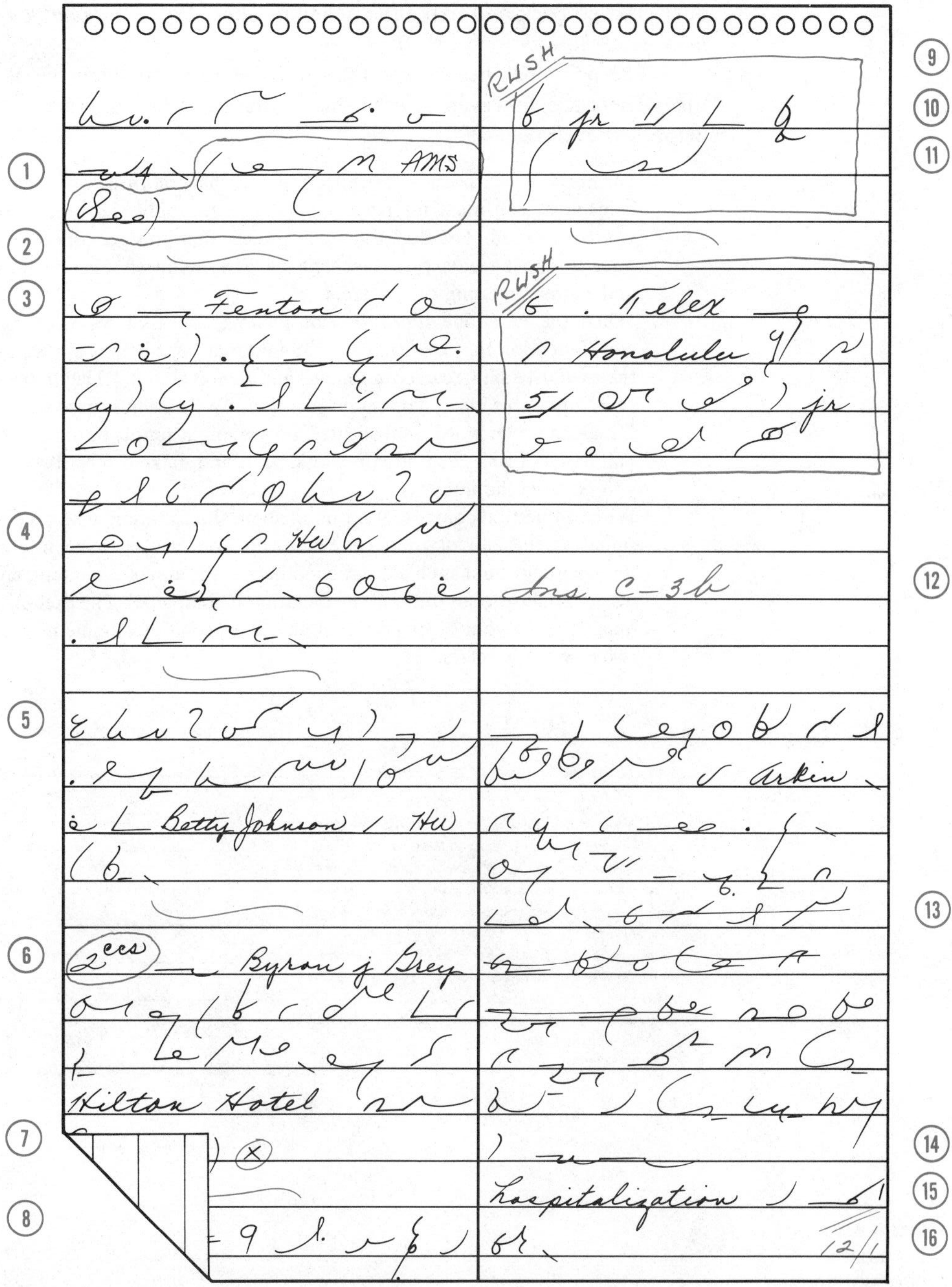

Illus. 8-3
These notes are keyed and signaled for accurate transcription. The notes are written in Century 21 shorthand.

out. Then go back and make the deletions later. *Do not rely on your memory to handle changes.*

The point has been made that you should be unobtrusive at dictation time. There are, however, at least three situations when interruptions may be helpful or even necessary.

1. When the executive is so far ahead of you that the thread of dictation is being lost, you must interrupt! Look up inquiringly and repeat the last words recorded. The dictator much prefers that you get complete notes, interrupting if necessary, rather than leave the dictation session with words and phrases missing or incorrect.

2. When the executive repeats a conspicuous multisyllabic word or root word, mention the repetition—if you find that your help is appreciated. If the executive said *"elaborate plans"* and then dictated, "They have *elaborated* upon this idea," you might mention, "We have just used *elaborate*." Usually another word is substituted, or you might simply be told, "Thanks; you fix it." From then on you would fix it and make a substitution when you go over the notes.

3. When a question comes to your mind about the dictation, insert a clear-up signal at the end of the line. Some dictators prefer to be interrupted immediately about such a question, others at the end of each item, and still others prefer to wait until all the dictation is completed. The executive will quickly learn your clear-up signal and at a propitious moment will often ask to what it refers.

WHAT THE DICTATOR SAID:

Take a letter to J. K. Kelly at Smith-Keller. We have been disturbed, Jim, by the recent rise in the price of uranium from blank dollars a ton to blank dollars a ton. Ask Henry to supply those figures. I think I am right, but I want to verify them before writing such an important letter. Since we are such a heavy user of your product, we wonder if you can't quote, no, offer, a better price on our next shipment, possibly a 5 percent discount on orders in excess of 2000 tons. If this is impossible, may I suggest that you agree to supply our needs for uranium at the present price for the next ten months.   Yours truly

WHAT THE SECRETARY WROTE:

Illus. 8-4
The most important practice in taking dictation is to *learn to listen.*

Unusual Dictation

A secretary is often asked to take unusual kinds of dictation, such as those discussed below.

Highly Confidential Dictation. Transcribe highly confidential dictation when there is little likelihood of anyone being around. Give the original and carbon copies to the executive as soon as possible and destroy the dictated notes. If the carbon paper retains an imprint of the typescript, destroy it also.

Telephone Dictation. Keep a separate shorthand notebook right at the telephone. In taking telephone dictation, you have the use of only one hand and may have to ask for phrases to be repeated. Since the dictator cannot see how fast you are taking notes, it helps if you say yes after you have completed each phrase. To avoid errors, read the entire set of notes back to the dictator.

Occasionally the executive may request you to monitor a telephone conversation and take notes. Unless you are unusually speedy you cannot hope to get every word, but you can take down the main points in the way one takes lecture notes. Transcribe such notes at once while they are still fresh in your mind.

Both sides of a telephone call can be recorded on a dictating machine placed near the telephone. Legally, however, the other person must be told that the conversation is being recorded. The recording may be kept for reference, or you may be asked to transcribe the entire conversation or to abstract the important points.

On-the-Spot Dictation. At times it is necessary to take dictation within a split second, while standing or working at a desk where there is no cleared space.

Illus. 8-5
During a conference, the executive has asked the secretary to come in and record comments on an advertising layout under consideration.

You may even have to take the notes on scratch paper. Practice taking dictation with a notebook on your knee or while standing using a scratch pad, in order to become accustomed to the awkwardness of such rush work. After transcription, date the notes, fold them to less than page size, and staple them to the first blank page in your dictation notebook.

Dictation at the Typewriter. Occasionally the executive may ask you to type something as it is being dictated to you. It helps to ask before starting whether the dictation will be long or short to determine the placement of the item on the page. A retyping, however, is often required, because in the majority of cases the placement is unsatisfactory and insertions or corrections have been necessary. Do not stop to erase errors as they are made. It is better to correct the errors or retype the page when the executive has finished dictating and has left your desk.

Printed Form Dictation. The answers to questions on a printed form are frequently dictated. The executive usually works from the form; therefore, the information given will seem sketchy and incomplete. If the dictator does not give the identifying numbers or letters of the items, ask for them so that you can type the information on the proper lines.

If only one copy is furnished, it may be well to make a photocopy of the completed form for the files. If completing printed forms is a new experience or you are unsure of the line spacing on the form, you could make a photocopy of the form and practice on it.

MACHINE DICTATION

Dictating machines are not replacing shorthand, but they are used extensively for processing communications by both the multifunctional secretary and the correspondence secretary. Today there are dozens of manufacturers of dictating equipment. Some of them are Dictaphone, Wang, IBM, Lanier, Vydec, and Norelco.

Dictating to the multifunctional secretary may take place from an executive's office, home, or even a telephone booth. The transcribing equipment is usually on the secretary's desk. Dictation to a correspondence secretary in a word processing center is transmitted to a word processing center from the word originator by either public or private telephone connections. The advantage of the private wire is that the dictation system does not tie up the telephones of either the dictator or the word processing center. Also, once installed, the telephone expense is diminished. Several recorders are located in the center; and, with the more sophisticated systems, a recorder not in use by another dictator is automatically selected and put into operation for the incoming dictation. The media on which the dictation is recorded vary from cassettes or a continuous loop of magnetic tape to magnetically coated disks.

Portable and Desk Models

The hand-sized, battery operated portable dictation unit was and is a boon to the traveling salesperson or executive, who can mail the recorded material to the secretary for transcription. A portable unit can be used in a car, in an airplane, or wherever it is convenient for the word originator. Many executives who like to work at home find this dictation unit indispensable for originating communications.

A desktop dictation unit is often located at the dictator's desk. The unit saves time if the originator dictates to a desktop machine while the secretary is freed to perform other tasks. Some units may also be used as transcribing machines. However, only one operation can be performed at a time—either transcribing or dictating—on a combination unit.

Endless Loop or Continuous Flow Systems

All the dictation machines described up to this point are called discrete media because they use a specific receiving medium, such as a disk, cassette, or belt. Such a medium can be stored, mailed, or switched from dictation machine to transcription machine. All portable and desktop units use discrete media that allow the dictator to play back the dictation and to make changes and corrections by dictating over the material to be erased. The endless loop-based system is used as an alternative to cassettes in the word processing

Illus. 8-6
The endless loop-based system is used as an alternative to cassettes in the word processing center.

center. Loops of magnetic tape, which are sealed inside a case or tank, go round and round for hours of use and reuse. Dictation is recorded on one tape head, and another head plays out the dictation for the correspondence secretary to transcribe. It is possible, then, for the correspondence secretary to start to transcribe while the dictator continues recording and thus to speed up rush work. The other advantage is that the encased tape requires no monitoring to see whether it should be reloaded with new recording media. Monitoring panels with visible dials show the supervisor at a glance which tanks are in use, which are idle, and how much untranscribed dictation has not yet been assigned to an operator. Some endless loop systems automatically send priority items to the front of the line for transcription first. Others indicate the length of an item for transcription.

RELATIONSHIP OF THE ADMINISTRATIVE SECRETARY TO THE WORD PROCESSING CENTER

In the organization of a typical word processing center, the administrative secretary will have these responsibilities for sending material to and receiving material back from the center:

1. Assemble attention-today items that require dictation.

2. Research special names and addresses, sending them to the center to supplement its records.

3. Keep the backup materials from which the dictation originated organized for possible reference.

4. Receive the completed work and inspect it to the extent of the employer's wishes, possibly even proofreading.

5. Present the work to the dictator for signature. Attach all appropriate enclosures and mail the material.

6. Return to the center any material to be corrected or revised.

7. Photocopy and distribute copies of signed material when the regulation number of copies provided is inadequate.

8. Follow up if the *turnaround* time (the time elapsed between dictation and delivery of transcript) is too long, requesting the completed material from the center.

9. Record and file the code numbers assigned to any material stored on permanent dictation media.

10. Dictate to the center.

LEARNING TO DICTATE

Both the multifunctional secretary and the administrative secretary will find that they can work more efficiently if they use dictation equipment. A deterrent to using dictation equipment is the reluctance of the dictator to organize both thoughts and materials before starting to speak. The principal also fears that the dictation will be imperfect, although all equipment provides for playback, correction of dictation, and some type of control with which to alert the transcriber to a transcription problem. Some secretaries, accustomed to transcribing and to speaking slowly and distinctly with logical phrasing, have less difficulty in dictating efficiently than do some executives.

To prepare for giving easily transcribed dictation, first study the instruction book for the equipment until you can operate all the controls. Dictate a practice item that contains tricky words and figures; wait until a later time; then see whether you can distinguish every word and figure.

An outline made before the dictation is a useful device in producing dictation of which you can be proud. And the more complex the letter, the more necessary the outline.

Illus. 8-7
When dictating, speak slowly and distinctly and give explicit instructions.

On the following page is an example of the way a dictator should record material. The accompanying transcript shows how the finished document should look when it is transcribed. You should study this material carefully and use the checklist when dictating.

DICTATION SCRIPT

OPERATOR, I'M BILL EVANS IN THE WORD PROCESSING CENTER. THIS IS A CHECKLIST FORM TO BE TYPED ON OUR COMPANY NAME LETTERHEAD FOR CAMERA READY COPY. THE FORM WILL HAVE A TITLE, THREE HEADINGS, AND A SERIES OF ENTRIES UNDER EACH HEADING, ONE AND ONE-HALF INCHES FROM THE TOP OF THE PAGE, PLEASE CENTER AND TYPE IN ALL CAPS THE TITLE, **Dictation Checklist**. TRIPLE SPACE, OPERATOR. ALL TYPING LINES SHOULD BEGIN FLUSH WITH THE LEFT MARGIN. PLEASE CAPITALIZE THE INITIAL LETTER OF EACH WORD IN THE HEADINGS. FOR THE ENTRIES BELOW EACH HEADING ALWAYS UNDERSCORE FIVE SPACES BEFORE TYPING THE ENTRY. TYPE EACH ENTRY ON A SEPARATE LINE, USING SINGLE SPACING, STARTING EACH ENTRY WITH A CAPITAL LETTER AND CLOSING IT WITH A PERIOD.

DICTATION FOLLOWS. THE FIRST HEADING IS **Before Dictation**. DOUBLE SPACE. THE FIRST ENTRY IS **Establish purpose and objectives**. NEXT LINE **Place reference material in clear view**. NEXT LINE **Outline material to be dictated**. NEXT LINE **Check condition of dictation equipment**. NEXT LINE **Turn recording machine on**.

TRIPLE SPACE, OPERATOR. THE NEXT HEADING IS **During Dictation**. DOUBLE SPACE. REMEMBER TO UNDERSCORE FIVE SPACES BEFORE EACH OF THE FOLLOWING ENTRIES. **Identify yourself by name** COMMA **title** COMMA **and department**. NEXT LINE **Dictate initial instructions**. NEXT LINE **State the priority of the document**. NEXT LINE **Identify the type of document**. NEXT LINE **Give format instructions**. NEXT LINE **Specify kind of stationery or form required**. NEXT LINE **Indicate the number of carbons wanted**. NEXT LINE **Dictate filing and retention** R E T E N T I O N **instructions**. NEXT LINE **State whether draft or final copy is expected**. NEXT LINE **Specify the date**. NEXT LINE **Spell addressee's** APOSTROPHE BEFORE S, **name and organization**. NEXT LINE **Announce beginning of new paragraphs**. NEXT LINE **Spell proper names and unusual terminology**. NEXT LINE **Dictate special punctuation and capitalization**. NEXT LINE **Repeat difficult numbers, plurals, and tenses**. NEXT LINE **Differentiate** D I F F E R E N T I A T E **clearly between instructions and text**. NEXT LINE **Backspace and make all desired corrections in dictation**. NEXT LINE **Dictate name** COMMA **title** COMMA **department** COMMA **and initials**. TRIPLE SPACE, THE LAST HEADING IS **After Dictation**. DOUBLE SPACE. ENTRIES FOLLOW. **Indicate special notations needed**. NEXT LINE **Specify distribution of transcribed material and supply any needed additional addresses**. NEXT LINE **Request extra photocopies desired**. NEXT LINE **Announce end of document**. OPERATOR, THIS IS THE END OF THE CHECKLIST.

SAMPLE

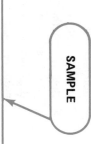

HOWELL PHARMACEUTICAL COMPANY

DICTATION CHECKLIST

Before Dictation

_____ Establish purpose and objectives.
_____ Place reference material in clear view.
_____ Outline material to be dictated.
_____ Check condition of dictation equipment.
_____ Turn recording machine on.

During Dictation

_____ Identify yourself by name, title, and department.
_____ Dictate initial instructions.
_____ State the priority of the document.
_____ Identify the type of document.
_____ Give format instructions.
_____ Specify kind of stationery or form required.
_____ Indicate the number of carbons wanted.
_____ Dictate filing or retention instructions.
_____ State whether draft or final copy is expected.
_____ Specify the date.
_____ Spell addressee's name and organization.
_____ Announce beginning of new paragraphs.
_____ Spell proper names and unusual terminology.
_____ Dictate special punctuation and capitalization.
_____ Repeat difficult numbers, plurals, and tenses.
_____ Differentiate clearly between instructions and text.
_____ Backspace and make all desired corrections in dictation.
_____ Dictate name, title, department, and initials.

After Dictation

_____ Indicate special notations needed.
_____ Specify distribution of transcribed material and supply any needed addresses.
_____ Request extra photocopies desired.
_____ Announce end of document.

Adapted from EXECUTIVE DICTATION FOR WORD PROCESSING (1978), Dictaphone Corporation, 120 Old Post Road, Rye, New York, 10580.

Illus. 8-8
Dictated script and checklist

DICTATION BY NUMBER

Since many situations covered by the dictator are recurring ones, it is a great time-saver to answer letters referring to a common situation by reproducing a numbered form letter; for example, Letter 19. If there is a slight variation in the circumstances, the dictator may consolidate several form paragraphs into a satisfactory answer, possibly adding an original paragraph or two.

In these circumstances, the originator, who has copies of form letters and paragraphs at the desk, may dictate something like this: Dear Henry, It was good to see you in Toledo last week. Paragraph 11, Paragraph 67, and Paragraph 3.

SUGGESTED READINGS

Dictaphone Corporation. *Executive Dictation for Word Processing.* Rye, N.Y.: Executive Corporation, 1978.

Gonzales, Jean. *The Complete Guide to Effective Dictation.* Boston: Kent Publishing Co., 1980.

International Business Machines. *First Time Final.* Franklin Lakes, N.J.: Office Products Division of International Business Machines, 1973.

Schrag, Adele Frisbie. *How to Dictate.* New York: McGraw-Hill Book Company, 1981.

South-Western Publishing Co. *Century 21* textbooks in shorthand. Cincinnati: South-Western Publishing Co. (College and high school textbooks have hints on handling dictation.)

Uris, Auren. *The Dictation Book.* Willow Grove, Pa.: International Information/Word Processing Association, 1980.

QUESTIONS FOR DISCUSSION

1. As a new secretary to the director of an agricultural chemical research laboratory, how would you familiarize yourself with the highly technical vocabulary?

2. What would you do if during dictation the executive:
   (a) Hands you a letter of invitation to speak at a professional meeting and asks you to reply stating that the pressure of business makes it impossible to prepare adequately for such a presentation and suggesting a substitute, Maria Savitsky?
   (b) Dictates a telegram?
   (c) Asks you to telephone for a plane reservation?
   (d) Tells you to put all interoffice memorandums on a form that follows the Modern Simplified Memorandum model (See Reference Guide Section.)?

(e) Dictates a three-page monthly report and asks you to rough it out?
(f) Asks you to substitute another name for the one dictated in the first paragraph?
(g) Dictates an unfamiliar technical word?

3. How would you handle the situation if the dictator:
(a) Uses out-of-date stereotyped phrases habitually?
(b) Makes obvious errors in grammar?
(c) Repeats the same conspicuous word several times in one business letter?
(d) Refers to secretaries as *she* and executives as *he* in all dictation although your company has a model affirmative action program in operation?
(e) Dictates even the most obvious punctuation although much of it is questionable?
(f) Mumbles?

4. What would you do if you were called to take dictation:
(a) At 11:45 and you had a luncheon engagement at 12:10?
(b) Just as you were in the midst of giving instructions to an assistant who would have no other work to do unless you finished the explanation?
(c) Just as you were putting the finishing touches on an important report that the executive had instructed you to complete before doing anything else?
(d) When as you were in the midst of reorganizing your card file?

5. How would you proceed if you dictated a letter to the word processing center that was transcribed in a format that did not conform to your instructions?

6. Type the preferred plural of each of the following words. Then use the Reference Guide to verify or correct your answers.
(a) attorney at law
(b) commander in chief
(c) cupful
(d) follow-up
(e) Fox (proper name)
(f) go-between
(g) higher-up
(h) judge advocate
(i) notary public
(j) runner-up

PROBLEMS

1. Dictate to a dictation machine the letter called for in Discussion Question 2a. Ask either a classmate or your instructor to criticize your first effort in using this equipment.

2. As a multifunctional secretary, you usually rough out your compositions before typing a final copy. Your firm changes to a word processing center, and you fear you may be unable to dictate perfect communica-

tions to the center. Outline a plan of action for becoming more confident.

3. Take office style dictation from your instructor or from a tape prepared by your instructor until you are confident that you have mastered the special techniques required. Then take three letters from dictation or tape to be transcribed as Problem 5, Chapter 9.

Quality Transcription

Transcription is a high order skill, often performed under rush conditions, involving competency in typewriting, English usage and punctuation, and decision making. The ultimate test of your ability to perform this complicated process is a quality transcript that will receive acceptance. This chapter concentrates on the techniques that a good transcriber uses whether working from shorthand notes or from machine dictation.

The chapter first discusses learning to use the special features of the typewriter available to you, for many new helpful controls are being added that simplify typewriting and save time. Then it describes the techniques that any good transcriber uses. Next the specialized work methods followed by the multifunctional secretary are covered. The final section is devoted to the transcription activities of the correspondence secretary or word processor and the responsibilities of the administrative secretary after receiving the completed transcript.

As you read the chapter, keep in mind that concern for cost reduction is bringing about today's changes in the methods of producing business communications. In whatever situation you expect to function as a secretary, vow to systematize your transcription practices so that your output will be of the highest quality and quantity. In this way you will contribute to a reduction in the spiraling costs of business documents.

YOUR EQUIPMENT

As soon as you take a secretarial position or receive new equipment, familiarize yourself with it. Examine your machine to see how many features are available to you. The more sophisticated equipment will be found in the word processing center, but as costs decrease and technology improves, the multifunctional secretary will increasingly have a number of timesaving features available.

How can you learn to operate the machines most efficiently? Vendors provide instruction either at their companies or yours. Your own company may offer training. Manufacturers often publish training materials and software packages for the operation of their equipment.

YOUR FUNDAMENTALS

To handle the vocabulary needed by a secretary requires at least a twelfth grade reading level according to a study of business communication. To improve your vocabulary, read the books and magazines about the type of business you work for; however, do not limit your reading to your specialized field. You should read widely in every area. The better background you have, the greater your chances for success. Above all, read the newspapers and news weeklies regularly, and use the dictionary often to learn the meanings of unfamiliar words.

Your tool of the trade as a secretary is your facility with the English language—your spelling, punctuation, word usage, typewriting style, and use of reference books. You must master the fundamentals so that you can transmit the dictator's ideas flawlessly. You—not necessarily the dictator—are the expert in this area; you are responsible for perfection in communication.

To master your spelling difficulties, compile and maintain your own list of troublesome words, perhaps using the blank inside cover pages of this book. If you persistently write down each misspelling that occurs in your writing and each uncertainty that you have to check in a dictionary, you will have a custom-made list for instant reference.

It may help you also to develop your own mnemonic devices. Many a secretary has clinched correct spellings by word associations or parallelisms that are easy to remember: *calendar* ends with the *a of day*; *privilege* has the *leg* that comes from *legal*; *all right* parallels *all wrong*, and so on.

A secretary must know the rules of punctuation as they apply to formal writing. Some office work is at that level. A paper that is to appear in print or a report to the board of directors must be punctuated with formal correctness. In routine business writing there is a trend to reduce the amount of punctuation, especially those marks that indicate pauses. Such punctuation is often omitted in the customary places in sentences which are clear in meaning. But whenever you are in doubt, punctuate fully. Comprehensive punctuation rules are given in the Reference Guide.

Grammar and usage are based on the relatively fixed standards used in communicating at a formal or educated level. Since most of the executive's writing is at that level, the secretary must have a mastery of grammar—a knowledge of grammatical construction for speaking and writing correctly.

Dictionaries vary—from the very British and formal *Oxford English Dictionary* to *Webster's Third New International Dictionary of the English Language*, which aroused a great furor among scholars of the English language when it first appeared. It contains new words that have crept into the language through usage but have never before been listed. Those willing to accept such words as *finalize*, who see a dictionary as a descriptive record of living language, will approve of the new *Third*. They will be guided by the designations *slang*, *substandard*, and *nonstandard* in their choice of a word. Those who look at a dictionary as a source of what the language *ought* to be, who believe that language should be a pure body of words revealed from on high, will believe that workaday forms are out of place. They will choose a more traditional reference.

Three recommended desk size dictionaries that have recently been revised are: *Webster's New Collegiate Dictionary* (1981), *The American Heritage Dictionary of the English Language* (College Edition, 1978), and *Random House College Dictionary* (1975). A desk dictionary should be replaced every five years or so with a current edition.

Turning to the dictionary at transcribing time, you want to learn:

1. The correct spelling of a word—such as *neophyte*
2. The correct spelling of an inflectional form—such as the past tense of *benefit*
3. The preferred form of variant spellings—such as *acknowledgment* or *acknowledgement, judgment* or *judgement*
4. Whether to use one word or two words—such as *highlight* or *high light*
5. Whether to treat a word as a foreign one and underline it—such as *bon voyage* and *carte blanche*
6. How to divide a word at the end of a line—*committal*, for example
7. Whether to use a hyphen to join a suffix or prefix to a word or to form one complete word without a hyphen: *pre-Socratic* and *preview; selfsame* and *self-control; businesslike* and *droll-like*

Unfortunately each of these seven situations is usually indicated in different ways in the entries in different dictionaries. The key to how they are indicated in your dictionary is given in the explanatory notes at the front of the dictionary. (Sometimes this section has a more explicit title, such as "Guide to the Use of the Dictionary.") One secretary hyphenated numerous words incorrectly because of confusing the mark denoting syllabication with the one indicating a hyphen. Careful reference to the explanatory notes will prevent such embarrassing mistakes.

When you do locate an important point in the explanatory notes, underline it or enclose it in a frame with pencil for easy reference. You thus save considerable time in the future.

A current and comprehensive secretarial handbook will help you with many transcription problems. At the end of this chapter several preferred ones are listed. There are also secretarial manuals for special fields: law, medicine, science and technology, and so on. These aids are listed at the end of this chapter to help you in case your work involves specialization. Reference books are discussed more fully in Chapter 18.

TRANSCRIPTION PROCEDURE

To assure efficient transcription, first make certain that all is in readiness: the typeface clean; the ribbon in good condition; the supply of letterheads, envelopes, and carbon paper adequate and carefully arranged for a flow of work without wasted motion; reference books within reach; a pencil at hand for use in editing the notes and a colored pencil for identifying or emphasizing instructions; and erasing and correcting supplies nearby. Familiarize yourself with any procedures that dictate company-wide styles or formats. About 90 percent of all documents can be arranged attractively if you leave 1" to 1½" left- and right-side margins. To help yourself estimate the space required for transcribing a letter from your shorthand notes, count the number of actual words in five or six lines of your notes. Find the average number of words per line. Multiply the average number of words per line by the number of lines in your notes to find the total words in the body of the letter. Use the total word count as your reference in determining the placement of the letter.

Order of Transcription

Transcribe the rush and top priority items in the order of their immediacy as indicated by your notes, instructions on the dictating equipment, or your supervisor. Telegrams, mailgrams, or cablegrams get first attention. Special delivery letters should be attended to next and, if urgent, presented immediately for signing and mailing. If there is an interoffice memorandum of great importance, it may take precedence over all the rest of the transcription items. Show your employer that you can make the right decisions as to priorities. Store in one regular place any transcription items that must be carried over until the next day.

Editing and Completing Dictated Items

Before starting to type an item, read through it intently; then edit until it is letter perfect and ready for smooth, continuous transcription. To read and rework your notes does not indicate incompetence but rather efficiency. As you read through each item:

Insert punctuation.	Make substitutions for repeated words.
Indicate paragraphs.	Rewrite poor sentences.
Correct errors in grammar.	Verify facts—prices, names, etc.
Correct errors in fact.	Write out difficult spellings.
Eliminate redundancies.	Fill in blanks left by executive.
Clarify ambiguities.	Find and insert needed information.

If the dictated sentence does not make sense to you, it probably will not be clear to the addressee. When in doubt, ask. If the dictator is in the next room, interrupt only at a propitious time. If your supervisor in a word processing center cannot clear up a transcription problem, telephone the originator. Only valid, sensible changes should be made in the dictation, as illustrated on the following page:

What the Executive Said

Let's meet in Chicago Wednesday morning, January 24. I'll arrive the night before the meeting. Please make a reservation for me at the Drake for the 24th.

What the Secretary Typed

Let's meet in Chicago Wednesday morning, January 24. I'll arrive the night before the meeting. Please make a reservation for me at the Drake for the 23rd.

It annoys a dictator for a secretary to change "We are sending you a selection of samples" to "A selection of samples is on its way to you," just because of a preference for the changed sentence. Don't be like the secretary who changed *criterion is to criteria is* because of unfamiliarity with the singular form and failure to check the dictated word.

The final step before the actual transcription of each item is to check any instructions in your notes or at the beginning of a machine dictated item as to format, number of copies, distribution, additions on certain copies, enclosures to be prepared, or whether final copy or rough draft is wanted. In making a rough draft, use wide margins and double or triple spacing to allow for editorial changes.

Stationery

Give some thought to the most efficient arrangement for your stationery so that you can locate the correct letterhead quickly.

Choice of Letterheads. More than likely you will use a variety of letterheads. There will be at least the regular business one, the interoffice one, and the executive's personal letterhead. If the employer serves as an officer or member of the board of an outside organization, that letterhead will probably be used too.

Waste of Stationery. Letterheads are expensive, and the waste of them is appalling. Office wastebaskets are full of letterheads discarded because of careless work and slovenly corrections. Transcribe carefully and become skillful at correcting. One company reduced the cost and waste of hasty transcribing with a huge sign like that shown at the left.

Number and Kinds of Copies

Some companies require two copies of every letter, one for the individual correspondence file, and another for a chronological file of all letters mailed each day. The materials in this chron file are kept at least a month for quick reference. Whether this copy is produced by carbon paper, a copying machine, or word processing equipment will depend on your organization's equipment or methods. Copies can now be obtained from computer input. As a secretary you will be delighted with the trend toward less and less use of time-consuming carbon copies.

IT TAKES LESS
TIME TO BE RIGHT
THAN TO REWRITE!

You will be asked to make and furnish certain individuals and departments with copies of every letter you type that relates to subjects of mutual interest. List in your desk manual the persons who should receive copies for each general subject. You can then make the correct number of copies and distribute them properly each time. Before beginning to transcribe, always check the notations or oral instructions which precede the item. These will usually tell you the number of copies needed.

Diacritical Marks

Add any necessary diacritical marks (in pencil or ink) after removing the sheet from the typewriter.

```
maître d'hôtel
résumé
garçon
señor
```

The Matter of Dating

Date every paper. Use the date of transcription if it differs from that of the dictation. It may be necessary to edit the dictation to make it conform, as "your visit *yesterday*," rather than "your visit *this morning*." On casual typewritten matter use the abbreviated form, as 8/28/—.

Letter and Envelope Styles

Many companies furnish form and style manuals for use with their correspondence. If you do not receive one, compile your own models from previous correspondence and from style authorities. Study the model letters and envelopes shown on pages 746–747.

The modified block letter is used most often because of its time-saving features. If you have the choice, you may want to use the simplified letter style. Study the post office recommended format for envelopes (shown in Chapter 11.) Use the latest forms of nonsexist salutations—or the omission of the salutation altogether. Note the new ways of indicating reference initials, especially those used for computer entered documents. Using whatever decision-making authority you have, try to modernize the format of your transcription—but never forget that the dictator is in charge.

Proofreading

Although sophisticated word processing equipment will detect a misspelled word or incorrect hyphenation, the machine cannot store all the words you may use. And most secretaries do not have such sophisticated equipment. You will be responsible for proofreading. No matter how beautiful a document looks, if there is a proofreading error, the desired reaction is destroyed. A memorandum from the publisher of secretarial materials stated: "The enclosed catalog will *aquaint* you with. . . ." Do you think any material was ordered? A ridiculous error such as reference to a *dump* truck driver as a *dumb* truck driver lost a valuable customer.

Although speed in producing transcription has increased strikingly, proofreading is not the place to strive for increased output; take your time and proceed painstakingly.

Common Transcription Errors. The top ten transcription errors are letters omitted, substitutions (-ing for -ed, for instance), space omitted, punctuation mark omitted (such as failure to close a quote), transpositions, words omitted, small letter for a capital letter, a full line omitted, a spelling error, or a capital letter for a small letter. Watch for them.

Good Proofreading Techniques. The following techniques are recommended:

1. Use the paperbail method. Roll back to the first line of the copy and use your paperbail as an eye guide as you read line by line.
2. Read the material once for content.
3. Read again for mechanical errors: grammar, spelling, and punctuation.
4. Read from right to left. (Sometimes a copy should be used because it is inked more heavily than the original and easier to follow.)
5. Wait thirty minutes and reread.
6. Check numbers, especially decimals, and names and addresses with extreme care.

If you are unsure of the accuracy of your proofreading, ask someone else to read aloud from the original as you proofread or ask someone else to proofread your work. (In some word processing centers proofreading is a particular function assigned to a specialist.)

Keeping It Confidential

There are always several persons in a large office who are inquisitive as to what is currently happening in the executive offices. Transcripts on secretaries' desks such as finished letters waiting to be signed, the letter being typed, and copies in viewing range are often fruitful sources of information. If someone comes to your desk while you are transcribing, roll the letter back into the typewriter, making your action as unobtrusive as possible. Keep the group of transcribed letters covered with a sheet of paper, in face down order, or inside a file folder. Copies are just as informative as originals, so treat them with the same respect. Many executives now use an electric wastebasket that shreds paper that might reveal company secrets.

Same Letter to Several Addressees

With a letter addressed to several persons but typed in one writing, type all the names in the address position. Treat each copy as an original, individual letter as indicated here.

1. Put a check mark above or beside the name of the person to whom the copy will be sent.

2. Address an envelope for that name; slip the envelope over that copy.

3. Present each checked letter with its addressed envelope for signing with the rest of the mail.

Reference Notations

Several types of information may be noted below the final signature line. These include reference initials, enclosure notations, copy notations, and filing codes for correspondence prepared in a word processing center.

Reference Initials. The reference initials are typed a double space below the last typed line in any of several ways.

ty or *TY* or *t* (transcriber only)
MP:TY or *MP:ty* or *mp/t* (dictator and transcriber)
MP:AG:TY (executive, actual composer of document, and transcriber)

Enclosure Notations. Type a double space below the reference initials at the left margin. Use *Enclosure* or *Enc.* when an item is to be sent in the envelope with the letter.

Copy Notations. Type the names or initials of copy recipients a double space below the enclosure notation. (The sender need not sign these communications.) If the sender does not want the recipient of the original correspondence to know that a copy is being sent to someone else, the sender should place a 5" × 3" card behind the original and type *bc* (blind copy) and the name or initials of the person receiving the copy before removing the pack from the typewriter. The notation *pc* stands for photocopy, and *cc* indicates a carbon copy.

Word Processing Codes. Codes are typed as reference notations to identify correspondence items prepared in a word processing center so that they can be located on magnetic media or hard copy. Such codes are not yet standardized, but the following example of a letter written by Lorene Mark shows possible handling:

LM/a 2.4

LM is the word originator; *a* is the word processor; *2* identifies Tuesday, the second day of the week; and *4* indicates the fourth document typed by *a* on Tuesday and identifies the fourth magnetic card or hard copy filed behind *Tuesday* in the center's file.

Envelopes

Before removing a letter from the typewriter, drop its envelope between the letter and the platen. When you remove the letter, the envelope will be positioned for addressing. After addressing the envelope and before removing it from the typewriter, check it against the original source document for accuracy. Then slip the addressed envelope, flap side up, over the top of the letter and its enclosures. The accumulated stack of correspondence is easy to handle, and your employer will find it easy to read and sign the letters. However, some employers prefer the addressed side up to facilitate matching the address on the envelope with the letter address in order to reduce address-ing errors. Some of the new typewriters are programmed so that a letter address once keyboarded can be retained for typing the envelope automati-cally.

Enclosures

Whenever an enclosure is mentioned in a letter, there is an implied instruction to someone to obtain the enclosure and attach it to the letter before submitting it for signature. That someone is the multifunctional secretary in the traditional office and the administrative secretary if a word processing center is used. If possible, collect all enclosures at the same time. Do not use

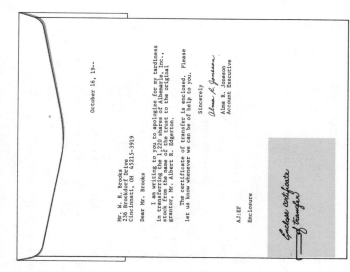

October 16, 19--

Mr. W. R. Brooks
236 Brookdorf Drive
Cincinnati, OH 45215-3919

Dear Mr. Brooks

I am writing to you to apologize for my tardiness in transferring the 1,220 shares of Albemarle, Inc., stock from the name of the trust to the original grantor, Mr. Albert R. Edgerton.

The certificate of transfer is enclosed. Please let us know whenever we can be of help to you.

Sincerely

Alma R. Joneson
Account Executive

AJ:EF
Enclosure

Enclose certificate
of transfer

Illus. 9-1
If an enclosure will be bulky or difficult for the signer to handle, the secretary attaches a note to the letter as a signal of awareness of the enclosure and as a self-reminder at mailing time.

as an enclosure either the file copy of a letter or the original copy of a letter received. Instead, prepare a copy on a copying machine or type a plain, identified copy of the letter.

If an enclosure is small enough not to cover the body of the letter, it is attached to the face. If larger, it is put at the back of the letter.

Should it be necessary to send in a letter for signature without its enclosures, clip a note to it listing the enclosures missing. The note will serve a dual purpose: it will inform the executive that you have not forgotten the items to be enclosed, and it will remind you not to mail the letter until the enclosures are at hand.

Separate Mail Items

Prepare or obtain material to be sent in a package or a mailing envelope and get it ready for mailing. If someone else is responsible for mailing, give complete instructions in writing to that person or department, and prepare a typewritten address label. Make a tickler item to check later on the material.

You may enclose a letter with a package sent by priority mail without additional postage (see Chapter 11). This procedure saves sending out a great deal of under-separate-cover mail and keeping track of it by tickler items.

Submitting the Correspondence for Signature

The secretary to only one executive submits the completed correspondence for signature, but in an organization with a word processing center the administrative secretary performs this function.

If rush items are involved, they are submitted as soon as completed. Some executives like to sign the mail at least twice a day. In other cases the mail is signed in the afternoon in time to meet the mail schedules (with which the secretary must become familiar). Learn and follow the executive's preferences in these matters.

The correct arrangement of transcribed material is as follows: the letter and its envelope on top, then the extra carbons, and the file copy with its notations. If the executive is there, present the letters face up. If not, turn the top letter face down to keep it clean and to prevent its being read.

Most secretaries arrange to be at the executive's desk for the signing session, for there are often questions and comments about the items to be signed and about the work ahead.

A frequent point of irritation between an executive and a transcriber is the difference between what the executive thinks was dictated and what has been transcribed. There is only one gracious way to handle these differences of opinion as to who is at fault. The secretary accepts responsibility for making all corrections and changes. It really does not make any difference who made a mistake. The important thing is to go about correcting it at once, cheerfully and willingly.

Secretarial Signatures

Both the multifunctional secretary and the administrative secretary in a word processing setup are frequently given authority to sign the transcribed letter. Recently, both men and women in either the executive or the secretarial role have chosen a signature that does not identify their sex, possibly adopting initials rather than the given name. Some women select the increasingly popular *Ms.* that does not reveal their marital status.

Because it has become the prerogative of the person involved in producing correspondence to exercise personal preference in choosing a business signature, the secretary should be guided by this preference and follow it meticulously.

The customary ways for a secretary to sign mail in the executive's absence or upon request are:

Very truly yours

*Helen Benton*MW

President

Sign the executive's name in your own handwriting and add your initials. Use a readable script of generous size.

Very truly yours

Helen Benton

President

Imitate the executive's signature.

Sincerely yours

Max Williams

Max Williams
Secretary to Ms. Benton

Sign your name and then type your name, title, and the name of the principal.

Preparing the Correspondence for Filing

The transcribed dictation is prepared for filing by the multifunctional secretary or, if there is a word processing center, by the administrative secretary. Staple the copy of each reply to the top of the incoming letter it answers. Staple the copies of letters originating at your desk into sets if the letters are longer than one page. Place pertinent letters in the pending file or make tickler items from the copies. Write each follow-up date on the copy of the letter itself to show that the date has been set and recorded. Add the filing notation before laying the correspondence aside. The matter of designating *where* to file each letter is taken up in Chapters 14 and 15. Increasingly the file notation is made by the dictator or transcriber and typed on the document at transcription time.

SENDING SIGNED MAIL

Before mailing, the secretary makes a final check. Has the material been signed? Are all enclosures attached? Is the envelope address the same as the address on the letter? Is the amount of postage correct? If stamps are used, are they securely affixed? In some large offices secretaries are relieved of the final work of sending out correspondence. Mail clerks collect the signed letters and the envelopes and fold, insert, seal, and stamp them. In small offices the secretary attends to every step of the routine.

Modern office equipment such as the folding machine makes the routine faster and easier, but the secretary should know the most efficient manual procedures as well.

Folding and Inserting Letters Manually

A letter is ready for mailing when it is signed and all enclosures are assembled. A secretary often folds and inserts the letters while waiting at the desk for the executive to read and sign the rest of the mail. Every letter should be folded in such a way that it will unfold naturally into reading position. The proper methods are shown in Illus. 9-3.

You can fold and insert a stack of letters very quickly at your own desk by developing a routine based on these steps.

1. Have a cleared space on the desk.
2. Take a letter from the stack of signed mail; place it before you on the desk and fold it neatly; insert it into the envelope at once.
3. Lay the envelope aside in a stack with the flap out flat (not folded over the envelope) and with the address side downward.

The routine that proves most efficient for you must be worked out. Experiment with some 20 or 30 large and small dummy envelopes and letters until you have developed a routine free of wasted motions.

Sealing Envelopes

When all the letters are enclosed, joggle the envelopes into a neat stack. All the address sides will be down and the flaps will be opened out. Now pick up the stack, grasp the flaps, and bend them back in order to make them flatter. Holding the short edges of the stack of envelopes between your hands, drop the envelopes off the bottom of the stack one at a time on the desk, so that only the gummed part of the flap of each envelope is visible. Then take a moistening tube, sponge, or wet paper towel, and with one swing of the arm start at the bottom and moisten all the flaps at once. Lay the tube aside on a blotter and start sealing the envelope nearest you by folding over the flap. Continue up the column. As you seal each envelope, pick it up and lay it in a stack, flap side up.

In the ceramic wheel type of moistener, a wide wheel passes through a shallow reservoir of water at the bottom. To use this moistener, turn the stack of envelopes over so that the address sides are up. Take the top envelope and, with both hands at the short edges, pull just the gummed part of the flap over

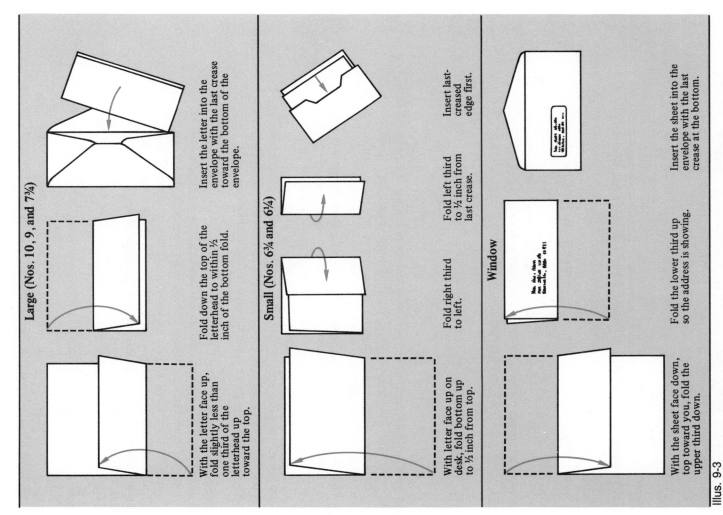

Large (Nos. 10, 9, and 7¾)

With the letter face up, fold slightly less than one third of the letterhead up toward the top.

Fold down the top of the letterhead to within ½ inch of the bottom fold.

Insert the letter into the envelope with the last crease toward the bottom of the envelope.

Small (Nos. 6¾ and 6¼)

With letter face up on desk, fold bottom up to ½ inch from top.

Fold right third to left.

Fold left third to ½ inch from last crease.

Insert last-creased edge first.

Window

With the sheet face down, top toward you, fold the upper third down.

Fold the lower third up so the address is showing.

Insert the sheet into the envelope with the last crease at the bottom.

Illus. 9-3
Examples of ways to fold letters

the rotating wheel. With the forefingers, fold the moistened flap down over the envelope and lay it aside, address side up.

Stamping

If the sealed envelopes are to be stamped by hand, first remove all those that require special stamping. Lay the rest of them out in columnar form with the address side up, leaving depth enough for the stamps to be pasted. Take a strip of stamps that are joined with the horizontal edges together, moisten one stamp at a time on a nearby sponge or moistener, and affix it to an envelope, working from the top envelope down. For strip stamps that are attached at the vertical edges, as rolled stamps are, lay the envelopes across the desk.

Envelopes requiring special stamping should be given individual attention. Those that are sent special delivery or to other countries and those that are too heavy for the minimum postage should be handled separately. Write in pencil in the stamp position the amount of postage needed. This penciled figure is later covered by the stamps.

Considerable loss is incurred from using excess postage. Every office should have some kind of postal scale. Weigh every piece of mail. When in doubt, weigh! Small scales for first-class mail are sensitive to fractions of an ounce. Check the accuracy of your scale periodically by placing nine *new* pennies on it and adjust until they weigh exactly one ounce. The post office no longer delivers unstamped mail; so check carefully to be sure all mail is stamped.

SPECIALIZED TRANSCRIBING TECHNIQUES FOR THE MULTIFUNCTIONAL SECRETARY

The following suggestions apply only to the multifunctional secretary transcribing from shorthand notes.

Positioning the Notebook

To hold your notebook in an upright position, attach a large button or tie a large knot at each end of a piece of string so that you can set the opened notebook between the buttons or knots.

Suggesting a Change

When you feel that a whole paragraph should be changed, type the dictated text on a separate sheet with your revision below. Take it in to the executive and say something like, "I roughed out a paragraph here. I thought you might want to change it because. . . ." If your revision is not approved, accept the decision matter-of-factly.

Transcribing a Rough Draft

Your employer will ask for a rough draft of any material that must be prepared with extreme care. Bulletin board announcements, memorandums to be widely circulated, reports, speeches, or publications may go through several revisions. (Sometimes you will transcribe these from longhand, and sometimes that longhand is difficult to decipher.)

Follow these suggestions for typing rough drafts:

1. Unless instructed otherwise, type only one copy on inexpensive paper that will take ink corrections, deletions, or additions. To identify rough drafts, you may prefer using colored paper. Use paper of the same size that you will use in the final copy.

2. If your typewriter uses mag cards or tape, prepare a hard copy while keying the rough draft. You will then need only retype the changes or additions and merge them with the original tape or card.

3. Type *DRAFT* near the top of the page so that you will mail the corrected copy, not the rough draft.

4. For a one-page item, single-space and arrange to resemble the completed document.

5. For a speech or report, double-space or triple-space. If the executive makes many changes habitually, triple-space.

6. If you are typing a complicated table, record the location of headings and tab stops so that you will figure them only once. A rough draft of a complicated table is often necessary for your own guidance.

7. Although you will try to prepare correct copy, X out errors and do not spend unnecessary time on corrections.

8. Keep all revisions of a long item in a separate, properly identified folder along with supporting data until the job is finished. If there are a number of revisions, number each one as you proceed, such as *Second Revision—page 2.*

9. Paste up revised copy to reduce the amount of retyping required. Use computer printouts of tables if they are available.

Indicating Completed Work or an Interruption During Transcription

You may not transcribe items in consecutive order. As you complete each item, draw a diagonal line through your shorthand notes. As dictation machines vary, follow the instructions given on the equipment for indicating the completion of an item on the recording media.

When shorthand transcription is interrupted, insert a conspicuous signal at the cutoff place in your notes, or you may have to reread the whole page to find your place.

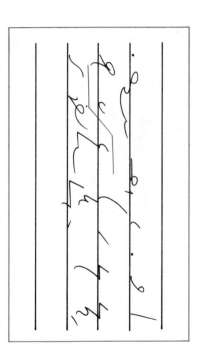

Systematizing Routine Mailings

You may be responsible for regular mailings to a specified list—40 branch managers every Thursday, for instance. You can save time by following this routine:

1. Type stencils of the addresses, 10 to the page.
2. Run off 52 copies from each stencil, using back paper.
3. Detach individual labels from each sheet and affix them to the appropriate envelopes.

Envelopes for the year's mailings are ready in three operations. If your organization has a word processing center, this is the type of routine work that can be sent there.

SPECIALIZED TRANSCRIBING FUNCTIONS OF THE CORRESPONDENCE SECRETARY

The correspondence secretary performs three steps in transcribing the dictated material:

1. Keyboarding the material dictated as rapidly as possible, not stopping for the correction of errors of any kind.
2. Editing the copy and making the necessary corrections and changes in format. Here is where your facility in spelling, punctuation, grammar, and word usage is put into play.
3. Playing out the corrected copy into a usable document.

Keyboarding the material is followed by correcting it. On the visual screen, the operator can see the copy and the corrections as they are made.

Most correspondence secretaries perform the first two steps, but some of them specialize in playing out the corrected copy only, from a mag card, tape, or disk that has been filed in the center. When a filed letter is used in producing a new letter, the operator either types the dictated address or merges the address from a stored tape with the body of the letter. If several paragraphs are to be combined to form the finished letter, the operator knows the proper controls to push in order to call up the needed data.

The correspondence secretary needs great skill in English and word usage in order to perform the first two steps. Equally or more important, however, is an interest in and an understanding of machine capabilities.

SUGGESTED READINGS

A basic reference that should accompany you to your first position is this textbook with its valuable reference section. The references which follow will also help the secretary in self-development.

DeVries, Mary A. *Secretary's Standard Reference Manual and Guide*. West Nyack, N.J.: Parker Publishing Co., 1977.

Doris, Lillian, and Besse May Miller. *Complete Secretary's Handbook*, 4th ed., revised by Mary A. DeVries. Englewood Cliffs, N.J.: Prentice-Hall, Inc., 1977.

Jordan, Lewis. *New York Times Manual of Style and Usage*. New York: New York Times, 1976.

A Manual of Style, 12th ed. Chicago: University of Chicago Press, 1969.

Miller, Besse May (ed.). *Private Secretary's Encyclopedia*. Englewood Cliffs, N.J.: Prentice-Hall, Inc., 1978.

Smith, Genevieve. *Genevieve Smith's DeLuxe Handbook for the Executive Secretary*. Englewood Cliffs, N.J.: Prentice-Hall, Inc., 1979.

Whelan, Doris. *Secretary's Handbook*. New York: Harcourt Brace Jovanovich, Inc., 1978.

Webster's Secretary's Handbook. Springfield, Mass.: G. & C. Merriam Company, 1976.

LEGAL SECRETARIAL AIDS

Bate, Marjorie Dunlap, and Mary C. Casey. *Legal Office Procedures*, 2d ed. New York: McGraw-Hill Book Company, 1981.

Dupree, Garland, and Dorothy S. Namanny. *Legal Office Typing*. Cincinnati: South-Western Publishing Co., 1975.

Ferrman, Marian. *Legal Secretary's Handbook*. West Nyack, N.J.: Parker Publishing Co., 1977.

Gordon, David, and Thomas Hemnes. *Legal Word Book*. Boston: Houghton Mifflin Company, 1978.

Knapp, Mary M. *Legal Terminology*. Skokie, Ill.: Stenograph Corp., 1981.

Morton, Joyce. *Legal Secretary's Procedures.* Englewood Cliffs, N.J.: Prentice-Hall, Inc., 1979.

Park, William R. (ed.). *Manual for Legal Assistants.* St. Paul: West Publishing Co., 1979.

Roderick, Wanda W. *Legal Studies, To Wit: Basic Legal Terminology and Transcription Course.* Cincinnati: South-Western Publishing Co., 1978.

MEDICAL SECRETARIAL AIDS

Atkinson, Philip. S. *Medical Office Practice,* 2d ed. A practice set. Cincinnati: South-Western Publishing Co., 1976.

Bredow, Miriam, Karonne J. Becklin, and Edith M. Sunnarborg. *Medical Office Procedures,* 2d ed. New York: McGraw-Hill Book Company, 1981.

Kutie, Rita, and Virginia Huffman. *Medi-Speller: A Transcription Aid.* Springfield, Ill.: Charles C. Thomas, Publisher, 1979.

Ehrlich, Ann. *Medical Office Procedures.* Champaign, Ill.: Colwell Company, 1977.

Saputo, Helen, and Nancy Gill. *Medical Secretary's Standard Reference Handbook.* Englewood Cliffs, N.J.: Prentice-Hall, Inc., 1980.

SUGGESTED QUICK REFERENCES

Dictionary (a recent one)

House, Clifford R., and Kathie Sigler. *Reference Manual for Office Personnel,* 6th ed. Cincinnati: South-Western Publishing Co., 1981.

Leslie, Louis. *20,000 Words,* 7th ed. New York: McGraw-Hill Book Company, 1977. (Spelling and word division reference.)

Montoya, Sarah. Monthly column in *The Secretary* magazine called "Word Watching."

Sabin, William. *Gregg Reference Manual,* 5th ed. New York: McGraw-Hill Book Company, 1977.

Silverthorn, J. E., and Devern J. Perry. *Word Division Manual,* 2d ed. Cincinnati: South-Western Publishing Co., 1970.

ZIP Code Directory

QUESTIONS FOR DISCUSSION

1. Would any of the following practices suggested in the chapter be unnecessary time-wasters for an experienced, competent secretary?
   (a) Making an outline of an item before dictating to dictation equipment?
   (b) Developing a bank of standard opening and closing sentences, paragraphs, and letters to answer recurring letters
   (c) Eliminating two proofreadings to detect errors
   (d) Prereading and editing notes before transcribing
2. Some executives dictate at the end of an item the number of extra copies

wanted. How can the transcriber be sure that the required number of copies is provided? Do you have a suggestion for changing the dictator's habit?

3. In what ways do the responsibilities for a dictated item differ for the administrative secretary, the correspondence secretary, and the multifunctional secretary?

4. What kinds of changes should the secretary make in dictation? What kinds should not be made?

5. What implied directions would you follow in transcribing:
   (a) A personal letter to a classmate in charge of a college reunion?
   (b) A letter about a discount improperly taken if the invoice in question is handed to you along with the customer's letter being answered?
   (c) A reply to a letter of complaint about the service given to a customer by a branch office?
   (d) A proposed contract for the construction of a new plant?

6. Retype any of the names and titles that are incorrect in form. Use the Reference Guide to verify your answers.
   (a) Mr. Floyd B. Smith, Jr., M.D.
   (b) Wallace P. Mundy, Esq., Ph.D.
   (c) The Hon. Hilda B. Kane
   (d) Dr. Louise Adams, M.D.
   (e) Dean Kelly P. Murphy, Ph.D.

PROBLEMS

1. On the inside cover of your own collegiate dictionary paste a typewritten list showing exactly:
   (a) *How* the following are shown in the dictionary:
   Foreign words
   Hyphenated words
   Inflectional forms
   Parts of speech
   Preferred spellings
   Syllabication
   (b) *Where* the following can be found in the dictionary:
   Abbreviations
   Adjective-and-noun terms (such as *blind alley*)
   Biographical names
   Place names
   Prepositional phrases (such as *on hand*)
   Punctuation
   Noun-and-noun terms (such as *band wagon*)
   Rules of grammar
   Having such a reference will save you much time in using the dictionary.

2. Be prepared to set up and demonstrate the following:
   (a) speed sealing of envelopes, using as many types of manual moisteners as possible
   (b) speed stamping

3. In typewritten form prepare answers to the following questions. Then correct your answers, using the reference books designated in the chapter and citing your authority.
   (a) What are synonyms for *agent, integrity, mediocrity?*
   (b) What is the correct salutation for a clergyman?
   (c) What are the state abbreviations, ad-

(f) Should *cooperate* and *reread* be hyphenated?

4. One of your greatest assets in producing quality transcripts is your ability to proof-read accurately. As a pretest of your competency in this area, type the letter below and check the errors, retyping a mailable copy if instructed to do so by your instructor. (You may need to refer to the Reference Guide.) Can you locate 20 errors?

5. Transcribe your notes from Problem 3, Chapter 8.

dresses, and ZIP Codes for the following letters?

Federal Reserve Bank, Kansas City, Missouri

Doctors Hospital, Seattle, Washington

El Paso (Texas) Chamber of Commerce

(d) Should there be a space after the first period in writing *Ph. D.?*

(e) How should the following sentence be punctuated?
Did he say Are you going

Drs. J. M. Miller & H. A Kahn
Medical Arts Bldg
Omaha, Nebr.

Gentlemen

We have no way of determing from your letter of Feb 10 you needs for additional X-ray equiptment.

We have ask our sales representative Manuel Alvarez to telephone you for an appointment before he attends next months state physicians convention in Omaha, and examine your present machines.

As you requested I reminded him not t1 call on you until after 4 p.m.; that being the end of your office hours.

In the mean time you may like to examine our latest catalog, so that you can see what is available from our company. It is enclosed

Yours Cordially

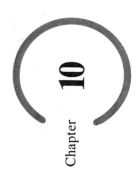

Chapter **10**

Composing Assignments

One of the most important contributions you will make to your employer will come from your ability to write effectively. Other than a face-to-face contact or personal call, the letter is the most effective way to communicate ideas in business. It is often the only contact the public will have with your firm. Your ability to express personal concern, build goodwill, and solve business problems through the written word will make you an invaluable employee.

Whether your first assignment is a simple reply to a request for a catalog or a letter to satisfy a sensitive customer complaint, you'll find that composition will give you the opportunity to display your writing ability and creativity. Good writing, however, is hard work. Each composing assignment will test your educational background and experience. To do a good job, you must produce communications that are clear, concise, natural, and friendly. To help you become *letter perfect* in your composing assignments, this chapter presents in capsule form the principles involved in producing the kinds of communications that bring a favorable reaction. Examples of typical business and personal letters that you may be asked to compose for your employer are also included.

THE BASICS

You may find it difficult at first to write in a style similar to that of the person who will sign the letter. However, when your employer says, "Type a reply for my signature," you will know he or she has confidence in your writing ability.

Successful writers know how to organize their thoughts in a logical fashion. They are also aware that written language has more impact upon the reader than the spoken word has upon the listener. In problem situations, they rewrite again and again until they have just the right combination of ideas, words, and sentences to convey the message that will make a lasting, favorable impression.

A review of the basic principles of good writing will help you recall the do's and dont's of composing clear, concise, correct communications that represent a modern approach to writing letters, memorandums, or any other forms of business correspondence.

The careful writer follows a plan. Before committing one word to paper, you should reread the letter or memo that is to be answered. You will want to ask yourself, What does the reader expect? Before you undertake a writing assignment, isolate the main purpose of your communication and build your message around it; focus on your reader by writing about things of interest to the reader; gather and verify the facts you want to include; outline the major points and place them in the most effective order; and then draft the letter, making sure that every sentence is clear and that you have given complete and correct information.

Set the Proper Tone

Tone makes communication human. It shows the attitude of the writer and should make the message seem cordial, tactful, positive, and courteous. By ignoring tone you may give your reader the feeling that you are blunt, impolite, superior, unfriendly, or given to high-pressure sales tactics. The effective writer controls the tone of correspondence by the careful choice of words. The reader's interpretation of your words will determine the nature of the response to your correspondence. To improve the tone of your letters, follow these suggestions:

Personalize Your Message. Even if your letter is written for a mass audience, make each reader feel that it was written to one person—the recipient.

Personal Tone

Welcome! We were all delighted, Mr. Lynn, that your name was on our list of initiates for last year. Your contributions as a new member will help us increase our many services to the community.

Impersonal Tone

Last year we initiated fifty new members, and our membership continues to grow. We are pleased to add your name to the list.

Most business communications suffer from too much attention to the writer's point of view and not enough emphasis on the reader. Such letters lack the *you* attitude. Instead of beginning a paragraph with *I* or *We*, reverse the order and begin with *you* as shown in the following examples:

Emphasis on the Reader	**Emphasis on the Writer**
For your convenience we have just opened a new branch office at the Village Shopping Center.	We have just opened a new branch office at the Village Shopping Center.

Using the reader's name is also a good way to put your reader in the picture. Don't overdo this, however, or you run the risk of sounding too familiar.

Personal	**Impersonal**
You will be glad to know, Mrs. Lane, that the Bank of Grundy has raised the interest rate on passbook savings to 9 percent.	The Bank of Grundy has raised the interest rate on passbook savings to 9 percent.

Humanize Your Message. Relax and let your letters reflect your personality. Business communications need not be dull and mechanical.

Friendly, Human Tone	**Dull, Monotonous Tone**
Thank you for your interest in a position in our Accounting Department. I have passed your application along to Mr. Moore, and he will be writing to you concerning openings in that department.	This will acknowledge receipt of your application for a job with our firm. I am forwarding it to our Accounting Department for consideration.

Encourage Your Reader. Accent the positive elements in your message. Tell your reader what you can do and not what you *can't* do. Bring out points favorable to your reader. If you have good news, tell it in the first sentence. If you have bad news, avoid dwelling on negative terms such as *error, mistake,* *inconvenience*, and *trouble*. Such words merely emphasize the problems you have caused.

Positive Tone	Negative Tone
Your programs for ARTS IN THE PARK will be delivered in time for the festival. Through careful scheduling, we will pick them up in Philadelphia, proof them there, and get them to you before the festival opens on Monday.	We regret to inform you that the programs you will need for ARTS IN THE PARK were erroneously shipped to Philadelphia. This unfortunate mistake means that we must pick them up in Philadelphia, proof them there, and deliver them just before the festival opens on Monday.

Be Natural—Write the Way You Talk. A business message should be a substitute for a visit or personal call and should be written in a conversational tone. If your letters or those of your employer contain hackneyed or stereotyped expressions that make them dull, substitute natural expressions as in the following examples:

Natural Expressions	Hackneyed Expressions
Here is or enclosed is	Enclosed herewith please find
By (specific date)	At your earliest convenience
Separately	Under separate cover
As you requested	As per your request
Your letter of (specific date)	Your letter of recent date
Now or presently	At the present writing
Because	Due to the fact that
Today, tomorrow, or specific date	In due course
In case	In the event that
As we agreed	Pursuant to our agreement
(omit)	Thanking you in advance
(omit)	Please be advised
(don't)	May we take the liberty of
(omit)	Permit me to say that
Please let us know	We would like to be advised
Until	Until such time as

Practice Tact. Tact is a keen sense of what to do or say to maintain good relations with others. It is essential in the tone of a letter that must tell a reader that a claim has been denied, a promotion disapproved, or that employment is being terminated.

Tactful Tone	**Tactless Tone**
Please indicate on the attached form the size and color you prefer so that we can ship your order before May 1.	You failed to indicate the proper size and color on your order blank.
Thank you for telling us that your hot water heater has not been properly repaired.	We have your letter in which you claim that we did not repair your hot water heater in accordance with the terms of your contract.

Never Write in Anger. No matter how hard you try, your words and expressions will give you away. Writing letters that destroy customer relations is something no business can afford. The best advice to follow is to cool off and wait a few days before responding. (If your employer violates this principle, you may take it upon yourself to hold the letter a few hours or even until the next day. Your employer knows this rule of thumb, too, and will appreciate and thank you for your good judgment.)

Improve Sentence Quality

Today's busy reader has little time for wasted words that contribute little if anything to the message. Every word should work. Your writing will improve considerably if you let each sentence express one idea. The following suggestions should help you improve the quality of your sentences:

Keep Your Sentences Short. Short sentences containing fewer than 15 words will give your message impact. They also carry your reader's interest from one set of ideas to another. Caution should be exercised, however, not to put too many short sentences together. Such an arrangement gives your writing a monotonous, jerky effect.

A sentence that expresses a thought briefly and clearly is concise, stripped of superfluous words, and thus easy to read and understand.

Conciseness is a mark of finesse and skill. It is important because it saves time—the writer's, the typist's and the reader's—and it can save paper. To achieve conciseness, state a fact only once. Cut out the superfluous words and phrases in each sentence. Beware, however, of the brusque tone that can be created through *abrupt* conciseness. For instance, "Be here at five," lacks the graciousness of "I'm looking forward to seeing you at five."

Keep Your Paragraphs Short. Your reader will be less likely to ignore your ideas if you present them in short paragraphs. Remember, though, that when you change the subject, begin a new paragraph.

Prefer the Short Word. A good vocabulary is essential to precise expression. As a general rule, however, the simple word will have a more powerful effect than a long one that your reader may have to look up. Small words express big ideas—*God, sun, sea, sky, joy, war.* A waiter is more likely to grasp your meaning if you ask, "Is the *tip* included in the price of the meal?" than if you ask, "Is the *gratuity* included in the price of the meal?"

The trend in business letters is toward short words that are used in conversation. They usually create a friendly, personal relationship between the writer and the reader; and they help the writer to relax and write naturally.

If a word is long, chances are you should change it to a shorter, more familiar one so that the meaning is clear. Avoid the use of colloquialisms, slang words, and coined phrases. There are readers, however, who are scholarly and intellectual. Visualize the reader and use the kind of words suitable to the position and probable education of the reader.

In the list that follows, look over the words commonly used in business writing, and their short, conversational counterparts. Would you say that the short ones are always preferable to the long ones? that the long ones are always preferable to the short ones?

ameliorate . . . . .improve	endeavor . . . . .try
ascertain . . . . .learn	equitable . . . .fair
cognizant of . . .aware of	initiate . . . . .begin
commitment . . .pledge, promise	modification . . .change
communication . .letter	procure . . . . .get
consummate . . .complete	remuneration . . .pay, salary
determine . . . .learn	submitted . . . .sent
disseminate . . .spread	utilization . . . .use
effectuate . . . .bring about	verification . . .proof

A handy reference for the secretary's desk is *Roget's International The-saurus in Dictionary Form*, a listing of synonyms, antonyms, and phrases.

Avoid Redundant Expressions. Too many words lengthen a communication unnecessarily and sap its vitality. When two or three words are used to express a thought that could be expressed with one word, your writing becomes redundant and has a tendency to cause the reader to lose interest.

Here are some examples of the redundant expressions that occur most frequently in business communications. In each of these examples only one of the words is needed—you need to build a *watch list* of needless words that creep into your correspondence:

each and every	rightly deserve	fill up
right and proper	finish up	absolutely free
first and foremost	first began	repeat again
full and complete	reduce down	true facts
over and done with	still remains	small in size
baffling and puzzling	later on	new innovation
one and the same	seldom ever	free gratis
free and unencumbered	quite unique	exactly identical
concur and agree	both alike	very complete
prompt and immediate	rather likely	joined together
consent and approval	just recently	continue on
promise and assure	very latest	refer back
trust and confidence	meet together	matinee performance
up until	past experience	invisible to the eye
very complete	close up	the only other alternative

Another common error often made by business writers is using comparative forms of words that have no degrees of comparison. If a task is *impossible*, it cannot be *most impossible*. Words such as *honest, fatal, mortal, final,* and *hazardous* are concepts that cannot be compared. Such expressions as a *completely honest* person and *very fatal* disease and *rather obvious* result merely in wasting your reader's time.

Strive for Clarity. It would be difficult to estimate the number of hours that are lost in business because of unclear statements—statements that leave the reader confused and uncertain and lead to inaction and lost business. A statement like, "All the citizens had a part in appointing the members of the committee, and they think that the project should continue," leaves serious doubt as to whether *they* refers to the citizens or the members of the committee. Such statements baffle even the brightest readers and could lead to serious misinterpretation. If there is any doubt that what you have written could be misinterpreted, rewrite it.

Use Active Verbs. To make a forceful impression, writers have found that the active rather than the passive voice is helpful. In the active voice, the subject is the doer of the action; whereas in the passive voice, the subject is acted upon. Therefore, passive voice tends to weaken a sentence. When *forcefulness* is not a factor, however, and the writer wants to concentrate on the you attitude, passive voice may be used to avoid *we* and *I*. Passive voice is also effective in eliminating sexist pronouns (his, her) in describing occupations, life-styles, and so forth.

The following sentences illustrate each of these principles:

Forceful

Weak

I have approved the
plan.

The plan was approved
by me.

Nonsexist

Sexist

The contractor must
be advised of any
changes in the
specifications.

He must advise the
contractor of any
changes in the
specifications.

Use Concrete Expressions. Vague expressions and ambiguous references cloud your meaning and detract from your message. Precise, specific terms will improve the clarity of your writing and make your sentences more forceful. Expressions such as a *good* salary, a *large* crowd, a *few* hours, a *big* sale, and *several* errors are vague and ambiguous. One reader may visualize a good salary as $10,000 while another would consider $25,000 a good salary. After you have written your first draft, check it for these or any other fuzzy expressions.

Avoid Negative Expressions. In every kind of communication, words of negative connotation are to be avoided. As one correspondent put it, negative words can turn a letter into a brink of war communiqué. Negative words in their kindest usage still have an unpleasant tinge. A starting list of negative reaction words is given here.

You can undoubtedly add others—and should!

alibi	failure
biased	fault
blame	impossible
can't	inconvenience
cheap	insist
claim	regret
complaint	reject
criticize	scheme
defend	so called
error	useless
evict	wrong

Words of positive connotation are tone helpers. Use them whenever possible. Compiling your own reference list of positive reaction words will help you to become alert to using them. Here are a few:

ability	good	pleasant
advantage	gratifying	please
benefit	happy	prominent
effective	help	recommend
enjoy	kind	responsible
fitting	lasting	thoughtful

Use a Forceful Beginning Sentence. Getting started is often the most difficult part of the letter-writing task. Your first sentence should be gracious and at the same time establish a point of contact with your reader. *Thank you* is always a good beginning when it is used appropriately and sincerely. When your reader has had previous correspondence with you and is expecting a specific reply, a good way to begin is by giving assurance in the first sentence. The following illustrations should be helpful:

Forceful

Thank you for your letter of April 14 requesting a list of last year's scholarship recipients. This information was destroyed at the end of the school year and is no longer available.

Weak

We regret to inform you that we have checked our files and cannot supply the information you requested.

Your check for $145 in payment of claim No. 1878 is in the mail.

In reference to your claim No. 1878 in the amount of $145, we have instructed our Accounting Department to mail you a check for same.

A copy of our booklet, Recycling for Profit, is on its way to you with our compliments.

This will acknowledge receipt of your letter of May 15 requesting a copy of our booklet, Recycling for Profit.

Many business writers are adopting the *dearless salutation* and the *salute opening* to begin their letters although the use of *Dear Mr., Miss, Mrs.,* or *Ms.*

combined with the last name is still the most popular form of salutation. Because of the nonsexist movement, *Dear Sir, Gentlemen,* and *Dear Madam* are disappearing as a form of salutation. The dearless salutation substitutes some other word for *dear,* and the salute opening incorporates the salutation in the first few words of the opening sentence as illustrated in the following examples:

Dearless Salutation

Hello, Mrs. Wilkins:

Salute Opening

Good Morning, Dr. Cortez:

You are right, Mrs. Wilkins, in assuming that the shipment was prepaid.

Congratulations, Dr. Cortez, on your recent appointment to the Finance Committee.

Use a Gracious Ending. The closing lines are your last chance for a good impression and a favorable reaction. Here are some important pointers on writing effective closing sentences:

1. Make the last sentence independent of the complimentary close. Avoid fragmented endings such as *hoping to hear from you soon, I remain.*
2. Omit meaningless phrases. If you have turned down an application for credit, it is meaningless to say, "Call on me again when I can be helpful."
3. Make it easy for your reader to reply to a specific request. Use statements such as "Return the postage free card" or "Sign the enclosed card, and we'll bill you later."
4. Look to the future. Resell your company, its products, and its people.
5. Ask for the action you want. If you want your reader to respond in a certain way, don't imply your expectations. When you can, point out the advantages the reader will gain by reacting favorably to your request.

Your future orders will be filled promptly, and you will receive the same courteous treatment that has made us the outstanding auto parts dealer in this area.

Sign the contract and return it to us before June 30 to ensure a fun-filled summer in your new Dune Buggy.

6. End on a positive note; but if you are answering a letter asking for an adjustment, don't apologize. Apologies and negative endings only remind the reader of inconvenience and error. A frank admission of error on your part may win your point, but too many negative words weaken your message.

7. Instead of writing "We regret the inconvenience this error has caused you, but mistakes are bound to occur in an organization as large as ours," use a positive approach: "The situation you described in your letter of October 15 has been corrected, and we look forward to working with you when you again need furniture for your new home."

8. Don't thank in advance. This is discourteous, and it presumes upon the reader's willingness to cooperate. It is appropriate to show appreciation in the closing sentence, but never make a statement such as "Thank you in advance."

9. Stop when you've said enough. In an attempt to be courteous, many letter writers drag their readers through a maze of words that add nothing to the message. Statements such as "Again, let me thank you for . . ." are redundant and weaken the effect of your letter.

TYPICAL LETTERS COMPOSED BY THE SECRETARY

The occasions when a secretary may be requested to compose material for the employer fall into two categories—assignments of a business nature and those of a personal nature. No matter what the orientation may be, a request to compose a letter for the employer's signature is to be regarded as a compliment—a compliment to your ability to do this high-level secretarial task.

Business Correspondence

Generally, experienced secretaries are asked to write drafts of reports, speeches, minutes of meetings, difficult letters, and memorandums. This material would probably require the employer's signature. Routine assignments, such as replies to requests for information, transmittal letters, special requests, messages, reservations, appointment letters, or acknowledgments might appropriately be signed by the secretary or administrative assistant.

If you are just beginning to assume these correspondence duties, you may wish to type a suggested reply to a letter and give it to your employer for editing. This is a good way to familiarize your employer with your ability as a correspondent. In the course of transcribing your employer's dictation, you may find it necessary to correct errors in grammar, dates, amounts, repetition of words, and sentence structure. Of course, you will do so tactfully and courteously. This is another instance where your knowledge of English fundamentals can be brought to your employer's attention. If you become recognized as an expert in this area, you may find yourself putting the finishing touches on much of your employer's business correspondence.

Acknowledgments. In general, every letter should be answered or acknowledged promptly, preferably the day it is received. In *answering* a letter, discuss the points raised. In *acknowledging* a letter or other materials, merely tell about its receipt and add any other necessary information. Acknowledgment letters may be sent to notify a customer that an order or a request for an appointment has been received. An effective acknowledgment letter will show appreciation; refer to the major points in the letter received; explain the action to be taken in the future; resell the customer on your firm, its products, and its service.

Thank you for your letter of October 4 indicating that your order was shipped to Memphis instead of Nashville as you requested (appreciation).

Your concern about receiving your merchandise in time for pre-Christmas sales is understandable (major point). Mr. Andrews, our sales manager, is in Atlanta this week; and I will notify him today to authorize a shipment to you from our Atlanta warehouse (specific action).

We will make every effort to provide you with prompt and courteous service to ensure that you receive your merchandise in time for your pre-Christmas promotions (resale of company service).

Covering Letters. A universal business practice is to inform the recipient when money or material is being sent separately. Such a covering letter tells, with a touch of personal interest, what is being sent, why, when, and how.

A letter of transmittal is a form of covering letter also and states that the material is enclosed and usually includes pertinent remarks about the enclosure.

When material is to be included in a letter, start with the direct approach. Indicate what is being sent and why. Tie in with the reader's personal interest if possible.

Today we mailed you separately a complete set of swatches of our latest collection of decorator fabrics (what is being sent and why). These should be helpful to you in selecting draperies for your new home (reader's personal interest).

Requests and Inquiries. Letters that request personal favors, information, or free materials should be courteous and complete in every detail. Let the reader know exactly what you want; support your requests with sound reasons why the reader should comply. Don't write in a demanding tone—keep in mind that you are the one who wants the favor. Make it easy to reply to your letter and express your gratitude and your willingness to return the favor.

In the November issue of the Office Male, I noticed an article outlining the many opportunities available to male secretaries. The article was both informative and timely, and I would like to have reprints for students who come to me for career counseling.

Enclosed is an addressed envelope. If there is a charge for these reprints, please bill me.

I appreciate your help in providing these informative articles. Your magazine is often helpful in assisting students in planning their careers.

Answers to Inquiries. When you write a letter in reply to an inquiry, try to give a satisfactory answer that will make your reader think that you are giving personal attention to the request. If you cannot provide the information requested (for whatever reason), tactfully state your refusal so that your reader will not be offended. Express appreciation for the letter and, when possible, give the information requested—don't make excuses. Offer additional help when appropriate—this is an excellent public relations tool.

Thank you for your letter of January 4 asking for a complimentary copy of our booklet on fund raising. The demand for this publication has been so heavy that we ran out before the end of the year. This booklet is being reprinted and will be available by February 1.

In the meantime, if you would like to have our Fund Raiser's Kit, which contains much of the same information plus some of the materials you will need to get started, just write your order on the bottom of this letter. Enclose $3 to cover mailing costs, and we will get a kit in the mail to you.

Reminder Letters. Every secretary keeps a tickler file of items that have to be completed. Answers awaited, reports due, goods to be received—all are recorded. When an item is overdue, the secretary sends a reminder. This is a routine procedure, and the secretary writes the note without being instructed to do so. Tactful phrasing is imperative, for no one likes to be reminded of negligence or lack of promptness.

To ensure that you are writing tactful reminder letters, never write in an accusing tone. Don't belittle by implying forgetfulness on the reader's part. Give complete information and close with a positive look to the future.

```
By July 24 we must complete our bids on the
new construction on Highway 77 North.  We
need the quotations that we requested on
June 1 to get our bids in on time.  Could
you possibly have this information sent to
our Chicago office by the first of next week?
A stamped envelope is enclosed for your
convenience.

Your help in securing this contract is
greatly appreciated, and we look forward to
working with you as the project progresses.
```

Negative Letters. Often a letter must be written on an unpleasant subject: *complaints or claims, refusals, mistakes.* These require special care in composing.

Complaint Letters. As a company employee, you believe that a complaint letter which you receive is antagonistic to the company and must not be taken lightly. A prompt, thorough investigation of the complaint is necessary. Often a company does not even know there is a reason for dissatisfaction; so a genuine complaint letter is generally appreciated.

But what about the situation in which *you* have a complaint? A good formula to follow in writing your letter is to begin with a positive reference to the trouble, continue with a detailed explanation and end with a courteous request for an adjustment. See if the following paragraphs meet these criteria:

```
On October 16 I ordered a solid cherry night-
stand to match the PROVANTIQUE bedroom group-
ing I purchased from you on August 29.  The
nightstand was delivered this morning in the
carton in which it was originally packed.
Upon opening the carton, I discovered that
```

the nightstand had been packed before the finish had completely dried. There were impressions of the cardboard packing on the top of the stand that no amount of cleaning will remove.

I am expecting guests for the Thanksgiving holidays and am eager to have the room completed before their arrival. Will you please have your truck pick up the nightstand, have it refinished, and return it to me before Thanksgiving? If this is not possible, could I please have another nightstand shipped from the factory?

I realize that this error was made at the factory, but I know you will take care of it in time for me to complete the room before my guests arrive.

Refusal Letters. One of the most severe tests of your ability to compose an effective letter will come when your employer asks you to write a letter of refusal. Banks often have to reject loans, employers have to turn down applications for positions, and your employer will sometimes have to refuse requests for favors. Since it is difficult to hold the reader's goodwill when you must refuse a request, letters of this type require special care.

When it is necessary to refuse a request, use the sandwich technique of placing the refusal between a positive opening statement and a positive closing statement. The positive opening statement is a buffer and will reduce the impact of the bad news. It should contain at least one element upon which both you and your reader agree, but it will not be effective if it sounds artificial or contrived. You should give a detailed explanation leading up to the refusal. Keep it practical and sympathetic. Avoid general statements that substitute for a detailed explanation. State the refusal, or imply it strongly. Leave no doubt in your reader's mind. Offer an alternative action if possible and resell your company, its products, and its services. Here is an example of a flat refusal:

The PROVANTIQUE bedroom suite that you purchased from us on August 29 is indeed one of the finest groupings our store has carried. We are sure it is especially beautiful in your new home (positive point of agreement).

The PROVANTIQUE grouping has been discontinued by the manufacturer, and no matching pieces are available. Our refinishing specialist tells us that all attempts to match the finish on the PROVANTIQUE grouping have proved unsuccessful (explanation leading to the refusal).

May we have John Hendricks, A.S.I.D., our interior designer, visit you at your convenience? We have explained your concern to him, and we are confident his suggestions will enable you to select a compatible piece of furniture to complement your PROVANTIQUE grouping and enhance your guest bedroom (alternative suggestion).

Our adjustment department will call you to make arrangements to pick up the nightstand. Of course, the full purchase price will be refunded, and we will offer you our most attractive price on any item you select as a replacement (resale of merchandise).

We appreciate the opportunity you have given us to help you furnish your new home. With the holidays approaching, we look forward to helping you select any accent pieces you may wish to acquire to beautify your home at this happy time of the year (positive closing).

Mistake Letters. As long as people and computers handle the affairs of business, mistakes will occur. These errors require letters that are tactful enough to soothe feelings and maintain harmonious relationships. When you write a letter about a mistake, admit that you are at fault without the use of pompous phrases and long words. Should you forget to put an enclosure in a letter, write a brief note of explanation to the addressee, attach the enclosure, and send a copy of the message in with the rest of the day's mail to be signed. This procedure lets your employer know that the enclosure was omitted from the original correspondence.

Psychologically it is human nature to want to help a person who admits a mistake—unless these mistakes occur too frequently with severe consequences. Compare your reactions to the mistake letters at the top of page 219:

Acceptable

After you called yesterday, I checked our file of October advertisements and found that we neglected to include yours. We are sorry that this happened, and we will give your advertisement preferred placement in our November issue.

Unacceptable

Pursuant to your telephone call of October 10, we immediately searched our records to determine what disposition had been made of your ad submitted for publication in the October issue of Edwardian Times. Apparently, through some inadvertent oversight on the part of our editorial department, your ad was omitted from this issue. We hope that delaying the ad for another month will not seriously inconvenience you.

Personal Correspondence

Occasionally your employer will ask you to write personal letters to business acquaintances. Some of these letters may be written without dictation and submitted to your employer for signature. It is especially important that these letters sound as though your employer had written them. Use the same salutation, complimentary close, and writing style that your employer uses. Personal correspondence should be typed on executive size stationery or on the executive's personal stationery, if available; otherwise, it should be typed on plain bond paper. You will want to draft your first attempt for approval. The types of personal business letters your employer may write are almost limitless —letters of appreciation, sympathy, recognition, congratulations, formal acceptances and regrets, letters of introduction, and letters accepting and declining invitations to speak. Often, because of their personal nature, your employer will dictate these letters; however, should he or she ask you to compose such a letter, you will want to consult an etiquette book or an up-to-date handbook on communications. The following examples of letters frequently delegated to the secretary for composition should prove helpful.

Letters of Appreciation. A busy executive in the office is usually just as busy on the outside with community activities. For instance, after a year of work on a civic project, your employer may ask you to write a note to the committee members acknowledging the contributions they made to the project. You may want to say the following:

```
The work is finally concluded, and it is
through your efforts and those of the other
members of the committee that we can mark
this project Complete.
```

```
Watching our dream become a reality will be
gratifying to each of us.  I hope we will
have the opportunity to work together on
another project for the betterment of our
community.
```

Letters of Recognition. In the course of your employment you will come to know many of your employer's friends and will recognize their names when you see them in print. If one of them has an article in a current magazine, you may scan the article and draft a letter complimenting the friend, using the executive's writing style, as in the following example:

```
I have just read your interesting article in
the current issue of Dynamics.  The article
is informative and shows your skill in or-
ganizing usually confusing ideas into a
clear, pro-and-con presentation that allows
valid conclusions to be drawn.  Your readers,
I know, will commend you for your treatment
of this complex subject.
```

Letters of Sympathy. If death or tragedy occurs in the family of one of the executive's friends, you can draft a sympathy note to be copied in longhand by the executive. A personal note is more thoughtful than a commercial card. It is sincere, and usually brief. The words *die* and *death* are seldom used in sympathy notes, for they seem to be lacking in consideration. Euphemistic phrases such as *your bereavement, fatal illness, tragic happening,* and *the obituary in the paper* are kinder.

```
I was sorry to read in    It is difficult to
this morning's paper       find words to express
of your mother's pass-     my feelings about
ing away.  My thoughts     yesterday's events.
are with you.              I am thinking of you
                           today, and my sym-
                           pathy is with you.
```

Letters of Congratulations. If there is publicity about the promotion or professional achievement of one of your employer's friends, you may want to draft a letter of congratulations.

Congratulations, Bob, on your appointment to
the vice-presidency. I should like to add
my sincere good wishes to the many others.
From our years of association, I know that
you will bring to the position the keen in-
tellect and the fine personal qualities that
the office requires.

Letters Accepting Invitations to Speak. Letters accepting invitations to speak should convey appreciation and enthusiasm. Details of the invitation might be repeated to assure the person issuing the invitation that the time, place, date, and other arrangements are clear. If your employer is a popular speaker, who receives numerous similar requests, it might be wise to put together a packet to include with the letter of acceptance—this could be a guide letter tailored to the specific occasion; material to be used in introducing your employer; a list of the special equipment your employer will need to make the presentation (projectors, recorders, screens, etc.); and a publicity photograph (to be sent only when requested). If your employer is to be accompanied by a spouse or other special guests, this information should be included in the letter of acceptance. This courtesy helps avoid a last minute rearrangement of the head table by your host. Give your reader as much information as possible in the letter of acceptance. This will eliminate the need for additional correspondence asking for a biographical sketch, a photograph, and a list of audiovisual equipment needed for the presentation.

Use the following example as a guide letter.

Thank you for including me in your plans for
the annual Employees' Banquet to be held at
the Mario Hotel in New Orleans on Monday,
November 14, at 7 p.m.

In keeping with your banquet theme, I have
entitled my remarks, "The Five A's of Job
Satisfaction." I will do my best to give
your employees an interesting twenty minutes.

My wife will accompany me and, as you suggested, we will meet you in the lobby of the
hotel at six o'clock.

I look forward to meeting you personally in
New Orleans.

Letters Declining an Invitation to Speak. Letters declining an invitation to speak should express appreciation for the invitation but at the same time express regret. A specific explanation of the circumstances that prevent acceptance should be given. Specific reasons are more sincere than statements such as "due to circumstances beyond my control," or "because of a previous engagement." These are flimsy excuses and have a ring of insincerity.

Acceptable

Thank you for inviting me to be your keynote speaker at the ARTISTS' FORUM on August 23 in Portland, Maine.

I regret that a teaching assignment at a print-making workshop during the entire month of August makes it impossible for me to accept.

It was thoughtful of you to include me in your plans, and I hope you will keep me in mind next summer when I will not be teaching.

Unacceptable

I regret exceedingly that I must decline your invitation to speak at the ARTISTS' FORUM on August 23.

Circumstances beyond my control make it impossible for me to accept.

Letters Canceling Previously Accepted Engagements. Canceling previous engagements often causes inconvenience, frustration, and ill will and should be done only when a genuine emergency arises. Despite careful planning, there may be occasions when it will be necessary for your employer to cancel a previously accepted engagement. The following model should be helpful in drafting a letter of this type:

This is a difficult letter to write because I know it can only cause you worry and inconvenience.

On Monday morning I was awakened at home to learn that our North Brattenborough plant had lost gallons of milk because of a leak in the filtering system. This morning our home office ordered everyone on site to direct a massive project to correct this situation. This unexpected emergency will, of course, make it impossible for me to speak before the National Symposium in Santa Fe next Saturday.

Guide Letters. You will soon discover that situations repeat themselves and that many of the letters you compose cover the same circumstances. When you find an especially effective sentence or terminology, preserve it for the next letter. You can do this by compiling a guide letter reference manual containing letters that reflect your employer's language and typical reactions. Although the preparation of such a reference takes time, it will be one of your greatest time-savers. Here is how to do it:

1. Keep an extra carbon copy of all outgoing letters for a month.

2. Reread them at the end of the month, all in one sitting. As you reread them objectively, you will recognize words, phrases, and ideas that recur.

3. Separate the letters into categories, making extra copies of those that fit several classifications; underline favorite phrases and other keys to your employer's ways of handling situations; and set up a file folder for each group. Ask yourself the reasons for variations among the letters in the amount of detail used, degree of cordiality, language, tone, and style.

4. Make an outline of the points usually covered in a letter in each category.

5. Pick out the best opening and closing sentences and the best key points tailored to specific situations.

6. Compile a letter guide, using a loose-leaf notebook. Type the model outline for the category on a heavy sheet to be used as the divider between categories of letters. Type model opening and closing sentences for the category on a separate sheet and model paragraphs on other sheets.

7. Code the index tabs for each section. For instance, "Congratulations" could be C and an especially good paragraph could be C4.

8. When you compose a letter, compare it with the outline to be sure that you have included all necessary parts.

9. Keep a record of the form used for each letter sent so that you will not again send the same letter to a person.

One of the capabilities of a word processing center is to store on magnetic tape or diskettes standard paragraphs which can be used in a variety of letters. It is the administrative secretary's responsibility to furnish paragraphs used often by the executive. When a letter is given to you for reply and standard paragraphs apply, all you need do is signify by number the paragraphs required. The word processing center will do the rest.

Summary of Letter-Writing Basics

This section has covered the basic principles of effective letter writing. Your adherence to these guidelines should assist you in avoiding the most common pitfalls that make letter writing dull and uninteresting. The next time you compose a letter, analyze it against the checklist in Illus. 10-1 to ensure that it conforms to the proper letter-writing techniques for making a favorable impression on your reader.

CHECKLIST FOR EFFECTIVE LETTER WRITING

Can you answer yes to all these questions?

_____ Is your letter long enough to give complete information but short enough to assure a thorough reading?

_____ Is it clear and easy to read so that your reader
will have no difficulty in understanding your
message?

_____ Does it present advantages to the reader that will
encourage the action you desire?

_____ Is it natural, friendly, and conversational?

_____ Is it neat and attractive, indicating that you care
about the impression it makes?

_____ Does it indicate a desire to help the reader?

_____ Is it courteous—free from unpleasant and negative
words or superior words and phrases that belittle
the reader?

_____ Is it forceful and interesting—free from dull,
hackneyed expressions? Have you used a variety of
word arrangements and sentence structures?

_____ Is it personalized, making use of the reader's name
and points of interest to the reader?

_____ Does it place most of the emphasis on the reader
through the avoidance of too many sentences that
begin with I, we, our, and my? Does it have the
you attitude?

_____ Is it free from sexist language that stereotypes
people in certain roles?

Illus. 10-1

If you can answer yes to most of these questions, your letter-writing ability is
above average.

Written communication among the staff of a company takes the form of an interoffice memorandum, a less formal style than the traditional letter. (See the illustration of an interoffice memorandum in the Reference Guide.) The secretary will have many opportunities to compose messages for intracompany distribution, such as ordering supplies, requesting temporary help, or setting the time and place for a meeting. Your writing approach to this correspondence should be direct and concise. If your employer requests that you write a memorandum to the staff scheduling a meeting, your notice might be as follows:

```
The meeting of the sales staff will be held
in Mr. Breese's office at 10 a.m. on May 4.
The items for discussion include the estab-
lishment of sales districts and quotas.
Please bring . . . .
```

News Releases

If in your company publicity is not the responsibility of an advertising department or an agency, you will at times be asked to compose or type brief articles for newspaper or magazine publication. News releases are unsolicited items which are sent to editors in the hope that they will be used. They must, therefore, be *newsworthy* and be of interest to readers.

Style. A good news item contains all the facts clearly stated *without* opinion. The italicized words in these expressions are opinions of a writer: *dire* emergency, everyone *should*, *noted* attorney, *signally* honored.

In composing a news release, answer the five *W's*—*who, what, when, where,* and *why*—plus the *how.* Put the vital facts in the first sentence, the second most important in the second, and so on. This journalistic style is for the convenience of the busy reader and the busy editor. If the release has to be shortened, the editor cuts out sentences beginning with the last and works upward. This leaves the important news intact without rewriting.

Typewritten Form. A company that submits numerous releases uses a special letterhead such as that shown in Illus. 10-2. Otherwise, an item is put on a regular letterhead or on an 8½- by 11-inch sheet of bond paper. If a plain sheet is used, the name, address, and telephone number of the company are typed across the top. In every case a person whom the editor can call for additional

```
┌─────────────┐
│ IBP         │        PUBLIC AFFAIRS DEPARTMENT
│ Corporation │        3915 N. Meridian Street
└─────────────┘        Indianapolis, IN 46208-8396
                       (812) 871-8811

                                              FOR IMMEDIATE
                                              RELEASE

     Chicago, November 21, 19--.   While addressing a stockholders'
meeting at the Convention Center, President Joseph Miller announced
April 21 as the date scheduled for IBP Corporation's ground-breaking
ceremonies for a 5-building headquarters complex estimated to cost
in excess of $75 million.  Site of the new development is company
owned acreage north of the present administration area.  Miller
also confirmed IBP's plans to expand its highly sophisticated com-
puter services operation by building an 8-floor addition to present
facilities.  Cost of the new building for computer operations is
projected to reach $43 million.

     IBP's plans for expansion of plant and operations reflect a
strong corporate optimism based, in part, on a strong commitment to
diversification of products and services.  Figures for the last
five years show IBP's sales to have grown 32 percent annually.  This
year the corporation anticipates 30 percent growth, and it hopes to
sustain a compound growth rate of 25-30 percent well into the next
decade.  Reaction by stockholders to the Miller announcements was
very supportive.

June Huybers

fe1

                              # # #
```

Illus. 10-2

In composing a news release, answer the five *W's*—*who, what, when, where,* and *why*—plus the *how.*

release to one page, if possible.

Number each page after the first one at the top center.

Type —*more*— at the bottom of all pages but the last.

Type # # # at the end of the release.

Send the original and type *Exclusive to* . . . on the release if it really is exclusive. A carbon copy indicates you are sending the same release to other publishers, and the editor may be one who will not use the release unless it appears to be exclusive.

Mail the release directly to the department editor.

Foreign Correspondence

Most corporations now do business abroad. Letter style for foreign correspondence is much more formal and traditional than for domestic correspondence. Such letters require a "flowery" style of writing. Social amenities must be observed meticulously. Although you will probably not compose many letters to foreign companies, you may be asked to have the message translated into the language of the recipient. Then you may have to retype it on your company's letterhead. That can be a real challenge even for the expert typist!

When addressing a letter to a foreign recipient, copy the address *exactly* as it is given. Here, too, style differs. In European and South American countries the street number *follows* the street name: Nassaustraat 7, not 7 Nassaustraat. In Japanese addresses there are many other designations in addition to the street name and number which are used to locate the prefecture and the section of the city; all are essential.

SUGGESTED READINGS

Bowman, Joel P., and Bernadine P. Branchaw. *Successful Communication in Business.* San Francisco: Harper & Row, Publishers, Inc., 1980.

Hunsinger, Marjorie, and Donna McComas. *Modern Business Correspondence.* 4th ed. New York: McGraw-Hill Book Company, 1979.

Whalen, Doris H. *Handbook for Business Writers.* Rev. Ed. New York: Harcourt Brace Jovanovich, Inc., 1978.

Wolf, Morris P., Dale F. Keyser, and Robert R. Aurner. *Effective Communication in Business,* 7th ed. Cincinnati: South-Western Publishing Co., 1979.

QUESTIONS FOR DISCUSSION

1. Your employer has been invited to be the keynote speaker for the state convention of Executive Women International. The date of May 5 conflicts with a scheduled presentation of a new line of products to a group of buyers in New York. Your employer asks you to respond. What information should you include in your letter?

2. When you were hired, your employer told you that every letter was an opportunity to build goodwill for the company. What are some of the steps you can take to ensure that the letters you compose build goodwill for the company?

3. If your employer is promoted to a position involving international trade, how can you help to write overseas business letters that build goodwill for your company?

4. Your employer says, "Subscribe to *Business Week* for me, please." These are the only details you have. How will you handle this task?

5. What is your reader response to these first sentences in letters?
   (a) This is in answer to your letter of July 10. Your ideas . . .
   (b) We cannot send the merchandise you want until we receive payment for the last shipment.
   (c) Your ball-point pens are lousy, and we are sending back the whole kit and caboodle of them express collect!
   (d) It is with extreme pleasure that we send you the catalog you so graciously requested in your welcome letter of May 7.

6. A former classmate of yours has applied for an executive secretarial position in the office of the comptroller of your firm. Your employer has the final word on personnel changes. Because of your friend's lack of accounting background and experience, another applicant was selected. Your employer is aware of your relationship to your classmate and has asked your help in drafting the letter turning down the application. Discuss the approach you would take in drafting such a letter.

7. Revise the following sentences to make them more euphonious. Then use the Reference Guide to check your answers.
   (a) The letter was too abrupt and tactless.
   (b) The job was just a job to the secretary.

PROBLEMS

1. Your employer, Ms. Perry, has just been promoted to the position of personnel manager for your firm. Ms. Perry is a recent college graduate and has a tendency to be verbose. On your return from a workshop in effective letter writing, you are asked to revise the following letter to conform to good letter-writing practice. Rewrite this letter.

We have your letter of March 16 for which we express our sincere thanks and appreciation. The information your office has kindly supplied us will be most helpful in helping us decide upon the choice of the individual who will make the most substantial contribution to this company.

In the event that any other information should come to your attention regarding the qualifications of this individual, we should appreciate your sending it along to us immediately.

We look forward with sincere pleasure to hearing from you further. In the meantime, if we can return your generous favor, please do not hesitate to call on us.

2. At a recent secretarial workshop the participants were asked to reduce the text of the following letter to the smallest possible number of words. One secretary got it down to eight words. Can you do as well?

Gentlemen

A copy of your pamphlet of "The Human Side" has been handed to the undersigned and in reading the contents we have been very much impressed and are wondering if this pamphlet can be secured by subscription and, if so, what are the charges for such subscription. Might we hear from you in this regard at your earliest convenience?

Yours truly

3. Mr. Stanley intercepts the following two letters written by his assistant. He asks you to write acceptable replacements for them. Type each on a half-sheet simulated letterhead.

(a)

Dear Mrs. Gau:

Concerning our conversation of last week, we regret the delay of shipment of your order.

We are at a loss to explain why your merchandise has not reached you. The delivery truck picked up the package as requested.

We value your business. Naturally, we will do everything in our power to regain the confidence you have in our company and our products.

Very respectfully yours,

(b)

Dear Mr. Franklin:

We are indeed pleased to send you a copy of our recent catalog. In addition, we have alerted our sales representative in your territory, Janet Brinkley, to call for an appointment in your office. You should be hearing from her soon.

In checking our records, we see that we have not yet received your January order. Please let us have the opportunity to continue being of service to you.

Sincerely,

Case Problems

Alice Barnes has been secretary to Don Morse, president of Morse-Jacobs, for eighteen years. During that time they have not changed their work habits, although other offices in the company have reorganized. Both are near retirement age. Mr. Morse regards Alice as his strong right arm, never relieving her of any part of her work for others to handle. Alice stays long after five o'clock and has always felt rushed during the day trying to live up to the expectations of her employer. Also, since she believes herself indispensable, she carries much of the burden of the office home with her.

Alice decided to discuss the situation with Mr. Morse, but three weeks passed before she had the opportunity to present her problem. One evening, just before five, she approached Mr. Morse to describe her problem and ask his advice. After one sentence, he broke in with, "Yes, Alice, I know you have too much to do. Why don't you get some of the people in word processing to help you? You could dictate some of the routine letters to them. I am sure you could use word processing more than you do. In fact, I think we are both being criticized for not setting a better example of utilizing it for nonconfidential material. I certainly don't want you to work so hard that you become ill. Just work things out. Anything you do will be fine with me. I want to catch the 5:25, so I'll have to hurry."

With that Mr. Morse took his briefcase and rushed from the office. In fact, Alice had the impression that he was somewhat annoyed that she had brought up the problem.

The next morning Alice dictated ten letters for transcription in the word processing center. However, she personally went to the center and asked the supervisor if she could speak with the transcribers. Consent was given rather icily. She told the operators that Mr. Morse preferred a letter style different from the standard format used by the center and that she would proofread the letters herself. The operators appeared annoyed, as did the supervisor.

The letters were delivered in good time, but three of them contained uncorrectable errors that rendered them unmailable. Alice stayed after five to retype the letters, took a pill for her ulcer, and grumbled: Well, *that* didn't help matters. I had to do the work myself after all. I don't know why these kids that we get here can't do anything right. **What principles of supervision has Alice Barnes violated? How could she have solved her problem?**

ployees, even she, were under suspicion. She was so shocked by the implication of her guilt that she could think of no reply.

In trying to assess the blame, she reviewed her relationships with the rest of the staff and remembered that when she returned from lunch one day she surprised Al Johnson, a recently hired junior chemist, as he was rummaging through her desk. His explanation was that he had misplaced the schedule of projects and knew she had another one in her desk.

She also remembered that, although she usually kept the top drawer of her desk locked and the key in her purse, she had neglected to lock the drawer that day. She was so sure that she knew the culprit that she decided to confront Al Johnson and insist that he tell Dr. Barton about his involvement and take full responsibility.

What steps would you take in this situation?

Case 3-3
CARELESSNESS IN MAILING CORRESPON-DENCE

J. J. Payhos, branch sales manager of a large national corporation, was concerned about the disappointing performance of a sales representative under his supervision. He and the corporate sales manager discussed termination of the sales representative's employment.

Mr. Payhos then dictated a stern but courteous memo to the sales representative telling him that he must meet next month's sales quota and increase the number of daily calls if he hoped to stay with the company. At the bottom of the carbon copy which was to be sent to the corporate sales manager, he wrote in longhand, "Hope I wasn't too hard on him, but he has been goofing off long enough. I'll keep you informed of developments."

Two days later Jim Protzman, the secretary who had transcribed the memo, was confronted by an irate Mr. Payhos: "Just look at this. See what you have done! You put the memos in the wrong envelopes. This is what happened." Jim was handed the memo intended for the corporate sales manager with a second notation at the bottom: "I resign. I never 'goofed off' in my life."

Jim now remembers that, when Mr. Payhos sent him on an emergency errand at 4:45, he gave the day's mail to the person assigned to him and asked him to insert the transcribed materials in the envelopes and see that they were dispatched.

What should Jim say to Mr. Payhos? How should he handle the error with the clerk? What principle is involved?

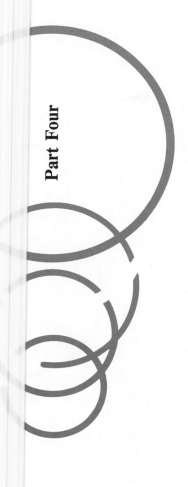

INFORMATION PROCESSING: TRANSMITTAL SERVICES

The secretary is in varying degrees responsible for postal and shipping services and for widespread communication by telephone and telegraph. Sending and receiving goods and information in the least expensive and most expeditious way are essential to good business operations.

The secretary who provides administrative support is now and will increasingly be actively involved in the exciting changes that are occurring in the field of transmittal services. Technological advances make it possible to transmit and receive data, image, and voice communications over networks that transform previously independent equipment into integrated information systems.

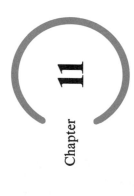

Chapter **11**

Postal and Shipping Services

Postal costs are a major expense in every company. Business is making conspicuous efforts to reduce this expense and also to improve postal service. In a large organization the secretary sends much of the outgoing mail to the mail department for dispatch but may also bypass this department by preparing and sending business mail, including packages, directly. In a small office, though, the secretary has complete responsibility for the mail. Transmittal expenses can be greatly reduced by a secretary who is familiar with postal information and services. Postal changes occur frequently, however, so that information must be constantly updated.

In 1970 legislation was passed to change the Postal Service, which had been a department of the federal government, into a quasi-independent corporation. The purpose of this reorganization was to provide a self-sufficient, more flexible service. The only regulator of the Postal Service is the Postal Rate Commission, a Congressional committee. The plan of the Postal Reorganization Act was to mechanize mail handling. Unfortunately, though, service has not improved measurably; and many companies are turning to alternative methods of mailing and shipping.

This chapter describes the domestic and international mail classifications and explains special mail services. It discusses mail collection, delivery, and the use of money orders to send money to other locations. Most important, it makes suggestions for speeding mail delivery and reducing postal expense.

DOMESTIC MAIL CLASSIFICATIONS

Domestic mail includes mail transmitted within, among, and between the United States, its territories and possessions, to Army (APO) and Navy (FPO) post offices, and to the United Nations in New York City. (APO refers to Army Post Office, and FPO refers to Fleet Post Office.) The separate armed services designations are now combined into a single Military Postal Service agency.

The Postal Service divides available domestic mail into the following general classes: first class, priority mail, express mail, second class, third class, fourth class, official mail and free mail for the blind and visually handicapped.

The best source of mailing information is the *Domestic Mail Manual*, which is updated regularly, and may be purchased from the Superintendent of Documents, U.S. Government Printing Office, Washington, D.C. 20402. General descriptions of each mail classification, taken from this manual, are given in this chapter. Rates and fees are not provided since they are subject to change. For current information, consult the publications available from your local post office.

First-Class Mail

Airmail as a domestic category has been discontinued, and all first-class mail has been upgraded to airmail status. If air service is not available, the first-class mail is sent by the fastest means available. First-class mail refers to items weighing no more than 12 ounces. Items weighing more than 12 ounces that are to be sent by fastest route are called priority mail, which is discussed below.

Among the kinds of mail sent by first class are letters in any form (typewritten, handwritten, carbon copy, or photocopy); post cards; business reply mail; and matter partly in written form, such as bills and checks. All first-class envelopes should be sealed.

Because of the need for mail to conform to automated sorting machine measurements, a surcharge is assessed on each piece of nonstandard-sized mail in addition to applicable postage and other fees. Items subject to this surcharge are first-class letter and postcard mail that is more than 6⅛ inches high, or 11½ inches in length, or more than ¼ inch thick, and also mail that is less than .007 inches thick or less than 3½ inches high or 5 inches long. All envelopes must be rectangular in shape.

Postage for first-class items is charged on the first ounce. If mail weighs more than one ounce, the rate for the second ounce is less than for the first —a fact not realized by many mailers.

Formerly mail deposited without a stamp was delivered to the addressee and postage collected at that point. Today such mail is not delivered.

Priority Mail

Priority mail is really another type of first-class mail but is given a separate classification by the Postal Service because it is relatively new and needs to be popularized. Priority mail refers to first-class mail weighing over 12 ounces. The maximum weight for priority mail is 70 pounds. The maximum size limit is 100 inches in length and girth combined. Packages sent by priority mail are given preferential handling and are shipped by air and selected ground transportation. Packages, either sealed or unsealed, can be mailed at any post office (not in mail collection boxes). Delivery is made within two or three days. Charges are assessed by zones; the longer the travel distance, the higher the rate. Even so, priority mail may be less expensive than overnight express service.

The mailer who wants to send large envelopes by either first-class or priority mail should designate the class of mail on both the front and back of the envelope to prevent its being handled as third-class mail. Even better are envelopes with green diamond borders for such first-class mail and red diamond borders for priority mail.

Express Mail

Express Mail Next Day Service is the fastest postal service available for sending both letters and packages. Delivery of an item deposited at the post office by 5 p.m. is *guaranteed* by 3 p.m. of the following day if the city of the addressee can be reached by surface and scheduled airline transportation within the required time. Naturally this service is limited by availability of transportation and is confined mostly to metropolitan areas. The addressee also has the option of picking up the shipment at the airport of destination by 10 a.m.

Second-Class Mail

Second-class mail includes printed newspapers and periodicals. Publishers and news agencies are granted second-class rates if they file the proper forms obtained from their local post office, pay the required fees, and comply with the regulations. Such mail must bear notice of second-class entry and be mailed in bulk lots.

You will probably not be responsible for such bulk mailings, but you may mail single copies of a second-class publication. The public may mail newspapers and other periodicals unsealed at the *transient*, or fourth-class, rate. To qualify for the transient rate, the entire publication must be mailed, and no writing can be included. To call attention to an article in a publication, the mailer writes *Marked Copy* on the wrapper. Slit an addressed envelope and roll it around the publication. Use the gummed flap of the envelope to seal the roll, but leave the ends of the publication exposed. Write *Second Class* on the wrapper above the address.

Third-Class Mail

Third-class mail is used for matter that cannot be classified as first- or second-class mail and that weighs less than 16 ounces. The same matter in

Mail that may be sent third class includes merchandise, printed matter, keys, advertising, and so on. Special rates also apply to books, manuscripts, music, sound recordings, films, and the like.

Fourth-Class Mail

The more common term for *fourth-class service* is *parcel post*. It includes all mailable matter not in first, second, or third class which weighs 16 ounces or over.

Parcel post rates are scaled according to the weight of the parcel and the distance it is being transported. Every local post office charts the country into eight zones. Zone charts showing the parcel post zone of any domestic post office in relation to the sender's post office may be obtained free from the sender's post office.

There are both weight and size limits for fourth-class packages according to delivery zones. Size limits are given in total inches of length and girth combined, as shown in Illus. 11-1. There are also special rates according to weight and zone for bound printed matter weighing 16 ounces or over. Size limits vary by class of post office at the destination. Consult your local post office.

Fourth-class packages may be sent unsealed or sealed. Mailing of sealed packages implies that the sender consents to inspection of the contents. This silent assent replaces the old written endorsement: *May Be Opened for Postal Inspection*. A sealed package is treated as parcel post by the postal sorters no matter what rate of postage has been paid unless the package is conspicuously marked *First Class*.

It is a good idea to include the name and address of both the addressee and the sender inside a parcel post package just in case the outside address is damaged or becomes unreadable. Also, if the contents of the package are perishable or fragile, put a label on the wrapper that says either *Perishable* or *Fragile*.

Recently the Postal Service made a move to recapture the lead in small shipments by establishing a billion dollar *National Bulk Mail System*. NBMS has more than 20 mechanized bulk mail facilities and offers two-day delivery for parcels picked up and delivered within the same NBMS zone. Each addi-

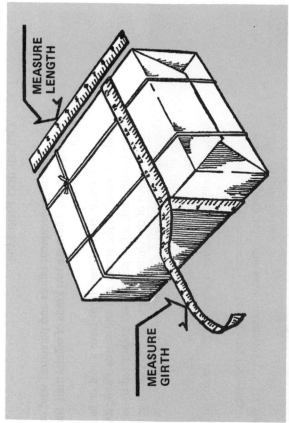

MEASURE LENGTH

MEASURE GIRTH

Postal Service Manual

Illus. 11-1

To determine the size of a parcel, measure the longest side to get the length; measure the distance around the parcel at its thickest part to get the girth; and add the two figures together. For example, a parcel 10 inches long, 8 inches wide, and 4½ inches high measures 35 inches in length and girth combined (length, 10 inches; girth, 25 inches: 4½ inches + 8 inches + 4½ inches + 8 inches). A free pamphlet on "Packaging for Mailing" may be obtained from your post office.

tional parcel post zone requires one extra day. Packages for city or suburban delivery are limited to 40 pounds and 84-inch combined girth and length; those for rural delivery to 70 pounds and 100 inches in combined girth and length.

Certain kinds of packaged mail are given special low rates as follows.

Books without advertising that contain at least 22 printed pages are eligible for a special fourth-class rate; so are manuscripts if labeled *Special Fourth-Class Mail.* The sender may, however, decide to send manuscripts by first-class mail because the rate difference is inconsequential.

The library rate applies to materials sent to or from libraries, schools, and certain nonprofit organizations. The secretary may use this rate when returning qualifying material to any of the organizations that are permitted to use this rate. The rate is the same to all zones and applies to books, periodicals, theses, microfilms, music, sound recordings, films, and other library materials. The package may be sealed, but it must be marked *Library Rate* conspicuously on the address side.

It is recommended that the sender consult the local post office before mailing special fourth-class mail or library materials.

Official and Free Mail

Federal government offices and personnel send out official mail without affixing postage. There are two kinds of official mail: franked mail and penalty mail.

A *franked* piece of mail used here is used to transmit operation of the sender in place of the stamp and the actual hand signature. *Free* on the address and Only a few are authorized to use this frank, such as the Vice-President of the United States, members and members-elect of Congress.

Resident Commissioners, the Secretary of the Senate, and the Sergeant at Arms of the Senate.

Penalty mail is used for official government correspondence. It travels in penalty envelopes or under penalty labels stating *Official Business—Penalty for Private Use.*

Free mail is sent without postage by the general public. It is limited to a few items such as census mail and absentee ballot envelopes from members of the Armed Forces.

Congress of the United States
House of Representatives
Washington, D.C. 20515

OFFICIAL BUSINESS

UNITED STATES POST OFFICE

LOCKLAND BR.
CINCINNATI, OH 45215

OFFICIAL BUSINESS
P-166

PENALTY FOR PRIVATE
USE TO AVOID PAYMENT
OF POSTAGE, $300

MR REX YOUNG
3788 WESTMONT DRIVE

MR REX YOUNG
3788 WESTMONT DRIVE
CINCINNATI OH 45204-4027

Illus. 11-2 Notice the difference between an official franked envelope and penalty envelope. A franked envelope must show a real or facsimile signature and carry the words OFFICIAL BUSINESS. A penalty envelope must carry the penalty warning and the words OFFICIAL BUSINESS under a return address.

Mixed Classes of Mail

Sometimes it is expedient and reflects better judgment to send two pieces of mail of different classes together as a single mailing to assure their delivery at the same time either by labeling the package *First-Class Mail Enclosed* or by attaching the letter to the outside of the mailing. Delivery time is determined by the mail classification of the package. Therefore, a first-class letter attached to a package will go as fourth-class mail.

Previously, if a piece of first-class material was attached to a second-, third-, or fourth-class mailing, the Postal Service required postage for both pieces. As the result of a recent ruling, a piece of first-class mail that is incidental (related) to the matter mailed via another class—except nonmerchandise third-class mail—does not require separate, additional postage.

Mail for the Blind

Some kinds of mail to and from the blind may be mailed free; other kinds may be mailed at nominal rates. If, as a secretary, your work involves sending letters and parcels to or from the blind, you will want to consult the local post office.

SPECIAL MAIL SERVICES

In addition to transmitting mail, the post office provides many special services. The sender should be aware, however, that fees for such services may be very expensive.

Registered and Insured Mail

A piece of important or valuable mail can be registered or insured, depending on its nature.

Registering Mail. First-class or priority mail can be registered. The full amount of the value of the contents must be declared on a piece of mail being registered because the fee charged is based on the full value. There are two sets of fees. The one used depends upon whether the sender has commercial insurance covering the matter being mailed. When the maximum liability of the post office is less than the value of the shipment, special private insurance is usually taken out by the sender for the specific shipment during transit.

Each piece of mail to be registered must be tightly sealed along all edges (transparent tape cannot be used) and must bear the complete addresses of both the sender and addressee. The sender takes it to the registry window where the postal clerk computes the fee.

The sender of the registered mail may instruct the Postal Service to change the address should it be necessary. For example, if you send a registered letter to a company sales representative in St. Louis and then learn that the person has moved to Kansas City, you should telephone the St. Louis post office and request that the address be changed.

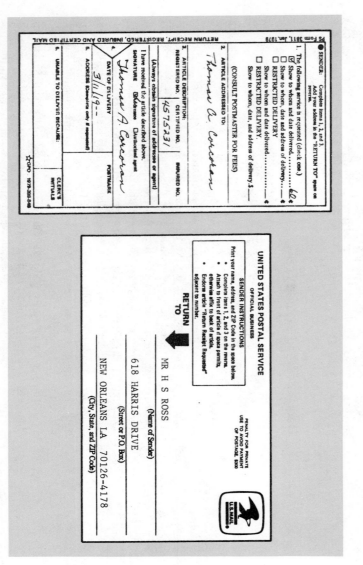

Insuring Mail. A piece of third- or fourth-class matter, or priority mail contain-ing third- or fourth-class matter, may be insured up to $400. The package is taken to the post office window where the clerk makes out a receipt for it. If any (An unnumbered receipt is given if the package is insured for $15 or less.) After paying the regular and insured postage on the package, the clerk gives the receipt to the sender for filing. If the package is lost or damaged, the post office reimburses the sender according to the amount of the fee.

may be more convenient to use a mailing book rather than file a separate receipt for each package. Mailing books, which are issued by the post office on request, provide pages for entering the description of parcels insured. The sheets of this book are officially endorsed at the time of mailing and become the sender's receipts.

Return Receipts and Restricted Delivery. The sender is always furnished with a receipt showing that the post office accepted the piece of insured or registered mail for transmittal and delivery. However, the sender often wants legal evi-dence that the piece of mail was also actually received by the addressee. For an added fee the sender may obtain a signed receipt, commonly called a *return*

Illus. 11-3   Ungummed side   Return receipt   Gummed side

receipt, on any piece of certified or registered mail or on any piece of mail insured for more than $15. This service is helpful when the address used is one of several years' duration or when there is reason to believe that the addressee may have moved.

A sender who wants a return receipt fills in the number of the receipt, name, and address on a postal card form supplied by the post office, and writes *Return Receipt Requested* on the front of the mail.

This card is pasted (face down) along its two gummed edges to the back of the envelope or package. At delivery the letter carrier removes the card, obtains the addressee's signature on the ungummed (reverse) side, fills in the information required, and mails the card to the sender.

For an added fee, delivery may be *restricted to the addressee* only if the piece of mail is registered, certified, or insured for more than $15. The charge for a return receipt is almost doubled if the receipt is requested after mailing.

COD Service

Merchandise may be sent to a purchaser *COD*—that is, *collect on delivery*—if the shipment is based on a bona fide order or on an agreement made with the addressee by the mailer. The sender prepays the postage on the shipment and the COD fees, but they may be included in the amount to be collected if agreeable to the addressee. Otherwise the addressee pays the amount due on the merchandise, plus the fee for the money order to return the money collected to the sender. The maximum amount collectible on one parcel is $400. If the sender alters the COD charges after the parcel is sent or designates a new addressee, an additional charge is made.

Certificates of Mailing

For a few cents a sender may obtain a very simple proof of having taken a piece of mail to the post office for dispatching. Such proof may be used for any kind of mail. The sender fills in the information required on a certificate blank, pastes on the appropriate stamp, and hands this certificate to the postal clerk with the piece of mail. The clerk cancels the stamp and hands the certificate back to the sender as evidence that the piece of mail was received at the post office.

This is an economical service for one who is mailing something that is of value to the addressee but who has no obligation or responsibility to pay the extra expense of having the material insured, registered, or certified. It also furnishes a sender with inexpensive proof of having mailed tax returns.

Certified Mail

Certified mail service requires that a record of delivery be maintained by the post office from which a letter is delivered. The carrier delivering the item

P27 4575232

RECEIPT FOR CERTIFIED MAIL

NO INSURANCE COVERAGE PROVIDED—
NOT FOR INTERNATIONAL MAIL

(See Reverse)

SENT TO

MR. WILLIAM STRONG

STREET AND NO.

19185 HENRY ROAD

P.O., STATE AND ZIP CODE

Cleveland, OH 44126-3117

POSTAGE	$	20 ¢
CERTIFIED FEE		75 ¢
	SPECIAL DELIVERY	¢
	RESTRICTED DELIVERY	¢
RETURN RECEIPT SERVICE	SHOW TO WHOM AND DATE DELIVERED	60 ¢
OPTIONAL SERVICES	SHOW TO WHOM, DATE AND ADDRESS OF DELIVERY	¢
CONSULT POSTMASTER FOR FEES	SHOW TO WHOM AND DATE DELIVERED WITH RESTRICTED DELIVERY	¢
	SHOW TO WHOM, DATE AND ADDRESS OF DELIVERY WITH RESTRICTED DELIVERY	¢
TOTAL POSTAGE AND FEES	$	1.55
POSTMARK OR DATE		

CINCINNATI OH
APR 13 19
LOCKLAND BR

CERTIFIED MAIL

P27 4575232

PS Form 3800, Apr. 1976

Illus. 11-4
Receipt for certified mail

Certified mail has the following advantages: (1) it provides the sender with a means of checking on the delivery of the letter; (2) it provides official evidence of mailing if a postmarked receipt is obtained; and (3) it gives the letter the appearance of importance and urgency, and for that reason it is frequently used by many collection agencies.

Special Delivery and Special Handling

The delivery of a piece of mail may be expedited by the use of special delivery or special handling services.

Special Delivery. *Special delivery service* provides the fastest handling—from mailer to addressee—for all classes of mail. Mail must be marked *Special Delivery* above the address. Immediate delivery is by messenger during prescribed hours to points within certain limits of any post office or delivery station. Do not send special delivery mail to post office box addresses, military installations, or other places where mail delivery will not be expedited after arrival.

Special Handling. Most people are not aware of *special handling* for third- and fourth-class mail—a service that is less expensive than special delivery. It provides the most expeditious handling and ground transportation practicable. Parcels move with first-class mail, but they do not receive special delivery at the destination post office.

Since all special delivery mail (including packages) is handled and transported in the same manner as first-class mail, it is not necessary to include special handling on a package being sent special delivery. The rate for special handling is high, and it is often less expensive to send third- or fourth-class mail first class unless it is very bulky.

Slugs for Hand Stamping

Bulky mail, called *slugs*, should be marked *Hand Stamp* in large red letters on both the front and back of the envelope. Unmarked slugs are often ruined during mail processing. Unless clearly marked for separation from other mail, slugs may be routinely placed in the canceling machine and may cause serious damage to it.

Stamps

Ordinary postage stamps are available in sheet, coil, or booklet form. Postage stamps can be exchanged at full value if stamps of the wrong denomination were purchased or if damaged stamps were received. Envelopes with imprinted stamps are also available.

Other Supplies Available from the Post Office. Stamped envelopes in various sizes, kinds, and denominations may be purchased at the post office individually or in quantity lots. For a nominal amount, the post office will have the sender's return request and name and address imprinted on them when the envelopes are ordered in quantity lots. Two lines of advertising material may also be included.

First-class postal cards are available in single or double form, the latter kind being used when a reply is desired on the attached card. To facilitate in-company printing of standard messages in batches, government postal cards are available in sheets of 40.

Unserviceable and spoiled stamped envelopes and cards (if uncanceled) may be exchanged at postage value. Such exchanges are made in stamps, stamped envelopes, or postal cards.

The post office also sells a combination mailer, which is a large envelope with a No. 10 envelope attached, in which to mail a third-class enclosure and a first-class letter. Also available are various shipping containers which are usually on display and can be purchased for packing your parcels.

Metered Postage

One of the quickest and most efficient ways of affixing postage to mail of any class is by means of a *postage meter* machine. The postage meter prints on each piece of mail the postmark and the proper amount of postage. Consequently, metered mail need not be canceled or postmarked when it reaches the post office. As a result, it often catches earlier trains, trucks, or planes than does other mail.

The meter machine may be fully automatic, not only printing the postage, postmark, and date of mailing but also feeding, sealing, and stacking the meter stamped envelopes. The imprint is usually red and may carry a line or two of advertising. Some models can also print the postage on gummed tape that can be pasted onto packages. The meter registers the amount of postage used on each piece of mail, the amount of postage remaining in the meter, and the number of pieces that have passed through the machine.

The machine itself is purchased outright, but the meter mechanism is leased. In order to use a postage meter, a company must first obtain a meter license by filing an application with the post office where its mail is handled. The application must tell the make and model of the meter. A record of use must be maintained in a *Meter Record Book* supplied by the post office.

The meter locks when the remaining postage supply reaches $10. The

Unfortunately mail does not always reach its final destination on first mailing. Some pieces must be forwarded, returned to the sender, or remailed. Additional postage may or may not be required.

Forwarding Mail. The secretary is often required to forward mail. The following information indicates the extra postage or fee required.

First-Class Mail Up to 12 Ounces—No additional postage required. Change the address and deposit in mail.

Second-Class Publications—Full postage must be paid at a single piece rate. Change address, affix postage, endorse *Second-Class Mail,* and deposit in mail.

Third-Class and Fourth-Class Mail—Additional postage at applicable rate must be paid. Change address, affix postage, and deposit in mail.

Registered, Certified, Insured, COD, and Special Handling Mail—Forwarded without payment of additional registry, insurance, COD, or special handling fees; however, ordinary forwarding postage charge, if any, must be paid.

Special Delivery Service—This mail will not receive special delivery service at second address unless a change-of-address card has been filed.

Return of Undeliverable Mail. An undeliverable first-class letter will be returned to the sender free of charge. For undeliverable third- or fourth-class parcels, the sender must pay full postage for the return service. To assure that third- and fourth-class packages are returned, place *Return Postage Guaranteed* conspicuously below the return address.

Undeliverable letters and packages without return addresses are sent to the dead letter office where they are examined. They may be opened to find a return address; so it is wise to enclose a completed address label in a package being mailed. Whenever an address is found, the mail is returned for a fee. Undeliverable dead mail is destroyed or sold.

Remailing Returned Mail. The secretary is always chagrined when mail is returned. Any piece of mail returned with the "pointing finger" rubber stamp RETURN TO SENDER and with the reason indicated must be put in a fresh, correctly addressed envelope, and postage paid again.

Change of Address

The post office serving you must be officially notified by letter or by one of its forms when you change your address. The old and the new address and the date when the new address is effective must be given. Correspondents should be notified of a new address promptly by special notices or by stickers attached to all outgoing mail. The post office will supply new address cards free for personal and business use.

Recalling Mail

Occasionally it may be necessary to recall a piece of mail that has been posted. This calls for fast action. Type an addressed envelope that duplicates the one mailed. Go to the post office in your mailing zone if the letter is local or to the central post office if the letter is an out-of-town mailing. Fill in *Sender's Application for Recall of Mail.*

If the mail is an undelivered local letter, on-the-spot return will be made. If the letter has left the post office for an out-of-town address, the post office (at the sender's request and expense) will wire or telephone the addressee's post office and ask that the letter be returned. If the mail has already been delivered, the sender is notified; but the addressee is not informed that a recall was requested.

MAIL COLLECTION AND DELIVERY

A number of plans have been inaugurated by the Postal Service to improve operations and reduce costs. An explanation of some of these plans follows.

Addressing Mail

The ZIP (Zone Improvement Plan) Code was designed to speed mail deliveries and to facilitate the use of automated equipment in the processing of mail. The ZIP Code originally conceived by the United States Postal Service in 1963 was five digits. In 1981 the Postal Service started a campaign to get businesses to use nine-digit ZIP Codes. The expanded ZIP Code includes not only the original five digits but four additional digits preceded by a hyphen. For example, an expanded ZIP Code might be 45227-1035. With four more digits, the Postal Service can pinpoint mail delivery and make ZIP Codes very precise, permitting the fine sorting of mail down to the individual carrier's route.

All bulk mailers of second- or third-class mail are required to include the ZIP Code on the address. Failure to do so may subject the mail to a higher

tion for each state and abbreviations for cities with long names. The two-letter abbreviations can be used on all mail if the ZIP Code is included. The list of approved abbreviations is presented on page 755 of this book.

Optical character readers that electronically scan addresses are used in many post offices. They are programmed to scan a specific area on all envelopes; so the address must be completely within this read zone, single-spaced, and blocked in style. The two-letter state abbreviations must be used. Acceptable placements for a No. 10 and a No. 6¾ envelope are shown below.

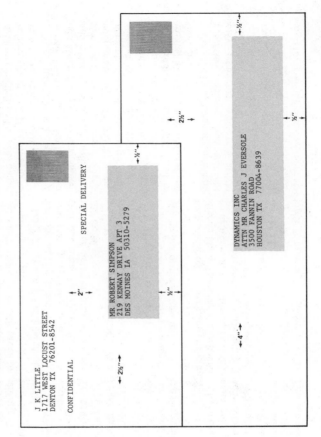

J K LITTLE
1717 WEST LOCUST STREET
DENTON TX   76201-8542

CONFIDENTIAL

SPECIAL DELIVERY

MR ROBERT SIMPSON
219 KENWAY DRIVE APT 3
DES MOINES IA   50310-5279

DYNAMICS INC
ATTN MR CHARLES J EVERSOLE
3500 FANNIN ROAD
HOUSTON TX   77004-8639

Illus. 11-5
Post office optical character readers are programmed to scan a specific area on all envelopes. The illustration shows the read zones within which the address must be typed on No. 6¾ and No. 10 envelopes.

Presorting Mail

To encourage large mailers to presort mail before depositing it, the Postal Service grants a reduction of a few cents in postage on each presorted piece. To qualify for the reduction, a minimum of 500 first-class pieces must be included in each mailing. For the specifics on presorting, you should contact your local post office.

Any business lives or dies on the bottom line. Yet every year businesses take the expense of delayed delivery or undeliverable mail straight to the bottom line. The cost runs into the thousands of dollars.

Proper addressing is not a mystery. By developing a check list for proper addressing, you can save time, money and trouble. When your mail meets size requirements, carries a correct address and ZIP Code and the proper amount of postage, it moves easily through the mechanized sorting process and saves you and the Postal Service time and money. When improperly addressed, mail is diverted to manual handling which is slower and more costly.

Here is a basic "anatomy of a well-addressed envelope" that will not only assure that your mail arrives where you want it delivered, but also will get it there in the fastest time at the lowest cost.

(1) It helps when you capitalize everything in the address, eliminate all punctuation and use the common address and state abbreviations. Though not mandatory, these three steps will make your mail easier to handle and to process.

(2) Single space the address block. Put one or two spaces between the character groups and at least two (but not more than five) spaces between the state abbreviation and the ZIP Code.

(3) If your company uses a data line unrelated to the address place it *above* the address.

(4) If you're mailing to a foreign country, place that country's name in the *last line* of the address block.

(5) If you desire, you may use both a post office box number and a street address. However, the mail will be delivered to the address, be it the box or street number, which appears *immediately* above the bottom line.

(6) The ZIP Code must be *correct* for the address given.

(7) If you're using, window envelopes, remember the address must be the only thing visible through the window. Make sure your addressed insert fits the envelope to prevent shifting. Try to keep 1/4" clearance between the address and the window edges.

(8) Typewritten or printed addresses can be handled more efficiently than handwritten addresses. Try to avoid italic or script types.

(9) When you address mail, don't forget the return address. Use your proper postage.

(10) Affix proper postage. Even the most carefully prepared mail can't reach its destination if it lacks the proper postage.

If you encounter an addressing situation that doesn't fit this standard address format, check with your local postal officials.

They'll be happy to help you with proper addressing practices and assist you in eliminating needless wastes of time and postage.

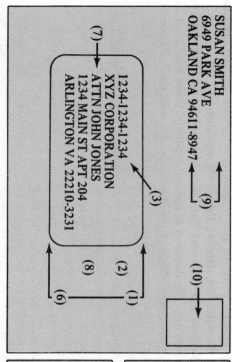

SUSAN SMITH
6949 PARK AVE
OAKLAND CA 94611-8947 ← (9)

1234-1234-1234 ← (3)
XYZ CORPORATION
ATTN JOHN JONES ← (7)
1234 MAIN ST APT 204 ← (8) (2)
ARLINGTON VA 22210-3231 ← (1)
(6) (10)

MINISTRY OF POSTS
OTTAWA ONTARIO
CANADA K1A 0B1 ← (4)

GRAND PRODUCTS INC
100 MAJOR ST
PO BOX 200
PORTLAND OR
97214-9653 ← (5)

Illus. 11-6
By developing a checklist for proper addressing, you can save time, money, and trouble.

Reprinted with permission, from *Memo to Mailers* (Jan. 1981) published by the U.S. Postal Service

Postal regulations require bundling and identifying five or more pieces of metered mail. Presorted bundles of metered mail are indicated by color-coded labels. For example, mail for the same state would be coded with an orange label bearing an *S*, and all mail for the same firm would carry a blue label with an *F* on it.

Mail presorted by ZIP Code moves faster. Large mailers can presort and forward mail to a specific ZIP Code or to a specific company in one bag. The post office furnishes trays for presorting in preparing mail for deposit at the post office.

The opportunity for postage reduction carries the implication that every mailer in the organization must cooperate in enabling the mail room to obtain such reductions. This means that mail should be sent to the mail room regularly during the day rather than following the practice now prevalent in which 75 percent of outgoing material reaches the mail room sometime in the late afternoon.

The secretary who is responsible for mailing material outside the company should presort mail for speedier handling by the post office. Before depositing mail, separate it into major categories such as local, out-of-town, precanceled, and metered. It can then bypass one or more preliminary handlings in the post office. Types of presorting vary with the types of individual mailings. For instance, if most of the mail goes to in-state addresses, this mail may be kept separate and identified as "All for (*State*)," thus eliminating one sorting operation and permitting immediate placement with the mail for that state.

Bar Codes

The post office uses bar code readers to automate sorting of the mail. A series of bars and half-bars found on some letter mail represents an address.

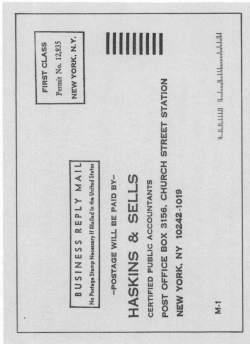

Illus. 11-7
Business reply envelope showing bar code

The series of bars below the address contains the ZIP Code and certain letters and numbers from the street address, city, and state. Envelopes bearing bar

Post Office Box

It is possible to rent a post office box where mail can be picked up at any time that the post office building is open. Mail can be obtained faster from the box than from the carrier.

Mailgram

The *mailgram* (see page 307) is the result of cooperation between the Postal Service and Western Union. Western Union owns and installs in post offices equipment that receives messages on a continuous roll of paper. A Postal Service employee tears off the message, inserts it in a window envelope, and dispatches it for guaranteed delivery with the next morning's mail.

Vertical Improved Mail (VIM)

Vertical Improved Mail (VIM) is a mail distribution system installed in many new large office buildings. In essence, VIM is the reverse of the familiar mail chute that channels mail dropped from the upper floors into a collection box. Under VIM all incoming mail is delivered to a central mail room in the building. There postal employees sort it into lockboxes by floors. These boxes are then placed on a conveyor belt and keyed to be ejected automatically to the right floor. There the office personnel pick up and deliver the mail. By this process the offices on each floor of the building can have continuous delivery of incoming mail. In buildings where lockboxes are not feasible, call windows can be used for frequent pickup of mail.

General Delivery

Mail may be addressed to individuals in care of the *General Delivery* window of main post offices. This service is convenient to transients and to individuals who have no definite address in a city. Such mail is held for a specified number of days and, if uncalled for, is then returned to the sender.

The executive on a touring vacation or a sales representative who is driving for several days and does not have specific hotel addresses frequently asks to have mail addressed in care of *General Delivery* to a city en route. The address can also include the words *Transient* or *To Be Called for.*

Such a letter would go to the main post office in a city and be held at the *General Delivery* window for the addressee for 10 days or up to 30 days

Postage Due Mailing Fees

The mailer can do a great deal to obtain information about changes of address by using first-class mail marked *Address Correction Requested, Return Postage Guaranteed* and paying a fee to the carrier delivering the returned mail.

The postmaster will correct any list of local mailing addresses at the expense of the mailer. Cards with the addresses of the "lost" addressees are distributed to the local carriers who fill in the correct addresses or explain other reasons why delivery cannot be made, such as *No Such Number*.

The list should be typed on cards about the size and quality of postal cards, with one address per card. The name of the owner of the list should be placed in the upper left corner of each card for identification purposes. Cards should be sent only to the post office that serves the address shown on the card.

Private Mail Delivery

Private carriers also transport letters. For example, Federal Express provides overnight letter delivery to most major United States markets. The maximum weight for an overnight letter is two ounces or the equivalent of ten 8½" × 11" folded pages. A special pouch is used to deliver the letter.

Some companies use their own employees for mail delivery of unstamped letters between their offices and companies with whom they conduct a large volume of business. Another time- and money-saving operation is hand delivery of bills. Some magazines now send issues to their news dealers for hand delivery.

Electronic Mail

The fastest growing segment of message transmittal is electronic mail. Growing numbers of manufacturers are producing electronic equipment that transmits messages faster than the traditional letter. Many organizations are converting to at least partial electronic message transmittal. The Postal Service itself is moving toward methods that will improve the transmittal of correspondence. Electronic Computer Originated Mail (E-COM Service) is a long-awaited service designed for such high volume mailings as credit card statements, overdue payment notices, letters, advertising messages, utility bills, and other common types of computer originated mail. This system will allow a company to send computerized messages over public telephone lines or via other private telecommunications carriers to Serving Post Offices (SPO's), which are located in the larger cities.

THE MECHANIZED MAIL ROOM

With rising costs and increased automation, businesses are interested in improving the capabilities of the mail room. An example of an advanced electronic mailing system is one manufactured by Pitney Bowes that provides instant rate information. The mailer can compare alternative methods of sending mail and choose the most advantageous rate. Letters and packages are weighed, the appropriate rate classification is entered, and metered postage is printed. When postal rates or fees change, a new rate module is entered, and the appropriate rate classification is entered, and metered postage is printed. When postal rates or fees change, a new rate module is sent to the user for plugging into the system. The document printer records the weight, date, shipping mode, zone, and charges on the shipping document and assigns a parcel identification number.

Pitney Bowes, Inc.

Illus. 11-8
Electronic
mailing
equipment

MONEY ORDERS

Money may be transferred from one person or business to another by use of a *money order*. There are instances in which money orders are the requested form of payment. They are also a convenience to individuals who do not have a checking account.

Domestic Money Orders

Postal money orders may be purchased at all post offices, branches, and stations. The maximum amount for a single *domestic money order* is $500. However, there is no limit on the number of money orders that may be purchased at one time. Money orders are also available at a low rate to depositors at savings banks and at other businesses, such as drugstores, supermarkets, etc.

REDUCING POSTAL EXPENSE

- Use paper and envelope weights that approximate the requirements for the class of mail involved. (One company that had been mailing first-class letters weighing slightly more than one ounce changed to a lighter weight paper that reduced each piece to less than one ounce and cut its first-class-mail bill almost in half.)
- Send some mail by classes other than first when it is not imperative that the material be delivered immediately. Compare the rates before making this decision.
- When unsure of the correct amount of postage, weigh the mail to avoid wasted postage or mail delayed by insufficient postage. Have the scales checked for accuracy periodically.
- Except for urgent items, combine in one mailing at the end of the day all mail addressed to the same person or the same branch office. (In a large company the mail room will do this for you.)
- Obtain up-to-date rate charts from the post office. Consult your mail room for new rates and regulations available from the local post office.
- If your employer approves, print reports and type long letters on both sides of the paper.
- Maintain up-to-date address lists, continually correcting all lists that may involve address changes.
- When sending reply requested mail, use business reply envelopes and postcards rather than stamped ones, thus paying postage only on those actually returned.
- Use *Special Handling* rather than *Special Delivery* for packages except in case of emergency.
- Send mail to the mail room regularly throughout the day so that it can be presorted for reduced postage rates.
- Use approved typing shortcuts such as the two-letter state abbreviations for addresses, solid capital envelope addresses, and the AMS simplified letter style.
- Use window envelopes when appropriate to save typing time.

International Money Orders

Money may be sent to a foreign country by means of an *international money order* procurable at the local post office. When buying such an order, you are given only a receipt for it by the postal clerk, who then arranges for

she is a single, married, or widowed. The purpose of the payment should also be stated.

SPEEDING MAIL DELIVERY

- Type addresses within the OCR read zone. Use single spacing and keep the address to three lines or, at the most, four.
- Type the room, suite, or apartment number on the second line *after* the street address when addressing mail to multiunit buildings.
- Use the *ZIP Code* on all mail.
- Use the services of the post office to correct mailing lists and to add ZIP Codes when the volume justifies the nominal expense.
- Bypass one or more preliminary handlings at the post office by presorting mail before depositing it.
- Mail early and often rather than all at once at the close of the business day. Establish an afternoon cutoff time for low priority first-class mail (usually 2 or 3 p.m.) and send it to the post office before the evening rush. Low priority first-class mail readied after this cutoff is then scheduled for deposit the following morning.
- Investigate the desirability of renting a *post office box.* Box holders can obtain mail more often and at irregular hours. Mailgrams can be obtained by the start of the working day.
- Consider express mail service, mailgrams, or facsimile mail (if available) when urgency is indicated.
- Double-check all addresses. It is easy to transpose numbers in street addresses and ZIP Codes.

INTERNATIONAL MAIL

Information regarding the rates, services, and regulations covering international mail may be obtained from the local post office or from the *International Mail Manual.*

Classifications of International Mail

International postal service provides *postal union mail* and *parcel post.*

Postal Union Mail. *Postal union mail* is divided into *LC Mail* and *AO Mail.*

   LC Mail (Letters and Cards)—letters, letter packages, air letters (aerogrammes), and postal cards

   AO Mail (Other Articles)—printed matter, merchandise samples without salable value, commercial papers, small packets, matter for the blind

The postage for letters and postal cards mailed to Canada and Mexico is the same as for the United States.

To all other countries the rates are higher and weights are limited. Letter packages (small, sealed packages sent at a letter rate of postage) are given letter treatment if they are marked *Letter*. A customs label identifying the contents must be attached to each letter package carrying dutiable merchandise.

Parcel Post. Parcels for transmission overseas are mailed by *parcel post* and must be packed even more carefully than those delivered within the continental United States. These packages may be registered or insured. Special handling services are also available. There is no international COD service. A *customs declaration* form must be attached to the parcel with an accurate and complete description of the contents. Since rates, weight limitations, and other regulations are not the same for all countries, the secretary should obtain information from the post office about requirements for a particular shipment.

International Air Postal Services

Rates on letters by air to foreign countries are charged at a fixed rate for a half ounce (except to Canada and Mexico where rates are the same as in the United States—a one-ounce basis for a fixed rate).

Air Letters (Aerogrammes). The post office sells an *air letter* sheet which may be mailed to any country with which we maintain airmail service. It is an airmail, prestamped, lightweight, single sheet that is folded into the form of an envelope and sealed. No enclosures, either paper or other kinds, are permitted. Firms engaged in international trade may print, subject to prior approval of the Postal Service, their own aerogramme letterheads.

AO Mail by Air. Many businesses are not aware of the cheapest and fastest of all international postal services—*AO mail by air*. No export forms are required for most shipments. This service is restricted to samples of such items as merchandise, maps, printed matter, and drawings; but it is ideal for shipping small articles and should be investigated by those companies using other air services.

International Air Parcel Post. A minimum of forms is required in shipping by *international air parcel post*. This service is available to nearly all countries and is rated on the first four ounces and each additional four ounces according to the country of destination.

Reply Postage

To enclose reply postage with mail going out of the country, use an international reply coupon, called *Coupon Response International*. It is pur-

SHIPPING SERVICES

Shipments are made by means other than the post office—by air, rail, ship, bus, and truck. The secretary needs to know the kinds of services rendered, the advantages of each, and the sources to investigate for current information. The following discussion deals with three shipping services—United Parcel Service, express, and freight.

United Parcel Service

United Parcel Service carries packages among all 50 states either by air or truck. It offers overnight ground delivery to points up to 150 miles from the place of origin, second day service to points up to 450 miles away, third day service up to 900 miles, and fourth day delivery up to 1,500 miles. Parcels are limited to 50 pounds and a combined girth and length of 108 inches. If a UPS driver is unable to make a delivery the first time, the driver will try twice more before a notice is issued to pick up the package at the local UPS office. Refused or undeliverable packages are returned to the sender at no extra charge. Rates are based on weights and delivery zones.

UPS also offers second day *Blue Label Service*, which is much cheaper than overnight fast freight service offered by companies owning their own fleets of planes. The cargo, like Express Mail, flies on passenger planes on a space available basis. UPS makes deliveries and will pick up shipments for a nominal fee.

Express Service

Express service is offered by rail, air, van, or bus. Each service offers advantages, and choice of service depends on specific shipping needs.

Rail Express. It is possible to ship a package by rail express by delivering the package to the station of any one of a few railroads that operate express service for short hauls. Amtrak operates an express service in many areas. Consult the Yellow Pages to see whether such service is available on railways in your vicinity.

Air Express. *Air express* is a highly competitive, growing service. It is expensive but it is the fastest means of transporting packages. Next day delivery is assured to most points in the United States. Pickup and delivery service is included in the fee. Companies such as Emery, Federal Express, and Purolator own their own air fleets and can provide faster service than those using commercial planes. Some airlines also offer express small parcel service.

Van Express. For deliveries to points not accessible by air, some express couriers offer van service from metropolitan areas. For example, Purolator supplements its air express service by using vans for shipping packages up to 70 pounds and no larger than 108 inches in length, width, and girth.

Bus Express. If speedy delivery of a package to a small town in another part of the state is necessary, the secretary should consider *bus express.* This service is particularly useful when destination points are located where there are no airports. Round-the-clock service is offered, including Sundays and holidays—and between many points, same day service. Pickup and delivery service is available at an extra charge. Most bus lines offer this type of shipping, the most widely known being Greyhound and Trailways. Items are insurable free up to $100, and a small charge is added beyond that value. The size of a package is limited to 100 pounds by Greyhound and 150 pounds by Trailways. A package must be no larger than 140 inches in combined length, width, and girth with a restriction of 5 feet in length by Greyhound and 6 feet by Trailways.

Choosing an Express Service. With so many choices, the shipper needs to make constant comparisons of costs and services. For current service and rates, call the agencies listed in the Yellow Pages that offer express service.

Freight Services

Freight is generally thought of as a shipment sent by any method other than mail or express. It is the most economical service used to transport heavy, bulky goods in large quantities. Because freight shipping is the most complex of all methods, the secretary will probably not be required to select the carrier and to route the shipments. Still, it is good to know a few of the salient facts.

Railroad Freight. Ordinarily when goods are shipped by *railroad freight,* they must be delivered by the shipper (consignor) to the local freight office. When the shipment arrives at its destination, the addressee (consignee) must arrange for delivery or must call for the shipment. Many railroads, however, have instituted store door delivery with trucks operated by the railway company in order to meet the competition of the door delivery service of trucking companies. More and more, the shipper loads the goods into containers at the home location and takes them to the carrier, who transports and delivers the shipment to the consignee with no further handling. Containerized shipping also offers the advantage of better security.

A service called *piggyback* is offered by the railroads to trucking firms for long-distance hauls. Here loaded truck trailers are driven to the railway depot in one city, detached from the tractor and placed on railroad flatcars, and moved by rail to another city where they can be unloaded and driven to their destinations. Thus towns and areas not on the regular railroad lines can be reached by this service.

To provide a less-than-carload freight service at a special rate, *freight-forwarding companies* assemble from several consignors shipments that are less than a carload and that are going to the same destination. This service allows shippers of small quantities to gain a carload rate from the railroads.

Motor Freight. *Motor freight* is used for both local and long-distance hauls. Truck companies operate coast-to-coast service and have connecting services with local trucking lines. As described above, they often work in conjunction with railroads. Sometimes shipments are held by trucking companies until they have a paying load destined for the same locality. Specialized trucks also carry single commodities such as milk, gasoline, new cars, chemicals, sand, and gravel in truckload quantities.

Air Freight. Businesses find that the high cost of air freight is partly offset by reduced costs in inventory and in warehouse space. There is also a saving in packing costs, since air shipments do not require the sturdy crating that surface shipments frequently demand.

Delivery service is provided without charge; however, there is a small charge for pickup service.

Water Freight. *Water freight* is usually considerably cheaper than any other means of freight transportation. River barges and other vessels on the inland waterways of the United States carry such commodities as lumber, coal, iron ore, and chemicals. Bulky items for overseas shipment are carried in freighters, while passenger lines carry mail and items packaged in crates. Information on services and rates can be obtained from shipping companies.

International Shipments

The market for American products is worldwide. International air cargo service makes it possible to deliver goods to most places in the world within a matter of hours. The bulk of tonnage to foreign markets, however, still moves via *surface* (ships).

International shipments present problems—special packing, complicated shipping procedures, marine insurance, foreign exchange—usually not encountered in domestic trade. The mere handling of communications with a foreign business firm can be a problem in itself. International time zone differences are discussed in Chapter 13.

Shipping Documents. A foreign shipment involves the preparation of a number of documents, such as forms to obtain an *export license* (some commodities), *ocean bill of lading, consular invoice* or *certificate of origin,* and *export customs declaration.* Large manufacturers doing extensive business abroad usually establish export departments (1) to market the products, (2) to execute the required export and shipping forms, and (3) to arrange for the actual shipments.

Many small firms use the services of an export broker or Combination Export Management (CEM) firm. This firm performs the same functions as an export department; namely, marketing, processing, and shipping of goods.

Some businesses prefer to use the services of a foreign freight forwarder or cargo agent, who specializes in processing foreign shipments. The agent executes the required report and shipping documents and arranges for the actual shipment.

International airlines and steamship companies also maintain departments that assist customers with their overseas shipments.

International Air Cargo. To send a shipment by *international air cargo,* whether you are sending one package or a carload, contact the office of an international airline. The airline will provide instructions on packaging and addressing the shipment and completing the necessary documents such as *bill of lading* and *customs declaration.* In many cases air freight or even express is less expensive than international parcel post.

SUGGESTED READINGS

Akers, Herbert W. *Modern Mail Room Management.* New York: McGraw-Hill Book Company, 1979.

Business Week, Administrative Management, The Office, Time, Newsweek, and newspapers carry reports on the postal service as changes are made.

Domestic Mail Manual. Washington, D. C. U. S. Government Printing Office. Replaces Chapter 1 of the *Postal Service Manual* describing domestic mail service and gives a detailed description of each class of mail and special services available to the public. Subscription basis only, with changes issued as required.

Gross, Edmund J. *Penny-Pinching Postal Pointers for Everyone.* Hollywood: Halls of Ivy Press, 1976.

Memo to Mailers. Washington, D. C.: Public and Employee Communications Department, U.S. Postal Service. Published monthly for customers originating significant quantities of mail.

National Directory of Addresses and Telephone Numbers. New York: The National Directory of Addresses and Telephone Numbers, (updated annually).

National ZIP Code and Post Office Directory. St. Louis Postal Data Center, P.O. Box 14872, St. Louis, MO 63180

QUESTIONS FOR DISCUSSION

1. In your opinion has service improved since the Postal Service is no longer a department of the federal government?

2. What alternative methods of sending mail have developed to compete with the Postal Service? How is the Postal Service attempting to combat this competition?

3. Discuss precautions that must be taken in the placement of the address on an envelope. Why?

4. Which considerations would influence you to choose certified mail over a certificate of mailing?

5. In what in-company ways can an organization speed the mail without increasing postage costs?

6. Your employer hands you an addressed and sealed envelope for stamping and mailing and says that it contains an income tax return. How will you go about obtaining legal evidence that the income tax return was mailed? (The federal government prosecutes a taxpayer whose return is not received, even though the taxpayer has a carbon copy of the return and makes a verbal claim that the return was filed by mail.)

7. You are sending a request for a free brochure published in Norway. How can you arrange to enclose with your request adequate postage for mailing the brochure?

8. There are three ways of sending a letter which tells that a parcel post package is being mailed out: separately, enclosed with the contents, or in an envelope fastened to the outside of the package. Which do you think is preferable and why?

9. Your employer asked you to mail an important letter to Germany. You are chagrined when it is returned for insufficient postage. The letter weighed one ounce, and you had affixed domestic postage. Why was it returned? How can you prevent a recurrence of such an error?

10. Mail from the home office reaches your city post office around 2 a.m. each morning. However, it is not delivered to your office until the time of the regular mail delivery at 10:30 a.m. Your employer wants to have the home office mail as early as possible so that district sales representatives can be told of price changes. What do you suggest to solve this problem?

11. When would you choose express mail over priority mail?

12. Why is a surcharge justified for mail that does not conform to size standards?

13. The post office recommendations for new address formats have been disregarded by many secretaries. Why? Should you follow them?

14. Why should the business organization assume the responsibility of presorting mail?

15. What are the advantages of containerized shipping?

16. Fill in the blanks in these sentences, selecting the correct use of numbers in parentheses following the sentence. Then use the Reference Guide to verify or correct your answers.

(a) Leave _____ blank spaces after all terminal marks of punctuation. (2)

(b) The _____ brochure is a complete guide to Canada. (66 page)

(c) The expressway is completed except for a _____ mile exit ramp. (¾)

(d) Send us your check for _____ to cover the cost of shipping. ($12.00)

(e) The _____ lengths of pipe were shipped on flatcars _____ long. (30', 50')

(f) We expect the temperature to reach _____ degrees below zero. (4)

(g) The course is listed as a _____ semester offering. (½)

(h) The interest was calculated for _____. (1 year, six months, and 9 days)

PROBLEMS

1. Assume that your employer is out of the city on a business trip. How would you go about forwarding each of the following unopened pieces of mail? State whether additional postage is required.

(a) A personal letter

(b) A piece of registered mail requiring a signed return receipt

(c) A letter mailed by your office to the employer but returned because of an insufficient address

(d) A special delivery letter you wish to have forwarded also by special delivery

(e) A parcel post package

2. Set up a three-column table with each column head indicating the information requested in (a), (b), and (c). In the appropriate columns enter the information required by Items 1–21.

(a) The class of postal service that should be used (If parcel post is chosen, indicate the zone.)

(b) The kinds of fees that must be paid in addition to postage

(c) Special requirements or secretarial procedures

(1) A carbon copy of a letter

(2) A pen corrected copy of a printed price list

(3) A library book you are returning by mail

(4) A letter addressed to a relative of the executive enclosing bonds valued at $500 and registered for full value, return receipt required showing address where delivery was made

(5) A magazine addressed to a city 30 miles distant and sent at the personal request of the executive

(6) An 18-ounce sealed package containing a printing plate and addressed to a city 550 miles distant, with special delivery service

(7) A seven-ounce unsealed package of candy sent special delivery

(8) A $20 money order addressed to a city 20 miles distant

(9) A box 3' long, 1½' wide, and 1½' high, weighing 40 pounds, addressed to a city 400 miles distant

(10) A sealed parcel weighing five ounces sent by priority mail

(11) A box of perishable bulbs weighing eight pounds

(12) A monthly statement of a department store to a customer in the same city

(13) A postal card to a city 300 miles away

(14) A one-pound parcel containing clothing sent to a city 95 miles

distant and insured for $15 with a return receipt requested at the time the parcel was mailed

(15) A check for $45 to a city 300 miles away

(16) Sixty individually addressed unsealed envelopes containing one-page mimeographed price lists

(17) A five-pound box containing automobile parts addressed to a city 250 miles distant where your employer is stranded in a disabled automobile

(18) A letter sent by certified mail with a postmarked receipt requested

(19) A one-pound sealed parcel containing costume jewelry insured for $75 and being transmitted 2,500 miles

(20) A certified letter containing notice to an heir to an estate with return receipt requested showing where the envelope was delivered

(21) Thirty mimeographed invitations in unsealed envelopes addressed to out-of-town members

3. Which service would you recommend to someone living in a metropolitan area in sending the following goods?

(a) An engine part for factory equipment that has broken down

(b) One thousand copies of a convention program for distribution in two weeks

(c) An antique desk inherited by an heir in New Orleans from a relative in St. Louis

(d) Ten dozen summer shirts ready for shipment on March 3

(e) A year's supply of letterheads for a branch office in Osaka

(f) Photographs for a resident of a town 30 miles away; the recipient is to take them on a vacation trip the following day

(g) Ten dozen summer shirts to replenish stock during a sale

Chapter 12

Basic Telephone and Telegraph Services

You have used the telephone for years and probably think that you are adept in handling this instrument used so frequently by the secretary. The business telephone is, however, quite different and much more complicated than the personal telephone. One of the common complaints about office personnel is the ineptitude of employees on the telephone. You yourself can recall many instances in which indifference, a long delay, or rudeness has created an unfavorable impression of the company to which you made a telephone call.

On the other hand, telephone effectiveness can win accolades for the secretary, for the employer, and for the organization. For instance, an executive who frequently spoke by phone with an outstanding secretary described her in this way, "Marjorie is just perfect on the telephone. She always makes me feel good. Her voice always has a lilt, and she is willing to help me. Not only is she willing, but she does help me. She knows more about her company than most of the people who work there. She is worth thousands of dollars in goodwill alone."

Any secretary who answers the telephone has an opportunity to make friends for the employer and for the company. The telephone is a vital link between you and the public and between you and your co-workers. It speeds up communication, often supplanting personal visits or letters.

Western Union, too, helps to accelerate business action and to get results when other means have failed. You must know how and when to use its services.

In this chapter the telephone equipment you will probably encounter in your environment is discussed. You will learn how to improve your telephone speech and adopt appropriate telephone etiquette. Techniques for answering incoming local and long-distance calls and for handling multibutton telephones are explained. You will understand how to take messages, how to record or summarize conversations, and how to send a telegram.

TELEPHONE EQUIPMENT

There is intense competition among manufacturers to provide telephones with increased capabilities. The Bell System, which is by far the largest company, and its manufacturing unit, Western Electric, constantly introduce new equipment. Other manufacturers, too, are competing for the telephone dollar, so it is hard to predict what telephone you will have on your desk or when it may be updated by a new one. Probably, though, you will use a telephone with at least some of the features described in this chapter.

Rotary Dial or Touch-Tone Telephone

You are probably accustomed to both the rotary dial and Touch-Tone telephones. The rotary dial telephone with ten holes for dialing is more easily manipulated with a special gadget with a ball on the end that fits the holes or with the eraser end of a pencil than with the index finger. The Touch-Tone telephone has twelve buttons, the two additional ones providing direct access

Illus. 12-1
The Touch-Tone telephone can be used for regular telephoning and also for tone transmission of data for entry into computers.

Reproduced with permission of A.T.&T. Co.

to a computing center, a dictating center, or other service center. The Touch-Tone telephone can be used for regular telephoning and also for tone transmission of data for entry into computers.

Key Telephone

Many office desks are provided with key telephones. The key telephone is equipped with lucite push buttons. This key telephone enables a person to make or take a number of calls simultaneously from both inside and outside the office. A key telephone in the hands of an inefficient secretary can create havoc with office procedure.

To answer a call:

1. Determine the line to be answered by the location of the ring, the tone, or the signal light on the bottom.
2. Depress the key for the line to be answered, remove the receiver, and speak.

To place a call:

1. Choose a line that is not in use (unlighted).
2. Push down the key for that line, remove the receiver, and make your call.
3. If you accidentally choose a line that is being held, depress the hold key to reestablish the hold.

To hold a call:

1. Ask the person to hold the line.
2. Depress the hold key for about two seconds to assure holding; both the line key and the hold key will return to normal position (with the light on).
3. Place or answer another call on another line. The person being held cannot overhear your other conversation.

The *Touch-a-matic* telephone adds an electronic memory in which frequently called numbers can be stored so that they can be dialed at the touch

Illus. 12-2
The
Touch-a-matic
telephone has
an electronic
memory in
which frequently
called numbers
can be sorted.

of a single button. A key telephone may also be equipped with a *Last-Person-Called* button which enables the user to recall the person last talked to by touching the button before a new number is called.

Key Telephone Systems

The key system permits each user to select an outside or intercom line. Com Key systems come with various capabilities.

Bell's Com Key 416 gives an ultimate capacity of 4 central office lines, 16 stations, and 2 intercom paths. It has distinctive ringing features so that the secretary is alerted to the type of call being answered. It is possible to set up multiline conferences among the phones in the system just by depressing the necessary buttons simultaneously. Two people may also converse with each other over the intercom.

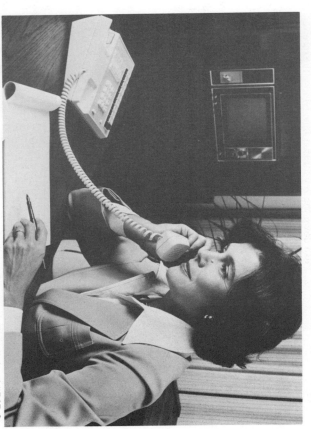

Reproduced with permission of A.T.&T. Co.

Illus. 12-3
Bell's Com Key
416 has a
capacity of 4
central office
lines, 16
stations, and 2
intercom paths.

When an in-company call is initiated, the buttons of the caller and the one being called on the Com Key are pressed down; and when the call is terminated, both buttons pop back up to signal that the lines are free. It is possible to summon personnel from any station in the system over wall-mounted loudspeakers. Incoming calls can be switched automatically to a predetermined alternate station. Background music can be piped to workers over the Com Key. If a message comes in while a phone is in use, the attendant can flash a light to alert the person at that phone to request the message.

PBX (Private Branch Exchange) Systems

Many businesses have sufficient phone traffic to justify some type of central switchboard. An attendant (operator) answers incoming calls and forwards them by touching a button on an electronic console (switchboard). To place outgoing calls, the caller dials 9 to get an outside line before dialing the phone number desired. The assistance of an attendant is not needed in making outgoing or internal calls.

Today's PBX systems are computer controlled. A computerized telephone system permits a company to acquire new features and calling capabilities through periodic enhancements to the computer program. These add-on features (enhancements) can be customized to fit the telephone arrangement in each organization.

Reproduced with permission of A.T.&T. Co.

Illus. 12-4
Today's PBX
systems are
computer
controlled.

Only the add-on features related to basic telephoning are discussed here, but Chapter 13 also refers to the elements of these electronic systems that extend telephone functions beyond basic services. Your telephone may have some of these features.

Call Pickup. As a secretary you may be a member of a group responsible for answering the other telephones if a member of the group is not at his or her desk. By dialing the code, you can answer the call without leaving your desk.

Speed Calling. The telephone will store up to 30 numbers that can then be called by dialing one or two digits, not 7 to 11 numbers. The telephone *remembers* the rest.

Repeat Number Call. The last number that was connected with a telephone is dialed by depressing only one button.

Call Forwarding. After a preset number of rings, a call is automatically forwarded to another preselected line or to the attendant. If an incoming call receives a busy signal, it is forwarded to a preselected telephone or to the attendant. A telephone can be programmed to transfer all incoming and outgoing calls within the system by flashing the proper button and dialing the desired telephone number. Other equipment can forward calls to telephones outside the system.

Call Hold. It is possible to place a call on hold and then originate and complete a second call before returning to the original caller. This feature is valuable if additional information is required to complete the original call.

Message Recorder. The telephone can be programmed to record an incoming message that can be played back later.

Camp-On Busy or Call Waiting. With a busy camp-on, the person who is using the telephone is notified that a call is waiting by a short audible tone that is not heard by the person at the other end of the line. When you hang up, the telephone is automatically rung and the call that was on hold is initiated.

Discriminating Ringing. A different ringing pattern is used for an incoming internal call, an outside call, or a long-distance call.

Centrex

One of the frustrations of the modern office is the difficulty of getting through the switchboard to the extension wanted. To circumvent this problem, many companies have installed *direct in-dialing* to the specific extension wanted (*Centrex*). After having been given the extension number and the company number, the frequent caller can dial the extension direct from an outside telephone. *After learning a Centrex number, record it in your directory.*

Additional features of Centrex are identification of all outgoing calls so that the accounting department can apportion long-distance calls to the right telephone, and no charge interoffice calls without attendant assistance. It is also possible to designate a centralized answering point so that one secretary can screen calls to several Centrex numbers. If your office has Centrex II-Plus or Centrex III, you may have access to helpful features such as call forwarding, speed calling, or call pickup.

TELEPHONE CONVERSATION

Some phase of at least 90 percent of all business transactions is conducted by telephone. That is why many personnel officers check the telephone performance of applicants before hiring them. It is also why companies frequently provide in-service telephone training for all office employees.

What the secretary says in carrying on the telephone conversation is important: tactful choice of words in contrast to blunt statements; offers of help in contrast to plain no's. Ease in conducting pleasant, effective conversations comes with experience and proper training.

The Voice with a Smile

Your voice over the phone reflects your personality. **Make it attractive to whoever is calling.** The person calling may be very important or, on the other hand, an unimportant person; you don't know so you cannot afford to answer indifferently. Here are seven simple rules to follow in developing a pleasant telephone voice:

1. Speak at a normal speed, with rising and falling inflections that avoid monotony.
2. Use a tone suitable for face-to-face-conversation, keeping the voice low-pitched.
3. Speak directly into the transmitter, which should be between half an inch and an inch from the lips.
4. Try to visualize and speak directly *to* the person calling—not *at* the telephone.
5. Try to convey a friendly, intelligent interest.
6. Show that you are wide awake and ready to help the person on the line.
7. Use simple, nontechnical language and avoid slang. The *bye-bye* at the end of a conversation leaves a distinctly bad impression.

Telephone callers are guests of the organizations we work with, and answering their calls places us in the unique position of host or hostess. Why not offer them the same friendly hospitality we give so freely to our own houseguests?

Your Telephone Personality
—The Economics Press

Telephone Etiquette

Rudeness that would never occur in face-to-face conversation is too often used in telephone encounters. "Minding your manners" is essential to telephone effectiveness. Follow these guidelines:

1. Answer the telephone before the third ring, even if you are in the midst of an important job. This practice will not only establish a good relationship with the caller but will also reassure your employer about your competence.
2. Avoid implying by your tone of voice any feeling that the call is an intrusion.
3. *Listen* until you know definitely what the caller wants. If in doubt, ask for a confirmation of your understanding. Nothing is more annoying than telling someone the purpose of a call and then realizing by the response that you were not understood. The listening technique is one of the most important communication skills, and in no place can you demonstrate better your mastery of listening skills than in your telephone conversations.
4. Establish yourself as a helpful person. Being able to speak confidently about your organization and being courteous as well as helpful, you can

rather quickly establish yourself as someone the caller can deal with and, most important, someone that your employer can trust. Here is a chance to widen your sphere of influence.

5. If you are required to terminate a conversation suddenly for any of several reasons, use a plausible excuse—the truth, tactfully worded—for example: "I'm sorry, Ms. Allen has just buzzed for me to come into her office," or "I'm sorry, someone is waiting for me in the reception room," or "I'm sorry, I must get out a rush letter for Mr. Barkley."

6. Sprinkle your conversations with *thank you* and *please*—not just superficial ones but genuine ones such as, "Thank you, *so much*, Mr. Rodrigues, for letting us know that."

7. Make the very flattering gesture of using the caller's name if you recognize the voice. In case of doubt, however, you should not risk the possibility of making an error in identification.

8. Follow through; don't leave the caller stranded. Go that last mile. Either get the information, transfer the call, or arrange for someone (maybe you) to call back, and then *do so*. Promises must be carried out.

9. Remember that offices are busy places, so keep all telephone calls as short as possible by eliminating chitchat and by planning conversations before placing calls. Some organizations do not permit any personal calls, but you may occasionally have to make one. In any case, keep personal calls to a minimum and *keep them short*.

10. Close the conversation courteously and graciously. Suggested wording of your last sentence might be:

> Thank you for calling, Mrs. Levinson.
> I'm glad I was able to help you. Goodbye.
> You're welcome, Mr. Rogers. Goodbye.

Enunciation

Sounds can be mistaken as they travel over the wires. Enunciation then becomes very important, for you will be giving and taking information over the telephone frequently. Watch for these frequent causes of inaccuracy: *F* and *S* are often confused, as are *P* and *B*, *T* and *D*, and *M* and *N*.

When word accuracy is needed, telephone spelling is used. To prevent mistakes, use any simple, easy-to-understand word to identify a letter, such as *D as in David*, *A as in Alice*, and so on. It is particularly important that the listener understand any numbers used in telephone conversation. The speaker should slightly exaggerate the enunciation; for example, "Th-r-ee" (strong *R* and long *EE*). Repeat the number; or, if there is still a question about one digit, give its preceding sequence, as "Three, four, *five*," emphasizing the final proper number.

The American Telephone and Telegraph Company recommends the following practice sentences to improve your diction. Read them aloud slowly, giving every sound its proper value. Think about them, too.

1. For distinct enunciation, every word, every syllable, every sound must be given its proper form and value.

2. Think of the mouth chamber as a mold in which the correct form must be given to every sound.

3. Move your lips noticeably.

4. Your teeth should never be kept closed while you are talking.

5. You may know what you are saying, but others won't unless you make it clear to them.

6. Through practice we can learn to speak more rapidly, but still with perfect distinctions.

7. The courtesy of face-to-face conversation, in which the smile is so important, can be conveyed by telephone only through a smiling voice.

INCOMING CALLS

There are specific techniques to follow in handling incoming calls. Because every executive has preferences, determine how calls are to be dealt with. Some want to answer their own calls; others want them screened. If you are working with several executives, who may be out of the office frequently, it is especially important to learn the wishes of each one. Armed with this information, you can then adopt appropriate procedures.

Identification

How you answer your telephone depends upon whether it is connected directly to an outside line or to the company switchboard, but you should always identify the company or the office and yourself. If your telephone is on an outside line, you may answer, "Allen and Lovell, John—'s office." If the call comes through the company switchboard, you will answer, "Ms. Allen's office, Susan —," because the switchboard attendant has already identified the company before ringing you. In no case do you say only hello or yes.

A method of identification at the switchboard that is increasing in popularity because of its friendliness is, "Thank you for calling XYZ Company," or even "Good morning. Thank you for calling XYZ Company." Some people believe, though, that these greetings are time consuming and counterproductive.

Screening Calls

When the employer prefers to have you answer, is away from the office, or is obviously too busy to answer, you will, of course, answer all calls.

If you answer a call from someone whose voice you recognize as that of a VIP, you automatically put the call through without question. When the caller provides no identification or you do not recognize the voice, you may be required to find out who is calling. This procedure requires skillful questioning. The abrupt question, "Who is calling?" sounds rude and discriminating. Tactful secretaries phrase their questions somewhat like these:

May I ask who is calling, please?

or

May I tell Ms. Wong who is calling, please?

Some executives prefer such screening of *all* calls so that they can immediately identify the caller by name.

When you do not let the caller talk with the executive, you need to give a plausible explanation and to suggest a substitute person or time. A typical explanation might be:

Mr. Graham, Mrs. Allen is attending an important conference. May I help you or transfer you to someone who can?

Executive Unavailable

The secretary has three responsibilities regarding incoming calls when the executive is not available for answering the telephone:

1. Giving helpful but not explicit information to the caller about the executive's time schedule and activities
2. Getting information from hesitant callers
3. Taking messages and keeping a record of incoming calls

Giving Information. When the executive is not available, the secretary is discreet about giving information. Definite information may be exactly what the executive does not want told to certain callers. *When in doubt, don't be specific.* Unless there is a known reason for being specific, the secretary tries to be helpful but not explicit. Note the differences in the following responses:

Specific	*Helpful But Not Explicit*
Miss Ettinger hasn't come in yet.	Miss Ettinger isn't at her desk. I expect her at ten o'clock.
Ms. Smith is in Chicago on business.	Ms. Smith is out of the city today.
Mr. Hubbard left early today to play golf.	Mr. Hubbard won't be in until tomorrow.

Getting Information. Getting information from an unidentified caller often presents a problem—and a challenge. How can you get both the name of the caller and the purpose of the call before the person says, "I'll call back," and then hangs up? You may have to use a rather oblique approach. The conversation might develop something like this:

You answer the call and say, "Ms. Allen is away today. I am her secretary; perhaps I can help you." Notice that you do not ask who is calling or what is wanted. If the caller is still hesitant, you might ask, "May I have her call you tomorrow?" If the answer is, "Yes, will you? This is Helen Fox, 621-6412," you might then ask, "Shall I give her any special message, Miss Fox?" Or you might ask, "Will Ms. Allen know what you are calling about?" A positive answer to any such question necessitates identification of the caller or the purpose of the call.

Tactful Requests	*Discourteous Requests*
May I say who's calling, please?	He wants to know who's calling.
He's in a meeting. May I take a message?	If you'll tell me who's calling, I'll see if I can locate him.
Will you please wait while I see if she is in?	Mrs. McDuff isn't taking any calls this morning.

Taking Messages. As you answer your telephone, pick up a pencil and push a pad of paper into place. *Keep these supplies handy at all times.* Always offer to take a message when your employer is out. Ask the caller to explain any details that you do not understand. Take time to repeat the message and verify all spelling. If a callback is indicated, say, "I'll ask Mrs. Brown to call you when she's free," rather than the tactless, "I'll have Mrs. Brown call you when she is free."

After you have recorded the message, complete the record by adding the date, the time the call came, the name and identity of the caller, and your

TELEPHONE MESSAGE

FOR _Mrs. McDuff_   DATE _8/4/--_

M_r_ _F. Jones_   OF _____

PHONE NO. _301-921-4108_   TIME _9:15_

✓	TELEPHONED		PLEASE PHONE	
	RETURNED YOUR CALL		WANTS TO SEE YOU	
	CAME TO SEE YOU		WILL CALL AGAIN	

MESSAGE _The meeting of the product managers has been postponed until next week._

BY _E.J.M._

Illus. 12-5
Telephone message form

initials. Some firms use small printed slips for this purpose. It is possible to buy books of telephone message forms interleaved with carbon sheets so that the original message can be put on the executive's desk and the carbon copy retained in the book for reference.

Even if there is no message to report, make a record of the call. When the executive is away, a helpful secretary keeps a complete telephone diary of all calls received and messages recorded.

With today's equipment, in some offices the written message may be put into the computer to be called up by the executive and read from a screen, or it may be voice recorded for oral transmission.

The administrative secretary may establish a *message island* which each executive can check regularly. In all cases relay the messages promptly.

Transferring Calls

When a call comes that someone else can handle better, transfer the call. The caller, however, may be justifiably annoyed if the call has already been transferred to you. Several techniques can be used to demonstrate that you and your organization want to be helpful. First, be sure that the person to whom you transfer the call can actually give the information sought. Here is an opportunity to demonstrate your understanding of your company's organization pattern, to show that you know who knows what. Second, tell the caller that you are transferring the call but if you are disconnected you can be reached again at—(extension number). Stay on the line until you are sure that someone else has answered the call. Third, consider the possibility of getting the information for the caller yourself and returning the call. Nothing is more important than your company's (and your own) image, nor more exasperating than a *I-couldn't-care-less, I-have-my-own-work-to-do* attitude.

Recording Complete or Summarized Telephone Conversations

Your employer may wish to record crucial telephone conversations. If so, the recorder must be equipped with a sound device that emits intermittent beeps to warn the other person in the conversation that the call is being recorded.

At other times you may be asked to summarize telephone conversations in which case a less complete record is available. The transcript can be condensed but should be typed in dialogue form as indicated on page 713 of the Reference Guide.

Answering a Second Telephone

You may work with an executive who has two or more telephones in the office. If both of them ring at the same time, answer one and ask the caller to excuse you for a moment while you answer the other one. Get approval before you put the caller on hold. If the second call is local, get the number and offer to call back, placing the call immediately after completing the first call.

If the second call is long distance, explain that you are handling another call and excuse yourself long enough to tell the first caller, "I'll be with you in a minute." Complete the long-distance call as quickly as possible and when you get back to the first caller express appreciation for waiting and apologize for the delay.

If you are on the telephone when the second call comes in, follow the same procedure.

Precautions for Receiving Long-Distance Calls

Long distance is used more and more often as travel costs rise, and you will receive many such calls. To reduce waiting time, a well-trained caller will immediately announce that this is a long-distance call. In that case a special effort should be made to get on the line immediately the person for whom the call is intended.

If the executive is not available, take great care in listening carefully and recording the message completely and accurately. If you receive a person-to-person call for your employer, give the long-distance operator full information as to when the call can be returned. The operator will ask you to have the executive return the call and will give you those details that will help in completing the return call, such as: "Please ask Miss Downey to call Operator 18 in Detroit and ask for 719-1380, Mr. Smith."

If your employer can be reached at another telephone, either locally or in another city, and you believe there will be no objection to receiving a call there, you should tell the operator where the call can be transferred.

If your telephone is equipped with call forwarding, press the call forwarding button and dial the number at which the executive can be reached. If the number is outside your organization, dial the code access number that has been assigned your telephone and then the local number of the telephone to which the call is to be transferred.

Message-Taking Services

New devices and services are available that assure that telephone calls are always answered, even when the telephone is not covered.

Answering, Recording, and Switching Devices. Automatic answering equipment can deliver any message that the user records. Before leaving the office, the executive (or the secretary) turns on the machine and makes a recording to tell callers the time of return and to ask them to leave a message. The person calling hears the announcement and then records a message. An innovation made possible by electronics is equipment that enables the executive to call in and revise the previous recording. Small businesses, such as real estate and insurance offices, find this service especially advantageous. This equipment has also been expanded to attract large users. For instance, up to six hours of recorded messages can capture overnight orders for a meat wholesaler.

Telephone Answering Services. Unlike the automatic recording device that merely recites impersonal messages, the attendant in a telephone answering service is able to exercise judgment and understanding in personally assisting the caller. Many business firms invest in such service as a way of personalizing their offices during the hours they are not open. The secretary in an office using such service should establish friendly relations with the answering service, check with the attendant immediately upon coming into the office after it has been closed, and provide complete information when the answering service takes over.

Taped Announcements. Almost every telephone user is familiar with taped announcements that may be dialed: time of day, weather, flight information, market information, movie schedules, and even prayers. It is possible for a business to develop such announcements possibly specifying office hours. Some organizations record advertising messages that are played while a caller is waiting for a busy line to become available.

Special Reverse Charge Toll Service

A business can make its services easily available by telephone in cities where it has no office with a special listing in the telephone directory of each of such cities. These listings permit the caller to make the call as a local one, and the toll charge is billed to the listed number. For instance, a Yonkers company would have a New York City number listed in the New York City directory as:

Acetate Box Co

   263 AshbrtnAv Ynkrs . . . . . . NYC Tel No—292-2435

On such incoming calls, the secretary provides complete and cordial help—without waste of long-distance time (see page 277).

OUTGOING CALLS

In addition to answering the telephone, the secretary will place local and long-distance calls. To do this well, a secretary must know how to get maximum service from telephone directories and telephone operators and how to make the appropriate choices of service.

Using Telephone Directories

Before placing a call, the secretary must locate the telephone number, and sometimes that takes quite a bit of skill. The telephone directory has two parts: the Alphabetical Directory (white pages) that contains a complete list of subscribers, their addresses, and telephone numbers; and the Yellow Pages (classified directory) containing the alphabetic listings of names of businesses under headings that are also arranged alphabetically by product or service. Metropolitan areas often publish two types of Yellow Pages, one for business and another for consumers.

Both directories print, in the upper outside corner, the first and last names or headings listed on each page. The conspicuous location of these guide words makes it possible to locate the proper page quickly.

The telephone directory is a mine of information, especially one for a metropolitan area. For instance, the New York City alphabetical directory contains in its introductory pages emergency numbers; community service numbers; instructions for telephoning locally, nationally, and overseas; area codes for major cities in the United States; explanations of various types of service; zones for assessing message unit rates (see page 282); a map showing area code distribution; a local postal zone map; long-distance rates to major cities and hours during which rates apply; facts about telephone services and their costs; helpful hints for finding numbers quickly and easily; explanations of billing; and money-saving tips. Part of these explanations may be repeated in a foreign language if there are enough people in a particular geographical area to justify the translation.

A corporation may find it advantageous to keep in a central location a collection of telephone directories from cities in which it conducts a large volume of business. It is also possible to find out-of-town directories of large cities in some hotels and major travel terminals.

The Alphabetical Directory. In the *alphabetical directory* the numbers are usually located quickly, but the exceptions make it necessary for the secretary to know the rules followed in arranging names in alphabetical sequence in filing. For example, there are 21 columns of the surname *Miller* in one metropolitan directory. Alternate spellings are suggested as, *Also see MILLAR.*

Locating various government offices and public services also requires a knowledge of the alphabetical listings. They are generally listed under their proper political subdivisions—city offices under the name of the municipality, county offices under the name of the county, state offices under the name of the state, and federal offices under *United States Government.* Government listings are found either in their alphabetic location or in a special blue section at the end of some directories. Public schools are usually listed under the municipality and then under Board of Education. Parochial schools are individually listed. Addresses of identical listings are in alphabetical order of street names followed by numbered streets in numerical order. (*Eighth Street* follows rather than precedes *Second Street.*)

The Yellow Pages Directory. The *Yellow Pages* directory of business listings is a very helpful source of reference for the secretary. In metropolitan areas a separate Yellow Pages directory contains all classified listings. The executive may want to talk with "that air conditioning firm on Church Street," but may not know its correct name. An alert secretary would look in the Yellow Pages under *Air Conditioning Equipment & Systems—Supplies & Parts* and find *Tuttle & Bailey, Inc.,* the only air conditioning firm on Church Street.

You should circle every frequently called telephone number in the directory for easy finding next time. You should also jot down the number you looked up just in case you get a busy signal when you first dial it. When a new number is obtained, it should be listed on the proper directory page or in a desk telephone directory.

Personal Telephone Directory. Every secretary keeps a *personal, up-to-date telephone directory.* In it are listed alphabetically the names of frequently called persons and firms and their telephone numbers. Any list becomes out of date quickly unless a system is devised that provides for additions and deletions. Most secretaries prefer a small rotary wheel file for mounting this directory.

Some kind of card listing or tab insertion scheme is preferable to a solid-typed list which makes no provision for the addition of names and changes of personnel or telephone numbers. A thoughtful secretary places a condensed list of such numbers at the back of the executive's daily calendar pad.

The time-and-motion-conscious secretary will be interested in the analysis by the telephone company: You can look up a number in your personal telephone directory in 10 seconds, about a third of the time required for a search of the large directory. A personal telephone booklet may be obtained from the telephone company for the asking, or the blank pages at the back of most directories can be used.

Some people prefer not to have their telephone number listed in the directory. This may cost them a few cents a month because of additional administrative costs. Usually Directory Assistance (Information) will not have the number in its records. Only in exceptional circumstances, and with the customer's own consent, will the telephone company arrange to complete the call. Keeping unlisted numbers in the personal directory becomes doubly important since they cannot be looked up.

Telephone numbers of frequent correspondents may be taken from letterheads and entered in the personal telephone directory for possible use.

Business Promotion Listings. A company may list its telephone number in several ways that will promote business.

One way is to list a special reverse charge toll number. An example is the area code 800 number on which charges are automatically billed to the called party without any oral acceptance of charges being required. Newspaper and television advertising frequently carries an 800 number to call for further information, and hotels and motels often use this listing nationally. The listing looks like this.

SHERATON HOTELS & MOTOR INNS—
Reservation Office StLouisMo
No Charge To Calling Party 800 325-3535

Another way to attract business is to maintain a number in the city in which the directory is printed. From this number the call will be switched to the out-of-town subscriber's location. (The subscriber pays for the call.) Such a listing looks like this:

SAFECO INSURANCE CO OF AMERICA—
Claims 175 GreatNeckRd
GrtNk------**NYC Tel No—895-7447**
Marketing 666 KindermackRd
RiverEdgeNJ---**NYC Tel No—524-2244**

Some companies also list their out-of-town numbers in the hope that they will promote business even if the caller has to pay for the call. An example of this listing is given below:

South-Western Publshng Co
925 SpringRd Pelhm----**914 738-3600**

Local Calls

The procedure in placing calls varies with the kind of telephone equipment in use. If the desk telephone is a direct outside line, give the number to the telephone operator or dial it. If the line goes through the office switchboard, you either dial 9 for an outside line or ask the PBX attendant for a line by saying, "Outside, please." When you get a dial tone, you dial the number.

You will regularly be making two kinds of local calls—reaching someone with whom your employer will talk and placing your own calls. In the first case, after getting the number desired, ask for the person wanted and immediately identify your employer as the caller, saying something like:

Mr. Norman, please. Ms. Allen, of Allen and Lovell, calling.

To avoid making the person wait on the line, always determine if the executive is ready to take the call before placing it. If the answering operator or secretary asks you to put your employer on the line first, be gracious and follow the request. The person who must waste a few seconds waiting for the other to respond should be the one who originated the call.

In making your own calls, you will find it advisable to jot down what you want to say before you get the person on the line. This will help to avoid the embarrassment of having to call back for a point forgotten. You will speak with more confidence and effectiveness, and you will make a better impression by knowing in advance what you are going to say.

Introduce yourself properly. Upon being connected, give your own name, and, if desirable, your firm name. For example, "This is Susan Baer, of Allen and Lovell, Ms. Allen's secretary." Making a good impression on people whom you telephone is just as important as making a good impression on those who call at your office.

Message Units

Within some metropolitan areas, calls between widely separated locations are not considered local calls or long-distance calls but are individually charged as message unit calls.

A *message unit* is a telephone term describing a standard base rate used in determining the cost of a call. The table of rates in the front of the directory shows the *number* of message units chargeable between telephone exchanges and the length of the overtime period that is charged as a message unit. For instance, from Manhattan Zone 3 to Westchester Zone 7 is four message units (four times the base rate of 8.2 cents) or 33 cents. Message units are automatically charged and billed in total—not itemized.

Long-Distance Calls

Every time you pick up your phone, you enter a hundred-billion-dollar network that connects nearly 200 million telephones in North America. Every day this network performs over a billion switching operations. The telephone network is truly a giant. Local or long-distance calls can be made to all telephones in a domestic system, as well as to most other countries and territories throughout the world.

Types of Long-Distance Calls. There are two general types of long-distance calls—*station-to-station* and *person-to-person*. The secretary is expected to know the relative costs, the recommended and permissible practices, and the situations in which to use each type.

Station-to-Station. Because of the time and money saved through direct distance dialing on *station-to-station* calls, businesses will probably tend to use this type of service more and more except in cases where there is a question of whether a specific person can be located readily.

The procedure for dialing a distant telephone number is as follows. You should dial station-to-station when you are willing to talk with anyone who answers the call or when you are reasonably sure the person wanted is within reach of the telephone. Charges begin at the time the called telephone or switchboard is answered, even if the person wanted is not available. No charge is made if no one answers at the number called.

Sometimes valuable minutes are wasted by the efforts of the answering attendant to locate the person wanted. If you are trying to reach Mrs. Katz, registered at a hotel, the hotel operator may have to page her in the lobby and the hotel restaurants. If the operator is unsuccessful in finding her, the call is still fully chargeable.

Person-to-Person. A person-to-person call is made when you must talk to a particular person or extension telephone. Charges begin when the called person or extension answers. The procedure for dialing a person-to-person call is given below.

Placing Long-Distance Calls. Long-distance calls may be made by direct distance dialing or through the long-distance operator. In either case, if the call is answered by someone other than the person for whom it is intended, say immediately that this is a long-distance call so that time and money are not wasted.

Direct Distance Dialing (DDD). Station-to-station long-distance calls are dialed direct, without assistance from the operator except in case of difficulty. Usually you dial 1 plus a three-digit *area code,* then the telephone number desired, except when you are dialing a number with your own area code.

Specific directions for DDD may be found in the front section of the telephone directory. The general procedures to be followed are described in the next two paragraphs.

Obtain the area code from the company letterhead (where it is often included with the address), your personal telephone directory, the front of the telephone directory, or the operator. If you have the area code but do not know the telephone number of the person to be called, dial the prefix 1 (where necessary), the area code, and the number 555-1212. After you identify to the directory assistance operator the city and individual or business you wish to call, you are given the number. If there is even a remote possibility of future calls, record both the area code and the telephone number in your personal directory.

Dial the number carefully; but if you reach the wrong number on any DDD call, obtain the name of the city you have reached and promptly report this information to the operator to avoid all charges for the call. If you are cut off before completing a call, inform the operator so that the charges can be adjusted. Sometimes you get a recorded message telling you that your call has not been completed and asking you to initiate it again. If it is evident that for some reason your call is not going through, dial the operator for help.

Operator Assisted Calls. If you know the area code and telephone number to be called but you wish to call person-to-person, collect, on a credit card, or wish the call to be charged to another number, you need only routine operator assistance. Follow this procedure:

1. Dial 0 (zero), the area code, and the telephone number.
2. When the operator answers, for a

   Person-to-person call, give the name of the person you are calling.

   Collect call, say, "Collect" and give your name.

   Credit card call, say, "Credit card call" and give your credit card number.

   Call charged to another number, say, "Bill to" and give the area code and telephone number to which the call is to be billed.

If you require special assistance, dial 0, state your problem, and give the operator whatever information you have. One secretary had to call an official in Washington, D.C., at two o'clock for an employer who expected to be in the local courthouse near another telephone at that time. The secretary explained the situation to the operator, who placed the call at two o'clock to the courthouse telephone but charged the call to the employer's office telephone. Another secretary was asked to get in touch with A. J. Dearing, who was staying at a Pittsburgh hotel. The secretary told the long-distance operator that the only clue to Dearing's whereabouts was that lodging would be at one of the better hotels. The operator checked the hotels until Dearing was located. The secretary need not hesitate to ask for this kind of service.

Time Zones. Time zones are very important to the secretary in placing long-distance calls. A New York office would not call San Francisco before 12 noon because there would be little likelihood of reaching anyone in the San Francisco office before 9 a.m. Conversely, a secretary in Los Angeles, California,

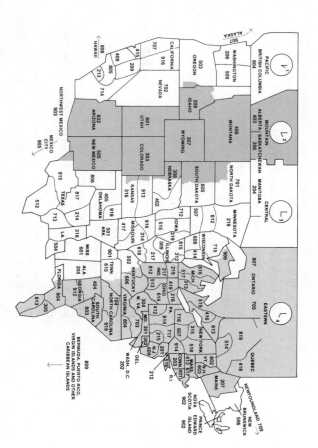

Illus. 12-6 This map shows telephone areas, area codes and time zones (Standard Time) in the continental United States and Canada.

would not place a call for Boston, Massachusetts, after 2 p.m., for very likely the office in Boston would be closed around 5 p.m. The secretary who places overseas calls should learn the time differences for the cities called.

The map that appears on page 284 indicates time zones in the continental United States and adjacent Canadian provinces so that the person placing a long-distance call can plan the call to coincide with the business day in the place called. The time zone map shows the area code to be used with the desired long-distance number. The time at the place where the call originates determines whether day, evening, or night rates apply.

Relative Costs. A study of the table in Illus. 12-7 shows that calls dialed directly are much cheaper than person-to-person calls and that having the

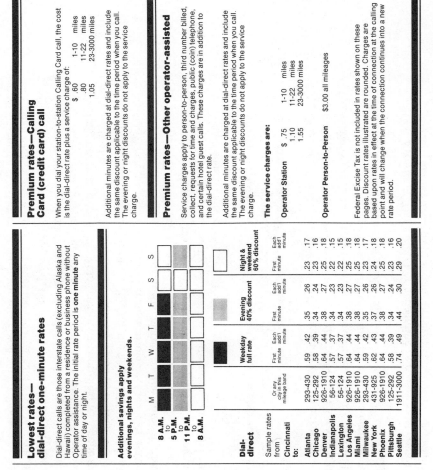

Lowest rates—dial-direct one-minute rates

Dial-direct calls are those interstate calls (excluding Alaska and Hawaii) completed from a residence or business phone without Operator assistance. The initial rate period is **one minute** any time of day or night.

Additional savings apply evenings, nights and weekends.

		M	T	W	T	F	S	S
8 A.M. to 5 P.M.		■	■	■	■	■	□	□
5 P.M. to 11 P.M.		▨	▨	▨	▨	▨	▨	□
11 P.M. to 8 A.M.		□	□	□	□	□	□	□

		Weekday full rate		Evening 40% discount		Night & weekend 60% discount	
Dial-direct Sample rates from Cincinnati to:	Or any city in this mileage band	First minute	Each add'l minute	First minute	Each add'l minute	First minute	Each add'l minute
Atlanta	293-430	.59	.42	.35	.26	.23	.17
Chicago	125-292	.58	.39	.34	.24	.23	.16
Denver	926-1910	.64	.44	.38	.27	.25	.18
Indianapolis	56-124	.57	.37	.34	.23	.22	.15
Lexington	56-124	.57	.37	.34	.23	.22	.15
Los Angeles	926-1910	.64	.44	.38	.27	.25	.18
Miami	926-1910	.64	.44	.38	.27	.25	.18
Milwaukee	293-430	.59	.42	.35	.26	.23	.17
New York	431-925	.62	.43	.37	.26	.24	.18
Phoenix	926-1910	.64	.44	.38	.27	.25	.18
Pittsburgh	125-292	.58	.39	.34	.24	.23	.16
Seattle	1911-3000	.74	.49	.44	.30	.29	.20

Premium rates—Calling Card (credit card) call

When you dial your station-to-station Calling Card call, the cost is the dial-direct rate plus a service charge of:

	$ .60	1-10	miles
	.80	11-22	miles
	1.05	23-3000	miles

Additional minutes are charged at dial-direct rates and include the same discount applicable to the time period when you call. The evening or night discounts do not apply to the service charge.

Premium rates—Other operator-assisted

Service charges apply to person-to-person, third number billed, collect, requests for time and charges, public (coin) telephone, and certain hotel guest calls. These charges are in addition to the dial-direct rate.

Additional minutes are charged at dial-direct rates and include the same discount applicable to the time period when you call. The evening or night discounts do not apply to the service charge.

The service charges are:

Operator Station	$ .75	1-10	miles
	1.10	11-22	miles
	1.55	23-3000	miles
Operator Person-to-Person	$3.00 all mileages		

Federal Excise Tax is not included in rates shown on these pages. Discount rates illustrated are rounded. Charges are based upon rates in effect at the time of connection at the calling point and will change when the connection continues into a new rate period.

Cincinnati Bell Inc.

Illus. 12-7

A table of long-distance rates to many cities is given in the front of every telephone directory.

number at hand and dialing the number yourself save a great deal of money. It also indicates that calling at night or on weekends is cheaper than calling during the business day.

Knowing relative costs of the different services enables the customer to use the telephone economically. For example, if an executive wanted to report a safe arrival in Cincinnati to the family in Seattle, a one-minute call could be made after 11 p.m. for 29 cents.

A table of long-distance rates to many cities is given in the front of every telephone directory. Rates to places not listed are obtainable from the long-distance operator.

You must often decide whether to use person-to-person or station-to-station service. You can arrive at the better choice only by considering every factor, including cost and whereabouts of the person called. If you were asked to reach a salesperson at the home office, you would choose a person-to-person call because the nature of a sales job requires field work, not office work, most of the time. On the other hand, the manager of a branch office is in the office most of the time and is usually available for a station-to-station call.

Several add-on features are available that relate to controlling costs of long-distance telephoning. Some computer controlled telephone systems automatically select the least expensive line for a call. If the least costly outside line is busy, the caller can be put in line for the first available line and then hang up. When the least costly line becomes available, the caller is rung back and the called number is automatically placed by the computerized telephone system. Thus, the caller gains a considerable amount of time lost to redialing a number. Other telephones automatically give priority to long-distance lines to the caller holding the highest rank so that valuable executive time spent on long-distance calls is reduced.

Paying for Long Distance. The secretary may be responsible for accepting long-distance charges, accounting for them, reversing them, or obtaining for the executive a credit card on which to charge calls.

Obtaining Charges on Toll Calls. Charges for long-distance calls are referred to as *toll charges.* If you need to know the cost of a call, request the operator *at the time the call is placed* to report the charges. The operator will then notify you after the call has been completed and the cost has been calculated. This service is not available on DDD calls.

Cost Records of Toll Calls. For accounting purposes most companies charge toll calls in their records to specific departments, clients, or jobs. With memorandum records kept at the secretary's desk showing the date, point called, and the person calling, the correct toll charges can be checked against the bill and charged to the proper departments. Modern equipment makes this allocation automatically.

The federal government levies on long-distance calls an excise tax which the telephone company collects from the subscriber. The tax rates are shown on the customer's bill. If the secretary is required to keep a cost record of each long-distance call for accounting purposes, the tax must be computed and added to the toll charge.

Collect Calls. A long-distance call (toll call) can be made *collect.* Charges on person-to-person and station-to-station calls can be reversed—that is, charged to the number called rather than to the one placing the call. The request to reverse the charges, however, must be made at the time of placing the call so that the person called can have an opportunity to accept or refuse the charge. Because collect calls are operator assisted, they are more expensive than direct-dialed calls.

Telephone Credit Cards. Executives who make a great many telephone calls away from the office may carry telephone credit cards on which they can charge these calls to their companies. These cards show a code number to be used when initiating a call through the operator. They also show the holder's name and business affiliation. Credit card calls cost more than DDD calls because they involve the operator. Monthly telephone bills identify credit card calls as such.

Service Charges. Service charges are applied to person-to-person, third number bills, collect, requests for time and charges, coin-operated telephone, credit card, and certain hotel guest calls. The continental United States is divided into mileage bands. The first band covers one to ten miles, the second band covers 11 to 22 miles, and the third band covers 23 to 3,000 miles. The service charges are determined by the distance covered by the call.

Alternatives to Established Public Systems

The Bell System and other trunk regional systems have had a virtual monopoly over the telephone industry since its initial development. The industry is now, however, becoming deregulated. In 1969 MCI Communications Corporation won the approval of the Federal Communications Commission to operate as a common carrier. MCI Corporation; United States Transmission Systems (City Call), a subsidiary of International Telephone and Telegraph; Western Union (Metro I); and Southern Pacific Communications (Sprint Ltd.) are competing in the long-distance telephone market.

Using these long-distance carriers is relatively simple. Basic service involves picking up a telephone, dialing a local number to contact the carrier's computer, obtaining a dial tone, entering an authorization code to identify yourself, and finally keying in the area code plus the number being called. Some systems offer optional features, such as abbreviated dialing, automatic dialing, off-peak hours service, travel cards (telephone credit cards), and numbers that allow systems access from outside the network. All systems provide complete accounting reports, including details of all calls and summaries for expense control.

Rates are lower than regular rates charged by the Bell System. Several employees can use these alternative systems simultaneously, and a variety of discounts are available each month depending on monthly usage. These systems can be used for both voice and data transmission.

SECRETARIAL RESPONSIBILITY FOR TELEGRAMS

Frequently it is necessary in business to send an urgent but brief message. In such instances a Western Union telegram is appropriate because of (1) its low cost, (2) the documentation that a written message provides, and (3) its attention-getting advantage over either a letter or a telephone call. The secretary will be expected to handle telegrams. A telegram might be used to confirm a bid or approve a contract. A personal opinion message might be sent to an elected state or national official to register a view on any issue if the telegram includes a signature and address.

There are two classes of telegrams, the regular telegram and the overnight telegram. The regular *telegram* can be sent at any time, day or night, any day of the week. The minimum charge is based on 15 words exclusive of address and signature; an additional charge is made for each additional word. Messenger delivery is assured at most points within five hours, but a delivery charge is assessed. Proof of delivery, in the form of the recipient's signature which is sent to the sender, is available for an additional fee. Usually, though, delivery by telephone within two hours is assured. A written confirmation copy of the message is mailed to the sender for an additional fee.

MS MERLE KATHERMAN POSITIVELY DELIVER
5.00 DLR
DLR HOMECRAFTS INC
721 COMFORT ST
LANSING, MI 48924-4045

PLEASE SHIP OUR ORDER 4773 BY 7/14 LATEST

ACME VENDING CO

Illus. 12-8
When for some reason a telegram must be delivered by messenger, there is a charge for the service. Note the words POSITIVELY DELIVER and the delivery charge notation immediately after the addressee's name.

The minimum charge for an *overnight telegram*, which costs considerably less than a regular telegram, is based on 100 words. Delivery of the overnight telegram is assured by 2 p.m. the following day.

If there is a chance that a telegram may be undeliverable at one location, an alternate address may be specified. If the message is of substantive importance, such as an order for bonds or confirmation of a contract, the sender may purchase insurance against an error in transmission.

If the message is to be written out for your communications center or delivered to a Western Union office, use either your company's or Western Union's form. Type the form, of course. Compose a message that is clear and brief. For example, avoid the ambiguous message, "Arrive Monday on the 3:30 flight." It does not indicate whether the time is morning or afternoon, the airport, or the airline. Use active verbs, avoid unnecessary adjectives, and use numbers instead of words when possible.

If you phone in the message, it will be typed by an operator as it is recorded. Collect complete information before making the call: correct spelling of all names, correct addresses (street, city, state, ZIP Code, and telephone number), and billing information.

If your office does not have telex or TWX but the addressee's office does, you can reduce expenses by sending the message as a telegram to the recipient's teletypewriter terminal. (The Western Union operator can obtain the telex or TWX number.) Telex and TWX are discussed in Chapter 13.

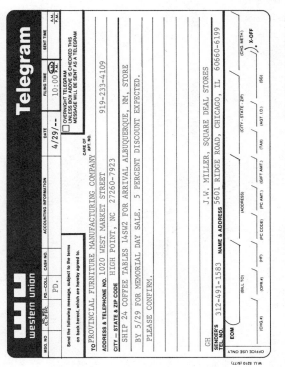

Illus. 12-9
Telegrams may be typed at your desk on plain paper or on a form provided by Western Union.

Western Union International, Inc.

Telegrams typed at your desk may be prepared either on blanks available without charge from Western Union or on plain paper. Follow these guidelines:

1. Prepare a file copy for every telegram phoned in or given to the TWX or telex operator. Whether phoned or typed, in most cases you will need a copy for the files, one for the accounting department, possibly one for your tickler file, and (if a confirmation copy is to be mailed) one for the addressee.

2. Indicate the type of service desired.

3. Include your reference initials in the lower left-hand corner.

4. Include in the address all essential information, including the telephone number, necessary in locating the recipient quickly. The address will not be charged for.

5. Omit the salutation and complimentary close.

6. To save money learn and follow Western Union practices for counting letters, words, and symbols:

   (a) Dictionary words in any language are counted as one word each, regardless of length.

   (b) Figures and nondictionary words such as *rehab, Solarbilt, scam,* or *Earthsafe* are counted at the rate of five characters to the word.

   (c) Personal names are counted according to the number of words and initials.

   (d) Punctuation marks are neither counted nor charged for regardless of where they appear in the message. Words such as *Stop* that are used instead of punctuation marks are charged as words.

   (e) Letters, figures, and symbols are counted as fewer characters if written without spaces. For example, NY is one character, but N Y or N. Y. is counted as two characters; 9a.m. is one character, but 9 a. m. is three words.

   (f) A signature may consist of *any two* of the following items: name of sender, title, name of department, or name of organization. This signature is sent without extra charge.

SUGGESTED READINGS

Greisinger, Frank. A column almost every month in *Administrative Management.*

Keeling, B. Lewis and Norman F. Kallaus. *Administrative Office Management,* 8th ed. Cincinnati: South-Western Publishing Co., 1983, Chapter 16.

Office Topics. A biweekly pamphlet sold in quantity to organizations for in-service training. Fairfield, Conn.: The Economics Press.

Telephone directory and Yellow Pages in your local community.

Traveler's Toll-Free Telephone Directory, a directory of 800-number listings updated annually. Burlington, Vt.: Landmark Publishing Co.

Your Telephone Personality. A biweekly pamphlet sold in quantity to organizations for in-service training. Fairfield, Conn.: The Economics Press.

QUESTIONS FOR DISCUSSION

1. Reword the following portions of conversations to reflect better telephone usage.

    (a) Sorry, I don't know where Miss Schwartz is. She should be at her desk. *Mrs. Schwartz is not at her desk now. May I take a message?*

    (b) We don't give that information out to the public.

    (c) You should have called the purchasing department for that information. *you need to call the purchaser, shall I, please hold &*

    (d) I don't know who handles employee insurance, but Mr. Wallenstein doesn't. *I'm not sure who handles that, please*

    (e) Miss Lombardi is in a conference with the tax consultant.

    (f) I haven't got time to look it up, Mr. Kenyon. I have to get this report ready for the committee meeting in 20 minutes.

    (g) I haven't the foggiest. I'll ask Marge to fill me in on what happened at that meeting.

    (h) Oh, I gave you the wrong information. I thought you were Professor Milligan of New State College who is writing a book on the same subject.

2. Think of business telephone calls in which you have taken part. Describe the techniques used by the other party that have pleased you and those that have annoyed you.

3. Examine your local telephone directory. What information is found in the introductory pages? in the Yellow Pages?

4. If your office is located in Philadelphia, between what office hours (yours) would you try to reach an office in Salt Lake City by long distance? If your office is in Salt Lake City, between what office hours (yours) would you try to reach a Philadelphia office?

5. Which class of long-distance service should you use in trying to reach each of the following persons?

    (a) A buyer in a department store

    (b) A lawyer who is pleading an important case

    (c) A politician who is staying in a hotel at which you made the reservation

    (d) Your employer's son who lives in a college dormitory not equipped with Centrex

    (e) The city editor of a newspaper

6. Do you think that organizations should adopt a no-personal-telephone-calls policy? Why?

7. Do you like the identification sentence, "Thank you for calling XYZ Company," or would you reserve this sentence for terminating the conversation?

PROBLEMS

1. Locate in the alphabetic section of your local telephone directory the numbers for the following. Type in tabular form a list showing for each item the organization or department wanted, the name under which the telephone is listed, and the telephone number.

   (a) City Hall
   (b) Western Union
   (c) Fire department
   (d) Park or recreation department
   (e) Police department
   (f) Post office
   (g) Public library
   (h) Your college or university
   (i) The local office of the state employment service
   (j) Telephone repair service
   (k) Weather information

2. The purpose of this problem is to familiarize you with the organization of your Yellow Pages. Type a list showing the heading in

the Yellow Pages under which you would find the names of subscribers for each of the following:

   (a) Office Supplies
   (b) Windshield Repair
   (c) Exercise Centers
   (d) Dry Cleaners

3. Type the following excerpts of conversation in acceptable form. Then use the Reference Guide to verify or correct your answers.

   (a) The opening part of a telephone conversation which occurred this Monday, shortly before noon. Mr. Lawrence Bell called Mr. Thomas Green.
   Bell—Tom, have you come to a decision yet? Green—No, I'd like a day or two more to think it over.
   Bell—Time is getting short, Tom. I have to know by Wednesday at the latest.
   Green—I'll sleep on it and let you know the first thing in the morning.

8. Search your local telephone directory for at least one of the following numbers: (a) an 800 number, (b) a local number that will switch the call to an out-of-town subscriber who pays for it, and (c) a listing of a business located in a nearby area that the caller must pay for. Why were these businesses willing to make this investment in this specialized service?

9. How much would a six-minute operator-assisted person-to-person call from Seattle to Cincinnati cost during business hours? If you cut the conversation to three minutes by careful planning and avoidance of chitchat, made the call during business hours, and used DDD station-to-station service, how much could you save?

10. Assuming that the following words come at the end of a typewritten page, indicate those words that you can correctly divide and show where you could make the divisions. Then check the Reference Guide to verify or correct your answers.

   (a) among
   (b) edited
   (c) couldn't
   (d) delicate
   (e) filling
   (f) September 20
   (g) self-starter

(b) A confidential memorandum to the president of the company, reporting on a conversation that occurred in the executive's office two weeks ago between Steve Douglas and Charlene Duncan:

This is the conversation as I recall it. Steve said I talked it over with Nelson, very confidentially of course, and he thought he could arrange a meeting before the end of this month. Charlene said do you think it was wise to expose our hand. Steve said I don't think talking it over with Nelson can be called exposing our hand. He's trustworthy. Charlene said well it's done now. What about the meeting?

4. Rewrite each of the following messages, using not more than 15 words so that the message may be sent as a regular telegram.

(a) THERE WILL BE A SALES MEETING SATURDAY MORNING IN THE OFFICE AT TEN O'CLOCK. PLEASE ARRANGE TO BE THERE. BRING REQUESTED ESTIMATES.

(b) MR. WILCOX WIRED SAYING HE WOULD BE HERE TOMORROW. IS IT POSSIBLE FOR YOU TO COME BACK? MUST KNOW BY THREE O'CLOCK.

(c) IN ANSWER YOUR TELEGRAM SUGGEST YOU OFFER A 40% DISCOUNT TERMS 2% 10 DAYS. DELIVERY TO BE MADE FOB NEW YORK.

5. Miss Mary Holmes, secretary to Harry Miller, handled the following telephone calls:

(a) Mr. Miller was attending a Kiwanis luncheon meeting at the Terrace Hotel and expected to be back at his desk at 1:30 p.m. At 12:15 a long-distance call came in from his superior, who was in Boston. Miss Holmes said, "Mr. Miller will not be back until 1:30 and cannot be reached until then."

(b) At closing time the long-distance operator had not reached a person with whom Mr. Miller must talk before the

next morning. Mr. Miller was going to dinner at his brother's home but would be at his own home until 7 p.m. Miss Holmes said, "Operator, try that number again and keep trying until 7 o'clock. Mr. Miller will be at 734-8973 in half an hour and will be there until seven."

(c) Mr. Miller was playing golf. The long-distance operator informed Miss Holmes that she had a call from Mr. Miller's New York broker, Mr. Adams, who wanted to talk to him as soon as possible. Miss Holmes said, "Mr. Miller is out of the office for the afternoon. If you will tell me where Mr. Adams can be reached, I will try to get in touch with Mr. Miller and ask him to call back immediately. I should be able to reach him within a hour."

(d) Mr. Miller was writing copy for an advertising circular and told Miss Holmes that he did not wish to be disturbed under any circumstances before four o'clock. A call came in from George Herman, his assistant, who was in Baltimore attending a sales conference. Mr. Herman was to leave Baltimore on a three o'clock plane. Miss Holmes said, "I am sorry, but Mr. Miller can't be reached this afternoon. Ask Mr. Herman if I can help him instead. I am Mr. Miller's secretary."

(e) Mr. Miller wanted to make a long-distance call from the office telephone, 623-2219, to Dr. L. K. Holthaus of New Orleans on a personal matter. Miss Holmes did not know Dr. Holthaus's number but knew that he was a noted ophthalmologist. She dialed the operator and said, "Operator, this is 623-2219. I want to call Dr. L. K. Holthaus in New Orleans. I do not have the number, but he is a well-known eye specialist. Will you give me the area code and the number, please, so that I can dial him direct."

(f) Mr. Miller wanted to call Ms. Houston in the purchasing department of the

Acme Company in White Plains, New York, area code 914. Mr. Miller wished to say that on Friday afternoon he would call on either Ms. Houston or her assistant about the new service contract. Could one of them be available for a conference? Miss Holmes made an operator-assisted call.

(g) Mr. Miller wanted to call his wife, who was visiting in Akron, Ohio. Her number was 864-0753 and the area code, 216. He said that it need not be a person-to-person call; but he wanted the call charged to his home number, 734-8973. Miss Holmes said, "Operator, this is 623-2219, Extension 62. I want to place a call to 864-0753 in Akron, Ohio. Don't charge the call to this number. It should be charged to 734-8973."

(h) Mr. Miller wanted to call Lawrence Taylor of the Lenox Supply Company in Los Angeles about the cancellation of an order. The number was 823-6501; the area code number, 213; the charges were to be reversed. Miss Holmes said, "Operator, this is 623-2219. I want to place a call to Lawrence Taylor of the Lenox Supply Company in Los Angeles. I don't know the number. Tell the switchboard operator there that Mr. Miller won't pay for the call because it is about an order he plans to cancel. Ask Mr. Taylor to pay for it."

(i) While Miss Holmes was on the button telephone, a second call came through. She excused herself and answered the second call, which was for Mr. Miller. She depressed the local button to ask Mr. Miller if he would take the call and then transferred it to his line. When she returned to the first call, she found that the caller had been disconnected.

Miss Holmes was surprised when Mr. Miller told her that he had arranged for her to take a five-hour course to improve her telephone technique. She had always thought that she was unusually proficient in this area. Criticize Miss Holmes's handling of the nine calls described above. Indicate what you would have done in the cases that were poorly handled.

Chapter **13**

Extended Telephone, Telegraph, and Other Communication Services

Chapter 13 describes the extension of traditional voice communication made possible by improved technology. It also describes how the various information-processing techniques described earlier in this textbook can be interconnected by means of the telephone and, more recently, computer and satellite networks to form information systems. These information systems can move, store, and retrieve information for either display on a screen or reproduction as hard copy. Output is in the form of *electronic mail.* Finally, the chapter analyzes how the installation of an information system affects office organization. The alert secretary will want to understand these technological and organizational changes in order to function well in the changing office environment.

THE STRUGGLE FOR CONTROL OF COMMUNICATIONS EQUIPMENT

The American Telephone & Telegraph Company had a virtual monopoly over telephone equipment until the 1968 Carterfone decision by the Federal Communications Commission. The Carterfone decision struck down the AT&T restriction against all "foreign attachments" (devices not owned by the telephone company) to the telephone system. Encouraged by this obvious motivation to competition, many companies arose to manufacture "interconnect" terminal equipment such as telephones, switchboards, and data transmission equipment.

During this period, however, users of foreign attachments were required to pay a service charge to the common carriers (telephone companies). This charge was for the installation and maintenance of a protective interface device that the telephone companies claimed was necessary to protect their equipment against damage by the attachment. In 1976 the courts removed the

295

requirement that the service charge be paid and that the interface device be required for most interconnect services.

Since 1976 the government has attempted to deregulate a number of competing federally controlled public services, including the communications industry. The common carriers, such as AT&T, are still engaging in an all-out political effort to prevent further encroachment of competing longline companies and equipment manufacturers. However, many interconnect services have emerged, more lawsuits have been instituted, and many new pieces of ancillary equipment have been attached. Obviously the battle is not over. It continues to be a fierce one that you will want to follow both as a consumer and as a business employee.

EXTENDED TELEPHONE SERVICES

In addition to basic telephone services, there are many additional telecommunication services available that directly affect the secretary. (The term *telecommunication* refers to any communication requiring the use of telephone or telegraph lines or satellite networks.)

Wide Area Telecommunications Service (WATS)

Wide Area Telecommunications Service (WATS) provides reduced rate long-distance service for subscribers with a high volume of voice or data transmission. *Inward WATS* (incoming calls) involves dialing an 800 or 1-800 toll free number as described on page 280. *Outward WATS* refers to calls made to persons outside the organization. Both types of WATS service may be purchased under either of two plans: a *flat rate* service covering the full business day (FBD) and including 240 hours of use a month or a *measured rate* service restricted to fewer hours and/or calling areas. Both inward and outward WATS can cover seven calling areas or "bands" that include the continental United States (five bands) plus Hawaii and Alaska, and Puerto Rico and the Virgin Islands. A subscriber may purchase access to all or part of these calling areas.

One type of company may need expanded long-distance service to only one or two areas, while another may need WATS service covering all seven areas. One company may want unlimited calls, while another may need only a limited number of calls and may want to restrict the length of calls.

Automatic Identification of Outward Dialing (AIOD)

Unfortunately many employees abuse the long-distance privilege. A check for a month in one company showed that 34 percent of its WATS calls were personal. *Automatic Identification of Outward Dialing (AIOD)* equipment in its simplest form enables a company to trace a dialed call back to the originating telephone station. This provides a control over unauthorized use of WATS and long-distance privileges.

Extended Area Service (EAS)

The concept of *Extended Area Service (EAS)* reflects the larger community of interest that exists in metropolitan areas. A business located in Washington, D.C., that needs "local" service to suburbs (such as Alexandria, Virginia, and Silver Springs, Maryland) could purchase reduced rate EAS at a flat monthly fee. The extent of use of such service is shown by the fact that more than a third of the calls handled as long distance 20 years ago now go through as local calls.

Leased Lines

It is possible for a company to lease from the telephone company or from a private company telegraph and telephone lines for its exclusive use. The tie line connects the various locations of a business complex in different parts of the same city or in different cities. It provides direct voice contact between separate units of a business and also transmits data. The tie line can connect switchboards, key telephones, and regular telephones. It provides unlimited calling at a fixed monthly charge and is always reserved for the exclusive use of the subscriber.

Many organizations lease telephone channels for calling their foreign branches or other companies. Volume of calls determines whether leasing lines is cost effective or efficient.

Foreign Exchange Service (FX)

A local telephone number in a site remote from plant or company headquarters can be listed so that a call made to the listed number goes through as a local call. The New York City directory might carry the number of a firm located in New Brunswick, New Jersey, as New York City Tel. No. 987-6604 (see page 278). FX does *not* refer to international calls.

The Speakerphone

The *speakerphone* has built-in transmitter and volume control so that both sides of a conversation can be amplified. The secretary can leave the telephone, walk to the opposite side of the office, look up information in a file, and read it to the caller from this location. The caller can be heard in various parts of the room; and, vice versa, the caller can hear comments and discussions among others in the room. This equipment expands opportunities for full communication during conference calls. It is also possible to telephone lectures that may be amplified for delivery to class and conference groups.

Illus. 13-1
The
speakerphone
has a built-in
transmitter and
volume control
so that both
sides of a
conversation
can be
amplified.

Conference Calls

Because of ever increasing expense of travel and the amount of executive time required for physical participation in meetings, conference calling is becoming popular. An electronic switchboard (see page 269) has conference call capability. If your organization does not have this equipment, however, it is still possible to set up conference calls. An executive may want to get a group opinion on an idea or to announce design or price changes or a policy decision. The secretary calls the number for long distance, asks for the conference operator, and gives the locations and names of persons to be included, sometimes specifying the time the call is to be put through. Several long-distance points can be connected for a *two-way* conference call. With special-ized equipment, such as a speakerphone or a loudspeaker, several persons may listen in on a call at any one location. Even more points can be connected for a *one-way* conference call (one in which the voice of only the caller is transmit-ted).

With recent innovations in equipment, it is sometimes possible to set up conference calls without the services of the operator. Also, with the add-on feature, a caller already engaged in a two-way conversation can add a third person to the call.

Mobile Service

Mobile telephone service is available for conversations between trucks, news services, planes, trains, and many other users. Anyone can make a call to mobile equipment from any telephone, and any telephone can receive a call from mobile equipment. To place a call to a mobile telephone, either dial the number (which is listed in the telephone directory) or contact the mobile service operator. The conversation travels partway by radio and partway by telephone wire.

Overseas Telephone Service

If your company has the proper attachments for International Direct Distance Dialing (IDDD), you may now reach numbers in 74 foreign countries by dialing directly. If you know the local number (possibly from the letterhead of the company being called) and have a directory from the Bell System with key numbers for the countries being called, you can sometimes save hours in getting a number. The correct procedure follows:

1. First, dial the international access code,
2. Next, dial the country code (a two- or three-digit number),
3. Then dial the city routing code (not necessary in small cities having only one code),
4. Finally, dial the local number.

For example, to dial London, dial 011 (the international access code) + 44 (the country code) + 1 (the city routing code) + 123456 (the local number). If you are using a Touch-Tone telephone, depress the # button after dialing the number to save connecting time. After dialing an international call, allow at least 45 seconds for the call to start. Because signals indicating ringing or busy differ somewhat from those in the United States, you will want to consult your local alphabetical directory or a special pamphlet available from your telephone company to keep yourself up to date on rates and special conditions in various countries.

If your telephone equipment is not capable of handling IDDD calls, dial the operator and give the country to be called, the name of the company wanted, and the name of the person to be reached. Of course, it is essential to consider the time zone and to check with the local operator or directory for the charges and times during which the various rates apply. All metropolitan telephone directories will probably have a chart on international rates.

A world time zone map will save valuable time in deciding when to place international calls. It will also prevent mistakes in calculating the time in countries called.

INTERNATIONAL TELEGRAPH COMMUNICATIONS

Overseas telegrams are sent by underwater cables or by satellite. International messages to land stations may be sent by companies that collect and distribute international messages, such as Western Union International, Inc., RCA Global Communications, International Telephone and Telegraph Corporation, TRT Telecommunications Corporation, and FTC Communications, Inc. Marine service is also available to send messages between ships and shore by radio.

All destinations are not served by all the overseas companies. To obtain the fastest service, check a routing chart for the most direct route before filing

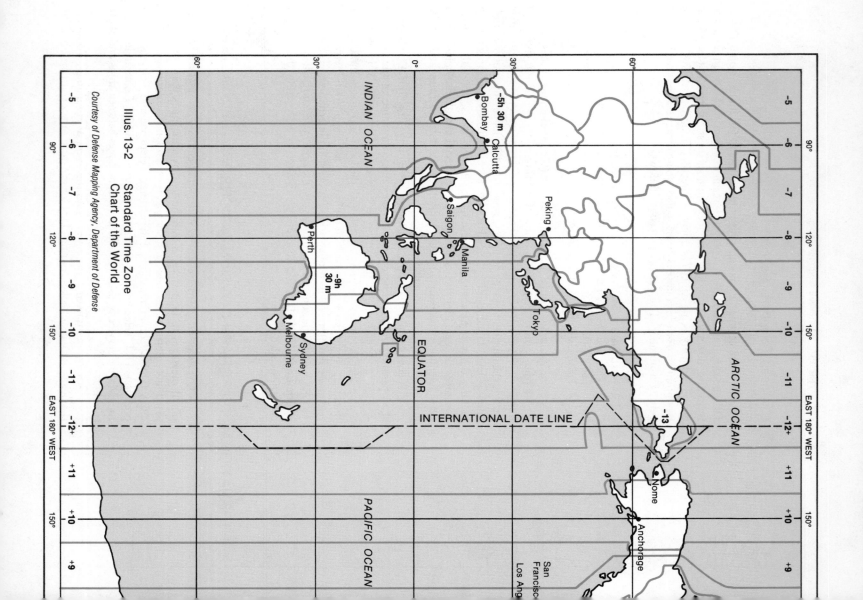

Illus. 13-2
Standard Time Zone
Chart of the World

Courtesy of Defense Mapping Agency, Department of Defense

INDIAN OCEAN

Bombay
-5h 30 m
Calcutta

Saigon

Perth

Manila

Peking

Tokyo

-9h
30 m

Melbourne
Sydney

EQUATOR

INTERNATIONAL DATE LINE

-13

ARCTIC OCEAN

Nome

San
Francisco
Los Ang

Anchorage

PACIFIC OCEAN

EAST 180° WEST

EAST 180° WEST

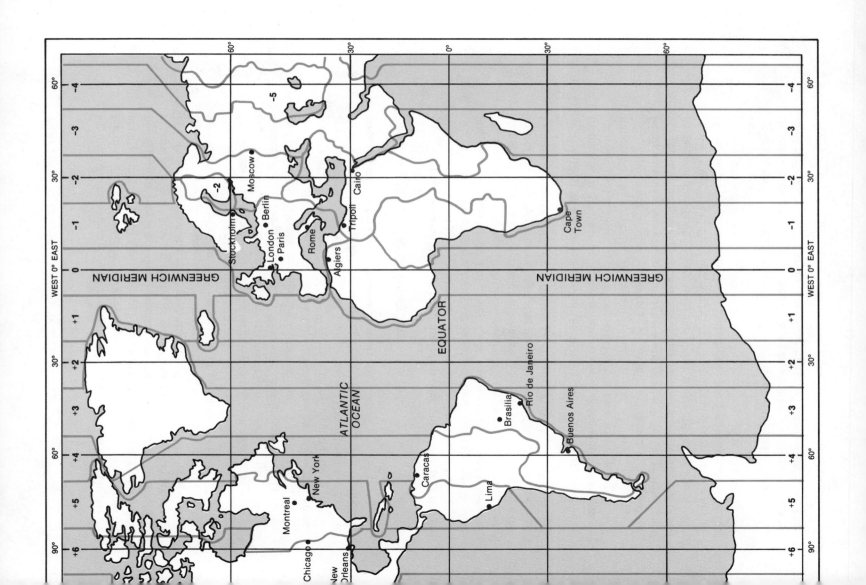

an international message with domestic Western Union. These charts are found in *The Pocket Guide to International Communications*, which may be obtained free from ITT (International Telephone and Telegraph) Communications, Inc., in New York, San Francisco, or Washington, D. C. When filing a message, if you know a preferred route, include the name of the carrier (via ITT, for example) on the message so that it will not be sent to a pool where messages are apportioned equally among carriers whether or not they represent the most direct route. The designation of carrier is not chargeable.

International messages may be sent by telex or TWX from your office, by telephone, or in person from your local Western Union office or an international office if there is one in your vicinity. Do not confuse the domestic Western Union Telegraph Co. with Western Union International. These are two completely separate and unrelated organizations.

The Federal Communications Commission has recently voted unanimously to end the monopoly of the Western Union Telegraph Co. over telegram and teleprinter service in the United States. The vote authorized the companies that now specialize in international service to begin providing domestic service between various American cities.

Classes of International Telegrams

There are two basic classes of international telegrams: *full rate* (FR) and *letter telegrams* (LT). These services are summarized in Illus. 13-3.

Because one code word may mean several plain language words, code language is frequently used in cables. Code words are composed entirely of letters. They may be real or artificial words, but they must not contain more than five letters. In an international message the use of code words lowers the cost of the message. For example, the one code word **KALOP** may be used to cover the statements: We authorize you to act for us. Will confirm this by mail.

A.B.C., Acme, Bentley's, and the Western Union codes are used most frequently. If you decide to use a private code, check with the telegraph company used in order to determine whether this code will be acceptable in the country to which the cablegram is sent.

Cipher words, used for secrecy, are usually composed of figures or of letters exceeding five per group. Cipher words do not fulfill the requirements of code or plain language. In a message that contains a combination of code, cipher, and plain language, the code and cipher words are charged at the rate of five characters to the word, while plain language is charged at the rate of fifteen letters to the word. Codes and ciphers are permissible only in the address and signature of a letter telegram but may be used in all parts of full rate messages.

Except for the destination country, each word in the name, address, and signature is counted as a chargeable word in a cablegram; therefore, a one-word cable address saves words in both incoming and outgoing messages. That is why one-word cable addresses are often printed on a company's letterhead. For a small annual charge a cable address may be registered at any telegraph office. It cannot duplicate another already on file.

	FULL RATE (FR)	LETTER TELEGRAM (LT)
Indicator Preceding Address	No indicator necessary	LT
Charge for Indicator	—	LT chargeable as 1 word; position immediately preceding the address
Precedence of Transmission	Takes precedence over all other messages	Delivery at destination next morning
Language	Plain language, secret (cipher or code), or a combination	Plain language, but code may be used in address and signature
Word Length	Plain language: 15 letters to a word Cipher or code language: 5 characters to a word	15 letters to a word
Minimum Number of Words	5	22
Relationship of Rates	Based on distance message is sent	One half of full rate

Illus. 13-3 A comparison of international full rate (FR) and letter telegrams (LT)

Frequently a firm in this country and its foreign correspondent will register an identical cable address and restrict its use to the exclusive exchange of messages between themselves. This procedure, known as a reversible address, eliminates the need for a signature on messages, thus saving the cost of one word.

Other International Services

As a secretary you will probably be concerned mostly with international telegrams. You should, however, know that your organization may also have international leased wires for telephoning and international telex for written message transmittal. These services will be performed by special attendants with whom you will work in sending messages.

Improved technology allows equipment used for message transmittal to serve different functions. During business hours this equipment can be used to transact regular international business, and during off hours it is used to transmit large volumes of data.

HOW TO PREPARE AN INTERNATIONAL TELEGRAM

	Type your city and state.
ATLANTA GA	
FR	Type FR (full rate, for immediate delivery) or LT (lower rate service, for next day delivery; not available to every country).
	Type the registered cable address or the addressee's name and address.
SMITHCO or SMITH COMPANY	
14 BAYSWATER ROAD	
LONDON (ENGLAND)	Type the overseas city and country. Enclose the country name in parentheses.
TEXT OF YOUR MESSAGE	Type the text of your message in caps.
NNNN	Type NNNN to indicate the end of your overseas message.

Note: In an international telegram, the following symbols must be transmitted in an equivalent form as illustrated.

In Place of:	Type:
Dollar Sign ($)	DOLLAR, DLRS, DOLS or DLS
Cent Sign (¢)	CENTS
Number Sign (#)	NUMBER or POUNDS
Ampersand (&)	AND
Percent Sign (%)	0/0 or PERCENT
Fractions (½)	Numbers with a slash (1/2)
Quotation Marks (")	Two apostrophe signs (''), or UNQUOTE
Semicolon (;)	SEMICOLON
@ Sign	AT
Roman Numerals	4, FOUR, or ROMAN 4
Lower case Letters	UPPER CASE LETTERS

Illus. 13-4
The preparation of an international telegram

ELECTRONIC MAIL AND VOICE MAIL

Communication that is sent electronically over telephone or telegraph lines or that is relayed by a satellite network is called electronic mail. The following forms of electronic mail will be described in this section: TWX and telex, mailgrams, facsimiles, communicating word processors, and data transmitters. In its simplest form, voice mail can be as basic as a telephone answering machine. Advanced voice mail systems use digital recordings, translating spoken messages into sets of numbers that the machine remembers. Digital memory allows more information to be stored in less space. All secretaries will not send or receive all such messages but will want the background to understand the technological developments. Others will find themselves provided with such extended services and will want to handle them capably.

Teletypewriter Messages

The *teletypewriter* combines the immediacy of the telephone with the documentation and accuracy of the letter. The teletypewriter can send and receive messages from another terminal. It is a relatively inexpensive means of providing fast communication in writing, 24 hours a day, 7 days a week.

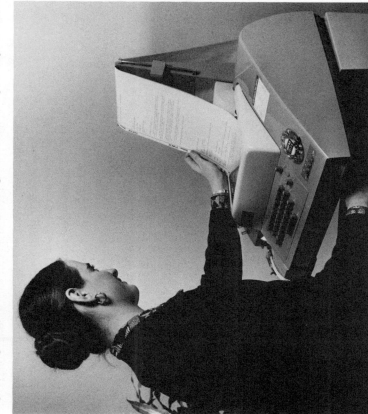

Courtesy of Western Union

Illus. 13-5
The teletypewriter combines the immediacy of the telephone with the documentation and accuracy of the letter.

There are two teletypewriter networks, *telex* and *TWX* (both owned by Western Union), that can be interconnected. These systems vary only slightly in how they work and in what they can do.

In addition to telex and TWX (pronounced *twix*) many large corporations also have their own teletypewriter systems for communicating with their foreign and domestic branches. These systems can be used to back up oral decisions, to secure a written record of a two-way "conversation," and to remind the recipient of an agreed upon action to be taken.

The teletypewriter is useful when an office in another time zone is closed, since a message can be received in the closed office and be acted upon the first thing the following morning. The teletypewriter has many uses: for a one-way call when no immediate response is needed, for requesting or providing information that will require a delayed answer, for communicating statistical information that must be accurately recorded in written form, or for notifying the recipient of an imminent telephone call involving an important matter. The teletypewriter is frequently used instead of letters, telegrams, and long-distance telephone calls.

Subscribers of telex and TWX are provided with a teletypewriter for their office use. If a message is to be sent from your organization's message center, type it on your company's forms for this purpose. By dialing a special code, you or an attendant can send messages on the teletypewriter. You or the message center attendant will get an automatic identification assuring you that you have reached the person wanted. The automatic identification may be repeated at the end of the transmission, confirming that the message has been received. In the actual sending process messages are punched on a paper tape

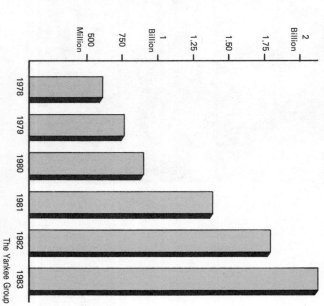

Illus. 13-6
The number of companies sending messages by electronic mail will continue to increase.

that can be corrected before transmission. Paper tapes should be retained for at least one business day in case the message must be re-sent because the transmitting lines were unavailable.

Teletypewriters are also used in sending mailgrams, telegrams, and cablegrams. Special applications are possible for an organization that frequently sends mailgrams to the same list of people. The addresses can be fed to the sending equipment from an address tape to be merged with the tape containing the message. An address list can be stored in Western Union's InfoMaster computer system from which it can be readily called into use. The InfoMaster can also be programmed for the type of delivery to be used for each message—telex-TWX, mailgram, domestic or international telegram.

Mailgrams

The mailgram, which was introduced in 1970, is a very popular service. It combines Western Union and post office services. Mailgram messages are sent over Western Union's computerized communications networks directly to the post office near the recipient's address. Any message that is directed to Western Union's computer is transmitted to a teletypewriter located at the post office nearest the receiver. The messages are typed on continuous rolls of paper. They are then torn off and inserted into distinctive blue-and-white

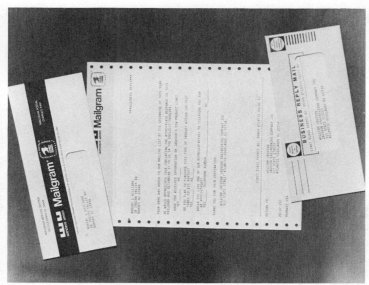

Western Union

Illus. 13-7
A business reply mailgram

envelopes for delivery the next business day by regular postal carriers. To receive mailgrams even earlier than the first delivery, some organizations rent post office boxes into which the messages are deposited as received.

Mailgrams offer several advantages over other forms of communication. They engender a sense of urgency and importance by their special envelopes and telegram format. They receive post office priority. When received, they are usually opened before the other mail. They are relatively low in cost. In 1981 the cost of a phone originated mailgram was $3.20 for the first 50 words.

Mailgrams may be sent to several people at different addresses simultaneously. For example, politicians use them widely to influence voters. They can be used to invite people to a function or to cancel one. They are often used in promoting sales. It is possible to detach a reply form at the bottom of a mailgram message, fill it in, and fold it into a business reply envelope to be mailed back to the sender postage free. In filing a mailgram, follow the instructions for preparing a telegram (see page 290).

Facsimiles

Facsimiles (exact copies of documents) can best be described as remote output copiers. They are virtually immune to errors. Equipment for facsimile transmission is connected with regular telephone circuits. Messages may be sent across town or thousands of miles. The most popular facsimile machine is the QWIP.

To send a facsimile message, place the copy to be sent in a sender or transceiver device that is identical with the equipment at the receiving location. (A *transceiver* is an instrument that can both send and receive messages.) To alert the recipient, dial the number to which the message is being sent. Place your telephone receiver in the coupler cradle and press the send button. (The coupler cradle is the resting place for the receiver that connects the two offices.)

To receive a document, place the handset (receiver) in the coupler cradle as soon as you receive the alert. Press the receive button. If you want to discuss the document that you have received, remove the handset from the receiving cradle and begin to talk.

A facsimile is chosen when only one copy of a typewritten page, chart, map, photo, or almost any other type of image is urgently required. Facsimile copy often does not reproduce clearly on office copiers, an important consideration with handwritten messages or statistical information.

A disadvantage of facsimiles has been the incompatibility of different manufacturers' equipment. Originally facsimiles could be transmitted from one point to another only via identical machines. New switched network services, made possible by powerful computer based systems, make previously incompatible facsimile machines capable of transmitting messages between different equipment and between more than two points.

Another disadvantage of facsimiles has been their high cost, since slow transmission time made the necessary telephone use expensive. Advanced

3M Company, Business Communication Products Division

Illus. 13-8
Facsimile
messages are
virtually immune
from errors and
can be sent
across town or
thousands of
miles.

technology now makes two- or three-minute transmission of a page possible, certainly an improvement over the six minutes or more often required with the early equipment. The computer equipment also includes store-and-forward capability. Messages can be retained and filed in the computer and recalled when wanted. These technological advances have made facsimile transmission a popular medium for utilizing electronic mail, with approximately 6.5 million messages a year estimated for 1983.

For best results in sending facsimile messages, clearly legible material is a must. Typewritten material generally transmits well as does handwritten material in black ballpoint pen or heavy pencil. Do not use facsimile messages for lengthy documents unless the cost involved is justified by urgency. Costs can be reduced by taking advantage of reduced night telephone rates. Be sure the office you are sending to has compatible equipment. Your company directory, telephone operator, or person in charge of communications can tell you this if you are sending an in-company message. A directory of organizations with facsimile equipment is planned.

Communicating Text Editors and Data Transmitters

Originally numerical data were sent from one location to another via attachments to touch telephones similar to those described for facsimile transmission. The most commonly used equipment was Data-phone or DataSpeed. The operator set up the machine by inserting the data to be sent, dialed the person to receive the message, and transmitted. Similarly, communicating text editors were linked via telephone lines; and sending and receiving text material were performed manually under operator control and supervision. These original methods are still used in many organizations.

Now it is possible to send both numerical and text material over the same machines. Because of lower night telephone rates, data are often sent at night for use the following business day, thus freeing the equipment for sending other electronic mail during the business day. The difficulty, though, is still compatibility of machines, a problem that is slowly being solved but is far from being completely eliminated. If machines are compatible, equipment from different manufacturers or different models from the same manufacturer can be connected. With compatible equipment, it is possible to use the same equipment for different functions.

Voice Mail

Voice mail is a store-and-forward system that combines three elements of communications equipment: the telephone, the computer, and the recording machine. It reduces the necessity of calling several times to reach people by telephone. The executive can record one-way telephone messages when free to record them, and they can be delivered when the person called is available to hear them. Voice mail is made possible by equipment attached to both a sending and a receiving telephone. Access into a voice mail system is gained by entering a code on the telephone. A recording then tells the user to dial the message and at the end of the message to dial the voice mail address of the recipient, which was supplied when the equipment was installed. The message is then converted to digital data, and the system will attempt to deliver it immediately. Failing this, the message is filed in the computer memory. Later, when the recipient dials into the system to obtain messages, the caller's voice is reconstructed.

ADVANCED COMMUNICATION NETWORKS

Developments in the field of electronics are evolving new and more efficient ways of circulating business information. When automation was introduced, the equipment performed only one function. The telephone transmitted only the voice. The computer processed only digital (numeric) data that was available at the source only. The correspondence secretary typed dictated items for executives in an immediate area, and the transcripts were sent by conventional means to another location. Reprographics equipment served only to reproduce information at one point.

Largely because of breakthroughs in communication equipment, the capabilities of formerly one-function machines have been merged. Messages can be composed, edited, transmitted, distributed, and filed in a fraction of the time it takes to send a business letter or even complete a typical telephone conversation. Mail can be picked up electronically from the equipment in which it is stored at the convenience of the recipient. It is possible not only to transmit voice, digital data, image, and text material to one or several locations electronically but to merge all four kinds of information at one receiving point.

Messages may appear on a VDT for reading, be stored in a computer's memory for later recall, or be printed out as hard copy. With appropriate sending equipment, all forms of information (handwritten or typed messages, processed/unprocessed data, charts, or voice messages) can be transmitted from point of origin to any distant point or points equipped with appropriate receiving equipment.

Although electronic mail can flash through the telecommunications chain in seconds, it could travel much faster if telephone lines were not involved. Satellites are beginning to replace the telephone for transmission of electronic mail. (A *satellite* is a man-made device launched from the earth into orbit around a planet or the sun.) Not only is satellite transmission faster, it is also less expensive for sending numeric, voice, video, and text between points if they are at least 700 miles apart. It is estimated that transmitting messages by satellite rather than telephone reduces costs by 40 percent.

Large organizations are the customers for satellite networks. Transceivers are placed in the customer's location where messages are originated. They are then beamed to a substation that transmits them to a satellite. At their destination they are again received by a substation and transmitted to a transceiver, where they are interfaced with equipment there and finally arrive at the user's terminal.

One of the first and largest satellite networks is Satellite Business Systems (SBS), which is jointly owned by International Business Machines, Comsat, and Aetna Life and Casualty Company. Other business equipment giants are joining this rapidly growing field.

THE POSTAL SERVICE AND ELECTRONIC MAIL

In 1982 the Postal Service's Electronic Computer-Originated Mail (E-COM) started. Users make an advance deposit and pay an annual fee. The E-COM system allows mailers to send three kinds of electronic messages: single-address messages (SAMs), common text messages for different addresses (COTs), and text-insert messages for different addresses (TIMs). A common carrier transmits the messages to specially equipped serving post offices (SPOs) in the addressee's localities. After receiving the electronic messages at an SPO, the postal service processes and prints the messages, inserts the copy into envelopes, and deposits the printout as First Class Mail.

MULTIFUNCTIONAL INFORMATION SYSTEMS

More and more data are being fed into computers that comprise the basis of *information systems*. Data can be inputted, processed, stored, retrieved, and outputted through use of the computer. The secretary can extract information from thousands of data processing records, merge it into word processing documents, communicate the information to other systems in the same building or around the world, print the information on high quality printers, or make a convenience copy. Illus. 13-9 shows a total information system built around IBM's 6670 Information Distributor.

As we enter the era of the automated and integrated office, we find intelligent copiers, such as the IBM 6670, taking on the new role of multifunction information coordinator and computer output device. The intelligent copier accepts input from one or more sources (text editor, computer, OCR unit, or magnetic media) and provides a variety of hard copy. Intelligent copiers utilize programming logic to perform many tasks (line justification, page numbering, etc.) on cue from a simple command. Though expensive, their speed, special features, programmability, and communications capabilities via telecommunication lines make intelligent copiers cost effective in the long run. Intelligent copiers have the potential to replace text editors, EDP printers, electronic mail, phototypesetters, duplicators, ordinary copiers, and addressing and labeling machines.

Management of Information Systems

As office work becomes more centered on information systems, controversy emerges among the various technicians now responsible for the functioning of the various components as to which group will be in charge of the total system. Since data processing arrived on the scene first, the computer group wants to take over. These managers believe that word processing is just an extension of their function. Word processors think that their activities are unique and not understood by data processing personnel and that they should be in charge. Those in reprographics and telecommunications believe that they should be chosen. The office management magazines, seminars, and training programs are all addressing this problem.

A consensus seems to be emerging that a generalist who understands the overall needs should be the information manager, supervising and coordinating the activities of the specialist technicians responsible for each of the functions. Of course, someone who was once a technician responsible for only one area might become this generalist, but the trend is toward hiring business administration graduates who understand communications, know how to use shared resources, and can fully utilize the various software programs.

The Secretary and Information Systems

For the most part the preceding discussion provides a look into the future. But tomorrow is now! Assuming, however, that you are in or will enter

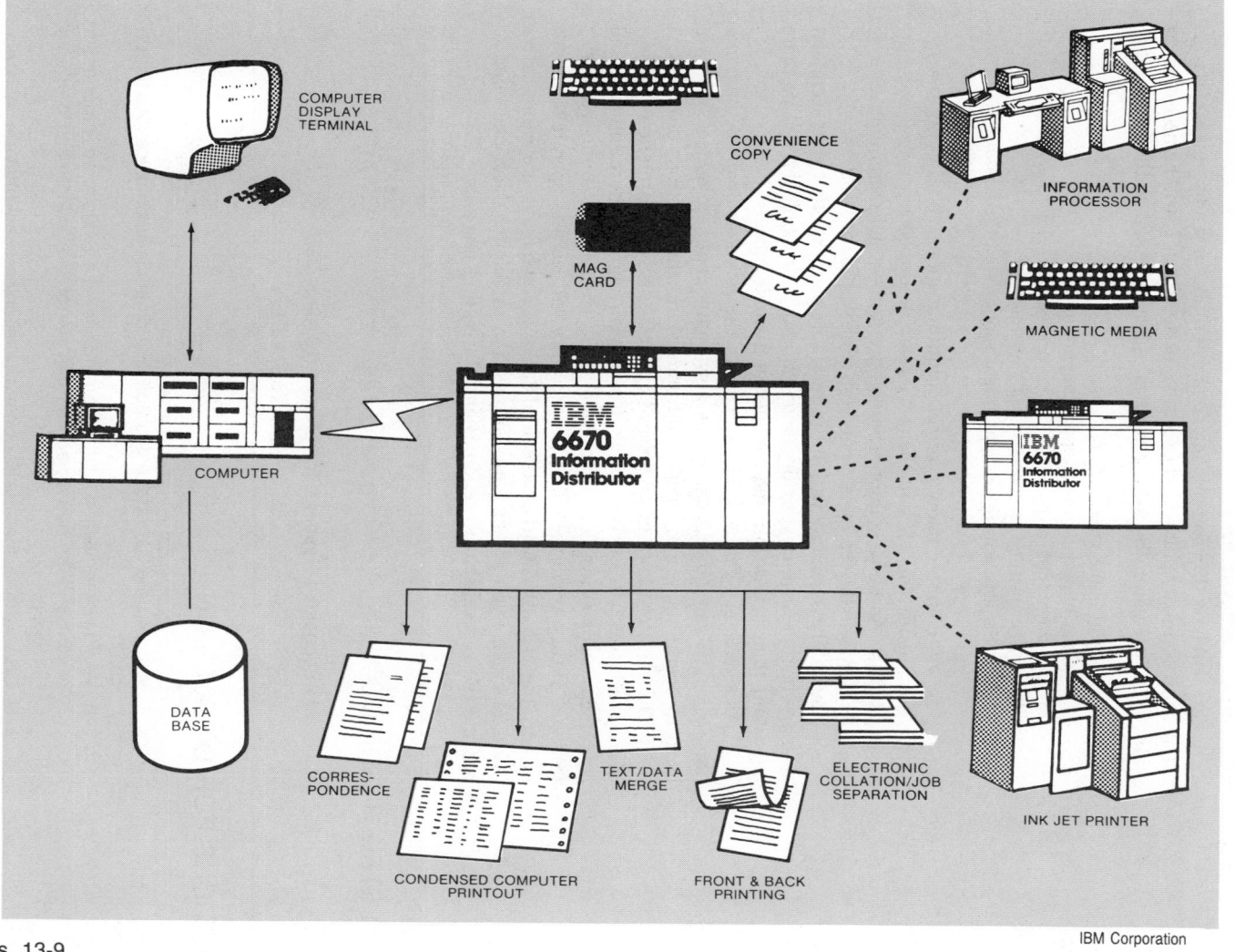

IBM Corporation

Illus. 13-9
Intelligent copiers are taking on the new role of multifunction information coordinator and computer output device.

a more or less traditional office, what does this chapter mean to you in performing your day-to-day duties?

You will have decision-making responsibilities for sending messages consistent with company policy and executive preferences. It will be necessary to evaluate each situation by asking yourself questions such as the following:

- How urgent is the message?
- Is a special impact on the recipient important?
- Are documentation or reference copies needed?
- Can another method save costly staff overtime?
- What is the least expensive, appropriate way to send the message?

You will compose many types of communications. In addition to originating documents, you will edit them. You will need to sharpen your communication skills. As more communications are sent via telecommunication or satellite, they should represent your best efforts at clarity and brevity.

You will be in contact with more and more people so that your secretarial image in representing your organization and your employer will be more important than it is within the confines of a single office.

As a secretary you will utilize many of the components of the information system. Your job will change as new components are added. You will learn to operate new components and understand the functions of others.

The wave of the future is toward executive use of information systems. More executives will work at home or while traveling as more sophisticated equipment becomes available. They will input their material to the secretary's terminal. If they are in the office, the secretary will learn to operate terminals on both the executive and the secretarial desks. If you have your eye on a career in management, you are in a unique position to acquire the background to become the generalist who becomes an information manager.

SUGGESTED READINGS

See Suggested Readings for Chapter 12, page 290.

QUESTIONS FOR DISCUSSION

1. Why was the Carterfone decision a landmark in communications legislation?
2. Why is deregulation of the communications industry so important to business? Why has it been so difficult for the government to achieve deregulation?
3. Do you think that the telephone companies should have a monopoly over communications equipment or do you favor free competition?

4. When should you choose a teletypewriter message over a telephone message? Why?

5. How can a company cut down on unauthorized long-distance telephone calls with special equipment? without special equipment? If the services are already paid for, should an employee hesitate to make an unauthorized long-distance call?

6. Under what circumstances would an organization subscribe to outward WATS? inward WATS?

7. Name a situation in which an organization would choose EAS leased lines, FX service.

8. Give three examples of ways in which the computer has contributed to improvement in telecommunications.

9. If you work for an international company, name a situation in which you would communicate with an overseas office by IDDD telephoning, by international telex, and by international telegram. How would you reduce costs of data transmission?

10. Why is it unlikely that technicians will control information systems? How could a technician qualify for a management position?

11. Capitalize the appropriate words in the following sentences. Then use the Reference Guide to verify or check your answers.

(a) Our high school provides the senior class with a free booklet on how to find a job.

(b) We will offer a special discount from august 1 through mid-October.

(c) Traffic is always heavy on labor day when students return to the university.

(d) He is known in the music industry as top-ten Martin.

(e) The only bureau in Washington that has current data on the subject is the bureau of labor statistics.

(f) Please include the material on line 6, page 12.

PROBLEMS

1. If you were employed by a well-equipped corporation headquarters, which type of communication would you probably choose in the following situations? Tell why you chose the medium you did.

(a) A message asking a governor to sign a bill

(b) A message to three sales managers in different locations (A reaction is necessary from each.)

(c) A message informing the payroll department in a branch office that data required for issuing paychecks have not been received

(d) A message containing detailed information about production schedules of a branch factory for the next two months

(e) A message to inquire about prices of a well-known office machine manufactured in a nearby suburb

(f) A message (about an important interview in London) to the president of the company en route to Europe by ship

(g) A message asking a salesperson 500 miles away to call on a prospective customer

(h) A message to the production manager in a distant branch factory

(i) A request for information from a bank in Englewood, New Jersey (across the Hudson River from your Manhattan office)

(j) A message that must reach 12 sales representatives in different locations by the following morning

(k) A message to the president of the company en route to Europe by ship (The message requires an immediate answer.)

(l) A message to the manager of a restaurant for which you supplied building materials, expressing good wishes on opening day

(m) A message that will be received after closing hours but must be available when the office opens the following morning

(n) A graph to be used tomorrow in a national sales meeting

2. Develop a bibliography of ten articles published within the past six months describing innovations in electronic equipment. Of what value was this investigation?

3. Visit a modern office and make a report to the class on one of the following topics (as your instructor directs): (a) an information system, (b) the company's internal and external telephone system, (c) TWX/telex, (d) facsimile transmission.

Part Four   Case Problems

Case 4-1
ABSENTEEISM IN
THE MAIL ROOM

Katherine McNamara was secretary to the personnel manager. At lunch with a group of co-workers, she heard a member of the mail room say to his friend, "Iz, I'm going to take this afternoon off. You sign out for me at five o'clock. Remember, I did the same for you on Monday."

Katherine had suspected that the mail department was loosely administered, but she had not believed it was possible to leave work without the absence being detected.

Since she worked in another department, she wondered about her responsibility.

Should she report the conversation to her employer? to the supervisor of the mail department? Should she speak to the young employees herself? Not wanting to tattle, should she ignore the situation entirely because it does not involve her?

Case 4-2
FOLLOWING A
CODE OF
ETHICS

Vera McKay was secretary to Helen Inness. When Miss Inness was on the telephone one day, she motioned to Vera and whispered, "Please turn on the recorder and take this conversation down verbatim, for it may mean trouble for the company."

Vera knew the Federal Communications Commission restriction against recording a telephone conversation without a receiver-connector containing a beep tone warning device. However, there was no time for discussion, so she did as directed.

When the call was terminated, however, Vera said, "Miss Inness, we are not permitted to record a conversation without telling the caller that it is being recorded and providing a beep tone."

Miss Inness replied, "Fiddlesticks. We have to protect ourselves, don't we?

What more should Vera do—if anything?

Case 4-3
BEING A ROLE
MODEL

Jane Edwards has developed a company-wide reputation for handling nuisance calls and for appeasing angry customers. Recognizing this ability, the receptionist, who has been in her position for only two months, has begun to transfer all such calls to Jane's desk. Jane realizes that this is a compliment to her tact and diplomacy, but she knows too that it keeps her from her assigned responsibilities. Her employer is unaware of the amount of time consumed in this activity.

Should Jane continue to take the calls, should she discuss the situation with her employer, or should she take other action?

Case 4-4
NECESSITY FOR
LEARNING
ABOUT MAIL
SERVICES

Louis Weldon had been secretary to an accounting firm for two weeks when he was given four items to mail on his way home from work: a signed income tax return of a client, a package of 200 handouts to be distributed by one of the partners when delivering a speech at a convention on Friday, a letter containing a check, and two magazines that had been borrowed from a colleague by a member accountant.

He sent the tax return and the check by first-class mail and the magazines and handouts by special handling. When he was reprimanded by his employer for his decisions, he said, "You didn't tell me how you wanted the items sent, and besides I was working overtime to get them in the mail anyway."

How should the materials have been sent? Why?
What principles did Louis violate by his actions?

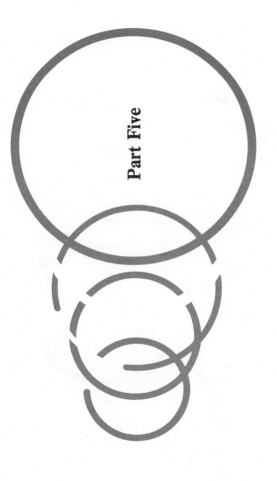

Part Five

ADMINISTRATIVE SUPPORT SERVICES: MANAGEMENT OF RECORDS

This section will discuss the secretary's challenging role in records control both within the immediate office and in relation to the organization-wide records management program. Some of the questions to be answered in this section are: What records should be kept? Where? How long? How can records be stored more effectively? How can records be made more readily accessible to management? How can records be protected against loss or accessibility to unauthorized personnel?

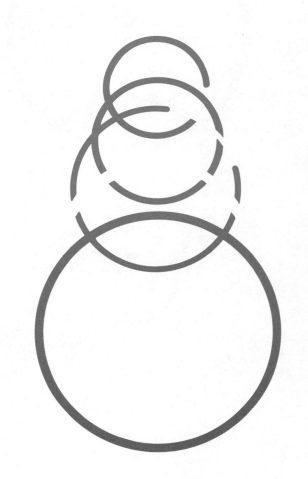

Chapter 14

Records Control

Each year more and more pieces of information are generated by business for filing. As more pieces of information are produced, the greater the necessity for making information available for decision making when needed and for destroying it when it is no longer useful. Consequently, the secretary needs to observe good filing practices and to insist that others with access to the files also observe them. Actually the secretary should regard filing a document as the last step in completing a work assignment. It is *not* an unrelated chore to be taken lightly.

This chapter discusses the secretary's filing responsibilities, the various filing methods for both paper and paperless offices, equipment and supplies, procedures for filing and retrieving records, the mechanics of good filing, retention and transfer of files to inactive status, and building company archives (historical records).

THE SECRETARY'S FILING RESPONSIBILITIES

Files are the memory of a business. They may be *centralized* in one location or *decentralized* in various departments or branches. Administrative and multifunctional secretaries will probably maintain decentralized (in-office) files and also send materials to and secure materials from a large central file.

The in-office files relate not only to the company business for which the executive is responsible but also to personal files kept in the office. The executive's personal in-office files should be separated from those concerning company business. The executive and the secretary need to plan together the in-office files if the filing system is to work well. Of course, the secretary will follow company procedures for borrowing and returning documents to the central file.

If the company has a records management program, the secretary will probably receive instructions about which materials are to be sent to the central file, which materials may be retained in the executive's files, and how long to keep certain records before destroying them or sending them to a low-cost storage area. Records managers are primarily concerned with reducing the amount of paper to be filed, and their work has been made more demanding by the accessibility of copying machines. The same document may be copied and filed in a half-dozen offices. Since office space is expensive and personnel costs are high, records managers want to prevent filing anything without reference value, to reduce duplication of copies in several locations, and to ensure that superseded material will be destroyed when a current replacement is filed. To save space, they frequently try to reduce executive files. On the other hand, executives, fearing that they cannot refer to items easily once the records have left their hands, build "little empires" that take up space and increase the expense of paperwork.

The secretary's task is one of reconciling the executive's habit of wanting to keep almost everything, with the need to reduce the executive's in-office files to a minimum. Consequently, the secretary needs to understand not only the executive's files but also the central filing system, so that material not available in the executive's files may be secured from the central file.

Designing the Files

There is a tendency to restrict one's concept of files to the typical vertical file cabinet conspicuous in every office. Actually the secretary usually works with many types of files—card files, project files, files of catalogs frequently consulted, magazine files, blueprint or other outsized material files, tape-cassette files, transparency files, files of computer printouts, microform files, open shelf files, and computerized files—in addition to the traditional drawer file with alphabetic, numeric, geographic, and subject captions. Each type of file has a unique function. The secretary's responsibility usually goes beyond maintaining existing files to include the designing and installation of various types of files that will best serve the executive's need for information. In planning files, three factors must always be considered: findability, confidentiality, and safety.

Findability. Unfortunately files are thought of first as places to *put* materials, not places to *find* materials. Yet the criterion for judging any file system is findability. The efficient secretary makes decisions about where to put an item after considering. How will it be requested? or How can I find it? Materials must be located with dispatch and only those actually wanted must be selected from a complete file. To do this, the secretary must understand what the executive needs and not provide 250 pages when only 10 are wanted. Placing materials in safekeeping is important, but being able to find them promptly when wanted is *vital.*

Confidentiality. The secretary is also responsible for the confidentiality of the employer's files. The degree of security required varies from the tight surveillance required over files and papers marked *Confidential, Secret, Vital,* or

Personal to the exercise of reasonable protection for the less sensitive materials that constitute the major portion of most files. If the executive is working in a highly sensitive area or industry, there should be a company policy as to who may have access to confidential and secret materials. In the absence of a company policy, the secretary working with the executive should establish such a policy for the executive's office.

Safety. Allied to the need for security is the secretary's ultimate responsibility for the safety of the records in the executive's office. Many of them may be irreplaceable. A safe practice is to lock all confidential items in a filing cabinet or vault before leaving at night as a safeguard against prying eyes or fire damage. Security systems that automatically lock the area and the file when not in use are built into many new files.

Developing an Index

The secretary in a new position may find an index of file captions for the executive's files already prepared. Chances are, though, none will be available, and the development of an index telling where in the files to look for materials will have a high priority. Even after the secretary has become familiar with the files, such a guide will prove advantageous, for it will help anyone (including the executive or a new assistant) locate material. A simple table of contents that indicates where to look for all types of records is shown on this page. Do not underestimate its value.

Communication between secretary and executive seems particularly weak in the filing area. Since the secretary is the one responsible for seeing that materials are placed in and retrieved from the files, there is the tendency to

FILE INDEX
NO. 89
CHEMICAL

	Location	
	File No.	Drawer No.
Correspondence		
Company	2	1
Government	2	2
Patents	2	3
Personnel Work		
Applications	1	2
Medical	1	3
Security	1	6
Reports		
Company	5	1
Outside	5	3

Illus. 14-1
A table of contents for locating filed material

FILING METHODS

Material should be filed according to the designation by which it will be sought and according to a method with an established procedure and set of rules that are understood by all who use the files. There are four basic filing methods—*alphabetic, subject, numeric,* and *geographic.*

Manufacturers of filing equipment have devised and patented improvements upon these four fundamental methods, such as color schemes to expedite sorting, filing, and finding procedures—or techniques for grouping names spelled differently but pronounced alike. Trade names such as *Wheeldex* or *Dataflie* refer to commercial systems. The word *system* is reserved for any filing plan devised by a filing equipment manufacturer.

Alphabetic Filing

Most, possibly as high as 80 percent, of all the filing done in the office is *alphabetical;* that is, the files are sequenced alphabetically. Furthermore, all filing systems are directly or indirectly based on the alphabetic system. Alphabetic filing is understood by everyone and the filing is *direct* (meaning that it is not necessary to consult a subordinate file before filing or finding). The method is based on the strict observance of the guides for alphabetic indexing that are presented in Chapter 15.

Phonetic indexing is a modification of alphabetic indexing. In phonetic indexing the names are arranged by their sound and not by their spelling. Thus, Burke and its variants—Burck, Berk, Berke, Birk, Bourke, Bork, Borck, and others—are filed together.

consider the files the secretary's private domain and not to involve the executive in planning them. Yet the filing system is a joint secretary-executive responsibility. If they work together in planning the system, the transfer of either of them to another office will not destroy the continuity of the files. A new secretary should not attempt to reorganize the files until considerable insight into the informational needs of the office has been acquired.

Ideas for setting up files may sometimes be obtained from professional organizations and publications. For example, a prefabricated administration file that contains main subjects and subclassifications printed on guide and folder tabs is available. The manufacturer claims this system will provide indexing applicable to 90 percent of all basic executive data.

It is also possible to buy prefabricated subject file systems for certain types of offices. For example, a prefabricated administration file that contains main subjects and subclassifications printed on guide and folder tabs is available. The manufacturer claims this system will provide indexing applicable to 90 percent of all basic executive data.

Subject Filing

The nature of some executives' work makes logical the filing of most of the correspondence, reports, and documents to be retained in the office under *subject headings* arranged in an alphabetic sequence in the files (actually an alphabetic file except that all captions refer to subjects or topics rather than to names of people or names of organizations).

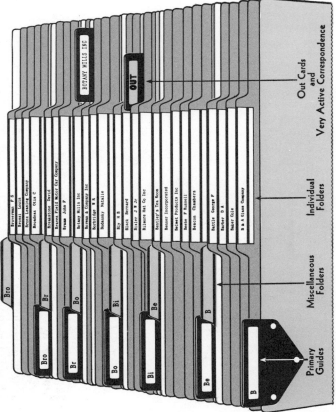

Remington Rand

Illus. 14-2
In this illustration of an alphabetic file, four positions are used for the captions.

Clear, concise, and mutually exclusive subject captions are essential to successful subject files. These captions are the key words used in locating filed material. To get an idea of the subjects used in subject filing, examine the Yellow Pages of your local telephone directory. For instance, in metropolitan Yellow Pages, you will see that Employment Agencies is cross-referenced to Employment Contractors and Temporary Help. Loans is cross-referenced to Banks, Financing, Credit Unions, Mortgages, Savings and Loan Associations, and Pawnbrokers.

Each piece of material is filed under *one subject caption*, but a *relative index* is prepared to support the subject file. This index is basically a cross-reference system. It lists all captions under which an item *may* be filed. To obtain an item from a subject file for which the subject caption is not known, the searcher first consults the relative index to identify all possible headings under which it may be stored.

The executive and the secretary may profitably spend time in developing the relative index—time that will be saved later when the executive asks for the material under a number of captions. If the executive asks for the file on wage-incentive plans of a rival company, the Green Corporation, the secretary may have it filed under: (1) fringe benefits, (2) incentive plans, (3) personnel, or (4) Green Corporation. Reference to the relative index will help locate the pamphlet.

A description of a portion of the subject file pictured below will perhaps best illustrate the principles. This illustration shows only one of the major headings with its subdivisions.

Each main heading has a number of subheadings. For instance, OFFICE EQUIPMENT is subdivided into several categories such as:

OFFICE EQUIPMENT: *Copying Machines*
OFFICE EQUIPMENT: *Duplicating Machines*
OFFICE EQUIPMENT: *Typewriters*

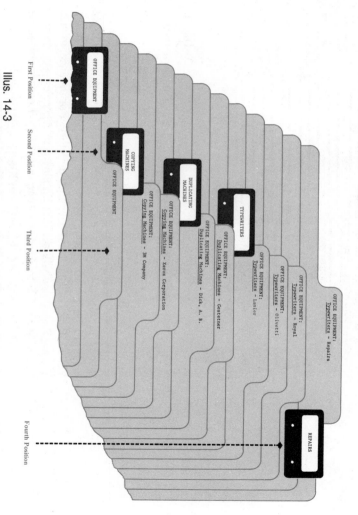

First Position

Second Position

Third Position

Fourth Position

OFFICE EQUIPMENT

COPYING MACHINES

OFFICE EQUIPMENT

DUPLICATING MACHINES

OFFICE EQUIPMENT:
Copying Machines – 3M Company

OFFICE EQUIPMENT:
Copying Machines – Xerox Corporation

TYPEWRITERS

OFFICE EQUIPMENT:
Duplicating Machines – Dick, A. B.

OFFICE EQUIPMENT:
Duplicating Machines – Gestetner

OFFICE EQUIPMENT:
Typewriters – Lanier

OFFICE EQUIPMENT:
Typewriters – Olivetti

OFFICE EQUIPMENT:
Typewriters – Royal

OFFICE EQUIPMENT:
Typewriters – Repairs

REPAIRS

Illus. 14-3
This subject file would be suitable for the purchasing agent or the office manager.

Some of these subdivisions may be further subdivided. For example, OFFICE EQUIPMENT: *Typewriters* is subdivided by manufacturer (IBM, Lanier, Olivetti, Wang, for example).

The subdivision *Typewriters* is further subdivided by the special classification guide REPAIRS in the fourth position. Additional classifications will depend on the needs of the user.

Subject filing presents special retrieval problems because material may be requested under any one of many titles. For this reason one management consultant said, "To do subject filing well, the secretary must think like the executive." No area of filing requires the exercise of better judgment on the part of the secretary than does arranging materials by titles that best indicate their content.

Numeric Filing

Lawyers, architects, engineers, accountants, realtors, insurance brokers, and contractors may assign a number for each project; and that number becomes the basis for the *numeric file.* Case records and confidential material where anonymity is desired are commonly filed numerically.

Illus. 14-4
In this file, alternate rather than consecutive numbers are assigned so that the appropriate intervening number can be assigned when a machine from another manufacturer is purchased.

CAPTIONS AND CORRESPONDING NUMBERS FOR A PORTION OF A NUMERIC SUBJECT FILE

Number	Heading	Division	Subdivision	Second Subdivision
100	Office Equipment			
110		Copying Machines		
112			3M	
114			Xerox	
116				
118				
120		Duplicating Machines		
122			Dick, A. B.	
124			Gestetner	
126				
128				
130		Typewriters		
132			IBM	
134			Lanier	
136			Olivetti	
138				Repairs

A numeric filing plan has four parts:

1. Alphabetic card index
2. Main numeric file
3. Miscellaneous alphabetic file for correspondence
4. *Accession* or number book, a record of the numbers that are already assigned

In the numeric file the alphabetic card index is first consulted to obtain the file number. The item is then located by number in the main numeric file. For a name or subject not shown in the card index, the miscellaneous alphabetic file is searched. Numeric filing is an *indirect* system, as one must refer to a card index before referring to the main numeric file.

If the subject file for a small operation (Illus. 14-3) were converted to a numeric subject file, the section for Office Equipment could be assigned the number 100 in the accession book and contain the numeric assignments (Illus. 14-4).

Advantages and Disadvantages. Numeric filing has both advantages and disadvantages. It is easy to learn. Misfiling is reduced because individually assigned numbers are less confusing than spelled names. Furthermore, extensive cross-referencing is possible in the alphabetic card index. A disadvantage is the necessity of consulting the card index before locating the material—a very time-consuming step. And when misfiling does occur, it is usually more difficult to locate the misfile than it is when an alphabetic file is used.

Illus. 14-5
In numeric filing, misfiling is reduced because individually assigned numbers are less confusing than are similarly spelled names.

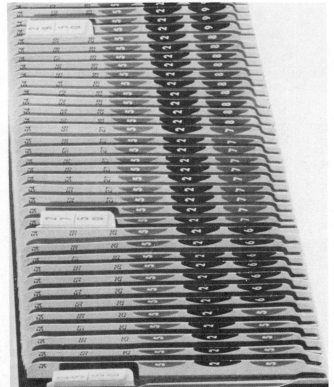

Terminal and Middle Digit Filing. In straight numeric filing, as the files increase, the numbers assigned to them become higher. Because most of the filing work deals with the most recent dates, the work involves the highest numbers. In a numeric file of insurance policies, for instance, the most recent policies would have the highest numbers. Chances are that the file clerk would work mostly with the higher numbered files.

Terminal digit filing avoids concentrating the bulk of the filing action in a small section of the files. This indexing method divides a number into pairs of digits. For example, insurance policy No. 412010 would be identified as 41 20 10. The last (terminal) digits would identify the drawer number; the second pair of digits to the left would indicate the guide number in the drawer; and the remaining digits would indicate the sequence of the folder behind the guide. Thus, policy No. 41 20 10 would be filed in Drawer 10, behind Guide 20, and in 41st sequence behind the guide (between policy No. 40 20 10 and policy No. 42 20 10).

To appreciate the advantage of terminal digit filing, visualize 100 file drawers, each labeled with a two-digit number (00, 01, 02, and so on through 99). Policy No. 2 12 00 would go in Drawer 00, while policy No. 2 12 01 would go in Drawer 01, and so on. As consecutive new policy numbers are assigned, the policy materials will be distributed throughout the 100 drawers.

Research shows that terminal digit filing saves up to 40 percent of file operation costs by assuring a uniform work load, better employee relations, unlimited expansion facilities, and fewer misfiles. This system has been adapted

Illus. 14-6
The terminal digit system assures easy filing and finding.

and modified into the triple terminal digit system (using the last three digits as the drawer number).

In *middle digit filing*, the two middle digits identify the drawer or section; the first two digits, the guide number in the drawer or section; and the final two digits, the sequence behind the guide.

Geographic Filing

Geographic filing keeps records by geographic units or territories. Divisions are made in a logical sequence: nations, states or provinces, cities, and so on. Guides are used for large divisions and subdivisions. Behind each guide, material is filed in miscellaneous folders alphabetically, usually by name of city and then by name of correspondent. Individual folders are filed alphabetically by location, then by name.

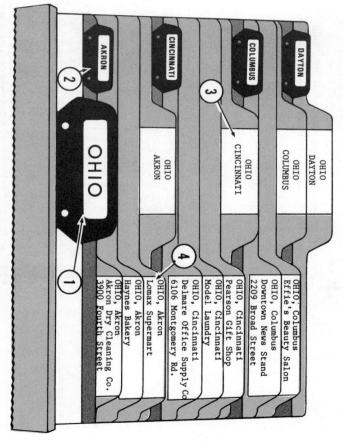

Illus. 14-7

In this geographic file papers are filed alphabetically by the geographical areas (see No. 1 and No. 2) indicated by the guides and folders. In the miscellaneous folder for each city (see No. 3), the papers are filed alphabetically by the names of the correspondents. Individual folders are used for correspondents who have enough communications to warrant a separate folder (see No. 4).

The geographic file is frequently supported by a card index in which names of companies are filed alphabetically. If the location of a company is forgotten, it may be obtained by reference to the alphabetic card index.

Selecting a Method

The basic filing methods used in your office should depend on how materials are identified. If they are identified by name (either personal or company), an alphabetic file system will probably be used. If each client, job, or project is identified by number, a numeric system is appropriate. When the identifying name for the item is a territory or a geographic location, the geographic method will be best. When items are categorized by subject, then a subject file should meet your office needs. In practice, it is not unusual to find all four filing systems in use in the same office.

The Secretary's Chronological File

A secretary who must send material to a centralized file usually keeps a chronological file as a ready in-office reference. This file, sometimes called a *reading* or *chron* (chronological) file, consists of a copy—carbon or photo —of each *outgoing* item of the day, filed in chronological order in a ring binder or topbound folder. Such a file can answer many questions—was a letter mailed, to whom was it addressed, when was it mailed, what price was quoted, and was an enclosure mentioned—all without the delay of consulting the central file.

To speed the locating of material in the reading file, some secretaries place a sheet with a date index tab between the copies to separate each day's work. It is also recommended that a notation be placed on each copy showing where the regular correspondence concerning that item is filed. The secretary retains materials in this file for a limited time only, perhaps six months to a year, each month discarding the materials for the earliest month.

FILING EQUIPMENT

Filing is an expensive operation largely because of space requirements. In fact, it costs $7 a year to maintain one inch of files. Naturally competition among manufacturers is keen in developing equipment that reduces costs.

Correspondence is filed in drawers or on shelves. It may be placed in regular folders that rest on the bottom of the drawer or in suspension folders that hang from a metal frame within the drawer or shelf. The advantage of the suspension folder is that heavily loaded folders do not sag and that folders open wide and slide smoothly on the hanger rail. Cards are filed in several ways: in drawers, in boxes, in trays, or in panels where the captions are visible immediately.

Vertical and Lateral Files

For many years the most often used type of filing equipment was the vertical file (with papers filed on the long edge) available in one- to six-drawer units in a wide variety of colors. Opening the drawers of these units requires at least three to four feet of space in front of the cabinet.

The conventional file cabinet that pulls forward the full depth of the drawer is rapidly being replaced by lateral files that require up to 50 percent less aisle space and provide up to 100 percent greater accessibility and visibility. The lateral file may be a drawer file that rolls out sideways, or it may be an open shelf file. In executive offices where attractive surroundings are important, the type of lateral file most often chosen has a closed front with either drawers that close or cabinets with doors that lift up, slide to one side, or pull down.

Open Shelf File

In open shelf filing the folders are placed vertically on open shelves with no drawers involved. Access to the folders is from the front. Since the shelves can extend to the ceiling, they can accommodate more material per square foot of floor space than the drawer file can; they require less floor and aisle space; they cost less; and they require less time to file and find records. In central filing departments open shelf filing is most often used.

The tabs identifying the contents of a shelf file folder project from the side of the folder, with the caption written on both front and back of the tab so that the searcher can locate a folder from either side. Color coding is frequently used with shelf files for easy visibility. If a whole section is color coded red, a folder with a green caption is obviously misfiled if it is in the red section.

Illus. 14-8
These open shelf files combine space-saving and ease-of-access features.

Mobile Files

Mobile files allow what is known as close support filing—putting the records at the point of use. The concept is to bring the highly active file unit to the operations area rather than forcing the worker to go to the file. Some mobile files are single units that are pushed around like carts. Others are multiple modules that roll on a suspension system from the ceiling. Some are stationary, like the tub file, with trays rotating to give operators access to needed material.

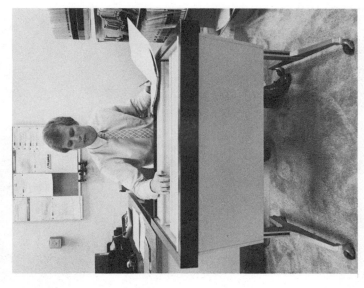

Illus. 14-9
Mobile files bring the highly active file unit to the operations area.

Files for Word Processing Centers

The array of equipment for housing magnetic media is almost as varied as it is for paper documents.

Floppy disks and magnetic cards are often filed in the plastic library boxes provided by the manufacturer when an order for supplies is delivered. These pop-up boxes hold the media upright on the operator's desk while in use and protect them against environmental contamination when closed.

Modular desk stands or rotary stands designed for flat magnetic media generally hold large amounts of material. One such module is comprised of panels, each of which holds ten floppy disks providing good visibility for easy indexing and accessing by the operator.

Ring King Visibles, Inc.

Illus. 14-10
Scan files for
appropriate disk.

Files for Computer Generated Material

Provision must be made for filing both computer tapes and computer printouts. The illustration of filed tapes in the central filing department of a large organization indicates the enormity of the problem and how one company solves it. Faced with a 15 to 20 percent annual growth in computer tapes, the company replaced fixed-in-place racks with automated mobile shelving. With fingertip pressure on a control button, the operator can move a bay of carriages sideways, right or left, over the tracks to open the desired aisle. The tapes have reference numbers and are logged in and out after every access.

Spacesaver Corporation

Illus. 14-11
Shelving
carriages shuttle
sideways to
eliminate aisles.

Oversize computer printouts are usually filed in special shelves that hold large suspension folders. The need for special shelves is minimized, though, by reprographic equipment that reduces the printouts to 8½"-by-11" size for filing in conventional equipment.

Horizontal Files

Horizontal files store in a flat position materials such as maps, drawings, or blueprints that normally are much larger than the materials filed in a vertical file drawer. They are most commonly found in engineering and architectural offices.

Rotary Card Files

The rotary wheel file is designed to make a limited amount of information available within arm's reach. The wheel can be small for desk use or motorized to hold large trays of cards, such as accounts receivable or credit information.

Delco Associates, Inc.

Illus. 14-12
The rotary file places a large volume of filed materials within arm's reach of the user. In this file the trays rotate independently.

Rolodex Corporation

Illus. 14-13
This rotary wheel file is designed for quick access to a limited amount of information. When the executive needs the addresses of several sales representatives, the secretary can furnish them quickly without leaving the desk.

Visible Card Files

In a visible card file, cards filed in a shallow metal tray or on upright stands show only the lower edge of each card. Flipping up the preceding card reveals the card desired. Cards can easily be inserted and removed from holders that are fastened so that the backs of cards can also be used for record keeping.

Kardex Systems, Inc.

Illus. 14-14
Visible card files are used extensively for situations in which information must be available quickly.

Visible card files are used extensively for perpetual inventories, accounting records of sales and purchases, personnel histories—those situations in which information must be available quickly, as in answer to a telephone inquiry. Colored signals provide a visible means of control; for example, a blue signal attached to the visible edge of a credit card may mean *Watch credit closely.*

MICROFILM

Today information can be reduced to the medium of microfilm, stored conveniently, and then retrieved quickly for reference and use. The rapid advances in micrographic technology have made microfilm systems much more efficient than paper record-keeping systems.

Microfilm—a fine grain, high resolution film containing an image considerably reduced in size from the original—is used extensively in business today. Since the cost of storing data in a computer is quite high, microfilm is used extensively in storing data from computers. Data in a computer can be converted to *computer output microfilm* (COM) for convenient off-line storage.

Off-line storage is independent of the computer's CPU. Through the use of microfilm, the saving in filing space is phenomenal. Only 200 feet of microfilm can carry the same amount of data as approximately 4,000 sheets of computer printout paper.

Types of Microfilm

Microfilm in reel or roll form was one of the first microforms. A wide variety of user needs and applications has given rise to a number of different forms in which microfilm is made, stored, and used. Some familiar microforms are described below.

Reels. Microfilm that has been greatly reduced in size from the original documents can be wound onto large reels that occupy relatively little space. The disadvantage is that material cannot be easily located on the reel and cannot be updated easily.

Cartridges. Cartridges are more convenient than reels for filing microfilm since each film may be wound onto a single cartridge. It is then easy to retrieve material. Cartridges can be self-threading; the manual threading necessary for reels is avoided. Microfilm on cartridges is well protected from fingerprints and other damage.

Cassettes. Cassettes are frequently used for filing microfilm. Each cassette contains two spools, the feed and the take-up, so that an already viewed film can be rewound easily. Microfilm on cassettes can be held in viewing position for reference at a later time.

Aperture Cards. Microfilm may be more convenient to use if the images are clipped from the film roll and mounted on cards that have an opening that fits the size of the image. These are called *aperture cards.* Data may be written on the card or coded by holes punched into the card that permit it to be filed and retrieved mechanically.

Microfiche. A sheet of film containing multiple images is called *microfiche* (pronounced *microfeesh*). As many as 96 images can be stored on one sheet. Thus, a 96-page report can be recorded on one 6-by-4 inch microfiche. Microfiche can be filed in a card file or in a specially designed book binder.

Jackets. Strips of film can be stored in a plastic carrier with sleeves designed to accept strips of film. Jackets can be updated easily with related information by adding single or multiple images. Images in a jacket can be copied or read directly from the jacket without removing the film. Jackets are commonly used for personnel applications, medical record files, and credit files.

Illus. 14-15
Microfilm is a fine grain, high resolution film containing an image considerably reduced in size from the original and is used extensively in business today.

Minolta Corporation

Microfilm Retrieval Systems

A number of retrieval techniques (manual, semiautomated, and automated) that direct the searcher to the information on microfilm have evolved over the years. High-speed microform indexing and retrieval systems use the computer. *Computer assisted retrieval* (CAR) has the capability to locate or identify microimages (a unit of information, such as a page of text, too small to be read without magnification) by commands initiated through a computer terminal. The computer manipulates an index at very high speeds and provides the necessary identification information for retrieving a desired document. An index serves not only to guide users to the location of the information being searched but also provides a basis for users to screen or select information. The operator of a terminal need only query the computer, and the image is automatically presented to the operator in a matter of seconds. In some systems the information can be displayed at the terminal, printed out as hard copy, or recorded onto microfilm.

FILING SUPPLIES

Some secretaries purchase their own filing supplies; some requisition them from the stockroom. In either case, a secretary needs to know what is available and how to describe each item correctly when ordering.

File Guides

File guides are rigid sheets that divide the file drawer into sections. They are frequently attached by a rod to the bottom of the drawer. They come in a variety of tab widths (tab *cuts*). A *one-fifth cut* means that the tab occupies one fifth of the top edge of the guide, permitting five tab positions. The positions are identified from left to right as *first position, second position,* and so on. An order for guides must specify the exact cut position or positions as one-fifth cut in second position or one-third cut in staggered positions.

Some guide captions are printed directly on the tab (frequently the case with alphabetic systems), or the tab may be a metal or plastic holder into which small typed or printed captions can be easily inserted.

Alphabetic guides with printed captions are available in sets ranging from the 23-unit sets used by small businesses to the sets of several hundred units used by large businesses.

File Folders

File folders come in various styles, weights, cuts, colors, and materials. Tab cuts range from full width to one fifth with *single* or *double* captions (depth of the cut). At the bottom front of the folder two or more horizontal scores or creases permit folding to form a flat bottom surface to adjust to the thickness of the contents.

Folders come in light, medium, heavy, and extra heavy weights; 11-point paper stock (a point is .001 inch) is medium weight. An innovation in this area is a folder made of thin, durable plastic. For bulky papers, pressboard folders with cloth expansion hinges at the bottom are best.

Also available are folders with built-in fasteners, with metal hooks for suspension from frames within the file drawer, and with printed captions. Folders with pockets for holding punched tape, punched cards, or standard size sheets can be obtained. It is also possible to purchase folders of different colors so that files can be color coded. Folders are available that have a tab calendar to which plastic markers can be attached to signal the date on which the contents should be acted on.

Orders for folders must specify weight and color of stock and size, position, and depth of cut. Orders for folders to hold any special type of material should contain complete information about the purpose for which the folder is to be used.

Folder Labels

Folder labels for captions come in continuous perforated rolls or in self-adhesive strips in a range of colors and in various widths to fit the tab cuts.

Colored labels and color-striped folders permit the use of a color code to divide the file into sections. Color coding increases filing accuracy, speeds the filing function, and reduces the time required to find misfiled folders.

Colored labels can also aid in transferring materials from active to inactive status. For instance, during a given year all useful material filed might be placed in folders with a blue-banded label. When files are to be reviewed for updating, only the blue-banded folders would be considered active.

Cross-Reference Sheets

Cross-reference sheets should be lightweight to conserve space. They should also be in color for easy identification in the folder. The secretary can purchase them or have them duplicated in the office.

FILING PROCEDURES

Many papers that should have been destroyed are filed. Letters of acknowledgment, letters of transmittal, announcements of meetings (noted on the desk calendar), forms and reports filed in another location, duplicate copies, and routine requests for catalogs and information fall into this category. (In some well-run organizations the original request is returned with the material.)

Any document that is superseded by another in the file should be removed. When filing a card giving a change in telephone number, remove the old one. When a new catalog is filed, destroy the old one.

A temporary file may be kept for materials having no permanent value. The paper is marked with a *T* and destroyed when the action involved is completed.

The government has developed this removal technique to a high level. In many departments of the government every document receives a date-of-destruction notation before it goes into the file. By continually purging the files of outdated material, the secretary can reduce the volume of material and keep the files up to date.

Preparing Materials for Filing

In addition to files for paper documents, files are maintained on computers and word processing media. The routines vary with the equipment, but in all cases appropriate indexing and coding and adequate cross referencing are at the heart of a successful system. The term *indexing* means deciding where to file a document; *coding* refers to adding that decision on the document so that it will always be placed in the same location when refiled.

The increase in the amount of information being filed has led to the development of index entries that include multiple keywords, such as document name, number, author, date, subject, operator, comments, revision level, and so on. The cross-references may be either on cross-reference sheets or on the document itself in order to prevent misfiles or problems in locating wanted filed material. Possible keywords and possible other captions should be used freely. A good secretary follows the rule: When in doubt, cross-reference.

In alphabetic filing, material usually is filed according to the most important name appearing on it. A letter to or from a business is usually coded and filed according to the name of that business. If the correspondent is an individual, that person's name is ordinarily used in coding. If, however, the person is writing as an agent of a business and the name of that business is known, the business name is used instead. Similarly, if a business letterhead is used by an individual to write a personal letter, the name of the individual is coded rather than the name of the business. Complete rules for alphabetic-filing sequence are given in Chapter 15.

In subject filing, the subject title must be determined from the body of the document which is then coded according to that title or a number that represents that subject. In numerical filing, the number to be used as a code is determined from a card-index file. In geographic filing, coding is done by state and city.

Most of the secretary's filing will probably still involve filing papers; so detailed steps are given for this operation.

Step 1. Conditioning Materials. To ready papers for filing, all pins and paper clips are removed, and related materials are stapled or welded together. Staple or weld the upper right corner so that other papers will not be inserted between the sheets in the file. Clippings or other materials smaller than page size should be attached to a regular sheet of paper with rubber cement. Damaged records should be mended or reinforced with tape. If they are not filed in special equipment, oversize papers should be folded to the dimensions of the folder and labeled to make it unnecessary to unfold them for identification.

Step 2. Releasing Materials. When the secretary places an incoming letter in the filing basket, it should bear a *release mark* indicating that it has been acted on and is ready for filing. This mark may be the executive's initials, a FILE stamp and the secretary's initials, a code or check mark, a diagonal mark across the sheet, or other agreed upon designation. A check of all attachments will indicate whether they belong to the document. A release mark is not necessary on a file copy of an outgoing letter or on an original of a letter to which a copy of a reply is attached. A file copy is usually of a distinctive color.

Step 3. Indexing and Coding. Once the secretary has decided where to file a document, coding may be done either by underlining or coding the name or words that are to be used as a basis for filing or by writing the appropriate name, words, or number in a prominent place. A colored pencil is commonly used for this purpose. In geographic filing coding may be done by merely underlining the city and state in the letterhead of an incoming letter or in the letter address or an in-house copy of the letter.

Step 4. Cross-Referencing. If there is a possibility that a filed letter may be sought under another caption, a cross-reference is made and filed in the second location. Cross-reference forms may be colored sheets imprinted with blanks that are to be filled in, or they may be tabbed, colored cards on which the reference information is listed. A photocopy or an extra copy of the letter (usually on paper of a different color from the file copy) can also be used as a cross-reference.

An example of a cross-reference sheet is given below to illustrate the handling of a letter received from the Modern Office Equipment Company regarding an exhibit at the Eastern Office Equipment Association convention in Baltimore. All correspondence about this meeting was filed under Eastern Office Equipment Association. However, a cross-reference sheet was made and filed under Modern Office Equipment Company. The secretary indicated that the item had been cross-referenced by placing an *X* (for cross-reference) near the name on the original letter.

Illus. 14-16 Cross-reference forms may be colored sheets imprinted with blanks that are to be filled in, or they may be tabbed, colored cards on which the reference information is listed.

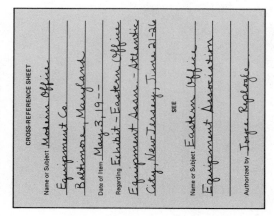

CROSS-REFERENCE SHEET

Name or Subject Modern Office

Equipment Co.

Baltimore, Maryland

Date of Item May 3, 19 --

Regarding Exhibit - Eastern Office

Equipment Assn. - Atlantic

City, New Jersey, June 21-26

SEE

Name or Subject Eastern Office

Equipment Association

Authorized by Joyce Replogle

Cross-reference correspondence or material that should be filed under more than one name. For instance, a letter from Allen Rothmore Company poses the problem: Is Allen a given name or a surname? A regular file should be set up for Rothmore Allen and filed under *Ro.* A cross-reference should be made to Allen, Rothmore.

A letter can be cross-referenced by subject. If inquiries have been mailed to several printers asking for quotations on new letterheads, a cross-reference sheet labeled "Letterhead Quotations" listing the firms written may be filed under *Le.* The correspondence with the printers may be filed alphabetically according to firm names.

Step 5. Sorting. Sorting is arranging the papers, including cross-reference sheets, in sequence for filing. When sorting material the secretary should first make one or two preliminary sortings before the final one. For example, in the first sorting all *A-E* papers are placed in one group. In the second sort they are put in *A, B, C, D,* and *E* order. It is a simple matter then to put each of these letter groups in correct alphabetic sequence. Sorting for a numeric file should follow a similar efficient procedure.

Step 6. Typing Labels. The one rule that should be observed in the format for typing file labels is the rule of uniformity. The following are useful suggestions:

1. Type the caption uniformly two or three spaces from the left edge of the label. Position the labels uniformly on the folders (see the illustration). This practice will prevent captions from being hidden in the file.

2. Type the primary reference on the top line in uppercase and lowercase letters. Uppercase and lowercase letters are easier to read than all capitals. If the title is too long for the width of the label, indent the carry-over words on the second line. Omit punctuation marks.

3. Type the secondary reference, such as city and state, on the second line blocked with the first line. If there is a street address, place it on the third line blocked with the preceding lines.

4. Spell out an abbreviation if the word is considered in filing. However, if the word is at the end of the name and is not needed for alphabetizing, it may be abbreviated.

Illus. 14-17
The captions at the left are inconsistent in style, punctuation, capitalization, and placement. Captions should be typed in uppercase and lowercase letters as shown at the right.

Techniques for Drawer Filing

Use an *individual folder* for letters and other materials to, from, or about one correspondent or subject. For each section, use a *Miscellaneous folder* for those individuals and businesses with whom correspondence is infrequent. When five records relating to a person or topic have accumulated in the *Miscellaneous folder*, open an individual folder. File material in the *Miscellaneous* folder in alphabetic order; then, within the alphabetic order, file in chronological order with the most recent date to the front of the folder. Adopt the timesaving guides which follow.

1. Set a definite time for filing every day.
2. File records face up, top edge to the left, with the most recent date to the

front of the folder. When material removed from the file is refiled, it should be placed in correct chronological sequence and not necessarily to the front of the folder.

3. Place individual folders immediately *behind* the guides.

4. Place a Miscellaneous folder at the end of each section of the file, just in front of the next guide. Check the Miscellaneous folders frequently to determine if additional individual folders are warranted. Usually an individual folder is made for a person or firm when the accumulated papers amount to five sheets.

5. Use a guide for every 6–8 folders (generally about 2.5 cm of drawer space), about 20–25 guides to each drawer.

6. Leave one fifth of the drawer for expansion and working space.

7. Keep no more than 20–25 sheets in one folder. With bulky files, use scored (creased-at-the-bottom) folders for expansion.

8. Break the files when the folder becomes crowded. Underscore the caption on the old folder in red so that all new material will be placed in the new folder. Date each folder and keep the folders filed together.

9. Use specially scored and reinforced folders for bulky materials such as catalogs.

10. Avoid accidents by opening only one file drawer at a time and closing it when the filing has been completed.

11. Lift the folder a little way out of the drawer before inserting material so that the sheets can drop down completely into the folder. When taking a folder out of the files for a short period, pull up the folder directly behind to serve as a marker in returning the folder.

12. Do not grasp guides and folders by their index tabs, or they will become dog-eared.

Filing Word Processing Materials

When materials are prepared on word processing equipment, documents stored on magnetic media are often indexed and coded for quick filing and retrieval. Confidential records containing personnel information, new patents, or proposed or in-progress projects, for example, are usually kept under strict security in their respective departments.

Handling Confidential Files

Security is always a problem with confidential material—whether in paper or paperless files. Confidential records containing personnel information, new patents, or proposed or in-progress projects, for example, are usually kept under strict security in their respective departments.

If confidential records are in a computerized file, there is always danger that information will become available to unauthorized personnel. To avoid this possibility, the person requesting the file is assigned a code number that must be entered into the computer before the file being requested is released.

Requesting Material from the Central Files

When the secretary releases to the central files material that will be needed at a definite future date, the item is marked or stamped with the notation *Follow-Up* or *Tickler* and the date on which it will be needed, or the file folder can be tabbed with the follow-up date. Frequently, however, the secretary will not know when the material will be needed. In these cases the material will be requested when needed by following the usual routine: by telephone, in person, or by a requisition card sent to the filing department. The entire contents of a folder or only specific items in a folder may be requested. A telephone request is faster than a requisition, especially if the information sought can be given orally.

Illus. 14-18
The secretary may request material from the central file on a standardized form such as this. The filing department records the two dates at the bottom of the card.

REQUEST FOR MATERIAL FROM FILES

Name or subject: Mohawk Supply Co.
Address: Boston, Mass.
Date of Material: Latter part of Feb.
Regarding: Adj. on Feb. Statement

Requested by: Date due: 4/6/--
Jeannette Morris   Charge date: 4/3/--

The more information the secretary can give the central files personnel about the wanted material (names, dates, subjects, addresses, file numbers, etc.), the faster the material can be located and delivered. Furthermore, the secretary who is familiar with the central filing system or systems can provide leads to the central files personnel as to where to locate what is wanted.

Materials should be returned to the central files promptly. A special problem arises when files that the secretary has received are transferred to someone in another department before they are returned to the filing department. In some companies, such transfers are to be reported to the filing department on a special form. In any case, the central files personnel should be informed of the location of the file.

Charge-Out Methods. When an entire folder is taken from the files or when separate items are removed from a folder, a record should be made so that others will be able to locate the materials.

Several charge-out methods are in common use. When an individual item is removed from the folder in a paper file, a *substitution card* is usually put in its place in the folder. This card indicates the nature of the material, the name of the person who has the material, and the date it was removed. When an entire folder is removed, an *out guide* may be substituted for the folder; or an out folder with a substitution card may be placed in the drawer to take the place of the regular folder. Sometimes the regular folder is retained in the file drawer, and the contents of the folder are transferred to a special *carrier folder*. This practice does not disrupt the filing of new material.

In some companies the original requisitioned material never leaves the central filing area. A photocopy is sent to the person making a requisition, and the copy is destroyed when the requesting person is finished with it. Since this practice is expensive and wasteful, it should be used only when it is essential for the original to remain in the central files.

Follow-Up Methods. The secretary may need to follow up on filed materials sent to other offices or departments. The daily calendar pad is frequently used for this purpose. The anticipated date for the return is jotted down as a notation on the future date page of the calendar. Another method is to write or type the needed data on a card and place it in a tickler file.

Reducing Misfiles

Manufacturers of filing equipment report it may cost as much as $80 in executive, secretarial, and clerical time to find a misfiled record. Furthermore, many companies experience a misfile rate of as much as 7 percent. Obviously the secretary should vow to avoid misfiling.

One cause of misfiling is carelessness—placing a record in a folder without scanning its contents to see if they are related to the document being filed, fastening materials together with paper clips which often also pick up unrelated papers, or putting one folder inside another one. Another cause of misfiling is not using supplies and equipment as recommended—too many or too few guides, overcrowded folders that sag so much that their tabs are hidden, drawers so overstuffed that there is inadequate work space, and miscellaneous folders crowded with papers for which individual folders should have been opened. The final cause of misfiling lies in coding—captions that are not mutually exclusive, choice of a wrong title, or too few cross-references.

If only one paper is lost, it is probably in the wrong folder. Check the folders in front and in back of the correct folder, check between folders, and check the bottom of the drawer. Look in charge-outs and in file baskets, and don't overlook your employer's desk and your own. Look in the index of files transferred to storage areas. Look under alternate spellings and anglicized forms of names and under similar numbers or titles. For instance, if the name is Brooks Allen, look under Allen Brooks. If 2309 is lost, look under 2390. Look in the relative index for other possible captions. If the file is not under CE, look under CA, CO, CU, since the second letter may have been misread.

If an exhaustive search does not locate an item, type on a sheet of paper all the information known about the missing item and the date on which the loss was discovered. File the sheet (perhaps in a folder labeled *Lost*) where the missing item should be. This practice forestalls a later search for the same item. Consider the possibility, also, of obtaining a copy of the lost item from its sender or source.

HOW TO APPRAISE YOUR FILES

Open a file drawer and answer these questions:

1. How crowded is it?

A tightly packed file drawer slows filing, causes paper cuts and torn cuticles, and increases the physical work of filing.

2. How many file guides have been used?

The purpose of the file guide is to direct the eye to the approximate location of the item sought. (See Guide 5, page 345.) Too few guides result in time spent in pushing, pulling, and fingering through the file. If you can place your hand halfway between guides and find the desired folder no more than three or four folders away, you have used an adequate number of guides.

3. How uniform are the folders?

An efficient file must have folders of uniform size and weight, uniformly tabbed, logically and consistently arranged. A conglomerate of folder sizes and tab styles is a sure indication of a sick file.

4. How have the folders been labeled?

Labels typed in uniform style not only give a neat appearance but save finding time. Time is wasted in reading labels that are handwritten, crossed out and retyped, or carelessly positioned on the folder.

5. How much material is filed in a single folder?

A folder properly scored (creased) and filled will normally hold three fourths of an inch of material. More material than that will cause papers to "ride up" and become torn or mutilated. Furthermore the label will be hidden; and when labels are hidden, filing speed is greatly reduced.

GOOD RECORDS MANAGEMENT PRACTICES

The purpose of records management is to identify and protect the important papers and documents of the company and to eliminate temporary, useless papers with the least possible delay. Experience has shown that a records management program usually results in 30 percent of the records being destroyed, 40 percent being transferred to a remote record (storage) center, and only the remaining 30 percent being retained in the office.

The emphasis, however, in records management is not only on the destruction of useless records but also on records preservation. The upsurge in government investigations of corporations and in antitrust and price-fixing legal actions has made it necessary for companies to be certain they have retained adequate records and that there is no gap in their documentation.

Archives

In addition to the files required for good management, it is necessary to preserve historical records, the *archives* of the organization. A secretary to a top executive is frequently responsible for seeing that such archives are kept permanently, usually separate from the records essential for conducting business.

Equipment is now available that can store on magnetic tape or floppy disks material that is no longer necessary in central files. The material transferred to such archives can still be indexed in the central files and can thus be located in remote storage. If archives are kept on paper, care should be taken to assure that high quality rag content paper is used. Archives of historical significance are often wanted on paper with a backup copy stored on microfilm or microfiche.

Retention Schedules

The most efficiently operated companies often have an overall file retention plan which the secretary should follow. The retention schedule of a company specifies how long a document can remain in the office flow; if and when it is to be removed to a separate, low-cost records center; and when it should be destroyed.

From among the various professionally organized retention plans available, an adaptation of recommended practices is presented.

1. File one month:
   General correspondence requiring no follow-up
2. File three months:
   Incoming and outgoing correspondence with customers and vendors on
      routine, promptly settled business
   Bank statements
   Stenographers' notebooks
   Expired insurance policies
3. File two years:
   Work sheets for financial statements
   Internal reports and summaries, including printouts from data processing
      equipment, and all magnetic tapes or disks
   Physical inventories
4. File in order to comply with the statute of limitations in the states affected:
   Canceled payroll checks and summaries

Invoices to customers and from vendors

Employee data, including accident reports

Completed contracts and leases, as well as other legal papers

Duplicate deposit tickets and checks, except as noted below

5. File permanently:

Books of accounts and minutes of stockholders' meetings

Capital stock ledgers and transfer records

Canceled checks, vouchers, and complete cost data on capital improvements

Tax returns and related papers

Perpetual agreements about pensions, group insurance, and other fringe benefits

All property records

Maps, specifications, plans

Organization charts and procedure manuals[1]

Because of the enormous volume of output materials, word processing centers usually have their own retention and disposal schedule. In one typical center these practices prevail:

1. Dictation media are retained one day only.
2. Magnetic media containing original letters that will not be repeated are kept for one week only.
3. Copies of completed material are sent back to the originator without retaining a copy in the center.
4. Each prestructured paragraph that is to be merged with other paragraphs to form a complete letter is reproduced on a separate magnetic medium and is retained until superseded.

Transferring Materials

Plans for storing files are made in relation to the importance of the material and the reduction of costs effected by storing infrequently needed documents in low-priced filing equipment in low-cost rental areas. The possibility of destruction of vital records by a disaster has caused concern for safe storage—in mountain vaults and caves in some instances and in widely dispersed units in others. Some companies have built storage centers, and others have rented file storage space from companies that specialize in providing ready access to stored materials.

Certain types of files can be handled under a perpetual transfer plan. When an undertaking is terminated or a project finished the file is closed and transferred. In other cases periodic transfer is made. By the one-period method all material is taken at a designated time from the active files and sent to transfer files. Although active files are established, it is all but impossible to

---

[1]Records Controls, Inc., Chicago, Illinois.

avoid consulting some old records. With a two-period transfer, however, the middle drawers are used for current materials; the upper and lower drawers, for semiactive materials. The semiactive materials are transferred in turn.

A variation of this plan is the maximum-minimum transfer. Only the inactive material is transferred at regular intervals. For instance, with a transfer date of June 30, 1982, materials filed from January 1, 1982, through June 30, 1982, would not be moved (they would remain in the active files). Materials dated from January 1, 1981, through December 31, 1981, however, would be transferred to storage. New materials would go into the active file until June 30, 1983. Then the files from January 1, 1982, through December 31, 1982, would be transferred, leaving the files for January 1, 1983, through June 30, 1983, in the active files. The secretary labels each transfer file with its contents, inclusive dates, and, in some firms, the discard date.

AUTOMATED FILING SYSTEMS AND THEIR EFFECT ON THE SECRETARY

To keep abreast of the phenomenal progress in office mechanization, filing methods have been changing rapidly. Just as their responsibilities in all areas have been affected by automation, secretaries may expect their filing activities to change. Electronic filing systems that eliminate paper shuffling are now in popular use in many offices. A comparison of a modern electronic filing system[2] with a paper filing method follows.

Paper Office	**System 90**
File drawers have folders for different subjects.	System 90 files have file categories for different subjects.
Documents are put into specific folders.	The STORE command puts the document into a category.
Documents are retrieved from files.	The GET command retrieves the document from a category.
Documents are copied and placed in another file.	The COPY command copies the document into another category.
Documents are moved from one file to another.	The MOVE command moves the document to another category.
Documents are thrown away.	The WASTEBASKET command puts the document into the wastebasket.

---

[2]System 90 Electronic Office, LBCI (formerly AXXA) Corporation, *Administrative Management* (November, 1980).

System 90

The SHRED option of the Wastebasket command deletes the document.

The ARCHIVE option files and retrieves documents to and from an archival floppy disk.

Paper Office

Documents are torn up.

Documents are put into warehouse storage.

SUGGESTED READINGS

Administrative Management—The Systems Magazine for Administrative Executives (Monthly). New York: Geyer-McAllister Publications. Select recent articles on records management and storage, micrographics, microfilm.

Bassett, Ernest D., David G. Goodman, and Joseph Fossman. *Business Records Control*, 5th ed. Cincinnati: South-Western Publishing Co., 1981.

Johnson, Mina M., and Norman F. Kallaus. *Records Management: A Collegiate Course in Filing Systems and Procedures*, 3d ed. Cincinnati: South-Western Publishing Co., 1982.

QUESTIONS FOR DISCUSSION

1. In what ways has your concept of the filing work of a secretary changed since reading this chapter?

2. Filing and records management are commonly used as synonymous terms. What distinction would you make between the two terms?

3. Do you agree with the concept that developing office files is a joint responsibility of the secretary and the executive, or do you think this is the secretary's responsibility alone?

4. How do you think computerized files will alter your secretarial responsibilities?

5. Any communication having reference value should be retained and filed. What are some of the communications that come into or are generated in the office that should be discarded relatively promptly?

6. Companies centralize files for economy and efficiency. Executives, however, tend to resist releasing materials to the central files, preferring to build up their in-office files. What can the secretary do to help resolve this conflict?

7. Your employer asks you to get from the central files any correspondence with a Mr. Beal that is available. Neither you nor your employer is sure of the spelling of the person's name, nor do you recall the initials. Several years ago, however, there was a person with a similar name involved in an infringement of patent suit against the company. You recall that this person lived in St. Louis. How would you state your request to the central files?

8. If you started to work in a position during a peak period and discovered that many materials were misfiled, the folders and drawers were overcrowded, the materials were not arranged chronologically in the folders, and the miscellaneous folders contained materials for which individual folders should have been opened, what would you do?

9. Suggest situations in which each of the following types of files will be advantageous:

alphabetic	subject	visible card file
numeric	geographic	chronological

10. Some people believe that an unusual word choice in a sentence is uncomplimentary to the intelligence of the reader and, in some cases, is sarcastic. Discuss the following italicized words. Would you use quotation marks with any of them in a business letter? Would you revise any of the sentences? Is any one of the italicized words an acronym?

   (a) We have heard his *famous* speech on absenteeism.
   (b) The *OCR* will save retyping time and eliminate errors.
   (c) Ms. Church was known as the company's most powerful *aggressee.*
   (d) Your absence will *wreck* our plans for an effective meeting.
   (e) Our new model will help us *murder* our competition.
   (f) Your directions were clear, but our shipping department *fouled up* your order.
   (g) She has one foot firmly planted in *NOW* and the other firmly planted in the past.

PROBLEMS

1. You are administrative assistant and secretary to the sales manager in an organization that has no automated filing equipment. The following items have been seen by the manager and are ready for action. Indicate what disposition you would make of each one. For instance, a notice of an interoffice meeting would be entered on the desk calendar and then destroyed. If an item is retained, indicate under what name or subject it would be filed. (A separate file is kept for the manager's personal items.)

   (a) A reminder notice for the next weekly meeting of the Sales Executives' Club
   (b) A new catalog from Brown and Brown, a firm that provides sales incentive plans (The old catalog is in the files.)
   (c) An application for a sales position from Wanda Higel
   (d) Copy for the *Weekly Sales Newsletter,*

   which is sent to the sales manager by Lloyd Giroux, editor, for final approval before it goes to the reprographic department
   (e) A letter from an applicant for a sales position thanking the manager for the initial interview
   (f) An announcement of fall courses at a local college (Employees who take job-related courses are reimbursed by the company for their tuition costs.)
   (g) A notice that the executive's office subscription to *Sales Management* has expired
   (h) A letter from Rosa Di Lorenzo asking to change her appointment from Wednesday to Friday at the same hour
   (i) A completed chapter for a book on *Prognosis of Sales Ability* (The name of the chapter is "Psychological Testing.")

(j) A copy of the manager's expense account for the preceding week

(k) A requisition for a new dictating unit for the manager's use.

(l) A car-rental contract covering automobiles for sales representatives in the Chicago area

(m) A quarterly report of Xerox Corporation in which the manager holds stock

(n) An interoffice memo from the president of the company approving the manager's request to hold a sales training conference at Lake Crystal on September 18–20

(o) A letter from an irate customer complaining about the treatment received from the Little Rock area salesman, Herman Beckwith

(p) A catalog from Hertz Company about its blanket quarterly service contract for company rentals

(q) Safety regulations applying to all departments in the home office

2. On July 18 your employer, Evelyn Forbes (credit manager), dictated the following letter to be sent to Mr. Frank W. Russo, 421 East Oak Street, Columbus, Ohio, 43210-3223.

"Dear Mr. Russo: On June 4 you wrote us that you had purchased the Oak Street Market in Columbus and that you would assume all the market's obligations. At that time the market owed us $86.15 on Invoice No. 3310. On June 13 you ordered more goods for $52.60 at 2/10, n/30. The old bill incurred by the Oak Street Market is now sixty days overdue and your own order of $52.60 remains unpaid. We wonder if something is wrong, Mr. Russo. Won't you write us at once, either enclosing your check for the two invoices or letting us know when we may expect payment. Yours very truly."

You are then told by the credit manager to follow up in ten days with Form Letter 5 if the account is still unpaid. If no action has been secured in 20 days, you are to send Form Letter 8.

(a) Type the letter and one carbon copy in good form so you can prepare the carbon copy for filing.

(b) Prepare a cross-reference sheet (see page 343) and cross-reference the letter.

(c) Release the letter for filing.

(d) Prepare the follow-up card for the tickler file.

Chapter 15

Alphabetic Indexing

With the many millions of documents filed in business, it is obvious that uniform rules are necessary for indexing each item that is filed alphabetically. Otherwise, the many people involved in filing would use different rules, and the result could be chaotic.

This chapter presents the generally accepted rules of alphabetic filing so that you and others with whom you work can easily find what is filed. Minor variations from the alphabetic rules presented are occasionally found in different organizations. Be sure to follow the rules that have been adopted at your place of work. The most important factor in alphabetic filing is consistency in applying the rules that have been established in your organization.

NAMES OF INDIVIDUALS

The first step in filing procedures is indexing. When you arrange names for filing purposes, you are indexing. The six rules that follow cover the indexing of individual names.

(1) Basic Order of Indexing Units

Each part of the name of an individual is an indexing unit. Consider the surname (last name) as the first unit, the first name or initial as the second unit, and the middle name or initial as the third unit. Arrange all names in A–Z sequence, comparing each letter in order until a point of difference is reached. *The letter that determines the order of any two names is the first letter that is different in the two names.* Consider first the first unit of each name. Consider the second units only when the first units are identical. Consider the third units only when the first and second units are identical. When further indexing is necessary to determine the relative position of two or more names that have exactly the same first, second, and third coding units, seniority abbreviations (*Jr., Sr., II, III, IV*) can be used to determine the filing order.

Illus. 15-1
Because the files were in order, this secretary was able to find a report she needed.

The Shaw-Walker Co.

Name	Index Order of Units		
	Unit 1	Unit 2	Unit 3
¹Joan Ander	Ander,	Joan	
Joan E. Ander	Ander,	Joan	E.
Louise Ander	Ander,	Louise	
Adam Anders	Anders,	Adam	
²John C. Anderson, Jr.	Anderson,	John	C. (Junior)
²John C. Anderson, Sr.	Anderson,	John	C. (Senior)
Anna Andersson	Andersson,	Anna	
Alma Lee Andrews	Andrews,	Alma	Lee
E. Bennett Andrews	Andrews,	E.	Bennett
³Soo On Bee	Bee,	Soo	On
⁴Eli J. Dorman, II	Dorman,	Eli	J. (II)
⁴Eli J. Dorman, III	Dorman,	Eli	J. (III)

Note 1: *Ander* precedes *Anders* because the *r* in *Ander* is not followed by any letter. This is an example of the rule that *nothing precedes something*.

Note 2: The abbreviations *Junior* (*Jr.*) and *Senior* (*Sr.*) are used in alphabetic sequence.

Note 3: An unusual or foreign personal name is indexed in the usual manner, with the last word considered to be the surname and therefore the first indexing unit.

Note 4: Titles *II* and *III* are used in numeric sequence.

(2) Surname Prefixes and Hyphenated Surnames

(A) A surname prefix is considered part of the first indexing unit. Among the common prefixes are *D', Da, De, Del, Des, El, Il, La, Le, Les, Los, Mac,*

Mc, O', Van, and *Von.* In some cases the first letter of a prefix is not capitalized. Spacing of the surname is not significant. (B) When compound (that is, hyphenated) surnames, such as *Martin-Ames,* or given names, such as *Jo-Mar,* occur in filing, each part of the name is considered a separate unit.

| Name | Index Order of Units | | |
	Unit 1	Unit 2	Unit 3
Catherine Lemate	Lemate,	Catherine	
Francis LeMate	LeMate,	Francis	
Ruth Martin-Ames	Martin-	Ames	Ruth
Wallace Martin	Martin,	Wallace	
Karen O'Bonner	O'Bonner,	Karen	
Jo-Mar Odell	Odell,	Jo-	Mar
¹Edith St. Marner	Saint	Marner,	Edith

Note 1: Even though *St.* is abbreviated in the name *Edith St. Marner,* it is indexed as if it were spelled in full and is considered the first unit. (A variation of this rule is to consider the prefix *Saint* and the part of the surname that follows it to be one unit.)
Note 2: A variation of Rule 2B above is to consider hyphenated surnames as one unit. Drop the hyphen and assume that the letters are continuous.

(3) Initials and Abbreviations

(A) An initial in an individual's name is considered as an indexing unit and precedes all names in the same unit beginning with the same letter as the initial. (B) An abbreviated first or middle name or a nickname is considered as if it were written in full.

| Name | Index Order of Units | | |
	Unit 1	Unit 2	Unit 3
Paula Cameron	Cameron,	Paula	
D. D. Crawford	Crawford,	D.	D.
Dale Crawford	Crawford,	Dale	
Jas. E. Dackman	Dackman,	James	E.
Jane Dackman	Dackman,	Jane	
¹Bob L. Davirro	Davirro,	Bob	L.
Robert Davirro	Davirro,	Robert	

Note 1: When the brief form of a given name is known to be used by an individual as a given name, this brief form name is treated as a unit.

(4) Titles

(A) A personal or professional title or degree is usually not considered in filing. When the name is written in index form, the title is placed in parentheses at the end of the name. (B) A title is considered as the first indexing unit only when it is followed by the given name alone or by the surname alone.

Name	Index Order of Units		
	Unit 1	Unit 2	Unit 3
Miss Mary J. Fatam	Fatam,	Mary	J. (Miss)
[1a]Father Delbert	Father	Delbert	
Rev. A. O. Hanson	Hanson,	A.	O. (Rev.)
Ralph Hanson, D. D.	Hanson,	Ralph (D. D.)	
[1b]Father Robert O. Hanson	Hanson,	Robert	O. (Father)
Madame Mavis	Madame	Mavis	
Capt. Orrin Mason	Mason,	Orrin (Capt.)	
Mrs. Ann Jones Milton	Milton,	Ann	Jones (Mrs.)
Dr. Diana Miltson	Miltson,	Diana (Dr.)	

Note 1: For names including the religious titles *Father, Brother,* and *Sister,* Rule 4B may be modified as follows:

(a) To group together within a filing system all names bearing one of these titles, consider the titles themselves of first importance in indexing, regardless of the names that follow them. Names that do not include a surname are indexed in the order written: *Father Delbert.* Names that include one or more given names and a surname are transposed after the title, as explained in Rule 1: *Hanson, Robert O. (Father).*

(b) To set up a separate section to include all such names in the files, consider the name or names following such titles as of first importance, and *disregard the title.* Names that do not include a surname are indexed in the order written. Names that include one or more given names and a surname are transposed. Indexing order for *Father Delbert* in such case would be *Delbert (Father); Father Robert O. Hanson* would be *Hanson, Robert O. (Father).*

(5) Names of Married Women

The name of a married woman is indexed as she writes it. Her last name is the main unit, her first name is the second unit, and her middle name or initial is the third unit. Mrs. or Ms. is placed in parentheses and is not considered in filing. Many married women are now using their maiden names, a hyphenated last name composed of their maiden and married names, or the names they used as their business names before they were married. If a married woman prefers to use her husband's first name and initial, her preference should be followed.

Name	Index Order of Units		
	Unit 1	Unit 2	Unit 3
Ms. Becky Jones Fritts	Fritts,	Becky	Jones (Ms.)
Mrs. Lucien (Becky Mae) Fritts	Fritts,	Becky	Mae (Mrs. Lucien)
Miss Becky Mae Jones	Jones,	Becky	Mae (Miss)
Mrs. Gerald V. Kingston	Kingston,	Gerald	V. (Mrs.)

(6) Identical Names

When the names of individuals are identical, their alphabetic order is determined by their addresses, starting with the city. Names of states are considered when the names of the cities are also alike. When the city and the state names as well as the full names of the individuals are alike, the alphabetic order is determined by street names; next, house and building numbers, with the lowest filed first.

Name	Unit 1	Index Order of Units		
		Unit 2	Unit 3	Unit 4
Janice Hess, 314 Elm Street, Toledo	Hess,	Janice	Toledo	Elm
Janice Hess, 92 Plum Avenue, Toledo	Hess,	Janice	Toledo	Plum
Edward Iglecia, Akron	Iglecia,	Edward	Akron	
Edward Iglecia, Columbus	Iglecia,	Edward	Columbus	
Edward Iglecia, Dayton	Iglecia,	Edward	Dayton	
Edward B. Iglecia	Iglecia,	Edward	B.	

NAMES OF BUSINESSES AND GROUPS

Business organization filing can sometimes present special indexing problems. A mastery of the following rules should give you the confidence you need when you have to file materials for other than names of individuals.

(7) Basic Order of Indexing Units

(A) Usually the indexing units of a business or group name are considered in the order in which they are written. (B) An exception is made to the usual rule when a business name includes the full name of an individual, such as *Sam Martin Garage.* In that case the units in the individual name are considered in the same order as if the individual name appeared independently, as shown below.

Name	Unit 1	Index Order of Units	
		Unit 2	Unit 3
S. Martin Hats	Martin,	S.	Hats
Sam Martin Garage	Martin,	Sam	Garage
Nelson Lumber Company	Nelson	Lumber	Company
¹Newsweek	Newsweek		
Jill Nobee News Corner	Nobee,	Jill	News
World Almanac	World	Almanac	

Note 1: The name of a magazine or book may be indexed according to these basic indexing rules for the name of a business.

(8) Articles, Conjunctions, and Prepositions

(A) Such words as *the, and, &, for, on, in, by,* and *of the* are generally disregarded in indexing and filing. However, they are placed in parentheses for coding purposes. An initial *the* is placed in parentheses after the last unit. (B) A word normally classified as a preposition but used as the first word in a business name, or as a modifying word, or as part of a compound name is considered a separate indexing unit.

Name	Index Order of Units		
	Unit 1	Unit 2	Unit 3
By the Lane Inn	By (the)	Lane	Inn
Charles of the Ritz	Charles (of the)	Ritz	
Committee on Departmental Reorganization	Committee (on)	Departmental	Reorganization
Emery & Frank Shoes	Emery (&)	Frank	Shoes
End of the Mile Tavern	End (of the)	Mile	Tavern
The Favorite Music Shop	Favorite	Music	Shop (The)

(9) Initials, Abbreviations, and Titles

(A) An initial or letter that is not a common abbreviation precedes a *word* beginning with that letter. (B) A known abbreviation, even though the abbreviation consists of a single letter without a period, is treated as if it were spelled in full, except *Mr.* and *Mrs.*, which are filed alphabetically as they are written. (C) A business name including a title followed by a given name, a surname, or a coined name is indexed in the order in which it is written.

Name	Index Order of Units		
	Unit 1	Unit 2	Unit 3
BB Brakes	B	B	Brakes
Ball Crank Co.	Ball	Crank	Company
B & O Railroad	Baltimore (&)	Ohio	Railroad
Bayard Co.	Bayard	Company	
C and C Dress Shoppe	C (and)	C	Dress
City Cleaners	City	Cleaners	
Dr. Footeze	Doctor	Footeze	
Miss Della Knits	Miss	Della	Knits
Monsieur Antoine Beauty Salon	Monsieur	Antoine	Beauty
Mr. Jim's Steak House	Mr.	Jim's	Steak

(10) Numbers and Symbols

(A) A number in a firm name is considered one word. It is indexed as one unit. Four-place numbers are expressed in hundreds (not in thousands) in order to consider a smaller number of letters in the indexing unit. (B) A symbol with the number is considered separately as a word.

Name	Index Order of Units		
	Unit 1	Unit 2	Unit 3
A 1 Garage	A	One	Garage
8th St. Bldg.	Eighth	Street	Building
1110 Choices Store	¹Elevenhundredten	Choices	Store
$5 Bargain Store	Five	Dollar	Bargain
Ft. Evans News	Fort	Evans	News
40th Avenue Laundry	²Fortieth	Avenue	Laundry
Fortilair Food Shop	Fortilair	Food	Shop

Note 1: Some file manuals omit the words *hundred* and *thousand* in considering the indexing unit—examples: *fiveten* for 510 and *twelveseventy* for 1270.

Note 2: When several names differ only in numeric designations, the order of those names may be based on the numeric sequence instead of the alphabetic order of those numbers written in words. For example, if several branch stores of the same company are numbered, it might be more convenient in an office to have the names arranged in numeric sequence.

(11) Hyphenated Names

The hyphenated parts of business names (including coined parts) are indexed and filed as separate words.

An exception is made to this rule when the hyphenated parts are shown in the dictionary as a single word or as a hyphenated word. Both parts are then considered together as one indexing unit.

Name	Index Order of Units		
	Unit 1	Unit 2	Unit 3
A-1 Retail Markets	A-	One	Retail
Read-N-Sew Studio	Read-	N-	Sew
Ready-Built Shelf Shop	Ready-	Built	Shelf
Reedy-Adam Corp.	Reedy-	Adam	Corporation
Charlene A. Reedy Corp.	Reedy,	Charlene	A.
Reedy-Miller Studios	Reedy-	Miller	Studios
Adam D. Reedy-Smith Corp.	Reedy-	Smith,	Adam
Self-Service Laundry	Self-Service	Laundry	
Self-Study Society	Self-Study	Society	
Selfton Voice Studio	Selfton	Voice	Studio

(12) One Versus Two Units

When separate words in a business name are shown in the dictionary as one word, the two should be treated as one indexing unit.

Name	Index Order of Units Unit 1	Unit 2	Unit 3
Semi-Trailer Rentals, Inc.	SemiTrailer	Rentals	Incorporated
Semi Weekly Cleaning Service	SemiWeekly	Cleaning	Service
Semiweekly Communication Review	Semiweekly	Communication	Review
Southwestern Machine Products	Southwestern	Machine	Products
South Western Office Supplies	SouthWestern	Office	Supplies
South-Western Publishing Co.	SouthWestern	Publishing	Company
Southwick Drug Service	Southwick	Drug	Service
Southwick Drug Store	Southwick	DrugStore	
Stephan's Super Repair Shop	Stephan's	Super	Repair
Stephan's Super Market Displays	Stephan's	SuperMarket	Displays

(13) Compound Geographic and Location Names

(A) Each English word in a compound geographic or location name is indexed as a separate unit. (B) A prefix or foreign article in such names is not considered as a separate indexing unit but is combined with the word that follows.

Name	Index Order of Units Unit 1	Unit 2	Unit 3
Le Mont Food Products	LeMont	Food	Products
Los Angeles Actors' Guild	Los Angeles	Actors'	Guild
North Dakota Curios	North	Dakota	Curios
Old Saybury R. R. Station	Old	Saybury	Railroad
St. Thomas Island Home	Saint	Thomas	Island
Saintbury Publishing Co.	Saintbury	Publishing	Company
[1]San Diego Greenhouses, Inc.	San	Diego	Greenhouses
[1]Santa Clara Lithographers	Santa	Clara	Lithographers

Note 1: The words *San* in *San Diego* and *Santa* in *Santa Clara* mean *Saint* and are therefore indexed separately according to their spelling.

(14) Possessives

When a word ends in *apostrophe s* ('s), the final *s* is not considered as part of the word for filing purposes, except when the *s* is part of a contraction.

When a word ends in *s apostrophe* (*s'*), however, the final *s* is considered.

Name	Index Order of Units		
	Unit 1	Unit 2	Unit 3
Girl Scouts of America	Girl	Scouts (of)	America
Girl's Sportswear	Girl('s	Sportswear	
Girls' Short Stories	Girls'	Short	Stories
Harper's Restaurant	Harper('s)	Restaurant	
Harpers	Harpers		
Harperston's Apparel	Harperston('s)	Apparel	
Harperston Bank	Harperston	Bank	

(15) Identical Business Names

(A) Identical names of businesses are arranged alphabetically by address, with address parts treated as identifying elements. (For this reason the word *City* should not be used in place of the name of the city for local correspondents.) (B) If the names of the cities are alike, filing arrangement depends upon names of states. (C) When two or more branches of a business are located in the same city, the names of the branches are arranged alphabetically by street names.

Name	Index Order of Units		
	Unit 1	Unit 2	Unit 3
Janicki Stationers, Decatur	Janicki	Stationers,	Decatur
Janicki Stationers, Eureka	Janicki	Stationers,	Eureka
Janicki Stationers, Sterling	Janicki	Stationers,	Sterling
Kastner's, 531 Main Street	Kastner('s),	Main	
Kastner's, 1024 Oak Street	Kastner('s),	Oak	

Note 1: The name of the building in which the firm is located should not be considered unless the name of the street is not provided or is identical for both branches.

MISCELLANEOUS ESTABLISHMENTS

In addition to individual names and business organization names, other establishments—financial institutions, publications, schools, hotels, churches, associations, and government offices—observe generally consistent rules in indexing and maintaining their filing systems.

(16) Financial Institutions

The names of financial institutions are indexed as written. If the names of financial institutions are identical, city, state, street, and building number are used to determine filing order.

Name	Unit 1	Unit 2	Unit 3	Unit 4	Unit 5
			Index Order of Units		
Bank of Atlanta	Bank (of)	Atlanta			
Bloomington Trust Co. Bloomington, Illinois	Bloomington	Trust	Company	¹Illinois	
Bloomington Trust Co. Bloomington, Indiana	Bloomington	Trust	Company	Indiana	
First Federal Savings Fairfield, California	First	Federal	Savings	Fairfield	California (CA)
First Federal Savings Fairfield, Connecticut	First	Federal	Savings	Fairfield	Connecticut (CT)

Note 1: If the name of the financial institution contains the name of the city or state, that geographic location is not repeated in the indexed form.

(17) Publications

The names of newspapers, magazines, and pamphlets are considered in the order written. The city of publication of a newspaper is usually the first word in the name of a newspaper.

Name	Unit 1	Unit 2	Unit 3
		Index Order of Units	
Business Week	Business	Week	
Wenatchee Times Wenatchee, Washington	Wenatchee	Times	
Times Herald Williamsport, Pennsylvania	Williamsport	Times	Herald

(18) Elementary and Secondary School Names

Elementary and secondary school names are considered in the order written, except that a person's name within a school name is transposed. In the case of identically named schools, city and state names are used to determine the filing order.

| | | Index Order of Units | | |
Name	Unit 1	Unit 2	Unit 3	Unit 4
Crispus Attucks High School Indianapolis, Indiana	Attucks	Crispus	High	School
			Unit 5: Indianapolis	
			Unit 6: Indiana	
Newport High School Newport, Rhode Island	Newport	High	School	Rhode Island
Newport High School Newport, Washington	Newport	High	School	Washington

(19) Colleges, Universities, Special Schools, Hotels, Motels, and Other Organizations

(A) When, through common usage, one part of a name more clearly identifies the organization, that part is used as the first indexing unit. Otherwise, names of organizations are indexed as they are generally written. (B) A city or state name as part of the organization name is considered an indexing unit or units. When the name of an organization is the same in two or more cities, city names are considered last as identifying elements.

| | Index Order of Units | | |
Name	Unit 1	Unit 2	Unit 3
1Howard Johnson's Motor Lodge	Howard	Johnson's	Motor
University of Idaho	Idaho,	University (of)	
Indiana University	Indiana	University	
Hotel Jolee Florists	Jolee,	Hotel,	Florists
Priest River Kiwanis Club	Kiwanis	Club,	Priest
Los Angeles City College	Los Angeles	City	College
Association of Lumbermen	Lumbermen,	Association (of)	
First Methodist Church	Methodist	Church,	First
1Martha Nelson Beauty College	Nelson,	Martha,	Beauty
2WLBC	Radio	Station	W
Venovich Motel	Venovich	Motel	

Note 1: An individual's name within the name of the organization is transposed in the usual manner unless the name is always considered as a unit.

Note 2: Preferable way to index a radio or television station is to consider *Radio Station* or *Television Station* as the first two units, followed by each call letter as a separate unit.

(20) Federal Government Offices

The name of a federal government office is considered for indexing in the following order: (1) United States Government (the first three indexing units), (2) principal word or words in the name of the department, (3) principal word or words in the name of the bureau, (4) principal word or words in the name of the division. Such words as *Department of; Bureau of;* and *Division of* are transposed, with the word *of* disregarded and so placed in parentheses.

When in doubt as to which United States government department a bureau, division, or office is attached, consult the *Government Manual.* This manual provides the latest available information on the administrative structure of the federal government.

Name	Index Order of Units				
	Unit 4	*Unit 5*	*Unit 6*	*Unit 7*	*Unit 8*
Bureau of the Census, U.S. Department of Commerce	Commerce, (of)	Department	Census, (of the)	Bureau	
National Oceanic and Atmospheric Administration, U.S. Department of Commerce	Commerce, (of)	Department	National	Oceanic (and)	Atmospheric — Unit 9: Administration
Social Security Administration, U.S. Department of Health and Human Services	Health (and)	Human Services	Department	Social	(of) — Unit 9: Security — Unit 10: Administration
Bureau of Indian Affairs, U.S. Department of the Interior	Interior, (of the)	Department	Indian	Affairs,	Bureau (of)
[1]Federal Bureau of Investigation, U.S. Department of Justice	Justice, (of)	Department	Federal	Bureau (of)	Investigation

Note 1: The Federal Bureau of Investigation is so well known by its full name and initials that the name is often filed as known.

(21) Other Government Offices

(A) The name of any other government office is considered in the following order: (1) principal word or words in the name of the political subdivision, followed by its state, county, or city classification, (2) principal word or words in the name of the department, board, or office. Such words as *Department of* and *Bureau of* are transposed, with the word *of* placed in parentheses. (B) If two or more political subdivisions have the same first indexing unit, the state name as an identifying unit is considered immediately after the first principal word in the political subdivision. This determines relative placement of items with identical first units.

| Name | Index Order of Units | | | | |
	Unit 1	Unit 2	Unit 3	Unit 4	Unit 5
Department of Public Safety California	California,	State (of)	Public	Safety	Department (of)
Board of Health Cincinnati	Cincinnati,	City (of)	Health	Board (of)	
Tax Collector Cook County	Cook,	County	Tax	Collector	

(22) Foreign Governments

Foreign language names are translated into English for indexing, and the distinctive English name of the foreign country is considered first. Next, divisions are considered in the same manner as are United States governmental units.

| Name | Index Order of Units | | | |
	Unit 1	Unit 2	Unit 3	Unit 4
[1]Republique Francaise Armée de l'Air	France	Air	Force	
Estados Unidos Mexicanos Secretaria de Industrio y Commercia	Mexico	Industry (and)	Commerce,	Secretary (of)

Note 1: The names of foreign countries may be uniformly filed according to the native spelling rather than the English translation.

CONCLUSION

To determine which of several possibilities of filing rules will best fit the needs of the office or organization, the secretary or the file supervisor should keep in mind major criteria of serviceability: (1) Which indexing procedure will provide for filing or refiling of materials with the least amount of error? (2) Which indexing procedure will provide for filing or withdrawing materials and for refiling materials with least time waste?

Once such a decision is made, definite steps must be taken to assure that, through the office manual and whatever other means might be helpful, the procedure will be communicated successfully to all concerned and will be followed consistently.

SUGGESTED READINGS

Bassett, Ernest D., David G. Goodman, and Joseph S. Fosegan. *Business Records Control*, 5th ed. Cincinnati: South-Western Publishing Co., 1981.

Johnson, Mina M., and Norman F. Kallaus. *Records Management—A Collegiate Course in Filing Systems and Procedures*, 3d ed. Cincinnati: South-Western Publishing Co., 1982.

QUESTIONS FOR DISCUSSION

1. If you are the only person with access to the in-office files, what difference would it make whether or not you follow an established set of indexing rules?

2. If all retained materials were stored on microfilm in a centralized filing department and no in-office files were maintained, would there be any reason for the secretary to be familiar with the rules of alphabetic indexing?

3. Why do rules for filing government units, banks, schools, churches, and other organizations differ from the other rules for indexing?

4. What is the major difference in indexing company names as opposed to indexing individual names?

5. Why should the word *City* not be used instead of the city name for local correspondents?

6. Refer to your Reference Guide. Give the correct salutation for a letter addressed to each of the following persons.

   (a) Mayor of a city
   (b) Governor of a state
   (c) Judge of a court
   (d) President of the United States
   (e) Member of the President's cabinet

7. In what order are the units of a federal governmental office considered for indexing?

PROBLEMS

1. Rewrite the following names of individuals in index form. Underline the first unit of the name once and the second unit of the name twice.

   (a) Wm. Mier, 381 Shady Lane, Louisville, Kentucky
   (b) Cheryl Mestes
   (c) Jas. C. Naber
   (d) Ms. Mary Messino
   (e) Mrs. Robt. (Debra L.) O'Brien, Akron
   (f) Tom M. O'Connell, Sr.
   (g) T. Kathleen MacNabb
   (h) Wm. Mier, 29 Parkland Avenue, Louisville, Kentucky

   (i) Mrs. J. Clarence Naber
   (j) Sister Norita
   (k) Mrs. Robt. (D. Lucille) O'Brien, Springfield
   (l) Tom M. O'Connell, Jr.
   (m) Thomas McNamara
   (n) Joe Manendez
   (o) J. L. Menio, Ph.D.

2. Rewrite the following business names in index form and alphabetical order. Underline the first unit of the name once and the second unit of the name twice.

   (a) Stoke's Paper Company
   (b) Mr. Tom's Fur Salon

(c) The Las Vegas Novelty Shop
(d) Tom & Joan's Bait Shop
(e) Top of the Mount Restaurant
(f) Russell Stone Camping Equipment
(g) 8th Street Garage
(h) Joanne Stokes and Daughters
(i) S & T Delicatessen
(j) Bureau of Labor Statistics, U.S. Department of Labor
(k) Stone's Grocery, No. 1
(l) South West Auto Supplies
(m) San Bernardino Rest Home
(n) Stone's Grocery, No. 2

3. You are to set up a portion of a file for the Sales Promotion Department of Ohio Bell Telephone, which is planning solicitation of all business organizations in a small Ohio city for a new type of push-button telephone. Arrange the following names in the correct filing form and order:

(a) First National Bank of Athens
(b) Saint Joseph's Church
(c) Martins' Service Station, Third Street
(d) South-Eastern Ohio Freezer Co.
(e) Bank of Ohio, Athens
(f) First Baptist Church of Athens
(g) Agricultural Extension Service (Federal Office)
(h) Board of Education, Athens
(i) Ohio University
(j) Rehabilitation Services Administration (Federal Office)
(k) Athens Chamber of Commerce
(l) State Highway Department
(m) C & O Railway
(n) Martin's Drive-in Theater
(o) First National Mortgage Co.
(p) Aaron Jones Retail Outlet
(q) Martins' Service Station, Elm Street
(r) Aaron-James Production Credit Corporation
(s) Cartinson Dress Shoppe

Group I

4. Group I is arranged alphabetically. File each Group II name in its proper position in Group I by placing the letter at the end of the line of the name it follows.

Group I

1. AAA Answering and Office Service
2. A & A Window Corporation
3. ABC Vending Corporation
4. A-1 Taxi Service
5. Abbey Floor Waxing Company
6. Abbott, A. C., Company, Inc.
7. Abraham & Straus
8. Abrahamson's Pharmacy
9. Abrams, Norma J. (Dr.)
10. Abrantes, Anthony (Jr.)
11. Academy Auto Wreckers
12. Accessory Shop
13. Ace Auto Service
14. Ackerman, Mary E.
15. Ackermann, Andrew J.
16. Acme Excavating Corporation
17. Acme-Standard Supply Company
18. Acorn Landscape Service
19. Acousticon of White Plains
20. Adam, Mary T.
21. Adano, Loretta C., Company
22. Addressograph-Multigraph Corporation
23. Adelman, Murray P.
24. Adelson, Maude
25. Air Dispatch Incorporated
26. Air-Way Travel Service
27. Al & Hazel's Restaurant
28. Albanese's Eastchester Inn
29. Albano Studio (The)
30. Alert Employment Agency
31. Alex's Radio & Television Service
32. Alfredo, A., Nurseries
33. Alitalia Airlines
34. All County Electric Service
35. Allen Brothers Incorporated
36. Allen-Keating Corporation
37. Allen's Supply Company
38. Allevi, Lillian (Mrs.)
39. Allied Van Lines, Incorporated
40. Allis-Chalmers Corporation

Group II

A. Accounting Associates
B. Addressing Machine & Equipment Company
C. A & A Automotive Company
D. Abrahamson Dress Shop
E. J. B. Allid
F. A-B-K Electric Company
G. Adler Shoes for Men

H. Acme Steel Company
I. Anita H. Alleva
J. Academy of Aeronautics
K. Air-Step Shoe Shop
L. Ms. Elizabeth Abbott
M. Alexander Carpet Company
N. A & P Food Co.

O. Al's Glass Service
P. Paul Allen Incorporated
Q. Aladdin's House of Beauty
R. Julie B. L. Allen
S. Alden Supply Company
T. The Alice Ackermann Shop
U. The Allen-Andrews Mailing Co.

Part Five   Case Problems

Case 5-1
BUILDING A GOOD RELATIONSHIP WITH RECORDS MANAGEMENT PERSONNEL

Marty Byrnes, secretary to Mark Janowitz, attorney in charge of shareholders' relations, was usually annoyed by the type of service she received from the records management administrator, Phyllis Downe. She thought that the department was inefficient and frequently slow in providing materials and often said so.

One day a crisis developed because of the possibility of a lawsuit instigated by a shareholder. Marty telephoned Ms. Downe to request records that had not been referred to in ten years. Ms. Downe told her that the files were, of course, on microfilm in the Records Center. It would be impossible to get them in fewer than four days because prior requests had to be taken care of first, and she was shorthanded and had nobody to locate the records by reading the microfilm.

Marty said, "But this is an emergency. Mr. Janowitz wants those records by four o'clock today." Ms. Downe replied, "Sorry, but that will be impossible unless Mr. Janowitz or you want to go 50 miles to the Records Center and get them yourselves."

What short-term action can be taken? what long-term action? What principles are involved?

Case 5-2
CONTROLLING THE FILES

Jacques Grenadier had to cope with the "generosity" of Madame Jeanne, one of the principals for whom he was administrative secretary in a large cosmetics company. Madame Jeanne frequently sent letters to colleagues with a penciled notation: "Please note and return" or "Let me have your comments, please."

Few of the letters or reports were ever returned for the file. Frequently Madame Jeanne wanted immediately a letter that could not be found. She would say, "But I must have that letter *now*. It has to be in your files. Where have you misfiled it this time?"

What reply should Jacques make? What system do you suggest to avoid recurrences of this perennial cause of contention?

Case 5-3
SECRETARIAL
ETHICS

Lisa Chiang was secretary to Conrad Justin, sales manager of the Jacobs Office Furniture Company. The company rented a list of sales prospects from Orville Evers, owner of a direct mail company, and used the list in a nationwide promotion.

In an independent personal effort, Mr. Justin obtained a patent for an electric wastepaper basket and started its manufacture in a small factory of his own.

Since distribution was his major problem, he used the sales prospect list rented by the Jacobs Office Furniture Company. He sent the advertising material out from his office, using the tapes containing the addresses that had been prepared for the Jacobs company. Lisa, of course, knew of this mailing.

While Mr. Justin was out of town, Orville Evers, owner of the direct mail company, stormed into the office with the advertising for the electric wastebasket and the envelope in which it had been mailed. He indignantly explained to Lisa that one address on his rented list was fictitious and contained a key word used to detect just such unauthorized uses.

Mr. Evers demanded the return of the list on the spot. He also insisted that Lisa give him the address tapes to take with him when he left the office.

What should Lisa do?
What is her responsibility to Mr. Justin? to the Jacobs Company?

Case 5-4
DEVELOPING
POSITIVE
ATTITUDES

Apartment Furniture, Inc., has a buddy system under which selected experienced employees are assigned on a one-to-one basis to help new workers adjust to their jobs. This assignment is considered a compliment to the experienced employee.

Blanche Woods, secretary to J. W. Mills, was delighted when Mr. Mills said to her, "Blanche, will you help me out? Ben Falk, who is buddy to Martica Joyer, wants to give up his assignment. Martica is a griper. She takes a negative attitude toward other employees and toward work assignments. Her supervisor and she are almost at swords' points, and she is becoming a misfit among her colleagues. Yet she does the best work that we have had from a beginner in months. She *could* become a real asset and is definitely worth saving. Personally, I like her.

"Ordinarily this situation would be handled by her supervisor, but you know as well as I do how rigid and inflexible Ms. Cruz is. I remember that you told me that you are interested in psychology, so why not give this assignment a fling?"

Blanche decides to accept the challenge, but needs help in developing a plan. What recommendations would you make to her?

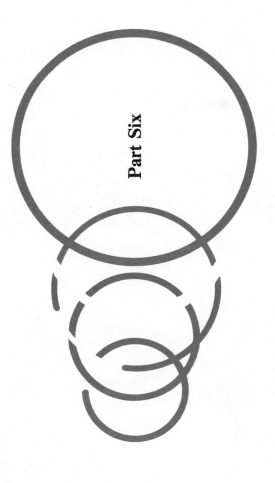

Part Six

ADMINISTRATIVE SUPPORT SERVICES: TRAVEL AND CONFERENCES

No two days are alike probably describes the working calendar of the administrative or the multifunctional secretary. Two responsibilities that require the ingenuity and resourcefulness of the secretary are expediting the travel arrangements of the executive and planning for and assisting at conferences. The secretary researches the most convenient schedules, procures tickets, prepares necessary material to be taken on the trip, and does the follow-up activities required after the trip. Whether a meeting or a conference, the secretary plans for its smooth operation, prepares a record, and reports the results.

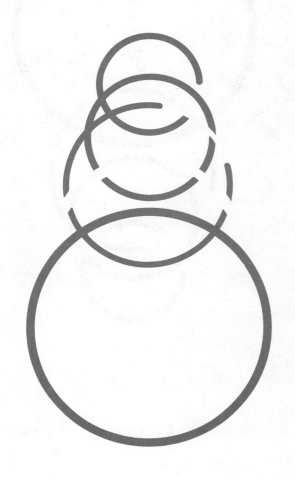

Chapter 16

Expediting
Travel Arrangements

In a recent survey of 300 executives 99 percent reported that they take business trips on a regular basis. For some, business travel meant over 50 trips a year, but the majority (61 percent) logged 15 trips a year. Unless the trip was under 300 miles, these executives generally traveled by air.

The administrative secretary or the multifunctional secretary, therefore, can expect the executive to say, "Tomorrow I must be in Chicago before 10 a.m., Wednesday and Thursday in Atlanta, and back here in the office early Friday morning." These directions set in motion arrangements for airlines, flights, hotels, and types of transportation from airports to hotels. Reservations that suit the executive's needs have to be made. The administrative or the multifunctional secretary researches the information, obtains the approval of the executive, and then completes the details for the trip following the company's travel policies. In addition, the secretary is responsible for running a smooth office while the executive is away.

Because transportation is such a highly competitive field, changes in equipment, services, and fares are being announced constantly. You cannot handle travel arrangements efficiently unless you keep up with these changes and incorporate them into your arrangements for your employer's travel. You will also need to know your company's policies about travel arrangements, which may change from time to time. You will want to learn your employer's preferences as to airlines, hotels, rented automobiles, and all facilities that will make strenuous but necessary trips as pleasant as possible.

COMPANY POLICIES REGARDING TRAVEL ARRANGEMENTS

The secretary's first concern in handling travel arrangements is to learn the company's policies. Who handles this responsibility? What airline, hotel, and other credit cards are issued, and what procedures are authorized for their use? How are tickets paid for? How are employees reimbursed for travel expenses? What restrictions does the company have as to per diem (per day) travel expenses? How are travel funds obtained?

Travel arrangements may be handled by a transportation department (or central travel section) within the company, by an outside travel agency, or by the secretary.

Transportation Department

In large organizations actual reservations for travel are expedited by a transportation department or central travel service that maintains close contact with all carriers, has on hand complete official guides for airlines and railroads, and deals with special reservation agents (at unlisted numbers) who serve only large volume buyers. The secretary informs the transportation department of a proposed trip and the time preferences of the executive; the department then suggests possible schedules to be approved by the executive. When the decision is made, the secretary completes a transportation voucher that is signed by the traveler and an authorizing official. This form is sent to the transportation department for its records. The department either issues or obtains the necessary tickets and distributes credit cards to authorized personnel.

Travel Agencies

In recent years the business world has turned increasingly to travel agencies to meet their travel requirements. By the very nature of its specialization, a reputable agency can cut through the maze of constantly changing fares, flight schedules, classes of service, and so forth. Some large companies, even those with transportation departments, use travel agencies exclusively to save employees' time and costs.

A client does not pay a travel agency for its service. Travel agencies are paid commissions by airlines, railroads, hotels, and other services booked for a client. To speed up their service and increase their knowledge, most travel agencies use computers or are in the process of installing them. They have at their disposal the same type of visual display terminals that ticketing agents have at airline counters.

Travel agencies offer their clients professional service in planning an itinerary, obtaining tickets, selecting and making hotel reservations, and arranging for rental cars. Some agencies extend credit. Most will accept major credit cards, such as Visa or American Express.

If you are asked to choose a travel agency to perform services for your employer, seek a recommendation from a satisfied traveler or look for the symbol indicating membership in the Institute of Certified Travel Agents (ICTA), American Society of Travel Agents, or Association of Retail Travel Agents.

The Secretary

If a business organization provides neither the services of an intracompany special transportation department nor the regular services of a travel agency, the secretary alone is responsible for handling all travel arrangements.

The alert secretary will soon discover the employer's preference for hotel chain, airline, or seat location. Consulting the executive about these preferences and remembering them from trip to trip can alleviate some of the mental and physical stress of the trip and thus contribute to its overall effectiveness.

AIR TRAVEL

Most people traveling on business prefer to fly, especially on long trips, because they save time. Today a passenger can breakfast in Chicago, lunch in San Francisco, and dine in New York. Supersonic transport planes cross the Atlantic from Washington to Paris in a little over three hours. The jet age has given the executive the advantage of keeping close contact with operations without being away from home base for too long a time.

Classes of Flights

Some people like to fly the jumbo 747's that connect the large cities of the United States with each other and with foreign cities. These planes are equipped with large away-from-seat lounges for both coach and first-class passengers. They also have in-flight movies and recorded entertainment. Other travelers prefer smaller planes, which also may provide movies and recorded entertainment in flight.

The major airlines are supported by regional lines that fly to cities too small for jet runways. A passenger traveling from a large city to a small one will probably fly on both jet planes and those of the regional airline.

Most planes have a first-class and a coach section. Generally the classes of flight are:

First Class. Serves complimentary meals during conventional mealtimes and generous refreshments. Has several attendants. Seats are wider, farther apart, and provide more legroom than those in the coach section. First-class fares are considerably higher (50 percent or more) than coach/economy fares.

Coach/Economy. Serves a complimentary meal or snack when the plane is aloft at mealtime. Beverage service for coffee, tea, or soft drinks is available at no charge. Coach passengers often sit three abreast, have less legroom, and occupy narrower seats than first class.

Many organizations have a policy that only high-ranking executives may travel first class, possibly only presidents, vice-presidents, and department heads. The secretary should learn these rules before making travel arrangements. Even though the executive may be entitled to first-class accommodations, coach reservations will probably be adequate for short trips. On a long trip, of course, the added comfort makes a first-class reservation desirable.

Meal services are diversified by competing airlines. Choices of up to three entrees in coach class are offered on certain domestic flights. Meals to accommodate special diets can be ordered.

Shuttle service is available between certain cities within the United States, such as New York/Boston, New York/Washington, and San Francisco/Los Angeles. Passengers board the plane without reservations, and the flights leave at frequent intervals or as soon as the plane is filled. Passengers pay their fares aloft with cash, credit card, or (with proper identification) personal check. Only carry-on luggage is accepted on some shuttle flights.

On most domestic flights each passenger is allowed three pieces of luggage: one measuring not more than 62 inches in girth, another measuring not more than 55 inches, and the third not more than 45 inches. Some luggage may be carried aboard without charge if it fits under the seat in front of the passenger. To avoid waiting for checked luggage at the destination, some airlines provide compartments inside the boarding door for bulky baggage. Passengers who bring on luggage in excess of the weight allowed are charged excess baggage rates in addition to the regular fare.

Air Fares

Air fares are constantly changing. In addition to first-class and coach fares, domestic airlines offer special rates for night flights, excursions that comprise a definite number of days, certain weekend trips, and tickets purchased a definite number of days before takeoff. Reduced rate night flights and excursions are not appropriate for most business travel. If your employer flies frequently, your office may wish to subscribe to the *FareSaver*,[1] a quick reference guide to discount fares that is published semimonthly. For the exact fare for a certain flight on a specific date, however, contact the airline directly or a travel agency.

Flight Schedules

Airlines publish flight schedules and make them available in airports, major hotels, and travel agencies. Schedules are not uniform in structure among airlines. Illus. 16-1, a sample schedule (not intended to be valid), shows the ease with which flight schedules can be read. The example is the schedule of all Trans World Airlines (TWA) flights between Albuquerque, New Mexico, and New York/Newark airports.

---

[1]*FareSaver,* Dept. CT, Box 40944, Washington, D.C. 20016

TWA

From:

ALBUQUERQUE, N.M. (ABQ)

Reservations:
Passenger: 243-8611
Freight: 505-842-4157

To: NEW YORK, N.Y. (JFK/LGA)/
NEWARK, N.J. (EWR)
AIRPORTS: L-LaGuardia J-Kennedy E-Newark

Freq.	Leave	Arrive	Flt No.	Stops
	8 05a	L 2 52p	170	1
	8 28a	L 3 52p	168/330	C
	8 28a	E 3 54p	168/464	C
	8 28a	J 4 38p	168/740	C
	8 28a	J 4 43p	168	2
	10 15a	L 5 15p	94/572	C
	10 15a	E 5 27p	94/56	C
	10 15a	J 5 40p	94/560	C
	10 50a	L 6 04p	290/338	C
X6	10 50a	E 6 24p	290/198	C
	12 45p	J 8 34p	106/82	C
	1 10p	L 8 10p	408	1

From:

NEW YORK, N.Y.
(JFK/LGA)/
NEWARK, N.J.
(EWR)

AIRPORTS: L-LaGuardia J-Kennedy E-Newark

To: ALBUQUERQUE, N.M. (ABQ)

Freq.	Leave	Arrive	Flt No.	Stops
	E 7 45a	11 45a	711/117	C
	L 8 00a	11 45a	303/117	C
	E 9 50a	1 32p	201/319	1
	L 10 00a	1 32p	319	1
	L 12 00n	3 49p	329/103	C
	L 12 55p	6 21p	295/239	C
	E 1 00p	6 21p	93/239	C
	L 3 25p	7 40p	477/105	C
	E 3 55p	7 40p	249/105	C
X67	L 4 30p	8 34p	345/449	C
	J 4 40p	8 34p	405/449	C
	E 4 55p	8 34p	3/449	C
	L 6 45p	9 51p	163	1

FREQUENCY CODES

1—Monday   3—Wednesday   5—Friday   7—Sunday
2—Tuesday   4—Thursday   6—Saturday   X—Except

C Connecting Flight

Illus. 16-1
This schedule of all TWA flights between Albuquerque and New York can be interpreted easily.

There are twelve flights daily from Albuquerque to New York with the exception of the 10:50 a.m. flight to LaGuardia Airport that does not operate on Saturdays. None of the flights is nonstop. Three flights show scheduled stops that do not require a change of airplane. These are called direct flights. Five flights land at LaGuardia Airport near downtown Manhattan, three land at Kennedy Airport, and four at Newark Airport in New Jersey just across the Hudson River from New York.

An executive planning a business trip to New York from Albuquerque most likely will prefer Flight 170, which has only one stop and no change of airplanes. The arrival time of 2:52 p.m. (local time) gives the executive time to check into a hotel and perhaps rest before an evening appointment or one the next morning. This TWA schedule does not indicate meal service; however, since the plane is aloft during mealtime, meal service most likely will be provided. Also, this schedule does not show that Albuquerque is on Mountain Standard Time. A passenger loses two hours in flying east from that time zone and gains two hours flying west from New York.

In returning to Albuquerque the executive has a choice among thirteen flights (with the exception of Flight 345, which does not operate on weekends) and three airports. Because of the convenience of Flight 319 leaving from LaGuardia at 10 a.m. and arriving in Albuquerque at 1:32 p.m. with only one intervening stop, this flight may be the likely choice. If the executive is an early riser and does not mind changing planes, Flight 303 leaving LaGuardia at 8 a.m. may be preferred. This flight will give the executive a half day of working time in Albuquerque.

In researching information on flights for an executive, the secretary should be aware that travelers normally have flight preferences in the following order:

- Nonstop flights to the destination
- Direct flights to the destination
- Connecting flights to destination using the same airline
- Connecting flights to destination using another airline (Airplane gates may be a considerable distance from each other, requiring a long walk, or in some airports a change in building or ride on an interconnecting bus or rail service.)

You should present possible flight schedules to the executive in this order. You should also be aware that, like New York City, many cities have more than one airport. In making connecting flight reservations, be especially careful to book the connecting flight from the same airport.

Flight Information

Because fares, services, and departure times change frequently, the secretary must be certain to use an up-to-date schedule. A call to the reservations and information number listed under the airline in the telephone directory will provide information not only about flights on that line but on others as well. For infrequent travel planning, this is a quick, convenient method. Certain air routes are so competitive that bargain fares are constantly being introduced. A call to the airline or travel agent will give you current information.

A transportation department—and in many cases an executive—will profit from a subscription to one of the airlines guides published by the Reuben H. Donnelley Corporation of Chicago: the monthly or semimonthly *Official Airline Guide, North American Edition*, the monthly *OAG Pocket Flight Guide*, or the quarterly *OAG Travel Planner & Hotel/Motel Guide*. Subscribers receive updated materials automatically. With one of these publications at hand, the secretary can research the most convenient flights available and present alternative plans for the employer's approval before initiating the actual reservations. These publications (according to their individual completeness) also give information about the airport facilities, the distance from the airport to the center of a city, limousine service (time, fares, and pickup points), hotels (Mobil ratings and rates), car rentals, and air taxi services available. The guides are simple to use once you understand the general method of presentation. The opening pages provide keys to the abbreviations and symbols used. Flight information is listed alphabetically by the destination city, then alphabetically by the cities from which flights to that city are available. A brief discussion on the use of the *Official Airline Guide* follows.

Suppose your employer is to fly from Kansas City, Missouri, to Tulsa, Oklahoma. Turn to the *To Tulsa* section (listed alphabetically under *T*). Under *To Tulsa*, locate the *From Kansas City, MO* listings (listed alphabetically under *K*). There you will find a flight schedule similar to that shown in Illus. 16-2.

Reading from the top of the table, you learn the following:

- Tulsa is on Central Daylight Time (CDT).
- TUL is the City/Airport code for Tulsa.
- Kansas City, Missouri, is also on Central Daylight Time.
- MKC is the City/Airport code for Kansas City, Missouri.
- The First Class (F) and Coach (Y) fares are shown. YM refers to Military Reservations.

Under the flight schedules, you quickly see that all the flights are non-stop, indicated by the *O* at the far right. Your selection of a flight will be based on your employer's time preference and the availability of the flight.

- The first flight of the day is at 9:40. This flight operates daily except Saturday and Sunday (X67).
- The flight leaves Kansas City International Airport (C).
- It arrives in Tulsa at 10:25 a.m.
- It is American Airlines Flight 25.
- Both first-class and coach are available.
- The aircraft is a Boeing 727.

Looking under the heading Connections, you find a listing of connecting flight fares for first class (F) and coach (Y). A listing of the connecting flights follows.

Illus. 16-2 This schedule taken from the *Official Airline Guide* should be of help in planning a business trip from Kansas City, Missouri, to Tulsa, Oklahoma.

CONNECTIONS SHOWN MAY NOT BE THE BEST FOR YOUR

To TULSA, OKLA.
From KANSAS CITY, MO.
K-MKC, C-MCI, F-KCK

											CDT TUL	CDT MKC
F	75.93	6.07									82.00	164.00
Y	58.33	4.67									63.00	126.00
YM	47.00											
X67	9:40a	C	10:25a T			AA	25	FY	CC		72S	0
	1:00p	C	1:45p T			AA	239	FY	JT		72S	0
	2:45p	C	3:30p T			AA	237	FY	CC		72S	0
X6	9:20p	C	10:05p T			AA	223	FY	CC		72S	0

CONNECTIONS

				F fare	Y fare	OKC						
A	150.00	12.00	162.00				F	CC				
B	117.59	9.41	127.00				F	JT				
C	117.59	9.41	127.00					CC				
D	101.85	8.15	110.00				Y	CC				
E	90.74	7.26	98.00					CC				
F	90.74	7.26	98.00				Y	JT				
G	90.74	7.26	98.00				Y	CC-T				
H	76.85	6.15	83.00				Y	CC-T				
X7	9:40a	C	10:35a OKC			OKC	AA	129	FY		727	0
(AGE)	11:10a OKC	11:42a T					AA	104	FYV		727	0
(BFF)	7:00p	C	8:48p OKC				AA	255	FY		727	1
	9:50p OKC	10:24p T					AA	438	FnYnV		707	0

If for some reason the executive wants to go to Oklahoma City first for a very brief conference at the airport, and then to Tulsa, it can be arranged.

- American Airlines Flight 129 leaves Kansas City at 9:40 a.m., arrives in Oklahoma City at 10:35.
- The connecting flight, American Airlines Flight 104, leaves Oklahoma City at 11:10 a.m., and arrives in Tulsa at 11:42.
- First-class, coach, and economy (V) service is available.
- The aircraft is a Boeing 727. It is a nonstop flight.

Flight Reservations and Ticketing

Reservations for air travel may be made by telephone, in person at the airport terminal, in the airline ticket office located in some business buildings or hotels in large cities, or at a travel agency. After choosing a flight, the traveler asks the airline reservations agent to check for the availability of space at the desired fare structure. Space availability is confirmed by means of computer equipment that records and stores reservations made for a flight from all ticketing stations. If your employer prefers to travel coach/economy, and that particular section of the plane is booked, first class may be available. If so, you should check with the executive to see if a first-class reservation should be made.

A ticket for an in-person reservation is issued at once; otherwise, it is issued and mailed to a specified address or held for pickup at the ticket office or airport. Payment can be made by cash, by check, or with an acceptable credit card for later billing. An organization having a transportation department usually has authority and supplies for issuing tickets in-house.

Even with a trip involving several destinations and airlines, only one ticket is issued (by the airline on which the flight originates). A passenger who does not know the continuing flights required can purchase an open ticket and make reservations later. Data for any changes in ticketed flights are merely attached to the original ticket.

When checking in for some flights, the passenger may reserve an aisle seat or a window seat; the smoking or nonsmoking section; or the front, back, or center section of the plane. On some airlines seat assignments can be made when the ticket is purchased.

Airlines allow a customer to make a telephone reservation and use a credit card or check for payment. If payment is by credit card, the secretary must know the credit card number and expiration date.

Air travel credit cards are issued to key personnel by many organizations. Other companies maintain charge accounts with the airlines and are billed regularly for authorized travel by employees.

Reconfirmations

Although reconfirmation on domestic flights is usually not required, it is always wise to reconfirm reservations for each part of a continuing air trip. This can be done on arrival at the airport. Giving the telephone number in that city at which the passenger can be reached is an assurance of a contact with the airline.

Redemption of Unused Plane Tickets

Unused tickets or unused portions of plane tickets can be redeemed by submitting them to the issuing airline or travel agency. If payment was through a credit card, the refund will be processed through the card account. If the ticket purchase was through a travel agency, the agent will process the refund. In the case of lost tickets, a waiting period of 120 days is imposed before a refund is made.

Airport Services

An airport limousine is available for transportation between downtown locations and the airport, usually at a lower rate than taxi service. In some cities the limousine calls for passengers at key hotels; in others it leaves from either a downtown ticket office or a downtown airline terminal. If the limousine leaves from a downtown airline terminal, the passenger checks in for the flight at the terminal. On arrival in some cases the traveler has only to board the plane. If the limousine leaves from a point other than a terminal, the passenger checks in at the airport.

Limousine service is also supplied between airports serving one city and between airlines within the same airport.

The airline timetable indicates whether helicopter service is available between airports in cities served by more than one facility or from the airport to downtown points.

Each major airline operates a flight club which any traveler can join on payment of a moderate annual fee. The executive who travels frequently finds waiting for planes less tedious in the club atmosphere of the flight club lounge.

Company Owned Planes

Many corporations own one or more planes. Business is taking to the air in its own craft to reduce travel time for executives even more than is possible by commercial aviation. Many companies, however, observe the precaution of limiting the number of top officials who can fly in the same plane (private or commercial) to protect continuity of management in case of an accident. Charter planes are also increasingly important, especially to areas not served by regional airlines.

TRAIN TRAVEL

Train travel for long distances is less and less attractive to business executives because of the time required and the reduction in services. Several

Here's a story one embarrassed secretary in Ohio tells: Her employer requested that she arrange for a charter business jet to fly him to Athens. She made all the arrangements for the flight, the plane took off as planned, and landed on schedule at Athens, Georgia. The problem? The executive meant Athens, Tennessee! The good-humored executive roared with laughter, saying, "It could be worse; we could be in Athens, Greece."

federally subsidized reorganizations of the railroads have been attempted to improve services on long trips. At first *Amtrak* and later *Conrail* (in the northeast only) attempted to provide a higher type of service than was possible on the financially depressed individual railroads, especially on routes connecting cities with high population concentrations. The efforts have not been entirely successful but are continuing.

Metroliners are available between Boston and Washington, D.C., and points between, offering improved services, new equipment, and fast schedules that enable the railroad to compete with airlines. On these special trains a seat is reserved when the ticket is purchased. Because of heavy demand, tickets must be bought well in advance.

Overnight trains between East Coast points and Florida and between Chicago and Florida are available with various kinds of sleeper service; extra fare, extra service trains are added during the winter season. Sleeping car and dining service is also available between Chicago and the West Coast.

The secretary can become familiar with the rail services by consulting the *Official Guide of the Railways.* The Guide is issued monthly and contains schedules of all railway and steamship lines in the United States, Canada, Mexico, and Puerto Rico.

The Panama Limited

April 27, 1980
READ DOWN

59 Daily		Km	Mi	Type of Service		READ UP 58 Daily
4 20 P ⊗		0	0	Dp Chicago, IL -Union Sta (C7) Ar		10 45 A
5 02 P		40	25	Homewood, IL		D 9 45 A
5 32 P		92	57	Kankakee, IL		9 04 A
6 22 P		185	115	Rantoul, IL		8 12 A
6 50 P		208	129	Champaign-Urbana, IL		7 56 A
7 32 P		280	174	Mattoon, IL		6 57 A
7 59 P		323	201	Effingham, IL		6 31 A
9 00 P		408	254	Centralia, IL		5 46 A
9 50 P		498	310	Ar Carbondale, IL Dp		4 50 A
10 05 P		498	310	Dp Carbondale, IL ◄— (St. Louis) Ar		4 35 A
11 13 P		584	363	Cairo, IL		3 29 A
12 15 A		653	406	Fulton, KY		2 32 A
1 07 A		725	451	Dyersburg, TN		1 32 A
2 50 A		850	528	Dp Memphis, TN Ar		11 55 P
3 05 A		850	528	Ar Memphis, TN Dp		11 40 P
4 17 A		947	589	Batesville, MS		10 22 P
5 05 A		1012	629	Grenada, MS		9 36 P
5 28 A		1049	652	Winona, MS		9 16 P
5 59 A		1097	682	Durant, MS		8 48 P
6 35 A		1154	717	Canton, MS		8 16 P
7 08 A		1191	740	Jackson, MS		7 43 P
7 39 A		1245	774	Hazlehurst, MS		7 04 P
8 01 A		1278	794	Brookhaven, MS		6 43 P
8 31 A		1316	818	McComb, MS		6 21 P
9 22 A		1400	870	Hammond, LA		5 30 P
10 35 A		1486	923	Ar New Orleans, LA (C7) Dp		4 30 P

For additional fares, see Amtrak Tariff Table 14.

Sample fares one-way

	Regular (1 adult)	Rmtte. (1 adult)	Bdm. (2 adults)
Chicago—			
Champaign, IL	12.50	119.65	139.30
Carbondale, IL	29.00	145.00	190.50
Memphis, TN	47.50	93.00	181.00
Jackson, MS	61.00	116.00	227.00
New Orleans, LA	75.00	134.00	261.00

Equipment
The Panama Limited
Chicago/New Orleans
Sleeping car . . . . roomettes/bedrooms
Amcoaches . . . . reserved
Amdinette . . . . tray meals & beverages/
  table service available

□ Checked baggage (except at Homewood, Effingham, Centralia, Cairo, Fulton, Dyersburg, Batesville, Winona, Hazlehurst and Brookhaven).

Reference marks
Ⓡ All reserved train.
Ⓢ Sleeping car accommodations.
Ⓧ Tray meal and beverage service.
□ Checked baggage handled, consult equipment listing for exceptions.
Ⓗ Tickets not on sale at station. This station does not have facilities to assist handicapped travelers.
◆ Ticket office not open at all train departure times.
Ⓔ Experimental stop. Subject to discontinuance.
D—Stops only to discharge passengers.
F—Stops only on signal to receive and discharge passengers. Please give advance notice.
24—Passengers not carried locally between this station and Chicago, except when connecting at Chicago to/or from other Amtrak trains.
CT—Central Time.

†Day seating only.
Sleeper fares shown include rail fare plus accommodation charge.
★ For details on family and children's rates, see Amtrak information page at the beginning of this section.
★ RWAO excursions available between select cities. Consult Amtrak.
★ RWO1 excursion fare available between select cities. Consult Amtrak.

Illus. 16-3
A railway schedule is easy to read as is illustrated in the Amtrak timetable appearing in the *Official Guide.*

This schedule illustrates the Chicago-Memphis-New Orleans route. The train is the Panama Limited No. 59 that leaves Chicago daily at 4:20 p.m. Intermediate stops and times are given. The types of services provided on the train are explained in the legend to the right of the schedule. Sample one-way fares are also given, but these change frequently, so they should be checked.

For those who commute by train daily from a suburb to a metropolitan area, monthly commuter tickets are generally available at a discount.

RENT-A-CAR TRAVEL

One thoughtful secretary sends expected visitors an area map showing the employer's office location and the location of recommended hotels, motels, and restaurants nearby, as well as the approximate driving time.

At times a business executive finds it convenient to travel by air or train and then to rent a car. Both airline and railroad timetable folders indicate those cities with rent-a-car service. Automobile rental companies publish directories of their rental agencies both here and abroad, giving the daily rates and mileage charges of each station. You can arrange for a rental car by calling the local office of the car rental agency, by using a toll free number given in the telephone book listing, or through the airlines. Since rates among agencies differ depending on the make of the car, the number of days required, weekdays or weekend, and the anticipated mileage, it is well to make a few telephone calls and present your findings to the executive for a decision.

When ordering the rental car indicate the date, the make and model of the car selected, the location where the executive will pick up the car, the number of days reserved, and the method of payment. Most car rental agencies will accept major credit cards, will help with local routes, where to eat and stay, and what to see.

The American Automobile Association provides its members with travel guides for any contemplated trip. Several oil companies and automobile insurance companies will map routes on request. Many handy dining and lodging guides are available at bookstores and travel agencies.

INTERNATIONAL TRAVEL

During the past three decades American business firms of almost every size have expanded their operations or at least their interests to include international ventures. These companies, known as multinational companies, generally have an international division within its organization and branch offices in foreign cities. A secretary to a top executive in a multinational firm will probably plan international as well as domestic travel.

General Considerations

Planning for foreign travel differs in several ways from planning for short, domestic trips. For instance, an executive traveling from New York to

London crosses five time zones, and travel experts estimate that it takes the human body *one* day to adapt fully for each time zone crossed. Body rhythms and cycles are disrupted, and changes in body temperature and heart rate occur. These bodily changes are the effects of *jet lag.* If possible, the secretary making international travel arrangements should schedule a flight that will allow the executive one day of rest before a scheduled meeting in London. For the return trip, two days are recommended for the traveler to adjust both physically and psychologically to the time differences. If this extra comfort time is not possible, at least schedule the flight to London that arrives at night, thus helping the executive to rest before a meeting. On the return schedule, choose a flight arriving either on a Friday or Saturday, giving the executive the weekend to rest.

Another difference between domestic and foreign travel is in arranging appointments. Both because of possible difficulties in getting around in a foreign city and because of the slower pace at which foreign business is conducted, the American visitor will want to keep appointments to two or three a day.

Holidays are different in each country. In planning the executive's trip, check to see if a holiday occurs during the period. For instance, in Italy many business firms close down for vacation the entire month of August.

Learning the customs of the countries to be visited is important to the success of a business visit. Most of the international airlines now publish guides for conducting business in Europe. In addition, the United States Department of State publishes a series of pamphlets entitled *Background Notes on the Countries of the World.* [2] which should be very useful to the secretary of a traveling executive. Another reference is *The 1980 Multinational Executive Travel Companion.* [3] Both publications contain dates of important trade fairs, holidays in each country, time differences, climate, hotel and restaurant information, addresses of important business contacts in each country, currency information, and invaluable hints for improving business contacts.

The business card is an important adjunct to the business call, perhaps a card with English on one side and the appropriate foreign language on the reverse side. A card is always presented by a caller; therefore, a business visitor can easily use up a supply of 200 cards while attending a business fair. The European business fair has no counterpart in this country. An entire year's output of a product may be sold during such a fair.

Abroad it pays to bring gifts—judiciously. There are as many subtleties to the art of international gift giving as there are differences in customs and business methods around the world. What pleases a customer in London may be offensive to a Tokyo counterpart. A present to the wife of a business contact in Europe will be accepted graciously, but a present to the wife of a Near

---

[2] Available from the Superintendent of Documents, U.S. Department of Printing, Washington, D.C.
[3] A pocket-sized guide published by World-Wide Business Centres, Inc., 575 Madison Avenue, New York, N. Y. 10022.

Eastern businessman is offensive. As with gifts, the practice of tipping may not be appropriate. Asking advice of a resident of the country being visited may be beneficial.

Services of a Travel Agency

A company's travel department or a travel agency can be of great help in planning a foreign trip. In lieu of a well-established company travel department, the secretary will find the following services of a travel agent almost indispensable.

- Making hotel and rent-a-car reservations
- Listing available transportation
- Suggesting an itinerary or itineraries and procuring tickets
- Notifying you of the required travel documents and how to obtain them
- Giving currency conversion rules and obtaining enough foreign currency for entering the first country on the itinerary
- Explaining baggage restrictions
- Obtaining insurance for traveler and baggage
- Listing port taxes levied (Most international airports charge from $1 to $3. An international transportation tax of $3 is imposed on each international passenger departing from the continental United States.)
- Providing information as to time limitations for visits
- Supplying free literature and services
- Arranging for the traveler to be met by a representative or a limousine
- Supplying information about vaccinations and inoculations required in each country to be visited, and supplying blanks for International Certificates of Vaccination
- Giving average temperatures to assist your employer in packing appropriate clothes

Passports

The first requisite for foreign travel is a *passport* issued by the Department of State. A passport is an official document granting permission to travel to the person specified in it and authenticating that person's right to protection. For travel in most countries outside the United States, a passport is necessary; but it is not required in Canada, Mexico, Bermuda, the West Indies, and Central American countries, although proof of citizenship may be requested. A visitor to Mexico must have a tourist card and carry proof of citizenship. Passport application forms can be obtained from the travel agent; from passport offices (Department of State) in Boston, Chicago, Los Angeles, Miami, New Orleans, New York, Philadelphia, San Francisco, Seattle, Honolulu, and Washington; from the passport office in local federal buildings; or from specific post offices. The booklet *Information for Passport Applicants* gives instructions about making an application for a passport and is available

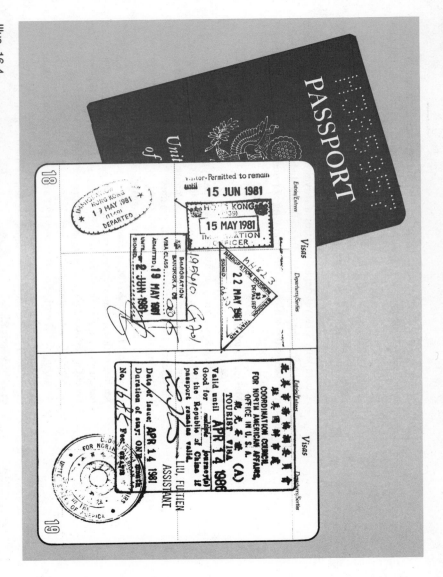

Illus. 16-4

This is a page from a valid passport. When a traveler enters a foreign country, an immigration officer of that country may stamp the immigrant's passport with a visa stamp (date of entry and allowable length of visit) and with an embarkation stamp when the visitor leaves the country.

at passport offices. For the first passport an applicant is required to appear in person before an agent of the passport office or a clerk of a federal court or a state court authorized by law to naturalize aliens. The applicant must present the following papers:

- The completed application.
- Proof of United States citizenship (birth certificate, baptismal certificate, or certificate of naturalization). If these proofs are not available, the applicant submits a notice by appropriate authorities that no birth record exists and such secondary evidence as census records, newspaper files, family bibles, school records, or affidavits of persons with personal knowledge of the applicant's birth. An identifying witness may also appear with the applicant.
- Proof of identification bearing signature and description, such as a driver's license.

- Two signed duplicate photographs *taken by a photographer* within the past six months.
- The passport fee.

If the applicant is going abroad on a government contract, a letter from the employing company is required showing the applicant's position, destination, purpose of travel, and proposed length of stay.

A person holding an expired passport must reapply for a current passport. A renewal application may be obtained from the nearest passport office or designated post office. Then the applicant completes the form, signs and dates the application, attaches two signed duplicate photographs taken within six months of the date of the application, and encloses the expired passport and the passport fee. These materials are mailed to the nearest passport office.

A passport is valid for five years from date of issue. Since processing a passport application may take three or four weeks, anyone contemplating foreign travel should keep the passport in order. The secretary to a traveling executive can be of assistance by noting the passport expiration date in the tickler file.

As soon as the passport is received, it should be signed and the information requested on the inside cover must be filled in. During overseas travel, a passport should always be carried on the person and *never* left in a hotel room, even in a locked suitcase. Loss of a passport should be reported immediately to the nearest passport office or, if abroad, to the nearest consulate. The business traveler should also carry a letter from the business organization represented—stating the where, when, why, and duration of the proposed visit.

Many Americans who travel abroad in the future will use a passport that can be read by a machine. When inserted in a special machine, the passport will display for an immigration officer examining it a coded symbol invisible to the unaided eye. These new electronic passports should speed the passage of travelers through red tape at borders and reduce the fraudulent use and counterfeiting of United States passports. A long-term goal of the system is the linking of the passport reading machines to a central computer that will keep track of international travelers.

Visas

A *visa* is a permit granted by a foreign government for a person to enter its territory. It usually appears as a stamped notation in a passport indicating that the bearer may enter the country for a certain purpose and for a specified period of time. Anyone in doubt as to the necessity of obtaining a travel visa for travel in any foreign country should consult the consul or a travel agent before leaving the United States. Consular representatives of most foreign countries are located in principal cities, and their addresses can be found in the *Congressional Directory*, available in many public libraries, or in the Yellow Pages under "Consulates." A traveler who intends to work in the country to be visited should check to see whether a work permit is required.

Vaccination and Inoculation Requirements

The travel agent or the consulate of the country to be visited can give information about *vaccinations* and *inoculations* required by the country visited. A vaccination record is no longer required for reentry to the United States. Records of these vaccinations and inoculations are signed by the physician and validated by the local or state health officer on the International Certificates of Vaccination form obtainable from the travel agent, the passport office, or in some cases, the physician.

Overseas Flights

International plane travel is basically the same as it is for domestic flights, with a preponderance of jumbo jets that seat more than 200 passengers. Innovations in services include large passenger lounges, a choice among several entrees at mealtime, and containerized baggage compartments in which baggage is always stored in an upright position and unloaded swiftly by bringing the containers to the customs area.

There are two classes of flights on most planes—first class and economy or tourist. Gourmet meals and beverages are served in first class. Beautiful china, crystal, and silver are used; and the service of flight attendants is outstanding. In tourist class, meals meet a lesser quality standard, but the passenger has a choice among entrees on some flights.

Baggage limitations vary with the airlines; so the secretary must check this information when making reservations. Passengers must reconfirm international flights within seventy-two hours.

Fares vary with the season of the year and according to the length of stay. The only way to keep abreast of air fares is to consult the airline reservation agent or the travel agent for any available special excursion rates. An international flight schedule of a foreign airline is more complicated than a domestic schedule. Timetables for foreign airlines are usually based on the 24-hour clock.

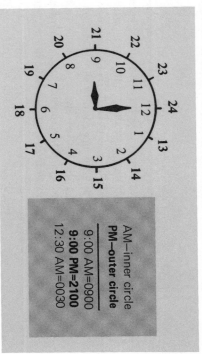

AM—inner circle
PM—outer circle

9:00 AM	=0900
9:00 PM	**=2100**
12:30 AM	=0030

Train Transportation

Most foreign railroads provide three classes of service: (1) *first-class* accommodations with four to six persons in a compartment, (2) *second-class* accommodations with six to eight persons, and (3) *third-class* accommodations where passengers sit on wooden, unupholstered seats. Seat reservations are necessary for first-class travel.

Passengers carry on their luggage to store on the train. For easy handling two small pieces of luggage, rather than one large bag, are recommended.

Sleeping accommodations on trains require first-class tickets. Sleeping cars are of the compartment type. Reservations well in advance of the trip are recommended, for it is often difficult to obtain sleeping car (*wagon-lit*) accommodations. Extra fare trains carrying first- and second-class sleepers only are available on the most important international routes. These deluxe trains with individual seats are also available for day travel.

Restaurant cars are attached to most express trains. Before the meal the dining car conductor comes through the train and takes reservations. The meal is served at an announced time at one seating only in most countries.

It is possible to buy a Eurail pass that entitles the holder to unlimited train travel in European countries during the length of time specified on the ticket. Several foreign railway systems maintain ticket and information offices in major cities in America. The Eurail pass must be purchased before a traveler leaves the United States.

Hotel Reservations

Hotel reservations can be made through the travel agent either in this country or abroad or through the airline used. Business guides indicate whether secretarial services or meeting rooms are available in listed hotels. Breakfast often is included in the hotel charge in Great Britain and frequently in the Netherlands. In other countries in Europe a continental breakfast, consisting of a hot beverage and a roll, may be included.

Automobile Rentals

Rented automobiles are as readily available in large foreign cities as in the United States. Flight schedules indicate whether this service is available at the airport. Rental can be arranged by the travel agent in this country, and it is usually possible to leave the car at a designated point rather than return it to the place of rental.

In most countries a United States driver's license is sufficient; but to be on the safe side, the traveler may obtain an American International Driving Permit from the American Automobile Association either here or in Europe for a small fee.

TRAVEL DETAILS HANDLED BY THE SECRETARY

The groundwork for planning a trip will probably be laid during a conference between the executive and the secretary. The executive will mention the places to be visited and the dates, and perhaps the names of preferred hotels. For example, if your employer in Omaha told you of a proposed business trip to visit the factory in Cleveland on Monday, March 2, keep appointments in Brussels on March 4, meet with an executive in Paris on March 5, return to Omaha by way of New York, have a one-hour conference at the New York airport, and be back in Omaha on the evening of March 9, you would arrange all the details of the trip.

Planning the Trip

Planning a trip requires checking transportation schedules, researching hotel information, and making necessary reservations. In the case just given, you would route the executive by air to Cleveland, from Cleveland to Brussels, from Brussels to Paris, from Paris to New York, and from New York back to Omaha. If your company has a transportation department, you should consult with someone in that department first. The transportation department, in all likelihood, will handle all reservations and make suggestions concerning hotels as well. If your company does not have a transportation department, you should obtain and study current timetables of airlines or discuss possible flights with airline reservation agents or travel agents. You should also obtain pertinent information about hotels or motels from a directory such as the *Hotel and Motel Red Book*[4] or regional directories published by the American Automobile Association or the oil companies. These directories give the number of rooms, the rates, and whether (in the case of a hotel) the lodging is operated on the European or the American plan. Under the European plan the rate represents the cost of the room only. Under the American plan the rate includes the cost of meals as well as the cost of the room. Most commercial hotels are European plan. A travel agency is especially helpful in choosing hotels.

Room rates quoted in a directory are for one night's lodging. Many hotels offer a reduced rate for occupancy of a room during the daytime only. This service is desirable for use as daytime headquarters when the traveler will be in the city for only a few hours. Since the time of arrival is often early morning, the executive may want to pay in advance and register for the previous night in order to be assured of accommodations before the midafternoon check-in hour.

If a rented automobile is needed, a motel may be preferable to a hotel. In any case, you should check distances from the airport to the accommoda-

---

[4]Published annually by the American Hotel Association Directory Corporation, 221 West 57th Street, New York 10019.

tions and to the meeting place. If a motel is chosen, it should be one that is near the destination. Nothing is more disconcerting than to find oneself across town from the appointment location.

A travel worksheet such as that shown in Illus. 16-6 can be useful in accumulating and finalizing trip plans. The executive's itinerary can be typed from the information on this form.

TRAVEL WORKSHEET

Employee _____   Date _____

Dates of Trip _____

Mode of Travel: Commercial Air _____   Company Plane _____   Train _____   Automobile _____

Date	Destination	Time (Local)		Flight/Train No.	Class of Service	Meals	Date Confirmed
		Departure	Arrival				

Ground Transportation Requirements (limousine, rental car, courtesy car):

Date	Time	Place	Type	Date Confirmed

Hotel Reservations:

Date	Destination	Estimated Arrival Time	Date of Departure	Name of Hotel/Motel	Date Confirmed

Travel Funds:

Cash Advance $ _____   Company Credit Cards Required?: Yes ____ No ____

Company Check $ _____   Specify: _____

Traveler's Checks $ _____   _____

Illus. 16-6
Travel worksheet

Making Reservations

When the executive has selected the flights to be used and the accommodations preferred, you can make the actual airline reservations—without outside assistance (not recommended for overseas trips), with the help of the transportation department in your company, or in cooperation with a travel agency.

If you make the reservations for lodging yourself, the requests should be specific, including the items listed below:

Kind of Room Desired—one room or a suite (location away from elevator, above a certain floor, with a view, etc.)

Kind of Accommodations—twin beds; studio; tub or shower bath

Approximate or Relative Rate—medium-priced or luxury-priced room

Names of Persons in the Party

Date and Approximate Time of Registration (If Known)—after 6 p.m., 9 p.m., etc. (If the executive may be late in arriving, a "guaranteed arrival" reservation can be made. The room will be held, but the guest will be billed even if the room is unoccupied).

Type of Transportation—available to and from the airport. If the hotel is known to have a courtesy car, provide flight number and arrival time.

Probable Length of Time Accommodation Is Needed

Method of Payment

There are several ways of making a reservation. Hotels and motels in a chain such as Hilton or Sheraton have communication systems for making reservations with other member hotels. A telephone call to the local hotel or motel assures the reservation in a member hotel. Out-of-town hotels sometimes maintain in major cities local offices where the reservation can be made. Once again, check the Yellow Pages, where toll free numbers can even be found for making reservations for hotels in Japan and Europe. A free worldwide directory can be obtained from American Express Reservations, Inc., Box G-10, 770 Broadway, New York City 10003. Most airlines also make hotel and motel reservations for their passengers. Some of them have a business tie-in with hotel chains. (Examples are United Airlines and Westin Hotels, TWA and Hilton Hotels.) The secretary in a company with teletypewriter equipment may ask its operator to request reservations; large hotels have teletypewriters. The secretary can write for a reservation if there is sufficient time or telephone or telegraph if not.

In requesting a hotel or motel reservation, it is important to mention the name of your company, since a special commercial rate may be involved. (Special rates are usually available to guests attending a convention.)

Confirmation policies differ; however, it is always safe to request a confirmation that the executive can have in hand when registering. Rooms are at a premium in many cities, and a confirmed reservation is a good precaution.

To simplify their accounting, some hotels and motels request that a deposit *not* be sent. Small operations may require a deposit.

Sometimes executives must cancel their entire trip or certain portions of their trip. In canceling hotel reservations, obtain the cancellation number for your records, particularly if the reservations are guaranteed.

Preparing the Itinerary

You can perform an important secretarial function by preparing a comprehensive itinerary for the executive to take on the trip. The usual itinerary (which is prepared by a travel agency if you use its services) covers only *when, where,* and *how* the traveler will go. An itinerary serves also as a daily appointment calendar. It contains helpful reminders and mentions the tickets and business papers taken along. The executive may request a number of copies for associates and family so that mail and messages can be forwarded and emergencies reported. Foresight and analysis are required to be able to prepare this type of itinerary.

A good way to start is to set up a file on the trip as soon as it enters the planning stage. In the file, place the travel worksheet prepared on convenient flights and trains (see Illus. 16-6), the purchased tickets, the reservations made, the confirmations received, the appointments obtained (Illus. 16-7), the factual material needed for scheduled meetings and appointments—in fact, everything that pertains to the trip. When it is time to prepare the itinerary, the items and notes can be sorted into chronological sequence according to the day and time each will come up. It is then an easy matter to list and describe each item in order. Illus. 16-8 shows the detail and thoroughness with which an itinerary should be prepared.

Some executives prefer to carry two documents: the itinerary prepared by the travel agency and an appointment schedule, as shown in Illus. 16-7. The

A P P O I N T M E N T   S C H E D U L E

City	Date/Time	GMT*	With	Telephone	Address of Appt.	Remarks
London	Thursday, 8/6, 9 a.m.		E. Morse	Mansion House 3312	To be arranged	Telephone Mrs. Morse on arrival. Folder A contains papers for meeting.
"	1 p.m.		H. Poling	Waterside Savoy 1113	"	Mr. Poling is arranging meeting with patent lawyer. Folder B contains patent information.

*Greenwich Mean Time

Illus. 16-7
Appointment schedule

ITINERARY FOR K. B. CUNNINGHAM

March 1-6, 19--

SUNDAY, MARCH 1   (Omaha to Philadelphia)   No direct flights available.

4:15 p.m.   Leave Omaha on American Flight 23.   Change in Chicago to United
             Flight 302 leaving at 6:15 p.m.

10:21 p.m.   Arrive in Philadelphia.   Guaranteed arrival reservation at Warwick
             Hotel (confirmation attached).

MONDAY, MARCH 2   (West Chester Plant)

Take Southeastern Pennsylvania Transportation Authority Conrail commuter train
from Penn Center Station.   Frequent service.   (Papers in briefcase.)

TUESDAY, MARCH 3   (En Route to Brussels)

9:00 a.m.   Leave Philadelphia on American Flight 2 to La Guardia Airport
             (New York) to connect with Sabena Flight 34 to Brussels.

11:00 a.m.   Leave for Brussels.

5:00 p.m.   Arrive in Brussels.   Reservation at Intercontinental Hotel (reser-
             vation attached).

WEDNESDAY, MARCH 4   (Brussels)

9:00 a.m.   Interview at La Societe Generale, Room 913, with Johann Schmidt
             about development of European office in Brussels (prospectus in
             briefcase).

1:00 p.m.   Lunch at La Maison du Cygne with Madame Helene Moal and three
             colleagues for same purpose (prospectus in briefcase).   (Confirm
             by telephone after 11:00 a.m.)

5:00 p.m.   Leave for Paris on Sabena Flight 711 to Le Bourget Airport.

6:21 p.m.   Arrive in Paris.   Reservation at the George V Hotel (reservation
             attached).

THURSDAY, MARCH 5   (Paris)

10:00 a.m.   Appointment with Martha Dillon at Citibank, 43 Rue de la Paix
             (financial statements in briefcase).

8:30 p.m.   Dinner at Maxim's with Roger Symonds (telephone 45-334).

FRIDAY, MARCH 6   (En Route to Omaha via New York)

12:00 Noon   Leave from Charles de Gaulle Airport on TWA Flight 803.

2:55 p.m.   Arrive at Kennedy Airport where Tom McQuiddy will meet your flight
             with a car.   Conference at International Hotel at airport (day-
             time reservation enclosed).   (Papers in McQuiddy folder.)

4:45 p.m.   Leave Kennedy Airport for Chicago on TWA Flight 347.

6:07 p.m.   Arrive at O'Hare Airport in Chicago.

6:45 p.m.   Leave Chicago on United Flight 779 for Omaha.

7:51 p.m.   Arrive at Omaha airport.

Illus. 16-8
This itinerary is a combination of travel and appointment records along with reminders.

appointment schedule will show the time, persons having appointments, how to get in touch with them, location of the appointment, and special notes about the meeting or the person.

Carrying Travel Funds

Often you must ask the executive whether you are to get money for the trip from the company's cashier or the bank. If it is an overseas trip, you determine whether there are any restrictions in the amount of currency that may be taken into the countries to be visited. You can order a $10 packet of foreign currencies for each country through the bank or a travel agent, or you can remind the executive to purchase one at the automatic vending machines in most international airports. It is always a good idea to provide a number of convenient $1 bills.

Traveler's Checks. You should remind the executive who plans to carry *traveler's checks* that they must be purchased by the person who will use them and by nobody else. Traveler's checks are issued in denominations of $10, $20, $50, and $100. Usually they cost $1 for each $100 of checks, but some banks issue them without charge especially during certain times of the year. An executive wishing to take $1,000 on a trip might take $300 in cash and the rest in traveler's checks.

Each traveler's check is numbered and printed on a special kind of paper. The purchaser signs each check on a line near the top before an agent of the issuing company. To cash one of the checks, the purchaser takes it to a business firm, bank, or hotel and signs the check again at the bottom in front of the person paying out the money. Such checks are as acceptable as cash and

American Express Company

Illus. 16-9
An illustration of an American Express Traveler's Check. The purchaser's signature and the payee have been blocked out. On purchasing the check the purchaser signs in the upper left-hand corner. On cashing this check the purchaser signs the check at the bottom left corner.

constitute almost personalized money, because anyone other than the purchaser must forge the purchaser's name on each check in the presence of another person in order to cash it. The secretary should prepare a record in duplicate of the numbers and amounts of the checks issued, one for the files and one for the executive to carry so that reimbursement can be immediate in case the checks are lost or stolen.

It is now possible for an American Express card holder to obtain a special personal identification number. This number can be inserted along with the American Express card into a dispenser located in large airports and the holder can obtain automatically up to $500 in American Express traveler's checks.

Money Orders. Sometimes the secretary acts as an advance money agent who supplies the traveling executives of the firm with company funds through express money orders. An express money order is similar to a postal money order except that it is issued by an express company, such as the American Express Company. Traveler's checks cannot be used for this purpose because they must be signed at the time of their purchase by the person who is to use them. In order to facilitate the cashing of express money orders, the American Express Company furnishes identification cards, which include the signature of the bearer.

The executive who is stranded without funds can always wire the secretary to send a money order by telegraph. The secretary usually takes cash or a cashier's check to the Western Union office, which in turn telegraphs the distant office to pay that amount to the designated person just as soon as an identification test is passed.

Illus. 16-10
An express money order is similar to a postal money order except that it is issued by an express company, such as the American Express Company.

Letters of Credit. Sometimes a letter of credit is used when extensive travel is involved or when the amount of travel funds required is relatively large. The cost for a large amount of money through a letter of credit is considerably less than the cost of traveler's checks. A letter of credit can be obtained from the local bank. It indicates the person to whom it is issued, and that person is identified by signature on an identification card. It also states the amount the holder is entitled to draw on the issuing bank. To obtain funds, the holder presents the letter of credit to any one of the designated banks in the city being visited. The amounts drawn are recorded on the letter of credit so that the balance that can still be drawn is always known.

Credit Cards. A recent trend is toward extensive use of multipurpose credit cards. Airline, railway, telephone, hotel, American Express, VISA, Master Card, Diners' Club, and similar credit cards permit the holder to charge practically any service or goods to a personal or company charge account. Credit cards should be carried in the wallet, ready for presentation when needed. Your only secretarial responsibility for credit cards is in requesting renewals on those that expire and in keeping the serial numbers on file. Credit card charges help the secretary in preparing expense reports and enable the executive to verify expenses.

Obtaining Insurance

The employing company sometimes buys blanket insurance policies covering executives while they are traveling on company business. In addition, it usually has rules governing the purchase of travel insurance at the airport. The secretary is expected to investigate company policy about travel insurance and follow through to see that the executive is appropriately covered.

Assisting in Departure

The secretary is frequently charged with packing the executive's briefcase. This is an important responsibility, for the effectiveness of any business trip is determined by the accessibility of relevant material when it is needed.

As soon as you learn of an impending trip start assembling materials and other necessary papers that must be taken along in order to avoid any last minute crisis. Start immediately to procure tickets and other required documents for the trip. Check the appointment book and ask how your employer wants to handle any scheduled appointments. Go through the tickler and pending files for matters to be handled in your employer's absence. Check all personal financial responsibilities (rent, insurance, or income tax payments) that may fall due before the trip is over and get instructions for handling them. Write any preliminary letters that will increase the effectiveness of the trip. You and your employer will decide how expected mail is to be handled. Find out *who* is responsible for *what* during the trip.

Just before departure, hand the executive all the documents procured, prepared, and kept safe:

- Travel tickets (also a schedule of alternate flights)
- Itinerary (both a detailed one and a thumbnail copy on a card)
- Attachments: Hotel and motel confirmations

Car rental arrangements

- Travel funds
- Address book (including addresses of any people to be visited in the area)
- A personal checkbook and expense account forms
- A company telephone directory
- A supply of business cards
- A supply of stamps (for domestic use only)
- Typed address labels, which can easily be attached to letters for known correspondents, such as the executive's family, secretary, or the president of the company
- Notebook, pen, pencil
- Dictation recorder and recording media
- Papers to be taken along (A separate envelope for each appointment is recommended, including copies of relevant correspondence, lists of people to be seen and their positions in their companies, and memorandums about matters to be discussed.)
- Personal items such as medication or extra eyeglasses
- Favorite reading materials, crossword puzzles
- Copies of company brochures, if requested
- Extra camera film, chewing gum, lifesavers

In addition to the above items, the following should be included for foreign travel:

- Money packets of foreign currency for the first stop and traveler's checks
- An American International Driving Permit (unless the secretary has determined that a United States driver's license is sufficient)
- Notes about reconfirming reservations for foreign flights at least 72 hours before departure
- Passport, International Certificates of Vaccination, and baggage identification labels for foreign travel

WHILE THE EXECUTIVE IS AWAY

While the executive is away, the secretary assumes increased responsibility for smooth operation of the office. But members of the management team also share the decision-making role involving problems usually handled by the employer. Sometimes it is better to discuss a perplexing situation with an executive who has been designated to handle crises than to assume too much authority. Routine matters, of course, should be taken care of promptly by the secretary.

The executive who wants to keep in touch with home base usually telephones the office daily, especially if the company uses WATS service. If you expect your employer to call you, you should keep notes about situations you want to discuss. Many secretaries keep a daily log of incoming calls, letters, and visitors, so that when the employer calls these can be discussed.

Your performance while the executive is away is just as important as it is when the executive is present. Other employees may be quick to notice whether you are busy or frittering away time, but the competent secretary will *automatically* have organized the work so that there is little idle time. This is the time to complete any tasks that you have not had time to do, such as reorganizing the files.

Upon return the executive will be grateful and pleased if you have taken care of routine matters, kept records of office activities for review, and arranged the matters that require attention in terms of their importance. The materials that have been accumulated should be separated into two groups: (1) matters already taken care of by you or others and (2) matters to be handled by the executive personally.

You should place the first group in a folder marked "Information Only." The second group goes into a folder marked "Important." Just before presenting the folders, you should arrange the materials in each folder in logical order, with the most important on top. A list of future appointments and engagements should be included in the "Important" folder.

If the trip is long, the executive may ask you to forward copies of documents that require personal attention (refer to pages 149–159 for proper processing of the mail). Two copies of mail may be sent to the traveler—one to the destination on the itinerary and one to the next point to be visited, in case mail service is slower than expected.

FOLLOW-UP ACTIVITIES

After the executive returns to the office, a flurry of activity is required to wind up the trip. First is the expense report.

Expense Report

Some firms advance funds for travel. Periodically, or when the trip is over, the executive submits a complete report on the results and the expenses incurred. In other companies executives advance their own funds and are reimbursed later in accordance with the expense report submitted and approved. In either case the executive must keep an accurate record of the dates and times of travel, the conveyances used, and the costs. Most organizations require receipts for hotel and other accommodations and for any expenses above an established minimum. The traveler's word is usually taken for the amount of taxi fares, meals, and tips; but such items must usually be listed or itemized. Receipts are required, however, for entertainment expenses over $25. In addition, the date, cost, place, nature of the entertainment, the business purpose, and the names of the persons included must be specified. For further information on allowable business expenses, you may want to consult a current copy of the Internal Revenue Service's Bulletin 463, *Travel, Entertainment, and Gift Expenses.*

Expense report forms are usually provided by the company and need only be filled in correctly and completely and totaled. The secretary should, however, check the executive's present accounting with previous reports to make sure that the amounts for such items as taxis and meals are reasonable and that the flight and rail fares are correct. Reimbursement is frequently held up until all items are in line and approved by the auditor's office.

Letters

Thank you letters must be sent to show appreciation for favors during the trip. The need for other letters will be generated by the nature of the trip.

Files

Materials will be unpacked and returned to the files. Duplicate files can be destroyed. Files will be updated by the secretary to reflect any changes originated by the trip.

SUGGESTED READINGS

Several of the airlines publish special periodicals that are available at no charge to possible business customers. Pan American's *Getting Around Overseas* is an example of a complimentary booklet as is Air Canada's *Business Traveler's Guide to Canada*. These and other booklets can be obtained from most travel agencies.

Doris, Lillian, and Besse May Miller. *Complete Secretary's Handbook,* 4th ed., revised by Mary A. DeVries. Englewood Cliffs, N.J.: Prentice-Hall, Inc., 1977.

Lehmann, Armin D. *Travel and Tourism.* Indianapolis: Bobbs-Merrill Educational Publishing Co., 1979.

North, Susanna. *Traveling Alone: A Practical Guide for Business Women.* New York: Sovereign Books, 1980.

QUESTIONS FOR DISCUSSION

1. What are the secretary's responsibilities for travel arrangements if there is an in-company transportation department?

2. In what ways can you inform yourself about current changes in air and rail travel? Just to show that you are alert to such changes, report any recent plan not described in the chapter.

3. If stranded without cash while on a business trip, what should a business executive do?

4. Just after your employer has left on a somewhat lengthy business trip by plane, you discover on your desk the itinerary, reservation letters, and appointment schedule. What should you do?

5. What procedures should be followed when the employer planning an overseas business trip requests the secretary to get a renewed passport, the necessary visas, and traveler's checks?

6. If your employer is planning to visit five countries overseas on a business trip, which types of information about the countries should you provide?

7. Why is it recommended that the services of a travel agency be enlisted in planning an overseas trip?

8. Your employer who is visiting a dissatisfied customer in a distant city telephones to ask you to mail at once the entire correspondence file relating to this customer. There is a strict company rule that no files can be taken from the building. What should you do?

9. While your employer is away from the office on an extended trip, how do you use your office time?

10. Type the following sentences. Then refer to the Reference Guide to verify or correct your answers.
   (a) The space age will provide modern man with a new frontier.
   (b) Reserve room 12 of the student center for our meeting.
   (c) U.S. route 64 runs east and west; U.S. route 77 runs north and south.
   (d) He is well known as a professor of asian culture and polynesian music.
   (e) Our Professor Griggs has taught history at the university of Texas for many years.
   (f) The students will hear president Mason speak at the first session on Monday.
   (g) We are unusually busy during the spring and summer months; most of the tourists are gone by early fall.

PROBLEMS

1. Working individually, or as a member of a team as your instructor directs, use travel schedules provided in your classroom. Recommend the best services available for a trip to Miami, Florida, for a two-day student convention.

2. You are secretary to T. M. Jonas, the sales manager of a corporation in St. Louis. You are to plan a visit to the five regional offices for your employer. The offices are located in Minneapolis, San Diego, Naugatuck (Connecticut), Portland (Oregon), and Birmingham (Alabama). It is your decision to establish the order in which the cities will be visited.

Planning and
Facilitating Meetings

Within a business organization the majority of decisions are made during or as a result of business meetings. A meeting can be an informal one among two or three staff members, a meeting of an entire department, or that of a committee charged with specific responsibilities. The meeting can be face to face in the same room or by telephone or closed circuit television hookup using today's technology.

Another type of meeting that generates decisions is the formal meeting of an organization, such as the annual stockholders' meeting, a special stockholders' meeting, or the regular or special meeting of the board of directors of a corporation. Another example is the multinational meeting where not all participants speak the same language—a challenging prospect to say the least.

Increasingly executives move from meeting to meeting in what seems like an endless succession. In today's business world more and more decisions involve group decision making; therefore, today's executives spend more time in meetings than at any time in the past.

In addition to these job-related meetings, executives participate in many organizations in the community, often assuming a leadership role. They also attend numerous workshops, symposia, and conventions where they exchange ideas with people with similar interests and learn new developments that will improve their job performance.

All types of secretaries are involved, too, in the many activities required to make all these meetings effective. The multifunctional secretary handles all the tasks described in this chapter. The administrative secretary helps with many of the preliminary activities and with follow-up duties. The correspondence secretary may have responsibility for sending notices of meetings and processing the reports that emerge from meetings.

COMMITTEE MEETINGS OR INFORMAL OFFICE CONFERENCES

Many office meetings do not involve complicated arrangements and may be scheduled or unscheduled. For scheduled meetings participants have been notified previously and should have a calendar notation to remind them of the time and place. If a member is late, the secretary should call the executive's secretary to determine if he or she plans to attend the meeting. For an unscheduled meeting the secretary may have to spend considerable time on the telephone with the secretaries of other executives trying to arrange a convenient meeting time. Once the time is agreed upon, a note confirming the time and place should be sent to all members.

If the meeting takes place in the executive's office, the secretary makes sure that the room is in good order with enough chairs available for all members and that all the materials needed are assembled. One way to create an atmosphere of relaxation is to provide refreshments—even if Styrofoam cups, plastic spoons, instant coffee or tea, and powdered cream are used.

During the meeting the secretary may be asked to take notes. Recommended conference procedure suggests that the chairperson summarize the actions and consensus of the meeting. The secretary reporting a meeting for such a chairperson is lucky. Many office conferences, however, are informal discussions where opinions are exchanged, conclusions are reached, and recommendations are made with no observance of protocol. In these cases the secretary, working alone, is expected to make a summary—subject to the executive's revision, of course—to be distributed to all participants. Certainly if, during the meeting, it is agreed that certain conferees take specific action, as a reminder the secretary should send each a copy of the report *with the agreed upon action underlined.*

Many departments have a weekly "stand up briefing" on Monday mornings. Because these meetings are intended to be short, the secretary need not make special provisions in the executive's office unless told otherwise. Generally no reporting of the briefing is required.

Teleconferencing

Using today's technology, meeting participants do not have to be in the same room to be in attendance. In fact, they do not have to be in the same city. In its simplest form a teleconference can be arranged using a phone or a speakerphone by dialing the parties, by using operator assistance to make the connections with other participants, or by means of a circuit where each participant dials a special access code and the connection is made. The secretary's role may include giving instructions to the operator, standing by until the conference is concluded, and taking minutes of the meeting.

Videoconferencing

Videoconferencing, an extension of teleconferencing, provides an added dimension: televised pictures of the participants. Sometimes one still photograph of each participant, called a *freeze frame,* is sufficient. In other situations

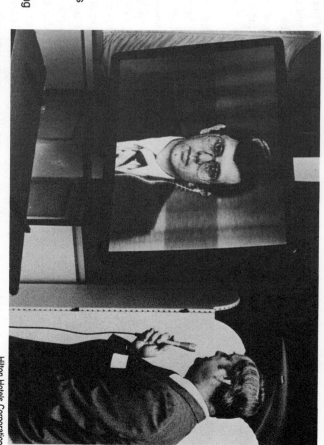

Illus. 17-1
Today's
technology allows
people to
exchange ideas
and information
without even being
in the same city.

full motion is used throughout the call because this method most closely approximates a face-to-face conference. During the verbal interchange, paper, visuals, and data can be sent back and forth via intelligent copiers (see page 312) and facsimile equipment (see page 308) positioned in the conference room. The secretary must contact the members for an agreed time and then schedule the equipment. For reporting or summary purposes, the secretary may be in attendance or replay the recording equipment at a later time.

Computer Conferencing

By the use of computer terminals, meetings can be held (either simultaneously or on a delayed basis) with groups of people geographically separated. Participants input messages to other members of the group on computer terminals linked by telephone on a national or international computer network. All records of discussions and document transmission are stored. It is like a business meeting except that everyone is not necessarily present at the same time. There may be discussion between two participants or a group discussion among several members. All participants do not have to be in a group at the same time. One could arrive at 9 a.m. and see what another member did at 11 p.m. the previous evening. Computer conferencing may include a range of graphic capabilities to support the views of members, such as slides, transparencies, sketches, and handwritten notes. A secretary's responsibilities may be to notify the executive as messages are received, to input messages as directed by the executive, to obtain additional information, and to call other executives for input to the meeting.

Multinational Meetings

A new experience for American business people is to attend and, even more so, to conduct a meeting where some of the members do not speak English. Secretaries to these executives may be asked to arrange for an interpreter to attend the meeting or to have the interpreter prepare audio tapes in the language of the non-English-speaking members. Another possibility is to have the secretary, with the help of the interpreter, prepare special overhead visuals and handouts in the foreign language or languages. Ensuring effective communication during this meeting will take a great deal of time and preparation on the part of the executive-secretary team.

If minutes of such a meeting are to be produced, the secretary should use a mechanical device such as a cassette or tape recorder for a verbatim recording and then consult with the interpreter and the executive in typing the report. Not all multinational meetings require this type of preparation. English is considered an international language. Although the foreign nationals may have knowledge of English, it is wise to use standard speech and writing, omitting slang and regional expressions.

FORMAL MEETINGS

Just as soon as you know that a meeting is to be called, you should set up a file folder, with the name of the meeting and the date as the tab caption. Into this folder goes every bit of relevant information that crosses your desk during the planning stages. When you prepare the agenda or later attend the meeting, you will derive much help from this folder.

If you are involved in planning a local meeting, the hotel personnel will make useful suggestions about facilities. For out-of-town meetings, you might inquire of the airlines and hotels involved whether they provide any type of planning service. Certainly they will coordinate the flight arrangements of the conferees and provide rooms, meals, and meeting rooms equipped with such necessary facilities as lecterns, chalkboards, or flip charts. Most international airlines provide conference facilities at airports for their passengers' use.

A hotel in which a convention is held customarily provides a complimentary room or suite for the president of the organization. In addition, conference attendees generally are given special room rates. The person making conference arrangements should also inquire as to whether or not meeting rooms are complimentary. These items should be included in the contract with the hotel. Some of the information in this section applies to informal meetings as well.

M E M O R A N D U M

October 21, 19--

TO: ✓R. Edison
    F. Marco
    J. Monroe
    S. Renberg

The Budget Committee met in Mr. Monroe's office on Monday, October 20, 19--, to discuss the group health plan and the parking lot resurfacing. All members were present.

Mr. Marco stated that the dental health plan is now in operation, and the anticipated premium for the year is $6,000.

Mr. Renberg has reviewed bids for resurfacing the company parking lot. The lowest bidder is Root Construction Company at $8,025. The work will begin Saturday, October 25.

Mr. Edison agreed to develop guidelines for budget forecasts and present them at the next meeting of the Committee.

Joyce Anderson
Joyce Anderson
Secretary to Mr. Monroe

Illus. 17-2
A summary of a meeting in memorandum form prepared and signed by the secretary.

Reserving the Meeting Room

The first detail the secretary takes care of is that of reserving the meeting room. This must be done before notices are sent out. What usually happens is something similar to this. The executive says, "Will you call a meeting on budget requests for next Wednesday afternoon at two?" Since these meetings have customarily been held in the conference room, you know that you are to check immediately to see that the room is available. You should sign with the person in charge of the room and give the name of the committee or group, the number attending, and the time period required. Nothing is more embarrassing to the chairperson—and more guaranteed to arouse animosity toward the secretary who is responsible—than to find that the conference room is already in use, or that the meeting must be cut short because of prior commitment for the room.

If the meeting is to be held in a hotel, the secretary reserves an adequate-sized room with seating facilities and posts the location and hour on the announcement board in the lobby and in the passenger elevators. If a meal is included, arrange with the hotel or restaurant banquet manager the menu, the serving time, the method of payment, and the number of guests. You will find that hotels and restaurants normally do not charge for meeting rooms if the conference includes meal service. In making these arrangements, keep a record of the names of hotel personnel you contact. This listing may be useful if at the last minute something must be done, such as requesting additional chairs for the conference room or an additional place setting at the dining table.

Notices of Meetings

The secretary's responsibility for taking care of the notices of a meeting frequently involves the five steps listed below:

1. Making the calendar notation
2. Preparing the mailing list
3. Composing the notice
4. Typing and sending the notices
5. Handling the follow-up work

Making the Calendar Notations. The secretary must make follow-up notations on the calendar as a self-reminder to prepare and send the notices. Make the notations on dates far enough ahead to allow time for the notices to be composed, reproduced, and delivered several days before the meeting. Notices that are too early may be forgotten. And while the notice for an office conference of staff personnel could be delivered the day before the meeting, an office conference of traveling salespeople might require two weeks' notice. You should also make a calendar notation for several days before the date of the meeting in order to confirm room reservations.

Preparing the Mailing List. Mailing lists of persons to receive notices are kept in several ways depending on the equipment available. If your organization has word processing equipment, the mailing lists can be put on one input medium and can be merged during the play-out with the notice itself from another input source. Even if the multifunctional secretary is outside the periphery of daily use of a word processing center, this is the type of routine work that might be handled easily in the center. Either the multifunctional secretary or the administrative secretary would be responsible for submitting alphabetized lists of names of those to receive notices for each type of meeting and for sending to the center changes in the mailing lists promptly as they occur. The correspondence secretary would be responsible for producing the properly addressed notices.

The multifunctional secretary and the administrative secretary should keep card files of the names, addresses, and telephone numbers of those who are to receive notices periodically. Type the addresses in either of two ways: Invert the name for easy filing (and follow with the address as it will appear on the notice), or type the entire item exactly as it will appear on the notice, perhaps underlining the last name as a filing aid. Type an identifying signal beside each address, such as *AMS* to indicate that the addressee belongs on the Administrative Management Society list. List or file by the last name of the addressee, using a systematic arrangement—straight alphabetic or alphabetically under geographic area, committee, group, or team.

How you prepare the address labels will depend on the type of equipment available. You may have an addressing machine for which you prepare address plates or you may run master copies of the address lists on a duplicator. During slack office periods address envelopes or cards so that one set is always ready for use.

An address list must be kept up to date. In addition to making changes as reported, once a year the secretary should send out double postcards for the

JONES, Maxwell

1501 Mirimar Street
Dayton, OH 45409-3528

513-429-3372

(AMS)

Illus. 17-3
A mailing list card showing the name inverted for easy filing and organization affiliation

membership to use in reporting their current addresses. When a change of address occurs, the secretary corrects the mailing list.

Composing the Notice. Simple notices can be composed by the secretary for approval by the executive. The notice of the previous meeting is a good model to follow if it specifies the day, the date, the time, the place, and either the purpose of a special meeting or the fact that it is a regularly scheduled one. The secretary who is required to prepare an agenda should send a request for agenda items along with the notice of the meeting.

Before a notice of an official meeting, such as a stockholders' meeting, is sent out, the legal department should check the organization's bylaws for any stipulations of certain information necessary for an item to be acted upon at the meeting. For instance, the bylaws may require that the notice include a statement that no dividends can be voted on unless the question of dividends is discussed at the meeting.

In preparing a notice for such a meeting, the secretary will be guided by the official secretary of the company, generally a lawyer. A form is included with the notice on which the shareholder may sign a proxy. Signing a proxy authorizes someone else to vote the stock if the shareholder is absent from the meeting. Because this notice must include a detailed list of the business to be transacted, the reasons for soliciting the proxy, and other information specifically required by law, it is usually prepared by the corporate legal department.

Typing and Sending the Notice. For small groups the notice is either typewritten or telephoned. For large meetings the notice is printed or reproduced by some duplicating process.

Postcard notices should be typed attractively, with the message neatly displayed. A simple, double-spaced form is acceptable for short notices. Some secretaries underline the important words.

Illus. 17-4
A duplicated notice of a meeting identifies all members of a committee with the name of the recipient checked off.

November 19, 19--

To the Budget Committee

Donald Wang
C. B. Newman
✓Marian Sternberg

The Budget Committee will meet in the Conference Room at 10 a.m. on November 24.

Please bring to this meeting comparisons of last year's budget with actual results in your division as of October 31 so that we can make preliminary estimates of changes that will be necessary next year.

J. F. Young

If the secretary is sending notices of regular meetings, a form may be printed or duplicated at the beginning of the club year so that the date, program topic, or other pertinent information is all that must be filled in to complete the form.

Some meetings or conferences are of such importance that the announcement is typed or duplicated on letterhead paper. If only a few names are involved, a tabular listing of the names of those to receive the letter may be typed in place of the usual single name, address, and salutation. With the tabular listing the salutation is a general one, such as "Dear Member," "Dear Committee Member," or "Dear . . . ," with the name to be filled in later. Modern usage permits the omission of the salutation entirely. An individual letter to each person is sometimes used, but that is a time-consuming procedure unless word processing equipment is available.

Because of the high cost of postage, many organizations have discontinued sending double postcards or return stamped envelopes that were formerly used to promote a high percentage of response.

Keeping a copy of the notice containing the date of mailing is a precautionary measure that the secretary should adopt.

Illus. 17-5 This notice is part of a double postcard. The return portion is preaddressed to the secretary and provides spaces for the recipient's name and number of reservations required for self and guests.

```
MEETING      The Personnel Directors Club of Oklahoma City

TIME         Monday, October 3, 19--

PLACE        Sheraton-Oklahoma Hotel (Room 421)
             228 West Sheridan Street

PANEL        Kevin Schwartz, Phillips Petroleum; Sandra
MEMBERS      Krey, Peoples Insurance; M. M. VanHorst,
             Methodist Hospital

TOPIC        "Meeting Affirmative Action Standards"

LUNCHEON     $8.50   (Make checks payable to PDC.)

             Please return your reservation card to reach the secre-
             tary by October 1. You must cancel reservations by 11 a.m.
             of the day of the meeting or be billed for the luncheon.

Telephone 834-5667 (Sarah Brown)
```

Handling the Follow-up Work. The secretary's follow-up duties consist chiefly of recording who and how many will or will not attend the meeting. If return postcards have been furnished, the notice follow-up is merely a matter of sorting the cards into the *will's* and *will not's*. But usually the follow-up means also telephoning several persons for a definite yes or no.

One executive who is secretary of a civic luncheon club in a large city sends out duplicated notices one week before the monthly meeting. Two days before the meeting the executive's secretary telephones to inquire of those who have not responded whether they plan to attend. An easy way to record attendance plans is to keep a three-column sheet on which names are listed along with acceptances and refusals. When this record is complete, the secretary telephones the hotel or restaurant, giving the number of reservations.

A helpful secretarial service, especially with a fairly small group, is to make reminder telephone calls to all persons expected or to their secretaries. A diplomatic way to do this is to inquire of the secretary if the executive plans to attend such and such a meeting called for such and such a time, adding in explanation that you are making a final check on probable attendance. Some members may be unable to attend for last-minute reasons; others may explain that they will be late. Fortified with such knowledge, the chairperson can call the meeting to order promptly.

Preparing the Order of Business (Agenda)

Every meeting should follow a systematic program that is planned and outlined before the meeting. In organized groups this program is usually called the *order of business*. It is called the *agenda* in academic and business meetings and conferences. *Calendar* is the term used at meetings of some legislative bodies, such as a city council. A review of the bylaws and of the minutes of previous meetings (properly indexed for easy cross-reference) will be of invaluable aid in preparing the order of business and in helping the presiding officer to carry out the agenda in an effective manner.

Sometime before the meeting you should remind the executive who is to preside over the meeting to prepare the order of business. If you know the purpose of the meeting, you can type the agenda in rough draft form using the order of business followed by the organization. Be sure to review the minutes of the last meeting to determine if any unfinished business items should be included on the agenda. Then submit this rough draft to the executive for revision or approval.

In some organizations a *tentative* agenda is distributed to the membership for their information and additions. If no additional items are submitted, the tentative agenda becomes the final order of business and is redistributed to all members. If additional items are submitted for consideration, a *final* agenda is prepared and sent to the membership. If the meeting includes a discussion of a proposed plan, a copy of the proposal should accompany the agenda. An example of an agenda is shown in Illus. 17-6.

The order of business may be set forth by the organization in its bylaws. If not, the usual order is as follows:

Call to order by presiding officer
Roll call—either oral or observed by secretary
Announcement of quorum (not always done)
Reading of minutes of previous meeting (Sometimes the minutes are circulated before the meeting, and this step is omitted.)
Approval of minutes

Reports of officers
Reports of standing committees ⎫
Reports of special committees   ⎬ Copies are usually given
Unfinished business (taken from previous minutes) ⎭ to the secretary.
New business
Appointment of committees
Nominations and elections
Date of next meeting
Adjournment

```
                    AGENDA FOR THE REGULAR MEETING

                               of the

                    COMMITTEE FOR A DOWNTOWN MALL

                            May 15, 19--


   I.  Call to Order         Randy Anderson, Chairperson

  II.  Reading of the Minutes  Alan Updike, Secretary

 III.  Treasurer's Report      Susan Novak, Treasurer

  IV.  Old Business

            Government Regulations, Walter Franks
            Special Funding Measures, Letitia Alberiche

   V.  New Business

            Architect's Concepts, William Chaney
            Rerouting Traffic, Officer Nelson
            The Tulsa Experience, Mayor LaFortune

  VI.  Adjournment
```

Illus. 17-6
Typical agenda

Last Minute Duties

The secretary's first duty on meeting day is to check the meeting room to see that the air in the room is fresh; that there are enough chairs, ashtrays, matches, paper, pencils, clips, and pins; and that any requested equipment such as a portable chalkboard, a tape recorder, an overhead projector or a VDT has arrived.

A group that is meeting for the first time appoints a temporary chairperson to preside and a temporary secretary. Later in the initial meeting the group elects permanent officers or appoints a committee to nominate officers and to draw up the constitution and bylaws.

You should next assemble materials in a file folder for the executive, arranging them in the order in which they will be needed as indicated on the agenda.

You should take to the meeting the minutes of previous meetings, a list of those who should attend, a copy of *Robert's Rules of Order* for your employer's reference, the bylaws, a seating chart, blank ballots, and aids similar to those shown in Illus. 17-7 for taking minutes.

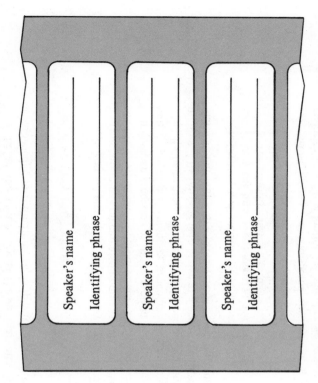

Illus. 17-7
To identify the speakers at a taped meeting, this form is helpful. It not only allows space for the name but also for the first phrase or sentence of that person's comments.

Many small business meetings and conferences are recorded on tape. If this is the case, the secretary should make arrangements for setting up the recording machine. One of your responsibilities at the meeting may be to operate the tape recorder as well as to take notes.

Unless you have previously done so, your next job is to assemble all the material that will be needed at the meeting—notebooks, pencils, pens, the minutes book, a list of standing and special committees, voting ballots, reports to be distributed to participants or perhaps a list of those attending, the companies they represent, and their addresses. It is most embarrassing to have to leave the meeting room several times for things that should already be there. It advertises that you are not very thorough. On the other hand, offering to get records or material on subjects that arise unexpectedly shows willingness to be of help. Before leaving a meeting room, however, the secretary must first get permission from the executive or the presiding officer. You are there to record data for the minutes, either through your own notes or through verbatim recordings of a professional reporter or a tape recorder (supplemented by your own notes taken as an aid in abstracting the important points from the mass of material later).

If you have noted beforehand from the order of business the names of those who are to present topics, you can record the names and topics easily at the meeting. You may also bring along or sketch a seating chart on which to fill in names as you hear them, thus being better able to match names with motions or discussions. If you miss a name, you can jot down some distinguishing characteristic of that person and ask your executive for help after the meeting.

Before the meeting opens, the secretary may have to make introductions, acknowledge introductions, or help with some last-minute arrangements.

Parliamentary Procedure

If you understand parliamentary procedure you can report meetings more accurately. You can also unobtrusively call the attention of the chairperson to any violations of parliamentary rules, such as voting on a motion before voting on an amendment to the motion. Therefore, you should review important points of parliamentary procedure before going to the meeting.

Parliamentary law has been defined as "common sense used in a gracious manner." Its purpose is to arrive at a group decision in an efficient and orderly manner. Parliamentary procedure is based on four principles:

1. Courtesy and justice must be accorded to all.
2. Only one topic is considered at one time.
3. The minority must be heard.
4. The majority must prevail.

Most business is transacted through main motions, which require a majority vote for adoption. A member addresses the chairperson, is recognized, and makes a motion. Another member seconds the motion. After the motion has been made and seconded, the chairperson states the motion, names both the one who made it and the one who seconded it, and calls for discussion. When the discussion ends, a vote is taken, usually by voice. The chairperson announces the result, "The motion is carried (or defeated)." If anyone calls "Division," the chairperson asks for a show of hands or a standing vote. If a majority demands it, the vote must be taken by ballot.

After a main motion has been made, a member of the body can propose an amendment to the motion. If the proposal is seconded, it is discussed. The proposed amendment must be voted upon before the main motion can again be considered. After announcing the action on a proposed amendment, the chairperson says, "The motion now before the house is . . ." and states the original motion plus the amendment, if the amendment carried. If the amendment lost, the original motion is acted upon.

If a motion involves two actions rather than one, a member can move that the question be divided for voting; then each part becomes a separate motion. If a motion is so bogged down that further discussion would seem to be a waste of time and if two thirds of the voting members agree, a member

RULES FOR HANDLING MOTIONS

Types of Motions	Order of Handling	Must Be Seconded	Can Be Discussed	Can Be Amended	Vote Required[1]	Vote Can Be Reconsidered[1]
MAIN MOTION						
To present a proposal to assembly[1]	Cannot be made if any other motions is pending	Yes	Yes	Yes	Majority	Yes
SUBSIDIARY MOTIONS[2]						
To postpone indefinitely action on a motion	Has precedence over above motion	Yes	Yes	No	Majority	Affirmative vote only
To amend [improve] a main motion	Has precedence over above motions	Yes, when motion is debatable	Yes, but only once	Majority	Yes
To refer motion to committee [for special consideration]	Has precedence over above motions	Yes	Yes	Yes	Majority	Yes
To postpone definitely [to certain time] action on a motion	Has precedence over above motions	Yes	Yes	Yes	Majority	Yes
To limit discussion to a certain time	Has precedence over above motions	Yes	No	Yes	2/3	Yes
To call for vote [to end discussion at once and vote]	Has precedence over above motions	Yes	No	No	2/3	No
To table motion [to lay it aside until later]	Has precedence over above motions	Yes	No	No	Majority	No
INCIDENTAL MOTIONS[3]						
To suspend a rule temporarily [e.g., to change order of business]	No definite precedence rule	Yes	No	No	2/3	No
To close nominations[4]		Yes	No	Yes	2/3	Negative vote only
To reopen nominations	These motions have precedence over motion to which they pertain	Yes	No	Yes	Majority	Negative vote only
To withdraw or modify a motion [to prevent vote or inclusion in minutes][5]		No	No	No	Majority	No
To rise to a point of order [to enforce rules or program][6]		No	No	No	No vote, chairman rules	No
To appeal from decision of the chair [must be made immediately][6]		Yes	Yes, when motion is debatable	No	Majority	Yes
PRIVILEGED MOTIONS						
To call for orders of the day [to keep meeting to program or order of business][6]	Has precedence over above motions	No	No	No	No vote required[7]	No
Questions of privilege [to bring up an urgent matter—concerning noise, discomfort, etc.]	Has precedence over above motions	No	No	No	Majority	No
To take a recess	Has precedence over above motions	Yes	Yes, if no motion is pending	Yes	Majority	No
To adjourn	Has precedence over above motions	Yes	No	No	Majority	No
To set next meeting time	Has precedence over above motions	Yes	Yes, if no motion is pending	As to time and place	Majority	Yes
UNCLASSIFIED MOTIONS						
To take motion from table [to bring up tabled motion for consideration][8]	Cannot be made if any other motion is pending	Yes	No	No	Majority	No
To reconsider [to bring up discussion and obtain vote on previously decided motion][9]		Yes	Yes, when motion is debatable	No	Majority	No
To rescind [repeal] decision on a motion[10]		Yes	Yes, when motion is debatable	No	Majority or 2/3	Yes

1. A tied vote is always lost except on a motion to appeal from the decision of the chair [see "Incidental Motions"] when a tied vote sustains the decision of the chair.
2. Subsidiary motions are motions that pertain to a main motion while it is pending.
3. Most incidental motions arise out of another question that is pending and must be decided before the question can be decided.
4. The chair opens nominations with "Nominations are now in order." Nominations may be made by a nominating committee, by a nominating ballot, or from the floor. A member may make a motion to close nominations, or the chair may declare nominations closed after assembly has been given a chance to make nominations. The voting is not limited to the nominees; every member is at liberty to vote for any member who is not declared ineligible by the bylaws.
5. The mover may request to withdraw or modify his motion without consent of anyone before the motion has been put to assembly for consideration. When motion is before the assembly and if there is no objection from anyone in the assembly, the chairman announces that the motion is withdrawn or modified. If anyone objects, the request is put to a vote.
6. A member may interrupt the speaker who has the floor to rise to a point of order or appeal, call for orders of the day, or raise a question of privilege.
7. Orders of the day may be changed by a motion to suspend the rules. [See "Incidental Motions."]
8. Motion can be taken from the table during the meeting when it was tabled or at the next meeting.
9. Motion to reconsider may be made only by one who voted on the prevailing side. A motion to reconsider must be made during the meeting when it was decided or on the next succeeding day of the same session.
10. It is impossible to rescind any action that has been taken as a result of a motion, but the unexecuted part may be rescinded. Notice must be given one meeting before the vote is taken, or if voted on immediately, a two-thirds vote to rescind is necessary.

Illus. 17-8
Compiled from Robert's Rules of Order

can "move the question," an action that forces an immediate vote. If the latter motion loses, discussion of the original motion continues.

A motion can be made to *table* a motion (to delay further discussion or action). A seconded motion to table must be voted upon at once. A successful motion to table permits the group to consider more important business and sometimes allows a motion to die—although a tabled motion may be taken from the table by a majority vote. (An even surer way to kill a motion is to move that the motion be postponed indefinitely.)

When it becomes obvious that further information is needed, a motion can be made to refer a matter to a committee, which is then named by the chairperson.

By unobtrusively calling the attention of the chairperson to a violation in parliamentary procedure, a secretary may prevent embarrassment to the employer occasioned by a member saying, "I rise to a point of order." When this statement is made, the presiding officer either must decide, without debate, whether the person raising the question is correct in claiming that the rules are being broken or must rely on the parliamentarian for advice. An error or omission in procedure can be pointed out by the secretary by a brief reminder note tactfully phrased.

Privileged motions have precedence over others. One of these is "to call for orders of the day," a motion that, without debate, forces the chairperson to follow the agenda.

The Secretary at the Meeting

If you are asked to take notes at a meeting, familiarize yourself ahead of time with matters that may be discussed by reading the minutes of previous meetings, the agenda, proposals, and other information that might be brought before the membership. This background information will be helpful to you in setting up the order of your note taking or in supplementing a recorder if the meeting is being taped. Select a chair next to the chairperson and concentrate on taking notes as unobtrusively as possible.

Your first duty may be to report whether a quorum (the required number of voting members) is present. A rapid check can be made by using a membership list. While taking notes, you may have to ask to have something repeated that you did not hear or were unable to get into note form. You may say, "I did not get that," or you may give a prearranged signal to the chairperson, such as raising your left hand slightly. Then the chairperson will ask that the point be repeated. The bylaws of some organizations require that the person making a motion submit the motion to the secretary in writing so that it will be exactly phrased in the minutes. Even here, though, you should take the oral motion down verbatim to be sure that the written motion conforms to the oral one. Copies of transcripts of involved presentations should be given to you to attach to the minutes.

You are not expected to take down the meeting word for word. Too many notes, however, are better than too few. No one turns to the secretary in a meeting and says, "Take this," or "You need not take this." You are simply held responsible for getting everything important in your notes, especially motions, amendments, pertinent discussion, and decisions. If you are afraid to decide at the instant whether statements are important, you should record them. They can be dropped from the final draft if they later seem inconsequential.

Some essential parts of the minutes may not be specifically recorded at the time of the meeting. The date, time, and place of the meeting and the name of the presiding officer may not be stated. The roll may be called; but if not the *secretary is expected to observe and to record* all the details of attendance —who attended, who did not attend, who arrived late, and who left early. The last two items of information are important in recording action on measures voted upon. (Those not wishing to go on record with their votes may absent themselves from a part of the session for just that reason.) To report as present a person who left the meeting during important transactions could have serious consequences.

BASIC METHODS OF VOTING

1. *Voice Vote* is the most common voting method since it is the easiest and fastest way of determining a vote outcome. If the vote is in doubt, another voice vote or show of hands may be taken. Responses in favor are either *yeas* or *ayes;* against, *nays* or *noes.*

2. *Show of Hands or Rising* is used when a motion requires a definite number of affirmative votes, such as two thirds. The secretary and possibly others appointed by the presiding officer are responsible for counting the votes.

3. *Roll Call* vote may be required by the bylaws of an organization for particular motions or may be decided upon by a motion from a member. The presiding officer states the responses to be used in voting for or against the motion. Members not voting may be asked to respond by saying, "Present" or "Abstain." Names are called in alphabetical order and the vote is given. The presiding officer is named last and only if the vote would affect the result. The roll call record is made a part of the minutes of the meeting.

4. *Ballot Vote* allows for a secret vote and is commonly used for elections or important matters brought before the organization. Printed ballots, as in the case of elections, generally are prepared before the meeting. For matters arising at the meeting requiring a ballot vote, slips of paper are distributed to the membership for voting use.

    Announcement of Results: The affirmative vote is given first, followed by a statement to the effect that the motion passed or the motion was defeated.

Illus. 17-9
Basic methods of voting

If you are depending on a taped report of the meeting as the source of minutes, you should have two recorders set up in the room, the second one to activate immediately after the first tape is used. In addition, you will need to make notes of *items that are not likely to appear in the recording:* the names of those attending, the official title of the speaker, who said what, the time of the meeting and adjournment, the names of those voting yes and no to motions, the names of those coming in late and leaving early, and possibly any difficult names and words that may cause confusion in transcription. If you outline the proceedings during the meeting, you can more easily make necessary insertions when you work with the verbatim report. Keep the tapes until the minutes have been signed and formally approved by the membership.

Number present _____

Excused (Names) _____
_____
_____

Absent (Names) _____
_____
_____

Things to do after meeting:

1. _____
_____

2. _____
_____

Motion _____
_____

Made by _____

Seconded by _____

Vote for _____ Against _____

Abstentions _____

Absent during voting _____

Summary of discussion:
_____
_____
_____

Illus. 17-10
Skeleton forms similar to those above are helpful in taking minutes. These forms may be consolidated on one page or placed on slips to be clipped to shorthand notes. If you list each item on the agenda, leaving after each item plenty of space for notes, you already have a guide for your minutes when the meeting starts.

If it is the secretary's duty to read the minutes of the last meeting, they should be read in an intelligible manner and in a voice loud enough that everyone in attendance will be able to hear what matters were considered and what decisions were made.

After the minutes are read, the presiding officer asks for corrections and additions. Usually this is a mere formality, and the vote approves the minutes as read. In some cases, however, corrections or additions are made. When this happens, the minutes should not be rewritten. The changes should be made in red ink on the copy of the minutes as they were originally written; and, of course, the corrections and additions become a part of the minutes of the meeting at which they are made. To save meeting time, some organizations have a Minutes Committee, whose function is to examine the minutes before the next meeting and report to the membership whether the minutes are in order or what changes should be made.

The order of business follows the agenda. The story of every motion, passed or defeated, must be recorded in the minutes. The name of the person making the motion, the complete motion exactly as stated, the name of the person seconding it, a summary of the pros and cons given, including the names of those speaking to the issue, and the decision by vote—all must go into the secretary's notes. Motions written out by their originators and written committee reports are important source documents.

After the business of the meeting is completed, the date of the next meeting is announced, usually just before adjournment. After the meeting has been adjourned, the secretary collects copies of all papers read and all committee reports so that they can be made a part of the minutes. (The committee reports are attached to the minutes.) Before leaving the meeting room, the secretary should check and verify all doubtful or incomplete notes, such as the correct spelling of names and the correct phrasing of a motion.

Follow-up Work after the Meeting

A great deal of work for the secretary always follows a meeting, aside from putting the meeting room back in order and writing the minutes or proceedings. Items that require future attention must be listed on both the executive's and the secretary's calendars. Individual letters must be written to those elected to membership and to those appointed to serve on committees or requested to perform certain tasks—even though they were at the meeting and are aware of the appointments or assignments. For expenses of participants to be paid by the organization, the secretary should see that necessary forms are completed and reimbursement made as soon as possible. (As a matter of courtesy, many executives send a summary of the meeting to the entire group.)

Resolutions. Often an organization wishes to send an expression of its opinion or will (such as a resolution expressing sympathy on the death of a member or concurrence in a stated objective) in the form of a resolution to a person or an association. A resolution may be presented at the meeting in writing, or the secretary may be instructed to prepare an appropriate resolution. After the meeting the secretary is responsible for composing or typing the resolution, having it signed and sent out, and incorporating it into the minutes.

Illus. 17-11
A resolution is
usually presented
as a formal
statement. Each
paragraph begins
with WHEREAS or
RESOLVED typed
in capital letters or
underlined.

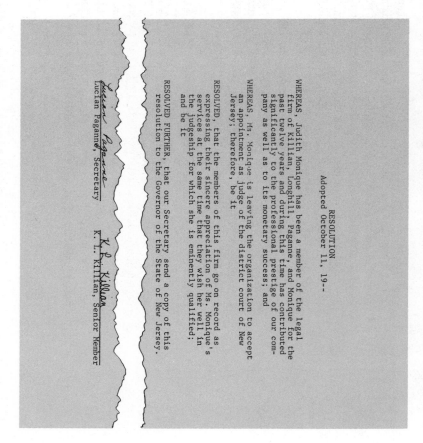

RESOLUTION
Adopted October 11, 19--

WHEREAS, Judith Monique has been a member of the legal firm of Killian, Longhill, Paganne, and Monique for the past twelve years and during this time has contributed significantly to the professional prestige of our company as well as to its monetary success; and

WHEREAS, Ms. Monique is leaving the organization to accept an appointment as Judge of the district court of New Jersey; therefore, be it

RESOLVED, that the members of this firm go on record as expressing their sincere appreciation of Ms. Monique's services at the same time that they wish her well in the judgeship for which she is eminently qualified; and be it

RESOLVED FURTHER, that our Secretary send a copy of this resolution to the Governor of the State of New Jersey.

Lucian Paganne, Secretary   K. L. Killian, Senior Member

Reporting the Meeting. The secretary sometimes encounters a problem in reporting what is *done* at a meeting, for the record reports only what is *said.* To winnow from the discussion the pertinent facts to serve as a record of *what has been decided* and as a guide to *what needs to be done by whom* challenges any secretary's best efforts.

Reports of meetings vary with the degree of formality required. For an office conference, the proceedings are compact and simple. For a meeting of an organization, the report customarily recognizes the efforts of individual members or refers to letters from former members, and, in addition, records the formal actions taken. The final minutes need not record the events in chronological order if the secretary finds that regrouping around a central theme is clearer. For *official minutes* of a formal nature (corporate minutes, for example), the proceedings are recorded in the order of occurrence in complete detail, including the exact wording of all motions or resolutions.

Sometimes the secretary places the original copy of the minutes in the secretary's book only. In other cases, however, it may be desirable to duplicate and distribute the minutes after they have been officially approved by the chairperson. If the minutes are to be referred to at subsequent meetings, duplicated minutes are often prepared with the line numbers typed at the left margin. It is then easy for a speaker to refer to *page 3, line 17*, and have the entire group follow the discussion easily.

The minutes should answer the journalistic questions: What? Where? When? Who? Why? Minutes should be written in the past tense and with complete sentences. The following suggestions apply to writing minutes of all kinds.

1. Use plain white paper.
2. Capitalize and center the heading that designates the official title or nature of the group which met, as *Committee V; Student Personnel Services; Recruitment, Guidance, and Placement*.
3. Single- or double-space the minutes and allow generous margins. There is a preference for double-spaced minutes. Indent paragraphs 5 to 10 spaces.
4. Prepare the minutes with subject captions for the various sections to expedite locating information. Record each different action in a separate paragraph.
5. Establish that the meeting was properly called and members notified properly. Indicate whether it was a regular or a special meeting.
6. Give the names of the presiding officer and the secretary.
7. Indicate whether a quorum was present, and provide a roll of those present. At official meetings and committee meetings list those absent.
8. Rough out the minutes with triple spacing for approval by your employer before preparing them in final form.

ORDER OF PRESENTATION
IN MINUTES

WHAT   1. Name of the committee, group, or organization

WHEN, WHERE   2. Date, time, place of the meeting

WHY   3. Type of meeting, regular or special; give purpose if special

WHO   4. Names of members, present and absent (if group is small)

    5. Names of presiding officer and secretary

    6. Identification of proceedings:

      Record all announcements, reports, resolutions

      (Reports can be appended to minutes)

      Record exact language of main motions, name of initiator and person who seconds motion

      A brief summary of the discussion on the motion

      Action taken

    7. Date of next meeting

    8. Time of adjournment

    9. Signature of secretary

    10. Date minutes are signed

MEETING OF THE COMMITTEE TO STANDARDIZE OFFICE FORMS

February 17, 19--

The Committee held its organization meeting in the private dining room in the company cafeteria at 12 noon.

Those present were Thomas Healey, L. D. Livovich, Margo Margolis, and Merville Perry. Madeleine Marshall was absent.

By unanimous vote Miss Margolis was elected chairperson, and Mr. Livovich was elected secretary.

The following actions were taken.

Collection of Forms Currently in Use. Using the corpora-tion organization chart, Mr. Healey will assign each member of the Committee a definite number of departments from which to collect all forms presently being used. These forms are to be collected by March 1.

Research on Forms Control. Mr. Livovich will obtain from the company librarian a list of books already available in our library on forms control. He will bring these books to the next meeting of the Committee so that members can volunteer to study those of greatest interest to them. He will also research books in print and request that the librarian purchase new books that would be useful. Mr. Perry suggested that the number of new books requested be kept to five, and the group concurred.

The meeting was adjourned at 1:15 p.m.

February 17, 19--
Date

L. D. Livovich
L. D. Livovich

9. Transcribe notes while they are still fresh in your memory. If that is impossible, you may find it desirable to take the notes home and read through them, securing them in mind for accurate transcription the next day. If minutes for a meeting that you did not attend are dictated to you, be sure that you get all the pertinent data from your employer at the time of the dictation along with any answers to questions.

10. Capitalize such words as *Board of Directors, Company, Corporation,* and *Committee* in the minutes when they refer to the group in session. Capitalize *Resolved* and *Whereas* in introducing resolutions.

11. Send official minutes to the secretary of the organization or presiding officer or both, for signatures. At the end of the minutes type a line for recording the date of their approval. *Respectfully submitted* or *Respectfully* may be used on formal minutes. The trend, however, is to omit these terms.

12. Use objective and businesslike language. Do not include personal opinions, interpretations, or comments. Record only business actions, not sentiments or feelings. Such phrases as *outstanding speech, brilliant re-*

port, or *provocative argument* are out of place in the minutes. Where gratitude or appreciation is to be expressed, it should take the form of a resolution.

13. Give the name of each speaker. Try to summarize the gist of each person's discussion about a motion, including reasons presented for and against its adoption. A recently formed organization interested in improving business records for historical purposes decries the lack of helpful information contained in the minutes of company meetings at all levels. This organization stresses the value of such summaries when later discussions of similar proposals are held.

14. Number pages at the bottom.

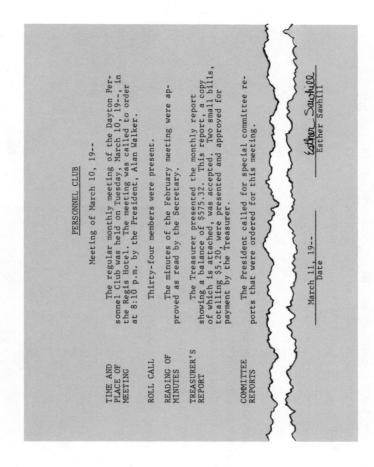

PERSONNEL CLUB

Meeting of March 10, 19--

TIME AND
PLACE OF
MEETING   The regular monthly meeting of the Dayton Personnel Club was held on Tuesday, March 10, 19--, in the Regis Hotel. The meeting was called to order at 8:10 p.m. by the President, Alan Walker.

ROLL CALL   Thirty-four members were present.

READING OF
MINUTES   The minutes of the February meeting were approved as read by the Secretary.

TREASURER'S
REPORT   The Treasurer presented the monthly report showing a balance of $575.32. This report, a copy of which is attached, was accepted. Two small bills, totalling $5.20, were presented and approved for payment by the Treasurer.

COMMITTEE
REPORTS   The President called for special committee reports that were ordered for this meeting.

March 11, 19--   *Esther Sawhill*
Date   Esther Sawhill

Illus. 17-13
Format 2
Example of captions in the margins

Indexing the Minutes. Because the composition of committees and organizations is constantly changing, sometimes groups find themselves in embarrassing situations because they do not know the regulations which they, as a body, have previously passed. They may take an action contrary to required procedure; they may violate their own regulations; or they may pass motions that contradict each other. The presiding officer may look at old books of minutes, which have been preserved since the beginning of the organization, and decide that it will be impossible to ferret out the separate actions on recurring problems. Nothing that you could do for the harassed officer could be more helpful than the preparation and maintenance of an index of the minutes by subject, giving the year and page number of each action taken. Sometimes a separate volume is used for the minutes of each year.

Writing captions in the margin of the minutes book beside the motions passed will facilitate preparing file cards for the index. The file cards should be captioned with the titles and possibly subtitles on which action was taken, along with the year in which the group acted and the page on which the decisions were recorded.

```
Minutes of the Budget Committee

Dental Care Plan

         January 13, 1982,  p. 1
         February 16, 1982,  p. 1
         March 16, 1982,  p. 1
```

Other Duties. The secretary should be especially diligent in processing all forms necessary for prompt payment of honoraria, fees, and expense accounts to those who were part of the program and to those who attended the meeting. A check should also be made to see that appropriate thank you notes and notifications of committee responsibilities resulting from the meeting are written.

Minutes of Corporations

Corporations are usually required by law to keep a minutes book for recording the minutes of meetings of stockholders and directors. Stockholders usually meet once a year, but directors' meetings are held more frequently. Minutes books are extremely important legal records. Recorded decisions must be carried out, for they constitute the regulations to which the management must conform.

The records of a corporation are kept by the corporation secretary, a full-time executive who is probably assisted by the secretary performing the types of duties described in this book. The stockholders' and directors' minutes are usually kept in separate books and are of immense legal significance. The minutes books must be carefully guarded against substitution or removal of pages by (a) the use of prenumbered pages, each signed and dated by the corporation secretary, (b) employing pages watermarked with a code symbol, or (c) a keylock binder that can be opened only with a carefully guarded key.

Illus. 17-14
An index card
concerning the
dental care plan
might look like
this.

Corrections resulting from the reading of the minutes at a subsequent meeting are written in and the incorrect portions ruled out in ink. These changes are initialed in the margin by those signing the minutes.

The minutes of a corporation identify the membership of the group, show the date and place of the meeting, tell whether the meeting is regular or special, give the names of those attending, and contain a complete record of the proceedings. The official secretary of the corporation has full responsibility for the completeness, accuracy, and legality for formal minutes even though a regular secretary may type them.

CONFERENCES AND CONVENTIONS

The executive is likely to participate in numerous conferences and conventions. A *conference* is a discussion or consultation on some important matter, often in a formal meeting. A *convention* is a formal meeting of delegates or members, often the annual assembly of a professional group. The executive's secretary is often involved in planning these events and in follow-up after the actual meeting.

Secretarial Planning Responsibilities

Some conferences and conventions require the full-time efforts of a secretary for an entire year. Weeks and months of painstaking work are required to handle details such as the following.

1. Arrange for speakers and tell them explicitly what they are to discuss and how long a time they will have for their presentations.
2. Obtain biographical material from speakers.
3. Ask each speaker the type of equipment and room arrangement required for the presentation. A form such as that shown in Illus. 17-15 is helpful in gathering this information. (The secretary to the executive who makes several conference presentations a year should have a packet of materials prepared for the conference coordinator including a biographical sketch, photograph, type of equipment required, and preferred room arrangement.)
4. Mail publicity material to prospective participants.
5. Prepare menus and plan social activities.
6. Prepare printed programs.
7. Prepare or maintain up-to-date mailing lists.
8. Obtain materials for the giveaway envelope given to each participant at registration.
9. Provide for the distribution of name tags.
10. Arrange for advance registrations by mail, if desirable; collect and deposit registration fees.
11. Publicize the conference or convention.

12. Contract for displays and exhibits.
13. Arrange hotel accommodations for speakers or distinguished persons.
14. Answer any inquiries concerning the conference.
15. Iron out the thousand-and-one necessary details as they present themselves.

EQUIPMENT REQUISITION

Session _____

Room _____   Date _____   Time _____

Room _____   Room Capacity _____

Seating Accommodations:

Speaker's Table _____

Chairs for Participants _____   Chairs _____

Equipment Required	Date Ordered	Operator Required
Tape/Cassette Recorder		
Chalkboard		
Easel for Chart		
Overhead Projector		
35 mm Projector		
Screen		
Videotape Recorder		
Slide Projector		
8 mm Projector		
Microphone		
Lectern		

Room Arrangement Preference (Indicate Preference):

Round Table _____   Horseshoe _____   Classroom Tables _____   Chairs _____

Illus. 17-15

A form such as this is helpful in gathering information on what type of equipment and room arrangement speakers will need.

Duties at the Conference

The secretary is challenged at every turn to perform efficiently during the conference; for, even with the best of planning, problems are bound to occur. You are responsible for seeing that the equipment specified by the speaker is in the room and is operable. You must arrange to have the projectionist on hand at the very minute the speaker wants to show films or slides. You must see that the room is darkened during the showing.

It is up to you to see that the microphones are operating and that service people are on hand during the presentations. This may involve checking on union regulations. It is you who must remember to send complimentary tickets for the spouse of the luncheon speaker, to position session signs, to have ice water at the lectern, to check the number of chairs on the platform, to check that the table is draped, and to provide place cards for the speakers' table and arrange them with a sense of protocol. Finally, it is you who must follow through with the gracious gestures that send the participants home happy.

Conference Reporting

At many conferences, the proceedings are of such value that they are preserved in permanent form. For example, the American Management Association may hold a conference on employee appraisal and later publish the proceedings as a service to its entire membership and to outside purchasers of the report. These meetings are usually reported by specially trained reporters. Here your function changes from reporter to coordinator. If you work in a situation where outside conference reporters are regularly used, you are expected to locate persons who can do excellent work. Keeping a file of possible reporters, printers, lithographers, and artists—along with an appraisal of the quality of their services—will be an invaluable aid.

As a secretary, you are responsible for all the conference groundwork and probably for all the follow-up work, just as you would be for any other meeting. You should not, however, be concerned with the writing of the conference report—only with the processing of it.

Often registrants at the conference want a copy of the proceedings. This service might be paid for by the registration fee, or an additional charge might be made. In any case the secretary may be responsible for securing mailing addresses of those entitled to the publication.

If papers are read at the conference, each speaker is usually asked to submit the paper prior to (or at) the meeting so that it can be either printed in its entirety or abstracted. Permission from the speaker must be obtained prior to publication. It is your responsibility to obtain a copy of this paper for publication.

The conference reporter needs to report only the discussion following the presentation of the paper—either from a tape recording or from summary notes. Sometimes the speaker is asked to prepare the summary. Then the reporter has to organize the material; edit it for uniformity of style; and write proper introductions, conclusions, or recommendations.

A final task for the secretary might be to compose recommendations for subsequent meetings, based on experience gained from this one.

SUGGESTED READINGS

Auger, Bertrand Y. *How to Run Better Business Meetings*, 8th ed. St. Paul, Minn.: Minnesota Mining and Manufacturing Company, 1979.

Carnes, William T. *Effective Meetings for Busy People*. New York: McGraw-Hill Book Company, 1980.

Cooper, Ken. *Nonverbal Communication for Business Success*. New York: AMACOM, 1979.

Doris, Lillian, and Besse May Miller. *Complete Secretary's Handbook*, 4th ed., revised by Mary A. DeVries. Englewood Cliffs, N.J.: Prentice-Hall, Inc., 1977.

Graham-Helwig, H. *How to Take Minutes*, 8th ed. Brooklyn Heights, N.Y.: Beekman Publishers, Inc., 1975.

Robert, Henry M. *Robert's Rules of Order Revised: 75th Anniversary Edition*. New York: William Morrow & Co., Inc., 1971.

QUESTIONS FOR DISCUSSION

1. How could an efficient secretary have improved the last organized meeting you attended:
   (a) before the meeting?
   (b) during the meeting?
   (c) after the session?

2. When should you send notices for the following meetings?
   (a) an informal office meeting
   (b) a bimonthly meeting of a professional organization
   (c) the annual meeting of the board of directors of the American Association of University Women at which reports from all committees are due

3. How are the secretary's responsibilities different in arranging a meeting for the executive and two company employees (a) over the telephone, (b) in the executive's office, (c) when one of the employees does not speak English, (d) through a computer network conference?

4. Contrast the methods of keeping mailing lists current when the secretary works alone and when the work is done by the correspondence secretary.

5. Your employer has planned a meeting with ten people in the company conference room. You have arranged for a recorder to tape the conference.

(a) Why is it a good practice to have two recorders in the room?

(b) What type of information will the recorder not provide for you in typing the minutes?

6. Why is it a better tactic for the secretary to take more materials or information to a meeting than might be needed or requested?

7. What should the secretary do:

(a) if an unidentified person makes a motion?

(b) if a person makes a motion that lacks clarity and that is changed several times in phraseology before it is voted on?

(c) if the chairperson entertains a new motion before the motion on the floor has been disposed of?

8. If a conference is being reported by a professional organization, what is the secretary's responsibility for the summary of the proceedings?

9. Retype the following sentences. Show the correct possessive form of the word in parentheses. Then refer to your Reference Guide to correct or verify your answers.

(a) Do you want copies of the (teacher) or the (student) handbook?

(b) We bought ($8) worth of stamps.

(c) I have not heard of anyone (else) dismissal.

(d) My (brother-in-law) business is for sale.

(e) The (Governor of Rhode Island) reelection will ensure progress for the state.

(f) Have you read the (Morgan company) report?

(g) There were several (women) groups in the parade.

PROBLEMS

1. You have been asked to prepare a resolution of appreciation of the services of Miss Janet Godfrey, who has just completed two terms as the first president of the Secretarial Department Club. She was instrumental in getting the College of Business to award a Top Secretary of the Year plaque at the annual awards banquet. She also represented the organization on the Council of Student Groups on campus.

2. After a recent conference for which you made most of the arrangements and wrote the minutes, the following complaints were made:

(a) A participant from 500 miles away could not locate the meeting room, which had been changed the morning of the meeting.

(b) Two participants were incorrectly identified in the minutes.

(c) One participant complained that the motion she made was incorrectly worded in the minutes.

(d) Two participants who were given specific post-conference responsibilities did not perform them and gave the excuse that they had forgotten what had transpired.

What should you do next time to prevent recurrence of these problems?

3. Your employer, Henry C. Campbell, is secretary of the Denver Credit Managers Association. The regular monthly meeting of that organization was held on Thursday, June 22, at 6:30 p.m., at the Palace Hotel. Mr. Campbell gives you the following notes for the minutes of that meeting. You are to type the minutes in good form, using headings in the margins for each paragraph.

Called to order — 8 p.m. by Ralph Riopelle, President.

Number of members present: 16. Charles Bairn, Vice-President, absent. Minutes of May meeting read by the secretary and approved.

Treas. report — present bal. $572.68. Accepted (copy of report given to you by Mr. Campbell). No bills presented for payment.

Budget Committee — Rene Betz, Chairperson. Motion to accept moved and seconded. No discussion. Motion carried.

Membership Comm. — Herbert Smith, Chairperson, introduced two new members, J. E. Gary and R. C. Baldwin.

James Steer introduced Donald Durst of Atlanta as speaker. Subject: "Trends in Installment Credit." Question and answer period followed.

Mr. Riopelle announced July 21 date of next regular meeting.

Motion for adjournment carried — 9:37 p.m.

Case Problems

Case 6-1
JUGGLING
EXPENSE
ACCOUNTS

Tony Alvarez, secretary to the sales manager of ASD Company, went to lunch with Mary Turner and Jack Lewis, sales representatives, who had just submitted their travel expense forms for a sales conference at Mount White Inn. The conference was held some distance from the home office, and each one had driven a car to get to the hotel. Jack said, "I hope that our mileage figures are somewhat alike, Mary. I added 75 miles and included a visit to a customer in Brookfield, though I must admit that I didn't make that call. I did get a telephone order from there that day, however. You know that, with today's inflation, we can't possibly live on the expense allowance that the company gives us."

Mary answered, "Yes, I know, Jack. We haven't had an adjustment in a year. I don't intend to lose money on my expenses either, so sometimes I have to juggle my figures a bit. I don't overestimate my actual travel expenses, but my expense accounts aren't exactly accurate either. Besides, everybody does it."

Then Jack said, "I know that we just had that memo from our sales manager asking us to cut down on travel expenses because our company has had such low third quarter earnings. I don't see much chance for a change in our travel allowance this year." He turned to Ken and said, "Tony, I have an idea. Why don't you suggest to Ms. Wolf that we be given a more reasonable figure?"

What should Tony say? What action, if any, should he take?

Case 6-2
LINES OF
AUTHORITY

Ms. Elverson came back from a trip complaining to her secretary, Lilli LiQuan, about the airline she had traveled on. Lilli had made the arrangements through Marie Koch in the Transportation Department. She knew that Marie usually chose the airline with which her principal had been displeased over others with parallel schedules.

Lilli had a friend who was an airline reservations clerk handling corporate travel accounts only. She decided that she would discuss with him the best schedules and accommodations for a trip to Chicago that three company executives were to make the following week. She decided on the round-trip flights, telephoned Marie to give her specific requests, and asked her to make the actual reservations.

Marie said indignantly, "Don't tell me which flights to choose. What are you trying to do—take my job away from me?"

Lilli tried to appease her by saying, "But Ms. Elverson didn't like her flight Wednesday and doesn't like to travel on the airline on which you always put our executives. I was just trying to be helpful."

What is the proper line of authority in this situation? What principle should Lilli follow in trying to handle the situation without troubling Ms. Elverson?

Case 6-3
EXPANDING
DUTIES

Frank Larson was secretary to Robert Holmes, manager of telecommunications for CXD. This multinational corporation had just purchased equipment for teleconferencing. Frank was asked to attend the briefings on the use of the equipment and was given all the instructional manuals connected with its use. He did not, however, study the manuals because of the pressure of his other duties.

The first tryout was to be a conference between the president of the company and its five regional vice-presidents. Mr. Holmes wanted this to be a stellar performance. Unfortunately the full motion video that was planned was unsatisfactory. Mr. Holmes asked Frank to supply freeze frames. Because he had not studied the material that had been given him, Frank did not know what a freeze frame was and had made no provision for obtaining the photographs.

After the pictureless conference, Mr. Holmes blamed Frank for not having had the backup pictures available. He pointed out that the instructions warn that they are necessary in case anything goes wrong with a conference as planned.

Frank replied, "I'm sorry, Mr. Holmes. However, I don't really think that I should be blamed. I'm a secretary, not an engineer, so I don't believe that I should have to know how to cope with that complicated equipment."

What principles are involved in Frank's reaction?

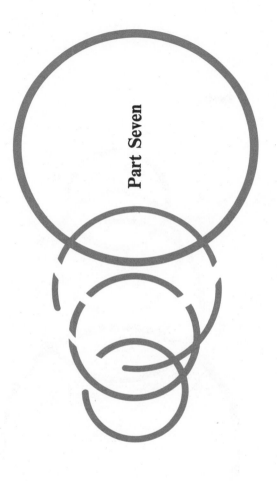

Part Seven

ADMINISTRATIVE SUPPORT SERVICES: RESEARCH AND ORGANIZATION OF BUSINESS DATA

A challenging area of secretarial responsibility is researching information for reports, presentations, or input to the computer. It provides an opportunity to increase one's knowledge as well as to demonstrate creativity in locating and organizing the information. For the secretary who types the final report there is the satisfaction of preparing a visually attractive and sometimes lengthy document with tables, charts, or other graphics.

In accomplishing these duties, the secretary may be working with new tools, such as the video display terminal of a computer or a microfilm reader. The professional secretary, therefore, must keep informed on advancements that will present new ways in which data and words are processed in the office.

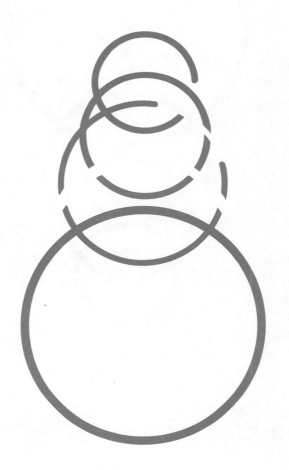

Chapter **18**

Collecting Business Information

An interesting and challenging responsibility of the administrative or multifunctional secretary is researching information for business reports. The secretary may find the information in the company records or may use outside sources such as a public or special library. Depending on the assignment, the information may be required by the executive or the secretary. Researching business information gives the secretary an opportunity to show initiative and work without supervision (an opportunity that often leads to recognition and promotion). The college-trained secretary should be particularly adept at knowing where to find information.

Here are typical examples of assignments for research of business information:

Verify the accuracy of data submitted in support of a proposal.
Gather the data the executive will need in preparing a proposal.
Examine possible solutions to a problem, advantages and disadvantages, opinions of authorities, ways others solve the problem.
Do the library research required by the executive in contributing to a project.
Gather and organize information the executive will need in preparing a speech or an article for a professional magazine.
Review personnel needs due to increased work load or establishment of new positions.
Research the financial condition of certain companies.
Compare product sales in a given category or territory.

In accomplishing these activities, the secretary locates the information and presents it in proper format. This chapter will assist you in becoming a knowledgeable researcher of business information. Chapters 19 and 20 discuss ways of organizing the data for effective presentation.

WHERE TO LOOK FOR INFORMATION

Needed information may be found in the *office of the executive* or of the *secretary*, in a *company library*, in an *outside library* or in a *computer data bank*. An executive undoubtedly subscribes to technical publications; other materials are collected through memberships in trade or professional organizations. The executive often acquires specialized reference books for a personal office library. The company also may provide reference materials for the desk of the secretary or office supervisor.

Libraries

Many large corporations maintain a company library staffed with a technically trained librarian. In addition to a librarian, many companies have a research staff that locates information requested by each office. In this case the function of the secretary is to provide an accurate and exact request for information. In other situations the secretary must locate the information in the company library.

It may be necessary to go outside the organization for needed information. The first logical outside source is the public library. A number of cities have public libraries with specialized business departments and branches that provide invaluable assistance to the business interests in their area.

The *specialized library* is another source of information. *The Directory of Special Libraries and Information Centers*, published by Gale Research Company of Detroit, lists special libraries, their location, size, and specialty. A local Chamber of Commerce will frequently have a library on commercial and industrial subjects. Many business, technical, and professional societies or associations maintain excellent libraries, generally limited to use by members. Law libraries are often located in county and federal court buildings or at the local university or college of law. Many cities provide municipal reference libraries for the public as well as for city employees. Hospitals and colleges of medicine maintain medical and surgical libraries. Art, history, and natural history museums have specialized libraries, as do colleges and universities. Some newspaper offices have large library collections that they may open to limited public use. The United States Department of Commerce maintains regional offices in the principal cities, making available the files of the publications of the Department.

Computer Data Banks

A relatively new information source to researchers is the computer data bank, where information on many different subjects (data bases) is stored. Information in many technical fields ranging from the environment to petroleum is now available for quick access from computers. A company with adequate computer facilities can subscribe to a particular service so that the data can be provided *in house.* A secretary researching information keys in a special code and, through instructions given, the information either appears on a CRT or is printed out.

Research and university libraries and some public libraries subscribe to one or more such services. An example of one of the services available is the *New York Times* Information Bank, which offers abstracts of the *New York Times* and thirteen other newspapers and over forty magazines. There is a charge, however, for the use of the computer. If a service is available at a public library, generally there is no charge or the charge is minimal.

USING THE LIBRARY

When a subject requires extensive searching or considerable listing and copying, the secretary usually goes to the library to do the work. If the secretary is unfamiliar with the library, a brief stop at the information or reference desk and a statement outlining the purpose of the visit can save considerable time. The reference librarian usually is very willing to assist researchers in locating the information sources they need.

Telephone Reference

A very valuable service to the business community is the reference librarian. A phone call to this specialist can give you the answer to most questions, trivial or practical. Some libraries have a telephone reference phone number listed for easy access to the services of reference librarians. The New York Library telephone reference number, for instance, takes up to one thousand calls a day. Reference librarians use fourteen hundred reference volumes to obtain their information.

In order to save time, callers should get straight to the point. Also, be sure to ask for the source of information if the librarian does not supply it. If your question is too specialized or too technical for a general telephone reference service, you will be referred to another library division or an outside source for assistance.

Finding the Information

The experienced researcher consults library indexes, guides, and catalogs as the first step in the process of finding information.

Books. The index of books is the *card catalog,* which can be either a card file or microform that requires a microfilm reader to locate a specific book. The card file shows the contents of the library just as a book index lists the topics treated in a book. In the catalog there are at least three index cards for each book: one card is filed by the author's name, one by title, and one or more by subject classification. Many of the cards contain *See also* notes, which indicate where similar or related information may be found. The cards are usually uniformly printed and available to libraries from the Library of Congress.

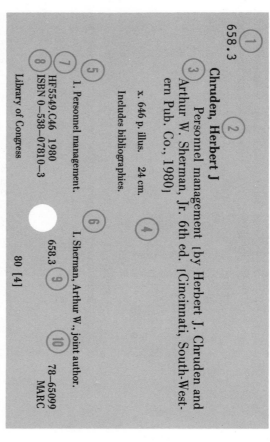

(1) 658.3

(3) **Chruden, Herbert J**
  Personnel management [by Herbert J. Chruden and Arthur W. Sherman, Jr. 6th ed. [Cincinnati, South-Western Pub. Co., 1980]

(4)   x, 646 p. illus.   24 cm.

  Includes bibliographies.

(5) 1. Personnel management. (6) I. Sherman, Arthur W., joint author.

(7) HF5549.C46 1980   (9) 658.3   (10) 78–65099

(8) ISBN 0–538–07810–3   MARC

Library of Congress   80 [4]

Illus. 18-1

An author's card in a library catalog shows the (1) classification (or call) number; (2) author's name; (3) title of the book, author or authors, edition, publisher, and date of publication; (4) text pages and size of the book in centimeters; (5) subject entry; (6) joint author entry; (7) Library of Congress classification number; (8) International Standard Book Number; (9) Dewey decimal classification number; and (10) serial number of the card.

Dewey Decimal System. The Dewey decimal system of classifying library collections is a type of subject filing and is used by most public libraries. The subjects are divided into not more than ten general classifications numbered in hundreds from 000 to 900 inclusive. Each major class may be divided by units of ten, such as 100, 110, and 120. These classes may be further subdivided by units of one, such as 110, 111, and 112. Subdividing can be continued indefinitely by using the decimal point—for example, 126.1, 126.2, 126.21, 126.211. Under this system, business information is found in the 650 groups.

Library of Congress System. Some research libraries use the Library of Congress designations (combination of letters and figures). With this system business information is found under the major category H (social sciences).

Published Indexes. An annual publication, *Books in Print,* in several volumes, lists all books included in publishers' catalogs, by author, title, and subject. The listings by subject headings are particularly helpful to the secretary in developing a bibliography of current books on a given topic. These books are normally shelved in the reference section of the library.

The *Cumulative Book Index* (or the CBI as it is familiarly identified) is an index of most of the books printed in English all over the world and still available from publishers. The CBI lists each book in three ways—author, title, and subject. These extra large volumes are normally shelved in the catalog department of the library or at the reference desk.

Other indexes that will help the secretary locate current information in special fields are the *Biological and Agricultural Index, Applied Science and Technology Index, Business Periodicals Index, Education Index, Social Sciences Index,* and *Engineering Index Annual.*

Pamphlets and Booklets. Much valuable information is now published in pamphlet, booklet, or leaflet form. Such material is cataloged by subject and title in the *Vertical File Index of Pamphlets* (a subject and title index to selected pamphlet material) which is published monthly. The following is a typical listing:

Illus. 18-2
Much valuable information is now published in pamphlet, booklet, or leaflet form. This example shows a typical listing from the *Vertical File Index of Pamphlets* (June 1980).

APPLICATIONS for positions
How to find a job: a woman's handbook, by Susan J. Jeffers and Ellen F. Carr. 62p '80 Jeffers/Carr associates 307 E 44th St. NY 10017 $2.95 send payment with order
   This booklet is written for women who are just entering or reentering the job market. As well as general advice, it includes ideas on fear, lack of experience, and a broader spectrum of opportunities for women today.
Looking for work. 29p '79 Smith associates Box 7543 Salem Or 97303 $4
   A practical guide for: locating job openings, preparing a job campaign, preparing a resume and interviewing.

This source of information can easily be missed during research because the material may not be indexed in the library's card catalog nor shelved. It is usually stored vertically in file drawers.

News. *Facts on File News Reference Service* is a weekly world news digest covering more than fifty United States and foreign newspapers and magazines. It is published as a one-volume, loose-leaf booklet with a cumulative subject index.

For newspaper references the *New York Times Index* should be consulted. Supplements of this index are published monthly, cumulative editions annually. Entries are arranged alphabetically under name of subject. *The Wall Street Journal* publishes a similar index.

Magazines. The best index on general magazines is the *Readers' Guide to Periodical Literature*—a cumulative author and subject index to articles appearing in periodicals that are on file in almost all main public libraries.

Preparing Bibliography Cards

The first consideration in selecting material for examination is its *date of publication.* If current information is desired, an article on laser beams published ten years ago would be of little value; but twenty- or thirty-year-old biographies of Benjamin Franklin would be worthwhile.

The second consideration is *content.* Some listings describe the types of information in the publications. Such descriptions help in selecting material to be researched.

For each reference selected for study, prepare a bibliography card. On a 5- by 3-inch card record the library call number, the author's name, the title of the publication (and article if it is in a periodical), the publisher, date of publication, and page reference.

Number the cards in the upper right corner in sequence, according to each new source used. The number that is thus assigned to a source is used to identify all notes that are taken from it. This method saves a great deal of time in identifying the sources when the references are copied or abstracted; besides, the bibliography cards serve as a permanent and detailed record of the sources used.

Illus. 18-3
The bibliography card (left) identifies the book as source No. 6. The card at the right shows pertinent material, organized and easy to use before writing the paper.

Taking Notes

The secretary is now ready to study, evaluate, accept or reject material, and record the references on individual sheets or on cards 6 by 4 inches or larger. By using cards or sheets of uniform size instead of a shorthand notebook, the complete set of references can be sorted for use in drafting the outline and the report.

Compiling Reference Cards. Each reference card should give the following information in a standard form similar to that in the illustration:

Page number—written in the upper left corner. (Do this first to avoid omitting it.)

Source—indicated by the number on its bibliography card.

Topic—described in a conspicuous position, giving the nature of the reference.

Information—written either as a direct quotation or as a summary statement. It is important that you make a distinction for your employer between what is a summary statement and what is a direct quotation from the information source. A direct quotation is written word for word and enclosed in quotation marks, and any omissions from the original are indicated by ellipses (. . .). Reproducing the author's work without express permission is in violation of the copyright laws. (See also Chapter 24.)

Abstracting. Abstracting is the process of taking the important ideas in a document and recording them in your own words. To prepare good abstracts, you must develop the ability to pick out the important points and express them in summary form. A secretary who is skillful in doing this can save the employer a great deal of reading time. A reference in abstract form should be identified as such, with the source and page number from which it is taken. Illus. 18-4 is an example of an abstract prepared by a secretary.

Illus. 18-4
To prepare good abstracts, you must be able to pick out the important points and express them in summary form.

ABSTRACT*

Murphy, Alma A. "Information Processing in the Modern Office." The Mechanized Office (October 10, 19--), p. 43.

Office work involves inputting, processing, and outputting information. Information is frequently inputted at the keyboard of a standalone text editor or a computer linked terminal. Information is processed through the use of hardware (computers and text editors) and software programs. Printed material, also called hard copy, is by far the most common form of output. Information can also be displayed on a CRT. Other forms of output are microfilm, magnetic tape and disks, and, in the case of word processing, the magnetic card. This article gives further evidence of the merger of data and word processing. More and more manufacturers are introducing equipment that performs both data and word processing functions.

*An abstract can be single- or double-spaced. Citation given is fictional.

SOURCES OF GENERAL INFORMATION

Copying Material. Fortunately most libraries provide researchers with typewriters and copying machines at a nominal cost. Because of the likelihood of errors in recording numerical data, statistical tables should be copied by machine.

When library publications can be borrowed, the material can be taken to the office and typed or reproduced on a copying machine. The librarian will, in fact, often lend the secretary a noncirculating copy for a limited time. Libraries are eager to cooperate with business people and to have them make full use of the library collections.

Information sources are being updated and revised constantly, and new materials are being published regularly. It is necessary, therefore, to update any guide (including this chapter) with current sources.

Atlases

An atlas is a collection of maps and statistical information regarding populations and geographic areas. *Rand McNally Commercial Atlas and Marketing Guide*, subscribed to by most libraries, contains not only geographic maps but also many economic maps with primary emphasis on the United States. The *New York Times Atlas of the World*, Comprehensive Edition, in addition to maps of every country in the world, includes sections on the solar system, world climate, and world energy resources.

Dictionaries

One would naturally expect a dictionary to be a frequently used reference source for the secretary. Even though the office has a large unabridged dictionary, the efficient secretary will want an up-to-date desk size dictionary within arm's reach. *Webster's New Collegiate Dictionary*, for example, is a valuable addition to the secretary's reference shelf. (See also Chapter 9.)

There are also innumerable specialized dictionaries: bilingual ones for use in writing and translating foreign correspondence and technical ones such as *A Dictionary for Accountants; Dictionary of Business and Management; Dictionary of Computers; Dictionary of Insurance; Dictionary of Occupational Titles; Dictionary of Education; Dictionary of Legal Words and Phrases; Black's Law Dictionary; Dictionary of Business, Finance, and Investment; Hackh's Chemical Dictionary; Modern Dictionary of Electronics; New Dictionary of Physics;* and *Black's Medical Dictionary.*

New developments outdate technical dictionaries rapidly. Only the most recent editions can be considered dependably up to date.

City Directories

A city directory gives a listing of residents of a city by name, address, and telephone number. City directories are not published by cities but by commercial enterprises for profit. Some large cities, such as New York City and Los Angeles, no longer have city directories.

A secretary to a lawyer or to an insurance agent may be asked to locate or trace the address of an individual by a search through city directories when the name of the person is not listed in the telephone directory. The secretary may have a phone number to call and not know the company name or person at that number. In such instance a city directory is extremely helpful since telephone numbers are given in numerical order.

Current and back issues of city directories are kept at libraries for the convenience of business users. The library collection of directories may contain the local city directory and also directories of all the cities in the state and of major cities throughout the country.

Special Directories

Hundreds of classified directories serve many fields—so many, in fact, that a special guide to directories is published. The *Directory of Directories*, an annual publication, lists more than 5,000 directories in industrial and professional fields. Some of them are listed below.

1. Those that list individuals engaged in the same occupation—for example, the *American Medical Directory*, which gives education and field of specialization of all physicians in the United States, Canada, Puerto Rico, and the Virgin Islands.

2. Those that provide biographical sketches of selected individuals. *Who's Who in America* is a biographical directory, reissued biennially, of notable living Americans prominent in science, politics, sports, or education. *Who's Who* is an international annual biographical dictionary. There are also many selective *Who's Who* references, such as *Who's Who in Insurance; Who's Who in the Office Machine Industry; Who's Who in the South and Southwest; Who's Who of American Women; Who's Who in American Politics;* and *World's Who's Who in Finance and Industry.*

3. Those that list all the businesses or service institutions engaged in similar or related enterprises in the United States, such as *Thomas' Register of American Manufacturers,* and *Standard & Poor's Register of Corporations, Directors and Executives. The Million Dollar Directory,* Volumes I and II, identifies the most important group of business buyers in the United States.

4. Those that list businesses in foreign countries, such as *Jane's Major Companies of Europe* and *Directory of American Firms Operating in Foreign Countries.*

5. Those that serve as buyers' and consumers' guides. The best known is *MacRae's Blue Book,* a buying guide published annually. This publication also lists trade names and firms owning such names.

6. Those that provide such information as the *Encyclopedia of Associations*, *Researcher's Guide to Washington*, *The New Guide to Study Abroad*, and the *Encyclopedia of Information Systems and Services*.

Encyclopedias

An excellent reference source is an encyclopedia. Only two are mentioned here. In addition to general information, the *Encyclopedia Americana* provides information on American cities and manufacturing and commerce. The *Encyclopaedia Britannica* is especially useful to obtain information on European countries and cities.

Government Publications

The United States government is a prolific publisher and a major source of information for the business executive. Some government publications may be subscribed to or purchased. Others will be found on file in the reference department or business section of the public library or in the municipal reference library of a city hall—depending on the subject matter. Large cities usually have a depository library designated by law to receive all or part of the material published by the government.

In *The Monthly Catalog of U.S. Government Publications* or the microfiche service, Government Printing Office Sales Publications Reference File, the secretary will find a comprehensive list of all publications issued by the various departments and agencies of the United States government. Included in this list are those for sale by the Superintendent of Documents and those for official use only. A semimonthly list of *Selected United States Government Publications* is sent free to persons requesting the Superintendent of Documents to include their names on the mailing list.

Proceedings and debates of Congress are given in *The Congressional Record*. The official directory of the United States Congress, *The Congressional Directory*, provides information on the legislative, judicial, and executive branches of the federal government. The *Congressional Staff Directory* publishes the names of staff personnel of the members of Congress in Washington and those serving on committees and subcommittees. The *United States Government Manual*, the official handbook of the federal government, provides information on the purposes and programs of most government agencies and lists top personnel of those agencies.

Publications of the Bureau of the Census of the United States Department of Commerce are based on data from censuses taken in various years including information on population, housing, business, manufacturing, and agriculture. Full census reports provide complete information. *The Statistical Abstract of the United States* (annual), however, presents summary statistics about area and population, vital statistics, education, climate, employment, military affairs, social security, income, prices, banking, transportation, agriculture, forests, fisheries, mining, manufacturing, and related fields.

The United States Department of Commerce publishes the *Survey of Current Business* (issued monthly), which reports on the industrial and business activities of the United States. Publications of the Department of Agriculture provide agricultural and marketing statistics and information for increasing production and agricultural efficiency. Department of Labor publications deal mostly with labor statistics, standards, and employment trends. The Department's official publication is the *Monthly Labor Review.*

Economic and agricultural data on many subjects may be acquired from various state governments. The secretary should address inquiries to the departments of health, geology or conservation, and highways; to the divisions of banks, insurance, and statistics; to industrial and public utilities commissions; or to the research bureaus of state universities. Pertinent information about executive, legislative, and judicial branches of state governments is given in the *Book of the States*, which is published every two years by the Council of State Governments.

Yearbooks

Yearbooks are annual reports of summaries of statistics and facts. *The World Almanac and Book of Facts*, which is the most popular book of this type, contains many pages of statistics and facts preceded by an excellent index. One reference librarian has said, "Give me a good dictionary and *The World Almanac*, and I can answer 80 percent of all questions asked me." It covers such items as stock and bond markets; notable events; political and financial statistics on states and cities; statistics on population, farm crops, prices, trade and commerce; educational data; and information on the postal services. Because of its wide coverage and low price, the secretary might request the executive to purchase a copy of *The World Almanac* each year for office use. Another yearbook of this type is the *Information Please Almanac, Atlas, and Yearbook*, published by Simon & Schuster.

The *Statesman's Yearbook* provides factual and statistical information on countries of the world. Data are provided under the following headings: type of government, area and population, religion, education, justice, defense, commerce and industry, and finance. The *International Yearbook and Statesmen's Who's Who* (one book) includes biographical sketches of over 10,000 political leaders and general information on international affairs and foreign relations.

SOURCES OF BUSINESS INFORMATION

Sources of business information, like general information, are constantly being revised, and new materials are being published regularly. This listing of specific business sources, therefore, is to serve as a guide and should be supplemented with new sources as they appear.

Abstracting Services

So vast is the volume of technical literature published in many areas that engineers, scientists, and business executives find it difficult to keep abreast of new developments. To help bridge this information gap, some large companies subscribe to an abstracting service that specializes in a specific field. An example is the American Petroleum Institute's Central Abstracting and Indexing Service. Highly trained specialists abstract thousands of journals, publications, and scientific papers from all parts of the world. The abstracts are distributed to subscribers.

Some of the abstracting services feed abstracts and selected references into a computer. The computer arranges the material alphabetically by subject. A computer driven phototypesetter prints out indexes periodically and can provide an immediate printout of all abstracts on a specific subject. The recipient can determine from the abstract whether to read the original and complete document.

General Subscription Information Services

Management often subscribes to information services relating to business conditions in general. These services present information from more direct and specialized sources than those found in the popular publications. A service may use loose-leaf form so that superseded pages can be destroyed and new and additional ones inserted easily. It may be the secretary's duty to see that the new material is filed in its proper place in the service, according to the instructions sent by the publisher. Services include the following:

Babson's Reports Inc. Two bulletins are issued: *Investment & Barometer Letter* (weekly) and the *Washington Forecast Letter* (weekly).

The Bureau of National Affairs, Inc. This privately owned company reports government actions affecting management, labor, law, taxes, finance, federal contracts, antitrust and trade regulations, international trade, and patent law. The bureau publishes a *Daily Report for Executives.*

The Kiplinger Washington Editors, Inc. A weekly confidential letter, *The Kiplinger Washington Letter*, analyzes and condenses economic and political news for subscribers.

The Conference Board, Inc. Over 4,000 subscribers support research in the fields of business economics, financial, personnel, and marketing administration, international operations and public affairs administration. Included in the service is a monthly magazine—*Across the Board.*

Research Institute of America. This company publishes *Research Institute Recommendations*, a weekly newsletter that analyzes economic and legislative developments and makes tax recommendations.

Predicasts, Inc. Over 2,000 English and non-English language publications are summarized in three indexes (United States, Europe, and International) published annually. These indexes are also available on computer terminals.

Specialized Subscription Information Services

The secretary should be acquainted with the subscription services for specialized fields described below:

Credit. Dun & Bradstreet Credit Service. This service collects, analyzes, and distributes credit information on retail, wholesale, and manufacturing companies.

Financial. (Most brokerage houses provide investment information to prospective and present customers.) Moody's Investors Service. This service publishes *Moody's Bond Survey, Moody's Dividend Record, Moody's Bond Record,* and *Moody's Handbook of Common Stocks.*

Standard & Poor's Services. Publications include *Analysts Handbook; Bond Guide; Called Bond Record; Commercial Paper Ratings Guide; Corporation Records; Current Market Perspectives; Daily Action Stock Charts; Dividend Record; Industry Surveys; Daily Stock Price Records; Register of Corporations, Directors and Executives; Review of Securities Regulations; Stock Guide; Stock Reports; Stock Summary.*

Labor. The Bureau of National Affairs, Inc., publishes a number of labor information services including the *Affirmative Action Compliance Manual, Equal Employment Opportunities Compliance Manual, Fair Employment Practice Service, Labor Relations Reporter,* and *Wages and Hours.*

Law, Tax. Commerce Clearing House Services. These services are especially useful to lawyers and accountants. The CCH *Topical Law Reports* (over 100 loose-leaf publications) provide assistance on such topics as federal tax, labor, trade regulation, state tax, social security, securities, bankruptcy, trusts, insurance, and aviation.

Prentice-Hall Services. These loose-leaf current publications cover the latest laws, rules, and regulations with interpretations and comments. Most aspects of federal and state laws with respect to business and taxation are covered. In addition, *Accountant's Weekly Report, Insurance and Tax News* (a biweekly newsletter), *Lawyer's Weekly Report,* and *Executive's Tax Report* (weekly) keep subscribers up to date.

Management. *Management Contents,* published biweekly, provides the table of contents of 285 United States and foreign journals and other information services.

Real Estate. A Prentice-Hall loose-leaf publication, *Real Estate Guide,* covers all practical aspects of real estate operation. Monthly supplements and replacement pages keep the guide up to date.

Trade. The Bureau of National Affairs, Inc. In addition to providing general business services, this organization publishes *Antitrust and Trade Regulation Report, Federal Contracts Report, International Trade Reporter,* and the *United States Patents Quarterly.*

Newspapers and Periodicals for Executives

Periodicals coming into the office can be divided into two types—general and specialized.

General Periodicals. The alert secretary scans general business magazines received at the office for material that may be of immediate or possible interest to the executive.

Typical business magazines are:

Barron's. A national business and financial weekly published by Dow Jones & Company, Inc.

Business Week. A weekly periodical published by McGraw-Hill, Inc, covering factors of national and international interest to the business executive. Statistics reflect current trends.

Dun's Review. This monthly magazine, which covers finance, credit, production, labor, sales, and distribution, is published by Dun & Bradstreet Publications, Inc.

Finance Facts. A monthly publication distributed by the National Consumer Finance Association on consumer financial behavior.

Forbes. A semimonthly magazine on corporate management for top executives published by Forbes, Inc., New York City.

Fortune. This monthly magazine published by Time, Inc., features articles on specific industries and business leaders. It also analyzes current business problems.

Nation's Business. Published monthly by the Chamber of Commerce of the United States, this business magazine concerns political and general topics.

Schools of Business Publications. The executive may subscribe to the business magazines published by some of the larger university schools of business. Well-known magazines of this type are the *Harvard Business Review* (bimonthly) and the *Journal of Business* (quarterly) of the University of Chicago.

Special Articles. In the business sections of such weeklies as *Time* and *Newsweek* and the special articles in *U.S. News and World Report,* the reader can learn a great deal about current business trends.

Newspapers. *The New York Times* is a daily newspaper covering world, domestic, and financial news and contains a special section on business in the daily editions. *The Wall Street Journal,* primarily an investor's newspaper, covers current business news and lists daily stock reports.

Specialized Periodicals. It is common for a company to belong to several trade associations, each of which helps the company with a different aspect of its business. In addition, the executive may belong to several professional associations. These associations issue regular magazines to their members, publishing articles and statistics of current interest. *The Standard Periodical Directory* lists over 65,000 United States and Canadian periodicals.

The Business Periodicals Index is the primary source of information on a wide range of articles appearing in business periodicals.

When seeking data on a specific magazine or newspaper, the secretary might consult *Ayer's Directory of Publications* (newspapers and periodicals, annual) or *Ulrich's International Periodicals Directory* providing such information as name of publication, editor, publisher, date established, technical data, and geographic area served. Another source of specialized magazines is the *Readers' Guide to Periodical Literature.* More than 100 well-known magazines (such as the *Architectural Record, Changing Times, Consumer Reports, Foreign Affairs, Monthly Labor Review,* and *Time*) are indexed in each issue and their articles cataloged under appropriate headings.

Handbooks

Handbooks have been published in many areas of business. They are highly factual and are written to give a general survey of knowledge about a field (with the minimum use of time and effort). A few of the many handbooks that have been published include *Handbook of Business Administration, Modern Accountant's Handbook, Handbook for Business and Advertising, AMA Management Handbook, Office Administration Handbook,* and the *Sales Manager's Handbook.*

Among a number of handbooks written for the secretary employed in a specialized office are those for the legal secretary, medical secretary, data processing secretary, real estate secretary, and others.

Secretary's Reference Shelf

In addition to the secretarial handbooks, this textbook, and reference materials needed for transcription, the secretary may collect other worthwhile reference books or may be asked by the executive to purchase them for the office. What is on the secretary's reference shelf should depend on the nature of the job and the background information needed. A useful, inexpensive reference is *How to Use the Business Library.* This manual is revised periodically and is a valuable adjunct to the office library or secretary's reference shelf. Among other sources of information are the following:

Abridged encyclopedias—such as *The Columbia Encyclopedia* (one volume), comprised of very brief articles. It is particularly strong on biography and geography.

An annual book of statistics—such as the *Statistical Abstract of the United States* or *The World Almanac and Book of Facts. The Guinness Book of World Records* also may be a valuable reference source.

An atlas or gazetteer—such as the *Rand McNally Illustrated World Atlas* or *Webster's New Geographical Dictionary.*

A thesaurus—such as *Webster's Collegiate Thesaurus.*

A book of quotations—such as *Bartlett's Familiar Quotations* or *The Home Book of Humorous Quotations.*

A book of etiquette—*The New Emily Post's Etiquette* or *Amy Vanderbilt's Complete Book of Etiquette Revised.*

A directory—such as the *National ZIP Code Directory.*

The secretary's reference shelf should surely include a technical handbook that covers the area of work of the executive.

A handbook of parliamentary procedure—*Robert's Rules of Order.*
A manual of style—such as *The Elements of Style,* by Strunk and White.
A communications manual—*Executive's Desk Manual of Modern Model Business Letters,* by Lloyd H. Geil.

SUGGESTED READINGS

Brownstone, David M., and Gorton Carruth. *Where to Find Business Information: A Worldwide Guide for Everyone Who Needs the Answers to Business Questions.* Somerset, N.J.: John Wiley & Sons, Inc., 1979.

Copeland, Amanda, and Lavelle Watkins. "Using Reference Materials," *Journal of Business Education* (November, 1979), pp. 70–71.

Gates, Jean K. *Guide to the Use of Books and Libraries,* 4th ed. New York: McGraw-Hill Book Company, 1979.

Johnson, H. Webster. *How to Use the Business Library,* 4th ed. Cincinnati: South-Western Publishing Co., 1981.

Weckesser, T. C., J. R. Whaley, and M. Whaley (eds.) *Business Services and Information: The Guide to the Federal Government.* Somerset, N.J.: John Wiley & Sons, Inc., 1979.

QUESTIONS FOR DISCUSSION

1. How would your approach differ in taking notes on a magazine article available on the library shelf and one available only in a computer data bank to which you have access?

2. What are the advantages of using a specialized subscription information service over a printed book as a reference source?

3. You have just been named supervisor of the new word processing center in your company. What general categories of reference books would you select for use by the correspondence secretaries? By what criteria did you make your selections?

4. If your employer asked you to go to the public library to obtain a copy of an article appearing in the *Journal of Business,* how would you locate the article?

5. In choosing a reference book, how can you be sure that you have the latest edition of the book?

6. Does the reference department of your public library offer telephone service? If so, what limitations are placed on it? Is there a special business department or branch? Where is the nearest depository of government publications?

7. If your employer is involved in scientific research and gives highly technical dictation, where would you turn for help in learning the vocabulary?

8. It is difficult to determine how long reference material should be retained in an office. In each of these cases, which factors would determine your decision?
   (a) Catalogs from suppliers
   (b) Back issues of professional and technical magazines
   (c) Advertisements of competitive items
   (d) House organs of your company
   (e) Copies of *Who's Who in America*

9. Decide whether you would use the italicized words in the following sentence dictated by your employer. Then check your Reference Guide to verify or correct your answers.
   (a) *Fewer* errors were made in the letter typed on the automatic typewriter.
   (b) New technology makes it possible to spend *less* hours on routine work.
   (c) *Less* work is required to operate the new copier.
   (d) There are *less* dollars in the budget this year.
   (e) A few *are* going to the conference.
   (f) Only a few *plans* to vote.

PROBLEMS

1. For Problem 4 in Chapter 20 you will be asked to prepare a business report on one of the following subjects. In preparation, you are now to do the necessary reading, prepare bibliography cards, and take the necessary notes.
   (a) Data processing versus word processing—who's to be in charge of administrative services?
   (b) Business behavior: assertiveness versus aggressiveness
   (c) Improving personal and records security in the office
   (d) The paperless office and how it works
   (e) Orientation training for the new office worker
   (f) The use of job-related tests in the selection of office employees
   (g) The privacy law and office records
   (h) How the supervisor supervises workers effectively
   (i) How well "Management by Objectives" works
   (j) The feasibility study for a word processing reorganization

2. Your employer has asked you to prepare an annotated bibliography on the productivity of the clerical office worker using only sources published within the last five years. Type the bibliography.

3. Assume that you are secretary to Randolph Parker, general counsel of one of the subsidiaries of a major manufacturing firm. Your employer has just been transferred to the home office and has just arrived in the office. He tells you that he has at least ten crates of books to be unpacked and arranged on his bookshelves. You are to supervise the arrangement of the books on the shelves. Also, he asks you to devise a system of control of these books, since he expects that many of the staff will want to use his materials. What is your plan of action for arranging the books on the shelves? Explain your system of control.

4. Assume that you are called upon to seek the following information. Prepare a list of your sources of information (identify by letter).

(a) Who is the chairperson of the board of American Telephone and Telegraph Company? Where will you find biographical data about this person?

(b) What is the address of the national headquarters of Administrative Management Society? What is the total membership?

(c) What was the population of Seattle, Washington, at the last official census?

(d) Who are the members of the Washington office staff of a senator from your state?

(e) What is the total circulation and the advertising rate of *Business Week*?

(f) What is the annual crude petroleum production of Saudi Arabia?

(g) What products are manufactured by Harold L. Palmer Company, Inc., Livonia, Michigan?

(h) What are the five principal business centers located in the state of Illinois?

(i) What is the London address of NCR Corporation?

(j) A quotation on the use of time.

Chapter 19

Presenting Statistical Information

Without a doubt computer technology has made a significant contribution to management decision making. Through the use of the computer, managers have at their fingertips quantitative (numerical) information that is pertinent to every facet of business operations. In virtually every organization computer technology has had its effect on the secretarial position. All secretaries—multifunctional, administrative, and correspondence—are working with numerical data more today than ever before. The voluminous output of the computer can be used by the secretary to produce appropriate tables, charts, or graphs for a business report or as visual media for a conference. In organizations equipped with computer graphics terminals the secretary may key a command to the computer to display a chart on the screen or produce a hard copy. A well-constructed table or chart can convey a picture of business operations more quickly and more clearly than words or numbers.

A good example is the annual sales conference of a company. Sales charts, graphs, and written communications including statistical data are commonplace. A speaker before the group usually uses overhead transparencies, flip charts, or a combination, to display quantitative information.

Giving life to figures, which well-planned tables and graphs really do, calls for a thorough knowledge of the techniques of table and graph construction, good planning, and imagination. The several steps involved in this type of work—compiling, classifying, and presenting data in tables and graphs—and the secretary's responsibility are discussed in this chapter.

THE SECRETARY'S RESPONSIBILITY

Chapter 18 pointed out that the secretary often has the task of gathering and organizing data for effective communication to others. This applies to both the multifunctional and administrative secretary. When a complicated chart, graph, or transparency is required, the person preparing it must know what

455

has to be said and what type of graph will best display the information. With these factors in mind, the secretary is better able either to (a) arrange for a graphic display to be made inside or outside the company or (b) prepare the graph either freehand or with commercial materials. When simple tables, graphs, or charts are involved, the multifunctional secretary most likely will prepare them. In an organization utilizing the word processing center concept, the correspondence secretary using typesetting equipment should be able to produce very professional tables and graphs.

Throughout this chapter the general term *secretary* will be used to indicate the individual who actually does the preparation of the graph.

COMPILING AND ORGANIZING DATA

The data with which the secretary works come from many sources. Some are compiled within the company. Other information, however, must be obtained from such secondary sources as magazines, yearbooks, and reports of outside agencies.

The data must be assembled onto a working form or forms so that totals can be obtained, averages and percentages calculated, and the information summarized. This process of transferring facts from the source documents to working forms is called *compiling* the data. The simplest compilation of data is a pencil written tabulation similar to the one illustrated below.

The Leisure and Recreation Corp.
Summary of Operations
For the Year Ended December 31, 19--

Sales and Revenues
(In Thousands)

Divisions	First Quarter	Second Quarter	Third Quarter	Fourth Quarter	Total for Year
Recreation					
Lawn and Garden	$25.6	$30.2	$39.4	$42.7	$137.9
Bicycles/Motorcycles	20.5	29.4	36.4	46.2	132.5
Sporting Goods	19.5	23.6	33.0	45.0	121.1
Marine Products	29.6	32.1	33.2	33.0	128.5
Total	$95.2	$115.9	$142.0	$166.9	$520.0
Recreational Vehicles					
Campers	$42.9	$45.2	$70.5	$90.2	$248.8

From Annual Report of the L + R Corp.
Compiled by R.C. 1/3/-- Checked by JM.

Illus. 19-1
A data work sheet should indicate the source, the compiler, and the checker. The work sheet should be filed with the completed tabulation, with the adding machine or calculator tape attached as proof of totals.

METHODS OF CLASSIFYING DATA

The objective in compiling data is to organize information into some type of meaningful classification. Data can be classified in any of five ways: (1) alphabetic sequence, (2) kind, (3) size, (4) location, or (5) time.

1. An *alphabetic sequence* of data is often used when the data are compiled for reference.

2. A *kind grouping* of data is used when the items are kinds of objects, characteristics, products, and so on. An example of kind grouping is a table entitled, "Retail Trade in U.S., 1982, by Kind Business." The number of stores and the year's sales are broken down into several main groups, such as food stores and apparel stores. Under each of these are listed the data for each of the types of stores included in the group.

3. *Size variations* may be shown in two ways: (a) in an *array*—that is, with the items listed in ascending or descending order, such as a table of the 50 greatest ports in the world with the ports arranged in the order of net tonnage in descending order; (b) in a *frequency distribution*—that is, according to the number in each size class. A frequency distribution is used instead of an array when the size classes can be grouped advantageously. Tables of age distribution are usually shown in this way; for example, the number of persons between the ages of 10 to 14, 15 to 19, and on as far as needed, instead of the number of persons 10 years old, 11 years old, and so on.

4. A *location listing* is used to show the data by geographic units—such as cities, states, and countries. Real estate data are often listed this way, as are commodity sales on a national scale.

5. *Time-of-occurrence or time series listings* are very common. The listing may be made by days, weeks, months, years, decades, and so on.

Illus. 19-2
In many offices, machine tabulation has supplanted manual compilation of data. From input media the computer calculates and prints the data on perforated, accordion folded sheets like that shown here.

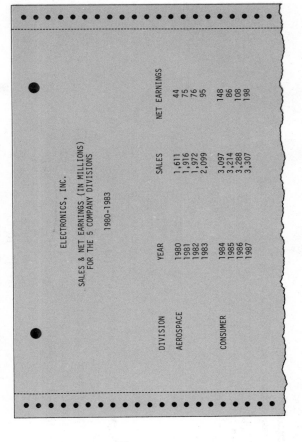

```
                ELECTRONICS, INC.

       SALES & NET EARNINGS (IN MILLIONS)
           FOR THE 5 COMPANY DIVISIONS

                   1980-1983


DIVISION      YEAR      SALES      NET EARNINGS

AEROSPACE     1980      1,611          44
              1981      1,916          75
              1982      1,972          76
              1983      2,099          95

CONSUMER      1984      3,097         148
              1985      3,214          86
              1986      3,288         108
              1987      3,307         198
```

After data have been collected, they may be translated into either averages or percentages so that comparisons can be made. To say that sales in Dallas were 35 percent greater this month than last month is easier to interpret than to say that sales last month were $50,000 and this month, $67,500.

In some instances, it may be more helpful to know the average salary of employees in the purchasing office than to know the highest and the lowest salary paid. The use to be made of the data determines which figures will be of most value.

Averages

One way to help the reader understand a set of figures is to compute an average. (An *average* is a single value used to represent a group.) But which of the three averages in common use should you choose? The one used most often is the *arithmetic average* or, more technically, *arithmetic mean*. It is determined by adding the values of the items and dividing that total by the number of items. If the weekly payroll for 120 employees is $33,000, for example, the average pay is $275.

The *mode* is a second kind of average. It is the value that recurs the greatest number of times. The data are arranged in a frequency distribution to determine the mode. For example, the mode in the following distribution is the class interval $250.01 to $260.00, because the greatest number of earned amounts fall in that range.

Weekly Earnings	No. of Employees
$240.01–$250.00	2
250.01– 260.00	26 ←MODE
260.01– 270.00	19
270.01– 280.00	9
280.01– 290.00	5

The *median* is an average of position; it is the midpoint in an array. In order to determine it, the data must be arranged in an array; that is, in either ascending or descending order. Then it is necessary only to count the number of items and find the mid one, which is the median. For example, assume that five students have the following amounts in their checking accounts:

Student A	$1,000
Student B	650
Student C	500 ←MEDIAN
Student D	100
Student E	10

The median is $500; on the other hand, the mean is $452. Obviously the mean is affected by extreme cases (the student with an abnormally large checking account and the one with almost nothing). This kind of influence is why the median is usually selected as the average that comes nearest to indicating the true state of affairs when there are extreme cases in the data.

Percentages

Percentages help in making numbers understandable and the relationship of various items to one another and to the total more easily grasped. In Illus. 19-5, page 463, the last column shows the percentage each cost factor represents of the total cost. The statement, "The secretarial cost in producing a business letter is $1.87" has less meaning than "The secretarial cost in producing a business letter is $1.87 or 28.21 percent of the total cost of producing the letter."

Percentage relatives or *index numbers* are used to compare the extent or degree of changes. They are relative because they are based on a value at a specific time and that base must be clearly defined. For example, in 1929 there were approximately 20,000,000 telephones in the United States; in 1940, 22,-000,000; in 1960, 66,500,000; and in 1976, 155,173,000. The percentage relatives, based on the 1929 figure as 100, are 110 for 1940, 332.5 for 1960, and 775.8 for the 1976 index.

PRESENTING DATA EFFECTIVELY

It is the secretary's responsibility to determine the most effective presentation of numeric data. Tables are preferable for exact representations and, when well constructed, are easy to read for making comparisons and reaching conclusions. Graphics (charts and graphs), on the other hand, are better when quick identification of relationships is important.

Tables

Three types of tables are used for writing business reports: *general purpose* tables—those to be used for reference; *special purpose* tables—those that direct the eye and mind to specific relationships of significance; and *spot (informal)* tables—unnumbered tables that appear within paragraphs of the report. General purpose tables are usually placed in the appendix and numbered consecutively. Most of the tables of statistical data included in business reports are special purpose tables. The tables on page 458 are spot tables.

A table should be self-explanatory. It should be kept simple and designed for rapid reading. The incorporation of too many elements in one table detracts from its readability and effectiveness. When planning a table, keep one question in mind: Precisely what is this table to show? All data that do not apply should be excluded.

After the table has been developed, it may be well to dramatize the material presented in it by a chart or graph. In other words, the chart does not replace the table; it supplements it. *Tables provide details; charts present relationships* but not minutiae and are not satisfactory to the reader who seeks exact data.

Planning the Table Layout

A well-balanced table can be typed perfectly the first time if the work is carefully planned. The facts and the figures to be tabulated must be analyzed carefully before the various headings and column arrangements are determined. The best method of planning a table is to make a penciled rough draft.

After this plan is drawn, the secretary can save time by using the backspace-from-center method when tabulating.

Suggestions for Typing Tables

Additional suggestions will help you plan and type an effective table that first time!

Table Captions. Most tables include the following sections: table number, main title, secondary heading, column or boxed headings, and stub (left column) headings. Only the main title is typed in all capital letters. The other headings are typed with initial capital letters only. Illus. 19-3 shows the important parts of a table.

Table Numbers. Tables should be numbered consecutively throughout a report. Arabic or Roman numerals can be used and follow the word *Table* typed in all capital letters or with an initial capital letter (Table 1, Table I, TABLE 1, TABLE I). The table number is the first caption line and the table title the second line, and both precede the body of the table.

Main Title. The title should be complete and clearly worded. The main title along with the other headings should make the table self-contained. If the data represent a period of time, the title or subheadings should indicate the period covered. Include internal punctuation in the title, but no terminal period.

If a title requires more than one line, break at a division of thought using single spacing. Avoid ending a line with a preposition. The title should be divided so that the second or third lines are shorter than the preceding line(s). The table title should not extend beyond the margins of the table.

POOR: The International Information/Word Processing Association
Annual Convention, Hyatt Regency Hotel, Houston, Texas, May
19–23, 19—

GOOD: The International Information/Word Processing Association
Annual Convention at the Hyatt Regency Hotel
Houston, Texas, May 19–23, 19—

Abbreviations. In order to save space, abbreviations may be used in column headings; but they should never be used in titles.

Columns. Each vertical column must have a heading. Column headings must clearly identify the items in the column and be centered over the column. For easy reference, the column headings may be numbered consecutively from left to right with the numbers enclosed in parentheses. Columns of related data should be placed closer together than other columns. Major divisions of groups of columns can be indicated by wider spaces or by double vertical rules between columns.

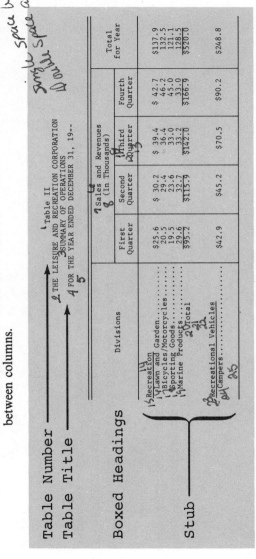

Illus. 19-3
This table was typed from the work sheet compilation shown in Illus 19-1. Leaders and skipped lines have been used to improve the readability of the table. To avoid confusion in reading large figures, the amounts are shown in thousands. Thus, $95,200 is shown as $95.2.

Alignment. In tabulated words and phrases, such as line headings in a table, the left margin should be kept even. In tabulated figures, the right margin must usually be kept straight. When decimal fractions involving different numbers of places to the right of the decimal point are listed, the decimal point must be kept in vertical alignment. Type $+$, $-$, and $\pm$ signs close to the number at the left. Use dashes, leader points, or a blank space to indicate omissions in a column.

CORRECT ALIGNMENT:

	MULTIPLY	BY	TO OBTAIN METRIC
	Miles per hour	1.6	Kilometers per hour
	Pounds	0.45	Kilograms
	Square feet	0.09	Square Meters
	Ounces	28.35	Grams

INCORRECT ALIGNMENT:

	Miles per hour	1.6	Kilometers per hour
	Pounds	0.45	Kilograms
	Square Feet	0.09	Square Meters
	Ounces	28.35	Grams

Amounts. A comma should be used to separate every three digits in amounts, but it should not be used with the digits after a decimal point. For example: *1,125.50* and *21.16184.*

For sums of money the dollar sign should be used with the first amount in a column and with each total. This also is true of columns of percentages or like symbols (pounds, kilograms, etc.)

	Correct:	Incorrect:
	$1,456.26	$1,456.26
	362.35	$ 362.35
	18.46	$ 18.46
	$1,837.07	$1,837.07

Leaders. Lines of periods, *leaders*, aid the reader by guiding the eyes across a wide expanse of space from one column to another. Leaders are usually typed with a single space between periods. Periods on successive lines should be in vertical alignment.

The time-saving method of aligning leaders is to notice whether you typed the periods in the first line on an odd or even number on the typing scale. If you typed the first period on an odd number, all subsequent numbers will begin on odd numbers. It may sometimes be necessary to leave an extra space at the beginning in order to align the periods. Your finished copy should look like this:

Night school classes	45
Art classes	47
Fashion design and clothing	52

Spacing. Tables can be entirely single-spaced, double-spaced, or a combination of single and double spacing. When long columns are single-spaced, skipping a line every three, four, or five rows improves readability.

Rulings. Rulings improve the appearance of a table. They may be typed with the underline key or made with pencil, a ball-point pen, or India ink.

Illus. 19-4
To rule lines on the typewriter, place the pencil or pen point at an angle in the cardholder notch. For horizontal lines, move the carriage from left to right. For vertical lines, release the variable line spacer and turn the platen forward or backward.

A double ruling the entire width of the table is made at the top of the table two lines below the title. Single rulings the width of the table should divide the stub and box headings from the rest of the table. A single ruling the same width should also end the table. If used, vertical rulings separate the columns and should extend from the double rulings at the top to the bottom single ruling.

Illus. 19-5
Vertical lines may be used to separate columns and the ends of the table may be left open. The footnotes are placed directly below the table and are identified by use of lowercase letters.

Table V
AVERAGE BUSINESS LETTER COSTS FOR THE YEAR 1981[a]

Cost Factor	Average Cost per Letter	Percentage of Total Cost
Secretarial Time	$1.87	28.21[b]
Fixed Charges[c]	1.88	28.36
Dictator's Time	1.75	26.39
Nonproductive Labor[d]	.54	8.14
Mailing Cost	.36	5.43
Materials	.23	3.47
Totals	$6.63	100.00

[a]Based on data supplied by the Dartnell Corporation, Chicago.
[b]Expressed to the nearest 1/100 of 1%.
[c]Depreciation, overhead, rent, light, and similar items.
[d]Time lost due to waiting, illness, vacation, and other causes.

Units. The unit designation of the data must be given (inches, pounds, and so forth). Generally this information is provided above the columns as a part of the heading or subheading.

Footnotes. If the meaning of any item in the table is not clear or must be qualified, an explanation should be given in the form of a footnote. Footnotes are also used to indicate the source of the data.

Footnotes are single spaced. The source footnote is typed first followed by any footnotes referring to specific items in the table.

To identify footnote references in numeric data, use symbols (24,961*) or lowercase letters (24,961[a]). A number used to reference a footnote (24,961[1]) can be confused as being part of the numeric data. Illus. 19-5, Table V, shows proper footnoting.

Reference. The name of the person responsible for the preparation of the table should be indicated on the file copy at least. When the data come from a secondary source, such as a publication, the source should be indicated as a footnote on the table.

Variety and Emphasis. Both variety and emphasis on relationships can be given to the typed copy by using italics, boldface (all capital letters), and type of different sizes and styles, by varying the placement of the column totals, or by using different colored ribbons. For instance, dual pitch typewriters (pica and elite options) can be used. Footnotes and column headings can be typed in elite type, and the body of the table typed in pica type. Changing the type style elements on an element typewriter can provide even wider variations. Also, a wide carriage typewriter and oversize paper can be used for a table that cannot be accommodated on standard equipment and paper.

Checking the Typed Table

Every typewritten table must be checked for accuracy. Proofreading requires the help of another person, who should read the original draft while the secretary checks the typed copy. Reading figures for checking is an oral technique that has a fairly definite prescribed routine, indicated by the examples given below. The words in the examples that are connected by a hyphen should be read as a group; the commas indicate pauses:

718	seven-one-eight
98,302	nine-eight, comma three-oh-two
24.76	two-four, point, seven-six
$313.00	three-one-three even (or no cents) dollars
77,000	seventy-seven thousand even

For copy in columnar form it is usually advisable to read down a column rather than across the page. This procedure provides a double check because, in most instances, the typing work has been done across the page. If the table includes totals, the amounts in each column should be added and checked against the total.

After the accuracy of the typed table has been verified and errors corrected, the original draft of the table should be filed in a personal folder kept by the secretary or attached to and filed with the typed file copy of the final draft. If anyone who reads the typed copy discovers an error, the filed copy of the original data will enable the secretary to determine whether the error occurred in the original material, which may have been supplied to the secretary, or whether the error was made in the process of typing the table.

Graphic Presentation

A graph is a statistical picture. It presents numerical data in visual form, making them more easily analyzed and remembered. The average person can remember a graph yet is unable to remember the columns of figures upon which the graph is based. Taking the hard facts of business and organizing them in visual form to make comparisons easy, to emphasize contrasts, and to bring out the full force of the message is a challenging opportunity.

Computer graphics equipment now permits people and machines to exchange graphic information at electronic speed. Some employees work directly with graphics, charts, curves, sketches, and drawings generated on a

CRT. The images can be recorded on film or, if a printer is attached, can be produced as hard copy. Another form of business charting is the magnetic wall chart used for displaying numeric data and qualitative information, such as scheduling of personnel. A wall chart is shown in Illus. 19-6.

Illus. 19-6
This wall chart is used for keeping track of jobs in process.

You can construct graphs on your typewriter or with the help of commercially available aids, such as Chartpak and Zipatone. These kits contain self-adhering bar and line tapes in various designs and colors. With these materials the amateur can make charts that are very effective—even dramatic. Professional chart makers can help with more complicated presentations.

Alphabet lettering packs, such as those offered by 3M, can also help the secretary produce an effective graphic presentation. The line graph in Illus. 19-7 was prepared by a secretary untrained in the art of using such materials. Lettering machines, available in large and in bold type, are ideal for overhead transparencies, printed presentations, and slides (see the discussion on Kroy-type in Chapter 6). The secretary needs a basic knowledge of the various types of graphs. An "Idea" folder can be set up in which examples of each type (both typewritten and commercially prepared) can be placed, with notes concerning their suitability for certain data.

Preparing Charts and Graphs

In making any chart or graph, no matter how simple, it is best to rough out a working copy first. The materials you will need include graph paper, protractor, ruler, compass, and a lettering guide. When the final copy is prepared, the graph should be framed on the paper. The bottom margin should be slightly larger than the top margin. The margins on the sides should be equal unless the pages are to be bound at the left. If the necessary guide points are marked lightly in pencil, they can be erased after the inking in is completed.

In a report having several charts or graphs it is common practice to number them consecutively. A chart or graph is labeled *Figure* to distinguish it from a table. The word *Figure* is typed using an initial capital letter followed by an Arabic number, for example, Figure 3. The title of the chart or graph follows the figure number with the main words typed with initial capital letters. The caption is generally typed below the chart or graph but can appear above the illustration. Also, numbering may not be necessary for an isolated chart or one used as a transparency during a presentation.

The source of the data and the date of compilation are placed below the chart. Even when this information is omitted from the presentation copy, it must be recorded on the working copy.

Line Graphs. A commonly used type of graph is the *line graph*. It is most effective in showing fluctuations in a value or a quantity over a period of time, such as variations in production, sales, costs, or profits over a period of months or years. Thus, the line graph is an effective way to depict a comparison of trends over a period of time.

The line graph shown in Illus. 19-7 emphasizes the positive relationship that existed between the total sales of foreign and domestic branches of a company over a five-year period.

Follow these suggestions for preparing line graphs:

1. Prepare a working copy on printed graph or coordinate paper and the final or presentation copy on 8½" × 11" plain paper.
2. Place periods of time on the horizontal scale at the bottom of the graph; record variations in quantities or numbers on the vertical scale.
3. Always show the *zero* point. To prevent the curve from occurring too high on the chart, show a "break" in the chart with two wavy horizontal lines to indicate the part that you have omitted.
4. To avoid distortions, plan the size of your graph. It is good practice to make the width at least *one and one-half and not more than one and three-fourths times the height.* A rise can be made to appear very steep and thus sharp or quite gradual, depending on the relation of height to width.
5. If possible, position all lettering horizontally on the chart.
6. Work with no more than four or five lines on a graph, giving each a legend or identification on the graph. Make each line distinctive in character by using different colors or by using these lines: heavy solid (—), light solid (—), broken (--), dots (. . .), or dot dash (—.—.—.).

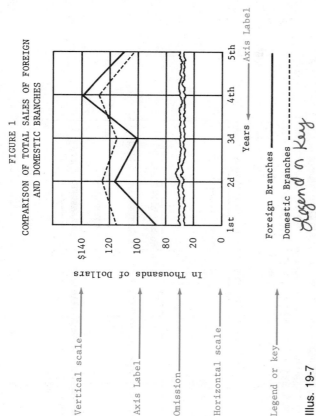

FIGURE 1

COMPARISON OF TOTAL SALES OF FOREIGN
AND DOMESTIC BRANCHES

Foreign Branches ――――――
Domestic Branches ----------

Legend or Key

Vertical scale

Axis Label

Omission

Horizontal scale

Legend or key

Illus. 19-7

This line graph shows the *zero* point, uses two wavy lines to indicate the omission that positions the significant data properly, and gives a key or legend identifying the two items being plotted. As many as four or five items can be plotted, provided the lines are not too close together.

Bar Graphs. The bar graph presents quantities by means of horizontal or vertical bars, both equally effective. Variations in quantity are indicated by the lengths of the bars. The width of the bars is the same. The bar graph is most effectively used to compare a limited number of values, generally not more than four or five. Bar graphs are used in time series and frequency distributions.

Follow these suggestions for preparing bar graphs:

1. For easy readability leave one-half to a whole bar width between single bars. Bars can be contiguous, having no spaces between them. This type of bar graph is called a *histogram.*

2. Except for time series, the quantities indicated on the chart should begin with *zero* (0). In a chart where starting at 0 makes the chart too tall or too wide, omit that portion after 0 on which all bars would appear and indicate the omitted portion by a pair of break lines as indicated in Illus. 19-7.

3. When possible, arrange bars in ascending or descending order. If they are arranged according to time, chart the earliest period first.

4. Bars may be in outline form or solid. If the bars represent different items, shade or color them for contrast.

5. To type a bar, use uppercase letters (X, W, N, $), a heavy strikeover (X over 0), or a combination of letters and characters. See Illus. 19-8.

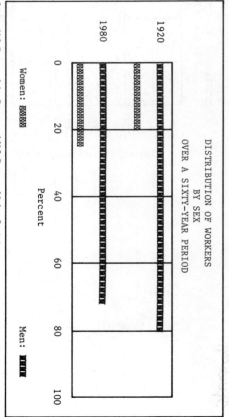

DISTRIBUTION OF WORKERS
BY SEX
OVER A SIXTY-YEAR PERIOD

Women: ▨▨▨▨   Men: ▮▮▮▮

Percent

0   20   40   60   80   100

1920

1980

Source: U.S. Bureau of the Census and U.S. Bureau of Labor Statistics

Illus. 19-8

For this typewritten horizontal bar graph, the heavy bar was typed by striking over uppercase *M, W, A,* and *V.* The light bar was typed by striking over uppercase *X* and *O.* Note that the chart is unnumbered and that the caption is at the top of the graph. This chart is for a transparency.

Circle Charts. The circle chart, sometimes called a *pie chart,* is an effective way to show the manner in which a given quantity is divided into parts. In this type of illustration the complete area of the circle represents the whole quantity, while the divisions within the circle represent the parts. Thus, the chart shows not only the relationship of each part to the whole but also of each part to every other part. A maximum of six parts is suggested so that all parts can be easily identified.

The circle chart may be used to present such data as how the sales dollar is spent; how taxes paid by a firm are divided among local, state, and federal governments; or the percentage of store purchases made by men compared with those made by women. Follow these suggestions for preparing circle charts:

1. Convert the data to be presented into percentage form. Let the circumference of the circle equal 100 percent.

2. Arrange the elements to be plotted according to size, largest first.

3. Mark the top center of the circumference of the circle the 12 o'clock position. From this point, moving in a clockwise direction, mark off that percentage of the total that each segment represents, beginning with the largest segment. The sequence may be changed, however, to permit emphasis on a specific element.

4. Determine the size of each segment. If a protractor is used, the circumference of the circle equals 360 degrees, or a total of 100 percent; thus a segment representing 10 percent would be 36 degrees. If a protractor is not

available, divide the circumference of the circle into four equal parts (each part representing 25 percent). Each fourth part may in turn be divided into halves (representing 12½ percent segments). Follow this division plan until the size of segment desired is obtained.

5. If space permits, identify each segment by a caption inside the segment. Shade or color the segments to provide contrast and to dramatize proportions.

6. Type the titles of the sections horizontally.

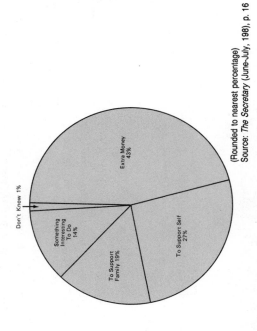

Don't Know 1%

Something Interesting To Do 14%

To Support Family 19%

To Support Self 27%

Extra Money 43%

(Rounded to nearest percentage)
Source: *The Secretary* (June–July, 198), p. 16

Illus. 19-9
Reasons for women working
Responses to 1980 Virginia
Slims Poll
If the researcher wanted to emphasize the need for women working in this circle chart, the categories *To Support Self* and *To Support Family* would be placed at the top of the circle.

Pictorial Charts. One of the more interesting developments in graphic representation is the use of pictorial charts, or pictographs. They are generally an

College Graduates Among Adults Over Age 25

1940   4.6%

1950   6.2%

1960   7.7%

1970   11.0%

1978   15.7%

Illus. 19-10
By means of an outstretched hand holding a diploma this illustration depicts the growing number of college graduates in the United States since 1940.

adaptation of one of the other types of graphs in which drawn symbols are used to represent the types of data being charted.

For example, a bar chart showing fire losses may be illustrated with a streaming fire hose, the length of the stream varying with the amount of the loss. The growth of telephone service may be shown by drawings of telephones arranged in a line, each telephone representing so many thousand telephones.

A secretary may not be expected to do the actual artwork for a pictorial chart but can be expected to devise a suitable chart by cutting and pasting appropriate symbols and then making a copy on a copy machine. When a chart is produced by a commercial artist the secretary is responsible for planning the graph and overseeing the work of the artist.

Map Charts. Maps are often used to depict quantitative information particularly when comparison is made of geographic areas. After the selection of the proper map, follow these suggestions in preparing the map chart:

1. Outline the geographic areas, by use of either color, shading, or crosshatching.
2. Provide a legend to explain the meanings given to the colors, shadings, or crosshatchings.
3. If quantities are involved, figures can be placed inside the geographic area. Other symbols representing quantities, such as dots, may also be used.

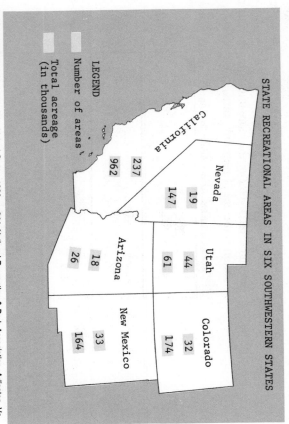

STATE RECREATIONAL AREAS IN SIX SOUTHWESTERN STATES

LEGEND
Number of areas
Total acreage (in thousands)

Illus. 19-11
To illustrate a report on recreational facilities, the secretary constructed this map chart, using color to give meaning to the figures presented on the chart.

Source: *Statistical Abstract of the United States*, 1980, p. 244. National Recreation & Park Association, Arlington, Va.

Limitations of Charts and Graphs

Although charts or graphs are useful in presenting comparative data, they have certain limitations. The number of facts presented on any one graph is usually limited to four or five. It is best to use a table when six or more items are involved. A second limitation is that only approximate values can be shown on most charts or graphs.

A third limitation is that it is possible for a graph to be drawn with mathematical accuracy and still give a distorted picture of the facts being presented. For example, the overall width of a line graph determines the angles of the plotted lines. A graph that is too narrow may indicate a much sharper rise and fall in the lines than the data indicate. In the same way, a graph that is too wide may tend to give the impression of a much more gradual fluctuation than may have actually occurred.

Flowcharts

One of the most widely used tools in office management is the flowchart. It traces a unit of work as it flows through the office. Symbols with connecting lines are used to trace a step-by-step sequence of the work from point of origin to point of completion. The basic symbols are shown in Illus. 19-12. A template

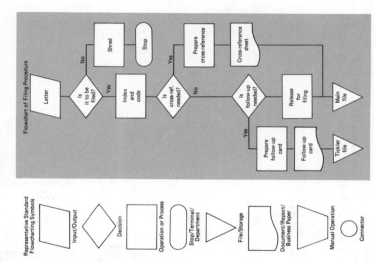

Illus. 19-12
A flowchart traces
a unit of work as it
flows through the
office.

can be purchased for drawing these symbols. While the meaning of each symbol has become fairly standardized, a key can be provided to prevent any misunderstanding.

Organization Charts

An organization chart is a graphic presentation of the organizational structure of a business. It points out responsibility relationships and answers two basic questions: (1) What are the lines of authority (who reports to whom)? (2) What are the functions of each unit (who is responsible for what)?

A business organization is seldom static. It is changed by new personnel, new divisions, new responsibilities, and realignment of old responsibilities. The

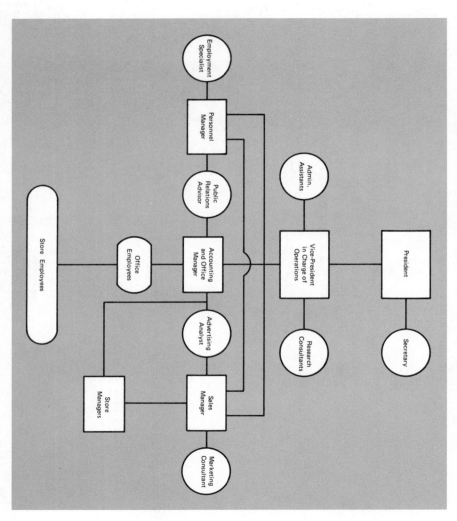

Illus. 19-13
On this organization chart, the four levels of administrative authority are clearly identified. The administrative staff is differentiated from the support staff. Note that the secretary to the president is not under the supervision of the office manager.

organization chart, therefore, is frequently revised. The technique of preparing and updating an organization chart is part of the know-how that every secretary needs. Following are some suggestions for preparing an organization chart.

1. The chart should be simple. A complex chart can confuse more than it can help.
2. Responsibility should flow downward in the chart with each level clearly identifiable. Lines of authority should be easily identified.
3. When the intersecting of a line is unavoidable, the *pass symbol* (a half-circle "detour" in an otherwise straight line) is used.
4. Different symbols differentiate policy-making positions (line) from support positions (staff).

Illus. 19-13 shows an organization chart of a line-and-staff relationship. Such a chart is supplemented with a functions chart on which the responsibilities of each position are identified. To show both authority relationships and functional responsibilities on one chart detracts from its visual simplicity.

SUGGESTED READINGS

Carlsen, R. et al. *Encyclopedia of Business Charts.* Englewood Cliffs, N.J.: Prentice-Hall, Inc., 1977.

Keithley, Erwin M., and Philip J. Schreiner. *A Manual of Style for the Preparation of Papers and Reports*, 3d ed. Cincinnati: South-Western Publishing Co., 1980.

Lesikar, Raymond V. *Report Writing for Business*, 6th ed. Homewood, Ill.: Richard D. Irwin, Inc., 1981.

Murphy, Herta A., and Charles E. Peck. *Effective Business Communications*, 3d ed. New York: McGraw-Hill Book Company, 1980.

Schmid, Calvin F., and Stanton E. Schmid. *The Handbook of Graphic Presentation*, 2d ed. Somerset, N.J.: John Wiley & Sons, Inc., 1979.

QUESTIONS FOR DISCUSSION

1. Give two examples based on college enrollment figures to illustrate the necessity for extracting information from raw data so that appropriate decisions can be made.
2. What kind of graph should be prepared to present the data in each of the following?
   (a) Proof that a company has initiated affirmative action programs within the past three years
   (b) The total yearly cost of going to college during the past five years
   (c) Tuition rates at state supported and private colleges over the past ten years

PROBLEMS

☆ 1. The total sales of four product lines of a women's wear company are $828,000 divided as follows:

Purses	$250,000
Millinery	125,000
Cosmetics	275,000
Hosiery	178,000

(a) Convert the amount of sales of each line to a percentage of total sales.

(b) Prepare a circle chart showing these percentages.

2. From your knowledge of the personnel composition of a word processing center (see Chapter 1), prepare a line organization chart.

☆ 3. The following figures represent the sales volume for Innovative Products for one year. Prepare a line graph of the data.

	First Year	Second Year
January	$86,857	$114,273
February	69,623	92,526
March	38,972	64,159
April	34,284	60,844
May	40,485	69,273
June	37,737	76,294
July	40,852	74,858
August	46,085	82,437
September	49,592	80,158
October	55,846	83,628
November	54,249	87,849
December	61,292	94,958

What implications can you give about seasonal fluctuations and general performance for the two years?

(d) Amounts spent on research in the six divisions of a large corporation over the past three years

(e) The division of energy costs among five departments of a firm

(f) The number of male employees as compared with the number of female employees of a company for each year of a five-year period

3. Corporations usually use graphs extensively in their annual reports to stockholders. Financial tables and statements, however, are generally used in presenting data to boards of directors and to banks. Why are graphs used in the one case and tables in the other?

4. The secretary to the vice-president in charge of research is often charged with the responsibility for reports written by the scientists in the division. The graphs can be made by using typewriter characters, by commercial materials for use in making improved charts, or by contracting for professional charts. Which factors will influence this secretary's decision?

5. A consultant firm with a total of 50 employees reported in a community wage study that its average wage (arithmetic mean) was $20,000. An examination of the records revealed that the firm had ten executives, each receiving $50,000 a year. What would be your criticism of the reported average wage figure?

6. In the following sentences insert the proper word for those enclosed in parentheses or revise the sentence so that there is no doubt as to the meaning. Then check your Reference Guide to verify or correct your answers.

(a) The state legislature meets _____ (every two years).

(b) The vacancies were posted _____ (twice a year).

(c) The board will meet _____ (every two months).

(d) We report to the home office _____ (twice a month).

4. Preparatory to establishing a policy on sick leave, your employer asks you to make a study of the number of days of absence from work because of illness and other causes (excluding vacations) of the 70 employees in the Des Moines office. From the records, you obtained the total number of days each employee was absent. They are as follows:

26	8	17	15	17	14	13
16	7	5	47	20	25	19
12	20	11	15	9	4	41
18	27	19	11	19	12	13
8	3	44	18	24	17	15
18	14	13	10	2	37	20
28	16	15	15	14	11	9
1	32	19	30	18	11	12
10	6	13	15	33	17	21
16	11	13	8	7	14	12

(a) Prepare a penciled frequency distribution of the days absent. Use a classification interval of five days (one work week), such as 1 to 5, 6 to 10, and so forth of the days absent. Determine the percentage of employees who were absent in each frequency interval.

(b) Type a table with an appropriate title and column headings.

5. The following amounts are the April sales per day of a product.

Amount	Amount
$118.23	$9.61
41.32	18.23
91.73	107.16
63.24	26.31
36.74	83.17
18.92	67.92
87.65	74.26
27.11	68.31
16.94	17.08
78.26	10.66
24.36	94.33
97.08	89.31

(a) Prepare in pencil a tabulation of the sales so that you can determine the median. What is the median sale for April?

(b) Calculate the arithmetic average or mean of the April sales.

Chapter 20

Assistance with Reports, Procedures Writing, and Publications

In this age of information processing, large and small businesses are depending heavily on data generated by the computer. Through the use of the computer, management has much more quantitative information available than ever before; and this increase in numerical data has led to more and different types of reports. Besides reports involving strictly quantitative data, organizations thrive on reports of a qualitative nature; for instance, studies of specific projects and proposals. It appears that business is following the principle of "the more information, the better management can function and make decisions affecting the company."

As business becomes more complex, so do management problems; and the weight of report writing and reports themselves increases. Every year millions of business reports are written—and generally it is management personnel who must digest and react to the information.

This chapter discusses the preparation and presentation of business reports, company procedures, and manuscripts for printing. It gives specific instructions for the organization of reports and illustrates techniques for making material attractive and interesting. This information is useful to secretaries in all job classifications.

REPORT WRITING

A business report transmits objective information to one or more persons and is written for a specific business purpose. A report is used to plan, organize, and implement business operations; it contains factual information presented in clear, concise language. It can be written by an employee of the firm for internal use of the company, or for a business client; it can also be prepared by a person independent of the company.

Reports written for internal use are *vertical* (up and down the company ranks) or *horizontal* (across management lines). They are formal (written) or informal (both written and oral). Written reports take the form of an interoffice memorandum, a letter, or a bound manuscript.

Report-Writing Routine

There is considerable difference in the routine for writing a report and the routine for writing a letter. The originator or an assistant follows these steps in preparing a business report:

1. Collects the information
2. Formulates an outline of the contents
3. Checks logic of content organization
4. Drafts the report for first typing
5. Rechecks the organization of material and edits sentence by sentence for clarity and correctness before the second typing
6. Checks again the organization and editing before final typing

The language of reports is objective, emphasizing factual information free of any personal bias or opinion. Reports are generally written in the third person without *I*'s, *we*'s, and *you*'s. Replacement nouns such as the *writer* or *researcher* are also frowned upon. An illustration of objective and personal style writing follows:

Objective	*Personal*
A *study* of office correspondence at Henderson Associates *supports* the need for a word processing center.	After making a study of office correspondence at Henderson Associates, we recommend establishing a word processing center.

The present verb tense or a combination of present and past tense is used. For example, a discussion of how the study was conducted or when investigations were made is written in the past tense because these actions are no longer in process. Some reports discuss all actions as having taken place in the past, in which case the past tense is used throughout the report.

Originators vary in their skill in writing reports. Every originator, however, edits and polishes successive drafts until the final report is as clear, concise, and logical as possible.

478

The Secretary's Responsibility

The multifunctional secretary, the administrative secretary, and the correspondence secretary play an important part in business report preparation. The multifunctional secretary's role follows closely the report-writing routine discussed previously. It is not unusual for the secretary to be involved in each step of the report preparation, from collecting information to the final typing of the report. The administrative secretary may participate in all steps with the exception of the actual typing of the report. The correspondence secretary, on the other hand, is responsible for the format and typing operations.

Naturally all three secretarial roles include the responsibility for editing the report for clear language, for eliminating repetitive words and phrases, for checking spellings and meanings of words, and for double-checking all figures. These are established contributions of the secretary to the report-writing process.

The Form of the Report

Depending on the nature and circulation of the report, the form can be a letter, an interoffice memorandum, or a formal bound manuscript. Some companies have developed style sheets for all or for special reports. If such is the case, the form indicated in the style sheets will be used as a standard practice. In other cases, the writer follows a consistent pattern.

Letter Reports. Letter reports are external reports prepared for clients outside the firm. These reports follow the letter format including all letter parts and are typed on letterhead stationery, single-spaced with one-inch side margins. Special headings, such as introduction, summary and/or conclusions and recommendations are common in letter reports. These headings are centered or typed at the left margin and should be underscored. Tables are used to display numerical data and, if provided, are introduced in the text. Tables should begin and end on the same page. As with most reports, the language is objective, written in the third person, and free of statements that show personal bias.

Interoffice Memorandum Reports. Memorandum reports are internal communications and follow the memorandum format with TO: FROM: SUBJECT: DATE: headings (see Illus. 20-1). These reports are single-spaced and may include side headings such as introduction, discussion, summary and/or conclusions and recommendations, and so forth. Tables and supporting data can be included as attachments to the memorandum. The language of memorandum reports can be a combination of first, second, and third person writing. The circulation of the report determines the writing style. For instance, a report for upward distribution probably would be written in objective, third person style; while one being distributed horizontally may be more informal.

Di Drayer Industries   Interoffice Memorandum

TO: Edward F. Bullard, President   DATE: October 10, 19--

FROM: Lucille Stanford

SUBJECT: Status Report--Employee Volunteer Program

To accomplish our goal for more community involvement by our company and
personnel, a study has been made of our community needs. In addition, a
survey of our staff has been made to determine the members' interest in
participating in volunteer community projects. A skeleton plan of such a
program follows:

Identification of Community Projects

Utilizing the interview technique, members of the Public Relations Department visited with local Chamber of Commerce officials, social welfare
agencies, independent agencies, and personnel in the mayor's office to
identify projects suitable for our proposed volunteer program. As of
today, a list of 150 projects, with their descriptions, has been identified. Some projects require group efforts, while others can be accomplished by one individual. One of the most pressing needs found in our
survey was the lack of fire protection services in Burday Township.
Attachment A provides a listing of projects and their descriptions.

Matching Employee Interests to Projects

When the program is finalized, information about the community projects
will be publicized in the company magazine and posted on all available
bulletin boards. Employees will be asked to apply for projects of interest to them. A volunteer coordinator will interview applicants and make
the assignment to specific projects.

Implementation of the Program

A volunteer coordinator will be selected to head the program. This
individual will devote full time to this project. Employees will be given
at least five hours of released time to fulfill their project duties. The
coordinator will be responsible for the appointment of the employee to the
selected project and evaluate the employee's contribution. The coordinator
in collaboration with employee volunteers will be responsible for preparing
a report at the conclusion of each project.

Policy Statements

The next step in our plan for a volunteer program for Drayer Industries is
to develop policy statements. These documents will be available for your
study by the first of next month.

LS:RT
Attachment A

Illus. 20-1
Example of an interoffice memorandum report

Formal Reports. A short formal report may consist of only the body or informative text. A long, formal report may have, in addition to the body, various introductory parts and appendixes in the following order:

Introductory Parts:	Sturdy cover or title page (or both)
	Preface or letter of transmittal, including acknowledgments
	Table of contents
	List of tables, charts, and illustrations
	Summary
Body of the Report:	Introduction, including purpose of the report
	Main body of the report
	Conclusions and recommendations
Supplementary Parts:	Appendix or reference section
	Bibliography
	Index

Notice that the summary *precedes* the main body of the report. This arrangement benefits the busy executive who may be interested in or have time to read only a synopsis of the report. Those who need or want complete information will read the entire report.

Of the three main parts of a report (introductory, body, and supplementary), the body is usually developed first and typed in all but final form before the other parts are prepared. For this reason, the development of the body of a report is discussed first here.

DEVELOPING THE BODY OF THE FORMAL REPORT

Certainly the originator of a report is responsible for what the report says and what it implies. The writer who has access to a secretary will sensibly and logically work with that individual as a team member in the report preparation.

The Outline

A methodical writer first sets up a topic outline or framework of the report containing all the important points that will be covered. The outline is usually submitted to a superior for approval. This outline may later serve as the table of contents and the heading framework for the report.

No main heading or subheading in an outline ever stands alone. For every *I* there is at least a *II*, for every *A* a *B*. (When an outline contains a single heading, a thoughtful reading will usually reveal that the heading actually is part of another point, or misplaced, or irrelevant.) The headings should be phrased accurately and concisely *in parallel style*. The main headings *I* and *II* should be parallel with each other. Subheadings under the same main heading should be parallel with each other. For example, under a first main heading, the subheadings may be noun phrases, while the subheadings under a second major heading may be verb phrases. Headings can be short constructions beginning with nouns, verbal nouns, or verbs; long constructions that tell the story; or complete sentences. Once the style is established, it must be consistent and parallel throughout.

```
DESIGNING A BUSINESS FORM

I   PURPOSE OF THE FORM

    A.  Systems Analysis

        1.  Definition of the Problem
        2.  Discussion of the Facts
        3.  Analysis of the Results of the Study
        4.  Recommendation

    B.  Preparation of the Proposal

        1.  Rationale for the Study
        2.  Discussion of the Systems Analysis

II  FORM DESIGN

    A.  Type of Information
    B.  Space Requirements
    C.  Sequence of Information
```

Illus. 20-2
Notice that in this outline describing the designing of a business form each heading is introduced by a noun (underscored).

The Rough Draft

A carefully written formal report is typed one or more times in rough-draft form. A rough draft is generously spaced and accurately transcribed with little thought of final form or appearance. The purpose of the rough draft is to get the writer's thoughts on paper—to provide something tangible to edit and improve. Rather than a waste of time, this is a vital step. In typing rough drafts, the secretary follows these practices:

1. The paper used is less than letterhead quality but is sufficiently strong to withstand erasing during the editing process. Many offices use colored paper.

2. Carbon copies are not made unless they are expressly requested. If an extra copy is needed for cutting into strips in reorganizing the material, a copy can be made on a copying machine.

3. Plenty of room for write-ins and transfer indications is provided by use of triple spacing and wide margins on all four sides.

4. Each successive draft is given a number and dated. Each page is numbered in sequence and sometimes carries the draft number and date also.

5. Each successive draft is carefully checked and proofread so that subsequent drafts will contain valid material.

6. Typing errors are X'd or lined out unless the machine has a correcting mechanism.

7. Quoted matter, if several lines in length, is single-spaced and indented in the same form as in the final copy because changes in quoted matter are unlikely.

8. Footnotes are typed at the bottom of the page, or on a separate sheet, or as shown in Illus. 20-3.

9. Material to be placed in the appendix should be typed in final form labeled Appendix (or Exhibit) A, B, and so forth and kept in a file folder for safekeeping until the report is completed.

Save all rough drafts until the report is completed and presented, even though they have been superseded, because the writer may decide to use material from an earlier draft.

A simple method of incorporating a footnote into a rough draft is shown in this example[1]--that is, to type the footnote immediately

----

[1] Estelle L. Popham, Rita Sloan Tilton, J. Howard Jackson, and J Marshall Hanna, Secretarial Procedures and Administration (8th ed.; Cincinnati: South-Western Publishing Co., 1983), p. 513.

----

below the line in which the reference number appears, separated from the textual matter above and below by lines across the page.

Illus. 20-3
Footnotes typed in this style in a rough draft will automatically be retained in correct position if copy is rearranged during editing.

TYPING THE BODY OF THE FORMAL REPORT

The final version of the report measures the originator's skill in concise, logical writing and the secretary's skill in sustained, attractive, meticulous typing and proofreading. To be sure that each page is uniformly typed, the secretary designs an attractive page layout and prepares a job guide sheet for use in the final typing. Margin and line spacing are planned to ensure readability of the document. If the secretary has an automatic typewriter, instructions can be programmed into the machine. A dictionary and a punctuation guide must be within easy reach of the typist.

Most reports require multiple copies. Today the tendency is to type the original on good quality paper and photocopy for distribution or type the original on a master for reproduction.

If carbon paper is used to make copies, keep the original and the carbon copy of each page together in the same order in which they were typed until they are ready to be proofread and corrected. Never leave the carbon paper in a set of typed pages because pressure exerted on the pack will cause unsightly offset marks on each copy. Do not fasten each set of pages together with a paper clip because the clip leaves crimp marks.

Place the bottom copy on top of the set to protect the choice ribbon copy. Since the bottom copy is used for proofreading and marking corrections, it will be ready without further handling of the set of pages. If the bottom set of carbon copies is used for proofreading, any illegibility will be revealed. In this way, an illegible copy will not be passed on inadvertently and be proved useless. If any figures on a set of pages are especially unclear, consider the set unusable.

Page Layouts

There are two kinds of typed page layouts: the *traditional*, which looks much like a standard printed page of a textbook; and the *nontraditional*, in which the units of typing are creatively arranged and displayed. The successful secretary must be alert to ways of presenting facts in nontraditional layouts as well as in traditional ones. By varying margins, line spacing, indentations, capitals and small letters, spacing between letters and words, underlining, placement of various parts, using white space generously, and devising charts, drawings, and graphs, the secretary can achieve results that will greatly enhance the effectiveness of a report.

Job Instructions. Typing a report of many pages, and often of many copies, must be organized in advance and controlled while in process so that it can be carried through to a consistent completion. To accomplish this task, set up a job instruction sheet covering every point about type style, form, placement, and format that may be needed. Try to answer in advance every question that will likely be raised. Include the items below and all others that might apply to the specific job.

1. Kind and size of paper to be used
2. Weight and finish of carbon paper to be used
3. Number of copies to be typed
4. Kind and type style of typewriter to be used
5. Page format:
   Paper guide scale number
   Left margin—number on typewriter scale
   Right margin—number on typewriter scale
   Top margin—number on line guide scale (see discussion page 484)
   Bottom margin—number on line guide scale (see discussion page 484)
   Single- or double-spaced typing
   Paragraph indentation—number of spaces

Tabulation indentation—number of spaces

Tabulation identification—I, A, (1), (a), etc.

Tabulation spacing—single-spaced or double-spaced

Headings—examples and placement (see discussion page 487)

Subheadings—examples and placement (see discussion page 487)

6. Placement of computer printouts, tables, graphs (see page 490)

7. Quotations (page 488)

8. Enumerations (page 489)

9. Footnotes (page 489)

10. Instructions for numbering pages (page 490)

11. Handling of typed pages awaiting assembly (see discussion page 490)

12. Instructions for proofreading (see discussion page 499)

13. Instructions for collating (see discussion page 499)

14. Instructions for binding (see discussion page 499)

15. Distribution of copies

16. Disposal of original draft pages

Indentations. Paragraphs may be typed flush with the left margin or indented 5, 10, 15, or even 20 spaces. Formal reports usually are double-spaced with paragraph indentations. For single-spaced reports blocked or with paragraph indentations, double-space between paragraphs. In blocked double-spaced work, triple-space between paragraphs. Indentations make for easy reading regardless of the line length of the body.

Margins. There are several techniques you can use to maintain even top and bottom margins in reports. For instance, if you are typing the entire report yourself, a *top and bottom margin guide* may be sufficient. You can make your own guide by typing line numbers down the extreme right edge of a second sheet. Place this guide at the back of the carbon pack or behind the top sheet with the line numbers showing along the right edge.

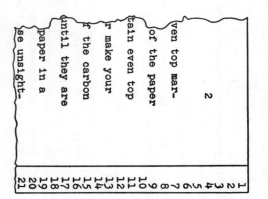

```
                                    1
                                    2
                                    3
                       ven top mar- 4
                                    5
                                    6
                        of the paper 7
                                    8
                                    9
                       tain even top 10
                                    11
                                    12
                        r make your  13
                                    14
                                    15
                        f the carbon 16
                                    17
                                    18
                       unt1l they are 19
                                    20
                        paper 1n a    21
                        se unsight-
                            2
```

Illus. 20-4
Number the lines in ascending order, 1-33, starting at the top to midpage. Starting at midpage, number the lines in descending order, 33-1, to the bottom of the page.

A device used to maintain even side, top, and bottom margins is a *special guide sheet*.[1] This guide is particularly useful when several typists are working on the report. The *special guide sheet* is typed on ordinary bond (or onionskin, if carbon copies are required) and is placed directly behind the page being typed.

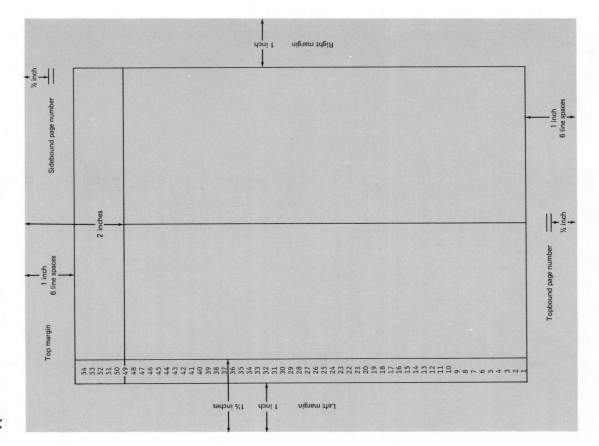

Illus. 20-5
A special guide
sheet

[1]Adapted from Erwin M. Keithley and Philip J. Schreiner, *A Manual of Style for the Preparation of Papers and Reports* (3d ed; Cincinnati: South-Western Publishing Co., 1980).

The guide sheet shown in Illus. 20-5 for a left-bound manuscript should be ruled with dark ink or colored pencil that will be visible through the top sheet.

1. In the *upper right corner* and *centered at the bottom* are short lines positioned so that a page number typed to rest on them will leave a ½-inch top and a 1-inch side margin, or a ½-inch bottom margin, as desired. Usually only topbound manuscripts are numbered at the foot of the page; but if a first page of an unbound or left-bound manuscript is to be numbered, the number is centered at the foot of the page as for a topbound manuscript.

2. The vertical rule 1½ inches from the left indicates the left margin setting. The extra ½ inch is for binding.

3. The vertical rule 1 inch from the right indicates the right margin of the copy. Keep the right margin as even as possible. No more than two or three letters should extend beyond the vertical line. Use a word division manual for speedy and correct decisions about end-of-line hyphenations. Avoid hyphenating words at the end of the first line on a page or at the end of more than two consecutive lines, and never end a page with a hyphenated word. Do not end or begin a line with a 1- or 2- letter syllable.

4. Two horizontal lines (1 inch and 2 inches from the top of the sheet) mark the top margins of the manuscript. The first page of a part (letter of transmittal, table of contents, chapter) begins on line 13, which leaves a 2-inch top margin. Subsequent pages start on line 7, which leaves a 1-inch top margin. (Position the typewriter cylinder to type on the first line of writing *below* the rules shown.)

5. The horizontal line one inch from the bottom edge of the paper indicates the last line available for typing. Plan to leave at least two lines of a paragraph on the page and carry at least two lines forward to the next page. Plan the last line of the body of the material to allow for any footnotes that go on that page.

6. The vertical center rule shows the horizontal centering point of the page, the point equidistant between the marginal rulings at left and right.

Titles. An attractively arranged title or an unconventional display of a title draws attention to the material, a respectable objective of a title page. Several variations of title placement are illustrated below.

1. One-line titles centered, underscoring optional:

TRADITIONAL TITLE

Uppercase and Lowercase

S P R E A D   H E A D I N G

EXTRA   SPACE   BETWEEN   WORDS

2. Three-line titles, framed, centered:

```
. . . . . . . . . . . . . .
.   A   T I T L E   .
.       F R A M E D   .
. D I S T I N C T I V E L Y .
. . . . . . . . . . . . . .
```

3. Distinctive arrangements, centered:

```
- - - A n   U n c o n v e n t i o n a l
            A r r a n g e m e n t
              o f   t h e   T i t l e - - -

                                              - - - A n   U n c o n v e n t i o n a l
                                                          A r r a n g e m e n t
                                                            o f   t h e   T i t l e - - -

- - - A n   U n c o n v e n t i o n a l
      A r r a n g e m e n t   o f   t h e
                  T i t l e - - -
```

Every typewritten title is a part of a picture. Therefore, select a style that is attractive in width and weight and that is in satisfying proportion to the dimensions of the typed page. It is hard to *visualize* which form of title is best. But you can try them out for size, weight, and appearance by typing several experimental arrangements of the title, cutting them out, and laying each one on a full page of similar typing. The best one will become evident.

Headings and Subheadings. Headings and subheadings are used to guide the reader through the report. The criteria for their wording is: Does the heading clarify the content and increase readability, and is the construction parallel to other headings?

In general, headings and subheadings parallel the outline. Note their arrangement in this book and their usefulness in preparing the reader and in showing the relative importance of subject matter. For example, centered and capitalized headings are superior to centered headings with capitals and lower-case letters (initial capitals). Also, centered headings are superior to side headings. With each heading there must be a discussion, such as an introduction or transition sentence to the information that follows.

Both headings and subheadings can be varied by placement, by use of initial capitals, and by indentations (often referred to as degree headings). Before typing the report, the multifunctional secretary prepares a job instruction sheet (see Illus. 20-6) indicating the form and position of each heading and subheading, of each margin and indentation, and of all line spacing.

PLACEMENT OF HEADINGS AND SUBHEADINGS

Caption	Placement
Title of Report or Chapter Number and/or Chapter Title	All capitals, underscoring optional Two inches from top of paper (elite type) One and one-half inches (pica type) Each line centered horizontally Triple space to first line of main heading
No. 1 (Main) Head	Initial capital letters, underscoring optional Each line centered horizontally Triple space to first line of typing
No. 2 (Sub) Head	Initial capital letters, underscored, flush with left margin Double-space to first line of typing
No. 3 (Sub) Head	Initial capital letters, underscored, typed at paragraph indentation point (five or more spaces)

Illus. 20-6
Portion of a job instruction
sheet

If the report is being typed in the word processing center and the original prefers a certain format, the administrative secretary prepares a guide sheet and sends it to the center with the manuscript.

Quoted Matter

Reports often quote material from other sources, either directly or indirectly, and must give credit to these sources. For indirect quotations or references, a footnote providing the source suffices. Direct quotations are handled in the following ways:

1. Quotations of *fewer than four lines* are typed in the body of the paragraph and enclosed in quotation marks.

2. Quotations of *four or more lines* are usually typed without quotation marks, single-spaced, and indented from the left margin or from both margins.

3. When a quotation of *several paragraphs* is not indented, quotation marks precede each paragraph and follow the final word in the last paragraph only.

4. A *quotation within a quotation* is enclosed in single quotation marks.

5. *Italicized words* in the quotation are underscored.

6. *Omissions* are shown by ellipses—three spaced (. . .) periods within a sentence, four periods at the end of a sentence.

7. *Inserted words* (*interpolations*) are enclosed in typewritten brackets using the underscore and diagonal: [ ]. Parentheses cannot be used, since they often occur naturally in the context and the reader will be unable to identify matter enclosed in them as inserted matter.

8. A *footnote reference* showing the source should be made for the quotation unless the source is identified adequately in the text.

Permission to quote copyrighted material must be obtained from the copyright holder when reports are to be printed or duplicated and given public circulation. Material published by a governmental agency is not copyrighted. Full information should be sent with the request including the following:

1. The text leading up to the quotation or a copy of the page that includes the quotation
2. The lines to be quoted, or lines underscored on the page as it will be published
3. The credit line or complete footnote reference
4. The title, publisher, and date of publication of the material in which the quoted matter will appear

Footnotes

Footnotes are numbered in sequence on each page, throughout each section, or throughout the entire report. There is an advantage in numbering footnotes anew with each page or section—if footnotes are inserted or deleted, only the numbers on the page or within the section need be changed. If a bibliography is part of the report, the footnote reference can be shortened to reflect the last name of the author, the name of the publication, and the page cited. Another possibility is to number the references in the bibliography. Then, in the body of the text next to the quotation, type in parentheses the number of the work, a colon, and the page number, such as (15:30) indicating the fifteenth reference in the bibliography and page 30. Styles of typing footnotes may be reviewed in the footnote and bibliography style guide in the Reference Guide.

Enumerations

In typing numbered sentences, align the first word of the second line with the first word in the previous line (called a *hanging indent*). Do not return to the left margin or begin under the number. For example:

1. Our recruiting program will begin in September, and our objective will be to hire as many qualified young women as we can find for the vacancies.

2. Our training program will run for one full year. The first three months will be devoted to the orientation of new employees.

Computer Printouts, Tables, and Graphs

Output from the computer can be incorporated into the body of the report with appropriate explanations. A table or graph can be used or the computer printout can be labeled as an exhibit and placed in the appendix section. Tables and graphs can be reduced on some copy machines. If this is the plan, make the reductions before typing the manuscript, so that proper space allowance can be made in the manuscript. Numerous computer tables or graphs detract from the readability of the discussion. Unless they are absolutely necessary to understand the text, lengthy tables should be in the appendix.

Numbering Pages

Usually the typist saves time by waiting until the body is typed in final form before typing page numbers. If making carbon copies, the typist numbers the top sheet of each carbon assembly in pencil as it is completed, thus keeping unpaged copy in order. After the supplementary sections and the preliminary pages have been typed, page numbers can be typed for the body of the report.

The title page of a report is considered the first page and is not numbered. Subsequent preliminary pages are numbered in small Roman numerals (letter of transmittal, summary) *ii, iii* at the bottom center. For left-bound manuscripts Arabic numerals without punctuation are used to number the pages of the body of the report and supplementary parts (appendix, bibliography, index). Numbers are typed one-half inch from the top at the upper right corner. After page one, pages are numbered consecutively throughout the report. Numbering the first page of a report is optional. If it is numbered, the number is centered one-half inch from the bottom of the page.

PREPARING AND TYPING THE OTHER PARTS

The order in which the other parts of a report are prepared varies, but inserting page numbers on the table of contents must be one of the last steps. In the following discussion the concluding supplementary parts and then the introductory parts are considered.

Appendix or Reference Section

In a formal report an *appendix* or *reference section* devoted to supplementary information, supporting tables and statistics, or reference material follows the body of the report. Items placed in the appendix are numbered Appendix A, B, and so forth and are shown in the Table of Contents.

Bibliography

All references mentioned in a report should be included in the bibliography. References used in the study, but not cited, should be in the bibliography also.

A report that is based on a study of published materials frequently includes a bibliography listing the source material. Such a bibliography is called a *selected bibliography*. Many business reports are based on factual information within the company, and there is no need to refer to outside source material.

Sometimes the multifunctional or administrative secretary is requested to prepare a *comprehensive bibliography* listing all the material published on a subject for a selected period of time. An *annotated bibliography* contains an evaluation or a brief explanation of the content of each reference. An example of one reference in an annotated bibliography follows:

Popham, Estelle L., Rita Sloan Tilton, J. Howard Jackson, and J Marshall Hanna. *Secretarial Procedures and Administration,* 8th ed. Cincinnati: South-Western Publishing Co., 1983.

This text is designed to prepare secretaries for job entry as well as advancement. Job functions of the multifunctional secretary, correspondence secretary, and administrative support secretary are covered. The text provides a comprehensive picture of present-day office technology. The Reference Guide appearing at the back of the book is invaluable to the secretary trainee and to the secretary on the job.

A bibliography reference is very similar in form to a footnote in that it cites the author's name, the title of the publication, the publisher, and the date. The name of an editor, a translator, or an illustrator may also be included. The price and complete details on the number of illustrations, plates, diagrams, and so on can be included if this information will be of value to those who will use the bibliography. Specific chapters or sections and their inclusive page numbers may be stated if the entry refers to only a certain part of the book or periodical; otherwise, page numbers are omitted.

Type the word *Bibliography* approximately two inches (one and one-half inches, if pica type is used) from the top of the page in capital letters. References are given in alphabetical order or by sections and then alphabetically. The first line is typed flush with the left margin with succeeding lines indented. Each reference is single-spaced with a double space between references. See Reference Guide for the proper presentation of the bibliography.

Index

An *index* is included only when it is felt that there will be occasion to use it. A detailed table of contents usually suffices. When an index is necessary, the secretary uses a copy of the report for underlining in colored pencil each item on each page that should be included in the index. Each underlined item and its page number are written on a separate slip. The completed slips are then sorted into alphabetic order, and a typed index is prepared from them.

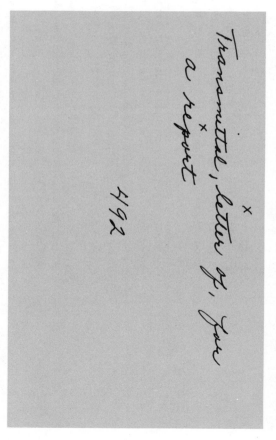

Transmittal, letter of, for
a report
×

492

Illus. 20-7
The index slip for an intern from this book is shown. The X's indicate that cross-reference slips were made and listed under *Letter of transmittal for a report* and *Report, letter of transmittal for.*

Letter of Transmittal

Frequently a *letter of transmittal* is bound into the report and performs a function similar to the preface of a book. It gives authorization for the report, details of its preparation, the period covered, acknowledgment of persons who contributed materials, and other such information to help the reader understand the depth and breadth of the report and arouse interest in studying it (see Illus. 20-9).

The language of the letter is more personal than the objective style of the report. The letter of transmittal is typed on the regular business letterhead and is signed in ink. It is reproduced on the same kind of paper used for the other pages of a duplicated or printed report, and the signature is duplicated rather than handwritten.

Summary

The summary is a concise review of the entire report and its findings. It includes a statement of the problem, its scope, the method of investigation, conclusions, and recommendations. It is objective in nature and is written to give the reader a clear understanding of the facts in the report. The length of the report determines the length of the summary; however, recommended style is to limit the summary to one page. The word *Summary* is typed two inches (one and one-half inches, if pica type is used) from the top of the page. Double-space the discussion using the same side margins as the report (see Illus. 20-11).

Title Page

Even a report of five or ten pages is improved with a *title page.* The title page designed by the secretary should be simple if the report is typed in traditional form. If the report is typed in nontraditional form, the secretary should try for distinction and artistic display of the information. Attractive borders can be made using the *m, x,*), (, * , ' , or " keys or a decorative key.

The title page must contain the essential facts for identifying the report: the title, for whom it is prepared, by whom it is submitted, the date, and the place of preparation. The essential facts vary with the contents and the readers of a report. An interoffice report may require only the title and the date. The writer should approve the content and arrangement of the title page.

Type the title centered in all capital letters approximately two inches from the top of the page. If the title must be divided, separate logically, since each line should express a complete thought. Double-space between lines. The remaining information is centered vertically and horizontally using initial capital letters with the last line typed two inches from the bottom of the page. Illus. 20-8 shows a well-balanced title page.

Table of Contents

After paging the report, the secretary prepares the table of contents that precedes the report. This table lists the preliminary parts, the main division, if applicable, the main topics or chapter titles, subheadings, and page numbers, Roman and Arabic. The word used for the major divisions of the report, such as *Section, Chapter, Part,* is typed in all capital letters at the left margin after the preliminary parts. Main headings begin at the left margin and subheadings are indented two or three spaces. Leaders (period, then space) are commonly used to aid in the readability of the table (see Illus. 20-10).

Rough out the table of contents to get an idea of its vertical length and the horizontal length of the items before deciding on the final style.

The next five pages present parts of a report typed in acceptable form.

```
                    ******************************************************

                                       A FEASIBILITY STUDY

                                               OF

                           WORD PROCESSING-ADMINISTRATIVE SUPPORT CENTERS

                         ***************************

                                         Prepared for

                                     Electro-Mag Company
                                   1606 North McVickers Street
                                       Chicago, Illinois

                       *****************************

                                         Submitted by

                                   Management Research, Inc.
                                2500 Diversey Parkway, West
                                     Chicago, Illinois

                                        June 30, 19--

          **********************************************
```

Illus. 20-8
Title page for a left-bound report

June 30, 19--

Mrs. Agnes B. Harper
Electro-Mag Company
1606 North McVickers Street
Chicago, IL 60639-5124

Dear Mrs. Harper:

The feasibility study, authorized by you on January 1 of this year, concerning the establishment of the word processing center concept in your organization is now complete.

The study included a thorough investigation of your company's written communications requirements and a series of conferences at random with management personnel and employees in the office. An attitude survey of the clerical staff was also made.

It is recommended that the Electro-Mag Company establish an experimental satellite word processing center in the Sales Department and that a work measurement procedure be adopted for this center. After a period of six months, it is suggested that an evaluation be made of the center's productivity. This evaluation will determine whether the concept should be implemented in the Accounting and Manufacturing Departments.

Working with you and your staff has been a pleasure. Our gratitude is expressed to the many employees of the Electro-Mag Company who cooperated with us in making this study.

Yours very truly,

Jean J. Torres

Jean J. Torres
Director of Research

ii

Illus. 20-9
Letter of transmittal for a left-bound report

Illus. 20-10
Table of Contents page for a left-bound report

TABLE OF CONTENTS

SUMMARY

The feasibility study of the word processing-administrative
support center concept for the Electro-Mag Company indicates the
desirability of implementation for the company. Immediate
advantages will be realized in the rapid delivery of error free
sales proposals, in the capability of sending original copies of
sales letters to prospective customers, and in the ability to meet
the deadlines faced by the company in many of its written reports.
The change to the system concept of producing written transcripts
will result in long-term reduction of clerical costs in terms of
personnel needs and supervisory time.

Therefore, the following recommendations are submitted:

1. The Electro-Mag Company establish an experimental
   satellite center in the Sales Department.

2. A work measurement study be made during the trial
   period of six months.

3. Six word processing stations be established in the
   center under the direction of two supervisory
   personnel.

4. An evaluation of the productivity of the center
   be made at the end of the trial period.

The results of the evaluation will determine whether additional
centers should be established in the Accounting and Manufacturing
Departments.

iv

Illus. 20-11
Summary page for a left-bound report.

A FEASIBILITY STUDY

OF

WORD PROCESSING-ADMINISTRATIVE SUPPORT CENTERS

<u>Introduction</u>

This section discusses in detail the problem of the study,
the purpose of the investigation, and the definitions of concepts
used throughout the report.

<u>The Problem</u>

The establishment of word processing-administrative support
centers in the Electro-Mag Company is explored to determine whether
the concept can meet the ever growing communication needs of the
company without an increase in per page costs. Random conferences
with management personnel and surveys of the clerical staff
are evaluated.

<u>Purpose of the Report</u>

Because of the increase in the written communication
requirements of the Electro-Mag Company and the need for a reduction
of clerical costs in this area, this feasibility study has been
undertaken to determine whether the word processing center
concept can accomplish these objectives. All factors involved in
the output of written communications are considered. These factors
are then studied in a cost analysis within each department of the
company.

Illus. 20-12
First page of a left-bound report

PROOFREADING, FINAL CHECKING, COLLATING, AND BINDING

After all the typing is finished, four important steps remain: proofreading, final checking of mechanics, collating, and binding. (All figures and computations would, of course, have been checked *before* the final typing.) If the report is typed in the word processing center, these activities are performed in the center. The administrative secretary also proofreads the report.

Proofreading

Each typed page of the final copy of the report is proofread word for word and figure for figure. A practical plan is to use a copy for checking, boldly marking all corrections on it, and filing it permanently. The careful worker goes through the material at least twice—the first time comparing the copy with the original for accuracy of typing and for omissions, and a second time for consistency of style and form. If possible, proofread the copy with the help of another person.

Final Checking

Use a final check sheet and go through the report once for each factor listed below. This final check has caught many an embarrassing error and is, in fact, a device that can well be used for all work involving detail and accuracy. Check the following items *on each set* of the report unless a copying machine has been used.

1. Indicated corrections made on every page
2. Correct references to page numbers, tables, or figures
3. Correct sequence of page numbers (necessary for each set even when a copying machine has been used)

Collating

The final report is submitted in complete sets, with the ribbon copy on top. The typed pages are assembled in reverse order—that is, the bottom page is laid out first, face up. In this way, you can see any blank or mutilated pages during assembly. When you have collated a complete set, joggle the pages horizontally and vertically until they are exactly aligned.

Binding

Binding is the last step in preparing a report. The most popular form of binding is the staple. When only one staple is required, position it diagonally in the upper left corner. When a wider margin has been left for binding at the

PREPARING COPY FOR THE PRINTER

Most of the duties associated with preparing a manuscript for a magazine or an outside printer are part of the multifunctional and administrative secretary's responsibilities. If a word processing center is available, the actual typing is done in the center. Since the copy is to be followed exactly, it is imperative that punctuation and spelling be correct. Of course, the office retains a file copy for ready reference.

If possible, the secretary should discuss styling with the person who is to be responsible for the work. Together they should develop a style sheet showing the type to be used for main headings and subheadings, for footnotes, for the bibliography, and for captions.

Manuscript

A manuscript to be typeset must meet the following important specifications:

1. Type all copy double-spaced on one side of 8½- by 11-inch sheets, with one or preferably two copies. Leave generous side margins. Quoted material or other text matter to be set apart should be single-spaced and indented on both sides.

2. Key all typewritten copy to its exact position on a page layout.

3. Number all sheets in the upper right corner. Two or more compositors may work on the same assignment; so correct numbering is imperative.

4. Type incidental changes, or write them clearly in ink, between the lines or in the margins.

5. Typewrite a long addition on a separate full-sized sheet and give it an inserted page number, such as 16a; indicate on page 16 the point at which the insertion is to be made.

6. Draw a heavy line through words to be omitted.

7. Give explicit directions. With the help of a compositor, specify size and style of type faces and amount of leading (space between lines) desired.

top or at the left, use two or three staples along the wide margin, parallel with the edge of the paper.

If a report that is to be stapled proves to be too thick, use double stapling, inserting the staples in proper position from the front and then inserting a second set in the same spots from the back.

Some offices prefer sturdier and more permanent types of binding. Some of these bindings require special supplies and equipment, such as metal eyelets, punches, wire spiral devices, or plastic combs. A convenient and attractive cover in transparent plastic with a snap-on spine is available.

8. Use a single underline to indicate *italics*, a double underline for SMALL CAPS, and a triple underline for REGULAR CAPS. To indicate bold face, use a wavy underline.

9. Number footnotes consecutively. They may be typed on the page to which they pertain; between full width rules directly under the line in which the reference occurs; at the bottom of the page but separated from the text by short line; or all in sequence on a separate sheet.

10. If a photograph is to be included, type the caption on a separate piece of paper and paste on the bottom edge of the picture.

11. Provide titles. Number tables and illustrations consecutively with Arabic numerals. Send with the manuscript a full list of all tables and illustrations.

12. Include a title page showing the title, the author's name and address, and perhaps the date.

13. Include the author's vita sheet, if requested.

14. Send the original copy to the printer. Do not fasten the sheets together. Keep them flat by placing them between strong cardboards or in a strong box.

15. Send the manuscript by first-class mail.

Magazine Articles and Press Releases

At times an executive may be asked to submit an article for magazine publication. The secretary simplifies the editor's job of judging the space needed for the copy by typing a sample paragraph from a recent issue of the magazine line for line. In this way average line length and the number of lines to an inch of printed material is determined. Headings for the copy should be consistent with those used in the magazine. This information becomes the style sheet for the article. A covering letter giving the approximate number of words in the article also aids the editor.

If the approximate length requirements of the article are provided by the publisher, the secretary types a rough draft version with double spacing in the average line length of the magazine copy. This copy is given to the executive with a close estimation of the amount of space presently accounted for. As revisions are made the executive can lengthen or shorten the article. Copies of the published material should be kept in a file so labeled.

Press releases should be addressed to the City Editor unless a definite person (such as the Financial Editor) is specified. Publicity and news releases are discussed in Chapter 10.

Reading Proof

It is customary for the printer to submit proofs. The secretary usually does the checking for errors, but the executive should be given an opportunity to approve revisions.

The first proof is usually in galley form—long sheets containing one column of printed copy, the column width as on the final printed page. Each kind of error or change to be made is indicated by a proofreader's mark (illustrated in the Reference Guide on page 758). The place of the correction is indicated in the text, and the kind of correction to be made is written in the margin on the same line. If there is more than one correction in a line, the proofreader's marks in the margin are separated by conspicuous diagonal lines.

The printer submits the second proof in page form. This new proof must be again meticulously read and corrected. Page numbers and page headings are shown in this proof and are usually checked as separate individual operations. This is often the final opportunity for the author to catch errors and to make changes.

PROCEDURES WRITING

Procedures writing has been called "verbal flowcharting." It lists step by step the logical sequence of activities involved in a given task. Procedures writing serves to control as well as to communicate. It controls how things are to be done as it instructs employees in the steps to follow in recurring operations.

Illus. 20-13
In all manner of writing—report, procedures preparation, or material for publication— careful research is the foundation for accurate information.

Writing good procedures seems deceptively simple, but to eliminate extraneous material is extremely difficult. Effective procedures writing is one of the most valuable forms of business writing because it saves time and money.

Writing procedures is a sophisticated process—so much so, in fact, that some companies assign one person to write procedures, thus maintaining uniformity. It is important that procedures be written in a simple, direct style, using terms easily understood by all who will be expected to interpret and follow them.

Procedures for a department or for an operation are usually collected in a loose-leaf notebook that can be updated by adding and deleting pages as new procedures are issued. The notebook is commonly known as a procedures manual. It is helpful to include an index in the manual for easy reference.

A Sample Procedure

The establishment of word processing centers in most large corporate headquarters has necessitated the development of procedures for submitting work to the centers. As an administrative secretary, you might be asked to write some of the procedures that affect your office. Assume that your input is requested for the submittal of material to the center. There are at least four formats that you can use in writing the procedures: traditional, improved traditional, job breakdown, and playscript. These formats are illustrated on the following pages.

```
The word originator who has a hard copy document to be typed
by the word processing center prepares the document in
readable form with complete instructions and attaches it
to Form 101 WP, Word Processing Center Job Ticket, and
sends to the Word Processing Center.

The Word Processing Manager enters the document on Form 102 WP,
Work Log, and notes the date and time on the Job Ticket.
The manager then assigns the work to one of the Correspondence
Secretaries.

The Correspondence Secretary types the final document in
appropriate form and makes the required number of copies
and then submits to the Word Processing Coordinator for
proofreading and distribution.  The messenger delivers the
completed work to the originator for signature and mailing.
```

Illus. 20-14
The traditional format features prose style writing and uses little spacing variation.

The word originator who has a <u>hard copy document</u> to be typed by the word processing center

1. completes Form 101 WP giving detailed instructions
2. attaches Form 101 WP to the document
3. sends to the word processing center

The Word Processing Manager enters the document on the Work Log, noting the date and time on Form 102 WP, and gives to a correspondence secretary for typing.

After typing the document, the correspondence secretary submits the work to the word processing <u>coordinator</u> for proofreading and distribution. A messenger delivers the work <u>to the</u> originator for signature and mailing.

Illus. 20-15
The improved traditional format uses variations in spacing, underlining, and tabulations to emphasize appropriate points.

Job Breakdown. With the job breakdown the logical sequence of action is reflected in the *Steps*. The *Key Points* represent cautions to the worker at the points where mistakes are likely. The *Steps* tell the worker what to do; the *Key Points* tell how to do it.

Every *Step* does not have to have a *Key Point*, and there may be more than one *Key Point* for one operation.

Steps	Key Points
1. Prepare hard copy document.	1. Be sure that the document is in readable form.
2. Attach to Form 101 WP, Word Processing Job Ticket.	2. Include complete instructions and all necessary information.
3. Send to Word Processing Center by messenger.	3. Note the time the work was picked up.
4. Receive completed work from the Word Processing Center.	4a. Check to see that directions were followed and all information included.
	4b. Verify number of copies.
	4c. Check to see if envelope is included and is the right size.
5. Sign and mail.	5. Any changes would require the return of the document to the Center.

Illus. 20-16
The job breakdown format

Playscript. The playscript format answers the question, "Who does what?" It utilizes the team approach in completing office tasks. The actor is easily identified, and what the actor does starts with an action verb in the present tense. According to the developer of this technique, playscript is really a form of flowchart. Any step that backflows rather than proceeds by forward action can immediately be spotted, and gaps in the logical steps can also be quickly detected, just as backflow is revealed in a flowchart.

Responsibility	Action
Word Originator	1. Prepares document in readable form including complete instructions.
	2. Attaches Form 101 WP, Word Processing Center Job Ticket, and sends to the Center.
Word Processing Manager	3. Enters the document of Form 102 WP, Work Log, noting the date and time on the Job Ticket.
	4. Assigns the work to a correspondence secretary.
Correspondence Secretary	5. Prepares final document in appropriate form and number of copies.
	6. Submits to word processing coordinator.
Word Processing Coordinator	7. Proofs work and prepares for distribution.
Messenger	8. Delivers to originator for signature and mailing.

Illus. 20-17
The playscript format

Selecting the Format

A traditional person or a traditional company probably will adopt the improved arrangement of the traditional format. A more venturesome author in search of eye-catching appeal probably will choose the job breakdown or the playscript. In a procedure involving one operator, the job breakdown might be chosen, for it has the advantage of cautioning against wrong moves. It looks more complicated than the playscript, however. The playscript probably will be selected for writing procedures involving more than one worker.

SUGGESTED READINGS

Carr-Ruffino, Norma. *Writing Short Business Reports.* New York: McGraw-Hill Book Company, 1980.

Keithley, Erwin M., and Philip J. Schreiner. *A Manual of Style for the Preparation of Papers and Reports*, 3d ed. Cincinnati: South-Western Publishing Co., 1980.

Matthies, Leslie H. *The New Playscript Procedure.* Stamford, Conn.: Office Publications., Inc., 1977.

QUESTIONS FOR DISCUSSION

1. Why is it important that a definite order of arrangement and mechanical rules be followed in report preparation?

2. If you were assigned the responsibility for typing a long report, which questions would you ask and what items would you decide for yourself before you started the typing?

3. Assume that you and two other multifunctional secretaries will type the final copy of a formal report for your immediate supervisor. How will you make sure that all pages are uniform in placement and follow proper format? How will you proofread the work?

4. How do the responsibilities of the administrative secretary, the correspondence secretary, and the multifunctional secretary differ in business report preparation for one word originator?

5. Reports written in the third person can be dull reading. How can a secretary assist the report writer in making the report interesting reading?

6. Who and what determine the format of the company procedures manual?

7. If you had obtained all the data available on a certain subject and an executive had drafted a report based on this information, what would you do if in the morning's mail you received a business magazine containing an article that covered a new angle of the subject? Would you call the executive's attention to the new material, knowing that it would mean a rewrite job?

8. Retype the following sentences. Express the numbers in parentheses correctly. Then check the Reference Guide to verify or correct your answers.

   (a) He held the check for _____ days. (7)

   (b) The check for _____ pays for a copier that is _____ years old. ($40, 12)

   (c) The typewriter was purchased approximately _____ years ago along with _____ drawer file cabinets. (12, 5, 3)

PROBLEMS

1. Type each of the following titles twice (eight different arrangements). Divide the titles into two or more lines if necessary, and center each line horizontally on the page. Allow six line spaces between titles. Indicate your preference of the resulting styles.

   (a) Career Paths in Word Processing Centers

(b) How Information Processing Creates Total Business Systems

(c) The Mature Woman Returns to Work in the Business Office

(d) The Increasing Ranks of the Male Secretary

2. To provide practice for yourself in using proofreaders' marks (see page 758 Reference Guide), indicate the method of marking (both in the text material and in the margins) the changes listed below. Set up three columns headed *Change Desired in Text*, *Proofreader's Mark in Text*, and *Proofreader's Mark in Margin*.

   (1) Insert the word *more*.
   (2) Change the word *readnig* to *reading*.
   (3) Delete the word *usually*.
   (4) Show a space in *ofthis*.
   (5) Even up the left margin where the letters have been set a space too far to the left in one line.
   (6) Write the word *think* in solid capitals.
   (7) Show an apostrophe in the word *womens*.
   (8) Capitalize the word *congressional*.
   (9) Insert a hyphen in *selfemployed*.
   (10) Indicate a new paragraph in the copy.
   (11) Italicize the word *usually*.
   (12) Use lowercase correctly for the words *History, Algebra, Social Studies,* and *English*.
   (13) In marking the copy for the preceding question, you inadvertently indicated that the word *English* should be written in lowercase too. Show that you want the original capitalization to stand.
   (14) Transpose *two only* to *only two*.
   (15) Use less space between words.
   (16) Use small caps for the paragraph heading, *Characteristics of the New Process*.
   (17) Use quotation marks around *shot in the arm*.
   (18) Indicate no paragraph.
   (19) Indicate that type does not match.
   (20) Delete the hyphen in *readilly-available service*.
   (21) Insert a comma between *pens and and*.
   (22) Center and type in solid caps the heading: *Introduction*.
   (23) Change *thimk* to *think*.
   (24) Indicate leaving more space after a colon.
   (25) Increase the amount of space between lines.
   (26) Move copy to the right to align.
   (27) Indicate correct spelling of *state room*.
   (28) Delete the apostrophe in *it's*.
   (29) In the title *A Manual of Style for the Preparation of Papers and Reports*, the words *and Reports* have been crossed out. Indicate that these two words should be retained.
   (30) Delete the comma: *He finished the report, and got it on his superior's desk before leaving the office that afternoon.*

3. Type an outline of an article on the topic of word processing appearing in any recent issue of *Administrative Management* or *Word Processing & Information Systems*.

4. From the bibliographical notes that you prepared for Problem 1 in Chapter 18, develop a business report on one of the ten topics given (or a topic of your own choice which your instructor has approved). Use graphs or tables if you think they will improve your presentation.

5. Assume that you are sharing the responsibility for typing the report in Problem 4 above with two other secretaries. Type a set of job instructions and a special guide sheet for you and your team to follow in typing the report.

6. Using information in the Reference Guide, type correctly as a footnote and as a bibliography item the following information:

   (a) An unsigned article, "Growing Market for Electronic Mail," on pp. 74–76 of *The Office*, August, 1980.
   (b) A book written by John T. Molloy entitled *The Woman's Dress for Success Book* published by Warner Books, New York, in 1978. The footnote refers to page 65.
   (c) A chapter written by Dennis L. Mott en-

titled "Time Management" in the National Business Education Yearbook, No. 18, *The Changing Office Environment,* edited by Margaret H. Johnson, published by the National Business Education Association, Reston, Virginia, in 1980. This chapter appears on pages 142–150.

(d) An article by Paula B. Cecil called "Write Your Own Word Processing Manual" in the February, 1980, issue of *Modern Office Procedures.* The material is on pages 135–140.

7. As administrative assistant in a government procurement office, you are assigned the supervision of two young assistants. You have given them the responsibility of opening and sorting the office mail. You decide to prepare a procedural statement in playscript style covering this activity. Before you begin writing, you analyze the cycle of the operation, determine the actors involved (the two assistants, mail messenger, and yourself), analyze each action in the operation, and identify any office forms used in the process. Write the statement of procedures. (You may wish to refer to Chapter 7).

Part Seven

Case Problems

Case 7-1
SECRETARIAL DECISIONS

Jim Harper has been secretary to Ms. Juanita Sanchez, branch manager, for five years. He has typed many reports for publication, sometimes adopting nontraditional formats to highlight important points and make the reports more attractive. Ms. Sanchez has accepted these changes, sometimes complimenting him on the innovative arrangements.

Jim is surprised, therefore, when he receives a memo from Ms. Sanchez stating that henceforth all reports for publication are to be typed in traditional styles. Jim is annoyed that the reasons behind this new directive were not discussed with him before the decision was made.

Should he accept the instructions without question, or should he ask to discuss it with Ms. Sanchez?

Case 7-2
DELEGATING WORK

Carmen Reynolds was put in charge of producing a 78-page medical report. She met with each of the three typists assigned to the job, gave instructions as to style, handed them a prepared guide sheet, and requested each typist to read Chapter 20 of this book. The work had to be completed within two days so that Dr. Johanna Spector, her employer, could take it to a meeting at which she was to be the featured speaker. Carmen received the completed work for assembling for presentation to Doctor Spector just two hours before the deadline.

She was horrified to discover that one typist had used a typewriter with pica type, although the other two had used elite type; one had put the footnotes in the center of the page following the material to which they referred; and one had typed paragraph headings in solid caps while the other two had capitalized only the important words in the title and had underscored the title.

She showed the variations to Doctor Spector and said, "I am just sick about the way this report looks. You would think that these typists could follow instructions. What can be done now?"

Doctor Spector replied icily, "Nothing, absolutely nothing. I will have to tell the people at the symposium that I will mail them a copy of the report next week. Heaven knows how I can get all the addresses. But, Carmen, I am very unhappy with the way you handled this. After all, you are the one in charge. I had thought that you could handle a simple assignment like this one."

Was Carmen at fault? What did she do wrong? If she talked with you about the problem, what advice would you give her for handling such a situation?

Case 7-3
UNETHICAL
BEHAVIOR OF
THE EXECUTIVE

Sally Fong is secretary to Harold Rose, vice-president, Research and Development, for Haskins Leather Processing Company. Mr. Rose has asked Sally to type a proposal to research the feasibility of producing a new type of automatic lock for suitcases.

The preceding week Sally had had dinner with her friend, Tom Lamston, who is also employed in the Research and Development unit. Tom had enthusiastically discussed a new automatic lock that he had invented and intended to patent.

At the office Sally looked carefully through Mr. Rose's proposal for mention of Tom as the inventor of the lock, but it was not there. Mr. Rose has taken full credit for the invention himself.

Where do Sally's loyalties lie?

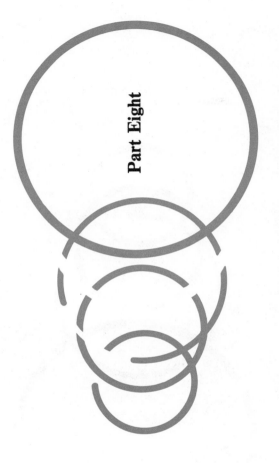

Part Eight

ADMINISTRATIVE SUPPORT SERVICES: FINANCIAL AND LEGAL ASSISTANCE

The extent to which a secretary is involved in the company and personal banking of the employer, in the employer's investment and insurance program, in payroll preparation, and in the production and processing of legal papers depends upon a number of variables. Among such variables are the size of the business or office, the function of the division in which the secretary is employed, and the specific job title of the secretary. In addition, the financial interests of the executive or executives for whom the secretary works will determine the scope of the functions performed.

The topics in Part Eight not only contribute to the secretary's job performance but also have personal values. As a wage earner and a financially responsible individual, the secretary needs to understand banking services, ways to record and audit investments and insurance policies, how to organize data for the preparation of income tax returns, and the significance of certain legal terminology and forms.

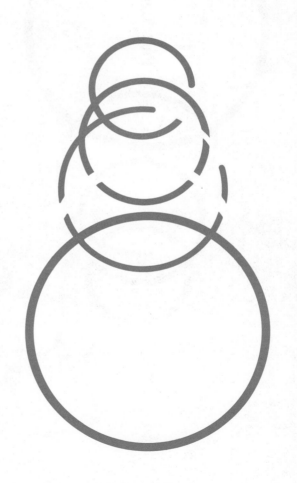

Chapter 21

Banking Responsibilities

The extent to which the administrative or multifunctional secretary will be responsible for the office banking or the executive's personal banking usually depends upon the size of the office. In the small office the secretary may keep all the financial records and do all the banking. In a large office these responsibilities are usually handled by others, but the secretary may keep the petty cash fund, use the special services provided by banks, approve bills for payment, arrange for foreign remittances, and perform other functions that relate to the company's bank accounts. In addition, many top executives expect their secretaries to assist with their personal financial records and banking.

Although the total time spent each day in performing these financial duties may be comparatively small, their importance must not be underestimated. They represent exacting and confidential responsibilities. They are exacting because they involve handling other people's money. They are confidential because financial data are always highly restricted pieces of information.

Whether your financial duties are extensive or limited, you may expect to perform some, if not all, of these functions: make bank deposits, write checks, cash checks, pay bills, reconcile bank statements, handle petty cash funds, and record incoming funds. Although specific practices and methods vary somewhat, basic banking procedures are similar.

FINANCIAL TRANSACTIONS

The new secretary with financial responsibilities must be identified at the bank as representing the employer. If the secretary is to sign checks for the withdrawal or payment of personal or company funds or to endorse and cash checks, the bank must be authorized to honor the secretary's signature. The employer may be required to sign a special authorization form or to arrange for the secretary's signature to be added to the signature card on file at the bank. Some banks require that the secretary be issued a power of attorney, described in Chapter 24, to perform these functions.

Accepting Checks

Accepting a check that is given in person or received through the mail requires precautions to assure that the check is valid—that it has been properly prepared. Examine these points: (1) date—to see that the check is not post-dated (dated later than current date), (2) amount—to determine that the amount of payment is correct, (3) figures—to be sure that the amount written in figures agrees with the amount written in words, and (4) endorsement—to see that an endorsement, if required, has been properly made. To have a deposited check returned by the bank because it was improperly written is time consuming and inconvenient. Before depositing a check and while the details are still available, be sure to record the information needed for the accounting records on a receipt form or in a record book.

Proving Cash

You might have the responsibility for receiving cash payments and making change and payments from a cash drawer. This responsibility will necessitate proving cash at the beginning or end of each business day. Since you will be held personally responsible for this money, it is essential that you follow a system for protecting these funds. Should you relinquish custody of the cash drawer to another employee, prove the cash before doing so and ask for a receipt to protect yourself.

To prove cash efficiently, use a form similar to the one shown below:

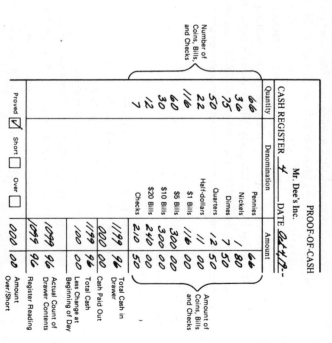

Depositing Funds

To make a deposit, the secretary presents to the bank teller a deposit ticket in duplicate listing the amounts being deposited (or a passbook). The deposit itself—consisting of currency, coin, endorsed checks, and money orders—should accompany the deposit ticket.

Coins and Bills for Deposit. Banks prefer that coins and bills, if in sufficient quantity, be put in the money wrappers that the banks furnish. Coins are packed in paper rolls as follows:

Denomination	Number of Coins to a Roll	Total Value of Coins in Roll
Pennies	50	$ .50
Nickels	40	2.00
Dimes	50	5.00
Quarters	40	10.00
Halves	20	10.00

Bills of each denomination are made into packages of $50, $100, and so forth. The packages are separated into all-of-a-kind groups with each bill laid right side up and top edge at the top. Torn bills are mended with tape. A paper bill wrapper—a narrow strip with the amount printed on it—is wrapped tightly around the bills and securely glued.

The depositor's name or account number should be stamped or written on each roll of coins and package of bills. Receiving tellers of banks do not stop to count packaged money when taking deposits, but someone counts it later in the day. If the depositor's name or account number appears on each roll or wrapper, mistakes can be easily traced.

Extra bills are counted and stacked, right side up, the largest denominations on the bottom and the smallest ones on top, and fastened with a rubber band. Extra coins are counted, placed in an envelope, identified, and sealed.

Checks for Deposit. In order to deposit a check or money order, the payee (person to whom the check is written) endorses it on the back; however, banks accept checks for deposit that are endorsed by a representative of the payee. In fact, a bank may accept an occasional check that lacks an endorsement. Some banks stamp the back of such a check with a statement such as, "Credited to account of payee named within—absence of endorsement guaranteed."

Notwithstanding the last sentence, it will be the secretary's responsibility to endorse every check for deposit. If the name of the payee is written on a check differently from the account name, endorse the check twice: first, as the name appears on the face of the check and, second, the exact way the account is carried. A rubber stamp endorsement (showing the name of the bank, the name of the account, and the account number), obtained from the bank where the employer banks or from an office supplies store, is the most timesaving method. Companies that receive a large number of checks can use a machine that will endorse checks at a high rate of speed. If a check is to be deposited, a pen signature need not be added to a rubber stamp or machine endorsement.

There are several standard endorsements:

1. *A restrictive endorsement* is one in which some condition attached to the endorsement restrains the negotiability of the check or renders the endorser liable only upon a specified condition or conditions, such as *For deposit*, or *Upon delivery of contract*. A restrictive endorsement is commonly used when checks are being deposited. A restrictive endorsement need not be signed personally by the depositor but can be endorsed or stamped by the secretary. The *For deposit* qualification automatically keeps the check from being used for any purpose other than for deposit to the account of the depositor whose name appears in the endorsement.

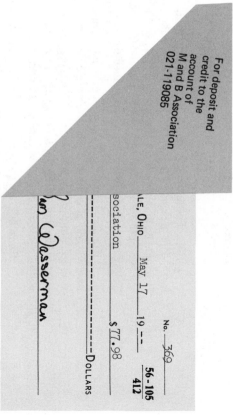

For deposit and
credit to the
account of
M and B Association
021-119085

LE, Ohio May 17___ 19 — — No. 369

56-105
412

sociation $77.98

——————————————— Dollars

Jim Wasserman

2. An *endorsement in full* or *special endorsement* (Illus 21-3) gives the name of a specified payee, written before the endorser's signature. This endorsement identifies the person or firm to which the instrument is transferred. A check endorsed in this way cannot be cashed by anyone without the specified payee's signature. The words *Pay to the order of Marilyn Royer* in the illustration identify the name of the person to whom the check is being transferred. For further transfer, Marilyn Royer must endorse the check again.

3. A *blank endorsement* consists simply of the signature of the payee, making the check payable to any holder. This endorsement, therefore, should never be used except at the bank immediately before the check is being deposited or cashed. A check should never be endorsed at the office or sent through the mail with a blank endorsement. If it is lost, the finder can turn it into cash.

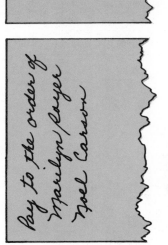

Illus. 21-3
Endorsement in full

Blank endorsement

The person or business that accepts an endorsed check (unless stated otherwise in the endorsement) assumes (1) that the check is genuine and valid, (2) that the endorser has received value for it, and (3) that, if necessary, the endorser will reimburse the holder of the check if the bank refuses to process it.

Magnetic Ink Numbers. The American Bankers Association has adopted a uniform system of MICR (magnetic ink character recognition) that provides for preprinting the bank's transit number and the depositor's account number in magnetic ink characters in a uniform position at the bottom of the checks. When a check is received at the bank, the date, amount of the check, and other coded information also are recorded in magnetic ink characters at the bottom of the check. Optical character recognition (OCR) equipment sorts the checks according to issuing bank and account numbers, computes totals, and posts to the depositors' accounts. This is done electronically.

Illus. 21-4 shows a preprinted deposit ticket for an MICR system; Illus. 21-5 shows a check identified by magnetic ink characters.

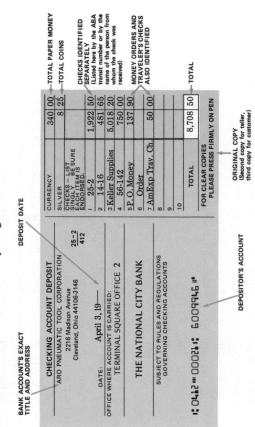

Illus. 21-4
Deposit ticket

Illus. 21-5
Note that the series of magnetic ink identification numbers at the bottom of this check are the same as those of the preprinted deposit ticket in Illus. 21-4.

No. 832	$325.27
Date	April 15, 19—
To	Apex Corp.
For	Machinery Parts

	Dollars	Cents
Bal Bro't For'd	8,604	81
Amt Deposited	9,13	40
Total	9,518	21
Amt This Check	325	27
Bal Car'd For'd	9,192	94

ARO PNEUMATIC TOOL CORPORATION
2216 Madison Avenue
Cleveland, Ohio 44106-3146

NO. 832

Date April 15, 19— — 25-2/412

PAY TO THE
ORDER OF Apex Corporation _____ $ 325.27

Three hundred twenty-five 27/100———————————— Dollars

TERMINAL SQUARE OFFICE 2
THE NATIONAL CITY BANK
Cleveland, Ohio

Marion T. Owen

⑆0442⑈0002⑆ 600494⑈

When an automated system is in use, the depositor can use only those deposit tickets and checks that have been printed with the account number. If a depositor does not have a deposit ticket or check at the time of a deposit or withdrawal, bank personnel will provide one.

Deposit Tickets. Many types of deposit tickets are used. Most banks have deposit tickets designed especially for use with automated equipment, usually in multiple sets with interleaved carbon or NCR coating. The deposit ticket shown in Illus. 21-4 is designed for automated processing.

If you wish to receive a portion of the total amount listed on the deposit slip as cash, you may "split" the deposit. This can be done, for example, when your employer asks you to deposit a salary check and bring back a specific amount of cash. Your employer should not restrict the endorsement in this case, since you are not depositing all the money.

Account Numbers. Each depositor has an account number with which the bank's automated equipment identifies the depositor's account; therefore, the account number must appear on the deposit ticket. This number is usually printed in small type in the upper right portion of the check. It identifies the depositor with a supply of deposit tickets either printed with the account number in magnetic ink characters or with space provided for the depositor to record the account number.

Check Numbers. Each bank in the United States has been assigned an ABA (American Bankers Association) transit number. This number is usually printed in small type in the upper right portion of the check. It identifies the bank for clearinghouse functions. Illustrated, the numbers mean:

City or State	25-2	Specific bank in the city or state
	412	(4) Federal Reserve District
		(1) Branch in the district
		(2) Number of days required to clear the check

Some banks require each check listed on the deposit ticket to be identified by using the two top ABA transit numbers, in this case 25-2, unless the check is drawn on the bank in which the deposit is made. In this case, the check is identified by the name of the maker of the check.

Listing Checks. When a large number of checks are regularly deposited, common practice is to list the checks on an adding machine and to attach the tape to the deposit ticket, listing only the total on the deposit ticket. Some banks, however, which prefer that all checks be shown on the deposit ticket, provide large deposit tickets for such use.

Listing Other Items. Money orders, bank drafts (Illus. 21-11), traveler's checks, and interest coupons are listed with the checks on the deposit ticket. Certain government, municipal, and company bonds provide interest coupons attached to the bond. On the due date the coupon can be detached from the bond, placed with a deposit ticket in an envelope provided by the bank, and deposited. A separate envelope must be used for each class of coupon.

Using the Night Depository

Some businesses use the *night* or *after-hours depository* for funds collected after banking hours. The bank provides the depositor with a bag in which to lock the deposit. The depositor then can drop the bag through a slot accessible from outside the bank at any time the bank is closed. On the next banking day, a bank teller unlocks the bag and makes the deposit. The depositor later stops at the bank to pick up the empty bag and deposit receipt. If the depositor prefers, however, the bank will leave the deposit bag locked until the depositor arrives to make the deposit personally. Branch banks and evening banking hours further add to the convenience of the depositor.

Banking by Mail

Depositing by mail has become very popular because of the time it saves. The secretary in a small office may make all or most of the bank deposits by mail. Various kinds of mail deposit tickets and envelopes are provided by different banks. All checks must be endorsed *Pay to the order of (name of bank)* or *For Deposit Only*, signed, and listed on the mail deposit slip. The deposit ticket and endorsed checks are placed in an envelope and mailed to the bank or are dropped in the night depository. Currency should never be deposited in this manner unless sent by registered mail. By return mail the bank sends the depositor a receipt, along with a new mail deposit ticket and envelope.

Using a Checking Account

Banks provide a variety of check forms: checks with attached stubs; pads of checks with interleaved copy sheets or with attached *vouchers* (a form used to record the purpose and other details of the payment). In companies where all disbursements must be made by check, voucher checks and a check register are used. A *check register* is a special journal containing a chronological and serial record of all voucher checks issued. Such a system ensures close control over cash disbursements. Many businesses use prenumbered checks imprinted with the name of the business. The secretary is responsible for ordering a new checkbook before the old one is completely used. Banks usually enclose an order sheet toward the back of the checkbook.

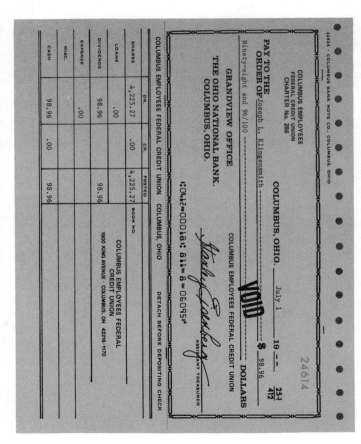

Illus. 21-6
A voucher check consists of the check and a detachable stub that shows the purpose of the check and various data necessary for record keeping.

Completing Check Stubs. Complete the stub *before* you write the check. Failure to do so frequently results in the details of a check being forgotten. In addition to showing the number of the check, the date, the name of the payee, and the amount, the stub should provide other data for classifying or breaking down the disbursement in the accounting or tax records. For example, if the check is for a part payment, an installment payment, or a final payment, that fact should be noted. If the amount covers several items (such as payment for two or more invoices), each should be listed. If the check is in payment of an insurance premium, the name of the insured and the policy number should be listed.

Writing Checks. A check is a negotiable instrument and imposes certain legal responsibilities on the maker. Therefore, it must be written with care to ensure that no unintended liability is created. For example, an altered check is not cashable. If a bank honors such a check, it must assume any resulting loss. However, if it can be shown that the maker failed to use reasonable precautions in writing the check, thus making alteration difficult to detect, the maker must assume any resulting loss. Consequently, always type checks or write them in ink (never pencil). Follow these steps:

1. Be sure that the *number* of the check corresponds with that on the stub. If the checks are not numbered in printing, number all checks and check stubs upon starting a new checkbook.

2. *Date* the check on the exact date that the check is being written. Occasionally checks are postdated—that is, dated ahead to a time when sufficient funds will be in the checking account. This is a questionable practice, however.

3. Write the name of the *payee* in full and spell the name correctly. For correct spelling, refer to bills, letterheads, or the telephone directory. Omit titles such as *Ms*, *Mr.*, *Mrs.*, *Miss*, and *Dr.* On checks written to a married woman, use her given name: *Ruth Hill*, not *Mrs. John R. Hill*.

4. In writing the *amount*, use large, bold figures written close to the dollar sign and sufficiently close together to prevent the insertion of other figures. In spelling out the amount, start at the extreme left, capitalizing the first letter only, and express cents as fractions of 100:

   To write a check for less than $1, circle the amount written in figures and write *Only* before the spelled-out amount. Cross out *Dollars* at the end of the line.

5. Fill any *blank space* before or after the amount with hyphens, periods, or a line.

6. The *purpose* of the check, such as *In Payment of Invoice 6824*, may be written in a corner of the check, if space permits, or across the end of the check.

Never cross out, erase, or change any part of a check. If you make an error, write *VOID* conspicuously across the face of both the check and the stub. Save a voided check and file it in numerical order with the canceled checks returned from the bank. Since it is easy to alter the impressions made by a worn ribbon, type checks with a fresh ribbon. Keep the checkbook in a safe place, and guard its confidentiality.

Writing Checks for Cash. A check for funds for the personal use of the account holder can be written to *Cash* as the payee and signed by the account holder. A check so written is highly negotiable. Anyone in possession of it can turn it into money. The cautious person, therefore, will use this form only when writing the check on the bank premises. (The bank asks the person receiving the money to endorse the check, even though the payee is *Cash*.)

The secretary may be expected to keep the executive supplied with cash. On banking days, the secretary simply asks, "Do you need money?" If so, the secretary writes the check and either presents it for the executive's signature or, if authorized, signs it. To cash a check made out to *Cash* and signed by the employer, the secretary will be required to endorse the check when it is presented at the bank. Checks made out to *Cash* are risky and if lost can be cashed by anyone. Unless the secretary is well known at the bank, positive identification will also be required. After cashing the check, the secretary should keep the currency separate from personal funds. Place the money in an envelope, seal it, and protect it until delivery.

As a special service some banks provide depositors with a check-cashing or bank check guarantee card. This card, which is a form of identification, guarantees that the bank will honor the card holder's check up to a specified amount. Check-cashing cards facilitate the cashing of personal checks at stores and at other banks.

Checking Accounts That Pay Interest. Funds deposited in checking accounts may draw interest. Banks and savings and loan associations nationwide offer NOW—short for Negotiable Order of Withdrawal—accounts. Some credit unions pay interest on share-draft accounts, which are like NOW accounts. Most financial institutions offering this service require a minimum balance. A service charge is imposed on accounts that fall below a minimum balance. For example, one financial institution may require you to keep a minimum balance of $500 in your checking account to earn interest. If your balance falls below $500, there is a flat $2 monthly maintenance fee plus 15 cents per check paid on the account. Before depositing money in an interest-earning checking account, you should investigate the offerings of several financial institutions. Some of the questions you will want to ask are: How much interest is earned? Will a minimum balance required? What if I go under the minimum? Will a traditional noninterest-bearing checking account serve my purposes just as well?

Stopping Payment on Checks

After a check has been issued, payment can be stopped unless the check has been cleared by the bank upon which it was drawn. This procedure may be necessary when a check has been lost, stolen, or incorrectly written. Most banks charge for this service.

To stop payment, telephone the stop payment desk of the bank and give the name of the maker, the date, number and amount of the check, the account number, the name of the payee, and the reason that payment is to be stopped. The bank teller will search the checks on hand to see if the item in question has cleared the bank. If it has not, the teller will process the request for a stop payment. Then you must dispatch either a letter of confirmation or a stop payment form supplied by the bank. When you are sure that the stop payment request is in effect, write a replacement check if necessary. Most banks will honor a request to stop payment for a limited time only. If additional time is needed, a new request must be filed with the bank.

Reconciling the Bank Balance

Each month the bank returns to the account holder the *canceled checks* (checks that have cleared during the month) along with a statement that lists each deposit and withdrawal and any other items, such as interest earned, a service charge, or stop payment charge. The account holder then checks the accuracy of the checkbook records and files the canceled checks as proof of payment.

When the statement and canceled checks are received, the final balance on the statement and the bank balance in the checkbook are compared and the difference between the two records accounted for. This process is called *reconciling the bank balance.*

Many banks print, on the back of the bank statement, instructions and a form for reconciling the bank balance. This printed form may be used, or the reconciliation may be typed on a separate sheet and attached to the bank statement.

Some banks offer a new service called *check truncation, check retention,* or *check safekeeping.* All three terms refer to the same practice—your bank keeps your canceled checks instead of returning them to you. You receive a monthly statement listing the number and amount of each check that has been canceled. You will also have the right to receive (some banks charge a fee) a copy of any check you need.

Making the Reconciliation. The following is a systematic procedure for making the reconciliation:

1. Arrange the canceled checks in numerical order.
2. Compare the amount of each canceled check returned by the bank with the amounts listed on the bank statement.
3. Compare the returned checks with the checkbook stubs. Make a distinctive check mark on the stubs of canceled checks. Compare also the amounts of deposits shown on the stubs with those shown on the bank statement. List and total any that were omitted.
4. List the outstanding checks, showing the check number, the payee, and the amount. Total the outstanding checks.
5. Add the total unlisted deposits to the bank balance; subtract the total amount of the outstanding checks. The remainder is the corrected bank balance.
6. The bank will list any service charges among the withdrawals on the bank statement. Subtract the amount of the service charges and any other deductions made by the bank from the balance shown on the last checkbook stub for the period being reconciled. The resulting figure should be the same amount as the corrected bank balance. If so, you must deduct the amount of the service charges from the balance on the checkbook stub that is currently the last one used. Any interest earned on the account may be shown on the statement. This amount should be added to the balance of the checkbook. The result will be the true current balance in the account.

As shown in the illustration at the left, an entry must now be made on the *current balance* (not the last stub of the reconciliation period) for any charges by the bank or interest earned.

No. 53	$49.95	
Date May 3	19—	
To *Yale Opticians*		
For *Prescription sunglasses*		
	DOLLARS	CENTS
Bal. Bro't For'd	1,168	33
Amt. Deposited	200	00
Amt. Deposited		
TOTAL	1,368	33
Amt. this Check	49	95
Bal. Car'd For'd	1,318	38
Int. Earned	1.	21
Card For'd	1,319	59

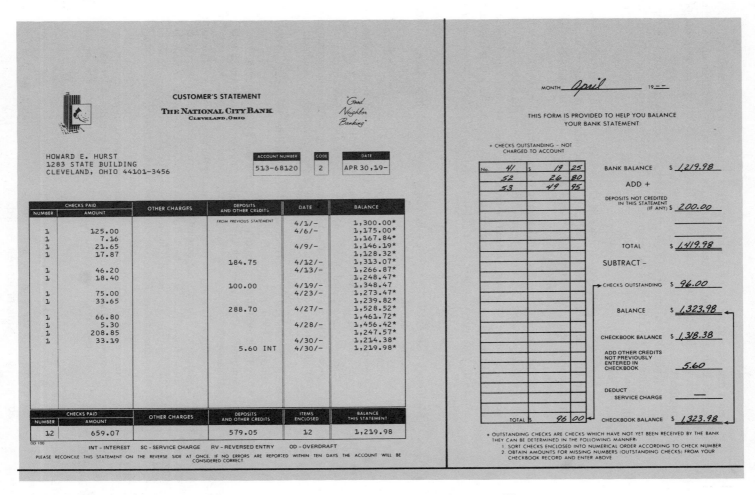

Illus. 21-7 (A)
The monthly bank statement shows the checks paid, the deposits received, interest paid, and any deductions made from the account.

Illus. 21-7 (B)
Printed on the back of many bank statements is a convenient form for reconciling the bank balance.

Locating Errors. If the two adjusted balances—statement and stub—do not agree, first check the computation on the reconciliation sheet to make sure there is no error. If there is none, make sure that:

No check has been omitted in the reconciliation. Go through the check stubs (one by one) and see that each one is included among the checks either cleared or outstanding. Also make sure that each check has a stub.

No deposit has been omitted. Cross check the deposits in the check stubs with those on the bank statement.

A deposit made by mail on the date that your bank statement is prepared will not appear on the statement. Add this deposit to the bank statement balance on the reconciliation sheet.

If there is still an error, either the bank has made an arithmetic error in the statement or, more likely, there is an error in the stubs. First check the accuracy of the *amounts forwarded* on each checkstub page. If these are correct, the arithmetic computations for each stub should be examined. When the error is located, mark the stub where it occurs:

"Error — should be $_____; corrected on Stub #_____."

Then make the compensating adjustment on the last stub.

Enter the amount of the error on the reconciliation statement and show where the error occurs and where it is corrected in the check stubs. After the proper check stub (the last transaction covered by the bank statement), write "Agrees with the bank statement *(date)*." Then you can easily find the starting point for the next month's reconciliation.

Filing Canceled Checks. File the bank reconciliation conveniently for the next reconciliation. You will need the records of checks now outstanding. Keep canceled checks inside the folded bank statements and file the statements chronologically, or file the bank statements chronologically and the checks numerically in a separate place. Save canceled checks, as they are evidences of payment; they constitute legal receipts. The retention period must be established by company policy.

Following Up on Outstanding Checks

Investigate any check that has not cleared through the bank within a few weeks of its date of issue. The payee may not have received the check or may have misplaced or lost it. A letter or telephone call to the payee will clarify the matter. If the check is apparently lost, cancel the old check in the checkbook, forward a stop payment order to the bank, and issue a new check.

Using a Safe-Deposit Box

Frequently the employer rents a *safe-deposit box* from the bank. This is a metal box locked by two keys into a small compartment in the bank's safe-deposit vault. The bank has very strict rules about access to safe-deposit boxes. The customer must register each time entry to the box is requested. A bank employee accompanies the customer to the box, opens one of the locks with the bank's key, and opens the other lock with the customer's key. The box itself is then removed and taken by the customer to a private room. Securities, wills, insurance policies, notes, gems, and other small valuable articles may be protected by safe deposit storage. Rent is usually billed annually and can be deducted directly from the customer's checking account.

The executive must sign a special banking form if the secretary is to have access to the safe-deposit box. The secretary may have two responsibilities relative to safe-deposit box work: (1) to maintain a perpetual inventory of its contents in duplicate, one copy to be kept in the box, the other in the office, and (2) to guard the key carefully.

Electronic Banking

Because millions of checks are processed by banks in the United States each year, a number of new procedures have been developed by the banking industry to reduce dependence on checks. Most of these new procedures employ electronic fund transfers (EFTs) which permit transfer of amounts from one depositor's account to another or cash withdrawals without the use of checks.

Computer and electronic technology has made EFT an acceptable substitute for checks and cash in many places. Each EFT service is designed to hold down the rising costs of handling checks and to provide a variety of banking conveniences. Most EFT services are available everywhere in one or more of the following forms.

Automatic Teller Machines. At shopping centers and convenient locations, automatic teller machines provide 24-hour banking. Automatic tellers are used

Illus. 21-8
A depositor
making a cash
withdrawal at an
automated teller

for cash withdrawals, to transfer funds, to make deposits, to make payments on certain loans and bank credit card accounts, to borrow funds in limited amounts, or to obtain the current balance of an account.

To use an automatic teller, the depositor inserts a plastic card and punches in a personal identification number (PIN). This number or code is known only to the depositor and the computer—unless the depositor reveals it to others. Federal law requires all automatic tellers to issue receipts.

Direct Deposits or Withdrawals. You may authorize specific deposits such as paychecks and social security checks to be credited automatically to your account on a regular basis. You can also arrange to have recurring bills such as insurance premiums and utility bills paid automatically. Employers may use EFT to deposit payroll checks directly to banks designated by the employee and eliminate the need to write large numbers of payroll checks each pay period. This service also saves the employee the inconvenience of a trip to the bank to make a deposit.

Pay-by-Phone Systems. After preauthorizing your bank to do so, you can call your bank (or other financial institution) and instruct it to pay certain bills or to transfer funds between accounts (for example, funds can be transferred automatically from checking to savings or vice versa). Each transaction will appear on a monthly statement from your bank.

Point-of-Sale Transfers. Such transfers let you pay for retail purchases with your EFT or debit card. This card is similar to a credit card with one important exception: the money for the purchase is immediately deducted from your bank account to the store's account. In other words, the amount of the purchase is deducted from the customer's checking account once the customer's identity and the availability of funds is confirmed.

Point-of-sale (POS) terminals permit transfer of amounts from a purchaser's bank account to the store's bank account without the use of the check. The terminal is connected by telephone circuits to the bank's computerized accounting data center. When a customer makes a purchase at the store, the store clerk or cash register operator inserts the customer's bank issued debit card into the store terminal. Using a telephone, the clerk dials the bank's computer storage facilities (this connects the store terminal to the bank's data center). The clerk then enters the amount of the purchase on the store's terminal keyboard. The customer keys in an individualized code number. The computer responds by authorizing the purchase, deducting the amount from the customer's checking account, and adding it to the merchant's account— all without a single piece of paper changing hands. The customer receives a monthly descriptive bank statement that describes checkless transactions in a form similar to the credit card statement.

The Impact of EFT on Secretarial Responsibilities. As a secretary, you will encounter EFT in one form or other as you transact routine banking for yourself or your employer. It behooves you to know your rights and responsibilities when handling EFTs.

Each time you initiate an EFT at a terminal (automated teller machines or point-of-sale transfers), you get a written receipt. Periodic statements must also be issued for all EFTs. Many banks use a single statement system that reports all transactions—deposits, withdrawals, savings, and EFTs on one form. You have 60 days from the date a problem or error appears on your statement or terminal receipt to notify your bank. If you fail to notify the bank within 60 days, you may find yourself without recourse. Under federal law the bank has no obligation to conduct an investigation if the 60-day deadline is missed.

If an error has been reported within 60 days, the bank must investigate the problem within ten business days after notification and tell you the results. If the bank needs more time, it may take up to 45 days to complete the investigation. In the meantime, however, the bank must replace the amount in dispute. The money is then available for the customer's use but must be paid back to the bank if the investigation reveals that no error was made.

If an EFT card is lost or stolen, notify the issuing bank within two business days after discovering the loss. You will then lose no more than $50 if someone else uses your card. If you do not notify the bank within two business days, you may lose as much as $500 if your card is used without your permission. The best way to protect yourself in case your card is lost or stolen is to notify your bank by telephone and follow up with a letter.

When you use EFT, the federal law gives you no right to stop payment. There is one case, however, where you can stop payment. If notice is given to the bank at least three days before the payment is scheduled, preauthorized payments, such as those for bills that are to be paid regularly out of your account, can be stopped. This right does not apply to bills you owe your bank, such as loan payments.

PAYING BILLS

An executive seldom turns over personal bill paying to a new secretary. It is one of the responsibilities that a secretary acquires or frequently assumes. First, the secretary may be asked to address the envelopes. Then, when rushed, the executive may say, "Will you please write these checks for me." It is then that the secretary can demonstrate capability in handling this responsibility. *Bill paying* consists of:

1. Verifying the items and checking the computations on each bill
2. Filling in the check stub (Be sure to itemize and identify the payment in order to use the stub in accounting processes or in preparing income tax returns.)
3. Making out the check
4. Writing on the face of the invoice or the statement the date, the number, and the amount of the check used in payment

5. Addressing the envelope
6. Tearing off the invoice or statement stub to be mailed with the check
7. Attaching the stub from the bill to the check and inserting both under the flap of an addressed envelope ready for presentation to the executive for signature

Verifying Bills

The secretary should verify the price, the terms, the extensions, and the additions on all bills. *Invoices* (itemized listings of goods purchased) must be checked against the quoted prices and terms or with records of previous prices paid. Monthly *statements* (details of accounts showing the amount due at the beginning of the month, purchases and payments made during the month, and the unpaid balance at the end of the month) can be verified by comparison with invoices and sales slips, check stubs, and other records of payments made on the account.

Bills for services (utility companies, for example) are usually accepted as they are, although the toll statement with the telephone bill is checked very carefully. You will wish to explore preauthorized bill payment service, if provided by your bank, to save your time in writing checks for utility bills. Before paying bills for professional services, the secretary should obtain the personal approval of the executive.

Credit Card Statements

To avoid carrying large amounts of cash or traveler's checks, many business and professional people use credit cards (such as American Express, Diners Club, VISA, MasterCard, and Carte Blanche) when traveling and when paying local entertainment expenses. Credit card statements also are helpful in preparing expense reports and in verifying travel and entertainment expenses for income tax reporting.

When making a purchase with a credit card, the purchaser signs a bill or receipt and receives a copy. A monthly statement for charges made to that card during the month is sent along with the signed receipts. The executive may delegate to the secretary the responsibility for checking the monthly credit card statement. This requires careful inspection of the signature on each receipt and a comparison of the amount on the enclosed receipt with that on the receipt given at the time of purchase.

Filing Paid Bills

A logical system should be set up for filing paid bills, for they provide the key to the canceled checks. If there are only ten to 20 bills each month, the secretary can place all of them in one file folder. If there are many, an

Rub the identification numbers on all credit cards with a heavy pencil. Lay all cards face down on the glass of a copying machine with space between them and make a one-page record. Write under each card on the copy the contact you must notify if the card is lost or stolen. File for ready reference.

alphabetic file may be set up; or a subject file may be used, keeping together all the utility bills, the insurance bills, the bills for supplies, and so on. Whenever a question arises concerning the payment of a bill, the secretary should be able to locate the annotated bill giving the check number and then to get the canceled check from the files for evidence.

Making Payments by Other Forms

Although most payments handled by the secretary will probably be made by ordinary check or electronic fund transfer, one of several special checks or money orders that can be obtained at the bank (usually at a nominal charge) may be used on occasion.

Certified Check. A regular depositor's check that is guaranteed by the bank on which it is drawn is called a certified check. To obtain such a check, the secretary takes the employer's personal check to the bank and asks that it be certified. After seeing that sufficient funds are in the account to cover the check, a bank official stamps on the face of the check "CERTIFIED," adds an official signature, and immediately charges the account with the amount of the check.

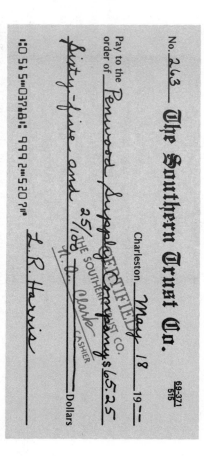

Official Check. A check written by the bank on its own funds is known as an *official check* (sometimes known as a cashier's or treasurer's check). Official checks may be used by depositors and by persons who do not have a checking account. The amount of the check plus a service fee is paid to the bank teller who then writes the check to the specified payee. Recommended practice is to

A certified check is used to accompany orders where cash is required and personal checks will not be accepted. A certified check may be required when bids or contracts are submitted for the purchase of state or federal property, for property settlements, and for other large purchases.

have the official check made payable to the purchaser of the check who must then endorse it in full to the ultimate payee. The canceled check then is proof of payment.

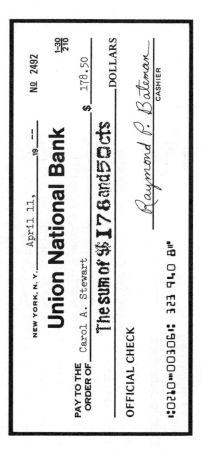

NEW YORK, N.Y. ____April 11,____ 19 __ __   No 2492

Union National Bank   1-30
                                                                 210

PAY TO THE
ORDER OF   Carol A. Stewart $ 178.50

The SUM of $ 178 and 50 cts   DOLLARS

OFFICIAL CHECK

                                        Raymond P. Bateman
                                                   CASHIER

⑈0210⑈00306⑈ 323 940 8⑈

Illus. 21-10
Official check

Bank Draft. A *bank draft* is a check written by the bank on its account in another bank located in the same or in another city. A purchaser pays the bank the exact amount of the draft plus a small fee for issuing the draft. Properly endorsed, the bank draft can then be cashed at the bank on which it is drawn. It differs from an official check only in that the bank draft is drawn by the bank on funds it has on deposit in another bank while an official check is drawn by the cashier on funds in the cashier's own bank.

The bank draft is used primarily for the transfer of large sums from one city to another specific city. The recipient of the draft can then be sure that the funds are in hand before taking certain action, such as releasing a shipment of merchandise, signing a deed, or starting work on a contract.

When there is need to transfer funds quickly, the bank communicates with its corresponding bank in another city directing it to transfer funds to a designated person or company.

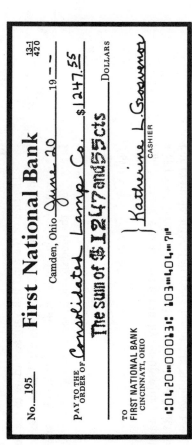

No. ___195___

First National Bank   13-1
                                                                420

Camden, Ohio ___June 20___ 19 __ __

PAY TO THE
ORDER OF   *Consolidated Lamp Co.* $ 1247.55

The Sum of $ 1247 and 55 cts   DOLLARS

TO
FIRST NATIONAL BANK
CINCINNATI, OHIO

                                        Katherine L. Grossman
                                                   CASHIER

⑈0420⑈00013⑈ 103⑈404⑈7⑈

Illus. 21-11
Bank draft

Bank Money Order. A *bank money order* or *registered check*) is similar to that issued by the post office. It is sold primarily to persons without a checking account who wish to send money through the mail. It can normally be cashed at any other bank—at home or abroad; it is negotiable and transferable by endorsement. The amount of a single bank money order generally is not more than $250, but there is no restriction on the number of bank money orders that may be issued to the same person to be sent to the same payee. The purchaser of a bank money order is given a receipt.

The bank money order is more frequently used than an official check or a bank draft when the amount of money transferred is relatively small. It differs from an official check in that the names of both the purchaser and the payee appear on the money order.

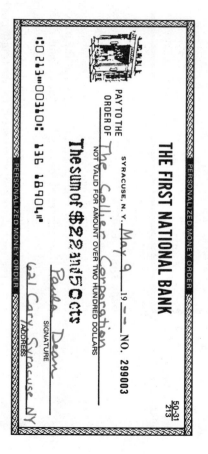

Illus. 21-12
Bank money order

THE PETTY CASH FUND

Payments of small amounts for postage, bus and taxi fares, collect telegrams, donations, delivery charges, and incidental office supplies are frequently made from a *petty cash fund*. In many instances the fund is entrusted to the secretary.

The size of the fund will vary according to the demands made on it. If the fund is large, it should be kept in a locked cash box and stored in the office safe or vault at night. If it is small, it can be kept in a small box or an envelope. In any event, the fund should be locked at night in a desk drawer, a file drawer, or the safe.

Petty Cash Records

The petty cash fund is usually set up with a stipulated amount, such as a $40 fund. Each replenishment of the depleted fund brings it up to $40 again. For example, after disbursements of $38.50 have been made from the fund, there should be $1.50 on hand. The reimbursement check to the petty cash fund is for $38.50. The employer may prefer to write a check for a full $40 each time or only for the amount of the cash disbursements. A purely personal fund can be of any size desired.

Petty Cash Report

In replenishing the petty cash fund, the secretary should prepare a summary report of all payments made.

Each expenditure should have a voucher covering it for an accounting record. If vouchers are used consistently, the total money in the cash box plus the total of the vouchers should equal the amount of the fund.

Keep a record of the receipts and the disbursements. Balance the record whenever the funds get low—or periodically, if the employer prefers. Some of the expenses itemized in a petty cash record may be tax deductible; file the records and examine them at tax return time. Make petty cash entries at once, for they are difficult to recall later. A practical petty cash voucher is shown in Illus. 21-13.

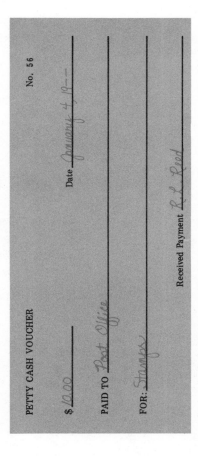

PETTY CASH VOUCHER   No. 56

Date _January 4 19 —_

$ _10.00_ _____

PAID TO _Post Office_ _____

FOR: _Stamps_ _____

Received Payment _R. L. Reed_

Illus. 21-13
Stationery stores sell pads of petty cash vouchers (or receipt forms).

THE TREASURER'S REPORT

The responsibilities of a treasurer will vary in different organizations; but the primary responsibility of this officer is to act as banker. This officer's duties, whether as treasurer of a corporation or a professional organization, are to receive and disburse funds and report the financial condition of an organization.

Prior to preparation of the report, you should file receipts for every payment in chronological order and pay particular attention to accuracy in accounting for money received.

The treasurer's report consists of a statement of the amount of money on hand at the beginning of the period, the amount received during that period, the amount paid out, and the balance at the end of the period.

The report is made for information of the members and should not contain detailed listings of separate payments for the same time. Too much detail is useless and makes the report difficult to understand.

Examples of treasurers' reports are shown in Illus. 21-14 and 21-15. These reports can be varied to fit the needs of most organizations. If the list

TREASURER'S REPORT

As Treasurer of the Oakland Chapter of AMS, I submit the following annual report:

The balance on hand at the beginning of the year was $1,150.76. Money received from all sources totalled $2,450.24. During the year expenses amounted to $1,250.00. The balance at the end of the year was $2,351.00.

An itemized statement of receipts and expenditures is attached.

Respectfully submitted,

Franklin P. Willis
Franklin P. Willis
Treasurer, AMS

Illus. 21-14
Treasurer's report (narrative form)

of receipts and expenditures is extremely long, a separate schedule of these can be attached to the report.

The treasurer's report may or may not be signed, but the treasurer's name should appear somewhere on the report. When the treasurer's report is submitted, it is referred to an auditing committee for examination and verification.

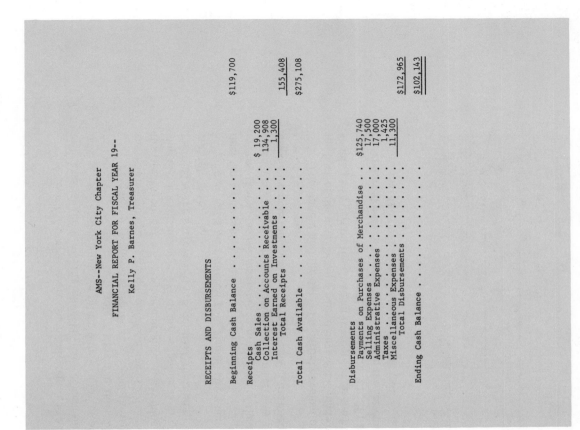

```
                    AMS--New York City Chapter

                 FINANCIAL REPORT FOR FISCAL YEAR 19--

                    Kelly P. Barnes, Treasurer



RECEIPTS AND DISBURSEMENTS

Beginning Cash Balance . . . . . . . . . .                    $119,700

Receipts
    Cash Sales . . . . . . . . . .        $ 19,200
    Collection on Accounts Receivable .    134,908
    Interest Earned on Investments .         1,300
        Total Receipts . . . . . .                            155,408

Total Cash Available . . . . . . .                           $275,108

Disbursements
    Payments on Purchases of Merchandise .  $125,740
    Selling Expenses . . . . . . .           17,500
    Administrative Expenses . . . .          17,000
    Taxes . . . . . . . . . . . .             1,425
    Miscellaneous Expenses . . . .           11,300
        Total Disbursements . . . .                          $172,965

Ending Cash Balance . . . . . . .                            $102,143
```

Illus. 21-15
Treasurer's report (statement form)

CREDIT AND COLLECTION INSTRUMENTS

The secretary's financial responsibilities may extend to such credit and collection instruments as notes, drafts, and certificates of deposit. Because these papers can be transferred or negotiated by the holder to someone else, they (together with checks and other substitutes for cash, such as bank drafts and money orders) are known as *negotiable instruments*.

Notes

A *promissory note*, more commonly referred to as a note, is a promise by one person (known as the *maker*) to pay a certain sum of money on demand or at a fixed or determinable future date to another person or party (known as the *payee*). A promissory note is shown in Illus. 21-16.

Frequently collateral is requested to pledge the payment of a note. In this case the instrument is called a *collateral note*. Collateral can be salable securities (stocks, bonds), a real estate mortgage, or anything that represents ownership and is exchangeable. When an obligation is fully paid, the collateral is returned to the borrower. If it is not paid, the creditor can convert the collateral into cash.

Some notes bear interest paid at maturity when the *face* of the note is due. On a discounted note, the loan-making agency deducts in advance the *interest* (known as the *discount*) from the face of the note. The remainder is called the *proceeds*. For instance, a borrower who receives a three-month discounted note for $1,000 will receive $960 if the discount is computed at the rate of 16 percent.

The amount and the date of a partial payment on a note are written on the back of the note. When a partial payment is made on a note, the secretary should make certain the payment is recorded on the back of the note, for the note is held by the lender until it is paid in full. If payment is made in full, the endorsed note should be turned over to the secretary, for then it is a legal record that the obligation has been discharged.

$ 660.00 _____ Phoenix, Ariz. August 7, 19 —

Four months _____ AFTER DATE _____ PROMISE TO PAY TO

THE ORDER OF James Bailey

Six hundred sixty 00/100 _____ DOLLARS

PAYABLE AT Second National Bank

VALUE RECEIVED WITH INTEREST AT 16 %

No. 13 _____ DUE Dec 7, 19 — _____ Monica Shaw

Illus. 21-16
Promissory note

Commercial Drafts

A draft is a written order by one person to another to pay a sum of money to a third person and is generally used as a collection device. In the commercial draft shown in Illus. 21-17, Ankromm and Son owe $539.62 to King and Wilson, who give this draft to their bank in Topeka for collection. The bank forwards the draft to its correspondent bank in St. Louis, which presents it for payment to Ankromm and Son. When the draft is paid, the proceeds are sent to the Topeka bank and then to King and Wilson.

Illus. 21-17 is a *sight draft*, for it stipulates payment "at sight." A *time draft* is payable at a future time and reads "thirty days after date" or some other stipulated period of time.

$539.62 _____   Topeka, Kansas, January 3, 19 —

_____ At sight _____ PAY TO THE

ORDER OF Ourselves _____

Nine hundred thirty-nine and 62/100 _____ DOLLARS

VALUE RECEIVED AND CHARGE TO ACCOUNT OF

TO C. B. Ankromm & Son   King and Wilson

No. 28   St. Louis, Missouri   L. B. King, Secretary

Illus. 21-17
Sight draft

Drafts are frequently used as a means of collecting before delivery for goods shipped by freight. The merchandise is shipped on a *bill of lading* (a written account of goods shipped) prepared in triplicate and signed by a freight agent. The original bill of lading with the draft attached is sent by the seller to the bank in the town of the buyer. When the merchandise arrives, the purchaser pays the draft at the bank, obtains the bill of lading, and then presents the bill of lading to the carrier (freight company) to obtain possession of the goods held at the local freight office.

Foreign Remittances

When a payment or remittance is to be made to a person or business firm in a foreign country, the following forms of payment may be used.

Currency. United States currency, or foreign currency purchasable through your local bank, may be sent abroad. Most foreign countries regulate the amount of currency that may be so transferred. Your bank will advise you as to the legal restrictions. Currency payments, of course, should be sent by registered mail.

Money Orders. Either your bank, local post office, Western Union, or American Express can arrange for money to be sent abroad for you. The money order is generally payable in the currency of the country to which it is sent. These money orders are speedy but can be expensive.

Foreign Bank Draft. A bank draft payable in a foreign currency can be purchased at your local bank. As with currency, most foreign countries limit the amount of money that may be transferred. The bank will arrange for the transfer of the draft, or the purchaser may transfer it by mail or other means. This method of payment or transfer of funds should be used when large amounts are involved.

SUGGESTED READINGS

Bowden, Elber V. *Revolution in Banking.* Richmond, Va.: Paul F. Dame, Inc., 1980.

Jessup, Paul F. *Modern Bank Management.* St. Paul, Minn.: West Publishing Co., 1980.

Kamerchen, David R. *Money and Banking.* Cincinnati: South-Western Publishing Co., 1980.

QUESTIONS FOR DISCUSSION

1. As Judith Hill was leaving for lunch, her supervisor, Edith Romero, asked her to deposit a customer's check in the bank. Mrs. Romero endorsed the check by writing the company name and her initials on the back of the check. Judith placed the check in her purse. During lunch and before the deposit was made, Judith's purse was either lost or stolen.
   (a) What poor business practices were evident in this situation?
   (b) Upon discovery of the loss, what should Judith do?

2. What precautions or safeguards should a secretary observe in writing checks? Explain why each precaution is important.

3. Many top level executives expect their secretaries to assist them with their personal financial records and banking. This may include writing checks to pay personal bills, keeping the executive's checking account, keeping records of the executive's investments, and so forth. Is this use of company paid secretarial time on the part of the corporate executive ethical? Is it the secretary's responsibility to conform or to refuse?

4. Your job requires that you accept cash payments and make change for customers. If a customer who has made a payment earlier in the day returns to your office telling you that the change received was $10 short, what action should you take before returning the money?

5. What is meant by electronic fund transfers? Why has this service been introduced by banks? What is the bank's responsibility to depositors who use EFT?

6. Your employer asks you to submit a plan for establishing and maintaining a petty cash fund in the office. What major topics or points will you include in your plan?

7. When a bank draft is purchased, it may be drawn in favor of the person or business to whom payment is being made or in favor of the person making the payment and endorsed by the purchaser to the creditor. Which do you think is the better method? Why?

8. Explain what shipping and payment procedure would be used to permit a fruit grower in California to receive payment for a rail shipment of fruit at the time of delivery to an Atlanta dealer. The fruit grower wants to permit the Atlanta dealer to be sure before making payment that the fruit arrives in Atlanta in accordance with the conditions of the order.

9. Retype the following sentences to indicate the writer's intentions as described in the parentheses at the end of each line. Then use the Reference Guide to check your answers.

(a) The enclosed questionnaire requires a ranking of every second question (2, 4, 6, etc.).

(b) These questions cover an endless list of items—materials, equipment, personnel, facilities (sentence unfinished).

(c) Excess (Access) to the highway was limited. (Show a correction.)

(d) We want *fourty* cases of bond paper. (Show a copied error.)

PROBLEMS

1. You bank at the First Trust Company. Your checking account number is 202-8558. On a sheet of paper write the endorsement you should use on your paycheck under each of the following conditions.

(a) You are depositing the check to your account by mail.

(b) You are at the bank and are converting the check to cash.

(c) You wish to transfer the check to Maas Brothers in payment on your charge account.

(d) You wish to have a rubber stamp made so you can deposit checks by stamp endorsement. Specify the endorsement.

2. Your office has a $50 cash fund that is stored in a small metal box and locked in a file cabinet at the end of the day. Entries are made in a petty cash book that contains the following columns: Cash Received, Cash Paid, Postage, Office Supplies, Donations, and Miscellaneous. The largest single expenditure permitted from the fund is $5. Prenumbered petty cash vouchers are used.

Since you are turning the responsibility for the fund over to an assistant, you prepare written directions, specifying details for:

(a) Safekeeping of the fund

(b) Making payments from the fund

(c) Replenishing the fund

Prepare the instructions.

3. You are asked to reconcile your employer's personal bank statement. You are given the canceled checks and the bank statement showing a bank balance on April 30 of $1,146.80. You compare the canceled checks and the deposits with the checkbook.

No. 110	$86.90
No. 115	12.80
No. 120	7.40
No. 121	74.55

A deposit for $586.80 made by mail on April 29 was not listed on the bank statement but was listed on the check stub. No interest is earned on this account. The bank had deducted the following charges from the account:

$15.00   Rent for safe deposit box

$ 8.90   Printing of personalized check-book

The checkbook balance carried forward at the end of Check Stub 121 was $1,575.85. Prepare a typed bank reconciliation statement.

4. Assume that you are completing the year as treasurer of your chapter of Professional Secretaries International. You must submit your annual report to the board of directors at the next meeting. Prepare the report from the following data (use the statement form):

You began the year with $522.42 in the bank. Receipts during the year consisted of $860, dues; dinners, $232; seminar ticket sales, $208.40. Disbursements consisted of: national dues, $516; printing, $46; postage, $7.50; paper and supplies, $25; jewelry, $41.81; dinners, $232; convention expense, $400.40.

5. The following checks, bills, and coins are to be deposited.

Checks

ABA Transit Number	Amount
43-45	$ 225.80
18-24	18.50
63-785	1,346.00
2-77	7.50

Bills

5	$20 bills
12	$10 bills
35	$ 5 bills
16	$ 2 bills
110	$ 1 bills

Coins

21	Halves
42	Quarters
52	Dimes
36	Nickels
76	Pennies

(a) Determine the total amount of the deposit.

(b) Indicate specifically how the checks, bills, and coins in the deposit should be prepared.

Chapter 22

Investments and Insurance

As an experienced secretary or administrative assistant, you may be required to maintain and supervise all records pertaining to securities, real estate, and insurance. These records are vital to the financial health of your company and are needed to determine property values, income and loss for tax purposes, and for settling insurance claims. Unless your employer's holdings are vast enough to justify the employment of a professional portfolio manager, you will need to understand the language of investments and the workings of the financial markets.

SECURITIES

A corporation can obtain capital by issuing stock or by borrowing money through bonds. *Stocks* are evidence of ownership in the corporation; *bonds* are evidence of creditorship—that is, of a loan to the corporation.

Stocks

Ownership in a corporation is divided into units known as *shares of stock.* A stockholder is an owner of one or more shares of stock, and this ownership is shown by a paper known as a *stock certificate.* The stockholder receives *dividends* in return for the investment in the corporation. Dividends are paid from the earnings of the company either in cash or in additional stock referred to as a *stock dividend.*

Kinds of Stock. Stocks fall into two general classes, *common* and *preferred.* Holders of common stock are usually the only ones who have the right to vote in the stockholders' meetings. The rate of dividends paid on common stock is not fixed.

Preferred stock usually has a fixed dividend rate and a preference over common stock in first payment of dividends and in the first distribution of assets if the company is liquidated. Preferred stock may be *cumulative* or *noncumulative.* With cumulative preferred stock, any unpaid preferred stock dividends accumulate and must be paid before any distribution can be made to holders of common stock. Noncumulative preferred stock does not contain a provision to pay dividends in arrears.

Preferred stock also may be *participating* or *nonparticipating*. It is participating only if the stockholder is entitled to share with the holders of common stock in any additional dividend disbursement after an agreed rate is paid on the common stock.

Some preferred stock is *convertible*; that is, the owner has the privilege of converting it into a specified number of shares of common stock at any time. Most preferred stocks are *callable*; that is, they are redeemable at the option of the issuing corporation at the redemption price specified in the stock certificate.

Stock may be *par value* or *no par value*. *Par value* means the value ($1, $5, $10, $100) printed on the stock certificate. This printed value has no significance in determining the market price of the stock, which is measured by the stock's earning power—past, present, and future. Many companies today, therefore, do not print any value on their common stock. It is then known as *no par value* stock.

Stockholders' Meetings. Stockholders' meetings are held annually. Members of the board of directors are elected at this meeting by the stockholders present in person or by proxy. The board, in turn, elects the officers of the company at one of its regular meetings.

A notice of the stockholders' meeting, accompanied by a proxy form and a proxy statement, is sent to each stockholder entitled to vote. The notice gives a description of the business that is to be transacted. A *proxy* is a legal instrument assigning one's voting privilege to a specified person or persons. If directors of the corporation are to be elected, the proxy statement indicates the names of the persons nominated for whom the stockholder's proxy will be voted. The stockholder may vote in person by attending the meeting or vote by mail by signing the proxy.

If the executive usually attends the stockholders' meeting, the date of the meeting should be recorded on the secretary's and executive's calendars. If the meeting is held out of town, the secretary may also be expected to make the travel arrangements. It may also be necessary to request a ticket to the meeting from the broker.

Annual Reports. Most companies send annual and, usually, quarterly, reports to stockholders. Such reports usually include a review of the company's activities and its financial statements.

Some executives study these reports carefully and then keep them. If this is your employer's habit, file them with other such reports or in the separate folder for that stock.

Bonds: Regular or Coupon

A *bond* is a certificate containing a written interest-bearing promise to pay a definite sum of money at a specified time and place. The interest due must be paid to bondholders before stockholders can share in the profits of the company, and for that reason bonds are considered safer investments than stocks. The ownership of bonds does not give the investor voting rights in the company.

There are two general classes of bonds—coupon bonds and registered bonds. *Coupon bonds* are payable to the person holding them. If the bond or the interest coupons are lost or stolen, they can be converted into cash by the holder. Coupon bonds, therefore, present a security responsibility to the secretary who is entrusted to care for them. Bonds should be kept in a safe deposit box.

Coupons are cut from the bonds on or after their due date and presented at a local bank for collection. Some banks make a small charge for this collection service. Bond coupons can be listed on a bank deposit ticket.

Registered bonds are decidedly less responsibility for the secretary. Such bonds are registered by the issuing corporation, which mails the interest and principal payments to the registered holders. If the bond is lost, the owner still receives the payments; and the bond certificate can be replaced.

Corporate bonds are usually issued in $1,000 units. The selling price, however, is quoted as a percentage of the par value. Thus, if a $1,000 bond is said to sell at 97⅝, it actually sells at $976.25, a discount of 2⅜ ($23.75) from its maturity value.

Interest on bonds issued by a municipality, a state, or certain other political subdivisions is exempt from federal income tax. These bonds are known as *tax exempt bonds*.

Stock Market Trading

Most stocks and bonds are purchased and sold through a stock exchange, such as the New York Stock Exchange, the American Stock Exchange (Amex), the Midwest (Chicago) Stock Exchange, the Pacific Coast Stock Exchange, and the Toronto Stock Exchange. A number of small organized exchanges are found in different parts of the country in large cities. On the New York Stock Exchange only securities listed on the exchange are traded; the American Stock Exchange and other exchanges permit trading in unlisted securities.

Some stocks and bonds are purchased in the *over-the-counter market*, which is not a place but a method of doing business; that is, the transaction is handled privately through a bank, a broker, or a securities dealer and does not go through any of the stock exchanges. A buyer or seller of the security is located, and the sale price is arrived at by negotiation. Most over-the-counter transactions are limited to unlisted securities (stocks and bonds of relatively small local companies that are not listed on an exchange).

Buying and selling of stocks and bonds on the stock exchange is handled through a *broker*. Stock certificates sold through brokers are not passed from owner to owner; the seller turns in the certificates to the broker who sends

The best kept secret in the American economy is how it works.

Robert L. Hielbroner

them to the transfer agent for cancellation. The transfer agent employed by the corporation is usually a bank, which keeps a record of the specific owners of stock certificates by names and numbers. The agent fills in a new certificate with the name supplied, writes in the number of shares the certificate represents, has it signed and countersigned, and forwards it to the broker for delivery to the new owner or for deposit to the credit of the owner's account at the brokerage firm. As a service some brokerage firms will hold all stocks and bonds owned by an investor and send a monthly statement or inventory of holdings, listing the amounts received as dividends or interest that month.

The term *mutual funds* is used to identify investment companies (or investment trusts). These investment companies sell shares to individual investors and use capital raised in this manner to purchase additional securities. These stocks and bonds are known as the *portfolio* of the investment company. The individual with limited funds is offered a chance to own (indirectly) an interest in many companies and types of securities because these investments are diversified among bonds, preferred stocks, and common stocks, and also among many corporations.

Mutual funds are available to investors wanting to purchase specialized securities—for instance, insurance, chemicals, or other stocks offering growth possibilities or high income.

Stock Market Information. The financial pages of leading newspapers report daily the stock transactions at major exchanges. The number of shares sold and the selling price for all stocks listed and traded in that day on each exchange are reported. Sales and prices of bonds are also reported in separate tables.

Stocks on which there was no trading—that is, no sales were made of the stock on the day being reported—are printed under a special "Bid and Asked" section. This section gives the closing bid and asking price for the stock. For example, AmFinani bid 42½, asked 44½. This means no American Finance stock was transferred and that there was an offer to buy at 42½ and an offer to sell at 44½.

In addition to the daily stock market report and financial news that appear in the newspapers, information on security prices, trends, and business conditions may be obtained from such sources as the *Wall Street Journal, Business Week, Barron's, Financial World, Forbes, The New York Stock Exchange Monthly Review, American Investor, Moody's Handbooks,* and *The Commercial and Financial Chronicle.* Several large brokerage firms and some banks also publish special reports on securities.

There are a number of investment advisory services. The most widely used services are those offered by Moody's Investors Service and Standard & Poor's Corporation. Most of these organizations analyze the stock market and for a fee provide investors with detailed information on companies, lists of stocks to watch, stocks that represent good buys, and stocks to sell. They also analyze the individual's stock holdings and provide other data that an investor may need. Such service is also available from the broker with whom an investor has an account.

Market Averages. A number of stock averages are designed to serve as barometers of the stock market—that is, to indicate whether the market is rising or falling. Probably the best known are the Standard & Poor's Index and the Dow-Jones Averages. The Standard and Poor's Index is based on the price of 500 stocks and is computed hourly each trading day. The Dow-Jones Averages include four separate averages—one for industrial (stocks of industrial corporations), one for rails, one for utilities, and a composite average of 65 stocks, intended to measure trends in all divisions of the market. The market averages are published in leading newspapers and are reported on television and by radio.

Market Terminology. Certain standard terminology is used in placing orders for the purchase or sale of stock.

Bid and Offer. The price at which a prospective buyer will purchase and the price at which a prospective seller will sell is called *bid and offer*. This quotation involves over-the-counter sales.

Day Order. The *day order* is good only for the day on which it is given; *GTW Order* is "good for this week"; a *GTM Order* is "good this month"; and a *GTC Order* (open order) is "good till canceled."

Discretionary Order. The *discretionary order* gives the broker the privilege of determining when to execute the order.

Ex Dividend. A company declares a dividend to be paid to all stockholders as of a given future date. Stock sold during the intervening period may be sold *ex dividend;* that is, the *seller* and not the *purchaser* of the stock will receive the unpaid declared dividend.

Limited Order. A *limited order* instructs the broker to buy or sell a security at a certain price only. If the transaction cannot be consummated at the designated price, the order is not executed.

Market Order. A *market order* instructs the broker to buy or sell a security at once. No price is indicated and the order is executed "at the market"; that is—at the best price obtainable.

Round and Odd Lots. Most stocks listed on the stock exchanges are traded in 100-share units, called *round lots*. An order for anything less than 100 shares is known as an *odd lot.* A small additional commission charge is made for handling *odd lot* transactions.

Short Sale. The investor sells short—that is, sells securities that he or she does not own in anticipation of buying them later at a lower price. To negotiate the sale, the broker borrows the stocks temporarily.

NEW YORK STOCK EXCHANGE COMPOSITE TRANSACTION*

1		2	3	4	5	6	7	8
19-- High	Low	Stock	P-E Ratio	Sales 100s	High	Low	Close	Net Chg.
55 1/2	37 1/4	AbbtLab 1	15	1357	46 1/4	45 1/2	46	- 3/4
53 1/4	36 1/4	AetnaLf pf 2	..	9	48 1/2	48 3/4	48 1/4	- 1/2
46 3/4	26 3/8	Boeing la	10	645	42	40 1/2	41 3/4	+1 3/8
7	5 1/2	CaroPw 1.72b	8	529	22 1/4	22 3/8	22 1/2	- 5/8
14 1/2	10 1/2	CloroxCo .52i	10	352	12 1/2	12 1/8	13 3/8	+ 1/8

Key*

1 The price range (high and low) of the stock in the year to date.

2 The name of the company and a description of the stock. The rate of annual dividend paid per share based on the last quarterly or semiannual declaration is listed next. Special and extra dividends are not included unless noted by a legend letter following the dividend rate. Check the legend at the end of the stock listing for interpretation of the letters. The following legends explain the letters used in the illustration above.

a—Also extra or extras   b—Annual rate plus stock dividend

i—Declared or paid after stock split   pf—preferred stock

3 Price-Earnings Ratio. The multiple shown in this column is the number of times the annual earnings per share that the current selling price of the stock represents.

4 The number of shares of stock sold during the day (in hundreds)

5 The highest price the stock reached during the day. Stock quotations are in eighths of a point (dollar). Thus 76⅛ means a price of $76.125 per share; 76¼ ($76.25); 76½ ($76.50); 76⅝ ($76.625).

6 The lowest price for which the stock sold during the day

7 The last (closing) price for the stock at the end of the day

8 The difference between today's last price and the last price of yesterday. The plus sign (+) indicates an increase in the last price of today over yesterday's last price; the minus sign (−) indicates a decrease.

Illus. 22-1

The illustration shown above provides the following information: To date this year, Abbott Laboratories common stock has sold at a high of $55.50 (55½) and a low of $37.25 (37¼). The stock paid $1.00 in dividends in the past twelve months. The price-earnings ratio is 15, meaning that the current selling price of the stock is 15 times the annual earnings per share. During the day 135,700 shares were sold. It reached a high of $46.25, and the lowest amount for which it sold was $45.50. The last sale for the day was at $46.00. This was down ¾ (75 cents) from yesterday's closing.

Stock Rights. When a corporation plans to sell additional stock, each existing stockholder may be given a stock warrant indicating the number of shares that the stockholder is entitled to purchase at a designated price, usually slightly below the market. A stockholder who chooses not to exercise stock purchase rights has the option of selling the rights to another party.

Stock Split. A company may split its stock to lower the market price. In a *stock split,* the company issues to each stockholder a specified number of additional shares for each share the stockholder now owns. For example, if it is a three-to-two split, the stockholder will receive three shares in exchange for each two shares owned.

Stop Order. The investor using a *stop order* instructs the broker to buy or sell "at the market" whenever the security moves to a specified quotation (price).

Stop-and-Limit Order. The *stop-and-limit order* sets the price at which the order may be executed after going through the stop. The limit price may be the same or different from the stop price.

Yield. The *yield* is the percentage of return for one year on one share of stock, computed at the current market price or at the price paid by an owner.

A Brokerage Transaction. To understand the procedure of a brokerage transaction, let us follow through a hypothetical one in which the secretary shares responsibility.

1. The purchaser or secretary places an order with the broker to buy 25 shares of U.S. Steel common *at the market* (generally by a telephone call). (The secretary makes a full memorandum of the order: the date, the time, and the order placed. The broker *executes* the order on that date—the trade date.)

2. When the broker has made the purchase through the stock exchange, an invoice called a *confirmation* for the purchase of the stock is sent to the buyer. (The invoice or bill for the purchase or sale of securities is called a *confirmation* because the broker is acting as an agent and is confirming by means of the invoice the instructions received. The confirmation lists the name of the stock and description, the number of shares purchased or sold, the price per share, extension, commission charge, tax, postage, and total. The secretary compares the confirmation with the memorandum of the order to make sure the order has been carried out correctly.)

3. The purchaser or secretary sends a check to the broker by the settlement date (which is five business days after the trade date).

4. The broker arranges for the transfer of the stock to the purchaser. (If the executive has the brokerage company retain the stock, the executive's account will be credited and the stock will be reported on the next monthly inventory statement. The broker may also collect dividends and interest, which will be shown on a detailed monthly report. This simplifies income tax preparation. If the executive retains his or her own stock certificates, the certificate will be forwarded by registered mail. If delivery is made to the executive, the secretary, upon receipt of the stock, records the stock

certificate number on the confirmation and transfers all the information from the confirmation to the executive's permanent record. The secretary may attach the confirmation to the stock certificate or file the confirmation chronologically under the broker's name so that it will be available when the stock is sold. The sales confirmation may be filed with the copy of the confirmation to the executive's income tax return.)

Delivery of Securities. When securities held personally by the executive are sold, they are ordinarily delivered to the broker's office by the secretary or by messenger or are sent by registered mail and insured, accompanied by a covering letter describing the securities in full. Include the owner's name and such items as the company name, amount, and certificate number for each stock certificate or bond enclosed. Request a return receipt.

Records of Securities. One good rule for the secretary to follow in keeping financial records for securities is to use a separate page or card for each lot.

JAN	FEB	MAR	APR	MAY	JUN	JUL	AUG	SEPT	OCT	NOV	DEC
					(Dividend Date)						

STOCK: Detroit Edison, common
BROKER: Merrill Lynch
FILED: Safe deposit box, City National

DIVIDENDS: Mar., June, Sept., Dec.

Date	Certificate Number	How Acquired	No. of Shares	Cost per Share	Total Cost*
1/18/--	H21601	Purchased	100	14 1/2	1,486.00
5/20/--	H29861	New cert. for H21601 after sale 40 shares	60		
12/4/--	H32504	5% stock dividend	3		

*Includes postage, insurance, and commission.

RECORD OF SALES					
Trading Date	Shares Sold	Selling Price	Gross Amount	Int. or State Tax	Commission Paid	Net Amt. Received
5/20/--	40	16 3/4	670.00	2.43	11.25	656.32

Illus. 22-2

A separate record card or sheet for stock transactions should be kept for each lot of securities. Purchases and sales are recorded on the front of the card as illustrated. Dividends are recorded on the ruled form on the back of the card. A metal tab can be used to indicate the dates on which to expect dividends. The card should show where the securities are kept.

Illustration 22-3 shows a convenient form and indicates the information that would be recorded on each group of securities.

The "where kept" notation is important information that should be recorded about any valuable paper. Papers tucked away in unusual safekeeping spots known only to the owner often remain hidden when they are desperately needed in the owner's absence.

Stock Certificate Numbers. When all the stock covered by one certificate is sold, the certificate is surrendered to the broker as part of the sale. When only a portion of a block of stock covered by one certificate is sold, the certificate is also turned over to the broker; but the investor receives a new certificate for a total of the unsold shares. This procedure requires a change in the certificate number on the stock records. For example, in the stock record shown in Illus. 22-2 the 40 shares that were sold were from the block of 100 shares covered by Certificate H21601. This fact was indicated. The new certificate number for the 60 unsold shares is also recorded.

LIST OF SECURITIES (CURRENT AS OF 5/17/--)

Date Purchased	Security	No. of Shares	Price per Share	Total Cost
1/18/82	Johns-Manville	240	13 3/4	$ 3,420.00
8/13/82	Mead Corp. Prf. 2.80	200	20	4,000.00
4/14/82	Pfizer	200	50 3/4	10,150.00

Illus. 22-3
The executive should have at hand a typed alphabetic list of securities. Usually the list is typed in triplicate: one copy for the executive's desk, one for the files, and one for the secretary's records. Each purchase of stock for a given company made on different days or at different prices should be listed separately.

United States Treasury Securities

The United States Treasury raises funds to finance the debt of the federal government by selling securities to the public through twelve Federal Reserve Banks and any of their branches. Treasury securities consist of bills, notes, and bonds.

Treasury securities may be purchased at a Federal Reserve Bank without charge. These banks take applications for securities from the public. Applications must be accompanied by full payment for the securities purchased. For a fee, Treasury securities may also be purchased from commercial banks or other financial institutions or a broker.

Treasury securities are backed by the full taxing power of the federal government; therefore, interest and return of the principal (face value of the security) are guaranteed. Interest earned on Treasury securities is exempt from state and local income taxes but subject to federal income tax.

United States Treasury Bills. A Treasury bill is a short-term security sold at auction on a regular basis by the United States Treasury. Treasury bills mature in 13, 26, or 52 weeks. Bills are sold in minimum amounts of $10,000 and in multiples of $5,000 above the minimum, such as $15,000, $20,000, $25,000, etc. Purchases are limited to $500,000 for each new offering. Purchasers receive a nonnegotiable receipt instead of an engraved certificate at the time the security is issued. This receipt is evidence of a book entry at the Treasury that establishes an account for the purchaser.

Interest is earned by purchasing Treasury bills at a discount and redeeming them at face value. For example, if your employer purchased a 26-week, $10,000 (face value) bill on June 1 for $9,556.36, the discount would be $443.64. A check for the amount of the discount would be mailed by the Federal Reserve Bank on the date the bills are issued.

Thirteen- and 26-week bills are auctioned every week on Monday, and the bills are issued on the following Thursday. Fifty-two week bills are offered and issued only once a month. At maturity the Treasury will mail a check for the face value of the bills unless your employer has requested an automatic reinvestment of the face value at maturity.

Treasury bills are among the best known and most popular short-term investments for corporate and individual investors. Because of their safety, liquidity, and exemption from state and local income taxes, your employer may well include Treasury bills in the company's portfolio of investments.

Treasury Notes and Bonds. Treasury notes and bonds have a longer maturity than Treasury bills. Notes have a fixed maturity of not less than one year and not more than ten years from date of issue. Bonds usually have a fixed maturity of more than ten years. Bonds are available in multiples of $1,000. Previously issued notes must be purchased in the securities market through a broker or commercial bank. Treasury notes and bonds are issued in either bearer or registered forms. If a *registered* security, the owner's name appears on the face of the security; the interest is paid only to the registered owner by a United States Treasury check. Notes or bonds in *bearer* form are payable to anyone who has possession of the securities. If in bearer form, a coupon is clipped from the note or bond for the collection of interest at any commercial bank or Federal Reserve Bank. Treasury notes and bonds pay owners a fixed rate of interest twice a year.

Savings Certificates

Investment certificates provide attractive alternatives for both individual and corporate investors. This form of investment is popular because the certificates are virtually risk free. Investment certificates provide a relatively high rate of return and can be purchased without the payment of fees, commissions, or administrative costs.

Institutions issuing certificates usually require that funds remain on deposit for a designated period of time. A substantial penalty is imposed for early withdrawal of the deposit. Interest is usually paid to the investor quarterly, semiannually, or annually. With some certificates the interest is paid monthly. Once the certificate has been purchased, the rate of interest is fixed until the certificate matures.

A minimum investment ranging from $100 to $10,000 is required by most financial institutions. The minimum required will depend upon the type of certificate and the issuing institution.

Six-Month Money Market Certificates. Commercial banks and savings and loan associations will issue to individuals and organizations six-month (182-day) money market certificates for a minimum deposit of $10,000. The interest rate paid on these certificates fluctuates weekly. These certificates are renewed automatically (unless the bank is notified that the holder does not wish the certificate renewed) at the interest rate in effect at the time of maturity. Interest is paid monthly, quarterly, or at maturity depending on the preference of the holder. Should your employer desire to cash a certificate, a written notice should be given to the bank fifteen days prior to the maturity date in some cases. Some certificates can be cashed at any time without prior notice.

These certificates are *not* negotiable—title cannot be transferred to another person. Lost certificates will be replaced if satisfactory proof of ownership can be provided. The holder of a certificate agrees to keep funds on deposit for a stated period of time. A certificate may, however, be redeemed prior to the maturity date; but a portion of the interest earned must be forfeited unless the holder has died or has been declared mentally incompetent.

Negotiable Certificates of Deposit (CD's). A negotiable certificate of deposit (CD) is a marketable receipt (can be sold to others) for funds that have been deposited in a bank for a specified time. Negotiable CD's are not the same as ordinary passbook savings accounts or time deposits. Negotiable CD's are offered by banks in the major money centers of the country in denominations ranging from $25,000 to $10,000,000. The original maturity period can range from one to eighteen months, but most have a maturity date of four months or less. Income from negotiable CD's is taxable at all levels of government; the rate of return is similar to that of Treasury bills. When the certificate matures, the owner receives the full amount deposited plus earned interest. Negotiable CD's may be obtained from financial institutions without the cost of a commission. These certificates are low risk, short term, and readily convertible to cash.

REAL ESTATE

A secretary may be commissioned to do all or any of the tasks related to the executive's real estate activities—to care for the valuable papers necessary to real estate transactions, to do the banking work, and to keep simple, complete records of income and expenses.

Buying Property

When real property is purchased, the title of ownership is transferred by means of a properly executed written instrument known as a *deed.*

Deeds. There are two types of deeds—warranty deeds and quit-claim deeds. In a *warranty deed* the grantor or seller warrants that he or she is the true and lawful owner with full power to convey the property and that the title is free, clear, and unencumbered. In a *quitclaim deed,* the grantor quits claim to the property; that is, the grantor relinquishes claim but does not warrant or guarantee the title.

A deed must be signed, witnessed, and acknowledged before a notary public. It should be *recorded*—that is, entered on public record at the courthouse in the county where the property is located. Deeds, mortgages, and leases are valuable legal documents and should be kept in a bank safe deposit box or in a fireproof vault or safe.

Legal Terms. Other legal terms frequently used when the title to real estate is transferred are:

1. *Amortization*—a mortgage or loan repayment plan that permits the borrower to retire the principal of the loan through regular payments at stated intervals

2. *Appurtenances*—rights of way or other types of easements that are properly used with the land, the title to which passes with the land

3. *Easements*—privileges regarding a special use of another person's property, such as right of way to pass over the land, to use a driveway, or to fish in a stream

4. *Fixtures*—those articles that are permanently attached to real estate, such as buildings, fences, and electrical wiring in a building.

5. *Foreclosure proceedings*—legal process used to satisfy the claim of the lender in case of default in payment of interest or principal on a mortgage

6. *Junior (second) mortgage*—a mortgage that is subordinate to a prior mortgage

7. *Land contract*—a method of payment for property whereby the buyer makes a small down payment and agrees to pay additional amounts at intervals (The buyer does not get a deed to the property until a substantial amount of the price of the property is paid.)

8. *Mortgage*—a formal written contract that transfers interest in property as security for the payment of the debt (Mortgages must be signed, witnessed, and recorded in the public records the same as a deed. The law considers the mortgagor [the borrower] as owner of the property during the period of the loan.)

9. *Option*—an agreement under which an owner of property gives another person the right to buy the property at a fixed price within a specified time.

Property Records

Permanent records of property owned are kept for several reasons: to determine the value of the property, to show the outstanding debt, to use in tax reporting, and to use as a basis for setting a satisfactory selling price.

A separate record should be kept for each piece of property owned and should include information similar to that shown in Illus. 24-4.

Illus. 22-4
Keep a property record similar to this form for each piece of property. At the end of each year all the income and expenses related to each piece of property can be conveniently organized for preparation of the income tax report.

Type and Location of Property	Commercial Property 127 North Webster Avenue Tucson, AZ 85715-8635		
Title in Name of:	Robert C. and Mary K. Folley		
Date Acquired:	2/21/--	Purchase Price:	$97,500
Mortgage(s):	Main Savings and Loan First Federal Bank		$40,000 5,000
Assessed Evaluation for Taxes:	$59,000		
Remarks:	Deed is filed in home safe		

Income from Rentals			Mortgage Payments Int. and Princ.			Expenses		
Date	Item	Amount	Date	Item	Amount	Date	Item	Amount
2/10	Rent	510.00	2/28	I.+P.	310.00	3/10	Taxes	500.00
3/10	Rent	510.00	3/31	I.+P.	310.00	3/10	Water	48.20
4/10	Rent	510.00	4/30	I.+P.	310.00	4/16	Plumb.	46.85

Investment Property. Property held for rental income or to be sold at a hoped-for profit is *investment property.* The secretary's employer may own several such pieces, or the business may be employed to manage such property for other owners, for which a service fee is received. Managing property means negotiating with the tenants, keeping the building in repair, and handling certain of the finances—collecting rents, paying expenses, and so on.

Tenants may be required to sign *leases* prepared by the secretary. Printed lease forms are available in stationery or legal supply stores. The pertinent facts must be filled in on the form and the signatures affixed. These forms should be checked with an attorney to be certain they set forth the exact conditions desired.

The secretary keeps detailed records of income and expenses on each piece of investment property because all income must be reported and all expenses are deductible on tax returns.

To keep accurate data on each unit, the secretary can follow the plan suggested here.

1. Set up an individual file folder for each rental unit, such as each suite of offices, each apartment in a building, or each house. Identify each unit on

APARTMENT LEASE

Date _February 10, 19—_

PARTIES
hereby leases to _Julia Diaz_ (hereinafter referred to as Lessor)
to as Lessee) the following described property: _Henry Nichols_ (hereinafter referred

PREMISES
Apartment No. _3_ at _301 Park Place_
in _Sussex, WI._ for use by resident as a private residence only.

TERM
This lease is for a term commencing on the _1_ day of _February_, 19—_,
19_—_, and ending on the last calendar day _March_.

AUTOMATIC
RENEWAL
If Lessee, or Lessor, desires that this lease terminate at the
expiration of its term, he or she must give to the other party
written notice at least 30 days prior to that date. Failure of
either party to give this required notice will automatically renew
this lease and all the terms thereof except that the term of the
lease will be for one month. This provision is a continuing one
and will apply at the expiration of the original term and at the
expiration of each subsequent term.

RENT
This lease is made for and in consideration of a monthly rental
of _($450) Four Hundred Fifty_ Dollars per month payable in
advance on or before the 1st day of each month at _504 Town_
Line Road.
If the rent is paid by the 5th of the
month, Lessee shall be entitled to a deduction of _($10) Ten_
Dollars per month or a net rental of _($440) Four Hundred Forty_ Dollars
per month; provided however that any monthly rental payment not received by the 5th of the month shall be considered delinquent. If
Lessee pays by check and said check is not honored on presentation
for any reason whatsoever, Lessee agrees to pay an additional sum
of $10.00 as a penalty.
In the event that the rent is not paid by the 10th of the month,
Lessee shall be deemed to be in default; and Lessor shall have the
option to cancel this lease effective on midnight of the 14th of
the month. On or before the termination date, Lessor shall deliver
written notice of Lessor's election to cancel this lease to Lessee's
premises.
Lessor acknowledges receipt from Lessee of the sum of _($440) Four_
Hundred Forty Dollars which is prorated rental for _30_ days
from the date of commencement of this lease to the first day of the
following month.

SECURITY
DEPOSIT
Upon execution of this lease contract, Lessee agrees to deposit
with Lessor, the receipt of which is hereby acknowledged, the sum
of _$(200) Two Hundred_ Dollars. This deposit, which
is noninterest bearing, is to be held by Lessor as security for
the full and faithful performance of all the terms and conditions
of this lease. This security deposit is not an advance rental and
Lessee may not deduct any portion of the deposit from rent due to
Lessor. This security deposit is not to be considered liquidated
damages. In the event of forfeiture of the security deposit due
to Lessee's failure to fully and faithfully perform all the terms
and conditions of the lease, Lessor retains all of his or her other
rights and remedies. Lessee does not have the right to cancel this
lease and avoid his or her obligations thereunder by forfeiting the
said security deposit. Deposit refund will be mailed.

Lessee shall be entitled to return of the said security deposit within 30 days after the premises have been vacated and inspected by Lessor provided said lease premises are returned to Lessor in as good condition as they were at the time Lessee first occupied same, subject only to normal wear and tear and after all keys are surrendered to Lessor. Lessor agrees to deliver the premises broom clean and free of trash at the beginning of this lease and Lessee agrees to return same in like condition at the termination of the lease.

Notwithstanding any other provisions expressed or implied herein, it is specifically understood and agreed that the entire security deposit aforesaid shall be automatically forfeited as liquidated damages should Lessee vacate or abandon the premises before the expiration of this lease, except where such abandonment occurs during the last month of the term of the lease, Lessee has paid all rent covering the entire term and either party has given the other timely written notice that this lease will not be renewed under its renewal provisions.

OCCUPANTS

The leased premises shall be occupied by the following persons only: _Henry Nichols_

PETS

No pets allowed to live on the premises at any time. However, this provision shall not preclude Lessor for modifying any lease to allow pets by mutual written agreement between Lessor and Lessee.

SUBLEASE

Lessee is not permitted to post any "For Rent" signs, rent, sublet or grant use or possession of the leased premises without the written consent of Lessor and then only in accordance with this lease.

DEFAULT OR ABANDONMENT

Should the Lessee fail to pay the rent or any other charges arising under this lease promptly as stipulated, should the premises be abandoned by Lessee or should Lessee begin to remove furniture or any substantial portion of Lessee's personal property to the detriment of Lessor's lien, or should voluntary or involuntary bankruptcy proceedings be commended by or against Lessee, or should Lessee make an assignment for the benefit of creditors, then in any of said events Lessee shall be ipso facto in default and the rent for the whole of the expired term of the lease together with the attorney's fees shall immediately become due. In the event of such cancellation and eviction, Lessee is obligated to pay any and all rent due and owing through the last day said premises are occupied.

In the event that during the term of this lease, or any renewal hereof, either the real estate taxes or the utility costs, or both, should increase above the amount being paid on the leased premises at the inception of this lease, the Lessee agrees to pay his or her proportionate share of such increase and any successive increases. Such payment or payments by Lessee shall be due monthly as increased rent throughout the remainder of Lessee's occupancy; and all such sums may be withheld from Lessee's security deposit if not fully paid at the time Lessee vacates the premises. A 30 day notice will be given to Lessee before any increase is made.

OTHER CONDITIONS

A temporary visitor is one who inhabits the property for no more than ten (10) days.

Executed in duplicate
at _301 Park Place_
this _10_ day of _February_, 19_____

_____
Julia Diaz
Lessor
Henry Nichols
Lessee

the file folder by number or address. (An alphabetic index of tenants' names giving their rental location will serve as a helpful cross-reference.) File in this folder everything pertaining to the unit of rental, such as correspondence, the lease, bills for repairs or improvements, lists of any special fixtures or furniture provided, rental amount.

2. Use a miscellaneous folder (or folders) for the building in general to take care of the items that cannot be charged to a specific rental unit, such as janitorial service, repairs to the exterior of the building or corridors, taxes, and other such items.

The record of all receipts and expenses paid can be written right on each folder, or on a card or sheet filed inside each folder. Preferably such records are kept on separate sheets in a loose-leaf book where the chance of their being lost is considerably reduced.

The banking of money collected from investment property and the payment of bills for such property should be handled carefully. It is extremely important that the deposit slips be completed so that every deposit can be identified and that every check stub be labeled to be charged against a specific rental unit or building.

Personal Property Records. To provide necessary information in event of death or other contingency the secretary is often asked to keep a file of the executive's personal property, such as an inventory of household goods, a description and the location of family jewels and heirlooms, insurance policies, and the names and addresses of certain key people involved in the executive's personal affairs. Such information and materials should be placed in sealed envelopes, labeled, and kept in a safe deposit box or fireproof office safe.

Tickler Card File

There are many recurring expenses on property, such as mortgage payments (usually due monthly), tax payments (due annually or semiannually), and insurance premiums (due annually). On income property the rent is usually due on a certain day each month. To make sure that income is received when due and that recurring expenses are paid on time, a tickler card should be prepared for each item so that the card can be used continually—refiled under the next pertinent date after it comes to the front on the current reminder date.

In addition to interest and mortgage payments, use tickler cards for

Taxes—Indicate for each kind of tax payment: kind of tax, payment date, amount, to whom to make the check payable, where to send the check, and whether or not a return must accompany the payment.

Insurance Premiums—See Illus. 22-8, page 560, for information to be shown.

Rent Receipts—For each rental unit show location, amount of rent, name and mailing address of tenant, and any special information regarding collection or interpretation of rent payment.

```
File date:    12th of each month

Mortgage payment due:   15th of each month
(Mail check no later than the 12th)

Duplex, 906 Seneca Street

Amount of check:   $225.00

Make check to:   Estate of Frank Foster
Send check to:   Willis and Thompson
                 148 Baker Bldg.
                 110 W. 7th Street
                 Fort Worth, TX  76102-6537

Final payment date:   April 15, 1988
```

Illus. 22-6
The tickler card for a monthly mortgage payment identifies the property, shows the file date, due date, amount of payment, to whom payment is to be made, and where the check is to be sent.

Source Materials

The employer who has extensive real estate holdings or is engaged in the real estate business may subscribe to an information service, such as the *Prentice-Hall Real Estate Service*. There are also a number of periodicals that specialize in providing current information on real estate, a few of which are *Real Estate Weekly, Building and Realty Record, National Real Estate Investor, Appraisal Journal, Journal of Property Management,* and *Construction Labor Report.*

INSURANCE

Insurance can be grouped into three general classes—personal, property, and liability. *Personal insurance* includes the many kinds of life, accident, and health insurance. *Property insurance* covers loss from impairment or destruction of property, such as fire, earthquake, burglary, and automobile collision. *Liability insurance* protects the insured against losses resulting from injury to another, such as public liability, workers' compensation, and employer's liability.

The individual or business purchasing the insurance is called the *policyholder.* The *policy* is the written contract that exists between the policyholder and the insurance company. The insurance company may be referred to as the insurer or the *underwriter.* The policyholder makes periodic payments to the insurance company for the policy. These payments are called insurance *premiums.*

In correspondence, be sure to include the *policy number*. If the correspondence relates to a claim, include the *claim number* assigned by the insurance company.

The secretary has three responsibilities regarding insurance; namely, to see that the premiums are paid promptly so that there will be no lapse in protection, to keep summary records on each kind of insurance for the executive's information, and to store the policies and related correspondence in a safe place.

Premium Payments and Renewals

Insurance premiums are payable in advance. Those on property insurance are usually paid annually or for a term of three or five years. Premiums on life insurance may be paid annually or in monthly, quarterly, or semiannual installments.

Many life insurance policies allow a 28- to 31-day grace period in making premium payments. If the premium is due and payable on August 16, payment of the premium may be made any time before September 16. If the premium notice does not specify the grace period, the secretary should inquire from the insurance company if a grace period is allowed.

Checks in payment of premiums must be drawn in sufficient time to have them signed and sent to the insurance company or agent before the expiration date. It is the secretary's responsibility to avoid any insurance policy lapse caused by failure to make a premium payment.

In addition to seeing that premiums are paid, the secretary should also arrange for the cancellation of policies when the protection is no longer needed. A policy can be canceled by telling the insurance company or agent of the cancellation and returning the policy. The premium for the unexpired period of the policy is refundable. The secretary should place a follow-up in the tickler file to check on the receipt of the premium refund.

Insurance Records

A beginning secretary may be fortunate enough to inherit a summary record of the employer's personal insurance commitments. More likely, however, no records will be available, and it will be necessary to compile the information from insurance policies on file in the office and from notices of premiums due as they are received in the mail.

Methods of keeping insurance records vary, but in general the records consist of an insurance register and a premium payment reminder, usually in the form of a tickler card. The register should contain information similar to that shown in Illus. 22-7, page 559. Some secretaries record insurance policies on separate sheets in a small loose-leaf notebook. Others prefer to use a separate register for each type of insurance: life, property, and liability. Certainly the executive's personal insurance and that of the business or office should be kept in separate registers.

TYPES OF INSURANCE

Personal Insurance—Protects against the results of illness, accident, and loss of income because of illness, accident, or death.

Life: Endowment   Health: Hospital care
        Limited payment life   Medical fees
        Ordinary life   Surgical fees
        Term   Loss of income

Property Insurance—Protects from financial loss resulting from damage to insured's property

Automobile collision   Marine: Barratry
Burglary and employee theft   Burning
Fire   Collision
Fire—Extended coverage (windstorm, lightning,   Mutiny
    riot, strike violence, smoke damage, falling air-   Piracy
    craft and vehicle damage, most explosions)   Sinking
Plate glass   Standing
Standard boiler
Valuable papers
Vandalism

Liability Insurance (Casualty)—Protects against claim of other people if insured
person causes injury or property damage to others

Automobile liability   Premise and operations liability
Bailee insurance   Public liability
Elevator insurance   Product insurance
Libel and slander   Workers' compensation

Credit, Fidelity, and Surety Insurance—Protects against losses from
Bad accounts (Credit)   Employee embezzlement
Title (Surety)   (Fidelity)

Illus. 22-7
Columns to provide appropriate information can be added to the insurance register as needed. When a policy expires, draw a line through the description to indicate that the policy is no longer in force.

INSURANCE REGISTER

Company and Name of Agent	Policy No.	Type and Amount	Date Issued	Amt. of Premium	Date Due	Grace Period
N.Y. LIFE V. Getty	29 22 84	Ord. Life on Mr. B. $50,000	3/2/55	$563.00 Semi-an	2/2 8/2	30-day
N.Y. LIFE V. Getty	37 86 21	Term $25,000 on Mrs. B.	1/9/68	$107.25 Annual	5/6	30-day
CONN. GEN. T. Ramsey	H261 162	Fire on household goods $25,000	1/12/72	$249 Annual	12/12	

Use a separate tickler card for each policy, and file the cards according to premium payment date. This helps to avoid the lapse of a policy or a penalty for late payment of a premium. Illus. 22-8, shows an insurance index card which provides all the information necessary.

```
File date:   December 26, 19--

Expiration date: January 4 each year

Type:  Fire insurance on office furniture

Amount: $15,000 With:  Mutual Insurance Co.
                       5352 First St., City

Policy No. X438832
Date of issue: January 5 each year
Premium: $117.20
Policy filed:  First National Bank
```

Illus. 22-8
File an index card for each insurance policy in a tickler file. This provides a convenient record of the insurance and serves as a reminder notice for renewals and premium payments.

Property Inventory

The importance of keeping an up-to-date property inventory can be fully appreciated only by someone who has experienced a fire or burglary loss. To present a claim for a loss, the insured must "furnish a complete inventory of the destroyed, lost, damaged, and undamaged property with cost and actual cash value." This is difficult to do after the loss has taken place. A property inventory also serves a second important purpose. It shows how much insurance should be carried. Property values change; and unless the inventory is updated periodically, property may be overinsured or underinsured.

The secretary in a small office can and should assume the responsibility for compiling an inventory of the furniture and equipment in the office. In addition, the executive should be encouraged to provide details for an inventory of the furniture and valuables at home. All inventories should be periodically updated.

Storage of Policies and Inventory Records

Since insurance policies must be examined occasionally for data on coverage, beneficiaries, rates, cash value, endorsements, and the like, the policies should be readily available—but in a safe place.

If the policies are kept in a file, you may find it convenient to remove them from their protective envelopes and place each policy in a separate folder. Identify the front of the folder with the name, address, and telephone number of the agent, and the policy number. Such a plan makes it possible to file with each policy any important correspondence, itemized lists of property covered, endorsements, and other pertinent data that affect the conditions of the insurance contract.

Since an insurance policy *is* a contract, you can discard it when it has expired and keep your file cleared. First, however, you should call or write the agent to make certain that no claim on the policy is pending and that it has no continuing value.

Fidelity Bonds

A *fidelity bond* is insurance on an employee's honesty. Most employers carry such insurance on those employees who handle large sums of money. The bonding company investigates the employee's character and the supervisory and control methods in force in the employer's business. No bond is sold if the applicant's character is questionable or if office conditions make it easy to embezzle company funds.

Blanket fidelity bonds covering the entire personnel are bought by banks and other financial institutions. They protect against losses by embezzlement, robbery, forgery, and so on.

To be asked to take out a fidelity bond is no reflection on your character. Actually it indicates that you are considered competent to be entrusted with company funds.

Action in Emergency

When disaster strikes, you will have an opportunity to prove that you are a cool-headed, responsible person who can think and act quickly. Others may be so excited and involved in the emergency that they fail to think of procedures. Insurance companies make these suggestions:

After a fire, as soon as the situation is under control, notify the insurance company immediately by phone and confirm the call by letter. The insurance company may be able to have an inspector on the scene to witness the damage and save a lot of paperwork later on.

Immediately report to the police any losses by theft.

Keep accurate and separate records for cleanup, repairs, and charges made by outside contractors. The items are all part of the insurance claim.

When an accident occurs, interview witnesses on the spot. Signed statements carry much weight and refresh memories in settling claims. If possible, take pictures at the scene.

When insurance policies are stored in the office, there is always the possibility of their loss by fire. As a precaution, type a list of the policy numbers, insuring company, coverage, and amount. Your employer should store this list in a safe at home. Thus, if the office records are destroyed, they can be more readily reconstructed.

WHERE-KEPT FILE

In the event of the sudden death of an executive, the family will need immediately certain financial information. The secretary can be of great assistance in such an emergency if a folder containing up-to-date information has been maintained. The following information might be included:

Bank Accounts—the name and address of each bank in which an account is kept, the type of account, the exact name of account, and the name of bank contact (if the executive has one)

Birth Certificate—where it can be found

Business Interests—list of the executive's business interests

Credit Cards—record of names and account numbers

Income Tax Record—where past returns are filed; the name and address of the tax consultant

Insurance Policies—location of insurance records (If these records do not contain detailed information on life, health and accident, hospitalization, and medical insurance policies, the information should be placed in the folder. The name and address of the insurance adviser should be filed also.)

Real Estate Investments—location of detailed property records

Passport—where it can be found

Safe-Deposit Box—the name of the bank, the box number, and location of key

Social Security—the social security number

Stocks and Bonds—location of detailed investment records

Tax Accountant—name

Will—location of the original and copies of the will; date of the latest will; name of attorney who prepared the will; executor's name and address

ADMINISTRATIVE FUNCTIONS

The secretary may be expected to perform a number of administrative functions related to the property, investments, and insurance coverage of the company and of the executive. The college-trained secretary has a background of courses in economics, accounting, business law, and, in some cases, real estate and insurance. All these courses contribute to your competency. As an administrative assistant you may be asked to

1. Prepare an investment prospectus on stocks that are under consideration for investment. This activity involves checking investment service reports for gathering data on products, past performance, background of company officials, forecasts for the area and for the company, comparison with competitors, and so forth. Such data are available in the business section of a public library and in special libraries.

2. Update the investment portfolio of the company or of the executive. The updating process involves analyzing (1) the rate of yield on each invest- ment, (2) profit trends, and (3) the outlook for the company. For some

classes of stock, charts showing the fluctuations in the market may need to be prepared and updated at regular intervals.

3. Supervise and follow through on repairs and improvements made to investment property. Frequent visits to the location of the property and careful study of the repair or construction contract are necessary.

4. Handle the details related to processing the sale or purchase of real estate. This activity involves such details as having the title searched for liens and mortgages, obtaining title insurance, and processing and recording the deed.

5. Review at regular intervals the insurance policies in force and arrange for revision in insurance coverage in keeping with changing values of the property. The responsibility includes canceling unneeded policies and being alert to new insurance needs.

6. Process an insurance claim. This responsibility involves compiling the records necessary to support a claim—cost records, appraisal of loss, and proof of loss.

SUGGESTED READINGS

Dow-Jones Educational Service Bureau, P.O. Box 300, Princeton, N.J. 08540, provides various publications that are available to educators. Write for information.

Greene, Mark R. *Risk and Insurance.* Cincinnati: South-Western Publishing Co., 1981.

Tucker, James F. *Buying Treasury Securities at Federal Reserve Banks.* Richmond, Va.: Federal Reserve Bank of Richmond, January, 1980.

Unger, Maurice A., and Ronald W. Melicher. *Real Estate Finance.* Cincinnati: South-Western Publishing Co., 1978.

The *Wall Street Journal, The National Observer, Barron's,* and *Changing Times* all contain articles of significance to investors.

QUESTIONS FOR DISCUSSION

1. A secretary whose employer invests in securities must know a number of stock market terms. What does each of the following terms mean? (Refer to outside sources for the meanings of terms with which you are not familiar.)

bear market	market value
blue-chip stocks	mutual fund
book value	option
bull market	over-the-counter
ex dividend	rails
growth stocks	sleeper
industrials	stock dividend
investment companies	stock split
margin	utilities

2. If a stockholder is dissatisfied with the way a corporation is being managed, what can he or she do?

3. Assume that you are treasurer of a professional organization that has accumulated $18,000 in a checking account. This amount represents a ten-year surplus of funds. Keep in mind that approximately $5,300 is required for annual operation, that in 18 months your chapter will host the national convention, and that funds must be withdrawn in advance to meet convention expenses. What would you suggest to the board of directors as a good investment?

4. Cite three major reasons for investing in Treasury bills rather than in common stocks.

5. Your employer is considering an investment in Xerox Corporation. You are asked to compile a report on the stock. What type of information would you include in the report? Indicate your information sources.

6. In addition to stock prices, what information does the financial section of the newspaper contain? Would you recommend that the secretary read this section regularly?

7. In the event of fire or theft, all financial records (including stock certificates, bonds, and insurance policies) may be lost. What precautions should a secretary take or suggest to the employer that will minimize such losses?

8. An owner of a small grocery store with six employees wishes to be protected against all possible insurable losses. Which types of insurance should be obtained? Include the building in which the store is located.

9. When the employer's automobile was involved in an accident, it was discovered that the insurance policy had lapsed because of nonpayment of premiums. The employer was extremely critical of the secretary. The secretary's defense was that the premium notices and follow-ups had been placed on the employer's desk. Furthermore, this was personal business and the employer's failure to act was not the secretary's responsibility. Do you agree with the secretary's position?

10. Consult the Reference Guide to verify your answers to the following.
  (a) Write the following years in Roman numerals: 1930, 1978, 2000, current year.
  (b) Convert these Roman numerals to Arabic numbers: CM; X; MMIX.
  (c) Show a shorter way to write the following amounts: $5,800,000; 7,600,000,000.

PROBLEMS

1. Your employer owns all the following securities:

200 shares . . . American Natural Resources, common, (ANatR)

100 shares . . . Coca Cola, common (CocaCol)

75 shares . . . Consolidated Edison, 5% preferred, (ConE pf 5)

5 bonds . . . New York Telephone, (NY Tel 4½s 91)

200 shares . . . Standard Oil of Indiana (StOInd)

500 shares . . . Union Oil of
Canada
(Union Oil)

(a) Prepare a report showing the current market value of your employer's security holdings. (Use the closing price of the security on the date of the report.)

(b) Your employer purchased the shares of American Natural Resources stock at 25. A quarterly dividend of 66 cents per share is declared. Determine the rate of yield that is received on the investment and the rate of yield at the current market price.

2. Your employer has investments in stock and carries several insurance policies. The insurance policies are on the employer's spouse, son, home, and automobile. You decide to set up a tickler file to assist you in keeping track of the securities and the insurance premiums and policies. Make a list of the type of information you would include on the card about each (a) security, (b) insurance policy.

3. Your employer owns a professional building that cost $220,000. The building houses 18 offices. Six offices rent for $600 a month, ten for $500, and the remaining two for $350 a month. All the offices were rented throughout the year except four of the $600 offices, which were vacant three months while being redecorated. The following expenses were incurred during the year in operating the building: management fee, 6% of the rental income; janitorial and maintenance service, $980 a month; supplies, $2,400; utilities, $4,400; taxes, $9,860; repairs, $13,835; redecorating, $11,250; and miscellaneous expenses, $975. Prepare a report showing the income, expenses, and net income for the year and the annual percentage of return on the investment in the building.

4. On a sheet of paper construct a form that will be convenient for recording the income as received and the expenses as paid out during the year for the professional building described in Problem 3.

Chapter 23

Payroll and Tax Records

Because every employee expects to receive pay at regular intervals, payroll functions must be performed. Time cards must be maintained, earnings and deductions computed, tax reports submitted, and payroll checks prepared. Payroll records must also be kept to comply with federal and state legislation; therefore, extreme accuracy is required of the secretary who has payroll responsibilities.

Payroll work in many firms has been computerized, and in large companies a special payroll department will handle much of the work. Nevertheless, the secretary is often responsible for input to the payroll system. The extent of your responsibilities for payroll work will, therefore, depend on the size and function of the office in which you work.

Whether or not your work includes payroll responsibilities, your employer will depend on you to assist in preparing annual income tax returns. This does not mean that you will be expected to be a tax expert. It does mean, however, that throughout the year you should collect pertinent income tax data so that they will be readily available at tax time. Your understanding of income tax procedures and knowledge of those items that will reduce your employer's taxes will be of invaluable assistance to the busy executive.

PAYROLL PROCEDURES

One of the most demanding responsibilities of the secretary in charge of payroll is the maintenance of essential pay records. These records are necessary to determine pensions, vacations, seniority, eligibility for company benefits, wage and salary increases, promotions, and employment references on former employees. They also enable the executive to determine when to hold performance reviews and to decide which employees to transfer or dismiss. In addition to maintaining these vital records, you should understand the forms and reports required by the Federal Insurance Contribution (Social Security) and Fair Labor Standards Acts as well as pertinent local legislation.

It is the secretary's responsibility to keep all payroll information confidential. From the calculation of the first time card to the writing of the payroll check, payroll facts must be protected. Computation sheets, carbon paper, and one-use typewriter ribbons must be destroyed to keep the inquisitive person from gaining payroll information that could damage morale. No matter how tempting, the professional secretary never discusses payroll information and is adept at dealing with co-workers who persist in inquiring about the income of others. If interrupted while working on the payroll, never leave your desk until you have placed all confidential information in a drawer and locked it.

Social Security

Under the social security system most business, farm, and household employees and self-employed persons are provided an income in old age and survivor benefits in event of death. Social security also provides a nationwide system of unemployment insurance and hospital and medical insurance benefits (known as Medicare) for persons of age 65 or over.

To pay most of these social security benefits, both employees and employers contribute an equal amount. Medical insurance (for persons of age 65 or over) is optional and is financed jointly by contributions from the retired insured person and also from the federal government.

Social Security Numbers. Each employer and employee must obtain a social security number for identification in the government records. For the employer the number is called an *identification number.*

To obtain a number, file an application form with the nearest social security office or post office. You will receive a card stamped with your number. If the card is lost, a duplicate can be obtained. If you change your name or need to make other changes, report them to the Social Security Administration. The secretary may find it convenient to have the following social security forms on hand:

Application for a Social Security Number (or Replacement of Lost Card)

Request for Change in Social Security Records

Request for Statement of Earnings

The Social Security Administration recommends that every three years each employee request a statement of earnings to make sure that individual earnings have been reported properly. This information can be obtained by sending a signed letter with your date of birth and social security number or Form OAR-7004 to SOCIAL SECURITY ADMINISTRATION, P.O. Box 57, Baltimore, MD 21203.

FICA Tax Deductions. Under the Social Security Act both the employer and employee pay *FICA* (Federal Insurance Contribution Act) *taxes* at the same rate. The present tax rates and those scheduled for the future (subject to change by Congress) are shown below.

PRESENT AND FUTURE FICA TAX RATES (Percentages)

Year	Employee	Employer	Self-Employed	Wage Base*
1982	6.70	6.70	9.35	$32,400
1983	6.70	6.70	9.35	Automatic
1984	6.70	6.70	9.35	cost of living
1985	7.05	7.05	9.90	adjustments in
1986	7.15	7.15	10.00	the wage base.

*Maximum earnings subject to FICA tax.

The FICA tax is deducted from the employee's wage each payday; these amounts are accumulated and forwarded together with the employer's FICA tax payment to the Internal Revenue Service Center for the region. To illustrate, assume that an employee earns $200 a week and is paid at the end of each week. At the rate of 6.70 percent, $13.40 is deducted for the employee's FICA tax and the employer contributes an equal amount. At the end of the quarter (13 weeks) the employer must remit to the government a total of $348.40.

Self-employed persons (such as farmers, architects, and contractors) are required to pay at a rate that is approximately three fourths of the total paid by the employer and the employee on the same income. Self-employed individuals report and pay their FICA tax simultaneously with their income tax.

Unemployment Compensation Tax

Employers are subject to a state unemployment tax. This tax provides funds from which unemployment compensation can be paid to unemployed workers. In most states the unemployment taxes are paid by the employer only.

Withholding (Income Tax) Deductions

The federal government requires employers to withhold an advance payment on income tax from the wages paid to an employee. The amounts withheld are remitted to the regional Internal Revenue Service Center at the time the FICA taxes are paid. The term *wages* used in this connection includes the total compensation paid for services, such as wages, salaries, commissions, bonuses, and vacation allowances.

The amount of income tax withheld depends on the amount of wages received and the number of personal exemptions the taxpayer claims. Each employee must file with the employer, immediately upon reporting to work, an Employee's Withholding Allowance Certificate (Form W-4) to indicate the number of personal exemptions which the employee claims. The following exemptions may be claimed:

1. An exemption for the employee

2. An exemption for the employee's spouse (unless the spouse claims his or her own exemption)

3. An exemption for each dependent (unless the employee's spouse claims them)

4. An additional exemption if the taxpayer or spouse is 65 years of age or more or is blind

The amount of tax withheld is then computed from a table provided by the Internal Revenue Service.

A number of cities and states tax personal income. The percentage of deduction and the form of payment vary; for example, one city may have the employer deduct 1 percent from every payroll check issued and remit the total deductions at the end of each quarter of a calendar year. Some states and cities require individuals to file annual income tax returns.

The following forms are needed for payroll records:

W-2 . . . . Wage and Tax Statement

W-3 . . . . Transmittal of Income and Tax Statements

W-4 . . . . Employee's Withholding Allowance Certificate

501 . . . . Federal Tax Deposit

940 . . . . Employer's Annual Federal Unemployment Tax Return

941 . . . . Employer's Quarterly Federal Tax Return

State Unemployment Return; other state and city report forms as required

Other Payroll Deductions

In addition to the deductions required by federal and state legislation, other payroll deductions—such as hospital care insurance (hospitalization), group insurance premiums, stock and bond purchases—may be made. In most firms these deductions are voluntary, and usually the authorizations may be canceled by the employee at any time.

Most employers furnish with each wage payment an itemized listing of all deductions made from the employee's wage. This information is usually provided on a form attached to the check, to be removed and retained by the

CALENDAR OF PAYROLL PROCEDURES

On Hiring a New Employee:

Have the employee complete *Form W-4 (Employee's Withholding Allowance Certificate)*. Record employee's social security number and number of exemptions. File the certificate in a safe place.

On Each Payment of Wages to an Employee:

Withhold the proper amount of income tax and FICA tax (refer to the instructions and tables supplied by the Internal Revenue Service and also to city and state information, if necessary). Make all other deductions.

As part of the payroll check or as a separate statement, a record of total wages, amount and kind of each deduction, and net amount should be given to the employee.

Within 15 Days after the Close of Each of the First Two Months of Any Calendar Quarter:

If income and employees' and employer's FICA taxes withheld total $200 or more, but less than $2,000, by the last day of the first month and/or by the last day of the second month in a calendar quarter, the full amount must be deposited in a Federal Reserve Bank or authorized bank by the 15th of the next month. Use *Form 501 (Federal Tax Deposit)*.

If the total amount of undeposited taxes is less than $200 by the last day of the second month of a calendar quarter, the full amount may be paid with the *Employer's Quarterly Tax Return (Form 941).*

On or Before Each April 30, July 31, October 31, and January 31:

File *Form 941 (Employer's Quarterly Federal Tax Return)* with the regional Internal Revenue Service Center. Remit with it the full amount due; that is, the total amount of income and employees' and employer's FICA taxes withheld during the quarter less total of *Federal Tax Deposit (Form 501)*.

The *State Unemployment Return* is usually filed at this time.

On or Before January 31 and at the End of an Employee's Employment:

Prepare *Form W-2 (Wage and Tax Statement)* showing the total wages, total wages subject to withholdings for income tax, the amount of income tax withheld, the total wage subject to FICA tax, and the amount of FICA tax withheld.

The government prepared Form W-2 consists of four copies—two copies given to the employee; one copy for the Internal Revenue Service Center, one copy for the employer's record. To save paperwork, many large firms print their own W-2 forms with five or six copies. The additional copies are given to the city and state (that is, for records of income tax withheld) if they require them.

On or Before January 31 of Each Year:

File *Form 940 (Employer's Annual Federal Unemployment Tax Return)* to report payment of federal unemployment taxes under the Federal Unemployment Tax Act. In general, employers are required to file state unemployment tax returns quarterly.

File *Form W-3 (Transmittal of Income and Tax Statements)* to provide a summary statement that enables a comparison of the total income taxes withheld as reported on all Form W-2's and the total amount of income tax withheld as reported on the four quarterly Forms 941.

Retain payroll records for a period of SEVEN YEARS.

employee when the check is cashed. At the end of each year, the employer is required to furnish each employee with a Wage and Tax Statement (Form W-2) that shows the total earnings and tax deductions. One copy of Form W-2 is attached to the individual's income tax return form.

Fair Labor Standards Act

There are primarily two classes of remuneration—*wages* at a rate per hour and *salaries* at a rate per week or month. Persons receiving wages are usually paid only for the hours they work; persons receiving salaries are usually paid for the full pay period even though they may be absent from work for brief periods. To differentiate, employees are called *hourly* and *salaried* employees respectively. Office employees are frequently paid salaries, although record-keeping requirements at times may make practical the payment of office employees on an hourly basis.

Most hourly and salaried employees come under the provisions of the *Fair Labor Standards Act,* which sets a minimum hourly wage and requires that each employer keep a record of the hours worked by each hourly employee and that each hourly employee be paid at least one and a half times the regular hourly rate for all time over 40 hours during a workweek. (For example, an employee who makes $10 an hour must be paid $15 an hour for overtime work.) Salaried workers and executives are excluded from the provisions of the Act.

Some companies pay overtime for all work beyond a specific number of hours a day. In other companies no overtime is paid salaried workers, but compensatory time off is given instead.

The Fair Labor Standards Act does not require the filing of overtime reports to any governmental office, but records must be kept on file for three years in the employer's office on nonexempt employees for perusal at any time a government examiner chooses to look them over. Detailed information about this legislation may be obtained from the nearest office of the Wage and Hour Division, Department of Labor.

Time Records

Hourly workers, such as factory and department store employees and some salaried workers, "punch in" and "punch out" each time they enter and leave their places of employment. The time is stamped on a time card. At the end of the payroll period the cards are collected and the pay is computed from the time stampings. Illus. 23-1 is an example of a time card.

Instead of using a time clock, salaried employees may sign in and out on a ruled sheet; or the secretary may be responsible for checking each person in and out daily on such a time sheet. Time records are not necessary in computing salaries, but it is advisable to keep them because such records may be the basis of paying overtime earnings or balancing compensatory time off with overtime worked. Then, too, there are various reports that require records of the overtime or compensatory time off of salaried employees.

SOC. SEC. NO. 696-44-2878			PAY PERIOD ENDING 4/30/--	
NAME Nancy Daniels			WITHHOLDING TAX EXEMPTIONS 1	
CLOCK NO. 12				
REG. HOURS 35½	RATE 4.10	AMOUNT 145.55	INC. TAX WITH. 9.95	TOTAL EARNINGS 170.15
O.T. HOURS 4	RATE 6.15	AMOUNT 24.60	F.I.C.A. TAX 26.80	TOTAL DEDUCTIONS 40.60
TOTAL HRS. 39½		AMOUNT	GROUP INS. .50	NET PAY 129.55
			HOSP. 3.35	
			OTHER	

Days	IN MORNING	OUT	IN AFTERNOON	OUT	IN OVERTIME	OUT	Total Hours
1	M 804	M 1201	M 1248	M 432			7¼
2	TU 754	TU 1202	TU 1252	TU 358			6¾
3	W 758	W 1130	W 1254	W 436			7
4	TH 759	TH 1203	TH 128	TH 431			7
5	FR 746	FR 1202	FR 1249	FR 430	FR 500	FR 905	11⅛
6							
7							
						TOTAL	39½

Illus. 23-1
Time card

Payroll Records

Federal legislation requires employers to keep payroll records. These usually include a payroll register similar to that shown in Illus. 23-2 to be completed each pay period. In addition, an employee's earning record (Illus. 23-3) is usually kept for *each* employee for at least seven years. (Pension records are usually retained permanently.) Data from the payroll register are transferred periodically to the employee's earning record. The employee's earning record provides quarterly totals for the required quarterly tax reports, as well as the annual total. Even though the laws affecting payroll taxes are changed from time to time, comprehensive records similar to those illustrated provide the basic data from which to compile almost any type of payroll tax report.

Requesting Salary Check

If a secretary is the lone employee in a firm, it may be necessary to remind the executive that it is payday—a somewhat embarrassing necessity for the

PAYROLL REGISTER

FOR PERIOD ENDING March 31, 19--

	EMPLOYEE	S M	EXEMP.	EARNINGS			DEDUCTIONS				NET PAY	
				REG.	OVER-TIME	TOTAL	F.I.C.A. TAX	WITH-TAX	HEALTH INS.	TOTAL	AMOUNT	CHECK NO.
1	Allen, Joanne	S	1	620.00	31.00	651.00	43.62	172.90	18.00	234.52	416.48	123
2	Bauer, Thomas	M	2	560.00		560.00	31.52	103.80	29.00	169.32	390.68	124
3	Cowan, Rhonda	S	1	480.00		480.00	32.16	110.00	18.00	160.16	319.84	125
19	Scott, Martha	M	2	520.00		520.00	34.84	91.40	28.00	154.24	365.76	141
20	Weyer, Louis	S	1	480.00	48.00	528.00	35.38	97.40	18.00	150.78	377.22	142
	TOTALS			10,340.00	1,059.00	11,399.00	763.73	2,246.80	424.00	3,434.17	7,964.47	

Illus. 23-2
A partial page from a basic payroll register. Standard forms may be purchased at a stationery store, or forms may be custom designed and duplicated. If requirements are large enough to justify having the form specially printed, the company will likely have a payroll department.

EMPLOYEE'S EARNINGS RECORD

PERIOD ENDING 19--	EARNINGS			DEDUCTIONS				NET PAY
	REG.	OVER-TIME	TOTAL	F.I.C.A. TAX	WITH-TAX	HEALTH INS.	TOTAL	AMOUNT
1 1/15	520.00		520.00	34.84	91.40	28.00	154.24	365.76
2 1/31	520.00		520.00	34.84	91.40	28.00	154.24	365.76
3 2/15	520.00	26.00	546.00	36.58	94.50	28.00	159.08	386.92
4 2/28	520.00		520.00	34.84	91.40	28.00	154.24	365.76
5 3/15	520.00		520.00	34.84	91.40	28.00	154.24	365.76
6 3/31	520.00		520.00	34.84	91.40	28.00	154.24	365.76
QUARTER TOTALS	3,120.00		3,146.00	210.78	551.50	168.00	930.28	2,215.72
YEARLY TOTALS								

NAME Scott, Martha	ADDRESS 261 Rose Avenue Atlanta, Georgia	SOC. SEC. NO. 561-245-4800	KIND OF WORK Secretary	DEPT. Sales
NO. DED. 2			MARITAL STATUS M	

Illus. 23-3
In addition to the payroll register shown in Illus. 23-2, an individual record for each employee must be kept. Specific requirements will determine the number of columns and the data to be recorded.

new or young secretary. A not-so-obvious way is to ask, "Shall I write out my salary check for your signature?" or "Do you want me to cash a check this noon for my salary?" Never wait until two minutes before leaving time and meekly and hesitatingly say, "This is payday." The lawyer, doctor, or branch office manager under whom the secretary is likely to be the only employee is a matter-of-fact business person who wants the secretary to be paid promptly but who may forget that important day and may not wish to be delayed at the last minute.

Administrative Responsibilities

The secretary may be involved in salary administration. For example, a secretary may be asked to perform such administrative functions as recommending promotions and salary increases for members of the office staff, assisting in determining compensation for office personnel, determining work standards, examining and proposing incentive plans for the office, evaluating office employees (see page 677, Chapter 27), and making recommendations for transfers and dismissals. The manner in which these functions are carried out plays an extremely important role in determining office morale.

An essential to a sound salary administration plan is that each employee be paid a fair and reasonable compensation for work done. This requires some form of job analysis. Before making recommendations involving salary administration, the secretary must be thoroughly familiar with the competencies required for each position and to have some measure of the quality and quantity of the work produced by each staff member. Job analysis and employee evaluation are two administrative areas in which the secretary may need to obtain background knowledge. The secretary also may find it helpful to be aware of union and legislative regulations regarding labor.

THE EXECUTIVE'S INCOME TAX

The secretary can assist the executive in the preparation of his or her annual income tax return by:

Being alert to items that the executive must report as income and items that may be taken as deductions, credits, and adjustments

Accumulating such items throughout the year with supporting papers and records for use at income tax time

Following up to see that returns are filed and payments are made

The performance of these duties demands certain basic understanding of what constitutes taxable income, which deductions are allowable, and how to organize the material to make it readily accessible.

Income Tax Files

The *income tax files* generally consist of income and deduction records, supporting computations and memorandums, previous years' tax returns, and a current income tax file folder or portfolio. To avoid the possibility of filing current tax materials with those of previous years, large expansion portfolios may be used and all the income tax material related to a given year filed in that portfolio and labeled "Federal Income Tax, 19——." All supporting records of income tax returns should be retained for several years.

At the beginning of each year a portfolio should be set up for income tax materials for the year, and all tax data (bills, canceled checks, reports, itemized listings, receipts) should go into it. Thus, when it is time to prepare the executive's tax return, all the essential records and reference materials will have been accumulated.

Records of Taxable Income

A record of the executive's personal income may be maintained in a special record book in which each item is individually recorded. In most instances, however, no separate record book will be kept. The tax information will consist mainly of deposit slips to which identifying notations have been attached, copies of receipts, statements of earnings and deductions, dividend distribution statements, statements of interest income on savings accounts, and other notations that the secretary files in the income tax portfolio. Since personal income may be derived from many sources and be received at irregular intervals, the secretary must be able to identify taxable income and must be alert in seeing that a notation on each income item gets into the tax portfolio.

The following items are *taxable income:*

Wages, Salaries, and Other Compensation. The gross amount (amount before deductions for such items as income tax, retirement contributions, employee pensions, hospitalization, and insurance) received from wages, salaries, commissions, fees, tips, and similar sources is taxable. In addition to these items, awards and prizes of money or merchandise, amounts received in reimbursement for expenses that are in excess of the actual business expenses incurred, and bonuses are also taxable income.

Dividends. Cash dividends over $100 per year on stock when paid in cash are generally taxable. Stock dividends, however, may or may not be taxable. Since some dividends may be wholly or partially exempt from taxation, a complete record of all dividends received should be maintained. Those dividends which are not taxable can be eliminated at the time the tax return is prepared.

At the beginning of the year, corporations usually send stockholders a form (Form 1099) stating the total amount of dividends paid to the addressed stockholder the previous year. Watch for and file this information in the income tax portfolio.

If your employer uses a broker to manage an investment portfolio, the broker will provide a detailed statement showing reportable dividends and interest. These statements are helpful in keeping track of income from investments and determining what is reportable at tax time.

Interest. With the exception of interest on tax exempt securities, all interest received is taxable. Thus, interest received from corporate bonds, mortgage bonds, notes, bank deposits, personal loans, accounts in savings and loan associations, and most United States government bonds should be itemized and recorded.

Gains on Sale or Exchange of Property. Profit from the sale of property (including home) is fully or partially taxable depending upon the length of time the property was owned and upon other circumstances. In order that the exact profit may be determined, it is essential that detailed property records be kept on each property item. Real estate, stocks, and other securities are property items.

Proceeds from Annuities and Endowment Life Insurance. A portion of income from annuities and endowment life insurance is taxable.

Rents Received. Income received from rents is taxable. The owner of property from which rents are received is entitled to deductions for depreciation, mortgage interest, taxes, repairs, insurance, agent's commission, and other ordinary and necessary expenses of operating the property. Property records should be kept on each rental unit owned. (See page 553.)

Royalties. Royalties include income received from writings, works of art, musical compositions, and inventions and patents. All expenses incurred in producing property (such as patents and books) that provide a royalty income are deductible.

Income from a Profession or a Personally Owned Business. All income from a profession or a personally owned business is taxable after deductions for all ordinary, necessary operating expenses have been made.

Nontaxable Income. Even with nontaxable items, the secretary should strive to keep as complete a record of all income as the working situation permits. The data will then be available when the tax return is being prepared. Incomes that are not taxable or incomes from which deductions are allowable can be examined and properly excluded or recorded by the tax consultant at the time of preparation of the tax return. The secretary should *not* assume the responsibility of judging whether or not income is taxable.

Records of Tax Credits and Deductions

A detailed record of each of the following allowable tax credits and deductions should be kept in the tax portfolio for aid in the preparation of the income tax return.

Alimony. Alimony or other payments in lieu of alimony under a decree of divorce or of separate maintenance are allowable as a personal deduction. Such deductions are taken in the year of payment by the spouse making the payment but are taxable income to the spouse receiving the payment. Child support payments, however, are neither deductible nor taxable.

Bad Debts. Nonbusiness bad debt losses are deductible as short-term capital losses if they are supported by document and are nonfamily loans.

Casualty and Theft Losses. Losses resulting from fire, storm, flood, or theft are deductible if not reimbursed by insurance. Damage to the taxpayer's automobile resulting from an accident would be deductible to the extent not covered by insurance. The taxpayer must absorb the first $100 of each casualty and theft loss.

Child and Dependent Care Credit. A tax credit for expenditures for child care (when parents are working) and for disabled dependents is allowed up to a designated amount and under certain conditions.

Contributions. Contributions to organizations or institutions devoted primarily to charitable, religious, educational, scientific, or literary purposes are deductible. Examples are contributions to schools and colleges, churches, hospitals, American Cancer Foundation, Girl Scouts, Salvation Army, and United Appeal. Charitable gifts to individuals, political organizations, social clubs, or labor unions are not deductible. Limited contributions to political parties are deductible.

Nonreimbursed expenses (use of automobile, postage, out-of-town telephone calls) incurred while serving in a campaign to collect funds for a charitable, religious, or educational organization are considered a contribution to the organization and are deductible as such.

Education. The cost of improving job-related competencies may be deductible depending upon meeting criteria established by the Internal Revenue Service. This includes expenses for tuition, books, and professional journals.

Interest. All interest paid on personal debts may be deducted. This deduction includes interest paid on such items as bank loans, home and property mortgages, installment loans on an automobile, and charges made on credit card purchases.

Medical and Dental Expenses. Medical and dental expenses are not restricted to those of the taxpayer but may also include the taxpayer's family and dependents. Medical care insurance up to a certain amount and medical expenses over a certain amount are deductible. To claim this deduction, the taxpayer is required to furnish the name and address of each person to whom such deductions were paid, the amount, and the approximate date of payment.

Taxes. Such personal taxes as the following are deductible: state or local income taxes, personal property taxes, real estate taxes, state or local sales taxes, and state transfer taxes on securities. Sales receipts and contracts should be kept in order to deduct sales tax on large purchases such as cars, boats, trucks, motorcycles, and motor homes. Tax on these items can, under certain conditions, be added to the amounts shown in the state sales tax tables provided by IRS.

The Executive's Business Expenses. *Traveling expenses* incurred when away from home in connection with one's business or profession and for which reimbursement is not received are deductible. These expenses include such items as airline tickets, excess baggage charges, airport transportation services, car rentals, automobile expenses, bus and subway fares, taxi fares, meals (only if away overnight), hotel/motel expenses, tips, telephone/telegraph expenses, laundry, and stenographic services.

Illus. 23-4
Travel expenses may be forgotten if they are not recorded promptly. At the completion of each business trip, the secretary should obtain from the executive the data needed to complete a report of travel expenses. Unless the expenses are reimbursed by the corporation, the report should be filed with attached receipts in the income tax portfolio.

TRAVEL EXPENSE REPORT

Date(s) Feb. 5-7, 19---

Purpose	To attend convention of National Dental Trade Association	
From/to	Houston to Chicago	
		Cost
Transportation	Air/coach	$292.00
Hotel	Conrad Hilton - 2 nights	128.00
Meals	2/5 $19.00	
	2/6 22.00	
	2/7 19.50	60.50
Other	Tips $ 9.00	
	Taxi 12.50	
	Convention reg. 12.00	
	Airport parking 8.00	41.50
	Total	$522.00

Receipts attached
    Hotel
    American Airlines
    Convention registration

Entertainment expenses for business purposes (customers, agents, clients, professional advisers) are deductible. The spouse of an out-of-town guest may also be included. Meals, including tips, theatre and other tickets are recognized entertainment costs. Even club dues are deductible, provided the club is used primarily for entertaining business guests. Deductions for entertainment, however, are subject to detailed examination by the Internal Revenue Service. Many companies place limits on executive travel expenses based upon the title of the executive. These limits include a daily amount for meals, lodging, and entertainment. Any verified amount that is spent by your employer for business purposes and not reimbursed by the company is deductible.

A detailed record similar to the one shown in Illus. 23-5 should be prepared, identifying each guest and the business connection, and supported by receipts if the total cost is $25 or more.

GRILL

SERVER	PERSONS	TABLE NO.	NUMBER 36234

McKenna's Restaurant

2	Onion Soup		3.20
3	Shrimp cocktail		9.00
2	Special salad bowl		8.00
2	Filet sole		8.00
1	Small steak		6.00
5	Coffee		5.75
3	Pie à la		4.50
	SUBTOTAL		44.45
	SALES TAX		2.22
	TIP	+ 15%	7.00
	TOTAL		53.67
	SIGNATURE	Betty Randall	

```
            GUEST LIST

        (Business Entertainment)

Date        April 10, 19--

Guest(s)    George Snyder
            Frank Fletcher
            Mary Lossi
            John Malinowski
            (All of V. M. Massey Co.)

Explanation Lunch at McKenna's to discuss
            contract renewal

Total cost  $46.67 plus 15% tip, $53.67
            Receipt attached.
```

Illus. 23-5
A record must support each entertainment expense. If the total cost is $25 or more, a receipt must be attached. At the end of each day the secretary should check the appointment book and flag any appointment that has involved deductible expenses. The next day the needed information can be obtained from the executive, the report prepared and filed with attached receipts in the income tax portfolio.

Gifts up to $25 in value per recipient per year are deductible when given for a business purpose. Each gift deduction, however, must be supported by a record showing date, cost, reason for giving, and the name and business connection of the recipient.

Many executives use credit cards in paying for travel and entertainment expenses. The secretary should identify each travel and entertainment expenditure on the monthly credit card statement and file it, or a copy, in the income tax portfolio.

Other Deductions. Other allowable deductions that apply in specific cases are safe-deposit box rental when income-producing items are stored in the box, subscriptions to investment publications, cost of uniforms and their upkeep when they are essential, union dues, moving expenses (within certain limitations), and cost of repairs to business property. The secretary should add to the master list of deductible items those items that are pertinent to the executive's situation.

Tax Guides and Forms

After studying an income tax guide, the secretary can be of more assistance to the executive in handling income tax materials. The secretary should

FORMS USED FOR FILING INDIVIDUAL INCOME TAX RETURNS

File on or before April 15 following the close of the calendar year:

Form 1040 (U.S. Individual Income Tax Return)—a two-page return (called the *long form*) that may be used for *any* amount of income. All deductions can be listed in full, and all computations are made by the taxpayer.

Form 1040-ES (Declaration of Estimated Tax for Individuals)—filed by every citizen who can reasonably expect to receive more than $500 from sources other than wages subject to withholding, or can reasonably expect gross income to exceed—

(1) $20,000 for a single individual, a head of household, or a widow or widower entitled to the special tax rates

(2) $20,000 for a married individual entitled to file a joint declaration with spouse, but only if the spouse has not received wages for the taxable year

(3) $10,000 for a married individual entitled to file a joint declaration with spouse, but only if both spouses have received wages for the taxable year

(4) $5,000 for a married individual not entitled to file a joint declaration with spouse

The estimated unpaid tax may be paid in full at the time of filing the declaration form; or it may be paid in four equal quarterly installments (payable on April 15, June 15, September 15, and January 15). The first installment payment must accompany the declaration.

also become familiar with the various tax forms, know how to choose the proper ones, and know where to find them.

Tax Guides. The following publications can be obtained from the office of the Internal Revenue Service free or for a nominal charge: *Your Federal Income Tax, Tax Guide for U.S. Citizens Abroad, Tax Information for Home Owners, Energy Credits for Individuals, Tax Guide for Small Business, Child and Disabled Dependent Care.* Inexpensive tax guides can also be obtained at bookstores.

Tax Forms. One set in duplicate of blank forms is mailed to each taxpayer; additional copies needed for drafting the return may be obtained from the local office of the Internal Revenue Service and usually from banks and post offices or reproduced on a copying machine. The Internal Revenue Service has ruled that reproduction of tax forms, schedules, and supporting data on office copying machines is acceptable. Forms may be prepared in pencil and reproduced on a copying machine, thus avoiding the necessity of recopying or typing the form.

Copies for the files should be made on a copying machine of all supplementary information and supporting data such as receipts, statements, expense reports, and other items that may be attached and mailed with the tax return.

Typing and Mailing Tax Returns

The tax return contains confidential information. It should be typed by the secretary, not by an assistant. Before typing, each figure must be checked for accuracy; then the return must be typed and proofread carefully. Before mailing the form, the secretary should check to see that it has been properly signed and that materials to accompany the return have been securely attached to the finished form as directed.

At the foot of the first page of the federal tax forms, space is provided for "Signature of preparer other than taxpayer." This does not mean the signature of the secretary who has merely collected tax data or typed the form. The signature is to be that of a tax consultant or attorney who has prepared the return and who assumes responsibility for its validity.

Since the mailing of all tax returns is a very important responsibility, the secretary should mail them personally. Do not put them in the regular office mail, send them through the mailing department, or trust them to a clerk or anyone else to post. The secretary should note on the file copy the exact time and place where each return was mailed. A certificate of mailing may be obtained from the post office as legal proof that the return was mailed. If such a certificate is obtained, attach it to the file copy of the return.

If a Declaration of Estimated Tax has been filed, the secretary must remind the employer when quarterly tax payments are due (June 15, September 15, and January 15). A good idea is to place cards in the tickler file at appropriate points.

A CHECKLIST FOR COMPUTING INCOME TAX

As you keep a tax portfolio or prepare the income tax return, check this list of common items that are deductible or nondeductible from adjusted gross income.

	Deductible	Nondeductible
Alimony and separate maintenance payments taxable to recipient	✓	
Automobile expenses (car used exclusively for pleasure)		
State gasoline taxes imposed on consumer	✓	
Interest on finance loans	✓	
License fees		✓
Ordinary upkeep and operating expenses		✓
Burglary losses exceeding $100 (if not covered by insurance)	✓	
Casualty losses not covered by insurance (fire, flood, windstorm, lightning, earthquakes, etc.)	✓	
Charitable contributions to approved institutions	✓	
Domestic servants (wages paid)		✓
Dues, social clubs for personal use		✓
Employment fees paid to agencies	✓	
Federal income taxes		✓
FICA taxes withheld by employer		✓
Fines for violation of laws and regulations		✓
Funeral expenses		✓
Gambling losses (to extent of gains only)	✓	
Gift taxes		✓
Gifts to relatives and other individuals		✓
Income tax imposed by city or state	✓	
Inheritance taxes		✓
Interest paid on personal loans	✓	
Life insurance premiums		✓
Medical Care Insurance Premiums (including Blue Cross and Blue Shield). Limited to 50% of premium cost with a $150 maximum	✓	
Medical expenses in excess of 3% of adjusted gross income (including the cost of artificial limbs, artificial teeth, eyeglasses, hearing aids, dental fees, hospital expenses, premiums on hospital or medical insurance) to extent not covered by insurance	✓	
Political campaign contribution up to prescribed limits	✓	
Property taxes, real and personal	✓	
Residence for personal use		
Improvements and street assessments		✓
Insurance		✓
Interest on mortgage loan	✓	
Loss from sale of		✓
Rent paid		✓
Repairs		✓
Taxes	✓	
Sales, taxes, state and local	✓	
Traveling expenses attending professional meetings	✓	
Traveling expenses to and from place of business or employment	✓	
Uniforms for personal use including cost and upkeep, if not adaptable for general use (nurses, police officers, jockeys, baseball players, etc.)	✓	
Union dues	✓	
Use taxes imposed on consumers under state law	✓	

Late Filing

The taxpayer who is late in filing a return is assessed a penalty. An individual, however, may obtain an automatic two-month extension for filing the return after the April 15 deadline by submitting an Application for Automatic Extension of Time to File U.S. Individual Income Tax Return. Further extensions are granted only under certain circumstances.

SUGGESTED READINGS

Bower, James B., and Harold Q. Langenderfer, *Income Tax Procedure*, issued annually. Cincinnati: South-Western Publishing Co.

Keeling, B. Lewis, and Bernard J. Beig. *Payroll Records and Accounting*, issued annually. Cincinnati: South-Western Publishing Co.

QUESTIONS FOR DISCUSSION

1. Does it build employee morale to make available to all employees the salaries paid employees in the company? Support your answer.

2. Why should a secretary not employed in the payroll department be familiar with payroll procedures and payroll taxes?

3. Why is the self-employed person taxed at a higher FICA tax rate than employees?

4. One of your assistants, who is your senior in age and tenure in the company, has the habit of arriving at work a few minutes late each morning. As a corrective measure you ask each member of your staff to sign in and out each day on a register sheet. There is opposition to your regulation by the other members of your staff on the grounds that they are salaried, not hourly, employees. What is the difference between a salaried and an hourly employee, and how would you respond to this objection?

5. What is the relationship between salary administration and job analysis, and why may a secretary need to have training in job analysis?

6. Assume you are employed in a small office (four employees) and your employer asks you to take complete charge of the payroll records, including preparing and submitting all payroll tax reports. Where could you obtain assistance to help you prepare for and carry out this assignment?

7. It is said that the secretary should play an assistance role in the preparation of the employer's income tax return. What does this mean to you?

8. The Internal Revenue Service requires a taxpayer to document all traveling and entertainment expenses for which a tax deduction is claimed. What is the secretary's role in compiling all of this important information?

9. What precautions should the secretary observe in typing and mailing the employer's income tax return?

10. If necessary, correct the following sentences. Then use the Reference Guide to check your answers.

   (a) The principle on the loan must be paid before June 1.

   (b) We must raise additional capitol for expansion of our new plant.

   (c) There is considerable disagreement between our many stockholders.

   (d) The contract's terms are precise.

   (e) Send us 35 8-column worksheets.

PROBLEMS

1. Obtain one of the following payroll forms, study the instructions for completing it, and be prepared to present to the class a description of the form and the method of completing it.

SS-4 . . . Application for Employer Identification Number

SS-5 . . . Application for a Social Security Number

941 . . . Employer's Quarterly Federal Tax Return

W-2 . . . Wage and Tax Statement

W-4 . . . Employee's Withholding Allowance Certificate

2. To accumulate information for a tax file, a secretary must have some understanding of taxable income and allowable deductions. From the following list, select those income items that are taxable and those expense items that are deductible. Arrange the items alphabetically and type them in a form convenient for reference. You may need to check reference sources to identify the tax status of certain items.

Income Items

Payment for writing magazine article

Interest from municipal bonds

Bonus from employer

Prize—paid vacation to a resort as a prize for the "Best Idea" contest

Rent received on property inherited from a relative

Dividends on corporation stock

Interest on U.S. government bonds

Merchandise received from employer

Interest on deposits in savings and loan association

Payments from accident insurance

Property inherited from a relative

Payment for a speech to a service club (not related to business)

Royalties received from a patent

Profit from sale of building lot originally planned for home

Expense Items

Contribution to an old friend

Tips paid for service while on business trip

Federal income tax paid during year

Interest on loan on family automobile

Contributions to Girl Scouts

Contribution of $25 to a political party

Interest on loan on home

Driver's license fee

State income tax

Property loss resulting from theft (not covered by insurance)

Federal Social Security tax

Retail sales tax (state)

Employment fees paid to agency

Life insurance premiums

Traveling expenses to and from the place of employment

Union dues

Repairs on home

Gift costing $25 given to a customer

Expenses incurred in acting as chairman of United Appeal fund drive

3. John O'Brian is paid $6.20 an hour and an overtime wage of one and one half times his hourly rate. All hours over 40 are considered overtime. He worked 48 hours during the last week in March.

(a) What are his gross earnings for the week?

(b) If the FICA tax rate is 6.7 percent and there is an $18.30 federal income tax deduction and a 2 percent state income tax deduction, what are his net earnings?

Chapter 24

Producing and Processing Legal Papers

Increased government regulations during the past two decades have made compliance with local, state, and federal legislation a matter of prime importance in most businesses. Laws pertaining to employee privacy, civil rights, malpractice, consumer protection, taxes, and environmental protection have influenced significantly the secretary's need for a knowledge of the law and legal procedures.

Obviously the scope and amount of legal work that the secretary performs varies from office to office. The secretary in the corporate office dealing with the nonlegal aspects of a business may perform only an occasional legally related function. On the other hand, the secretary in a legal office works full time in an environment where legal terminology, documents, and procedures are the core of the activity. The work is so specialized that legal secretaries have their own association that administers a training and certification program to give preparation and prestige to their profession. In large law offices, word processing technology is having a dramatic impact on the functions of the legal secretary. Much of the repetitive typing, copying, and proofreading that formerly constituted a significant part of the work of the legal secretary is now being done by automatic typewriters, computer printout terminals, and copying machines. This makes legal secretarial work less clerical and more professional and enables some legal secretaries to be upgraded to legal assistants or researchers.

This chapter introduces the secretary to the processing of legal papers. It describes some of the more commonly used legal documents, discusses the secretarial procedures related to preparing them, outlines some legislation with which secretaries should be familiar, and suggests reference sources to which the secretary may turn for assistance.

You may find legal work attractive and decide to become a trainee in a law firm, the legal department of a large corporation, or the government. In that case, you can build upon the content of this chapter with a specialized training program to become a Professional Legal Secretary (PLS), paralegal, or legal assistant. You may even decide to study law and prepare for the bar.

FREQUENTLY USED LEGAL DOCUMENTS

Business transactions frequently involve parties from different states. Complexities and problems arise in preparing the legal documents to cover conflicting laws of the federal government and the fifty states. To expedite legal procedures, a number of uniform statutes (laws) have been enacted, the most recent and most important one from a business standpoint being the Uniform Commercial Code. The legal documents described here conform to this Code.

Contracts

Many people are concerned with the legalities of buying and selling goods, property, and services. Every buying and selling activity constitutes a contract between or among those concerned. A *contract* is an enforceable agreement, either oral or written, which involves legal rights and responsibilities. A contract may be in the form of an oral agreement, sales slip, a memorandum, a promissory note, a letter, or a contract form. Some contracts, such as those for the purchase of real estate, must be in writing; but *all* important contracts should be written, although this is not a legal requirement.

Content. In typing a contract, the secretary should see if the following essential information is included:

Date and place of agreement

Names of parties entering into the agreement

Purpose of the contract

Duties of each party

A statement of the money, the goods, or the services given in consideration (as payment for) of the agreement

Time element or duration involved

Signatures of the parties

Prepare enough copies of a contract so that each party will have a file copy. (If the contract is prepared in a law office, an additional copy is made for the law office files.) When the executive sells his or her services by contract (as do engineers, architects, builders, and real estate representatives), the secretary may have a standard form to use as a model; but usually there are items peculiar to each contract that make it necessary to vary the fill-ins each time. Printed forms are available for most common legal documents. Since some contracts must follow a statutory model or must contain specified provisions, it is recommended that the secretary use a printed form or follow legal advice when preparing specified provisions.

Care Before Signing. All contracts should be carefully read by all parties before they are signed. Not only will mistakes, misunderstandings, and fraud be avoided but also content will be clarified with regard to (1) what responsibilities are assumed by each party, (2) exactly what is offered at what price, (3) how payment is to be made, (4) whether or not material can be returned, and (5) when and how the contract can be terminated.

Contracts Made by the Secretary. As has already been pointed out, the secretary often acts (in a legal sense) as the deputy of the executive; that is, the secretary knowingly—and sometimes even unknowingly—executes contracts. This situation places responsibility on the secretary to exercise caution in making commitments; in requesting work to be done by outside agencies; in quoting prices or making offers to purchase; and in signing purchase or repair orders, sales orders, or agreements on the secretary's own initiative, for such commitments may be contractual.

When signing an agreement (contract) generated by the secretary, the executive usually relies on the secretary's recommendation. The mere fact that the secretary presents a contract to an executive for signature implies the secretary's endorsement of its content. For example, the secretary may make all the arrangements for the purchase of a new machine. The executive signs the contract on the presumption that the secretary has checked all details and has verified that the contract is correct, understood, and proper. By attaching an annotation of the important points to a contract, the secretary can save the employer the time of reading "the fine print."

A contract copy should be filed carefully, for it is a legal instrument necessary when prosecuting any deviation from the contract. It is well to place the contract in a No. 10 envelope and mark plainly on the outside, "Signed contract between...." The contract can be filed permanently in the company's or person's file, in a separate "Signed Contracts" file, or, if it is important enough, in a safe-deposit box. In some companies, such legal papers are kept in asbestos envelopes as a protection against fire.

Wills and Codicils

The requirements regarding the drawing of wills and codicils are rather technical and vary among the states. Hence, they should not be drawn without proper legal supervision or direction.

Wills. A will is a legal instrument whereby a person provides for the disposition of property after death. A *testator* (man) or *testatrix* (woman) is the one who makes the will. One who dies without having made a will is said to die *intestate.* A *nuncupative* will is an oral one and is valid only as to personal property; land may not be devised by a nuncupative will. A will in the handwriting of the testator is called a *holographic* will. A *joint* will is one executed by two or more persons. A will that sets forth provisions conditional upon the occurrence of a specified event is called a *conditional* will. Such a will might be written before a person undergoes a serious operation.

A will may be *revoked* by mutilation, alteration, cancellation, destruction, or the execution of a new will. Every will should contain a provision stating that any and all previous wills are revoked even though the testator does not remember ever having made another will.

To *probate* a will is to prove its validity to the court for the purpose of carrying out its provisions. An *executor* (man) or *executrix* (woman) is the one named by the testator to carry out the provisions of a will. If a person dies intestate, the courts will appoint an *administrator* (man) or *administratrix* (woman) to settle the estate of the deceased.

Codicils. A *codicil* is a supplement that makes a change in the will, deletes or adds something to it, or explains it. It must be signed and witnessed with all the formalities of the original will.

A person asked to *attest* (witness) a will or codicil need not read the provisions and, of course, does not try. The attestant is merely witnessing the signature of the testator and assuring the beneficiaries that the testator was in sound mind when the will was signed. A will presented for witnessing should have only the signature area visible, thus preventing any chance reading of the contents.

Copyrights

Creative work reproduced for sale or public distribution may be *copyrighted.* Copyrighting applies not only to printed matter, such as books and periodicals, but also to photographs, pictorial illustrations, musical compositions, maps, paintings, and movies.

To copyright is to register a claim with the federal government to a piece of original literary or artistic work. A copyright grants the exclusive right to reproduce a creative work or to perform it publicly. Registering is done either by the originator of the work or the one reproducing and marketing copies. Copyrighting tends to prevent a dishonest or careless person from stealing another's creative work and marketing it. The copyright law allows the duration of a copyright for the life of the author plus fifty years after the author's death, ensures that public broadcasters and others cannot use the work of writers without their consent, and provides guidelines under which classroom and library copying of material is permitted. A copyright can be obtained by filing an application for copyright with the Copyright office, Library of Congress, Washington, D.C. 20559.

Affidavits

An *affidavit* is a written declaration made under oath that the facts set forth are sworn to be true and correct. The word itself means "he has made oath." An affidavit, made by an *affiant*, must be sworn to before a public officer (such as a notary, judge, or a justice of the peace).

For example, evidence of citizenship is required before an applicant can obtain a United States passport. If the person seeking a passport has no birth certificate, an affidavit from a relative declaring that the passport applicant was born in the United States may be used.

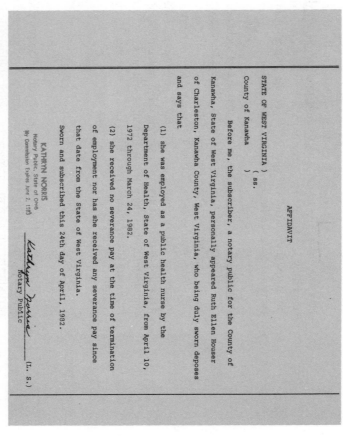

Illus. 24-1
An affidavit may be typed on ruled legal paper, as illustrated here, or it may be typed on unruled paper. It must be signed by a notary public, judge, or justice of the peace.

AFFIDAVIT

STATE OF WEST VIRGINIA)
) ss.
County of Kanawha   )

Before me, the subscriber, a notary public for the County of Kanawha, State of West Virginia, personally appeared Ruth Ellen Houser of Charleston, Kanawha County, West Virginia, who being duly sworn deposes and says that

(1) she was employed as a public health nurse by the Department of Health, State of West Virginia, from April 10, 1972 through March 24, 1982.

(2) she received no severance pay at the time of termination of employment nor has she received any severance pay since that date from the State of West Virginia.

Sworn and subscribed this 24th day of April, 1982.

Kathryn Norris   (L. S.)
Notary Public

KATHRYN NORRIS
Notary Public, State of Ohio
My Commission Expires June 2, 1985

Power of Attorney

A legal instrument authorizing one to act as agent for another is known as *power of attorney*. Often a secretary may be given power of attorney by the employer to act in the name and on behalf of the employer in performing certain specified functions set forth in the document. For example, the secretary may be authorized to sign checks and other legal documents for the executive. It may be made for an indefinite period, for a specific period, or for a specific purpose only. Only a secretary whose business integrity is unquestioned earns this decidedly weighty responsibility of acting as the employer's agent.

Power of Attorney
Know All Men By These Presents

That Henry Thomas Aske of the City of Akron, Summit County, State of Ohio has made, constituted and appointed, and by these presents do es make, constitute and appoint Raymond Henry Petroskey of the City of Seattle, State of Washington true and lawful attorney for me and in my name, place and stead to negotiate for the purchase of the structure and property situated at 112 West Third Street, City of Seattle, King County, State of Washington, known as Hidalgo Towers——

giving and granting unto Raymond Henry Petroskey said attorney full power and authority to do and perform all and every act and thing whatsoever requisite and necessary to be done in and about the premises as fully, to all intents and purposes, as I might or could do if personally present, with full power of substitution and revocation, hereby ratifying and confirming all that Raymond Henry Petroskey said attorney or his substitute shall lawfully do or cause to be done by virtue hereof.

In Witness Whereof, I have hereunto set my hand and seal the Third day of October , in the year one thousand nine hundred and eighty-three.

Sealed and delivered in the presence of

......................................(L. S.)

Illus. 24-2
A Power of Attorney is notarized in a form similar to that shown in Illus. 24-3.

Should the executive have power of attorney for someone else, the secretary sets up a special file and records all executions. These records will not only protect your employer but will serve as a vital source of information to the person who granted your employer power of attorney.

Patents

A patent [*obtained by an inventor, a discoverer for something useful*] may be obtained by a person who has "invented or discovered a new and useful art, machine, manufacture, or composition of matter, or any new and useful improvement thereof—not known or used by others in this country before. . . ." Literature on the procedure for securing a patent can be obtained from the Superintendent of Documents, U.S. Government Printing Office, Washington, D.C. 20402.

Legal specialists usually are employed to prepare the patent application, the first step in negotiations between the Patent and Trademark Office and the inventor.

A patent grant gives the exclusive right to make, use, and sell the patent. A patent must be applied for by the inventor. After the patent has been granted, it can be sold outright or leased, in which case the inventor is paid a royalty for its use. A patent expires at the end of seventeen years and can be renewed only by an Act of Congress.

Trademarks

The Patent and Trademark Office also registers trademarks for goods moved in interstate commerce, giving evidence of the validity and ownership of the mark by the registrant and of the right to use the mark. The registration term covers twenty years. However, during the sixth year of registration, an affidavit must be filed with the Patent and Trademark Office showing that the trademark is being used or that its nonuse does not signify intention to abandon the mark.

RESPONSIBILITIES FOR LEGAL PAPERS

The secretary may type legal papers, fill in printed legal forms, and witness the signing of the completed papers. To complete the work, it may be necessary to have the papers notarized; that is, acknowledged by a notary public. A notary public acknowledges that a document was actually executed by the person or persons who sign it. For convenience, it may be practical for the secretary to become a notary public, thus avoiding the inconvenience of having to go outside the office for this service. Finally, the secretary may be responsible for the recording of the legal paper.

Notary Public

Notarial commissions are issued by the secretary of state, the governor, or other designated official in the various state capitals. Application blanks will be furnished upon request by the appropriate official in the state in which the commission is sought, or they may be bought at a stationery store. There are usually a fee, an examination, and certain citizenship qualifications. Most states also require bond, which may be applied for on forms obtained along with the application. A notary public can purchase Error and Omission insurance to protect against financial liability.

The notary's appointment states the county or counties in which he or she has authority to notarize and the date of expiration of commission. It is necessary to buy a notary public seal and a rubber stamp. The former is used to press into the document the seal showing the name of the county in which the notary is commissioned to act and the seal of the state. The rubber stamp shows the date when the commission expires. Each notary receives local rules and instructions that must be observed.

A notary does not scrutinize the document being certified. The notary gives the oath and verifies that the signature or signatures are genuine. If you should become a notary, remember not to be curious about what is in the paper you are certifying.

If the secretary is not a notary public, a responsibility may be to arrange for the details related to having papers notarized. The names of two or three notaries public convenient to the office should be obtained. Sometimes it may be necessary to arrange a meeting time with the notary public and to notify all parties involved.

The notary public witnesses affidavits and signs *acknowledgments* and *verifications* that are executed under oath. In an acknowledgment the person swears that the signature appearing on a document is genuine and was made of free will. A verification is a sworn and signed statement of the truth and correctness of the content of a document. All necessary signatures must be completed before the notary public signs the document.

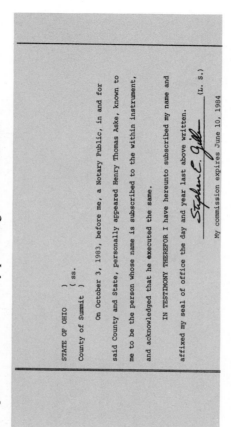

STATE OF OHIO)
) ss.
County of Summit)

On October 3, 1983, before me, a Notary Public, in and for said County and state, personally appeared Henry Thomas Aske, known to me to be the person whose name is subscribed to the within instrument, and acknowledged that he executed the same.

IN TESTIMONY THEREFOR I have hereunto subscribed my name and affixed my seal of office the day and year last above written.

Stephen E. Gill (L. S.)

My commission expires June 10, 1984

Illus. 24-3
An acknowledgment of a notary public

Preparation of Legal Papers

Legal papers can be divided into two classes:

1. *Court Documents.* These vary considerably and must follow the specifications of the particular court in the city, county, state, and federal government. They include such documents as *complaints, answers, demurrers, notices, motions, affidavits, summonses,* and *subpoenas.*

2. *Noncourt Legal Documents.* These include such legal papers as contracts, wills, leases, powers of attorney, agreements, and many others. They give formal expression to legal acts and are legal evidence if court action or litigation becomes necessary.

The form of legal papers is standardized in some respects; in others, it varies with the wishes of the court and with the personal preference of the employer.

Paper Size. Traditionally all legal documents were typed on 8½- by 13- or 14-inch hard-to-tear white paper called *legal cap*. Legal cap is printed with a red or blue vertical double rule 1⅜ inches from the left edge and a single rule ⅜ inch from the right edge. *Brief* paper, 8½ by 10½ inches, also with ruled margins, was used for legal briefs and memorandums; for some documents each line on a sheet was numbered. Although some courts still require legal cap for court documents, there is a trend toward using the standard 8½- by 11-inch sheet because this size can be microfilmed easily for storage in court files. Before typing a court document, the secretary should learn the requirements of the particular court.

Copies. Multiple copies of legal documents are usually required. For example, all parties to a contract receive a copy, file copies are necessary, and the attorney retains one or more copies for the office. Copies can be made on the copying machine; and, if so, the secretary types only the original and makes the copies from the original on the copier. In some offices the secretary types the original and, on color coded tissue weight paper, a file copy. All other copies are made from the original on the copier.

Copies can be used and referred to as *duplicate originals* if they are signed and made to *conform* in all respects to the original (to contain all the copy shown on the original).

After the paper has been *executed* (the original and duplicate originals made valid by necessary procedures, such as signing, witnessing, perhaps notarizing, and recording), all the distribution copies and the office file copy must be *conformed* by typing in the signatures, dates, and all other data that were added in executing the paper.

Type. For legal papers, pica type is preferred and may be required for court documents. In any case, do not use typefaces such as script, italic, or gothic.

Margins, Spacing, and Centered Titles. On paper with printed marginal rules, type within the rules by one or two spaces. On unruled paper, use 1½-inch left and at least ½-inch right margins. Top margins are 2 inches on the first page and 1½ inches on subsequent pages. Bottom margins are 1 inch.

For most legal papers, use double spacing, with a triple space above side headings. Some legal secretaries recommend that a triple space be made between paragraphs to provide flexibility for limited changes on any page without making it necessary to retype the entire instrument. Very long documents are sometimes single spaced to avoid exceptional bulkiness.

Two inches from the top of the first page, type the title of the paper in all capitals, centered between the rules. Divide at a logical point and double-space a heading that is too long for one line. Leave two blank line spaces below the title.

Stapling and Punching. Legal documents protected by legal backs should be stapled on each side at the lower edge of the top fold of the legal back about one inch from the side of the backing sheet. Staple legal documents prepared without legal backs, regardless of whether the document is an original or copy, one inch from the top of the page on both corners (see Illus. 24-4.). Try to avoid removing staples from documents fastened to a legal back.

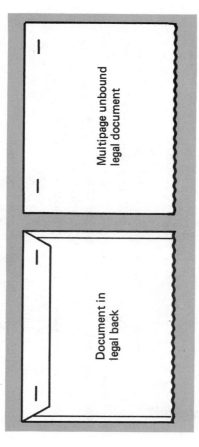

Document in legal back

Multipage unbound legal document

Illus. 24-4
Proper stapling of legal document

Once a will has been stapled, it becomes invalid if taken apart unless each page has been initialed in the handwriting of the one who makes the will.

A two-hole punch with the punches set 2¾ inches apart is used in legal offices to prepare documents for filing. All pages to be filed should be punched at the top center.

Hyphenation. Learn the preference for your particular situation. Sometimes the last word on a page must not be hyphenated; sometimes a divided last word is recommended to make the unwarranted insertion of pages more difficult. Avoid dividing words at the end of other lines.

Paragraphs. Indent ten spaces for paragraphs. To make difficult any unwarranted insertion of pages, do not end a page with the last line of a paragraph. Carry over two or more lines to the next page.

Quoted Matter and Land Descriptions. For quoted matter and land descriptions, indent five to ten spaces from the left margin; retain the right margin if desired, or indent five spaces. Indent another five spaces for a new paragraph in the quoted material. Indented quotations may be single spaced.

Page Numbers. Legal documents frequently go through a series of drafts before the final one. Number and date each draft: the first typing, *First draft*, (date); the second, *Second draft*, (date), and so on. Keep all drafts until the final document has been typed and processed.

Center page numbers one-half inch from the bottom edge. Always number the first and last page of every document.

Dates. Spell out single digit *ordinal* dates and type the year to conform: *the first day of June, nineteen hundred and eighty-three* (but *the 15th day of June, 1983*). Date every legal paper. If the last paragraph does not include the date, type the date on the last line immediately preceding the signature lines.

Numbers. Numbers with legal significance (amounts of money, periods of time) have traditionally been written in both words *and* figures. For example, *Five Thousand Dollars ($5,000)* or *Ten (10) barrels of oil* or *Sixty (60) days* (but a *six-month period*). (For general number usage, follow the style preferred by your employer.)

Use the dollar sign with a number in conformity with the spelled-out version: *Sixty Dollars ($60)*, but *Sixty (60) Dollars*. Capitalize all words of an amount except *and*: *Three Hundred Seventy-Five and* ⁴⁵/₁₀₀ *Dollars ($375.45)*. Some offices type dollar amounts in all capitals.

Reference Notations. On the first page of the file copy in the upper left corner, type the full names of the recipients of all copies of the document.

Names and Signature Lines. If you know the exact signature that is to be used, type it in the body of the document in exactly that way. If you do not know the form of the signature, use the legal name—the full two or three names of the person without abbreviations or initials. The legal signature of a married woman combines her maiden name with her married name, such as Dorothy Keller Brown—not Dorothy Ann Brown. Personal titles (*Mr., Mrs., Ms., Miss*) are not used; ordinarily neither are professional titles. To permit easy reference and identification, it is common practice to type in all capitals the names of individuals, businesses, agencies, and institutions named in a legal document.

At the end of a legal paper, type the lines for required signatures. These signature lines cannot stand alone on a page; arrange the body of the instrument so that at least two lines of text will appear on the page with the signatures. The lines extend from the center to the right margin, with two or three blank line spaces between them. Signature lines for witnesses begin at the left margin and extend to the page center.

Some secretaries lightly pencil in the respective initials at the beginnings of the lines on which each is to sign. Other secretaries use a small *X* to mark the spot. In some jurisdictions the names must be typed under the signature lines. Names are typed on file copy signature lines after some indication for *signed,* such as *Sgd.*

Seals. The abbreviation *L.S. (locus sigilli,* meaning "place of the seal") frequently appears at the end of lines on which parties to a paper sign their names. These letters have the legal significance of a wax seal. State laws determine whether or not a legal paper requires a seal.

Insertions. At the time of signing a legal paper, an insertion may be requested. An insertion is valid if the signers endorse it by writing their initials in ink near

---

An *ordinal* number is one that signifies rank or place in a sequence: first, second, tenth, etc. A *cardinal* number is used in simple counting to indicate how many: one, two, ten, thirty, etc.

TIME-SAVER. After preparing multiple copies of a legal paper that requires many signatures, attach a colored file flag at the appropriate point for each signer, using a different color for each one.

CONTRACT

THIS CONTRACT made and entered into this 4th day of January,

1983, by and between ROBERT LEYLAND ROBINS of the City of Tampa, County of

Hillsborough, State of Florida, doing business under the name of ADORN

MANUFACTURING COMPANY, and referred to as the firm in this contract, and

JANICE WEBBER LOGAL of Bradenton, Manatee County, State of Florida,

WITNESSETH:

1.   JANICE WEBBER LOGAL shall enter the services of the said

firm as a products representative for them in their business of manufac-

turing cosmetics for the period of one year from the 12th day of October,

1983, subject to the general control of said firm.

2.   The said products representative shall devote the whole of

her time, attention, and energies to the performance of her duties as such

representative, and shall not either directly or indirectly, alone or in

partnership, be connected with or concerned in any other business or pur-

suit whatsoever during the said term of one year.

3.   The said products representative shall, subject to the control

of the said firm, keep proper books of account and make due and correct

entries of the price of all goods sold and of all transactions and dealings

of and in relation to the said business, and shall serve the firm diligent-

ly and according to the best abilities of all respects.

4.   The fixed salary of the said products representative shall

be ten thousand dollars ($10,000) per annum, payable in equal semimonthly

installments.

Date: January 4, 1983   /s/ _____
                                   Adorn Manufacturing Company

                              /s/ _____
                                   Janice Webber Logal

Illus. 24-5
Observe that the copy is double spaced, and paragraphs have been indented ten spaces, names of the parties to the contract are in all caps, and dates conform to suggested patterns for legal papers.

it. At the time of typing, however, an omission may not be inserted between the lines to avoid retyping the page.

Erasures and Corrections. Each page should be typed accurately, for an erased and corrected error can cast doubt on the validity of an item if it occurs in a vital phrase. For example, "*four* thousand acres" erased and changed to "*forty* thousand acres" (or *June 6* changed to June 5) may raise a question of validity. An error in a single word in the straight text can usually be erased and corrected without question, but avoid erasing figures, dates, names, and places. If they must be erased, have the correction initialed.

Proofreading. The secretary who is unfamiliar with legal work should be particularly careful in proofreading and in questioning terms that are not understood. Novices have typed "the plaintiff praise" for "the plaintiff prays" and referred to the *Court of Common Please* or the *Court of Common Police* rather than the Court of Common Pleas. They have embarrassed themselves by referring to a *notary republic*. If you are not sure, find out!

Property descriptions, quoted material, and all figures and dates that appear in legal documents should be proofread twice because a minor discrepancy can be the basis of a litigation. Read a second time aloud to another person. Identify all capital letters, punctuation marks, and abbreviations.

Standard Legal Forms

Undoubtedly your employer will engage legal counsel when preparing important legal papers. If, however, certain types of papers are often used, such as leases or deeds, the forms given in legal reference books can be used as guides. Avoid indiscriminate copying of such forms because the laws vary from state to state, and laws also change.

Legal Forms. Stationery stores that supply legal offices carry printed legal forms that concur with local laws. These are called *legal forms* or law blanks. Look in the Yellow Pages under the heading *legal forms* for sources of supply for printed blanks of such common documents as affidavits, agreements, deeds, leases, powers of attorney, and wills.

Many printed legal forms consist of four pages, printed on both sides of one sheet of 8½- by 28-inch paper and folded once to make four pages of 8½ by 14 inches. The form for the endorsement is printed on the fourth page. With this arrangement, binding of the pages at the top is unnecessary, and a cover is not used. When the front page (page 1) is turned, pages 2 and 3 will read as one continuous page down the full inside length of the document.

Fill-Ins on Legal Blanks. Fill-ins may range from a single letter or figure to words, phrases, or long lines of text. Printed lines are usually not provided in the blank spaces; the typist, therefore, must align the typing line with the

REMINDER. Some legal forms are purchased in pads. Insert a reorder reminder approximately three fourths of the way through each new pad.

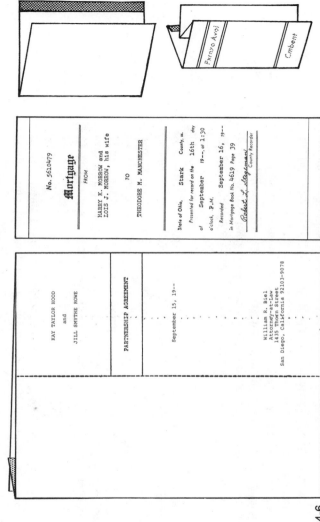

No. 5610479

Mortgage

FROM

HARRY K. MORROW and
LOIS J. MORROW, his wife

TO

THEODORE M. MANCHESTER

State of Ohio, Stark County, ss.
Presented for record on the 16th day
of September 19--, at 1:30
o'clock, P.M.
Recorded September 16, 19--
in Mortgage Book No. 4619 Page 39

Robert L. Hagerman
County Recorder

KAY TAYLOR HOOD
and
JILL SMYTHE ROWE

PARTNERSHIP AGREEMENT

September 15, 19--

William R. Biel
Attorney-at-Law
1435 Thorn Street
San Diego, California 92103-9078

Illus. 24-6

The *endorsement* (a description of the legal paper within) is typed on the outside of a cover as illustrated at the left above, or on a printed legal back as shown in the center. The correct folding of a legal back is shown at the right. Some offices file the folded documents in tall, narrow files with the endorsements in view; others use file drawers 16 inches wide and file unfolded legal papers with the first page to the front and the endorsements not visible.

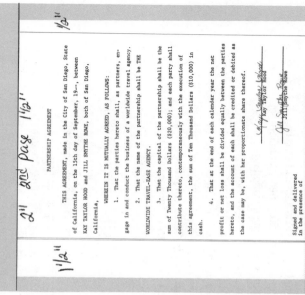

2" 2nd Page 1½"
½"
1½"

PARTNERSHIP AGREEMENT

THIS AGREEMENT, made in the City of San Diego, State of California, on the 15th day of September, 19--, between KAY TAYLOR HOOD and JILL SMYTHE ROWE, both of San Diego, California,

WHEREIN IT IS MUTUALLY AGREED, AS FOLLOWS:

1. That the parties hereto shall, as partners, engage in and conduct the business of a worldwide travel agency.

2. That the name of the partnership shall be THE WORLDWIDE TRAVEL-EASE AGENCY.

3. That the capital of the partnership shall be the sum of Twenty Thousand Dollars ($20,000); and each party shall contribute thereto, contemporaneously with the execution of this agreement, the sum of Ten Thousand Dollars ($10,000) in cash.

4. That at the end of each calendar year the net profit or net loss shall be divided equally between the parties hereto, and the account of each shall be credited or debited as the case may be, with her proportionate share thereof.

Signed and delivered
in the presence of

Kay Taylor Hood
Kay Taylor Hood

Jill Smythe Rowe
Jill Smythe Rowe

½" page # Continued

Illus. 24-7

To protect a legal document, use a single backing sheet (legal back or cover) with dimensions that are about one inch wider and 1½ inches longer than the instrument. This sheet is a high-grade, heavy quality paper, and is usually blue. After the back has been properly folded and reopened, the endorsement is typed. The typed pages are then inserted under the one-inch fold at the top of the backing sheet, and an eyelet or staple is placed at each side (about one inch from the top and the sides). Backing sheets may be color coded to differentiate types of documents.

printing line. Use the printed margins for typing full lines. As a precaution, rule a Z in ink to fill deep unused space. (See Illus. 24-2, page 591, Power of Attorney.)

Carbon Copies of Legal Blanks. To ensure the best possible alignment on carbon copies of printed forms, check the forms to be sure that all copies were printed at the same time. The legend 60M 7/6/—indicates that 60,000 copies were printed on July 6, 19—. Roll the matched set carefully into the typewriter and then insert the carbons (as shown on page 88). Because aligning is difficult, you may prefer to type each blank individually, checking each one against the source document. If you do this, type *COPY* on all but the one to be used as the original.

Riders. When the space allotted for filling in conditional clauses or other provisions in a legal blank is not large enough for the typewritten material, leave sufficient space after the last line to permit a slip of paper containing the rest of the typewritten material (called a *rider*) to be pasted to the document. Use legal cap for the rider, and cut off any unused part of the sheet. Fasten the rider (legal paper) securely to the document and fold the rider to fit neatly within the backing sheet.

Forms File. Many legal documents that the secretary types are adaptations of previous ones. A forms file of commonly typed legal documents, therefore, can be an important time-saver. Accumulate this file by making an extra carbon or photocopy of representative legal documents at the time of the first typing. In the margin, add helpful notes such as the number of copies to be prepared, the distribution of the copies, and other pertinent data. In time, the file will contain most, if not all, of the legal documents produced in the office. You can then consult the file to determine the exact procedure for any document contained therein. Legal secretaries consider their forms file to be their most valuable reference source.

WORD PROCESSING AND THE LEGAL OFFICE

Most large and many small legal offices are equipped with automated word processing equipment. There are several reasons for this.

Standard paragraphs that have been court tested make up a significant portion of many legal documents. By having these paragraphs on magnetic media and by using magnetic media activated typewriters, the paragraphs can be typed automatically, quickly, and error free. This leaves the operator the task of filling in the variable materials only.

Typographical errors and erasures in certain critical places in a legal document can disqualify the document for court purposes. Automated type-writers produce error free typing. This saves many hours of proofreading time.

Computer networks have been established to service legal offices. These networks have large banks of stored legal material—cases, decisions, opinions, and reviews—carefully indexed. For a fee a legal office can have access to this vast amount of stored information and save hours of research. For example, the computer network can be instructed to print out all the court decisions dealing with a specific point of law. This information usually comes into the legal office to subscribers via some form of computer terminal. In many cases this terminal is an automated typewriter that serves a dual purpose: reproducing materials stored on magnetic media within the legal office and receiving output from the legal computer network in response to a request.

THE PARALEGAL/LEGAL ASSISTANT

In the early 1970's when the American Bar Association recognized the need for administrative support personnel to free attorneys of many of the details associated with the practice of law, the position of paralegal or legal assistant was created. There is no difference in the meaning of the titles—the title depends upon the attorney's preference; the paralegal and the legal assistant perform the same duties.

A paralegal/legal assistant is an individual who works under the supervision of a licensed member of the legal profession. An attorney utilizes the services of a paralegal and legal assistant in much the same way as a physician would use those of a nurse. Some of the duties performed by a paralegal may be as follows:

1. To conduct the initial client interview
2. To follow up on an investigation of factual information
3. To research the law pertaining to litigation
4. To draft legal documents
5. To prepare various legal motions
6. To handle exhibits used in court
7. To prepare documents for the dissolution of a marriage, to collect accounts, handle claims, and probate wills

The duties performed will, of course, depend on the nature of the law practice and the needs of the attorneys. To be a paralegal, you must be willing to accept professional responsibility, have an interest in and an aptitude for the law, and be completely oriented toward serving the attorney who employs you. Your work must be of unquestioned accuracy.

The educational background required to become a paralegal varies widely. Since the program is relatively new, there are various programs designed to train paralegals. Some of these are degree programs offered by colleges and universities. Others are six-month courses offered by special schools throughout the country—there were approximately 225 schools offering paralegal programs in 1980. Some states offer a certification program

THE SECRETARY'S KNOWLEDGE OF THE LAW

leading to the professional designation Certified Attorney's Assistant. To obtain this certificate, a paralegal must pass a qualifying examination. Local state bar associations have details on paralegal programs offered in the various states. The paralegal field is growing in demand and prestige. It offers an excellent career opportunity for the secretary with a special interest in the law and could serve as excellent preparation for law school.

In 1981 the National Association of Legal Assistants (NALA) established a Certified Legal Assistant (CLA) program to promote high standards and professionalism among legal assistants. The CLA program involves the successful completion of a two-day examination; evidence of continuing education must be submitted to NALA periodically in order to maintain certified status.

Information on the CLA examination may be obtained from NALA Headquarters, 3005 East Skelly Drive, Tulsa, OK 74105.

Regardless of the type of business that employs you, some elements of business law will affect the day-to-day operations of the office. Because of the importance of your role as a guardian of information, a working knowledge of the laws that directly pertain to your company will add to your efficiency and prevent costly litigation. Business law is extensive and complex, and the secretary is not expected to be an authority on legal matters. However, most companies have established policies that govern the handling of information pertaining to the company, its clients, and its employees.

It is not uncommon for executives and secretaries to unknowingly violate legislation safeguarding equal employment opportunities and the privacy of personnel information. It is essential that every secretary be familiar with the company's policies and federal legislation regarding these areas.

Equal Employment Regulations

A secretary who works closely with the personnel department of a company should be especially familiar with regulations concerning recruiting, screening, hiring, and terminating employees, since these regulations are frequently violated. If you share the responsibilities for interviewing and selecting employees, you should know about the discriminatory nature of certain questions. Before asking any preemployment question, consider these two points: Is the question job related? Does the question eliminate a disproportionate number of minorities? If the answer to either or these questions is *yes* or *possibly,* omit the question.

Because the regulations change rapidly, it is necessary that you keep up to date. The three most significant regulations governing equal employment are:

1. Every employer who is engaged in interstate commerce and employing at least fifteen people is required to make employment decisions without consideration of race, creed, color, sex, religion, or national origin. Additionally, an employer may not segregate or classify employees or applicants in any discriminatory way. This prevents advertising jobs as male jobs or female jobs.

2. All employers of twenty or more persons are prevented from making employment decisions based on age for persons between 40 and 65.

3. Employers must provide equal pay for men and women working in the same business at jobs requiring equal skill, effort, and responsibility under similar conditions.

The Equal Employment Opportunity Commission, Washington, D.C. 20507 issues periodic guidelines for employers about equal employment.

Employee Information and Privacy Legislation

With the increasing sophistication of computerized record keeping systems, the public has become concerned about the kinds of information being collected, how the information is used, and who has access to it. The federal government responded to these concerns by passing the Freedom of Information Act in 1966 (FOIA) and amending it in 1974 with the Privacy Act. Both of these acts apply only to records kept by federal agencies, but it is possible that national legislation will be passed to ensure the privacy of employee records in private industry as well. Some states have already passed legislation to permit employees access to their own personal records.

The collection, dispersal, and access to personnel information is usually covered by company policy. The secretary should have a copy of these policies and be alert to requests from outsiders. Upon request, some companies will give only directory information to outsiders. Directory information consists of the employee's job title and dates of employment.

Knowing what you are permitted to tell a caller about personnel can save your employer the cost and inconvenience of a lawsuit if the wrong information should be given. Personnel and payroll records must be made available only to authorized users. If in doubt about what information can or cannot be given, always refer an inquiry to a higher authority.

SUGGESTED READINGS

Bate, Marjorie Dunlap, and Mary Casey. *Legal Office Procedures*. New York: McGraw-Hill Book Company, 1981.

Black's Law Dictionary. St. Paul: West Publishing Co., 1979.

Local Law Bulletin (daily or weekly), a record of court calls and current news about meetings of interest to the legal profession.

Martindale-Hubbel Law Dictionary. A four-volume reference published annually listing lawyers and their addresses, a digest of the laws of the fifty states and patent, copyright, and trademark laws.

NALS *Docket,* a bimonthly magazine published for members of the National Association of Legal Secretaries, 3005 E. Skelly Drive, Suite 120, Tulsa, OK 74105.

National Association of Legal Secretaries. *Manual for the Legal Secretarial Profession,* 2d ed. St. Paul: West Publishing Co., 1974.

Oran, Daniel. *Law Dictionary for Non-Lawyers.* St. Paul: West Publishing Co., 1980.

Reilly, Theresa M. *Legal Secretary's Word Finder and Desk Book.* Englewood Cliffs, N.J.: Prentice-Hall, Inc. 1974.

QUESTIONS FOR DISCUSSION

1. Answer the following questions relating to the preparation of a power of attorney.
   (a) What variable data are usually typed on a power of attorney form?
   (b) What may be done to prevent the fraudulent insertion of additions after the power of attorney form has been signed?
   (c) If the power of attorney is to authorize the bank to accept checks drawn on the company bank account when signed by the secretary, how many copies should be made of the document itself?
   (d) How can you be sure that all copies of a printed legal form are identical?

2. How does legal typing differ from manuscript typing in (a) the use of the hyphen in dividing words? (b) numbering of pages? (c) ending of a page with the last line of a paragraph? (d) acceptability of erasures and corrections?

3. Assume that you are a notary public. In what way do your responsibilities differ when you sign an agreement for monthly machine repair service and when you notarize an affidavit?

4. The secretary in an adjacent office asks you to witness the signatures on a contract. When you reach the office, you find that the signatures have already been affixed and you are asked to sign as a witness. What do you do?

5. Your employer asks you to rush out a legal paper that must be signed by persons waiting in the office. You type it quickly, check it even more quickly, and hand it in. After the signers leave, you notice you have made a serious error in a date. What do you do?

6. What precautions are required regarding signatures on legal documents?

7. One reference source states: "When making photocopies of the Will or Codicil, IT IS NEVER TO BE UNSTAPLED OR TAKEN APART." What is a codicil? Why should not the will or codicil be unstapled when preparing copies?

8. Many Latin words and phrases are used in legal documents. What is the English translation of each of the following Latin terms?

corpus juris   *quasi*
de jure   *quod erat demonstrandum (Q.E.D.)*
loco citato   *scilicet (ss)*
prima facie   *sic*
pro tempore (or *pro tem*)   *et al.*

If necessary, consult one of the references given on pages 603-604 for the correct translation.

9. Why would an employee want access to information kept in a personnel file?

10. A *conversion* is the unconventional use of a word, such as using a noun as an adjective or a verb as a noun. Select the words in the following sentences that have been converted to unconventional parts of speech. Consult the Reference Guide to check your answers.

(a) The Board railroaded the appointment of the chairman.
(b) Many performers skyrocket to fame after their first appearance in Las Vegas.
(c) We bicycled all over Europe.
(d) Her peaches-and-cream complexion is envied by all her friends.

PROBLEMS

 1. It has been recommended that a secretary accumulate a file of legal forms for reference purposes. Prepare a typing instruction sheet that could be inserted in the front of such a file. Include typing instructions for:

(a) Margins
(b) Spacing
(c) Paragraph indentation
(d) Writing dates
(e) Paging
(f) Writing figures
(g) Typing names
(h) Typing quoted matter
(i) Preparing forms for signatures
(j) Fill-ins in legal blanks
(k) Correction of errors

2. Assume that you wish to become a notary public in your state.

(a) From your library, from a notary public, or from some other source obtain the name and address of the designated official in your state who issues notary public commissions.

(b) Obtain from the designated official the specific requirements for the commission in your state. Type a summary list of these various requirements.

3. You are a notary public commissioned in Storey County, Nevada. Mr. Toni Nuvamsa asks you to prepare an affidavit for his signature stating that he, Toni Nuvamsa, is a member of the Apache Indian tribe and has resided for the past eighteen years at 2323 North Canyon Drive, Reno, Nevada. Prepare the affidavit using the one shown in Illus. 24-1 as a guide. Use the current date. You are to sign the form as the notary public.

4. Mr. Edward Thomas Stanek, who lives at 134 North 10th Street, Cleveland, Ohio, owns a building located at 3150 North Platt Street, Orlando, Florida. Mr. Stanek wishes to give Rebecca Mary Ploeger of 86 Professional Drive, Orlando, authority to sell the building and land for him and to execute in his behalf all papers necessary for the transfer of the property. Prepare the

power of attorney. Use the form in Illus. 24-2 as a guide. Your form, however, will be typewritten in place of using a printed form as illustrated. Use the current date. Complete the notary public statement that constitutes part of the power of attorney.

5. Using the partnership agreement shown in Illus. 24-7 type an original and two carbons of the partnership agreement for Helen

Bates Royzet and Martin Charles Cassi, both residents of Columbia, South Carolina. They are forming a partnership to operate a tax accounting service to be known as the Star Tax Service. Each agrees to invest $25,000 in the business. Profits and losses are to be distributed annually and divided equally between the partners. Use the current date.

Part Eight Case Problems

Case 8-1
CHECK AND DOUBLE-CHECK

John Sanchez was recently transferred from the personnel department to become secretary to Elizabeth Chou, manager of the accounting department. John was responsible for duplicating the quarterly financial report for the board of directors' meeting on Friday from rough-draft copy handed him on Wednesday morning by his employer. On Thursday afternoon he typed the offset master and took it to the reprographics department along with an order form for the duplicating job.

First thing Friday morning he put the copies on Ms. Chou's desk. Ten minutes later—and just fifteen minutes before the meeting—Ms. Chou stormed up to John's desk, shouting, "Look at this! Didn't you proofread this before you had it run? Don't you know that you always have to check your totals? Every good accountant does! You'd have seen that the total of every single column is wrong. The complete report is worthless, and the board is due in the conference room right now. You've made me look stupid! What can I do at this late date?"

Referring to the original rough draft, the two discovered together that Ms. Chou's 1's had a tail on them which John had read as 7's, a mistake that was repeated throughout the statement.

What can be done? Whose fault was the error? What changes should John make in his procedures?

Case 8-2
WORK ORGANIZATION

Norma Wilson was secretary to the dean of the School of Business at XYZ University. The dean was to present a paper on Friday in a distant city, and the 30-page paper was then to be submitted for publication in the proceedings of the symposium.

On Thursday Norma planned to type the final draft of the paper, for which she had done much of the research herself. As she settled down to the typing, the registrar called to remind her that all teaching schedules for the following semester were due by five o'clock that day. On Monday she had sent a rough copy of proposed schedules to all members of the division with a request from the dean that each member initial the schedule if approved or submit by Wednesday evening a request for revision and the reason for asking for the change. In checking the returned schedules, she found that Professor Lawler, a usually dissident faculty member, had not been heard from. She called his secretary, who said, "Professor Lawler is never in on Thursday. That's the day he works at the Research Council. It's on his class schedule filed in your office."

Norma then telephoned the registrar that the dean's material would be delayed until Monday at 10:30 because all of the faculty members had not responded. Just as she was starting on the report, the dean called an emergency meeting involving a disciplinary matter; and, as was customary, Norma was asked to take notes. Since both the meeting and the report were short, Norma transcribed her notes as soon as she returned to her desk.

At 11:30 Norma started on the research paper again. She discovered that she had omitted two page references on footnotes when researching the information. Instead of taking her lunch hour, she made a quick trip to the library to secure the missing information. Before resuming her typing, she telephoned to ask Professor Lawler's secretary to bring the missing schedule to her office just as soon as the professor came in on Friday. Then she placed a note on the dean's desk that the schedules would be delayed until Monday and asked if the schedules should be approved before she typed them. (The dean attended the Council for Deans at ten o'clock every Monday.)

A constant stream of faculty and student visitors delayed the report even more. At three o'clock the dean rushed to Norma's desk saying, "May I have the manuscript so that I can familiarize myself with it this afternoon? I want to read it smoothly tomorrow, and that requires practice."

Norma had to admit, "It's not ready yet, dean. There's just too much work in this office for one person. I can give you a rough draft in about twenty minutes, and I can mail the final corrected manuscript tomorrow afternoon if you give me the name and address of the editor of the proceedings."

The dean, visibly annoyed, retreated, muttering, "I gave it to you on Wednesday morning. You knew I had to have it today. Maybe you should try to plan your work better."

What errors in work organization did Norma commit?

Joyce Newman is secretary to the company comptroller. Her job involves handling confidential payroll information. She often has lunch with Connie Vernon, who is secretary to Marvin Keller, an inquisitive junior executive in the sales department. Mr. Keller sometimes joins the secretaries for lunch in the company cafeteria. Each time he has indirectly asked Joyce to divulge salaries of certain employees.

If you were in Joyce's position, how would you handle this situation?

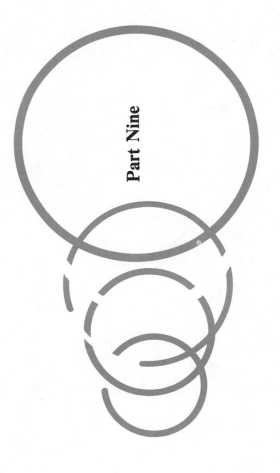

Part Nine

YOUR PROFESSION: PLACEMENT AND ADVANCEMENT

You are now ready to determine your future in the secretarial profession. Because of the many areas of specialization, selecting the right secretarial position requires self-evaluation and career planning. The secretarial position is still one of the best avenues to an administrative position. By making significant contributions to the job and to the employer, you can advance to a position of increased responsibility. With continued education you can aspire to a position involving the supervision of others. A career ladder in the secretarial profession does exist. As you enter the field, set your career goals and work toward them diligently so that you, too, can reap the dividends found in added prestige, greater responsibility, and financial remuneration.

Chapter **25**

Selecting the Right Position

You are now approaching the end of this textbook and perhaps your final term of formal secretarial preparation. Now is the time for you to begin to make fundamental decisions about your career. As you prepare for employment, you will find many career options available to you, and, therefore, many decisions to make in selecting the right position. For example, in large organizations new technology is providing new career paths in word processing center environments or in administrative support areas. Also, there are fields of specialization for the secretary, such as medical, legal, government, education, and technical. You have the choice of working in small or large companies and working for one person or several. The geographical location of the office may also affect your decision. You may prefer to work in the heart of downtown or in the expanse of suburbia. You may want to be a secretary in your own hometown, in a distant city, or even in a distant land. It's really up to you. All these decisions are yours. As a well-qualified applicant, you will have no difficulty getting the secretarial position you want in the office, location, and specialization of your choice.

This chapter will prepare you to make some of these decisions. Steps in the employment process—preparation of the personal data sheet and application forms and interview techniques—are discussed. The chapter concludes with a section for the experienced job seeker, giving useful suggestions for job hunting and preparing a personal data sheet.

TYPES OF OFFICES

The size of an office and its location will determine the type and extent of the benefits afforded employees. Although many secretaries work in the downtown areas of cities, where salaries are usually higher than those in outlying districts, attractive positions are open in the suburbs and in small outlying towns. From a secretary's viewpoint each type of office and location offers certain advantages.

Small Offices

Many secretaries prefer to work in small offices because they are able to perform a wide variety of duties. The small office is an excellent training ground for all facets of secretarial work. There is no one else to answer the telephone, greet callers, to do the filing, handle the petty cash, duplicate materials, sort and send out the mail, and purchase supplies. Examples of one-secretary offices are those maintained by attorneys, architects, engineers, accountants, doctors, dentists, insurance agencies, schools, and company branches.

Personnel Policies. One of the advantages of working in a small office is the freedom offered. The hours of work are usually established, but the secretary knows the volume of work and when time permits, or personal circumstances require, may extend the lunch hour or leave early.

Small offices usually have general personnel policies rather than clearly defined ones. This may or may not be to the advantage of the secretary. There may be no limit to sick leaves and emergency absences, or there may be no provision at all for them.

There are, however, a few definite disadvantages to working in a small office. Generally there is a limit to the salary a small office can pay. The ceiling may be set by circumstances of the business and not by the competence of the secretary. Instead of giving specified salary increases at definite intervals, the employer is likely to consider each salary increase individually. Another disadvantage is the absence of social opportunities in the work environment.

Administrative Opportunities. In some small offices, the secretary assumes a great deal of administrative responsibility but rarely is given an administrative title. Advancement is in terms of salary, not title. By working as a team, the employer soon learns the capabilities of the secretary and will increasingly expand that position to include more and more responsibility. Depending upon the nature of the work, the employer may be out of the office much of the time, and then the secretary virtually runs the office.

An office with three and four secretaries frequently provides excellent opportunities to gain supervisory experience. In such situations, the senior secretary may supervise the work of the office staff in addition to other duties of the job.

Large Offices

The work of the secretary in the large office tends to differ in many respects from that of the secretary in the small office. In the large office many of the business routines are performed by special departments. Telephone duties are handled by switchboard operators; postal and shipping chores, by the mailing and shipping departments; ordering supplies by the purchasing department—to mention a few. On the other hand, in addition to communication responsibilities, the secretary in the large office may handle travel details, research business information for the executive, draft reports, sit in on conferences and write the proceedings, and may perform other important services.

In some offices the typing and nontyping duties of the secretarial position may be separated, with the word processing center assuming the correspondence responsibilities. The secretary may choose whether to follow the career paths available in the center or those in the administrative support areas. In both options the secretary enjoys the benefits of membership in a large organization.

Personnel Policies. Personnel policies must be clearly defined and followed in large offices. Singling out an individual employee for special privileges can be damaging to office morale. The personnel policies of a large company usually cover such matters as the following:

Hours of work, lunch hour, and rest periods

Overtime pay or compensatory time off

Eligibility for vacation; length of vacation

Number of days allowed annually for emergency sick leave

Days considered as holidays (days off with pay)

Salary range for each job; frequency and extent of salary increases

Fringe benefits

Job descriptions

Job classifications

Job Classifications. There is opportunity for advancement in a large organization. Supervisory and administrative positions exist to which the secretary can advance. Secretaries to top management are frequently administrative assistants in both duties and title.

Fringe Benefits. Many businesses and government agencies offer fringe benefits to their employees. They are called *fringe* because they are outside the realm of salary, and sometimes outside the realm of taxable income. In some instances, these benefits cost the organization an additional 30 to 50 percent of the wages paid.

The most common benefits are:

Group life insurance

Medical examinations

Medical and hospitalization insurance

Long-term disability benefits

Company stock purchase plan

Profit-sharing plans

Pension fund

Bonuses

Employee credit union

Company educational seminars and conferences

Reimbursed tuition for job-related course work

Membership expenses in professional organizations

Company subsidized cafeteria

Recreational facilities

Dental insurance

A company may pay for all or part of the insurance premiums, make substantial contributions to the pension fund, and provide office space for the employee operated credit union. Some companies allow employees to choose their own package of benefits. Generous vacations, holidays, and sick leave periods are becoming more and more common. Liberal maternity benefits have been written into many company policies. Finally, firms dealing in a product or service, such as retailers and commercial airlines, offer attractive purchase discounts or travel plans to their employees.

OPPORTUNITIES FOR SPECIALIZATION

There are unlimited opportunities for the qualified secretary to specialize in a particular field. For most secretaries, a decision to specialize usually comes after some experience in general office work. Some office experience, training in business fundamentals and secretarial skills, and an interest in the area of specialization are necessary prerequisites for making this decision. Although there are many areas of specialization, this book can discuss only a few of them. In each field the typical duties of the position are mentioned.

The Medical Secretary

A long-established and rapidly growing area of secretarial specialization is that of the medical secretary. You may work in a doctor's or dentist's office, or for a clinic, a hospital, a pharmaceutical company, a public health facility, or even an insurance company.

Although desirable, special training is not essential; learning on the job is always possible. A knowledge of Latin, however, is a distinct help in understanding the terminology. Courses in German also will prove helpful. Independent business schools, community colleges, technical colleges and institutes, and some four-year colleges and universities offer programs for training the medical secretary. Besides training in office skills and medical dictation, curriculums include a number of science courses, the study of medical terminology, records management, and accounting procedures common to medical offices. Specialized handbooks are available to the medical secretary and to the secretary who is contemplating this field.

In the one-doctor office, the secretary may serve as receptionist, bookkeeper, transcriber of case histories, secretary, and office manager. Routine technical duties like sterilizing instruments or taking temperatures may be required. The secretary who is the only employee must perform all the office duties and must assume responsibility for running a smooth office. In the process, the principles of medical ethics are followed by keeping patients' medical records confidential.

In large offices and in hospitals, the work will consist of transcribing patients' records, either from shorthand or machine dictation, and of the myriad details involved in smoothly, pleasantly, and comfortingly handling the patients in today's busy medical office. But, regardless of the size of the office or organization, the secretary must be familiar with medical terms—both the meaning and the spelling—and with professional office procedures as well as medical and hospital insurance forms.

To keep current in the field, the medical secretary should join the American Association of Medical Assistants, a professional organization for the office staff, nurses, technicians, and assistants who are employed by physicians or accredited hospitals. This organization sponsors a certification program (Certified Medical Assistant-Administrative), publishes a bimonthly magazine called *The Professional Medical Assistant*, and holds an annual convention.

To be eligible to take the certification examination, candidates must meet certain requirements of training acquired in a medical assisting program or have experience in the field. The examination consists of two parts:

Basic Certification—covers medical terminology, basic anatomy and physiology, psychology, medical law and ethics, and office and clinical procedures

Administrative Specialty—covers oral and written communications, bookkeeping and insurance, and administrative procedures

The Legal Secretary

The legal secretary must have a command of the English language and excellent typewriting and transcription proficiencies. The work of the law office is exacting; an inaccurate record can be extremely expensive. Working long hours—most of them under pressure—the secretary must have a thorough knowledge of legal procedures and a real interest in the law. Most law offices today are equipped with some type of word processing equipment which reduces the need for retyping of legal documents.

The National Association of Legal Secretaries (International) holds an annual convention and offers its membership a bimonthly publication, NALS *Docket.* This organization sponsors through its chapters free training programs, an employment service, and a Professional Legal Secretary examination and certification program. To be eligible for the PLS examination, an applicant must have had at least five years' experience as a legal secretary and must provide the names of two attorneys as references. The two-day examination consists of seven parts: Written Communication Skills and Knowledge; Human Relations and Ethics; Legal Secretarial Procedures; Legal Secretarial Accounting; Legal Terminology, Techniques, and Procedures; Exercise of Judgment; and Legal Secretarial Skills.

Many of the peculiarities of the work of the legal secretary were described in Chapter 24. Actually the legal secretary's work is highly varied and involves extensive contacts with people—the clients of the law office. Occasionally secretaries become so fascinated with the profession that they study law in evening classes, pass the bar examination, and proudly change the desk plate from *Secretary* to *Attorney.*

The Educational Secretary

Every community offers employment opportunities for educational secretaries in work that varies widely among positions. The secretary to the top school officials of a large city system will have duties similar to those of the secretary in business and industry. On the other hand, the secretary in the office of a small local school will perform vastly different duties. Some examples are taking dictation, keeping records, ordering materials and supplies, supervising student aides, scheduling facilities, working on master schedules, and planning group meetings. This secretary will also meet school visitors and have close contacts with students, teachers, and parents.

The National Association of Educational Office Personnel is the professional organization for secretaries in this field. The organization upgrades the profession by sponsoring a continuing academic program, conducting conferences, and distributing three publications (*The National Educational Secretary, Beam,* and *Crossroads*) and pertinent information. The NAEOP also sponsors a Professional Standards Program that issues seven kinds of certificates (basic, associate professional, advanced I, II, III, bachelor, and master) based on education, experience, and professional activity. A college degree is required for the bachelor's certificate and a master's degree for the master's certificate. To be eligible for the examination, an applicant must be a member of the association.

The Technical Secretary

The technical secretary serves the engineer and the scientist—those who are at home in the laboratory but not in the office. To conserve the time of

TECHNICAL SECRETARY

Dynamic young medical research institute needs qualified technical secretary to support quality control division. Highly proficient in all phases of office procedures with top skills. Must be able to work without supervision. Background in mathematics and sciences helpful. Salary commensurate with ability. Excellent benefits. Call Ms. Alvarez at 641-6782 for appointment.

TRIANGLE RESEARCH INSTITUTE

5770 Waycross Drive
Bala Cynwyd, PA 19004-2139

Illus. 25-1
Advertisement for
a technical
secretary

highly paid scientific and engineering personnel, many companies provide each top-level scientist and engineer with assistants to perform routine functions and free the scientist for creative work. The secretary is the member of this team who assumes the office burden and minimizes the distractions and interruptions necessitated by office responsibilities. Imagine the personal fulfillment of the secretary who is a team member working on a cure for cancer or a new source of energy.

The technical secretary is probably as much an administrative assistant as a secretary. The work includes not only the usual secretarial duties but such

Illus. 25-2
The work of a
technical secretary
is demanding, but
financially
rewarding.

additional responsibilities as handling all or most of the correspondence from composition to mailing, maintaining the office technical library, at times gathering materials from other library resources, and proofreading and frequently editing scientific papers, as well as handling all details incident to their publication. The secretary prepares engineering reports, checks materials against specifications and standards, and orders materials in compliance with specifications. The work is demanding and exacting, but the pay is exceedingly rewarding. A strong background in mathematics, science, and technical terminology is a definite asset; advancement in the position requires continued study.

When you work as a technical secretary, you can expect to undergo security clearance if you are to be employed in a company having contracts with the United States Department of Defense. The maintenance of strict security control is becoming important to other companies as well, because of the possibility of the pirating of formulas, research findings, advanced designs, and so forth. The secretary must know how security is maintained for each classification from restricted data to top secret.

The Public Stenographer

As the title implies, the public stenographer works for the public—that is, for people (usually traveling executives) who need someone for dictation and transcription or an important job that can be handled in a minimum of time. For this reason, the office is usually located in a hotel, off the main foyer of a large office building, or at an airport facility. The public stenographer charges by the hour or job and may work for as many as a dozen persons each day. The work ranges from taking highly technical dictation to recording speeches and testimony of witnesses, to typing legal documents, to running errands for a busy executive. A public stenographer usually is a notary public as well.

Highly qualified persons usually find public stenography gratifying and exciting. A word of caution is needed, however: Only someone with a broad education, a wealth of office experience, the temperament to cope with the pressure of deadlines, and the highest level of skills should attempt to enter the field.

In the right location, the income is high; but much of the work is performed under time pressure.

Word Processing and Administrative Secretaries

The concept of word processing has provided two distinct career paths for the secretary employed in most large organizations. The word processing specialist or correspondence secretary (see Chapter 1) enjoys being a part of the most innovative change in today's office. Armed with the basic skills of typing, grammar, punctuation, and spelling, the specialist operates the newest of text-editing equipment in a teamwork environment. Word processing specialists tell of their fascination with the equipment and the daily challenge in learning the capabilities of the machines. The production of perfect typewritten lines and the assignment of confidential material or an entire job from start to finish are means by which the secretary is given more responsibility.

In addition to the basic skills, particular attributes for success in the center include flexibility, a good vocabulary, the desire to work with machines, the ability to think logically, to proofread and edit copy, to handle revisions, to listen and follow instructions, to work with others to get the job done, and to organize work so that it is completed in order of priority.

Since the concept of word processing is relatively new, the experienced word processor is in demand. Experience can lead to advancement to word processing coordinator or manager as new centers are opened up in a company. The word processor who intends to move up the career ladder must be equipped with managerial ability. This training can be acquired independently or as part of a company training program.

The traditional nontyping activities of the secretarial position are accomplished by administrative secretaries (see Chapter 1). These secretaries handle the work required of several employers and coordinate the material sent to the center. They may also dictate to the center.

Administrative secretaries must enjoy meeting the public in person and over the telephone. The ability to organize work and determine priority is crucial when a number of principals are served. Advancement opportunities may be greater than those of a multifunctional secretary because of the opportunity to work with a variety of executives.

The Temporary Service Secretary

One of the fastest growing services today is that of providing part-time office help. Kelly Services, Inc., Olsten Temporary Services, and Manpower, Inc., are but a few of the organizations specializing in this service. Others are listed in the Yellow Pages and are widely advertised in general publications. These organizations offer a corps of temporary workers to be deployed wherever required. It is estimated that over two million people work as temporaries each year. They help the office that experiences intermittent periods of heavy work load, they fill in for employees who are on vacation or ill, and they provide the one-half secretary for the one-and-a-half-secretary office.

In addition to rendering a service to business, these organizations provide a means of organized part-time employment to a large number of persons who are unable, because of family obligations or other duties, to devote themselves to year-round, full-time jobs. A temporary position permits a flexible schedule and the choice of job locations close to home. It also enables a person to acquire the needed experience before applying for a full-time job or reentering the job market after a long absence. To be happy in temporary work, the secretary must be flexible, confident, and adaptable to change.

The work of the temporary is as varied as is business. Calls for assistance come from all types of offices. The agency attempts to match the requirements of the job with the competencies of the temporary worker. Many a secretarial trainee in college has found that being an office temporary for the summer is one way to gain a wide variety of experience in a short time.

The Government Secretary

More secretaries work for the government than for any other type of business or organization. Government positions offer certain advantages, such as assured annual increments, job security, a sound retirement system, and the opportunity for advancement based on merit. A secretary trained in office administration, who has initiative and ambition, can advance to a position of great responsibility in government service. Being a government employee does not necessarily mean working in Washington, D.C., or for the federal government. Wherever there is a military installation, veterans' hospital, weather station, or federal bureau office, there are federal employees, including secretaries. State and local governments (combined) employ far more office workers than does the federal government. Thus, government jobs are found in towns and cities in America and in foreign countries.

The federal government, all states, and many municipal governments have a civil (meaning civilian) service merit system in which jobs are classified and appointments are made on the basis of examination results. As a student, you can obtain a certificate of proficiency in typing and shorthand from your college, but you must take the written examination of verbal and clerical abilities. The federal government is now following the practice of *self-certification* in typewriting. An applicant who certifies a typewriting skill of 40 or more words a minute does not take a typing test.

Stenographic posts are classified in the federal government as GS3 (General Schedule 3) through GS6, and it is possible for a secretary to advance to GS7 and 8. There is a standard base salary, with annual increments, for each GS rating. For high-cost areas, such as Alaska and Hawaii, cost-of-living increases are given.

For the first year of government service, an employee is considered on probation; after three years the status changes to *career permanent*. This classification means that you can apply to any federal agency without further testing. Also, if you leave government service and return within three years from the date of your termination, you do not lose accumulated sick leave. In addition, unused sick leave hours count toward an early retirement date.

The United States is divided into ten regions with an Office of Personnel Management in each. Also, there are 110 Federal Job Information Centers. These centers are listed in telephone directories under United States Government. If a center is not listed in your directory, the toll free number for the center in your state can be obtained by dialing 800-555-1212. To obtain information about a position, write to the regional office in which you wish to obtain employment or telephone your local center. If you are interested in working in Washington, D.C., write to the Office of Personnel Management (formerly U. S. Civil Service Commission), 1900 E Street, N.W., Washington, D.C. 20415.

The Foreign Service Secretary

Does the prospect of serving as a secretary in the American Legation in Berlin, Tokyo, Paris, Buenos Aires, or Copenhagen interest you? If so, you should examine the employment opportunities in the Foreign Service of the Department of State, United States Information Agency (USIA), Agency for International Development (AID), and the Departments of Army, Navy, and Air Force.[1] The Department of State has offices in over 300 cities worldwide.

Work in a foreign country can be thrilling, but also exacting. It calls for a special kind of person—one who is willing to live in an exemplary fashion, for our foreign service personnel are on display 24 hours a day. Each staff member represents the United States and contributes to the success of our program. The Department of State, USIA, and AID, therefore, carefully screen all foreign service personnel; and requirements are high. The basic requirements for a secretarial position in the Foreign Service of the Department of State are as follows:

21 years of age

United States citizen

High school graduate or equivalent

High score on a qualifying examination covering clerical ability, spelling, typing, shorthand

Good health

Minimum of one year of continuous general experience and one year of continuous office experience using shorthand (A year in college is usually considered equal to a year of work experience; however, a minimum of one year of full-time shorthand experience is always required.)

Competency in a foreign language is not required. If, however, you should have ambitions to advance to the position of a foreign service staff officer in the Department of State, ability to speak and write a foreign language is required. Extensive study of a foreign language in college will be a strong plus factor when your application is evaluated.

The pay is comparatively good, with additional allowances for housing, cost of living, and special compensation for hardship posts.

---

[1] Information about foreign employment through the United States Information Agency and the Agency for International Development can be obtained by writing to these agencies in Washington, D.C.

SURVEY OF EMPLOYMENT OPPORTUNITIES

A review of the help wanted advertisements in most newspapers will show that the highly qualified, college-trained secretary is in a position to pick and choose. The problem, then, is one of job selection. There are many dimensions to the selection process, as these questions reveal:

1. Do you want to work in your local community, or do you hope to find employment in a new location—a large city, a different part of the country, or abroad?

2. Which organizations relate to your special interests in art, music, sports, medicine, accounting, social work, research, writing, politics?

3. How do your education and skills match job requirements of your career goal?

4. Would you prefer to work in a one-secretary office or in a large group surrounding?

5. Are you fascinated with the new information systems equipment? Would you consider working with machines a challenge?

6. What are you looking for in a job? Security? No pressure? Competition? Responsibility?

7. What is the average salary for the position you are seeking?

Psychologists say that the key items in job satisfaction are a sense of responsibility, satisfaction of achievement, opportunity for growth, recognition from employer, and a feeling of being needed. The right choice is not the result of luck but of careful analysis and action.

Before you begin your job search, take a few minutes to prepare a job prospect list. Decide how you will evaluate a company. Set goals and objectives for yourself. Then begin to execute your plan.

Developing a Job Prospect List

No good sales campaign is ready for action without a *prospect list*. Your job prospect list should include potential employers who can offer the kind of employment opportunity you are seeking in terms of location, size, interest appeal, permanence, and job satisfaction.

College Placement Office. The placement office of the college you have attended for your secretarial training can give you expert help in developing your prospect list and can assist you in making job contacts. Complete all forms necessary for registration promptly. Get acquainted with the placement office

For information, write to the United States Department of State, Foreign Service Personnel Office, *Foreign Service Secretaries Brochure*, Washington, D.C. 20520.

personnel. Discuss your employment needs with them freely and often. If they arrange a job interview for you, always report to them after the interview. Solicit their advice and let them know you appreciate their assistance.

Free Employment Agencies. Employment agencies are a good source of prospective positions. Any person seeking employment may register without charge with one of the state employment offices. Registration includes a comprehensive interview and a skills test so that you can be properly classified according to your abilities, personality traits, training, and experience. In order to keep on its active list, you must communicate with that office regularly.

Other free employment services are available in some metropolitan areas. Consult the classified section of your newspaper for their listings.

Private Employment Agencies. A private employment agency performs three functions. It acts as an agent for the job seeker, as a recruiter for the employer, and as a job market information center which charges a fee for these services. In about two thirds of the jobs listed, employers pay the fee. In some states regulatory bodies set limits on fees charged by agencies. An applicant registering with an agency signs a contract in which the fee terms are stated. At that time the applicant is assigned a counselor. Inform the counselor of all employers you have contacted before coming to the agency so that you will not be obligated for the fee if a job arises from your previous contacts. A major advantage of a good agency is that it carries out a complete job hunt for the applicant, thus relieving the job seeker of much of the repetitive detail work involved in job hunting. Another advantage is that the agency serves as a third party representative for the applicant with prospective employers.

Private employment agencies perform a valuable service for the employer as well. The staff of the agency can expertly screen, test, and interview each applicant. The company then interviews only those who meet the company's specified qualifications. Because many businesses use private agencies exclusively, keep in mind that many desirable positions are available only through such agencies.

A private employment agency should be selected carefully. Don't hesitate to interview the agency to determine its professionalism. For a directory of reputable agencies, write to the National Association of Personnel Consultants, 1012 14th Street, N.W., Washington, D.C. 20006. The directory will be especially helpful in locating an agency in a distant city where you would like to obtain employment. Some agencies are a part of a recruiting network which can put you in touch with member agencies in other cities. Agencies listed in the directory subscribe to a code of ethical practices. You might also contact the Better Business Bureau in that city to determine if any agency has been reported for unethical practices.

Newspaper Advertisements. The classified section of the newspaper is an excellent source of information for the job seeker. Besides the employment picture of the community, skill requirements and the current pay rates for secretarial positions are often stated. You do not need to meet every specification of an advertisement, only most of them. If a particular advertisement appeals to you, follow carefully the directions given for making an application.

In reviewing the help wanted section, you will soon notice that these advertisements do not specify male or female or in any way indicate a preferred age of an applicant. Federal law prohibits employers and employment agencies from classifying jobs by sex (unless a realistic occupational qualification) or by preferred ethnic group or age level. In fact, some advertisements will state that the company is *An Equal Opportunity Employer*.

Firms that advertise for help in the classified columns sometimes use a blind advertisement (see Illus. 25-3). A *blind advertisement* is one in which a key or box number is used for your reply and the firm name is not mentioned. A legitimate blind advertisement is usually inserted that way because the firm does not want to be bothered with interviewing large numbers of applicants. Most employers notify present employees before running a blind advertisement. This prevents the possibility of an employee applying for the job and being embarrassed for doing so. Blind advertisements are sometimes used just to get names of sales prospects by someone who has something to sell.

Illus. 25-3
Blind
advertisement

TOP DRAWER

Interested in art, music, theater, sports? A new magazine that will cover all aspects of life in the exciting city of Chicago is looking for an exceptional secretary. You must have excellent skills, good judgment, be able to supervise the support staff, work effectively under pressure, and be eager to accept challenges and responsibility. Opportunities for creativity in the areas of writing, photography, graphics, and design abound. Strong background in English a must. This position offers you a ground floor opportunity to go as far as your abilities will take you.

Send resume to Box 119, Sun Times, Chicago, IL 60601-5047

Friends, Relatives, and Associates. Include friends, friends of your family, business people with whom you have had some kind of contact, student alumni groups, and former instructors on your job prospect list. Inform them that you are seeking a position and that you would appreciate their help. Naturally you will not want to make a nuisance of yourself. Another source is a professional organization, such as the National Federation of Business and Professional Women's Clubs, which maintains a Talent Bank of members for referral to employers seeking women to fill middle- to top-level management jobs. Special interest groups, such as Forty Plus, provide employment information. If someone refers you to an opening, it is a matter of courtesy to let that person know the outcome.

Other Sources. The Yellow Pages of your telephone book provide a classified list of the local businesses to which you might apply. Make a list of those companies where you would like to work. Take the initiative to visit their personnel offices. This is a most effective way of securing employment. For instance, if you are interested in a position in an insurance company, you will find listed under Insurance all the local companies. Make an appointment for an interview or send your personal data sheet and letter of application to the personnel department.

Do not forget that the government is a major employer. You will find federal and state employment offices listed in the telephone directory.

Become an avid reader of the daily newspaper and watch all news items that give clues to possible job contacts. New businesses are constantly opening, and items relating to jobs, changes, or expansions in business often appear in the newspaper.

Job Prospects in Other Locations. A number of information sources may be used to obtain job prospects in a distant city or area. In addition to the directory of the National Association of Personnel Consultants (see page 623), copies of the leading newspapers in the city or area can be examined at your local library. Names of companies can be obtained from the Yellow Pages. Telephone directories for major cities are kept in many public libraries. Trade association directories are helpful in providing addresses of companies.

Learning about a Company

You should exhaust all means of getting information on each of the firms on your prospect list. Telephone to find out the employment manager's name. Inquire of your friends, acquaintances, and instructors about the firm. Check library reference materials, such as Standard & Poor's, to learn of the company's financial condition. Examine the company's advertisements in papers and magazines. Study the annual report of the firm. A copy can usually be obtained by sending a request to the company.

Many large companies publish brochures describing job opportunities and employment policies of the company. Your college placement office may have them on file. If not, send a request to the company. If it is a small firm, you may inquire of its reputation from the Chamber of Commerce and the Better Business Bureau. Use separate file folders to accumulate pertinent material on each company.

Many firms will be eliminated as you proceed in this information-gathering campaign. When your prospect list is as complete as you can make it, check it and group your prospects by the jobs you are best fitted to fill. Select the prospects with which you think you have the best chances for employment and which will provide an interesting future.

Evaluating a Company

How do you judge a company as a potential employer? There is no sure test, but answers to the following questions may help.

What is the reputation of the company in the community? The community image of a company is the sum of many things—employee relationships, reputation for progressive management, sponsorship of community projects, fair employment practices, and general leadership in civic and business activities.

Is the company an equal opportunity employer? Is it known to discriminate in employment in the areas of race, creed, color, national origin, or sex?

How satisfactory are the employer-employee relationships (company morale)? Do the employees seem to have a common bond of enthusiasm, or are there undercurrents of distrust and backbiting?

Is the business financially stable? A business that is not economically sound cannot give its employees a sense of financial security. Its wage policies and employee benefits will always depend on the profit picture.

Is the company expanding? A growing organization usually offers opportunities for advancement.

What opportunities for training and advancement are provided? Companies that provide special training programs or pay tuition in local universities and colleges merit special consideration.

Don't overlook the opportunities in the small office—you may be happier there—or in the new company that is just getting under way. Being on the beginning team can be exciting and rewarding.

PREPARATION OF AN APPLICATION

A fundamental step in preparing to make an application for a position is to take an inventory of your knowledge, skills, strengths, and weaknesses in terms of the requirements of that particular position. What skills, understandings, and special qualities will the employer be seeking? What type of experience will be expected? Do you have unique qualities that would be an asset in the position? What weaknesses in your preparation or background might the employer note? What plan do you have to correct these weaknesses? The preparation of your personal data sheet will assist you in making this analysis.

Your Personal Data Sheet

Sometimes called a *résumé* or *personal history,* a personal data sheet is a concise, positive presentation of your background and abilities. Because your purpose is to gain a personal interview with the employer, your data sheet must arouse interest in your unique qualifications. It must be short, preferably one page; if too long, it dulls the interest. It must be a reflection of you, not a copy from a textbook, or one written by a friend.

Some large employment agencies and corporations code and enter information furnished on an applicant's data sheet in their computer system. When an opening occurs, the computer is searched for the names of applicants meeting the specific requirements of the job.

There are two types of personal data sheets: a chronological data sheet, which is a record of your work history, and a functional data sheet, which emphasizes job titles and job descriptions. In the latter, a summary statement of experience is given, followed by a list of functions and their descriptions. The names of employers and dates of employment follow this section or can be omitted.

Authorities do not agree on the merit of attaching a photograph to the data sheet. Some believe that a photograph places the personnel officer in a position of possible discrimination, since the photograph illustrates age, sex, and race. Yet other authorities think that a photograph can be of assistance in getting the interview. If you decide that a photograph will be helpful, be sure that it is a businesslike pose of approximately billfold size.

You will use your data sheet in a number of ways. Send it with your letter of application (discussed in the next section). Give copies to friends, relatives, and business acquaintances to pass on to prospective employers. Your college placement office will need one or more copies. Always take a copy to an interview. Use it to list accomplishments and some of the extras that are not included in an application form.

Make sure that your data sheet is expertly typed on good quality paper. Use wide margins and leave plenty of blank spaces between sections. These techniques add to the readability of your data sheet. Its appearance says as much about you as does the content. Many an applicant has lost the opportunity for an interview because of messy corrections, poor format, misspelled words, or grammatical errors on the data sheet or accompanying application letter.

Although an original copy of the data sheet is preferred for each mailing or interview, a copy made on a good quality copier is acceptable. Carbon copies are frowned upon by interviewers.

Personal Data. Every data sheet must have the name, address, telephone number, and permanent address, if appropriate, of the job seeker. This identification should appear as a heading for the information that follows.

It is no longer necessary to provide such personal information as age, height, weight, sex, marital status, or social security number. If, however, you consider it to your advantage to include this information, then do so.

Objective. This section gives you the opportunity to identify the specific position you seek, your long-range career goals, or both. If you have varied experience and can qualify for a number of office jobs, you should not give so much detail that it may disqualify you for positions that are open and for which you would like to be considered. From the reader's standpoint, an objective statement provides instant knowledge of the sort of job you are seeking.

Education. Include complete pertinent information about your educational background. Begin with facts about your most recent educational experience.

Schools Attended. List all the colleges and universities that you have attended and the high school from which you were graduated. List the most recent schools first and give dates of graduation, diplomas received, degrees conferred, awards, and scholarships.

Major Subjects. The business courses that you completed should be listed. Include also courses related specifically to the position for which you are applying. For example, in applying for a secretarial position in an advertising office, you would list the English, art, and psychology courses taken.

Secretarial Skills and Abilities. Give your speed in shorthand dictation and transcription. Indicate by manufacturer's name the electronic equipment you have used in your work experience and list separately the business machines that you can operate, stating your operating ability. Overrating your ability, however, may give your application a tone of superiority that may impress your potential employer unfavorably.

Work Experience. List your work experience in the order of recency (on a chronological data sheet) or in the order of its importance to the position in question (on a functional data sheet). For example, in applying for a secretarial position, list office experience (full and part-time) first, giving inclusive dates of employment, the name and address of the employer, the title of the position held, and a brief description of it. If your work involved the supervision of others, be sure to include the fact. And don't forget to mention promotions.

If you are like most college students whose experience is limited to part-time and summer employment that was not office work, you should include the dates and description of the work on your data sheet.

Special Interests, Abilities, and Accomplishments. Your extracurricular activities, special interests, and achievements may give the prospective employer an indication of what kind of person you are and how you would fit into the office; therefore, you should list:

1. *The extracurricular activities in which you have participated and the offices you have held.* Holding responsible offices in one or more activities or groups may be more impressive than parading evidence of membership in virtually every organization on the campus.

2. *Special honors received.* Recognition by awards and scholarships is evidence of your ability and perseverance.

Illus. 25-4 Letter of application

2925 Mirimar Street
Dayton, OH 45432-3237
April 10, 1983

Mr. Howard Edmunds, Personnel Director
Harmon Manufacturing Company
1604 Stanley Avenue
Dayton, OH 45432-3239

Dear Mr. Edmunds:

(tells why you are writing)
The Placement Office at Sinclair Community College has told me of the opening in your office for an associate degree graduate with some stenographic experience. I understand that the position requires a large volume of dictation in addition to routine office duties and provides an opportunity to assume administrative responsibilities. I believe I have the necessary qualifications; therefore, I would like to be considered for this position.

(tells why you are interested in this company)
While taking secretarial training at Sinclair, I had the opportunity to tour a number of industrial firms in our city. Of those that I visited, your company offices, your operations, and the friendliness of the staff impressed me the most. My hope is to become a part of that organization.

(refers to data sheet)
You will see from the enclosed data sheet that I have acquired a high level of stenographic skills and have the ability to operate a number of office machines including the Wang text editor. You will also note that I have supplemented my course work at Sinclair with on-the-job experience during the summers.

(action requests)
Since it may be difficult to reach me by telephone during working hours, I shall take the liberty of calling your office next Tuesday for an appointment. I am looking forward to discussing this position with you.

Yours very truly,

Lee M. Palmer

Lee M. Palmer

Enclosure

Illus. 25-5 A chronological data sheet

DATA SHEET

Lee M. Palmer
2925 Mirimar Street
Dayton, OH 45432-3237
(513) 555-9309

Career Objective: A secretarial position with opportunities to use shorthand skills, display initiative, and assume responsibility.

EDUCATION

Sinclair Community College   Associate Degree Major: Secretarial Studies
444 West Third Street   June, 1983
Dayton, OH 45430-3234

Major Courses:
Accounting   Office Management
Data Processing
Economics   Secretarial Procedures
Business Communications
Business Law   Word Processing I
                          Office Machines

Secretarial Skills: Shorthand dictation rate, 120 words a minute
Shorthand transcription rate, 35 words a minute
Typewriting straight-copy rate, 75 words a minute

Office Machines: Mimeograph, direct-process, and offset duplicators; Key-driven and electronic calculators; adding machines; and Wang text editor.

Belmont High School   Diploma (5th in class of 174), June, 1981
2323 Mapleview Avenue
Dayton, OH 45430-3236

WORK EXPERIENCE

Office of the Dean   Stenographer (typing, shorthand, filing)
Division of Business   1982-83 (part-time)
Sinclair Community College

Defense Electronic Supply Center   Correspondence Secretary (Word Processing Center)
Dayton, Ohio   Summers 1981-82

EXTRACURRICULAR ACTIVITIES

Office Education Association Club   President
Future Business Leaders of America Member

REFERENCES   Available upon request

3. *Special achievements if they have implications for the position you are seeking.* Your ability to read or speak a foreign language, awards for English composition or original writing, or special training in some field of science may be the specific point that influences the employer in your favor.

References. You will need to have at least three references in mind when you begin your job search. The longer and better they have known you, the more valid will be their evaluation of your abilities.

If you have had no experience, consider using instructors of business subjects or administrators who have firsthand knowledge of your training for a job and who can evaluate your work potential. Avoid using the names of close relatives for a work reference. You must secure permission to use anyone's name as a reference before submitting it to a prospective employer.

Upon leaving a job, you may request your employer to give you a letter of reference. This letter may be especially helpful to you if you are moving to another city or state.

On the data sheet indicate that references are available upon request. The names and addresses of your references are to be furnished during the interview or when you are completing an application blank.

Other Information. You may also wish to include on your data sheet the date that you can be available for employment and also information about your willingness to relocate. *Save for the interview matters concerning salary and your reasons for leaving previous employment.*

Your Application Letter

An application letter is another document used by the job seeker to obtain a personal interview. It may be the only document to describe your qualifications, or it may be a two-part document—the application letter with the data sheet attached. Like the data sheet, the application letter should be individually and faultlessly typed and limited to one page. It highlights the details given on the data sheet and emphasizes experience that is related to the job in question. Bear in mind, too, that your letter is but one of many that the employer receives. Thus, it should be unique in order to set it apart from all the rest.

Solicited and Unsolicited Application Letters. An application letter is *solicited* if you are responding to a help wanted advertisement or are writing at the request of an employer (frequently a part of the screening process). A personal data sheet should accompany a solicited letter. The letter will expand on your special qualifications for the position and will indicate why you are interested in the company.

Unsolicited application letters can be written to discover an opening or to follow up a reported opportunity. The same unsolicited letter format can

be used repeatedly with carefully made adaptations to meet special requirements. An unsolicited application letter need not include the data sheet. The
letter should include a summary of your previous experience and a discussion
of your capabilities and how they relate to the position you are seeking. If you
are granted an interview, then you can present your data sheet tailored specifically to the position available.

Basic Parts of an Application Letter. Whether solicited or unsolicited, your
letter should include the following parts:

1. An interesting first paragraph which tells why you are writing.

> The position of secretary described in your advertisement
> in today's issue of the Sentinel is a challenging opportunity.
> May I be considered for the position?

> Mr. Grant Lehman of your Sales Department suggested that
> I write to inquire whether you have. . . .

> Mr. Ron Radtke, Head of the Secretarial Science Department
> at Eastern Community College, tells me that you have a secre-
> tarial position open for a graduate with stenographic and word
> processing training. Will you please consider me an applicant.

2. A statement indicating why you are interested in joining the company (if
the name of the company is known), or in lieu of that, an expansion on
what you know about the requirements of the position you are seeking.
Note the use of the same words appearing in the advertisement.

> Your company is well known in our community for its
> superior products, recent plant expansion, and the benefits
> to employees. From what I have learned about LKM Company, I
> would be proud to be part of your future growth.

> Words such as "responsible" and "administrative ability"
> in the description of the position available immediately
> appealed to me. These words mean that you are looking for
> an individual who can show initiative, work without super-
> vision, and assume some of the administrative tasks of the
> employer. I believe that my training at Madison Technical
> College has qualified me to say "I am up to the tasks."

3. A closing paragraph suggesting an appointment and definite action.

> Because I cannot be called by telephone during business
> hours, I shall telephone your office on Friday morning to ask
> for an appointment for an interview.

> I should like very much to come to your office to talk
> with you about the position. When I telephone you on
> Wednesday morning, will you please let me know a time that
> would be convenient for you to see me?

Guides for Writing Application Letters. There is no one formula for writing
an effective application letter, but observance of these guides will be of great
aid.

1. *Address letter to an individual.* A letter directed "To Whom It May Concern" may never concern anyone. Find out the name and title of the person in charge of employment and use them. This information may be obtained from the switchboard operator of the company. The use of the name (correctly spelled) and title personalizes the letter and makes a favorable first impression.

   Obviously you cannot address your letter to an individual when you are replying to a blind advertisement. The correct address form and salutation for such a letter is shown at the left.

2. *Use the you approach.* Your application letter is a sales letter, and the product is you. You must convince the prospective employer how you can serve that company. Certainly you do so by telling about yourself, but this must be done from the perspective of the employer. Avoid terms such as *I want, I did this,* and *I did that.* Show that you understand the requirements of the position and demonstrate how your qualifications meet the employer's needs.

3. *Be honest, confident, and enthusiastic.* Your application letter can show a proper but not overemphasized appreciation of your ability. Above all, be *honest.* Your letter should be neither boastful nor deprecating. Employers are experts in detecting insincerity. Be specific about the position you want and the things you can do, but do not exaggerate. You may be called upon to prove your claims.

   Do not be apologetic. If your experience is limited, you need not call attention to the fact. Concentrate on your positive qualities.

4. *Be concise.* If you enclose your personal data sheet, omit in your letter a detailed treatment of your education and experience. Your letter then must be an invitation to read the data sheet. The statement, "I am enclosing information about my training and experience," does little to persuade the reader to continue to your data sheet. Stimulate interest by such statements as, "An examination of my personal data sheet will show that I am well prepared by training and experience for secretarial work," or "My extracurricular activities, described in the enclosed personal data sheet, have prepared me to work with other people."

5. *Make action easy.* You are more likely to win an interview by saying, "I shall call you on Friday morning to see if you wish to arrange a personal interview," instead of saying, "May I hear from you?" The purpose of the application letter is to get an interview. If you obtain one, your letter has done as much as you can expect it to do.

6. *Give the letter eye appeal.* Make your letter attractive and absolutely faultless in conformity with the best rules of business letter writing. Anything you say will be worthless if your message contains a typographical error. There must be no flaws in spelling, grammar, punctuation, typing, arrangement, spacing, placement, or wording. You should use a good quality bond paper of standard letter size. Your envelope should match the paper in quality. Letterhead paper should not be used, but your complete address (but no name) should be typed in the heading.

7. *File a copy of each application letter that you write.* It is a good idea also to keep records of the companies you interviewed, with whom you interviewed, and your evaluation of your performance.

Box H-816 Observer
Charlotte, NC 28202-2555

Ladies and Gentlemen:

Good Morning!

Personnel Department
    not
Personnel
Personnell
Personell
Personall

THE INTERVIEW

In a company's hiring process, there are usually two interviews—the first takes place in the personnel department, and the second within the department where the position is available. An invitation for the initial interview gives you an opportunity to learn more about the company and the position, as well as to discuss your career aspirations, training, and specific skills related to the position available. Go to the interview armed with information about the company, its products, and its reputation in the community.

This *first interview* typically lasts half an hour, which is ample time to exchange information and questions. During this period you must make a good impression. The interviewer will form opinions based on your general appearance, your voice, diction, posture, attitude, and personality. Your enthusiasm for your career will be noted. Certainly the interviewer will evaluate how you answer questions and how your abilities match the company's requirements. In short, your performance during this first interview, plus your data sheet and application form, provide a volume of information about you. If you are interested in the position, you will want an invitation for the second interview at the departmental level.

A successful interview doesn't just happen. The job seeker must prepare well to make that good first impression. This section will help you do just that. If you are asked to return for a *second interview*, you can be sure that you have the interviewer's interest.

Guides to a Successful Interview

Tend toward the conservative side in dress and appearance. Men should wear business suits; women, a suit or tailored dress. Nails should be clean and well manicured. Hair should be clean, trimmed, and styled simply. Make sure that you are satisfied with your appearance before you leave for the interview. It is a good idea to get a good night's rest and to hold a dress rehearsal prior to the interview.

A card, a letter, or a note of introduction to someone in the organization can be helpful. It may be a referral card from your placement or employment agency office or a note on the back of a personal card. This communication should put you in contact with the one you want to see.

Anticipate the questions the interviewer may ask. If you have thought through the possible questions, you will be less likely to be caught off your guard during the interview. So plan your answers to talk not too much nor too little; strive for the happy medium. Have a positive attitude. Remember, first impressions are extremely important.

Before the interview, use the pre-interview checklist shown on page 635 to be sure you are well prepared.

The Application Blank. You may be asked to complete an application blank before you are interviewed. The application blank is as vital a part of your application as the interview. Many applicants are eliminated entirely on the basis of the way they fill out the application. Therefore, never treat it casually. Read it through carefully before you begin to fill it out.

Application forms are usually planned with care. Every question serves a purpose for the interviewer. By law you need not reveal your age, marital status, number of dependents, and so forth.

In completing an application, be careful that you follow instructions. For instance, print your name when the instructions tell you to print; put your last name first if you are so requested. The way you fill out the form reveals far more about you than you realize.

The general neatness of the form is important. Good handwriting is desirable because there is always need for longhand writing in office work, and no one in any office wants to decipher a scrawly, illegible hand. An application form to be typed may be a disguised part of the typing test, so it should represent your best work.

The Interviewer's Method. The employment director of a company or a member of the staff conducts the preliminary interview. If a favorable impression is made, the interviewer sends the applicant to the immediate supervisor of the available position for the second interview. In talking with applicants, the initial interviewer follows a set pattern:

1. Establishes rapport with the applicant
2. Indicates who will make the final selection
3. Reviews the applicant's work experience record

Illus. 25-6
Make sure that you are pleased with your appearance before the interview.

A PRE-INTERVIEW CHECKLIST

1. Are you properly dressed and groomed?
2. Have you gathered all the information you need about the company—its products, its policies, its status in the community?
3. Do you know the interviewer's name? If not, obtain it from the receptionist before the interview.
4. Have you mentally formulated answers to the usual factual questions and also to possible unusual questions that the interviewer may ask?
5. Have you practiced the interview with a friend?
6. Are you prepared for an interview? Be sure to take the following items:
   a. Your personal data sheet
   b. Your social security card
   c. A complete school record showing dates of attendance
   d. A tabulated summary of your college courses
   e. A record of your business skills and personal accomplishments (unless included on personal data sheet)
   f. Letters of reference (Some personnel experts question the value of open letters of recommendation. You may decide to omit them.)
   g. List of personal references
   h. Your employment record, including dates, names, addresses of employers, duties performed, names of immediate supervisors, and salaries
   i. List of questions you wish to ask the interviewer
   j. A pen and well-sharpened pencils
   k. A small notebook for dictation (you may be asked to take an employment test)
   l. A good pocket-size dictionary
   m. Correction materials

DURING THE INTERVIEW

Leave your coat in the reception area.

Wait to sit down until invited to do so.

Refrain from smoking and chewing gum during an interview.

Keep your voice well modulated.

Look directly at the interviewer when speaking or listening.

Control your nervous actions and maintain good posture.

Refrain from overtalking or undertalking.

Avoid interrupting the interviewer.

Be pleasant to everyone you meet in the office.

At the end of the interview, thank the interviewer for the time and consideration and leave at once. Thank the receptionist also when you leave.

4. Asks questions related to the available job
5. Leads into the closing of the interview

The interviewer will question you to encourage you to talk. Many of the questions will be routine and, although answered on your personal data sheet, may be asked again merely to put you at ease and to give you an opportunity to express yourself. Be sure to listen to the questions. You can ask for a clarification if you do not understand the question. Some of the usual questions are:

What is your education?

What is your special training for this work?

What business experience have you had? By what firms have you been employed? Why did you leave them—particularly the last one?

Why do you want to work for this company? (What an opportunity to show that you know something about it)

Two laws (Title VII of the Civil Rights Act and the Age Discrimination in Employment Act) prohibit the interviewer from asking questions of a personal nature, such as race, ethnic origin, religion, age, marital status. You may wish to volunteer this information, since it may give you the leverage you need to obtain the position. A good rule to follow is to provide those facts that are to your advantage.

In addition to the typical questions, the interviewer may include a few that will take the applicant off guard. Some of these questions may seem unusual and perhaps presumptuous, but they are all part of the interview technique and have a purpose. Some questions of this nature and examples of answers are shown on page 637.

If you have had business experience, it is quite logical that your previous employment will be a point of discussion in the interview. You will probably be asked why you left your last position. Be prepared to answer this question and be sure to emphasize positive—not negative factors. Be truthful but brief. It is tactless and unethical for you to say anything detrimental about any former employer or firm for which you have worked, regardless of any personal feelings you may have. Always speak well of former employers. Nothing is gained by doing otherwise.

The Salary Question. Salary is always important, but don't pass up an interesting position for one that pays a few dollars a week more. If your work is challenging, your performance will soon merit a salary increase.

Your college placement office can obtain information about salaries. The International Information/Word Processing Association publishes an annual salary survey. The Administrative Management Society publishes an annual survey of office salaries, fringe benefits, and working hours. The United States

Some things interviewers dislike:
Messy application
Untidy appearance
Weak handshake
Exaggerations
Irrelevant questions
Incessant talker
Job pleader

QUESTIONS

If you were starting college over again, what courses would you take?

How much money do you hope to make by the age of 30?

What do you plan to be doing in your career five to ten years from now?

Do you prefer to accomplish work with others or by yourself?

Do you think you have done the best scholastic work of which you are capable?

What special interests do you have?

What have you learned from some of the positions you have held?

What are your future educational plans?

What personal characteristics do you believe are important in your field?

What do you think determines a person's progress within a company?

Why did you choose the secretarial field?

POSSIBLE ANSWERS*

I would major in the same field.

At least 50 percent more than my entry level salary today.

I plan to hold a CPS and be an administrative assistant to an executive.

This depends on the nature of the work (then provide an example).

(This answer will vary. Be honest.)

Sports, reading, cooking.

To work under pressure and to work with many types of individuals.

To prepare for the CPS examination.

Pleasant personality, cooperation, willingness to accept responsibility.

Performance on the job.

I like the office environment; I enjoy the skills required in the secretarial field.

_____

*Replies are reduced due to space limitations.

Additional Questions:

What do you expect your references to say about you when I call them?
How well do you work under pressure? Give an example.
What goals would you hope to achieve with our company?
How would you describe yourself?
What people have influenced your life? How?
Why should we hire you?
What two or three accomplishments have given you the greatest satisfaction?
Describe a typical day on your last job.
What do you consider your strengths? your weaknesses? (Give positive weaknesses, such as impatience, exacting, etc., which are terms often used by employers to describe good workers.)

Department of Labor makes an annual occupational wage survey in large cities. The survey reports may be obtained from the regional office of the Bureau of Labor Statistics. Some newspaper advertisements give local salary figures.

Most large businesses have a salary schedule about which you can become informed before applying for a position. When the salary question comes up in the interview—and it usually does—the best response is "I am willing to start at your scheduled salary for a person with my background."

If, before leaving the interview, you are not told what the starting salary is, it is appropriate to inquire "What is the starting salary for this position?" If the application blank asks "Salary Desired?" you should supply the standard range for that position.

Asking Questions. An interview is a two-way street, and you will be expected to ask questions. In fact, your failure to do so may be interpreted as indicating a lack of genuine interest on your part. What will be the scope of your work? With whom will you be working? What opportunities will the position provide for advancement? Does the company promote from within? What is the rate of employee turnover? Is there a company training program for self-improvement? These are all thoughtful, intelligent questions that concern you. Questions about working hours, vacation schedules, coffee breaks, and so forth are appropriate *if* you take care to give the impression that you are more interested in giving than in what you will get. Don't open yourself, however, to the criticism, "The applicant interviewed me."

Concluding the Interview. You will probably know quite definitely when the interview is coming to an end. If the interviewer has shown interest and in any way has encouraged you but has not made a definite commitment about a position, it is permissible to ask directly, "When will your decision be made?" If this does not seem to be a fitting question, you might ask, "May I call you on Friday at two?" If you are offered the job on the spot and you want it, accept the offer. If you need more time, ask for a delay. Do not say that you need time to discuss the job with your spouse or parents. That reply suggests that you are not a decision maker and could give the wrong impression to the interviewer.

The interviewer may rise, and that will indicate that the interview is at an end. You should rise too and thank the interviewer for the opportunity to discuss the position. Make no attempt to prolong the visit. Leave at once, pleasantly and with dignity. Remember to thank the receptionist as you leave.

Tests for Selecting Employees

If you have gained favorable consideration, you may be asked to take some form of test. By law, any test must be job related. For a secretarial position, a job-related test may be merely a letter or two to ascertain your ability in shorthand, typewriting, and spelling. It may be the operation of sophisticated equipment, such as a text-editor. It may be a test to determine your mathematical ability. Some employers request a more general test or one designed to detect a wide variety of abilities. The main thing to remember is that you know how to do what is asked and to do it quietly, confidently, and efficiently.

You may be asked, however, to take a psychological test or a lie detector test. You can refuse to take the test; but if you do for all practical purposes you have removed yourself from any consideration for the position.

Examples of types of tests and questions follow:

Type of Test	Questions
Personal Preference (occupational test) There are no right or wrong answers. An occupational preference can be learned by the answers to a series of statements.	Of these three activities indicate which you like the most and the least: Most Least Work with detail —— —— Operate office machines —— —— Sell office equipment —— ——
Clerical Ability Test Consists of Spelling Arithmetic Proofreading Meaning of Words Reasoning Problems	accomodate Right—— Wrong—— 33-⅓% of .50 = $2,459.35 (correct) $2,549.35 (error) ethics ——principles ——etiquette ——signs Blue is to black as tan is to ——green ——brown ——grey
General Employment Test Very similar to clerical ability test.	Which number in this series is out of order? 2 4 6 8 10 11 12 14 If three notebooks cost $2.25, how many can you buy for $10? The opposite of sit is ——.

Evaluation of the Interview

A good practice after leaving is to evaluate your performance and attitude, and note any changes you will make in the future.

Were your answers logical?

Did your conversation ramble?

Were you completely honest?

Were you convincing in your sales approach?

Did you keep your eyes directed to the interviewer?

Were you always courteous and positive in your replies?

What did you learn about the position?

Which questions did you handle well? poorly?

Can you do anything else to increase your chances of obtaining the position sought?

Besides evaluating your own behavior, it is important that you decide whether this is the best job for you. Refer to the section "Evaluating a Company" on page 626 to assist you in your decision.

Follow-Up of the Interview

If you decide you are interested in the position, a follow-up letter, arriving within two or three days after the interview, may put your application on top. A good follow-up letter includes an expression of appreciation for the meeting, a statement reaffirming your interest in the position, and additional selling points, such as qualifications not completely covered during the visit.

For some reason you may decide not to accept a position that has been offered. Certainly this situation demands a prompt, courteous, and straightforward letter of explanation. The day may come when you need the goodwill of that company or person.

Job Hunting Within the Company

Most companies have internal policies covering promotions. These policies specify the job levels that can be considered for certain positions. In some companies job vacancies are posted on bulletin boards. Generally, when a vacancy occurs, those holding positions at the required job levels are notified and asked to interview. Other factors, such as education and seniority, will be considered. For these reasons, you should make an effort to keep your personnel file up to date, including additional courses you have taken, offices you have held in your professional organization, and other pertinent information. Keeping a diary of your accomplishments in your current position will provide impressive information to bring to the interview.

If a job that represents a promotion for you becomes available, you should discuss it with your employer first, then make an appointment for the interview. An approach *not* recommended is to go directly to the executive for whom the opening exists. Follow the procedures set up by the company so that you will not be subject to criticism by your fellow workers, and possibly your present supervisor as well.

TERMINATION OF EMPLOYMENT

As you grow in your career, if you are like many office workers, you may decide to terminate a position. Perhaps you become unhappy with your job or your salary is not commensurate with your responsibilities or with the local salary levels. Another reason may be that the fringe benefits are better elsewhere. Never leave a job on impulse or for the wrong reasons.

Once you decide to resign, do so the right way by following the written or understood rules of convention. If the company has a manual, you will find the proper procedures given there. Otherwise give notice first verbally and then in written form (if requested). A resignation letter specifies the date of notice, the last day of employment, and the reason for leaving. It should also include a summary statement about the pleasant associations you have enjoyed with the firm. While still on the job, inquire about any benefits to which you are entitled, such as insurance options or unused vacation. After the notice period (usually two weeks unless you have made special arrangements), simply go pleasantly.

In the event that your employer initiates the termination you should be entitled to advance notice or severance pay. Before you leave, determine what benefits you have and whether you can expect a good reference from the company.

Regardless of the reason for termination, your exit should be an amicable one. Avoid expressing ill will toward the company or attempting to make fellow workers dissatisfied with the company and their jobs.

FOR THE MATURE JOB SEEKER

None is so old as the person who has outlived enthusiasm.
Henry Thoreau

The Age Discrimination in Employment Act of 1967 protects those workers in the 40–65 age bracket. Basically, employers cannot discriminate against workers or applicants because of their age.

The mature job seeker has much to offer a company: work experience, the prospect of a good attendance record, and the ability to learn as well as young persons. Probably the only reservation lies in the cost of benefits of the mature recruit. Retirement benefits, for instance, begin much sooner than for a young person.

If you are told you are overqualified for the job, the interviewer usually considers you too old or too high priced. You can turn this reaction into an advantage by emphasizing that your experience will lessen the training time required for the job. As for salary, you can stress that the salary scale is acceptable.

The reentry secretary must devote some time to preparation for employment. Dormant office skills must be revitalized by taking a refresher course or an individualized instructional program. The next step is to make a survey of employment opportunities. Temporary service agencies and companies that require part-time workers should be included. Finally, the reentry job seeker should prepare a personal data sheet and letters of application. Include all your work experience, both paid and volunteer.

A last word of advice for all job seekers: Don't be in a hurry to accept your first job offer. Evaluate each company and position in terms of your own goals and interests. Accepting a job you don't really want may prevent your later accepting the very job that you were seeking. The next interview just might be that right position for you.

```
                                    RESUME

                        Pat L. Swenson
                        8209 West 13th Street
                        Vancouver, WA 98661-9873
                        (206) 555-2247

CAREER OBJECTIVE        A secretarial position requiring a high level
                        of stenographic skills and administrative abilities

SUMMARY                 Five years of full-time secretarial experience in
                        the paper industry and three years of part-time
                        stenographic experience in the medical field

EDUCATION               Associate Degree, Secretarial Studies, Santa Rosa
                        Junior College, Santa Rosa, California

EXPERIENCE
  Secretary to          As secretary to the Administrative Vice-President of
  Executive             St. Regis Paper Company, I coordinated the efforts
                        of the clerical personnel in the section in addition
                        to accomplishing the varied duties of the position.
                        In a typical day it was not unusual for me to
                        type fifty letters from shorthand dictation. Routine
                        recordkeeping was necessary to control the volume of
                        mail entering the office each day. Maintaining
                        confidential files was a responsibility of this
                        position.

  Stenographer          During my college training, I held a part-time
                        stenographic post at the Santa Rosa Medical Clinic.
                        My major responsibilities included transcribing
                        medical records from a voice recording machine
                        and assisting with posting charges and credits to
                        patients' accounts.

SPECIAL QUALIFICATIONS  Ability to handle a wide variety of secretarial
                        responsibilities and supervise clerical workers.
                        Especially capable in the area of human relations.
                        Health and stamina to work under pressure of time.

MEMBERSHIPS             Professional Secretaries International
                        Word Processing Society, Inc.
                        President, Parent-Teachers Assn., John F.
                        Kennedy School

REFERENCES              Can be provided upon request
```

Illus. 25-7
This functional data sheet gives no dates of employment and places emphasis on the duties of former positions and the applicant's accomplishments.

SUGGESTED READINGS

Berliner, Don. *Want a Job? Get Some Experience. Want Experience? Get a Job.* New York: Amacom, 1978.

Bolles, Richard Nelson. *What Color Is Your Parachute? A Practical Manual for Job Hunters and Career-Changers.* Berkeley: Ten Speed Press, 1981.

Bostwick, Burdette E. *Finding the Job You've Always Wanted,* 2d ed. New York: John Wiley & Sons, Inc., 1980.

Cowle, Jerry. *How to Survive Getting Fired—and Win!* Anderson, Ind.: Warner Books, Inc., 1979.

Hawkins, James E. *The Uncle Sam Connection: An Insider's Guide to Federal Employment,* revised and updated. Chicago: Follett Publishing Company, 1978.

Rust, H. Lee. *Job Search: The Complete Manual for Job Seekers.* New York: Amacom, 1979.

Stanat, Kirby W., with Patrick Reardon. *Job Hunting Secrets and Tactics.* Piscataway, N. J.: New Century Publications, Inc., 1977.

QUESTIONS FOR DISCUSSION

1. Although there are many fine opportunities for employment in the suburbs of large cities, why is it that most young secretaries prefer to work in offices located downtown?

2. Why must a public stenographer be highly skilled and have a wealth of business background in order to be successful?

3. After carefully considering your training, interests, and special aptitudes, would you choose a specialization in the secretarial field (for example, legal, medical, technical, or educational)? If so, which one? Give reasons for your choice.

4. What advantages can you give for working as a secretary for a temporary employment agency?

5. What circumstances would make it desirable for a secretarial applicant to register with a private employment agency?

6. Certain questions of a personal nature cannot by law be asked in an interview, even though the information is of concern to the interviewer. Recognizing this situation, how can a female applicant obtain a possible advantage over other applicants when interviewing for a position?

7. What personal information, if any, would you provide on a personal data sheet if you are

   (a) male, 26 years old, married, one son, height 6'1", 170 lbs., willing to relocate?

   (b) female, 40 years old, divorced, two small children at home, 20 years of office experience?

   (c) male, 52 years old, divorced, excellent health?

   Which data sheet format would you select in each example?

8. What questions do you think an interviewer would ask of your former employer?

9. In addition to those questions listed in the textbook on page 638, what other questions could be asked by the *applicant* during an interview?

10. Is it ethical to accept, without informing your potential employer, a position which she or he considers permanent but which you consider temporary? Examples are a job for the summer only, one you intend to keep

PROBLEMS

1. Assume that you are seeking a position as a secretary. Prepare a data sheet and an application letter in reply to one of the following newspaper advertisements.

CORRESPONDENCE SECRETARY

Busy nationwide company is looking for a secretary for an entry level position in the word processing center. Typing minimum 50 wpm. Excellent benefits. Send letter and data sheet to Box 1853, JOURNAL.

SECRETARY

Needed: a secretary with better-than-average communication skills; shorthand 100 wpm; typing 60 wpm. Position involves maintaining a large volume of correspondence, telephone work, and customer assistance. Salary commensurate with ability. Reply Box 2100, JOURNAL.

2. When applying for a specific position, you are asked the following questions. Type your replies on a sheet of paper. In prepar-

ing your answers, try to analyze the motive behind the question.

(a) What are your career plans?
(b) How do you spend your spare time?
(c) Why do you want to work for this company?
(d) Are you willing to relocate?
(e) Do you like to work with office machines?
(f) Do your interests lie in the area of data processing?
(g) What do you consider a good starting salary for this position?
(h) Do you think your college grades reflect your true ability?
(i) Are you willing to work overtime when the situation warrants?
(j) What qualifications do you have that you believe will make you successful in your chosen career?
(k) Do you plan to join a professional organization?

3. Just before completing your secretarial training, you decide to survey the secretarial openings in your community by sending

only until another comes along, or one to gain experience to qualify for a position in another company.

11. Assume that you work for a large company. The position of secretary to the vice-president becomes vacant, and you and your colleagues in your job classification are in line. Why will you antagonize your fellow workers and possibly your supervisor by going directly to the executive and asking for consideration for the position instead of going through company channels?

12. In terminating employment, why is it good practice to avoid creating ill will toward your employer and the company?

13. A compound word may be written as a solid word, joined with a hyphen, or written as individual words. Explain why the following groups are written as shown. Then consult the Reference Guide to verify or correct your answers.

(a) forty-four, twenty-six, thirty-five, one-third
(b) re-cover, re-form, re-collect, re-creation, fruit-less diet
(c) four-day conference, up-to-date buildings, first-class accommodations
(d) ex-Ambassador, pro-British, pre-Christmas, anti-American

out a number of unsolicited letters of application. Using your own data and the names of local companies, prepare the letter, making sure that it is appropriate for each of the companies.

4. On a sheet of paper make three vertical columns with these headings: *Duties, Eval-uation, Improvement.* Describe the perfect job for you by listing at least ten duties of that position in the *Duties* column. For each task, rate yourself poor, fair, good, or superior. If improvement is needed, specify what action you should take in the *Im-provement* column.

Planning for Your Professional Future

You have learned about the many career paths open to secretaries, studied the performance of various secretarial duties, and been briefed on how to get the position you seek. You are now ready to consider your long-range goal—to become a successful secretary.

This chapter discusses the personal characteristics requisite to success as a secretary and the means at your disposal for getting off to the right start and growing professionally. It deals with some of the difficulties you will encounter and how you can cope with them to assure the professional future to which you aspire.

USING YOUR PERSONAL ATTRIBUTES

New secretaries enter the job market with varying degrees of competence in the skills necessary to perform the job. The same is true of personal qualities. One secretary may have all the characteristics that contribute to a successful career, while another may be weak in one or more of them.

Successful secretaries, those who are proficient in their work and who enjoy satisfaction and recognition in their careers, suggest certain prerequisites to achievement. Some are innate to the individual, and some can be learned on the job. They are:

1. *Initiative* in performing your work
2. *Flexibility* in your approach to office needs and operations
3. *Awareness* of the business and of your employer
4. Ability to build *positive human relationships*

Displaying Initiative

A new secretary may be reluctant to do work without being told or to assume new responsibilities not understood as part of the job description. Displaying initiative comes with confidence in one's ability to do the job. It may be difficult, however, to show initiative if you are assigned to an executive who expects no more than performance of habitual, routine tasks; or you may follow a predecessor who undertook only assigned jobs. Also, routinization of tasks in many offices reduces, if not eliminates, the opportunity to show enterprise or creativity or to do anything out of the ordinary. You may have to start slowly, but you can overcome resistance to using initiative if you demonstrate how much you can increase your effectiveness and that of your employer by extending your activities to include responsible tasks. Taking initiative, unfortunately, means taking risks. Use your judgment in taking action. Then review what you have done with your employer. If you have acted in error, you can profit from what you have learned and apply this new knowledge to a similar situation in the future.

There are many opportunities in the secretarial position to use initiative. In fact, making independent decisions and taking actions soon become a daily exercise. A secretary who composes a reply to a letter without the employer's requesting it is displaying initiative. A secretary who obtains information for an employer before being asked to do so is using initiative. You, the college-trained secretary, should feel comfortable in displaying your initiative. You have the background to be successful in making decisions on your own.

Being Flexible

You probably have heard the observation, "Nothing is more certain than change." For years the functions of the office were accomplished in the same way and with the same equipment. Today technology has revolutionized the way we communicate, the way we calculate, and the way we send correspondence. Secretaries have had to learn to cope with change. The look of the office has changed; and, for some secretaries, a choice has had to be made between specializing in correspondence or in the administrative support tasks of the secretarial position. An ambitious person entering the business world must be flexible. That person must be able to adjust to tomorrow's office and tomorrow's duties quickly.

Offices usually have their own routines, their own ways of working with information and getting jobs done. A new secretary must be willing to learn from others. On occasion the employer may request that you work a half hour longer or on a Saturday. Although this is a disruption of your regular schedule, if you are flexible you will be willing to make alterations in your work schedule and personal life schedule.

One very sensitive area in an office community is the promotion or shift of personnel. The secretary may be transferred to another department with a new set of co-workers and tasks, may be assigned a new employer or employers, or may have to learn to operate new equipment or adopt new office procedures. These changes are a way of life in all organizations. Whether you like or dislike, approve or disapprove, you must maintain a positive attitude. An employee who is flexible will make the most of these changes.

Developing Awareness

Being able to look at the office and its operations is one thing, but seeing what is there is quite another matter. Awareness is the capacity to draw accurate inferences from what is seen, heard, and learned. A secretary must be aware of how each person fits into the work scheme. Naturally, as a secretary, you must see quickly the part your employer plays and thus how your work contributes to the organization. *Listen and watch* may be a good motto for you to follow during your initial weeks on the job.

A college-trained secretary should have little difficulty in developing this trait. In college you studied business principles and organization, you understood office costs, and you learned the meaning of profit. With this background, *see* what you can do to assist the growth of your company, your employer, and yourself. (A word of caution is needed here: Temper any feelings of superiority you may have over your co-workers because of your college training.)

Building Positive Human Relations

To be happy and to grow in your secretarial position, you must feel good about going to the office each day. One reason a secretary may feel content about being in an office is the people in it. Good working relationships with one's supervisor, co-workers, and subordinates play an extremely important role in the well-being of a secretary. Expect to like everyone whom you work with and expect to be liked in return. One may have the highest of secretarial skills to offer the employer. Yet without the ability to maintain good working relationships this same secretary can soon become dispensable.

The golden rule approach with co-workers is worth considering. If you have been successful in establishing friendships throughout your life, you will be sensitive to the needs of others. For instance, you will play your part in making a new office colleague feel a member of the group. You will cooperate with others. You will treat each person courteously.

Your relations with executives, the ones to whom you report and others, are especially important to your success. Showing that you are a good team member will enhance your opportunities to *be* a real member of the team. Be cheerful even when you are called on to go beyond the call of duty. Maintain a smiling countenance and a voice with a smile. Avoid emotionality, especially when you are under pressure. Remain calm. Respect confidentiality. Reveal neither organization nor executive secrets. The word *secretary* is derived from the word *secret*. Never say anything in the office that you would not want displayed on the office bulletin board. People repeat what is said in confidence.

Carry your good human relations attitudes over to the public that deals with your organization. Every office or telephone visitor is important, and often you are the contact with the outside world that makes the difference in how your company is perceived.

BECOMING ACCLIMATED TO THE JOB

That first week or two on the job can be overwhelming. Everything will be new to you—the people, the office, and the work. This section gives you some clues on how to survive this first week of getting to know the office staff and learning about the company.

Some companies have well-planned programs for inducting new employees. If you obtain a position in such a firm, someone will be assigned to welcome you, introduce you to your colleagues, show you your work area, perhaps take you to lunch, tell you something of the history of the organization, possibly show you a movie about your new company, and provide you with booklets describing company policies and benefits.

Many companies, however, have no organized orientation program. If you are fortunate, the secretary whose place you are taking will remain on the job for a few days to train you. In many cases, though, you will report to an employer whose secretary has already left, and you sink or swim alone.

One of the first decisions you will have to make on the job is to determine priorities of duties. You will have to decide what work must be done immediately, what must be done by the end of the day, and what can be done at some later time. This will be especially difficult if you report to more than one executive.

Creating a Good First Impression

Everyone in the office will form first impressions of you, just as you will of them. Because you were hired, you can assume that you made a satisfactory impression on your employer. Now you must make a satisfactory impression on those with whom you work—and strive to make this impression a permanent one.

You will be under critical and detailed inspection that first day. Your dress, your grooming, and everything you do and say will be observed. At this point, exercise good judgment by first being an attentive *listener*. It is a human trait to be defensive toward an outsider or a newcomer until that person wins one's goodwill and approval. Don't be disconcerted by this; if you understand it, you will be encouraged to make your associates like and accept you. Remember that their approval is most important to your future welfare and your happiness.

Begin your first day on time, allowing plenty of time for the things that fate seems to have in store for that first trip to a new job! Being even a few minutes late will require an explanation to your employer, a situation that you will find uncomfortable.

Learning Names

Certainly one way to create a good first impression is to learn promptly and pronounce correctly the names of those with whom you work. Associate the name with a mental picture of the person when you are introduced or as soon as possible. An effective plan is to write the name and practice pronouncing it. Then address the person by name at every appropriate occasion. Drawing a floor plan to show the location of the desks and the names of their occupants will help you through that first week.

Observing Ground Rules

New employees are expected to learn quickly the company's regulations relative to rest periods, lunch hours, personal telephone calls, coffee breaks, smoking, and other similar activities. Some of these rules may be in writing; others will have been established by custom but are nonetheless binding. One of the surest ways to get off to a poor start is to be a rule breaker. Ignorance is a poor excuse. The only safe policy is to find out the rules and customs of the office and observe them. Some organizations even test new employees on the content of company manuals.

Living Up to a Code of Ethics

At its annual convention in 1977 the National Secretaries Association (International) announced a program to develop a code of ethics for secretaries. This activity was launched because business in general is under pressure to raise its ethical standards and because secretaries are trying to raise their professional status.

A continued series of monthly articles on the topic were printed in the NSA magazine, *The Secretary*. Chapters held programs or discussions on secretarial ethics during a two-year period, and international association leaders developed a code. At its 1980 convention the association (now called Professional Secretaries International) adopted a Code of Ethics for the Professional Secretary, which is available from its headquarters for a fee. The introduction to the Code states:

The development of a code of ethics demonstrates that the secretarial profession accepts the obligation to engage in self-discipline and accepts the responsibility and trust earned by secretaries throughout past generations.

Each secretary has a personal obligation to support and follow the *Code*, recognizing that the greatest penalty possible for its violation is loss of the respect of professional colleagues and the trust of employers, clients, and society.

The broad principles are embodied in four standards which are clarified in subheadings showing how each standard is applied to office behavior:

I. The secretary shall act as a trusted agent in professional relations, implementing responsibilities in the most competent manner and exercising knowledge and skill to promote the interests of the immediate and corporate employer.

II. The secretary shall strive to maintain and enhance the dignity, status, competence, and standards of the profession and its practitioners.

III. The secretary shall insist that judgments concerning continued employment, compensation, and promotion be based upon professional knowledge, ability, experience, and performance.

IV. The secretary must consider the promotion and preservation of the safety and welfare of the public to be the paramount duty.

In addition to observing this Code as well as company rules and policies, you will want to observe an unwritten work code. This code includes an appreciation of what belongs to your employer. For instance, you have agreed to work a certain number of hours a week. You have agreed also to the length of the workday. Any abuses of this time which is to be devoted to your work is in violation of your work code. You may be surprised to learn that employee tardiness and absenteeism cost one employer almost $500 a year per employee. In addition, have respect for the equipment and supplies which belong to your employer. This means a concerted effort to reduce waste and to maintain the security of these materials in the office.

Developing Office Friendships

Many secretaries make a distinction between their work lives and their personal lives. They try to avoid socializing with members of the office staff outside office hours. They believe this separation makes them immune from office gossip and office cliques.

Of course, these same secretaries recognize that office friendships are beneficial. Certainly the secretary who has friends throughout the company is better able to serve the employer. Through these friendships the secretary also gains a better understanding of the company and the functions of the various departments as parts of the total unit, the company.

Friendliness should extend to all employment levels—the goodwill of the office messenger, the custodian, and the reprographics operator is important to your success.

Coping with Sexual Harassment

Secretaries work in close contact with principals and co-workers. Sometimes employers or co-workers engage in sexual harassment. In 1980 the Equal Employment Opportunity Commission (EEOC) defined sexual harassment and adopted final guidelines for employers to deal with the problem. Sexual harassment, according to EEOC, is "unwelcome sexual advances, requests for sexual favors, and other verbal or physical conduct of a sexual nature" that take place under any of the following circumstances:

1. When submission to the sexual advance is a condition of keeping or getting a job, whether expressed in explicit or implicit terms

2. When a supervisor or employer makes a personnel decision based on an employee's submission to or rejection of sexual advances

3. When sexual conduct unreasonably interferes with a person's work performance or creates an intimidation, hostile, or offensive work environment

Professional Secretaries International explains the term *sexual harassment* as "any unwanted sexual advances, looks, jokes, innuendoes, etc., from someone in the workplace who makes you uncomfortable and/or causes you problems on your job. It is being judged by your body and looks rather than your ability, experience, or job performance."[1]

Sexual harassment in the office ranging from suggestive speech to actual physical attack and threats of withholding promotions or even dismissal have been widely exposed in motion pictures and news media. It has aroused public outcry by many people, especially women's groups.

Handling sexual harassment is especially perplexing for the young secretary in a new position who is eager to please associates. The problem becomes even more difficult because of the informality of today's office contrasted with the office even ten years ago. Still, much of what happens depends on the secretary's deportment. Maintain cordial but not too familiar relationships. Ignoring suggestive words and actions will often discourage them. Do not make an issue of one isolated incident. These are certainly the best solutions —if they work. If not, the secretary should speak unemotionally, asking the offender to refrain from such actions. If this does not stop the harassment, you should report the situation to your superior—or even ask for a transfer.

Undoubtedly there are many justified complaints that can and should be redressed, but the secretary can prove skill in human relationships by maintaining dignity and poise while solving a problem of this type alone. Armed with verifiable proof of infractions, though, the secretary may show equal poise in reporting an intolerable situation.

Learning about the Company

From the first moment, your overall program will be to learn as much as you can, about everything you can, as soon as you can. This is a sizable order for the new employee, but it can be done.

In some companies a job analysis, job description, or job specifications for your new position will be available in a company manual and will give you an idea of the scope of your duties. To serve your employer effectively you need to learn about the organization quickly so that you can interpret any request and carry out directions without asking for elementary information.

Learn as quickly as possible the names of customers, the names of your employer's close associates, the most frequently used telephone numbers, the most frequently used terminology in dictation, and the technical language of

---

[1]*The Secretary*, May, 1979, p. 12.

the company. The more you know and the more ready you are with the information, the quicker you will become valuable to your employer and the organization.

Company Manuals. Most organizations have one or more company manuals or instruction sheets for office routine. A general office manual will usually explain the organization of the company, the relationships of the various offices and departments, the general rules and regulations, and information that affects all employees—the date and method of distributing paychecks, descriptions of company benefits, and a list of the holidays observed by the company. Some manuals give directions for the work of all departments (or merely one department); others are procedural manuals for initiating and completing specific activities of the company.

Operating manuals are often available for the various machines and equipment in the office, and most large companies have style manuals or other forms of direction for setting up correspondence and company forms. If your office has such a manual, spend many of your spare moments studying and thoroughly digesting everything that has a bearing on your work—almost to the point of memorizing important facts.

If it is permissible for you to take some of these materials home for study, you should do so. Devoting an hour or so of quiet time at home may reduce considerably the amount of learning time required in the office.

The Office Files. The office files offer a wealth of information to the new secretary. Previous correspondence, incoming and outgoing, will indicate the type of correspondence you can expect and will also be an excellent source of terminology and technical language. As you look through the files, list the terms with which you are unfamiliar. Note your employer's letter-writing style and proper title, and where and how to file letters and records. Become familiar with the various forms and types of stationery of the company.

Other Sources of Information. Special types of records are often available to the secretary: Scrapbooks or collections of clippings about the executive, the company, or its products are sources of background information. Many organizations publish a periodical (known as a *house organ*) written by and about its employees. Back issues of these will tell you a great deal, as will journals of the particular industry.

One way to determine the actual scope of your position is to acquaint yourself with the duties of other company employees. Seeing how your job relates to theirs will help you understand not only your own job but also the total functions of the office.

Questions. Of course you must ask questions; but make them few and make them count. There are two kinds of questions. *Learning* questions help you find out things you need to know; they are excellent questions. *Leaning* questions are those about something you really should know or can research yourself; they are the kind that you should avoid.

There is a time and place for questioning. During the first few days of your work, whenever possible, accumulate your problems and questions by making notes, and ask them all at a logical time in one session with the employer or with your temporary mentor. As you compile your list, however, be sure that it does not include a problem that you could have solved yourself.

The other employees will usually be helpful in answering questions, but you must remember that they have full-time work to do themselves. Sometime later you will probably have an opportunity to repay those who have helped you by returning the favor when they need extra help.

Developing a Desk Manual

A helpful organizer for the secretary in a new job is the desk manual. If you have inherited one, you will find in this loose-leaf notebook explanations of company procedures, examples of company forms, and instructions for handling the duties peculiar to your job. If one is not available, begin at once to compile the information for your desk manual.

You can start some sections, such as correct letter form and mailing procedures, immediately. Accumulating others will require time and experience. You may want to prepare a breakdown of your duties by time periods: daily, weekly, monthly, and annually. If you are always busy during the day, take the time to do the bulk of the preparation after office hours. The first draft will be the most time-consuming; once written and thoughtfully indexed, the manual can be updated quickly and easily.

Procedures Sections. Undoubtedly one of the first sections you will prepare is the one that explains how to handle various secretarial duties. The topic outline on pages 656–657 is suggested in organizing this part of the manual. If you are an administrative secretary in a company with a word processing center, you will add to Section II the Part D given in the insert at the bottom of page 658. The correspondence secretary will want to prepare a desk manual also. A suggested format appears at the top of page 658.

In addition to these procedural sections, the secretary will include information of a general nature concerning the company, directories of important employer contacts, customers, or projects. A personal data section giving information about the employer is appropriate for the manual. If a secretary reports to several principals, it is a good idea to have specific information for each in the manual.

Company Information. One section of the manual will consist of pertinent company information, such as an organizational chart showing the lines of authority and the person in each executive and supervisory position. In addition the following information should be helpful to the secretary new on the job:

Addresses and telephone numbers of branch offices and subsidiaries

Names and titles of supervisory personnel at the branch offices and subsidiaries

Company rules and regulations—hours of work, lunch hour, coffee breaks, and the like

Company policies (vacations, sick leave, insurance, and other fringe benefits) in summary form

Telephone numbers of specific office services

Who's Who Directory. Another section of the manual will likely be a directory of the persons with whom the employer has frequent contacts. Individual circumstances will determine whether to subdivide into *in-company* and *outside* listings. At any rate, the list should include the following:

1. Those with whom the employer frequently corresponds or holds telephone conversations
2. Frequent office visitors
3. The names of professional or service people (attorney, doctor, broker, automobile service agencies)

To build a list of names for the directory, jot down each one as it comes to your attention. Then prepare a card for each name including the following information: correct spelling, company affiliation and address, telephone number, salutation and complimentary close for correspondence (Dear Charles, not Dear Mr. Jones, as you learn the relationship of the correspondent to the executive). Cross-reference the affiliations and identifications. For example, if you have Mr. Ericson's name as advertising manager of Acme Metal Company and Ms. Curry as sales manager of the same company, make a card for Acme and list the names of both executives. Likewise, if Ms. Roberta Nolan is your employer's attorney, make one card for Roberta Nolan, Attorney, and a cross-reference card for Attorney, Roberta Nolan. Copy the cards onto loose-leaf sheets and insert in the manual. (Some secretaries prefer to use the card file.) Update changes by typing and pasting the change over the original entry.

Clients and Projects Directory. When your employer works with a succession of important clients, customers, projects, or jobs, a special section in the manual is necessary. Provide a page for each person or project, listing such information as the title of the job, the work to be performed, pertinent data, terms, and special procedures that the secretary must follow. A list of all persons importantly connected with the job is also helpful. Here, too, cross-referencing should be freely used.

Personal Data Section. In addition to the major items that comprise the basic desk manual, many secretaries add a personal section. This section contains

TOPIC OUTLINE FOR PROCEDURES SECTION
OF THE DESK MANUAL

I. INCOMING MAIL
   A. Mail register
      1. Explanation of posting procedure
      2. Sample form
   B. Distribution of the mail

II. CORRESPONDENCE
   A. Interoffice correspondence
      1. Model interoffice memorandum forms
      2. Number and distribution of copies
   B. Outside correspondence
      1. Model letter forms
      2. Stationery examples
      3. Number and distribution of copies
   C. Mail schedules

III. COMPANY FORMS
   A. Models of all forms
   B. Instructions for completing
   C. Number and distribution of copies

IV. FILING
   A. Centralized filing system
      1. Materials that go to centralized file
      2. Procedure for reconciling the bank statement
      3. Procedure for obtaining materials from filing
   B. Secretary's file (full explanation of filing system)
   C. Transfer and storage policies

V. FINANCIAL DUTIES
   A. Bank account
      1. Procedure for making deposits
      2. Procedure for reconciling the bank statement
      3. Disposition of canceled checks and bank statements
      4. Location of bankbook and checkbook
   B. Payments of recurring expenses like membership dues and mis-
      cellaneous fees
      1. Dates of payments
      2. Procedures for payments
   C. Petty cash
      1. Location of fund
      2. Regulations covering expenditures from fund
      3. Filing of receipts
      4. Procedure for replenishing fund

VI. INFORMATION SYSTEM AND ELECTRONIC EQUIPMENT AVAILABLE WITHIN THE
    ORGANIZATION
   A. Locations
   B. Instructions for using services
   C. When to use

VII. OFFICE MACHINES
      A. Inventory of machines in office (serial numbers and purchase
          dates of all machines)
      B. Repair services (service contracts, name and telephone num-
          ber of each service)

VIII. SUPPLIES
      A. List of supplies to be stocked
          1. Quantities of each to be ordered
          2. Names and addresses (or telephone numbers) of suppliers
      B. Procedure for obtaining supplies
      C. Procedure for controlling supplies

IX.   SUBSCRIPTIONS TO PUBLICATIONS
      A. Names, number of copies, renewal dates
      B. Procedure for renewal
      C. Routing of publications in office

X.   PUBLIC RELATIONS
      A. News releases
      B. Announcements

XI.   TELEPHONE PROCEDURES
      A. Types of services available
      B. Regulations for use of various types
      C. Procedures for reporting toll charges
      D. Special instructions relating to use of equipment

XII. TELECOMMUNICATIONS
      A. Examples of telegrams, TELEX, TWX, FAX
      B. Number and distribution of copies
      C. Procedure for sending
          1. Determination of method used
          2. Time restrictions
      D. Procedure for recording charges

XIII. TRAVEL
      A. Employer's travel and hotel preferences
      B. Names and telephone numbers of persons in travel agency
          or airlines office
      C. Locations of timetables
      D. Model itinerary
      E. Method of ticket pickup
      F. Expense report form
          1. Number and distribution of copies
          2. Receipts required

XIV. REFERENCE SECTION
      A. Form letters
      B. Guide letter paragraphs
      C. Vocabulary list

WORD PROCESSING CENTER

Every word processing center will have a procedures manual which applies to all the operations and all the correspondence secretaries. In addition, the correspondence secretary may compile a desk manual that will include:

I. MACHINE OPERATIONS
   A. Machine codes (Menus)
   B. Machine capabilities
II. CORRESPONDENCE AND REPORTS
   A. Authorization for rush items and turnaround time
   B. Distribution of copies
   C. Filing
   D. Storage
   E. Standard proofreading marks
III. DIRECTORY OF CUSTOMERS, CLIENTS
   A. Names and addresses
   B. Selective salutations and complimentary closings
IV. COMPANY INFORMATION
   A. Organization chart
   B. List of administrative secretaries
V. COMPANY FORMS
   A. Signature authorizations
   B. Distribution of copies
VI. WORD PROCESSING REPORTING PROCEDURES
   A. Production report
   B. Transcription report

———————

Administrative Support

The administrative secretary's desk manual may include all the sections given on pages 656-657. In Section II the following additions are appropriate:

   D. Word processing center
      1. Dictation instructions
      2. Forms
         a. dictated material
         b. hard copy
         c. review sheet
         d. rush work
         e. form letters
      3. Proofreading/copying responsibilities
      4. File retention procedures

the unusual reminders—dates and events of special significance to the employer or employers and any personal information known by the secretary, such as:

Biography of employer or a complete listing of educational achievements, employment records, awards, and community services

Important numbers—social security, passport, and credit cards

Insurance policies—numbers, amounts, and payment dates (unless already in an insurance register)

Memberships in professional and civic organizations—offices held, meeting dates, dues, committee assignments, and so on

MOVING UP IN YOUR SECRETARIAL POSITION

After you have demonstrated your competence, you can hope for promotion. Your advancement will depend on your performance and your professional growth while in your present position.

Making Job-Enhancing Efforts

The secretarial profession is exactly what you make it. If you stay in your own little niche, doing only the work that has been assigned to you, you are likely to remain in the same position and at about the same salary indefinitely. Many employees who do not represent the standards set throughout this textbook carry the title of secretary. Some employers do not recognize the potential of their secretaries and limit their activities to routine tasks. Advancement is very much up to you. Each time you find a way to free your employer of some task, you will become more valuable. Each time you assume a new responsibility and prove yourself equal to the task, you will be better qualified for that coveted advancement.

This statement does not mean that you use aggressive tactics or that you infringe on the work of your co-workers—sure ways to ensure your being thoroughly disliked—but it does mean that if you expect to get ahead, you must be a self-starter, alert to opportunities to prove your value by assuming more responsibility.

In your rush to get ahead, don't overlook the fact that there is no substitute for competence. Competence comes at a high price—a price paid in hard work, study, and dedication. A capacity for growth must be coupled with the self-discipline necessary to carry out a sustained effort toward growing with a job.

Build an impressive record of service to your employer and to others. Continue to promote your own individuality by maintaining a wholesome balance between business and social life, by developing interests and hobbies, and by cultivating friendships. Be well informed about business practices as well as the world around you.

Assertiveness, not Aggressiveness. In today's society everybody is encouraged to speak out more forcefully, to express viewpoints more freely, to assume a leadership role instead of following blindly decisions with which they do not agree or that affect them adversely.

With the growth of affirmative action programs, interest in assertiveness has extended to the office, and various groups promote assertiveness training that enables employees to express their views when fair employment practices are not followed. College courses, workshops, and seminars abound to train employees to practice assertiveness effectively. Techniques learned help employees not only reduce employment abuses but also improve job effectiveness in all areas.

If you have a well-documented case that should be brought to the attention of management, you are completely justified in calling the situation to the attention of appropriate personnel. If, for example, you believe that you have been passed over for a raise or promotion, tell your employer, not your colleagues. A frank discussion of your job evaluation with your employer is usually fruitful.

There is, though, quite a difference between assertiveness and aggressiveness. Assertiveness (desirable) is a part of aggressiveness but can spill over into excessive aggressiveness (undesirable). Excessive aggressiveness may label you as pushy and work against your moving up in the organization. It may alienate management and even other groups that could become useful allies in achieving your goals. In other words, recognize and respect the fine line between assertiveness and aggressiveness.

Job Descriptions. Work for the establishment and utilization of improved personnel practices. Most large organizations have adopted job descriptions, which should be prepared and updated periodically by cooperation between the executive and the secretary. Have any expanded responsibilities put into writing; for example, setting up the conference room for a meeting may be your responsibility. But if you also organize the meeting, write the agenda, and prepare the report of the proceedings, make certain that these latter responsibilities are included in your job description. Upward mobility may be limited if you let the job description limit creativity and initiative. Performance beyond that called for in the job description often results in a salary increase greater than the standard increase given most employees.

Authority for Giving Executive Orders. Employers exercise a great deal of authority. Sometimes they forget that their secretaries do not have the same authority and will say, "Tell Ms. Montgomery to give me a report on the bid by Thursday." Unfortunately, your authority to give the order has not been established by your superior, and your request, although tactfully worded, may be resented by Ms. Montgomery. If you are having a problem of this kind, ask the executive to establish your authority to make such requests.

Growing Professionally

Your activities while you are in the office will determine in part your development toward professional status. You will need to learn all that you can on the job, but you can also make your out-of-the-office activities contribute to your growth.

Participation in organizations is one way you can grow professionally. Taking part in professional groups is important to all employees. Many advancements are secured because of contacts made in both social and professional groups. Because women formerly had access to fewer such organizations than men, they have established *networking* groups for the exchange of information leading to professional advancement. *U.S. News & World Report* estimates that more than 1,400 networking organizations developed in this country between 1979 and 1981.

Many professional organizations, available to both sexes, promote personal development by providing information, contacts, and support. They keep members updated on equipment and organizational changes, and enable them to work as part of a larger team and to learn new work styles, opportunities often not available in their employment environments.

Professional Organizations. The largest professional organization for secretaries is Professional Secretaries International which has chapters in the United States and foreign countries. Probably the fastest growing related organization is the International Information/Word Processing Association (IWP), formerly the International Word Processing Association. It has more than 12,000 members and about a hundred chapters.

Certification Programs. Several organizations sponsor difficult certification programs. Anyone passing these examinations demonstrates superior competency in the field. The certification programs of the American Association of Medical Assistants, the National Association of Legal Secretaries (International), and the National Association of Educational Office Personnel are described in Chapter 25.

The capstone of Professional Secretaries International is its Certified Professional Secretary certificate awarded to those who pass a two-day examination and have the required amount of verified secretarial experience. About 15,000 secretaries have qualified for the certificate since its inception in 1951.

The examination is divided into six sections: Behavioral Science in Business, Business Law, Economics and Management, Accounting, Communications Applications, and Office Administration and Technology. It is prepared by the Institute for Certifying Secretaries and is given every May in more than 100 testing centers in the United States, Canada, Puerto Rico, and Jamaica.

Students may take the examination near the end of their college program; but if they pass all sections, they will not be certified until they complete the experience requirement. Specific information about qualifying is not included here since it changes from year to year. It is available from Professional

662

Secretaries International, Crown Center, Suite G-10, 2440 Pershing Road, Kansas City, MO 64108.

To prepare for the examination, you may obtain the following materials from PSI for a minimal fee: *CPS Outline and Bibliography; CPS, a Sampling of Questions; Part V from Past Examinations;* and *Time Schedule for CPS Review.*

Unfortunately management is not as well informed about the CPS program as secretaries wish they were. There are notable exceptions, however. The governors of Indiana and Illinois have issued policy statements indicating that CPS holders will receive special consideration for promotions. A number of colleges grant college credit to holders of the CPS certificate. A model response of management to the advantages of the program is that of Valley National Bank of Phoenix, one of the largest banks in the Southwest. By 1979 quite a few of its secretaries had become CPS's. Nineteen had moved into supervisory management career paths, and eighteen were secretaries to senior management. Secretaries who indicate interest in the examination are carefully screened by the executive committee of the local secretaries' association. The bank spends approximately $500 in financing the educational preparation of each candidate who has demonstrated a potential for professional growth, and a new CPS receives a $400 bonus and a gold CPS key.

Seminars and Courses for Secretaries. Several professional organizations offer seminars and courses to improve secretarial performance. The local chapters of Professional Secretaries International conduct workshops, seminars, and CPS preparation courses. Private organizations such as the Dartnell Institute of Management sponsor seminars in major cities of the United States. Management organizations offer special seminars for secretaries, the Administrative Management Society and the American Management Association, to name only two. Colleges include such programs in their adult education offerings.

Many companies send their secretaries to these programs. If you are interested in attending any of them, you may request financial support from your immediate employer. If your request is granted, arrangements for time off from work and payment of registration can be made with your employer.

A study of companies with 500 or more employees shows that 75 percent of them offer some in-house courses, with one eighth of all employees participating, mostly during working hours. Many of these courses are designed to improve secretarial performance. It is obvious that educational opportunities are available to those ambitious enough to take advantage of them.

Promoting Your Employer

The more important your employer appears in the eyes of others—company executives, customers, clients, friends—the more important you appear, too. Here are some suggestions which will help in keeping you both in the limelight.

1. Keep your employer's personal data sheet up to date. Many employers have a prepared data sheet which they may submit when applying for membership in a professional organization or when supplying a biographical sketch prior to a speech or publication. This sheet needs to be updated regularly.

2. Watch the newspaper and magazines for press notices that mention your employer. See that they are clipped, identified, and filed. They can be rubber cemented into a scrapbook. Many people are too modest to handle or supervise such a task; so the secretary should take the initiative. Incidentally, posting clippings about your employer on the bulletin board is one way of letting everyone in the office know that your employer, too, is important.

3. Keep your employer's committee folders in good order and up to date. This important assistance will assure that your employer presents a good image in the eyes of other company personnel.

4. Watch the news for items concerning your employer's business associates and friends. When they are honored or promoted, draft a letter of congratulations for your employer's signature and submit it with the clipping.

5. Look for news reports about new firms or plants that may be potential customers. Your employer will be watching for these items also, but it does no harm for you to say "Did you happen to see this in yesterday's paper?"

As a secretary, however, do not forget that there is no better way to promote the image of your employer than to see that all work going out of the office is flawless and is turned out with dispatch. Mistakes, delays, and sloppiness are not the marks of a professional secretary.

If you have worked with an executive for a period of time, you should be able to assess whether or not that person is on the way up the company ladder. Kanter[2] points out that executive positions are extremely competitive. It is a cruel fact that many bright young executives do not make the grade and are destined for dead-end jobs that are secure but lead nowhere. She also emphasizes that nearly always people who get ahead in business are helped by a mentor (sponsor), someone who pushes not only for their own self-advancement but for yours, too. If you are attached to an executive whose promotional opportunities are nonexistent or who is not your mentor, you may decide that the best thing for you is to move out since you will probably not be moving up. You can ask for a transfer or change to another organization.

This is dangerous advice to the beginner, who is not always willing to wait until a sound judgment of the situation can be made, and many mistakes have been made. Nothing is more questionable on your employment record than proof that you are a job-hopper. However, an honest appraisal of your employer is valuable in planning your professional future. If you should decide on a move after you have been in a position long enough to establish that you were successful in it, leave with poise and dignity and without animosity.

---

[2]Rosabeth Moss Kanter, *Men and Women of the Corporation* (New York: Basic Books, Inc., 1977), Chapters 6 and 7.

Anything derogatory could haunt you for a long time after you are gone. A letter of resignation will help to keep a good relationship.

Identifying Yourself with Management

The position of secretary to a major official of the business is not one that you step into or inherit because you have completed a degree or technical program. These positions must be earned and are usually filled from the inside. Therefore, you will probably start on a lower level, but your goal is eventually to associate yourself with top management.

To work effectively on this level, the secretary must develop the ability to look at problems from the management point of view. This trait requires an orientation into management thinking through reading the same magazines that management reads, such as *Fortune, Nation's Business, Business Week, Wall Street Journal, Forbes, The Office, Administrative Management,* and others; through becoming concerned with management problems; and through studying management books and taking management courses, if available.

The emphasis of much of your secretarial training has been on following instructions, observing directives, carrying through on decisions that have been made, and assuming the initiative in a relatively narrow range of operation only. The management point of view, however, involves determining courses of action, making decisions, giving directions, and delegating authority and responsibility. To shift to the management outlook, the secretary must view problems basically from the other side of the desk. This transition requires a carefully planned program of self-education, orientation, and discipline.

You will need to grow every day of your working life. If the time comes when you cannot keep up with your employer, be assured that you will be replaced by someone who can. If you continue to grow with the job, you will have a position as long as you want it; and the possibilities for advancement become limitless.

As you grow into your management role, you will gradually be performing more supervisory functions. The higher up the management ladder you climb, the greater your supervisory responsibilities will be. Chapter 27, the final chapter in this text, will discuss management and supervisory problems.

SUGGESTED READINGS

Code of Ethics and CPS study materials. Kansas City: Professional Secretaries International.

Grizzard, Elizabeth S. and Barbara L. Hurless. "Talking It Out Within an Organization," *The Secretary,* October–May, 1979–80.

Kanter, Rosabeth Moss, *Men and Women of the Corporation.* Basic Books paperback and Harper *Colophon* hard cover, 1979. Every secretary or prospective secretary should read Chapter 4, pp. 69–103, "Secretaries," a discussion of how secretarial tasks and attitudes can be self-defeating and limiting. Also read the section on mentors, pp. 181–184, and Chapter 6, "Opportunity," pp. 129–163, about potential executives who do not make the grade.

Kennedy, Marilyn Moats. *Office Politics: Seizing Power, Wielding Clout.* Chicago: Association Press-Follett, 1980.

Kriett, Carolyn. *The Successful Creative Secretary.* West Nyack, N.J.: Parker Publishing Company, 1978.

Welch, Mary Scott. *Networking.* New York: Harcourt Brace Jovanovich, 1980.

QUESTIONS FOR DISCUSSION

1. Cite three additional examples of a new secretary showing initiative that is desirable. Cite three other examples in which you think that the secretary exceeded his/her authority.

2. What recommendations would you make to a co-worker who asks your advice on how to grow in the secretarial profession?

3. In what ways can a secretary profit from joining a local chapter of a professional organization?

4. Assume that you are employed to replace the secretary to a department manager in a large company and that the secretary has already left when you report. Where would you obtain the following information?
   (a) Your job description
   (b) Your employer's proper title
   (c) The lines of authority in the office
   (d) The letter style preferred by your employer
   (e) The name of the company president's secretary
   (f) The branch offices of the company
   (g) Your employer's professional memberships

5. Do you think a new secretary should be willing to take company manuals and work material home for study when first learning a new job? Why? Why not?

6. As a new employee, you are asked to learn the functions of other closely related jobs in your office. What are the advantages of this practice? Are there any disadvantages?

7. What do you think about the theory of some secretaries that professional work life should remain separate from personal life?

8. In today's office, why should a secretary have a code of ethics, while some other employees may not?

9. Personnel changes in company organization have resulted in your being assigned a second employer. In your own mind you question whether you can handle the work of another person. What attitude should you take with your present employer and the new one?

10. What factors might influence a secretary to leave an organization? Why could this decision be a risky one?

11. Retype the following sentences using the correct words from those in parentheses. Then check the Reference Guide to verify or correct your answers.

(a) Please (pardon, excuse) the slight flaw in the paper.

(b) Embarrassing (oneself, one's self) by using poor grammar is inexcusable.

(c) She is the (older, oldest) of the two partners.

(d) We must take at least two members (off, off of) the project.

(e) He (lead, led) the company in sales that month.

(f) (Later, Latter) in the year we will take up the (later, latter) of the two proposals.

PROBLEMS

1. Prepare a report on one of the following topics:

(a) What you believe are the personal contributions a secretary makes to the office, to co-workers, and to secretarial work

(b) How you plan to meet the challenge of new office technology in secretarial work

2. Select a professional organization that has a chapter in your area. Make arrangements to attend one of the meetings or interview one of the members. Give an oral report to the class including a description of the organization, its objectives, activities, membership requirements, and services to members.

Chapter **27**

Fulfilling Your Administrative Role

At some point in your career you may want to look beyond the secretarial position and explore the possibilities of moving into management. As you grow in experience, intellectual curiosity, and in your ability to solve problems and make decisions, you will find increased opportunities for jobs that will broaden your business perspective, increase your authority, and permit you to make major decisions. This increased knowledge and experience will strengthen your confidence in your ability to motivate and to lead others in the achievement of common goals.

Your contribution to your employer as a secretary will permit you to exhibit your managerial talent; it can also give you an indication as to whether you will make an effective manager. Study the job ahead. If you believe you have the ability to accomplish results through the work of others, start now to direct your professional development toward a management position.

This chapter will focus on the fundamentals of the management process and the basic qualifications for effective administration and supervision. Throughout this book some of the secretary's administrative duties have been discussed as an integral part of the secretarial position. This chapter goes beyond the administrative duties performed by the secretary by outlining the functions of management and the popular styles of leadership, and by giving some suggestions for continuing your professional growth as a manager.

APPRAISING YOUR MANAGEMENT POTENTIAL

In many offices secretaries perform a dual role; that is, their secretarial duties are combined with the supervision of other employees. Often these employees work for and answer to someone other than the secretary. Therefore, the secretary's authority is limited, and extreme tact and ability are required to keep the work flowing smoothly. Because the secretary's lines of authority are hazy under such an arrangement, frustration sometimes results; however, handling this dual role of secretary-supervisor successfully can prove your ability as a potential manager.

As you expand your horizons beyond the support functions associated with your secretarial position, focus on a particular job and analyze it. Ask yourself: What does the management job offer that my present job lacks? What qualifications does a manager need that are different from those required on my present job? Am I willing to let go the technical details of my present job to take on broader responsibilities? Have I trained someone to take my place so that the transition will be a smooth one? What are the negative aspects of being a manager? Do I really want to assume the responsibility associated with a management job, or would I rather remain at the support level with close

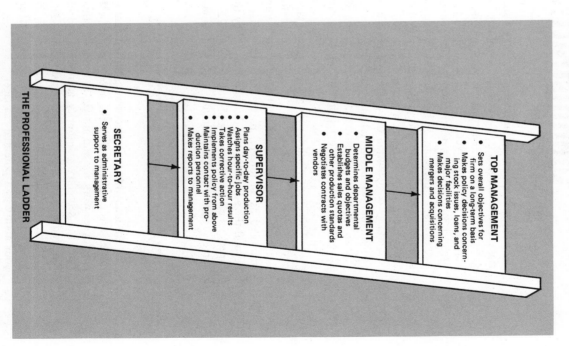

THE PROFESSIONAL LADDER

SECRETARY
- Serves as administrative support to management

SUPERVISOR
- Plans day-to-day production
- Assigns specific jobs
- Watches hour-to-hour results
- Takes corrective action
- Implements policy from above
- Maintains contact with production personnel
- Makes reports to management

MIDDLE MANAGEMENT
- Determines departmental budgets and objectives
- Establishes sales quotas and other production standards
- Negotiates contracts with vendors

TOP MANAGEMENT
- Sets overall objectives for firm on a long-term basis
- Makes policy decisions concerning stock issues, loans, and major facilities
- Makes decisions concerning mergers and acquisitions

Illus. 27-1
The professional ladder

association with my peers? If you can answer yes to most of these questions, you show promise as a successful executive.

UNDERSTANDING THE MANAGEMENT FUNCTIONS

Management is executive leadership or the ability to obtain desired results through the use of the resources of an organization and the efforts of others. The success of every organized activity depends on the managerial skills of its leaders. Although some managers seem to be born with the ability to lead, others must acquire management skills through reading, specialized courses and seminars, experience, and observation of successful executives.

The functions of management at all levels involve planning, organizing, controlling, and directing. To become an effective manager, you must understand each of these functions and how it contributes to the total organization.

Planning

Planning is the primary management function. Before anything worthwhile can happen in an organization, goals must be set, objectives established, and checkpoints and target dates defined. This is the essence of planning—the function essential to providing the course of action for the organization.

Plans may be made for the long term (more than one year) or for the short range (one year or less). Long-range plans are general in nature, since they must anticipate changes in social, economic, and political climates that can affect outcomes over a five-year or ten-year period. Short-range plans are spelled out in detail, and in some cases may be used to guide a specific, nonrecurring project. For example, as a manager you might make a short-range plan to conduct a feasibility study for installing a word processing unit in your company. Once the decision is made and the equipment is installed, there is no further need for the plan.

Good plans are not too rigid. Some flexibility is built in to allow for the uncertainties of the future so that slight adjustments can be made without major deviation from the requirements of the plan.

Organizing

Once plans have been formulated, a structure must be developed within which the plans can be carried out. Tasks must be divided among personnel. Each worker and supervisor must know who is to perform each task as well as when and how the work is to be done. The organizational function defines duties, assigns responsibilities (the obligation to perform a task), delegates authority (the power to make decisions related to the work), and establishes staff relationships—who reports to whom. In an effective organization employees answer to one supervisor. Imagine your dilemma, for example, in working as secretary to four executives, each of whom feels that his or her work should be given priority. Violation of this important principle, although not uncommon in many offices, is a cause of frustration, low morale, and high turnover.

Good organizational structure adheres to the principle of *span of control*. This refers to the number of employees who report to a single supervisor. The manager who supervises too many employees will not be able to perform all the supervisory duties effectively. On the other hand, supervision of too few employees is a waste of executive time. As a general rule, the lower the level of management, the larger the span of control can be. For example, a supervisor of a word processing center might supervise twelve correspondence secretaries effectively, but it would be difficult for an administrative manager to be responsible for more than five supervisors of operations (such as word processing, mail room, reprographics, records, credits and collections) because of the complex nature of their jobs.

Business responsibilities may be organized in a number of ways. However, the major types of organizational structures used in business are *line* and *line and staff* organization.

Line Organization. *Line organization* means that authority flows in a straight line from the top official in the company to the lowest administrative segment of the organization. A popular device for illustrating the line form of organization is the *organization chart*, which shows relationships among members of the organization and their areas of responsibility. A chart illustrating line organization is shown on page 28 (Chapter 2).

Line and Staff Organization. The line and staff concept of organization originated in the military. Business has adopted it as a means of coping with expanding relationships that accompany growing organizations. Most large

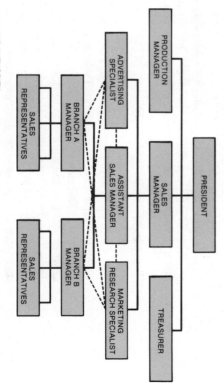

—— LINE AUTHORITY
--- STAFF ADVICE

PRESIDENT

PRODUCTION MANAGER

SALES MANAGER

TREASURER

ADVERTISING SPECIALIST

ASSISTANT SALES MANAGER

MARKETING RESEARCH SPECIALIST

BRANCH A MANAGER

BRANCH B MANAGER

SALES REPRESENTATIVES

SALES REPRESENTATIVES

companies today use line and staff organization because the structure permits the use of staff specialists for advice and assistance. The term *staff* refers to support activities of two kinds—specialist and personal. Staff specialists serve in an advisory capacity only—that is, they have no authority over line personnel. Their relationships to line personnel are indicated on organization charts by broken lines. Illus. 27-2 shows a line and staff organization.

Controlling

Control is the monitoring function that ensures that the work performed meets specifications. Control must be exercised to ensure that the work is of the proper quality, produced in expected quantities, at the most economical cost according to predetermined schedules, policies, and procedures.

Cost Control and Work Measurement. Two major types of control exist in every type of organized activity—cost control and production control. Your effectiveness in cutting costs—reflected in your ability to reduce the cost of supplies, overtime, absenteeism, etc.—is one of the best measures of your competence as a manager.

The other area of control in which the supervisor must be especially skillful is the area of production. In this regard work measurement techniques of several kinds are employed by supervisors as a basis on which to set production standards and arrive at pay scales for employees. Measuring the production of factory workers engaged in routine assembly line operations has been practiced for many years; until recently, however, measuring office work has not been practiced on a large scale.

In evaluating your work and that of your subordinates, you will need a set of criteria on which to base your judgments. Output in highly repetitive office operations has been successfully measured, and realistic quantitative standards have been established. In word processing centers line and page count are commonly being used to measure worker productivity and the success of the center concept itself. In the management literature you can find standards for such processes as straight copy and letter typing, addressing envelopes, filling in form letters, or cutting stencils. Your own systems and procedures staff will help you in setting standards. Qualitative standards are not as easy; just remember that the quality of all the work from your department is your responsibility.

Corrective Action. In spite of adequate planning, efficient organization, and proper control, something will occasionally go wrong. A subordinate may not perform up to the standards expected or external delays and errors may prevent the completion of a project on time. When this happens the supervisor must take corrective action. Corrective action, when taken promptly, can prevent more serious problems later on and help keep morale and productivity high. Problems, such as computer down time, failure of a printer to deliver forms, careless employees who make serious errors, and the like, must be dealt with by the supervisor decisively, calmly, and as soon as possible.

Directing

An effective manager leads employees in such a way that organizational goals are achieved. This is the function of directing. Expanding government regulations, new technology, and increased costs have magnified the importance of this management function. Employee turnover is expensive, and top management in every organization is aware that the key to managing through people is to have the best possible people through whom to manage. As a leader, you must motivate employees to work efficiently and attempt to boost morale by providing an environment conducive to job satisfaction.

SUPERVISING OTHERS

Effective supervision is the ability to get people to do *what* you want done, *when* you want it done, the *way* you want it done because they *want* to do it. Supervision is the first level of management, and as you move up professionally you will probably find yourself in a supervisory position. As a supervisor you will be a member of the management team responsible for getting the work done. What's more, you will be the communication link between top and middle management and those you supervise. Your job will be a multifaceted one. You will report to top and middle management, interpret management policies to those you supervise, and coordinate with other supervisors to facilitate the flow of work throughout the organization. You will be promoting teamwork.

The amount of supervision needed depends on the quality of the orientation process and subsequent training on the job. If the employee has received an in-depth orientation and adequate training, the need for supervision is considerably lessened. After the initial training period, the right amount of supervision becomes important—too much gives the employee the feeling of being policed; too little leads to confusion.

As a supervisor, your duties will consist of all or some of the following tasks:

DUTIES OF THE SUPERVISOR

- Helping select the right people for the job
- Controlling attendance—absences and tardiness
- Inspecting and proofing work
- Keeping workers informed
- Carrying out objectives and instructions of management
- Keeping track of hours worked
- Maintaining office discipline
- Planning, assigning, and scheduling work
- Controlling office costs
- Promoting teamwork and cooperation

- Listening to employees' problems
- Providing and caring for equipment and supplies
- Training employees
- Handling employee discipline problems
- Keeping records and making reports to management
- Maintaining high quality and quantity of production
- Maintaining high morale among workers
- Improving work methods
- Maintaining safe, clean working conditions
- Evaluating employees for raises and promotions
- Orienting new employees to the job
- Handling matters of compensation
- Delegating work to others
- Interpreting employees' needs to management
- Interpreting management's needs to employees

Fulfilling your role as a successful supervisor will require more than job competence and hard work. It will also require the ability to recognize and select outstanding employees and to develop their potential for making a contribution to the company and the department to which they are assigned.

Recruiting

The actual recruitment is usually the responsibility of the staff of the personnel department. Before they begin any recruiting, however, they study the complete job description and the educational, work experience, and skill requirements for the position. Later, potential employees who have met screening standards are sent to the immediate supervisor for final approval or rejection. (Note the word *rejection*. The supervisor, being close to the job, may recognize valid reasons why the proposed candidate would not be effective in the work situation. It is best to say no now and avoid later trouble.)

An objective of every company is promotion from within; as an effective supervisor or administrator you should include as one of your objectives the development of replacements and personnel for new jobs. In fact, without a well-trained replacement, you may not be considered for a promotion.

Assisting employees in reaching their potential begins with the orientation to the job. The better the orientation process, the less supervision required, and thus you have more time to accomplish your work.

Orienting

Large organizations have a formal orientation program for new employees. Films, slides, and lectures acquaint the new employee with the history, products, and fringe benefits of the company. Information related to the specific job, however, is left to the immediate supervisor. As this supervisor, it is your responsibility to explain and demonstrate the tasks of the job.

Included in your discussion must be how and when the employee will be evaluated and how this evaluation is tied to salary increments. The supervisor also introduces new employees to the office workers and conducts a tour of the office facilities. In a small organization, the secretary-supervisor provides the entire orientation program—from general information about the company to specific information about the job.

Many supervisors develop an induction checklist to follow in orienting a new employee to the company and to the position. This list may include 50 to 100 items, whatever it takes to explain the job. Supplementary materials such as an organization chart and the office telephone directory are useful in outlining the office hierarchy and office procedures.

Training

Before employees can perform effectively as team members, a basic understanding of procedures, policies, and technology is essential. It is the rare employee who can learn a complex job merely by observing. One of your supervisory duties will be to provide sufficient training to make the employee fully productive as soon after induction as possible. Too little training is expensive when it leads to errors, employee insecurity, and low productivity. On the other hand, training programs that prolong the time before an employee takes full responsibility for a job are also costly. To help determine the types and length of training an employee needs, the supervisor may find a list of specific duties and responsibilities of the job helpful in training new employees. It is also suggested that the supervisor follow these guidelines:

1. Focus attention on what the employee is to do. First, have the employee observe as you complete a task. Then check the employee's understanding by having the trainee work through the process step by step. Allow more time for the more difficult concepts.

2. Discuss the purposes behind each task and encourage questions. Explain the *who, what, where, when, why,* and *how* of each task. Suggest that the employee compile a list of instructions. For more complicated tasks it is a good practice for the supervisor to provide a written set of instructions. Use materials and office forms that are part of the job in your explanations.

3. Allow the employee some quiet time to digest this information.

4. Assist the employee in seeing what tasks are important and those which are not so important. Emphasize the key steps in each job task.

5. Provide feedback to the employee on the work that has been done. You may have to reteach certain points which may have been misunderstood by the employee or overlooked in your explanation.

After an employee has been in the office long enough to learn the assigned job, continue your teaching responsibility by training the employee to do other jobs in the department. This technique is called *cross training.* Cross training has merit for the supervisor and for the employee. When an employee is absent because of sickness or vacation, another employee can assume the duties of the position. Cross training makes the employee more valuable to the department in addition to increasing the employee's job skills.

An example of cross training can be found in the administrative support/ word processing center concept. Many companies train the administrative support secretaries on word processing equipment to provide for better understanding of the center's function as well as to provide greater flexibility of personnel. Within the center itself, correspondence secretaries, while being assigned to one specific piece of equipment, might be trained on all equipment available for the same reason—staff flexibility.

Delegating

You must delegate to survive the avalanche of paperwork that characterizes the modern office and to get the job done accurately and on time. As your responsibilities expand, you must let go of details and assign them to others. Working frantically from one crisis to another and attempting to do everything yourself will lead to fatigue and inefficiency and do little to develop the potential of those you supervise. As a supervisor you will be judged by your ability to develop productive employees. By delegating some of your duties, you can give those you supervise added experience. Start your task of delegation simply —delegate routine tasks such as filling out reports and forms, checking materials and supplies, and composing routine correspondence.

As you begin your supervisory duties, you may find that you are not very skillful in delegating work to others. Many supervisors admit that early in their careers they labored under the false notion that it is easier to do a job than to explain it to someone else, or that they were afraid to risk employee error on an important job. These are common misgivings; but, if you are to become effective as a supervisor, you must become effective at delegating work. Don't make the mistake of keeping busy with lots of routine details. Delegate the routine jobs that can free you to do the major management functions—planning, organizing, controlling, and directing.

Motivating

A supervisor has the obligation to obtain the best results from employees. The ability to inspire people to undertake a job enthusiastically, to work as productive team members, and to exercise initiative is the hallmark of successful management. It is essential that you understand why some people do superior work while others do as little as possible. Hundreds of books have been written on the subject of motivation, and the behavioral scientists are still seeking answers on how to motivate people effectively.

Closely allied to job motivation is the need for job satisfaction. Each individual has a set of needs applying to the job situation that must be satisfied. In the past, money has been used as the major motivation in the workplace. The assumption that people worked only for money has been debunked by recent motivational research. Studies have revealed that, after a certain level of income, money ceases to be a significant motivator for many employees.

Research studies by behavioral scientists such as Abraham Maslow and Frederick Herzberg have helped management personnel to determine the needs of employees. Maslow identified a *hierarchy* of human needs: physiological (food, clothing, shelter), safety, belonging, esteem, and self-actualization. He indicated that once a lower need is fairly well satisfied, a worker can be motivated only by a desire to satisfy the next higher need. His work suggests that managers must help employees to realize their upper level needs (belonging, esteem, self-actualization) before complete job satisfaction—and thus higher productivity—can be obtained. In the office, *belonging,* the third level, refers to acceptance and achievement of status with one's peers. The fourth level, *esteem,* is the need for prestige, recognition, and achievement. *Self-actualization,* the highest level, emphasizes becoming whatever a person must be, reaching one's full potential.

The supervisor can assist subordinates in achieving a degree of the higher level needs by:

- Giving each employee complete responsibility for the preparation of one section of a report or one unit of work

- Granting increased authority in the accomplishment of office tasks

- Allowing employees to participate in making decisions that affect their work

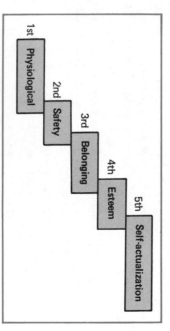

1st Physiological
2nd Safety
3rd Belonging
4th Esteem
5th Self-actualization

Frederick Herzberg took another approach to understanding employee morale. His research to determine which factors result in employee satisfaction and dissatisfaction on the job have been helpful to managers in their attempts to reduce employee turnover and increase productivity.

Herzberg's major findings revealed that task related experiences—achievement, recognition, interesting work, growth, advancement, and responsibility—caused people to be satisfied on the job. He called these experiences *satisfiers.* On the other hand, he found that those experiences that cause employees to be unhappy on their jobs were related to the job environment—working conditions, company policies and administration, supervision, money, status, job security, and interpersonal relationships. Herzberg classified these as *dissatisfiers.*

You will probably face the problems of tardiness, absenteeism, careless-ness, and errors. These are barriers to productivity, and as a supervisor you will be the catalyst who motivates and inspires employees to overcome these barriers. Some ways in which you can help your subordinates become success-ful in their work are given here:

1. Set specific objectives for each major undertaking. Set a reasonable stan-dard and give clear instructions.
2. Make employees feel that every job is important.
3. Make employees feel that they are important contributors to your team.
4. Ask employees for assistance, advice, and suggestions.
5. Let employees express their own ideas.
6. Train your employees and then trust them by giving them the freedom to work on their own.
7. Judge your employees' actions by the results obtained.
8. Suggest and request rather than demand.
9. Praise employees publicly when praise is deserved, but reprimand pri-vately.
10. Give credit where credit is due.
11. Listen to learn what is important to your employees.
12. Reward those who achieve and use their accomplishments to inspire others.
13. Look in on employees occasionally to check progress, offer help, answer questions, or boost confidence.
14. Don't assign a job that you don't know how to do.
15. Find out why employees do poor work.
16. Don't do the work yourself if the subordinate gets into deep water; let him or her learn from the experience.
17. Remember that employees put their best effort where the supervisor's emphasis is placed. Don't be a stickler for just one aspect of the job.
18. Put your critics to work. When you detect a complainer, delegate an important task to that person.

Evaluating

Periodically the secretary-supervisor must evaluate subordinates' work. In addition to being an organization's requirement, your evaluation is wanted and needed by the employee. Your evaluation can be either formal or informal (See Chapter 2).

In order to assess an employee's job performance you must:

- Be thoroughly familiar with the work involved.
- Have a set of job performance criteria.
- Be aware of individual differences in performing the tasks required by the position.
- Consider such factors as accuracy, neatness, and quantity of the employee's production.
- Be able to communicate your evaluation.
- Praise the work, not the person who performed it.

The importance to an employee of an evaluation cannot be overstated. Assume that you are responsible for the yearly evaluation of a subordinate. It is time for the first year evaluation, and you know that, in general, the person has done a good job. In the past few weeks, however, you have noticed a change in performance and in attitude. The person is cooperative but sullen; the work is not up to former standards. Reluctant to make negative statements on record, you decide to disregard the last few weeks' performance and complete the form on the basis of the previous record, confident that something personal is bothering the person and that it will work out in time. Also, you decide not to mention these points in your conference with the person.

Is this the best course of action? Surprisingly, many supervisors in this situation react in exactly the same way, tending to avoid possible unpleasant incidents and, in general, not wanting to become involved in the personal problems of employees. Yet it is the supervisor's responsibility to maintain the work level in the department or group and to assist the employee in every way to be a happy and effective worker. An unpleasant situation should be faced and an attempt made to resolve any problems as soon as possible.

A supplement to a formal yearly evaluation of employees is a list to determine an employee's cooperativeness at specific points during the year. Such a checkup may point out problem areas for you to investigate. For example, here are some activities you can review.

- Does the employee accept instructions and assignments willingly?
- Does the employee perform as directed?
- Does the employee assume responsibility for work, inform the supervisor if something goes wrong, call relevant matters to the supervisor's attention?
- Does the employee volunteer for special assignments?
- Does the employee give the job better than average attention?

The result of such an approach might be to commend the high performers, encourage the average group, and possibly work more closely with those who appear to need it.

Enriching the Job

Increased automation, the lack of diversity in many office jobs, and perhaps the monotony of some office tasks have brought a new challenge to the supervisor. More managers are beginning to give attention to the concept of job enrichment—an attempt to bridge the gap between the employee's capabilities and job responsibilities. This is done by providing greater challenge, more of a sense of accomplishment, and job responsibilities. Techniques such as flexible hours (employees choose within limits when to begin working hours), job rotation, cross training, full responsibility for an entire project, and pleasant working environment are being used in many organizations to provide job enrichment. In many companies jobs are being redesigned to fill this need.

After all is said and done, however, unless actual benefits accrue to the worker, job enrichment techniques will become ineffective. Artificial measures, unfortunately, cannot replace the need for training and promotion procedures designed to move employees through the hierarchy of an organization.

MAKING DECISIONS

One of the best gauges of your potential as a manager will be your ability to make effective decisions. Decisions are a part of every manager's job, and your survival as a supervisor will depend on your ability to weigh facts, consider alternate courses of action, foresee outcomes, and decide what to do. Deciding on the day-to-day activities can be done quickly and without much thought. Major decisions, however, require much thought, time, and effort. Deciding what to do in a crisis can be a traumatic experience for the worker who has always referred problems upward to a superior. As you grow in your knowledge of your job, you will learn what decisions you can make on your own and which ones you should refer to your superior. To arrive at the proper course of action, successful decision makers:

- Determine exactly what the problem is and write it down
- Develop a list of alternative solutions to the problem
- Examine the advantages and disadvantages of each possible solution
- Select the best solution and review all the ramifications of this choice
- Implement (and later evaluate) the chosen course of action

Further evidence of your management potential is your reluctance to dump your problems in the lap of your superior for solution. On the army staff, all problem interviews are handled on a "staff-work-accomplished" basis. The person with the problem is required to present all data along with a recommendation of at least one solution, but preferably several alternate ones—not a bad technique for business to follow too. After a problem is identified, the person closest to it should be in the best position to work out a solution and to recommend action.

My advice to managers is try leadership. Take one step forward. Think, and say what you think. Be out front. You may fall flat on your face. You may be wrong. You may take some outrageous slings and arrows, but you will never know the job of leading until you have stopped following.

H. Justin Davidson
Cornell University

MAINTAINING A COMMUNICATION NETWORK

It is estimated that 85 percent of a successful manager's job lies in the area of interpersonal communication skills. The ability to communicate effectively with employees is essential to the productivity of the office and to the well-being of its staff. This qualification is also important for the secretary-supervisor. The secretary must develop and maintain open channels of communication between and among subordinates, other supervisors, and company executives. Within an organization a communication network must be available for work instructions, problem solving, and work and information flow. Basic to the establishment of this network is the understanding of how communications are generated in the office.

Organizational Communications

Very little work can be accomplished in an office without communication. Through communication, information is furnished to management for use in decision making and control. Communication also serves to motivate and influence employees to higher productivity with which to meet the goals of the company.

Organizational communication takes many forms. It can be oral—on a one-to-one basis—or in a group. It can be written in correspondence, reports, forms, a company magazine, newsletters, an employee suggestion system, or bulletin boards.

Organizational communication can take several different directions. It can be upward to the company hierarchy; it can be horizontal to those on the same managerial level; and it can be downward to supervisees.

Office communicators—and everyone in the office qualifies—have an obligation to speak, write, and listen as the situation dictates so that the message is understood. This is the only way interpersonal communication activities can be of benefit to the company and to its employees.

Barriers to Communication

No two people enter the office with exactly the same educational, economic, and ethnic background. Yet many office managers, and secretaries as well, make the assumption that, if an individual has the skills to do the job, adaptation to the work, people, procedures, and equipment will come in due time. The fallacy in this assumption, of course, is with the important variable, people, and whether they communicate successfully with each other.

There are several reasons why communication between two people in the office can fail. Perhaps the most important one is *semantics,* the meanings of words and the changes in the meanings of words. *Lack of common knowledge* is another. A secretary who uses words that can be easily misinterpreted or uses a technical vocabulary with a new employee is essentially wasting training time. Miscommunication can occur also because of the mere fact that the employee is new and the secretary represents rank in the company.

Other barriers to effective communication are physical distance between desks or between offices and the noise level and distractions in an office. The secretary must recognize these as potential barriers and attempt to make changes or overcome them.

Communicating Effectively

In order to be successful in your supervisory role, you must communicate honestly, sincerely, and directly with your subordinates. Employees tend to be more responsive to the manager who creates an atmosphere of understanding and trust.

A chief executive who has done an amazing job of transforming a rundown company into an outstanding success instructs each department head to submit every Monday morning a report of all the *good* things that have happened in the department during the preceding week.

Effective communication is a two-way street. The sender and receiver must come away from the discussion or the written message with an understanding of what was related. In your supervisory capacity you will learn quickly the advantages of listening to employees. By doing so, you can establish a common ground on which to base further communications. You can also learn to know your subordinates so that a climate of mutual respect is possible.

Two areas in which the secretary can demonstrate interpersonal communication skills are the explanation of work instructions and the interpretation of personnel policies to subordinates.

Work Instructions. Work instructions can be given orally or in writing. Oral instructions have certain advantages over written ones in that the secretary knows immediately whether a subordinate understands the instruction, using the employee's facial expression and questions as clues. If the instructions are complicated, it is recommended that they be given both orally and in writing.

Often the supervisor needs to write job instructions or work procedures in order to update a procedural manual or to see that instructions are available, understood, and followed. Two important points to remember are: (1) how to perform a certain procedure and (2) why that specific type of procedure is desirable and important.

Personnel Policies. As a supervisor, you will be responsible for interpreting management policy to workers in such a way that whatever conformity is needed you will obtain. Usually this means explaining the reasons behind such policy and the benefits that will accrue from its enactment. Whether you are in sympathy with the policy or not, you have an unavoidable obligation to support all company personnel policies. Conversely, you have an equal obligation to communicate to management suggestions for change—either your own or those under your supervision.

DEVELOPING A LEADERSHIP STYLE

In every business organization certain men and women have risen to positions of leadership and responsibility only to find that their previous positions had not prepared them to deal comfortably with their new managerial roles. A significant number of these managers have developed an effective leadership style by imitating those who have supervised them in the past. Because managers use different leadership styles to get the job done, you will want to be aware of the various methods and the disadvantages of each. A leadership style that works for one manager may be totally ineffective for another. Much has been done to make managers aware of the various leadership styles. You should study them to discover one that will help you exercise leadership in a manner that is compatible with your personality and temperament.

Theory X and Theory Y

One classic philosophy of human behavior is Douglas McGregor's Theory X and Theory Y. McGregor maintains that most managers have based their leadership on the mistaken concept that employees work only for reward and punishment. Theory X assumes that the average worker is lazy, self-centered, lacks ambition, resists change, and is indifferent to company objectives. Theory X managers also believe that the average worker will do as little as possible to get by, is not very bright, and prefers to be told what to do rather than to think independently. Theory Y managers take the opposite view. They believe that all people have the potential for development, that they are not naturally lazy, and most workers have the capacity to focus their behavior toward achieving company goals. Theory Y managers believe that the primary task of management is to provide an environment that will allow workers to achieve personal goals while working to achieve the goals of the organization that employs them.

Management by Objectives (MBO)

A popular leadership style that uses the participative approach (Theory Y) and one that is highly recommended by behavioral scientists is Management by Objectives (MBO). Using this approach, the manager and the subordinate agree on the objectives they wish to accomplish in a specified time and the standards that will be used to measure the performance. Once these are agreed on, the objectives are put in writing. Under MBO leadership, the employee has complete freedom to accomplish the objectives. The manager will check progress at regular intervals and evaluate the employee's progress relative to predetermined goals. MBO, when properly administered, involves the entire organization by integrating goals, plans, and evaluations from the top echelon of management to the lowest work unit. MBO is the purest form of participative leadership because objectives, and how they are measured, are determined with the subordinate. To implement MBO, at least three steps should be followed:

1. A superior meets with a subordinate, and together they work out realistic performance objectives concerning the subordinate's work.
2. They agree on the means by which the employee is to reach the specified results.
3. At the end of a given time period, the superior and the employee compare actual results with expected results and then make appropriate decisions concerning future action.

If you are working in such an environment, you will be required to establish with your employer goals concerning your area of responsibility. The goals agreed upon will be specific, measurable, and time-bounded. Once the goals are identified, you begin to make plans to achieve them. Then, as a supervisor, you meet with your subordinates to determine their objectives. After a specified length of time, you may be evaluated in terms of the results you and your subordinates have achieved.

CONTINUING YOUR PROFESSIONAL GROWTH

Whether or not you seek a management position at some point in your career, you will want to continue your professional growth to ensure your job satisfaction and to increase your value to your employer. As a conclusion to this book, some additional suggestions are offered for improving your managerial skills and for growing professionally.

THIRTEEN CAREER COMMANDMENTS

1. Remember that good performance is the basic foundation of success.
2. Manage your career by actively influencing decisions about you.
3. Strive for positions that have high visibility.
4. Find a senior executive who can be your sponsor.
5. Learn your job quickly and train a replacement.
6. Nominate yourself for other positions.
7. Accept promotions that draw on your strengths, not weaknesses.
8. Leave at your convenience and on good terms.
9. Don't be trapped by formal, narrow job descriptions.
10. Recognize and work within office politics.
11. Get out of management if you can't stand dependency on others and having them dependent on you.
12. Recognize that you may face ethical dilemmas.
13. Stick to your personal values.

Source: Ross A. Weber, "The Three Dilemmas of Career Growth," *MBA* (May, 1975).

Nurturing Creativity

Many people think that only a chosen few, those in artistic fields, are creative. They believe that creativity is a talent and that one must be born with it to have it. Every day in the business world these people are proved wrong. Creativity can be present in many people in many occupational fields and can take many forms. Anyone who has an idea and develops it is being creative. Successful business people had to be creative to be successful. You can be creative, too. You can become a contributor in the business office, a creator of ideas and actions.

Where to begin? Start by having an open mind. Ideas are born in imagination, perhaps in nonconformist alternatives to office problems. Build a kit of ideas; and, as you do, experiment with them. Consider that a little idea can be expanded to a bigger or better idea.

Be an active observer of management functions. Look for *questions* surely, but also seek *answers*. Look for ways to improve work and information flow. Be a sounding board for your superior, and let the ideas happen.

Most people have a certain time of the day when they operate at their best level. For some people it may be the early morning hours; for others, it may be at twilight. Determine when you operate best, then set your mind to action. A mind can be alert only if it and its physical home are well rested. Adequate leisure time and proper eating habits are stimulants to creative brain activity.

A last note on creativity is a suggestion that you welcome new office experiences. In themselves, they are found to enlarge your visionary powers from which ideas and actions will come. There seems to be little question— a person who wants to can be creative. It is, therefore, up to you.

Improving Your Communication Skills

You will try to improve your communication skills, for even presidents of companies and countries continue to search for clearer and more persuasive ways of telling their stories.

You will find yourself on committees where you will want to influence the actions of others. Keep in mind the staff-work-accomplished approach, and make sure that when you speak you are making a constructive suggestion.

Plan what you are to say: Your well-presented communication will reduce your superior's reading time. Write and rewrite to reduce verbiage. Abstract material and present it graphically. Arrange material to highlight all the salient points. Become a master at presenting the heart of the matter in one succinct paragraph.

Consider the possibility of expressing your ideas in articles and talks. Too many people are afraid to attempt public speaking or writing for publication. Yet these are tremendous aids to personal development and creativity; they make you clarify and organize your thoughts effectively. Public speaking teaches you to think on your feet. You can learn to judge the reactions of your listeners and emphasize or rephrase a point according to your interpretation of your listeners' reactions.

Developing Personal Specialties

Work to develop one or more specialties for which you are known throughout the organization. For instance, you may be an expert in personnel work, state tax laws, or company pricing policies. Through your training of subordinates in your office, your reputation as a superior teacher may be known. Because of this recognition, you may be asked to develop and teach a company sponsored secretarial training course. Your desk manual may lead to the development of an office procedures manual. You may be considered a resource person, the person who knows the answers to questions frequently asked in the office. Or, if you have become acquainted with word processing, you may be asked to participate in a feasibility study for your office. Whatever your inclination, your specialty or specialties can work to the company's advantage and to your own.

Meeting the Challenge of Technology

As a professional in your field you must keep up with the technological developments that will affect you and your office. You must think positively and see the applications which can be put into effect. No other behavior is acceptable for the professional. Read these magazines religiously: *Administrative Management, The Secretary,* and *Modern Office Procedures.* Attend office equipment exhibits. While you do, put your creative mind to work. This is the way to meet the challenge of the eighties.

Taking Advantage of Professional Growth Opportunities

As you look ahead at management opportunities in the firm where you work, you may feel the need for additional education. Most colleges and universities offer a variety of evening courses that lead to advanced degrees in management, marketing, accounting, information systems, and economics. Should you want to specialize in an area that you feel promises a bright future, make your employer aware of your interest in additional education. In many cases, company financial support for your efforts is available.

Special seminars sponsored by universities, consulting firms, equipment vendors, publishing houses, and your own company's training department also offer excellent opportunities for self-improvement. Many of these seminars feature outstanding consultants in every major area of administration and management and are helpful in keeping your management skills up to date.

Membership in a professional organization can provide you with valuable contacts with those who share your business problems and professional interests. Through your association with other professionals you will enhance your management skills and strengthen your influence in the business community.

The spectrum of useful professional organizations will broaden as you move up. Every major segment of business (accounting, sales, personnel, records, etc.) has a professional organization structured to bring people together periodically to share new ideas and opportunities. The Administrative Management Society (AMS), the International Information/Word Processing Association, the Data Processing Management Association (DPMA), and Executive Women International are just a few of the many organizations that will offer you opportunities for leadership, creativity, and professional growth. (You will want to investigate the advantages of membership in a local chapter of an appropriate organization.)

Professional accreditation is another way to improve your upward mobility as a manager at the same time you upgrade your management skills. In much the same way that the CPS represents the capstone of your secretarial preparation, other certification programs are also available to the manager. One of these is the Certified Administrative Manager (C.A.M.) program sponsored by the AMS. It consists of a series of five examinations in personnel, finance, administrative services, information systems, and management concepts. In addition to the five examinations, a sixth examination, a management case study, is given to measure a candidate's ability to integrate and apply the material covered in the first five examinations. Candidates must also meet experience, leadership, communications, and character qualifications.

Only a few of the many opportunities for professional growth have been presented in this chapter. As you gain experience and improve your management skills, your opportunities to move up will become more frequent and more attractive. Your professional growth, therefore, will become a continuing part of your work life.

SUGGESTED READINGS

Business and Professional Women's Supply Service. *The Woman Manager in the United States.* 11722 Parklawn Drive, Rockville, Md. 20852, 1981.

Everard, Kenneth E., and Bernard A. Shilt. *Business Principles and Management.* Cincinnati: South-Western Publishing Co., 1979.

Haimann, Theo, and Raymond Heigert. *Supervision: Concepts and Practices of Management,* 3d ed. Cincinnati: South-Western Publishing Co., 1982.

Hennig, Margaret, and Ann Jardin. *The Managerial Woman.* Garden City, N.Y.: Anchor Press/Doubleday & Co., Inc., 1977.

Keeling, B. Lewis, and Norman Kallaus. *Administrative Office Management,* 8th ed. Cincinnati: South-Western Publishing Co., 1983.

Minor, Robert S., and Clark W. Fetridge (eds.) *Office Administration Handbook,* 5th ed. Chicago: The Dartnell Corporation, 1979.

Vocational Guidance Manuals, National Textbook Publishing Co., Skokie, Ill., 1980.

Williams, J. Clifton. *Human Behavior in Organizations,* 2d ed. Cincinnati: South-Western Publishing Co., 1982.

QUESTIONS FOR DISCUSSION

1. A manager must sometimes make decisions that are unpopular with subordinates. Give some examples of unpopular decisions that an office supervisor might have to make.

2. Why is supervision considered the first level of management, and why is it so important in the organizational structure?

3. Which type of manager is most effective—Theory X or Theory Y? Why?

4. You believe that your experience and education as a secretary have prepared you for a particular management position. What evidence can you give management to support your feelings?

5. As a secretary you have had many tasks delegated to you, but when you move into a management position you will need to delegate to others. How can you do this without causing resentment among your subordinates?

6. Why might a secretary who does not have a well-trained replacement not be considered for a promotion?

7. Why is the orientation process for new employees so important?

8. Your company usually follows the policy of promoting from within. As the office manager you find it necessary on one occasion to recruit a replacement from outside the company. What is your responsibility to the employees in your office?

9. What is meant by the term *cross training?* How is it of benefit to the employer? to the employee?

10. As a supervisor what contributions can you make to assist subordinates in reaching their full potential?

11. What qualifications must a person have in order to evaluate the job performance of another employee?

12. Why is job enrichment so important in today's business office?

13. Assume that you are working as a secretary in an organization which follows the MBO leadership style. How does this affect your position?

14. Why is creativity so important to the secretary who seeks promotion and advancement in the profession?

15. What specialty do you have that might be developed into a plus factor in your job?

16. Retype the following sentences. Capitalize the appropriate words in each line. Then refer to the Reference Guide to verify or correct your answers.

    (a) This is the space age—an era of Amazing Communication technology.

    (b) Every successful executive has studied accounting, marketing, finance, and economics.

    (c) A biblical reference is often used to begin a speech.

    (d) If you understand latin or other languages, you will probably excel in english and spelling.

    (e) Washingtonians who live in the district are very helpful to tourists.

PROBLEMS

1. In developing a feasibility study for a word processing center, your employer requests that you compare letter costs in your office with those reported in the national study shown in the table on page 463. Your employer asks that you collect and report the data.

To obtain data, you keep a production record for one week for Miss Wright, who devotes full time to taking dictation and transcribing. She recorded and transcribed 120 letters during the week.

The cost division of the Accounting Department provides you with the following cost information:

Miss Wright's salary...... $300 a week

Dictator's time........ 14 hours, costing $15 an hour

Fixed charges (depreciation, supervision, rent, light, interest, taxes, insurance, pension, and similar overhead)........ 40% of labor cost

Nonproductive cost (time lost by Miss Wright and dictator due to waiting, illness, vacation, and other causes)........ 15% of labor cost

Labor cost: Miss Wright's salary plus cost of dictator's time

Mailing cost for 120 letters (postage and labor)........ $38.40

Materials (amount used during week)........ $32.60

Filing cost for 120 letters (labor and materials)........ $32.60

Prepare a memo containing the total cost of producing the 120 letters and the cost per letter with a breakdown showing the amount and percentage of the cost that each factor represents. Include in your memo a discussion of the experiences of other companies that have word processing centers.

2. Your employer, Mr. Luna, is concerned about the loss caused the company by employee absenteeism. He gives you the following chart and asks you to compute cost figures. Further, he requests that you include in your report (for his investigation) general categories for some possible causes of excessive absenteeism (such as inadequate recruitment procedures).

Total sick days paid previous 12 months _____

Average daily pay multiplied by total sick days _____

Annual cost _____

Total accrued 5-year expense _____

You learn from the Accounting Department that in the last year 2,450 sick days have been paid and that the average daily pay is $40.

3. Assume that in your current secretarial position you have learned all that you can about the job and you see little possibility for advancement. You decide to seek another position. Before you begin, develop a career plan by compiling the following data:

(a) A description of the next job you wish to hold

(b) Status of the job market

(c) The size of the organization that will best assist you in your professional development now, three years from now, and six years from now

(d) The working conditions of those organizations listed in (c)

Type your analysis in memorandum form.

Part Nine   Case Problems

Case 9-1
FLEXIBILITY

When Joanne Nelson applied for a position at Beacon Industries at the end of her secretarial training program, she took an extensive series of tests in English mechanics, typewriting, and machine transcription. After the tests were checked, the personnel director told her that her scores in spelling, grammar, and punctuation were superior and offered her a position as a word processor.

Joanne said that she really expected to work as a secretary for one principal and that she felt that word processing centers were just a new term used to describe typing pools. She also said that she wanted closer association with management than she could get in the position offered.

The personnel manager presented the arguments that secretarial work is being automated, that the best opportunities for advancement probably lie within the new organizational pattern, and that she would have an opportunity to work with several executives and have better opportunities for advancement. The personnel manager also pointed out that flexibility and acceptance of new equipment and new methods are probably the most important qualifications of today's employee.

Joanne asked for time to think over the offer but promised to report her decision three days later.

What factors, personal and related to modern business practices, should Joanne consider? How should she proceed to reach the decision? What do you think her decision should be?

Case 9-2
STAFF WORK
ACCOMPLISHED

Karl Tremont was a new supervisor in the word processing center. He had had little experience in supervision and had been chosen because of his interest in the machine capabilities of the equipment and for his facility in English grammar. Things were not going well, and he decided to go to the director of administrative services, Morton Pope, lay his problems on the table, and ask for help.

When Mr. Pope asked what the difficulty was, he replied, "Just about everything. The word processors need more training in English mechanics. Only one of them has reached my production goals. Three principals don't like to dictate to a telephone and are continuing to use their secretaries for dictation although these employees have been given new titles as administrative secretaries. I am having a dreadful time, too, in getting service from the manufacturers. I guess I am just not cut out for supervision. I thought maybe you would work out my problems and tell me what to do."

Mr. Pope, who believed that developing the people under his supervision was one of his most important functions, said, "You know, Karl, I am an old army man. One of the first things we learned was the concept of 'staff work accomplished.' All the problems you have reported are really your problems, you know. In the army we were required to bring along with every problem one or two solutions and an analysis of the consequences of each solution. We would present the problem and then discuss these possible solutions with our superior officer. It worked out pretty well for the Army, and I have found that it works well for me here. Suppose you go back to your office and think through your situation. Come back on Monday with staff work accomplished, and maybe I can help you. Anyway I'll be glad to try."

Assuming Karl's role, work out a plan for the next visit to Mr. Pope.

Helen Fisher was attending the annual out-of-town sales meeting with her employer, George Crane, vice-president, sales. At Mr. Crane's request, she went to lunch with three regional sales representatives and her employer so that she could summarize the conversation. One of the sales representatives was a woman.

As the luncheon progressed, two of the sales representatives began to tell off-color stories, each topping the other in crudity. Helen became more and more uncomfortable.

Was she in a position to do anything about the situation? What?

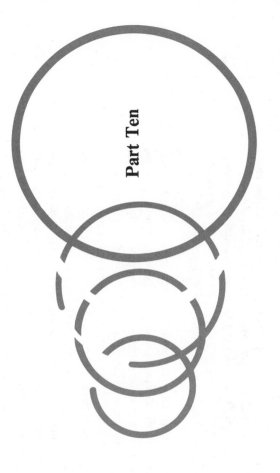

Part Ten

REFERENCE GUIDE

The English language is ever changing in its adaptations to advances in technology, science, business, and all aspects of the complex society in which we live. The study of this multifaceted language is fascinating and challenging. No part of this text should be of more help to the secretary than the Reference Guide, particularly those sections devoted to English usage and punctuation.

Handbooks and dictionaries *report* usage at different levels but are not definitive authorities. Nor does this Guide purport to be the final authority. It, too, *reports* current, acceptable business usages. When more than one usage is reported in this Guide, it is because opinion is *divided*—dictionaries and handbooks do not agree. A secretary, therefore, cannot presume that one reference book stands alone as supreme authority on usage. But once a selection of form has been made, that form should be used consistently.

Formal English usually is found in reports, important letters, papers for publication, and the like. Colloquial English is for the most part customary in business letters. (A term designated *colloquial* in the dictionary means that it occurs in English conversation at an educated level.)

Business correspondence often is direct and to the point; economy in the use of words saves times for the writer and for the reader. Frequently, however, the purpose of a business letter is to obtain a favorable result or to create a friendly reaction. Purposes such as these can often best be served by using informal conversational English. Thus, colloquial English can be appropriate and at times even desirable in business writing.

Industry and science often provide new meanings for commonplace terms and adapt them to colorful, specific meanings; for example, *power your engine, all systems go,* to mention only two. Business people often coin needed words: *flowchart, reprography, software,* to mention three that have been accepted by industry and by the publishers of *Webster's New Collegiate Dictionary.* When confronted with a coined word or expression, the secretary must recognize it and know how to call attention to it in a letter or report.

The trend in punctuation is toward less punctuation at the informal level; however, complete and accurate punctuation is still required at the formal level. The purpose of punctuation is to help make the meaning of the written word clear to the reader. Standard, accepted punctuation usage will attain this objective.

The purpose of this Guide is to help you acquire expertise and confidence as you fulfill your secretarial responsibilities. It should provide a handy and easy-to-use reference when needed in transferring your employer's thoughts from shorthand notebook or word processing equipment to final form or in any original writing you may be required to do.

CONTENTS

PUNCTUATION

Effective writing expresses precisely the author's intended meaning. Punctuation aids the understanding of meaning as a system of symbols that are familiar to the reader. While punctuation usage may vary in some instances, many fundamental rules are accepted and are generally adhered to in written English. The following pages present these rules along with examples that should illustrate the rules in a precise yet simple manner.

THE APOSTROPHE

1. Use an apostrophe to designate the possessive of nouns and indefinite pronouns.

(a) To form the possessive of a singular or plural noun or indefinite pronoun which does not end in a sibilant sound (s, x, z), add an apostrophe and an s.

dog's leash	William's coat
horse's bridle	children's coats
man's coat	Marivaux's plays (silent x)
men's coats	one's coat

(b) To form the possessive of a plural noun or indefinite pronoun ending in a sibilant sound, add only an apostrophe.

dogs' leashes	three years' work
girls' coats	the Thomases' house
ten dollars' worth	others' ills

(c) To form the possessive of a singular noun ending in a sibilant sound, add an apostrophe and an s.

Burns's poems	the fox's tail
Jones's store	Liz's idea

Exception: *If the singular noun has two or more syllables and if the last syllable is not accented and is preceded by a sibilant sound, add only the apostrophe for ease of pronunciation.*

Moses' law	Jesus' nativity
Ulysses' voyage	Demosthenes' orations
conscience' sake	

(d) To denote joint ownership, add the apostrophe or the apostrophe and *s* after the second noun only. Individual ownership is shown by making both elements possessive.

John and Amy's store (one store, owned by John and Amy)
John's and Amy's stores (two stores, one John's and one Amy's)
Waterfords and Tuckers' annual picnic

(e) To form the possessive of compound nouns and indefinite pronouns, add the apostrophe or apostrophe and *s* after the last element of the compound.

daughter-in-law's	daughters-in-law's
father-in-law's	fathers-in-law's
everyone else's	

2. Use an apostrophe to denote the omission of letters or figures.

It's too far to go. (Contraction of *It is*)
They haven't been here today.
The class of '75 had its reunion this year.
Who's going? (contraction of *Who is*)

3. Use an apostrophe to designate plurals of figures, letters, signs, and words to which special allusion is made.

If there are no 6's left in this type, use 9's turned upside down. Your *T*'s and *F*'s are too much alike, and so are your *u*'s and *v*'s. Use +'s and −'s to denote whether the sentences are correct or not. When *and*'s and *the*'s are used in titles, they should not be capitalized, unless they are the first word.

BRACKETS

The use of brackets is generally confined to writing of a technical or scholarly nature.

1. Use brackets to enclose information—an editorial interpolation, correction, explanation, or comment—which the writer wishes to include in quoted material.

"In 1630 [a typographical error for 1603] James came to the throne."

In applying for the job, he wrote, "I am very good in athletics [*sic*], and I can teach mathematics [*sic*]."

"These [the free silver Democrats] asserted that the artificial ratio could be maintained indefinitely."

Note: *The term* sic, Latin *for* thus, *is inserted to show that a misspelling or other error appeared in the original and is not an error by the person quoting.*

2. Use brackets when it is necessary to place parenthetical material within parentheses; however, such complicated usage should be avoided.

At 10:30 A.M. (the time agreed upon to have the meeting [see the correspondence of Ms. Blair and Mr. Williams]) only five of the ten committee members were present.

Note: *In the use of other punctuation marks with brackets, the same rules apply as for parentheses.*

THE COLON

The colon is a mark of introduction or anticipation. In general it denotes formality. The colon indicates a break in continuity that is greater than that requiring a semicolon and less than that requiring a period. It may be used to expand or emphasize a thought or to amplify in a second clause an idea contained in the first clause.

1. Use a colon to introduce a long or formal quotation.

Winston Churchill, in his opening statement as Prime Minister, declared to the House of Commons: "Victory at all costs, victory in spite of all terror, victory however long and hard the road may be; for without victory there is no survival."

John F. Kennedy, on conferring honorary citizenship on Sir Winston Churchill, said: "He mobilized the English language and sent it into battle."

2. Use a colon to introduce an example or a formal list; that is, a list preceded by a summarizing term.

A check payable to a married woman should include her given name, not her husband's: *Joan Ritson* rather than *Mrs. Harry Ritson.*

The following items are put on the check stub: the amount of the check, the date, the person or business to whom the check is payable, and the purpose of the check.

Exception: *Do not use a colon to introduce a brief, informal list when the colon would immediately follow a verb or a preposition.*

The only major types of coverage which cannot be written on an SMP policy are automobile, workers' compensation, surety bonds, and life or health insurance.

3. Use a colon between independent clauses or independent sentences when the second clause amplifies the first or when the second gives a concrete illustration of a general statement in the first. (Notice that the first word of an independent clause after a colon is capitalized.)

In time, however, one of her favorite contentions was justified: In the long run people who are conscientious, set goals, and work diligently will achieve the position for which they are best qualified.

George Washington, in a letter to the captains of the Virginia Regiment, said that discipline is the soul of an army: It makes small numbers formidable and procures success to the weak and esteem to all.

4. Use a colon after terms such as *the following* or *as follows* when these terms precede a list of enumerated items, a tabulation, a computation, etc.

You will need the following:
1. Typewriter
2. Transcription equipment
3. Stationery

Their actions were as follows: They went to the supermarket, purchased a number of items, returned to their car, and drove away.

Each category of liability should be listed and the total amount of liabilities presented in the following manner:

Liabilities

Notes payable	$1,500
Accounts payable	1,100
Salaries payable	300
Total liabilities	$2,900

5. By common acceptance, a colon is used in the following instances:

(a) After the salutation in certain styles of formal or business letters

Ladies and Gentlemen: Dear Ms. McDaniel:

Dear Sir: Dear Professor Gordon:

(b) Between the hour and the minute when time is expressed in figures

12:15 a.m.   2:30 p.m.

(c) Between chapter and verse in references to the Bible and between volume and page reference

Genesis 9:10   *Papers of James Madison* 1:16

THE COMMA

Since studies have indicated that three fourths of all punctuation errors are in the use of the comma, knowledge and correct use of the comma are necessary in order to convey ideas in a concise and clear manner.

1. Use a comma to separate independent clauses that are linked by the coordinating conjunctions *and, but, for, or,* and *nor.*

It was a beautiful June day, and the fragrance of the roses permeated the air.
The man was not afraid, nor was he upset by the news.

Exception: *When two or more verbs have the same subject, no comma is used between the parts of the compound predicate.*

The liquidity preference falls with an increase in prices and rises with a decline in prices.

When the clauses are short and closely related, no comma is required between the clauses.

The chairperson called for order and everyone sat down.

2. Use a comma to separate each item when three or more elements form a series without linking words between the elements.

They brought sandwiches, potato salad, baked beans, and soft drinks to the picnic.

The new secretary is aggressive but not offensive, efficient but not officious, and friendly but not servile.

The woman was either 21, 22, or 23 years old.

Note: *Although the use of etc. is discouraged, this abbreviation should be set off by commas when it is used.*

The store sold clothing, housewares, furniture, food, pharmaceuticals, linens, etc., at its Seventh Street location.

Exception: *When the elements in a series are simple and are joined by conjunctions, omit the commas.*

I cannot remember if that symphony was composed by Bach or Beethoven or Brahms.

3. Use a comma to separate coordinate adjectives which modify a noun. (Adjectives are coordinate if *and* can be used between them.)

The gaudy, tasteless decorations detracted from the appearance of the room. (The gaudy and tasteless decorations)

An old straw hat was lying in the street. (NOT An old *and* straw hat)

The late Senator Humphrey was a prominent public official. (NOT The late Senator Humphrey was a prominent *and* public official.)

4. Use a comma to separate elements which might be misread if the comma were omitted.

Abruptly the car stopped, throwing her forward.
As I approached, Mary held out her hand.
To John, Smith was an enigma.

5. Use commas to set off nonrestrictive clauses, phrases, and appositives (clauses, phrases, and appositives that are not essential to the meaning of a sentence).

Dr. Mary Towne, the eminent surgeon, was the principal speaker.

Effective listening, a major ingredient of empathetic communication, is a skill in which people differ greatly.

Restrictive clauses, phrases, and appositives are necessary to the meaning of the sentence and are not set off by commas.

The place *to be blunt* is at the meeting.

Those executives *planning to attend the conference* must register in advance.

John Wayne *the actor* starred in many movies; John Wayne *the doctor* is my neighbor.

Notes: *The conjunction or may appear with an appositive.*

The instructions, or information for correct use, were printed on the warranty card.

In some cases, only the writer knows if a clause is restrictive or nonrestrictive.

My brother, who is on the team this year, is a senior.
(The writer has only one brother.)

My brother who is on the team this year is a senior.
(The writer has more than one brother.)

6. Use commas to set off complementary or antithetical[1] elements.

The unjust, though at the same time necessary, restriction was placed on all members of the class.

(a) Commas should set off an antithetical clause or phrase introduced by *not* if the modified element is complete without it.

The dignitaries hoped that the president herself, not the vice-president, would attend the ceremony.

Betty went to the concert, not to hear the orchestra, but to observe the soloist.

(b) Commas should separate interdependent antithetical clauses.

The more Maria read about Greece, the deeper became her resolve to visit that historic land.

Exception: *Short antithetical phrases should not be separated by commas.*

(See examples at top of page 701.)

---

[1] *contrasting, opposing.*

The bigger the better.
The more the merrier.

7. Use a comma to separate an introductory adverbial clause or phrase from the rest of the sentence.

Where the opportunities are available, first line supervisors should be encouraged to move into higher management.

Because of the unusual circumstances, the president of the company addressed the assembled employees.

8. Commas set off an adverbial phrase or clause located between a subject and a predicate.

Olga, after receiving the award, left immediately for home.

Exceptions: *If a dependent adverbial clause follows a main clause and is restrictive, it should not be set off by a comma.*

Annette was surprised when she heard the news.

A comma is not used after a short introductory adverbial phrase if the clarity of the sentence does not suffer.

On Wednesday the group attended the meeting.

A comma is not used following an introductory adverbial phrase that immediately precedes the verb it modifies.

On the beach stood a man, a woman, and a child.

9. Use commas to set off introductory absolute, participial, infinitive, and gerund phrases.

That being true, Paul had nothing more to say.

After winning the election, the president addressed the students.

In order to succeed, one must work hard.

Driving as fast as traffic would allow, he arrived just in time.

10. An omitted word or omitted words are replaced by a comma.

The Imbus Corporation has long had a reputation for integrity and social responsibility; Hall and Hall, for questionable methods. (The comma takes the place of the words *has long had a reputation.*)

11. Use commas with the following parenthetical elements:

(a) To separate items of address and geographical names

Margaret stopped at 1673 Cedar Avenue, Cincinnati, Ohio, to see a friend. Princeton, New Jersey, is now her home.

(b) To separate dates

Stephen Foster was born on July 4, 1826, in Pittsburgh.

(c) To separate items in a reference

In *Hamlet*, II, ii, 255, you will find the reference under discussion.

(d) To set off words used in direct address

Is it true, Ann, that you are going to Switzerland?

(e) To set off introductory expressions and those used to mark transitions

To tell the truth, the employer was very generous.

The restrictive clause, on the other hand, limits the main clause.

(f) To set off parenthetical words, phrases, and clauses

The secretary, it was believed, turned the problem over to the Sales Department.

Note: *Do not use a comma to set off a quotation that is an integral part of the sentence.*

He shouted as he ran toward the house, "No one on the peninsula has a boat."

12. Use a comma to separate a short direct quotation from the statement that precedes or follows it. (A long or formal quotation is introduced by a colon.)

He said that his racing car would "do two hundred miles an hour" and he was "going to let it out."

13. A comma may be used to separate two identical words or phrases, even though the grammatical construction does not require the separation.

What is done, is done.

They marched in, in pairs.

14. Use a comma to separate unrelated adjacent numbers.

In 1978, 175 new books were published.

Note: *It is preferable to rewrite the sentence to avoid the foregoing construction.*

The company published 175 new books in 1978.

15. Use commas with numerals in the following instances:

(a) With figures of 1,000 or more, between every group of three digits, counting from the right

1,456   11,420   117,560,000

Note: *The comma is frequently omitted in writing four-digit numbers not in-*

cluded in a set containing numbers of five or more digits. If a text contains a great quantity of numerical matter, it is advisable to choose a consistent use for that text.

(b) With time divisions

November, 1989   New Year's Day, 1960

Exceptions: *Do not use commas with historical references, page numbers, dimensions, weights, measures, time, policy numbers, room numbers, telephone numbers, and most serial numbers.*

2200 B.C.	3 feet 6 inches
page 1463	4 pounds 2 ounces
806423518	2 hours 4 minutes

16. Use a comma after *that is, i.e.,* and *namely.* The punctuation mark preceding such expressions is determined by the importance or length of the interruption. If the interruption is minor, use a comma. If the interruption is important or lengthy, use a semicolon. Always use a semicolon if the expression is followed by an independent clause.

He came up through the ranks, that is, through hard work.

The editor persuaded the author to change the direction of his manuscript; i.e., she convinced him that his book should appeal to management's interest in current ideas and practices rather than in historical methods of operating business firms.

She submitted the problem to three of her friends, namely, Carlos, Evelyn, and Rosemary.

He said that he was going to give consideration to the three options the company presented to him; namely, to transfer to Duluth, to accept the production management position at the home office in Chicago, or to expand the branch office in Louisville of which he is presently manager.

THE DASH

The dash should not be confused with the hyphen. For purposes of typewriting manuscript, the dash consists of two hyphens (--) placed together with no space preceding or following them.

1. Use a dash when a sentence is interrupted abruptly and an entirely different sentence or thought is added.

The game will be—by the way, are you going to the game?

Robert's lawyer—she spent most of the night working on the case—looked tired and pale when she entered the courtroom.

2. Use a dash to indicate the omission of words or letters.

Little acorns—great oaks, you know.
Mary J—, of C—Street, was the witness.

3. Use a dash before a word or statement which summarizes a preceding series or which is an emphatic repetition of the preceding statement.

Verdi, Puccini, Rossini—these were the most popular operatic composers at that time.

The editor stated that the author's work was original and scholarly—original and scholarly in the sense that it presented new information that had been well researched.

4. Use a dash to set off appositives that have internal punctuation or that are used for emphasis.

All friends of the fine arts—civic leaders, professional and business people, concerned citizens—cooperate to make the annual Fine Arts Fund drive a success.

The most realistic view of supervisors is that to varying degrees they are a special class of managers—they are strategically placed management representatives. (replaces a semicolon)

5. When strong emphasis is desired, the dash may be used in place of the comma, the colon, the semicolon, or parentheses.

Consultants rely heavily upon their authority of competence—the right of a person to influence others by virtue of recognized ability and expertise. (replaces a comma)

THE ELLIPSIS MARK

The ellipsis mark—three periods with a space before, after, and between each period (. . .)—is used to show the omission of a passage that is being quoted. If the omitted passage comes at the end of the sentence a period is added, making four periods.

In Illus. 13-3, if the calculations have been made correctly, the materials and parts needed . . . will be ready at the same time. Adequate time for delivery and production will be allowed, and in most cases . . . spare time must be allowed so that there will be no costly delay in assembling the final product simply because one part was not ordered early enough . . . . The problems outlined here are particularly true of certain types of products made on special orders for special purposes.

THE EXCLAMATION POINT

The exclamation point has two basic uses: after an exclamatory sentence and after words that express strong emotion or feeling.

Then the captain shouted, "Cast off!"

Look out! You'll fall!

Exclamation points should be used sparingly; they should not be used in parentheses to express humor or irony.

THE HYPHEN

The hyphen has two chief uses: to mark the division of a word that appears at the end of a line and to designate certain compound words. As to the first use, words should be divided between syllables according to *Webster's New Collegiate Dictionary.* Never divide words of one syllable.

In typewriting manuscript, in order to avoid confusion for the typesetter, do not hyphenate words at the end of a line; let long words run into the right margin.

In forming compound words, it is always wise to consult *Webster's New Collegiate Dictionary,* since there are wide variations in styling compounds and numerous exceptions to the rules. For example, *vice-president* is hyphenated, but *vice admiral* is two words; *vice-presidency* is hyphenated, but *viceroyalty* is one word.

A few general rules apply to the use of hyphens in forming compounds.

1. Use a hyphen between a prefix and a root word under these circumstances:

(a) When the combination is a prefix and a proper name

un-American   pro-Canadian

(b) When the combination of the prefix and root word constitutes a homonym[2]

recover, re-cover   reform, re-form

(c) When the combination is a prefix ending in a vowel and a root word beginning with a vowel, if the omission of the hyphen will cause misreading

re-ink   co-op

Note: *The prefixes* ex-, self-, half-, *and* all- *are often used with a hyphen.*

ex-manager   half-baked
self-control   all-around

(d) When figures, letters, or numbers are compounded with words to form a single idea

---

[2] One of two or more words that are pronounced alike but are different in meaning: *right, write; piece, peace; sail, sale; stationary, stationery.*

two-year period
25-foot stick

T-shaped rod
U-turn

2. Use a hyphen between two or more words that precede a noun and act as a compound adjective.

long-established custom
coarse-grained wood
well-known speaker

up-to-date method
high-priced goods
off-the-record comment

Exception: *This usage does not apply when one of the words is an adverb ending in ly, when the words form a comparative or superlative compound adjective, or when the words follow the noun.*

highly paid executive
better known speaker
The company's operations were up to date.

3. Use a hyphen between the spelled-out numbers twenty-one through ninety-nine.

4. Use a hyphen in compounds formed from a noun or a verb and a preposition.

set-to
head-on

house-to-house
give-and-take

5. Use a hyphen in writing fractions which are single adjectives before a noun.

a one-fourth share

a two-thirds majority vote

Exception: *Do not use a hyphen when the fraction consists of an adjective plus a noun or when the numerator or denominator already contains a hyphen.*

three fourths of the population
two thirds of a mile
twenty-one hundredths (21/100)
twenty one-hundredths (20/100)

6. Use a hyphen after each word or number in a series that modifies the same noun (suspended hyphenation). Notice the use of the space following the hyphen.

six- or eight-cylinder engine
first-, second-, or third-class mail

7. Use a hyphen in compounding capitalized words.

the New York-Chicago flight

8. Use a hyphen to indicate continuing or inclusive numbers—dates, times, or reference numbers.

1981-1985
May-June, 1982

10:00 a.m.-5:00 p.m.
See pages 451-455.

PARENTHESES

1. Use parentheses to enclose nonessential information which interrupts the flow of a sentence or is incidental to the topic of a paragraph. Parentheses usually deemphasize information rather than emphasize it as is the case with dashes.

At 10:30 a.m. (the time agreed upon to have the meeting) only five of the ten committee members were present.

By using a captive insurer, the parent may be able to deduct such premiums paid to a captive and thus handle the loss reserve need with funds that are tax deductible. (The Internal Revenue Service has ruled that certain conditions must be met before premiums paid to a captive are tax deductible.)

2. Use parentheses to enclose letters or numbers in an enumeration that is not shown in list format.

The professor issued these instructions: (1) smoking is allowed only in designated areas, (2) punctuality in attending classes is expected of all students, and (3) completed assignments are to be submitted on time.

3. Use parentheses to enclose signs, numbers, and words when accuracy is essential.

Make out the check for the exact amount ($45.50).

The cash drawer was over by $200 (two hundred dollars).

An asterisk (*) was placed at the end of the sentence to indicate the footnote.

4. Parentheses are frequently used in text to enclose references to other parts of the text.

The current worth of this loss is $79,995 (see Table 31-1).

See Chapter 10 (pages 64-75) for complete coverage.

Note: Before *a parenthesis within a sentence, no punctuation mark is used.*

After parentheses within a sentence, no punctuation mark is used unless it would be required if the parenthetical material were removed; then whatever mark would be normally required follows the closing parenthesis.

Within parentheses inside a sentence, the punctuation is the same as if the material were a separate sentence. However, when it is a complete sentence, no capital is used at the beginning and no period at the end— although a question mark or exclamation point is used if one is required.

Parentheses may enclose a separate sentence, in which case the ordinary rules for using the capital and period apply.

THE PERIOD

A period is used to mark the end of a declarative or imperative sentence, a legitimate fragmentary sentence, or a run-in heading. It is also used to mark an abbreviation.

1. When a period is used after an abbreviation, it is followed (except at the end of a sentence) by whatever punctuation mark would normally be used there.

Washington, D.C., is the capital.

Breakfast is served at 8 a.m., lunch at 12:30 p.m., and dinner at 6:30 p.m.

2. Examples of legitimate fragmentary sentences follow.

(a) A transition sentence

Now for the second cause.

(b) Questions and answers

Who says this? The man who only four years ago said exactly the opposite.

(c) Sentences reporting direct discourse where there is no chance of mistaking the speaker.

"Ramona was at the meeting."
"No!"
"With her partner."
"Not Pedro?"
"No one else."
"What a surprise!"

3. A period may be used after a rhetorical question.

Will the audience please rise.

May I take this opportunity to express my thanks.

4. A run-in heading is one which is followed on the same line by text material. A period or other appropriate end-of-sentence punctuation ends the run-in heading.

The Authority of Organized Labor. The National Labor Relations Act of 1935 for the first time clearly legitimized at the national level the authority of organized labor . . . .

Note: *The design of a publication may call for the period to be omitted in typeset copy, but the author should always include the period in typewritten manuscript.*

5. Use a period in enumerated lists if the individual items are complete sentences. If the items are single words, short phrases, or incomplete sentences, use no period.

The main arguments for decentralized filing are:

1. The confidential nature of the material suggests that it be kept from the majority of employees.

2. Unnecessary delay in getting papers from the centralized department is avoided.

3. The papers filed will not be required by any other department.

The office manager should have available information about each of the following:

1. Principal types of furniture and equipment and reputable suppliers for each

2. Reliable statistics for comparing the effectiveness of competing brands of equipment and furniture

3. Suppliers' catalogs and current prices

4. Possibilities for standardizing equipment throughout the firm

Note: *The placement of the period with quotation marks, parentheses, and brackets is discussed under these headings.*

THE QUESTION MARK

1. Use a question mark after a direct question.

What are you doing?

Where are you going?

When will you return?

Note: *Do not use a question mark after an indirect question.*

She asked what you are doing.

He asked where you are going.

Placing a question mark at the end of a declarative or imperative sentence transposes such a structure into an interrogative remark.

This is where you are going to stay?

2. In a series of questions within an interrogative sentence, a question mark may follow each question. When used in this way, the question mark substitutes for a comma; the second and subsequent elements are preceded by one space and begin with a lowercase letter.

Where is my shorthand book? my pencil? my paper?

Our questions are: When will you arrive? where will you stay? will you have transportation?

3. Use a question mark in parentheses (?) to express doubt or uncertainty.

Nathaniel Bacon, the Virginia patriot, was born in 1642(?).

Note: *Do not use a question mark to make a joke or to be ironical, since such usage questions the reader's intelligence.*

Jack, you know, is the most studious(?) member of the family.

QUOTATION MARKS

The main function of quotation marks is to enclose matter quoted from any source, either spoken or written. Other functions are to enclose words used in a special manner and to enclose certain titles.

1. Use quotation marks to enclose direct quotations.

The manufacturing superintendent, in a heated discussion with the director of personnel, said, "I've had it with your job enrichment propaganda. It has taken me years to set up an assembly line that works smoothly and efficiently. Productivity is high, quality is on standard, and nobody is complaining. So why rock the boat?"

2. Use quotation marks to enclose the title of (a) a chapter in a book; (b) an individual poem, essay, or story in a volume; and (c) any item from a book or magazine. (Titles of books and magazines are italicized.)

The poems "Emerson" and "Lands End" appear in the volume *More People* by Edgar Lee Masters.

For information about how the actions of the Federal Reserve Board affect you personally, read "ABC's of How Federal Reserve Works" in *U.S. News & World Report*, January 9, 1978.

3. Use quotation marks to enclose words used in a special manner or words coined for special, limited use. Discretion should be practiced in using quotation marks in these instances. Only if readers are unfamiliar with the term should quotation marks be used to suggest that its status in the language is tentative.

The Federal Reserve Board controls the amount of reserves by use of a tool known as the "open market operation."

The speaker described his opponent's principal problem as the "ineptitude of innocence."

Note: *Quotation marks should be used sparingly for coined words, words used in a special manner, colloquialisms, irony, and slang, and then only if the word is foreign to the reader.*

4. The following general rules should be observed relative to the use of quotation marks:

(a) When several different speakers are quoted, each person's remarks are enclosed in quotation marks.

When Mark returned from the football game, everyone shouted questions at once: "Who won?" "What was the score?" "What did Jim do?" "Was there much passing?"

(b) When quoting a fragment of a sentence, do not begin the quotation with a capital letter unless the quoted passage began with a capital.

Senator Margaret Hall said that "the machinations of a corrupt political machine would have to stop."

(c) Quotations within quotations use single quotation marks. Quotations within single quotations use double quotation marks.

In a letter the new student wrote: "I have been following the advice of my instructor who said, 'When I decide to write something, I first read Pope's "An Essay on Criticism" to inspire me to do my best'; but I find that it doesn't help me at all."

Note: *The procedure for handling lengthy quotations is discussed in Exception 7, below.*

Exceptions:

1. Do not use quotation marks for proverbs, phrases, or figures of speech that are known to everyone.

He was honest, not because he believed that honesty was the best policy, but because honesty was inherent in his character.

Absence makes the heart grow fonder, but out of sight out of mind was her usual experience.

Silence is golden when one has much studying to do.

2. Do not use quotation marks to label your own humor or irony.

3. Do not use quotation marks for statements which are not quoted from someone else but are quotations in form only.

She thought, Shall I wear gloves to go on my interview?

He said to himself, I think I'm going to make manager this year.

4. Do not use quotation marks with the term so-called. *The term* so-called *is sufficient to mark off the usage as a special one.*

The so-called easy way sometimes turns out to be the most difficult and longest way to get results.

5. Do not quote the words yes *and* no *except in direct discourse.*

Many persons have difficulty saying no, so they frequently answer yes against their better judgment.

6. *Do not use quotation marks where the name of a speaker introduces the speech.*

> JEAN GROBE: It appears to me that we should give this experiment a chance before discarding the whole idea.
>
> MARK WHITE: A good suggestion, except that we have spent entirely too much time and money already on trying to solve this problem.

7. *Do not use quotation marks to enclose material that is set off as a block quotation. Block quotations of one long paragraph or several short paragraphs are usually set in smaller type than the text and are indented—usually on both right and left sides. Any quoted matter within a block quotation should be enclosed in double quotation marks, even if the source quoted uses single quotation marks.*

8. *Do not use quotation marks to enclose an indirect quotation.*

> Cynthia said that she was leaving because she wanted to arrive home before dark.

Other Punctuation with Quotation Marks

The rules for punctuating sentences containing direct quotations are illustrated below:

1. Introductory expression preceding the quotation

> She called, "Where are you going?"

2. Explanatory expression interrupting the quotation

> "It is not," she interrupted, "my habit to change my mind so quickly."
>
> "This is my idea," Bob declared; "therefore, I won't have you stealing it."

3. Explanatory expression after the quotation

> "What are you going to do about it?" she inquired.

Note: *A comma or a period precedes the closing quotation marks, including single quotation marks. A semicolon or a colon follows the closing quotation marks. The position of a question mark or an exclamation point depends on the content of the sentence; place before the quotation mark if it applies only to the quotation, or after the quotation mark if it applies to the entire sentence.*

> "Are you coming to the dance?" he asked.
>
> Have you ever heard her say, "I don't play bridge"?
>
> "What a wonderful day!" he exclaimed.

How generous of her to say, "You may take my new car"!

The professor was not shocked when the young instructor said, "I was dismayed at having one of my students define *salutary* as 'one who salutes.'"

Recording Telephone Conversations

Word-for-word personal or business telephone conversations are typed in any quickly typed, easily read style. All speakers must be fully identified.

Telephone call, 6/10/82, 2:50 p.m., Mr. Alan King to Mr. Willis Burt.

K Hello, Willis, how are you?

B Fine, Alan. What can I do for you?

It is not necessary to use quotation marks, since the identification of the speaker precedes each comment during the recorded telephone conversation.

THE SEMICOLON

If a comma indicates the smallest interruption in continuity of thought, the semicolon then stands midway between the functions of the comma and the period. The semicolon substitutes at times for the comma, at times for the period. But when it replaces either, there must be a logical basis for the substitution. The following guides cover the most typical uses of the semicolon.

1. Use a semicolon to separate independent clauses of a compound sentence that have a close, logical relationship when they are not connected by a coordinate conjunction.

The plane was overdue; it arrived three hours behind schedule.

She did not let her emotions sway her; she considered the various alternatives objectively.

2. Use a semicolon between independent clauses when a conjunctive adverb joins the clauses. The semicolon precedes the conjunctive adverb. The most common conjunctive adverbs are *therefore, nevertheless, however, moreover, consequently, so, also, thus, hence, then, still, accordingly, besides, furthermore, likewise,* and *otherwise.* These connecting words are generally followed by a comma.

The farmer used a new method of cultivation; therefore, the yield was larger.

The roads were impassable; consequently, the schools were closed.

3. A semicolon precedes a coordinate conjunction (*and, but, for, or,* and *nor*) between two independent clauses when either or both contain internal punctuation.

On their trip they went to Rome, which they found awesome; and then they went to Florence, Venice, and Assisi, which they considered the pearls of the Italian peninsula.

The office manager ordered pencils, shorthand notebooks, dictating tapes, and typewriter ribbons for the staff; but the order was lost in the mail.

4. A semicolon separates items in a series which are long and complex or which involve internal punctuation. (A comma is used between items in a series if a word or words are omitted.)

The defendant, in justification of his act, pleaded that (1) he was despondent over the death of his wife; (2) he was without employment, a place to live, and warm clothing; (3) he was rejected by his only son, who had moved to Alabama; and (4) he was under the influence of potent medication that had impaired his judgment.

When the vote was tabulated, Alvarez won first place; O'Connor, second place; and Schmidt, third place.

The speaker holds that democracy, although slow moving and inefficient, is the best form of government; that the freedom we possess, although bought with war and death, is worth the cost; and that our form of government is worth living for, fighting for, and if need be dying for.

5. A semicolon is used before such expressions as *for example (e.g.)*, *for instance, that is (i.e.)*, and *namely (viz.)*, depending upon the importance and length of the interruption.

Some pairs of words are bothersome to students; for example, *affect* and *effect, loose and lose, sit and set.*

Every punctuation rule suggests three acts on your part; namely, learn it, use it, and check your writing to see if you have used it correctly.

The professor spoke with authority; i.e., she set down the rules and stated that she expected them to be observed.

6. A semicolon follows the closing quotation mark if it would be used normally at the place the interruption comes.

The president shouted, "The motion is carried!"; nevertheless, pandemonium erupted in the crowded hall.

ACCEPTED USAGE IN WRITING

Rules concerning capitalization, italics, abbreviations, and numbers have evolved from writing practices found to be economical and effective, rather than from fundamental laws of language. Although all rules covering writing mechanics do not have the same degree of acceptance, those presented here are basically accepted and should be followed.

CAPITALIZATION

The tendency today is to capitalize as little as possible; hence a good practice is not to capitalize unless a rule exists for its use.

1. Capitalize the first word of a sentence.

2. Capitalize the first word of a direct quotation.

3. Capitalize all proper nouns and adjectives; for example,

(a) Names and initials of individuals

When a name includes particles such as *de, du, la, l', della, von, van, van der,* and *ten,* observe carefully the way the name is written and extend the courtesy of spelling the individual's name accurately.

Mary Van Reck	Charles de Gaulle
John von Bruckner	Lee De Forest

(b) Epithets, nicknames, and titles used as part of the name

Honest Abe	Stonewall Jackson
Blondy Gordon	Catherine the Great

(c) All words referring to the deity, the Bible, the books of the Bible, and other sacred books

the Trinity	the Supreme Being
Talmud	the Koran

(d) Names of months, days of the week, holidays, holy days, and periods of history

October	Epiphany
Tuesday	Yom Kippur
Fourth of July	the Ice Age

(e) Names of organizations, political parties, and religious bodies

Boy Scouts   the Republican party
the Democrats   the Methodist Church

(f) Names of geographic sections and places: continents, countries, states, cities, rivers, mountains, lakes, and islands

Africa   Rocky Mountains
Carson City   Missouri River
Portage Lake   Long Island
Lakes Michigan and Huron   the South

Exceptions: *Directions are not capitalized, nor are generic terms preceding a proper noun.*

He drove south on I-75.
city of Dallas

(g) Names of divisions of a college or university

Department of Chemistry
the College of Medicine
the School of Business Administration

(h) Names of specific historical events, specific laws, treaties, and departments of government

World War II   Treaty of Versailles
the Bill of Rights   Department of Justice

(i) Titles that precede the names of individuals and abbreviations after a name

General Douglas MacArthur
Professor Gordon Robinson, A.B., A.M., Ph.D.
the Reverend William Hammerstein
Father O'Toole
J. A. Hempstead, D.D.S.

(j) Names of streets, avenues, buildings, churches, hotels, parks, and theaters

the DuBois Tower   St. Thomas Church
First Avenue   the Astor Hotel

(k) Derivatives of proper nouns which are used as adjectives

Elizabethan play   Mexican music

(l) Personifications

Spring's warm touch

4. Capitalize the first word and all other words—except articles, conjunctions, and prepositions—in titles of books, magazines, newspaper articles, stories,

poems, musical compositions, theatrical productions, and chapters or subdivisions of books and periodicals.

Book Review Section of the *New York Times* (newspaper)
The Enjoyment of Drama (book)

5. Capitalize the words *Whereas* and *Resolved* in formal resolutions, and the first word following either of these.

6. Capitalize words before figures (except *page, line,* and *note*).

Chapter 12   Figure 14   Check 213   Invoice 92A

7. Capitalize registered trademarks and trade names.

Coca-Cola   Orlon   Laundromat

8. When two independent clauses are separated by a colon and the second amplifies an idea presented in the first, capitalize the first word of the second independent clause.

Thomas Carlyle has said that he who first shortened the labor of copyists by devising movable type was disbanding hired armies, and cashiering most kings and senates, and creating a whole new democratic world: He had invented the art of printing.

Exceptions: *Do not capitalize for emphasis.*

Do not capitalize the names of the seasons of the year unless personified.

Do not capitalize prefixes to proper names.

pre-Revolutionary colony   non-European country

Do not capitalize the names of college classes (freshman, sophomore, etc.) unless the class is referred to as a specific organization.

Do not capitalize words which were once proper nouns but which through common usage have become common nouns.

macadam   venetian blinds   panama hat

boycott   turkish towel   manila envelope

ITALICS

Discretion should be exercised in the use of italics for emphasis. The trend among good writers is to attain emphasis through sentence structure rather than through the use of italics.

In typewriting manuscript, indicate that material should be typeset in italics by underlining once.

1. Italicize to designate a key term in a discussion, a term with a special meaning, a technical term, or a term that is accompanied by a definition.

In expectancy theory, *valence* refers to the value a person places on a particular *outcome* (consequence of an action).

2. Italicize titles of books, pamphlets, newspapers, magazines, plays, lengthy poems, musical compositions, motion pictures, paintings, drawings, and statues.

3. Italicize letters used as letters and words used as words.

Note: *Parts of complete works, such as chapters of a book or articles in a magazine, are placed in quotation marks.*

The information is found in "The Management of Conflict and Stress" on page 346 of *Human Behavior in Organizations.*

Always dot your *i*'s and cross your *t*'s.

The word *thane* refers to one of superior rank.

Do not write *and* and *the* slantwise across the line.

4. Italicize foreign words or phrases that have not yet been adapted to everyday English usage.

Most businesses realize that a permanent clientele cannot be built upon the principle of *caveat emptor.*

If demand rises *ceteris paribus,* it is hypothesized that price will rise.

Exceptions: *Many abbreviations that in the past were italicized are now used so frequently that it is customary to use roman type in printing and to omit the underline in typing.*

| c. | et al. | etc. | e.g. | ibid. | idem | i.e. |
| loc. cit. | | op. cit. | q.v. | viz. | passim | |

However, because of its unique use with quoted matter, sic is still italicized and enclosed in brackets.

5. Italicize the names of ships, trains, aircraft, and spacecraft.

S.S. *Stella Solaris* (S.S. is not italicized.)
Lindbergh's *Spirit of St. Louis*
Gemini VI

6. Italicize the names of legal cases (plaintiff and defendant) but not *v.* (versus). when cited in text. Do not italicize the names of legal cases in footnote citations.

Labor leaders were disappointed when in 1921 the Supreme Court held in *Duplex Printing Press Company* v. *Deering* that the Sherman Act applied to unions under certain conditions.

[1] Ertel v. Radio Corporation of America (IndApp) 297 NE2d 446.

7. Italicize the word *Resolved* in formal resolutions.

8. Italicize the words *See* and *See also* in index cross-references.

9. Italicize such phrases as *Continued on page 000, Continued from page 000,* and *To be continued.*

ABBREVIATIONS

Although abbreviations are used infrequently in formal and general writing, advancing technology has resulted in an increased use of abbreviations and symbols in scientific and technical writing. This section will treat only the general use of abbreviations. The following are generally accepted practices regarding abbreviations in current use.

1. The personal titles *Mr., Mrs., Ms., Messrs., Dr.,* and *St.* (Saint) are abbreviated with proper names, whether initials or first names are included.

Mr. Brainard   Messrs. Whitney and Fleming
Mrs. Alice Meyer   Dr. A. E. Kraus
Ms. Jones   St. Francis of Assisi

2. Other personal titles such as *Rev., Hon., Prof., Gen., Col., Capt.,* and *Lieut.* are abbreviated when they precede the full name—surname and given name. When only the surname is used, these titles should be spelled out.

Prof. John McDaniels, A.B., Ph.D.
Professor McDaniels
General MacArthur

Note: *The titles Reverend and Honorable are spelled out if preceded by the.*

the Reverend Martha Graham
Rev. Martha Graham
Hon. Charles H. Percy

3. Abbreviate titles and academic degrees used after a person's name.

Abner Thorp, Jr.   Francis Mixter III, LL.D.
Ralph A. Phillips, Sr.   Rev. Josephus Martin II

Notice that Jr. and Sr. are preceded by a comma, II and III are not. (Personal preference as to the use of the comma between the name and the abbreviation should be respected.)

4. The abbreviations *B.C., A.D., a.m., p.m., No.* (for *number*), and the dollar sign ($) may be used with numerals.

559 B.C. (before Christ) (B.C. follows the year cited.)

A.D. 33 (in the year of the Lord) (A.D. precedes the year cited.)

5. The abbreviations *Bro.*, *Bros.*, *Co.*, *Corp.*, *Inc.*, *Ltd.*, and *&* are sometimes used as part of a company name; however, it is recommended that the official spelling of the company name be determined and that usage followed.

6. Names of government agencies, network broadcasting companies, associations, fraternal and service organizations, unions, and other groups are often abbreviated. The first time the name of the organization is used in a manuscript or text it is spelled out with the abbreviation in parentheses—Federal Bureau of Investigation (FBI). Subsequently use the abbreviation in all capitals with no periods and no space between the letters.

FTC	UNESCO	NATO
WAKW	AFL-CIO	USMC
FOE	NBC	YWCA

Note: *Avoid abbreviating the following categories of words within text, except in tabulations or enumerations:*

Names of territories and possessions of the United States, countries, states, and cities

Names of months

Days of the week

Given names, such as Chas. for Charles, Jas. for James

Words such as avenue, boulevard, court, street, drive, lane, parkway, place, road, square, terrace, building

Parts of geographic names, such as Ft. (Fort), Pt. (Port), Mt. (Mountain)

Parts of company names, such as Bro., Bros., Co., and Corp., unless they are abbreviated in the official company name.

Compass directions when they are part of an address—North, South, East, West (Exceptions are NW, NE, SE, and SW after a street name.)

NUMBERS

Since there is no simple, uniform style for the use of numbers under all circumstances, the decision to use a figure or a word can sometimes be perplexing. This section presents general guidelines covering current usage and should answer almost all puzzling questions that may arise.

Exact Numbers

1. Generally numbers from one through ten are spelled out unless the sentence contains a series of numbers that are over ten.

Since only eight people gathered for the meeting, it was canceled.

The employees of that department include a manager, two supervisors, and seven clerks.

The team won 17 games in 1979, 14 games in 1980, 10 games in 1981, and only 8 games in 1982.

Exception: *If the numbers contained in a sentence or paragraph are in different categories, use consistency in treating them in context.*

In the past ten years, the company acquired three subsidiaries employing 212 people—one, 103; another, 99; and a third, 10—of whom 150 have at least eight years of service.

2. Spell out any number that begins a sentence; however, in most instances restructuring the sentence to avoid starting with a number is preferred.

Round Numbers

3. Spell out round numbers that can be expressed in one or two words. Round numbers over one million may be expressed as a combination of words and numerals.

about two thousand employees
a population of three million
3.2 billion items of merchandise
$170 million

Note: *A round number such as 1,500 is expressed in hundreds rather than in thousands.*

fifteen hundred members (not one thousand five hundred members)

Adjacent Numbers

4. When one of two adjacent numbers is part of a compound adjective, spell out the smaller number.

25 twenty-cent stamps
ten 20-cent stamps
twelve 25-inch pipes

Separate unrelated adjacent numbers by a comma.

In 1979, 2,560,479 fans attended the baseball games in the new stadium.

Ordinal Numbers[3]

5. Spell out isolated ordinal numbers of less than one hundred. Ordinals of one hundred or more should be written in figures.

The company is marking the twenty-fifth anniversary of its founding.

For the 120th time, an employee is retiring under the company's pension plan.

They had a ninety-nine-year lease.

Addresses

6. Express federal, state, and interstate highways in figures.

U.S. Route 41 (U.S. 41)
Ohio 50
Interstate 75 (I-75)

7. Spell out numbered street names from one through ten. When figures are used for numbered street names, a hyphen with a space on both sides should separate the house number from the numbered street name. Use *d, st,* or *th* where necessary with a numbered street name.

345 Fifth Street
345 West Fifth Street
345 - 21st Street
345 West 21st Street

8. Express house numbers in figures, except *One* which is spelled out.

One Fourth Avenue

Dates

9. Use figures to designate the day and year after a month.

November 22, 1983

Use a figure to express the day of the month plus *d, st,* or *th* when it stands alone or precedes the month.

On the 22d of July we will fly to Athens.

Her letter dated the 14th did not arrive until last Monday.

It is also acceptable, although more formal, to spell out the day of the month.

The events of the twenty-second of November, 1963, are still a source of controversy.

---

[3]See page 745 for listing of ordinal, cardinal, and Roman numerals

10. Spell out, in lowercase letters, references to particular centuries and decades.

during the sixties and seventies

twentieth century

BUT the 1980s (Plurals of figures are formed by adding an *s* alone, unless used in a special context. See page 696.)

Money

11. Except in legal documents, sums of money (whether in dollars or foreign denominations) should be typed in figures. Whole dollar amounts are set with ciphers after the decimal point when they appear in the same context with fractional amounts. Even sums of money do not require the decimal point and ciphers.

The book was $20.50, but the store offered a discount of $2.00.

The discount of $2 was a temptation the customer could not resist.

12. In legal documents use capitalized words to express sums of money followed by figures in parentheses.

I agree to pay the sum of Seven Hundred Fifty-Five Dollars ($755).

I agree to pay the sum of Seven Hundred Fifty-Five (755) Dollars.

13. Amounts of money less than one dollar are typed or set in figures with the word *cents* spelled out.

The bottle of lotion was on sale for 89 cents.

14. A sum of money used as an adjective should be spelled out and hyphenated.

She bought a ten-dollar purse.

Time

15. To designate time, use a number with *a.m.* or *p.m.* When using *o'clock,* spell out the number.

8:00 p.m.

10:45 in the morning (Do not use *a.m.* or *p.m.* with *morning* or *evening.*)

nine o'clock

12:00 M. (noon)

12:00 p.m. (midnight)

16. The time of day may be spelled out in text matter.

The Senator left the office at five.

The Senate hearing was expected to last until half-past six.

Fractions, Decimals, and Percentages

17. Spell out isolated simple fractions in words. Write mixed fractions and decimals in figures. When a decimal fraction is not preceded by a whole number, a cipher is often used before the decimal point.

The bakery held one-half dozen doughnuts for us.

She was only 7 1/2 years old when she made her debut with the Dallas Symphony Orchestra.

Almost all the students arrived at 0.611 as the answer.

18. A percentage is written as a number with the word *percent* spelled out, except in statistical copy where the symbol % is used.

Only 3 percent of the loans were paid off.

Quantities, Measures, Weights, and Dimensions

19. In mathematical, statistical, technical, or scientific text, express physical quantities such as distances, lengths, areas, volumes, pressures, and so on in figures.

55 miles   250 volts

3 cubic feet   6 meters

20. Designate measures, weights, and dimensions in figures without commas.

Bob is 6 ft. 4 in. tall.

The package weighs 7 lbs. 4 oz.

The editor specified 8½-by-11-inch paper. (In technical matter x is used instead of by in expressing dimensions.)

Governmental Designations

21. The name of a governing body, political division, military unit, and the like is designated by a spelled-out ordinal number preceding the noun. Ordinals that require more than two words are expressed in numbers according to **Rule 5.**

Ninetieth Congress

Court of Appeals for the Tenth Circuit

Fifth Ward

Second Naval District

Fifth Army

Third Battalion, 122d Artillery

GLOSSARY OF ENGLISH USAGE

The following glossary is intended as a guide to acceptable usage as well as a reference to which the reader may turn when a question of diction arises. For the most part this glossary provides information that is not found in standard dictionaries but which is sometimes needed by those involved in spoken and written communication.

A or *an* before *h*. Use *a* if the *h* is sounded; *an* if the word begins with a vowel sound: a historic novel, a humorous story, a hotel, a hysterical person; an hour's drive, an heir, an herb, an honest opinion.

Ability to plus verb (*ability to influence*); not *of* (*ability of influencing*).

Accept, except. Accept is always a verb meaning *to receive; except* is a verb meaning *to exclude*, but is usually a preposition meaning *with the exception of.*

Acquiesce in (not *to*). He acquiesced in the matter of the bonus.

Adapt, adopt, adept. To adapt means *to change* or *make suitable. To adopt* means *to accept* or *put into practice. To be adept* means *to be expert.* They adapted to the harsh change in weather. They adopted the proposal. He is adept at training beginners. (*Adept* may be used with *at* or *in*.)

Adhere, adherent. Adhere (hold fast) *to,* as *to adhere to our policy;* an adherent *of,* as *an adherent of that policy.*

Advice, advise. Advice is a noun meaning a *recommendation; advise* is a verb meaning *to counsel.* I can advise you, but will you follow my advice?

Adverse, averse. Adverse means *antagonistic, hostile; averse* means *having a dislike* or *distaste for.* Use *to* with both words. She was adverse to racism. Joseph is averse to manual labor.

Affect, effect. Affect is a verb meaning *to influence. Effect* is also a verb meaning *to accomplish or produce.* The weather affected our sales. *Effect* is a noun meaning *result* or *consequence.* The weather had an adverse effect on our sales. The delegates effected a compromise.

Aggravate, irritate. To aggravate means *to make worse; to irritate* means *to annoy.* The thunder irritated me, but it aggravated my headache.

All, any, none, some, more, most. These words may be either singular or plural, depending on intended meaning. None of the money has been collected. None of the bills have been paid.

All of. Use *all; of* is redundant. If a pronoun follows *all,* reword the sentence. Check all the reports. They are all going. Not: All of them are going.

All right. This is the only correct usage. *Alright* is incorrect.

All together, altogether. All together means *in a group; altogether* is an adverb meaning *entirely.* The correspondence is all together in one folder. He is altogether too casual in his manner.

Allude, elude. Allude means *to refer indirectly; elude* means *to avoid.* They alluded to a possible wage increase, but a real settlement eluded them.

Allusion, illusion. Allusion means *an indirect reference to; illusion* means *a false impression.*

Already, all ready. Already is an adverb meaning *previously; all ready* is an adverb-adjective compound meaning *completely ready.* Ms. Adams has already left. Are you all ready to go?

Altar, alter. Altar is a noun meaning *a raised structure which serves as a center of worship or ritual.* They decorated the altar. *Alter* is a verb meaning *to change.* The tailor altered Mr. Davis's suit.

Alumna, alumnae, alumnus, alumni. An *alumna* is *a woman graduate or former student* (plural, *alumnae*). An *alumnus* is *a man graduate or former student* (plural, *alumni*). *Graduate, graduates* are good substitute words.

Among, between. Between implies two, whereas *among* implies more than two. There is quite a bit of feeling between my brother and sister. There is a great deal of rivalry among the women at the club.

Amount, number. Amount is usually used when referring to money and to that which cannot be counted; *number* generally refers to things that can be counted. The unusually large number of speculators accounted for the large amount of speculation.

Angry. One is angry *at an action; with a person.* She is sure to be angry with Mr. Lane about the oversight.

Anxious, eager. Anxious connotes distress, fear, uneasiness, worry. *Eager* connotes enthusiasm, anticipation, impatient desire or interest. We are eager to start on our trip. We are anxious to meet your requirements (but worried that we may fail). We are angry at having to wait. He is sure to be angry with Mr. Lane about the oversight.

Any. Use singular or plural verbs and pronouns according to the intended meaning. Was any of the dessert left? Are any of the students eligible for the prize?

Any place, every place, no place, some place are illiterate expressions to be replaced by *anywhere, everywhere, nowhere,* and *somewhere.*

Appraise, apprise. Appraise means *to set a value on; apprise* means *to inform.* The adjuster will appraise the damage and will apprise you of the estimate.

Apt, like, liable. Apt suggests habitual predisposition, suitable or qualified; *likely* emphasizes the idea of probability; the two are extremely close and commonly confused. *Liable* means *susceptible or something unpleasant or responsible.* A short-sighted person is apt to make mistakes in financial planning. It is likely that it will rain tomorrow. She was liable for damages according to the contract.

As, As should not be used for *that* or *whether.* Never say: I don't know *as* I can go today (use *that*).

As . . . as, not so . . . as. In making comparisons use *as . . . as. She is not so tall as me* may pass colloquially but should not be used in writing.

Awful, awfully. As a synonym for *extreme, extremely,* or *very* these words are overused. Incorrect: She was *awfully* confused. Correct: She was *very* confused.

Back of, in back of. Colloquial for *behind* or *at the back of:* "The garden is *behind* the house," not "*in back of* the house."

Bad, badly. Bad is a predicate adjective and should be used after verbs of sensing when used as linking verbs. *Badly* is an adverb. He feels bad about losing. She looks bad. The news sounds bad. But: He played badly in the tournament. He was injured badly in the accident. The home team played the game badly; the loss made them feel bad.

Balance, remainder, Balance is usually used as an accounting or banking term. *Remainder* connotes something that is left over. The balance in her account was substantial. Ship the remainder of the order.

Bases, basis. Bases is the plural of *base* and *basis.*

Between. See *Among.*

Biannual, biennial, semiannual. Biannual means *twice a year; biennial, once in two years; semiannual, every half year.*

Bimonthly, semimonthly. Bimonthly means *every two months; semimonthly, twice a month.*

Can, may. Can means *to be able to; may* means *to have permission.* This model can be used for heating and air conditioning. Tell him that he may leave when he is finished.

Canvas, canvass. Canvas is a noun (cloth). *Canvass* is a verb meaning *to survey* or *solicit.* The cartons were covered with canvas. Mr. Lindsay will canvass the employees for their reactions.

Capital, capitol. Use *capital* unless you are talking about the building that houses a government. Capitalize *capitol* only when it is part of a proper name. The United States Capitol is located on Capitol Hill.

Cite, sight, site. Cite means *to quote; sight* means *vision; site* means *location.* She cited some good examples in her lecture. They sighted another ship on the horizon. We chose the site for our new branch plant.

Claim. Claim is not a synonym for *maintain. Claim* means *to demand something that is due.* She maintained that she was correct. He intends to claim his inheritance.

Complected, complexioned. Complected is a provincialism for *complexioned.* A dark-complexioned person.

Complement, compliment. Complement means *to complete, fill,* or *make perfect; compliment* means *to praise.* Her attention to detail complements his energetic professionalism. He complimented Miss Shelley on her good work.

Consensus of opinion. Although there has been much discussion about the redundancy of this phrase, most dictionaries remain silent about it.

Considerable. Although *Webster's New Collegiate Dictionary* recognizes this term as a noun, it is considered a colloquialism by most writers. We lost *much* in the hurricane (rather than *considerable*).

Consist of, consist in. Consist of means *composed of; consist in* means *to lie, reside.* The mixture consists of four kinds of herbs. Liberty consists in the absence of obstruction.

Consul, council, counsel. A *consul* is a representative. A *council* is an assembly. *Counsel* is advice. When used as a verb *counsel* means *to advise.*

Consult. Consult *about* something or merely consult (*with* is redundant). The heirs consulted the lawyer about the will.

Contact. Although business usage has placed this term in general use as a verb, its preferred usage is as a noun. Please contact the dealer's office. Preferred: We wish to establish a business contact in Brazil.

Continual, continuous. Continual means *occurring in rapid succession; continuous* means *without break.* There were continual interruptions. The machine has been in continuous use for the past three hours.

Credible means *believable; creditable, praiseworthy; credulous, ready to believe on weak evidence.*

Data is the plural form of the Latin *datum. Data* should be used with a plural verb. Data are processed electronically at incredible speeds.

Descendant, descendent. Avoid possible misspelling by using *descendant* which can be either a noun or an adjective. (*Descendent* is only an adjective.)

Differ. One thing differs *from* another; persons differ *with* each other. One author's style differs from that of another in many ways. He differs with us on that point.

Different from. This usage is correct. *Different than* is incorrect. The circumstances were different from those he recalled.

Disinterested, uninterested. Disinterested means *an impersonal, unbiased,* or *unprejudiced interest;*

uninterested means *lacking in* or *absence of any interest.* The ethics of CPA's requires that they be disinterested in the success of their clients. She is uninterested in books of fiction.

Doubt. To express doubt, use *if* or *whether.* To express lack of doubt, use a negative and *that.* I doubt if there is time. He doubts whether she will attend. I do not doubt that there is time. I have no doubt that there is time.

Due to. An adjective construction that should not be used adverbially. Use *because of.* Due to faulty brakes, we drove slowly. (Say *Because of.*)

Each other, one another. Each other refers to two persons; *one another* to more than two. George and Mary are very fond of each other. All the men on the team like one another.

Eager. See *Anxious, eager.*

Effect. See *Affect, effect.*

Either, neither used as adjectives or pronouns take singular verbs. Either day is correct. Neither has replied to my letter.

Either . . . or, neither . . . nor. When these connectives join subject words, the *word that is nearer the verb* determines the use of singular or plural verb. Usually place the plural word near the verb. Either Mr. Lance or his associates are going. Neither the reports nor the book is here.

Else. Add apostrophe *s* to form the possessive. I saw no one else's grade. Matthew took someone else's coat inadvertently.

Eminent, imminent. Eminent means *high, lofty, distinguished; imminent* means *impending* or *threatening.*

Ensure, insure. Ensure means *to make certain* or *safe; insure* means *to give, take,* or *procure insurance* (used in a financial sense). Snow tires will ensure safe driving in the snow. Every automobile owner should insure his or her vehicle in case of accident.

Enthuse. This verb is a back-formation of the noun *enthusiasm.* Has been considered colloquial and/or informal. *Enthuse* should not be used in formal writing; *to be enthusiastic* is better usage even in conversation. She was enthusiastic about the plan.

Etc. Etc. is an abbreviation for *et cetera,* which means *and other things.* If *et cetera* is dictated, the secretary usually transcribes it as *and so forth.* To avoid using either *and so forth* or *etc.,* substitute *and the like. Etc.* should never be used when referring to persons. We must have all sales reports, expense reports, budgets, and the like, by the tenth of the month.

Ethics. Ethics is a plural noun but may be used in both plural and singular constructions. Professional ethics (singular) prohibits our advertising. In some instances his ethics (plural) have been questionable.

Except. See *Accept.*

Farther, further. Farther refers to distance or space; *further* refers to time, quantity, or degree. The airport is a mile farther on this road. We can go into the matter further tomorrow.

Female. Female is used in records and statistics but is not acceptable as a synonym for *woman, lady,* or *feminine.*

Fewer, less. Fewer refers to number; *less* to degree, quantity. There are fewer people living in single homes than formerly. She has less money this year.

Fine, well. Fine is used too often and too carelessly. It is a dubious colloquialism. Use *well.* The motor works well (not *fine*).

Good, well. To *feel good* and to *feel well* are not synonymous. Both *good* and *well* are adjectives, and *feel* (in this usage) is a linking verb. Use *well* to mean *in fine health*; use *good* to mean *pleasant* or *attractive*. When you feel well, you usually look good. I feel well and energetic. She feels good about her promotion.

Got, gotten. *Got* is preferred to *gotten* as the past participle of *get*. It is colloquial when used for *must* or *ought*: I've got to leave at once. Improved: I must leave at once.

Graduated. Use either *graduated from* or *was graduated from*. In letters of application, use the latter form—in case your reader is a purist. Formal: He was graduated from Indiana University. Informal: He graduated from Indiana University.

Hopefully. *Hopefully* generally is misused. It is an adverb and should be used as such. It is not a synonym for *it is hoped* or *I hope/we hope*. Use: We hope Miss James will do a good job. Avoid: Hopefully Miss James will do a good job.

Hope phrases. Do not use *in hopes of* and *no hopes of*. Use the singular form. We sent the letter to Fairbanks, Alaska, in the hope of reaching Ms. Hanna.

However. Avoid starting a sentence with *however* as a transitional word. Used as an adverb, *however* can start a sentence. Transitional: We waited for hours; however, he . . . . Adverb: However you advised him, he did not . . . .

Identical with. To compare likeness, use *identical with*, not *identical to*.

Illusion, allusion. *Illusion* means *a deceptive appearance*; *allusion* means something *referred to*.

Imply, infer. To *imply* means to *give a certain impression*; to *infer* means to *receive a certain impression*. Your question implies that you don't understand. I infer from your question that you don't understand.

In, into. *Into* is a preposition implying *motion*. *In* is a preposition implying *place in which*. She was diving into the pool (but was not yet in the pool). She was swimming in the pool (she is already in the pool).

Inconsistent. Use with *in* or *with*. He is inconsistent in his arguments. Her statements were inconsistent with her record.

Incredible, incredulous. *Incredible* means *unbelievable*; *incredulous* means *unbelieving*. The story is incredible; and, frankly, I'm incredulous.

Inferior to. Use *inferior to*; not *inferior than*.

Ingenious, ingenuous. *Ingenious* means *inventive*; *ingenuous* means *candid* or *artless*.

Inside of. Colloquial for *within*.

Irregardless. Illiterate. Use *regardless*.

Its, it's. The possessive case of pronouns takes no apostrophe. *It's* is a contraction of *It is*.

Job, position. Both words mean a post of employment, but with this distinction: A laborer who uses physical effort has a *job* and is paid *wages* at an hourly rate. A worker with special training or ability has a *position* and is paid a weekly or monthly *salary*. In personnel terminology, *job* is used for both because it is short; for example, a *clerical job*. (*Job* is also used for a unit of work.)

Junior, Senior, Jr., Sr., Junior is usually dropped after the death of the father of the same name. *Senior* or *Sr.* is unnecessary and is almost never used unless the two identical names are closely associated (such as business partners) or unless each is so well known that a distinction is needed.

Kind, kinds. Use singular verbs and pronouns with *kind,* plural with *kinds.* This applies also to *type, types; class, classes,* etc. That kind of machine performs well. The two types of machines used were suitable. Avoid: That kind of a machine performs well.

Later, latter. Later means *after a time; latter* means the *second of two things.* I shall reply later. I prefer the latter.

Latest, last. Although these words can be synonymous, a common distinction is to use *last* to mean at the end in time or place; *latest,* to mean following all others in time only, but not necessarily being the end. This is the latest edition of the book. It is not the last edition because we have started to work on the next edition.

Lay, lie. Lay means *to put something in place; lie* means *to recline or rest on.* Principal parts of *lay* are *lay, laid, laid.* Principal parts of *lie* are *lie, lay, lain.* Lay the mail down. He laid the mail down. The mail lies on the table. It lay there yesterday.

Lead, led. The past tense of *lead* is *led.* He led the opposition.

Leave, let. Leave means to depart; *let,* to permit or allow.

Less. See *Fewer, less.*

Like. Like should not be used for *as, as if,* or *as though.* Incorrect: The report looks like he took pains with it. Correct: The report looks as though he took pains with it.

Loan, lend. Although some writers use *loan* as a noun only, some dictionaries show both *loan* and *lend* as verbs. The principal parts are *loan, loaned, loaned; lend, lent, lent.* (*Webster's New Collegiate Dictionary* shows *loan* as second usage as a verb, with *lend* as a verb preferred usage.)

Loose, lose. These words are frequently confused. *Loose* means *to be free of restraint; lose* means *forget* or *misplace* or *to suffer a loss.* It is easy to lose a loose button.

Lots of. Colloquial for *many, much, a great many, a considerable number.*

Marital, marital, marshall. Marital means *pertaining to marriage; marital* means *warlike or military; marshall* (noun) means *an official,* (verb) *to rally.*

May. See *Can.*

Might of. Misused for *might have.*

Neither . . . nor. See *Either . . . or.*

None. See *All, any, none, some, more, most.*

Not, and not. When either of these two introduces a phrase in contrast to the subject, the subject determines whether the verb is singular or plural. Results, not wishful thinking, count.

Not only, but also. In this construction the noun closest to the verb determines whether the latter is singular or plural. When used with independent clauses, this construction is separated by commas. Not only the reports but also his report was due. Not only was it their first visit here, but also it was their first trip by air.

Off, off of. Use *off* only. The part fell off the machine. The girl jumped off the wall.

On, on to. She drove *on* the expressway berm (implies position and movement over). He stepped *onto* the porch (implies motion). They went *on to* the next town. (*On* is an adverb in the verb phrase *went on; to* is a preposition.)

Oneself. Preferred to *one's self.* Taking oneself too seriously is a foolish practice.

Only. Only should be placed as close as possible to the word or clause that it modifies. Alan types only form letters requested by the sales department. Alan types form letters only when he has spare time. Do not substitute *only* for *except* or *but.* Incorrect: No one is interested only Mr. Lane.

Oral, verbal. Oral means *spoken; verbal* means *relating to or consisting of words.* Although both are commonly used for spoken, use the dictionary meaning in formal writing. . . . an oral agreement; . . . a verbal contract.

Out loud. Colloquial for *aloud.*

Other. Use *than* after *no other.* Incorrect: It was no other but Jane. Correct: It was no other than Jane.

Outside of. Ungrammatical for *except* or *besides.*

Pair. The preferred plural of *pair* is *pairs,* although *Webster's New Collegiate Dictionary* shows *pair* as a second usage for the plural of this word.

Preferable. Follow by *to,* not by *than.*

Passed, past, pastime. Passed is the past tense and past participle of the verb *to pass. Past* is a noun or an adjective meaning *previously,* a preposition, or an adverb. *Pastime* (often misspelled *passtime* or *pasttime*) is a diversion. They passed the time by reading. Go two blocks past Elm Street. In the past my favorite pastime was reading.

Percent, percentage. Percent is one word. *Percentage* is also one word and should not be used with a number. *Percentage* is a dubious colloquialism when used for *proportion.* A large proportion (rather than *percentage*) of the fish were cod.

Person, individual, personage, party, people. A *person* is a human being; an *individual* is one apart from a group; a *personage* is a person of importance; a *party* is a legal term for person (other usage is slang). Use *persons* for small numbers, *people* for large masses.

Personal, personnel. Personal means *private; personnel* means *a body of persons usually employed (as in a factory, office, or organization).*

Personally, in person. These terms intensify meaning. Avoid using them in formal writing. I personally guarantee each one. Mr. Lane made the award in person.

Politics. This term is commonly used with singular verbs.

Position. See *Job, position.*

Practical, practicable. Practical means *sensible, efficient, or useful. Practicable* implies something that can be put into practice. My practical secretary has suggested a practicable method for handling follow-ups.

Precedence, precedents, precedent. Precedence means *priority or preference; precedents* is the plural of the noun *precedent* and means *an earlier occurrence; precedent* (preSEEdent) is an adjective and means *earlier in order.* Completing the school year took precedence over her desire to take the trip. There are several precedents for that decision. The precedent decisions that apply to this case must be considered.

Prerequisite As a noun, a *prerequisite for;* as an adjective, to be *prerequisite to.*

Principal, principle. Principal may be a noun or an adjective. As a noun it means *a person who has controlling authority or is in a leading position.* It also means *a capital sum of money.* As an adjective, *principal* means *chief. Principle* is a noun meaning *a law, a doctrine, a rule or code of conduct.* The principals in the legal case are present. The principal actor was outstanding in his part. Mrs. Palmer invested the principal of the trust fund and used the interest for living expenses. Mr. Palmer was always a man of principle, but he was principal of the school.

Proposition. Correctly used as a noun, *proposition* means an *assertion* or *dignified proposal*. Do not use this word as a verb.

Proved, proven. Although either word may be used as the past participle of *prove, proved* is preferred. *Proven* is better confined to use as an adjective. You have proved your point. It was a proven fact.

Raise, increase, increment. In business *raise* and *increase* may be used interchangeably when referring to wage or salary. *Raise* is the popular term, but *increase* is a more dignified term. *Increment* is generally used in personnel offices.

Real. Real should not be used for the adverb *very*. She made a very attractive appearance (not real attractive).

Remainder. See *Balance.*

Retroactive. Retroactive is always used with the preposition *to* not *from*. The price increase is retroactive to July 1.

Salary. See *Job, position.*

Set, sit, Set means *to put or place something, Sit* means *to place yourself.* She set the cup and saucer on the table. She sits on the porch every evening.

Species. Species means *a class of individuals having common attributes and designated by a common name.* It is spelled the same in the singular and plural. *Specie* is money in the form of coins.

Stationary, stationery. Stationary means *stable or fixed; stationery* is writing paper.

Statistics. Use the plural form except when referring to the science of statistics.

Stimulus, stimulant. Stimulus means *a mental goad; stimulant* means *a physical goad.* (In medicine these two words are used synonymously.)

Superior. Use *superior to,* not *superior than.*

Sure, surely. Sure is an adjective; *surely* is a modifying adverb. Are you sure? That was surely record time.

Tantamount. Use with *to.* His actions were tantamount (equivalent) to betrayal.

These kind, those kind. Ungrammatical. Use *this kind, these kinds.*

Till, until. Until is preferred at the beginning of a sentence.

Try and. This usage should be avoided. Use *to* with the infinitive: try to listen.

Type. Type is a noun or verb; do not use it as an adjective. This type of process is new. Not: This type process is new.

Uninterested. See *Disinterested, uninterested.*

Unique. Unique means *the only one of its kind.* It does not mean *rare* or *odd.* It is incorrect to say, "She is the most unique person I know."

United States. Use *the* before *United States,* rephrasing if necessary to avoid an awkward construction. (If necessary, substitute *American.*) Poor: According to United States laws . . . ; preferred: According to the laws of the United States . . . .

Until. See *Till.*

Up. Avoid the use of *up* with verbs such as *connect, divide, end, open, rest, settle, finish.*

Verbal. See *Oral, verbal.*

Very. *Very* should not be used to modify a past participle. It may modify an adjective directly. Incorrect: She was very interested in the position. Correct: She was very much interested in the position.

View. As a verb use *to view with;* as a noun use *in view of* or *with a view to.* We view it with indifference. In view of the time, we will adjourn.

Vulnerable. To be vulnerable (assailable) *to* something *in* some way or place. He was vulnerable to criticism in his business practices.

Wages. See *Job, position.*

Well. See *Good, well.*

Where compounds. *Anywhere, everywhere, nowhere,* and *somewhere* are adverbs and are written as one word.

Whether. In indirect questions, *whether* is preferred to *if.* They asked whether he had come. Not: They asked if he had come.

Whether . . . or, whether or not. For alternatives, use *whether . . . or* or *whether or not.* Avoid awkwardness. State whether you will go or stay. State whether or not you will go. Not: State whether you will go or not.

While, awhile. Use *while* as a connective for time or as a noun. *Awhile,* an adverb, is written as one word. While Mrs. Lambert was out, her caller arrived. Once in a while, we find that . . . . He left awhile ago.

While can be used for *although,* but it should not be used for *and.* While we see your point, we do not agree. Not: We order nails from the H & P Company, while we order hammers from Black and Burns.

QUICK GRAMMAR REMINDERS

These quick grammar reminders are not intended to be a substitute for a comprehensive grammar book. They are meant to be quick references to jog the reader's memory or quickly clarify a point of confusion that may arise when composing letters, preparing reports, drafting speeches, or performing any of the multitudinous writing tasks that beset the executive and secretary.

ACRONYMS

Acronyms are words from the initial letters or syllable of two or more words. They are neither enclosed in quotes nor underlined. Plurals, possessives, and tenses are formed regularly.

WAC, snafu, NATO

ACTION VERBS

See Transitive (Action) Verbs

AND IN COMPOUND SUBJECTS

Compound subjects of two or more words joined by *and* take plural verbs and pronouns unless the words together comprise a single element.

Our sales manager and our advertising director have sent in their reports.
Our sales manager and advertising director has sent in his report.
A pen and a pencil were found after the meeting.
A matching pen and pencil makes a welcome gift.

COMPOUND WORDS

Compound words fall into three groups: hyphenated compounds, one-word compounds, and two-word compounds. Information about the two latter groups can generally be found in *Webster's New Collegiate Dictionary* or any other standard dictionary. Compounds formed with prefixes and suffixes are treated in this section under "Prefixes, Joined" and under "Suffixes." For information about hyphenated compounds *see* "Punctuation: The Hyphen."

EUPHEMISMS

Euphemisms are softened, tactful phrases for blunt or harsh facts. Some common euphemisms are:

For *buried*: laid to rest
For *discharged*: left our employ
For *died*: passed away
For *claim*: think or believe

EUPHONY

Euphony (pleasing speech sounds) can be achieved by

(a) Avoiding the harsh or ugly sounds (*f*'s, *b*'s, *ch*'s, *t*'s, *ug*'s, *og*'s)
(b) Repeating pleasant sounds
(c) Using rhythmically accented syllables

Choppy: We are glad indeed to be able to advise you . . . .
Euphonious: We are pleased that we can tell you. . . . The record of all receipts and expenses . . . .

GERUND

(a) A gerund is a verbal (ending in *ing*) used as a noun. Gerunds can be used in all noun usages.

Subject: You learn that editing takes time.
Object: She learned editing from the senior editor.

(b) In formal writing a possessive is used with a gerund.

His editing included Chapter 10.
The team's winning made the crowd happy.

Exception: *The possessive form is not necessary with a compound or inanimate modifier.*

The No. 2 mill breaking down caused a delay.
The mill (*or* mill's) breaking down caused a delay.

IDIOMS

(a) An *idiom* is an expression or phrase that is somehow peculiar—an arbitrary grouping of words that is often illogical in construction or meaning but which is acceptable. Some common American idioms are *to make ends meet, to take pains, laid up with a virus, by and large,* and *to catch a cold or bug.*

(b) A prepositional idiom is one in which the combination of words has a special meaning; for example, *to live up to, to live down* something, *to put up with* something, *to set up, to set about* something, *to hand over, to bring up* a point.

INFINITIVES

An infinitive is the first principal part of any verb, is usually introduced by *to,* and is used as a noun, adjective, or adverb.

Noun, subject: To go will be a privilege.
Noun, object: He wants *to talk* with you.
Adjective: The place *to go* is Spain.
Adverb: He saved his graduation checks *to go* to Spain.

The *to* is usually omitted after the following verbs: *hear, feel, watch, let, dare, help, see, make, please, bid, need,* and *do.*

Help me (to) carry the luggage.
They bid us (to) leave immediately.
There was nothing to do but (to) read.

A split infinitive occurs when a word or phrase separates *to* and the verb. Use a split infinitive only when necessary for clarity or emphasis. Notice in the examples below how the meaning changes subtly with a shift of the infinitive.

The attorney invited them to *first* consider . . .

The attorney invited them to consider first . . . .

INTRANSITIVE VERBS

See "Transitive (Action) Verbs."

LINKING VERBS

See also "Transitive (Action) Verbs." These verbs *connect* a subject with a predicate noun or adjective.

to be (am, is, was, has been, etc.), act, appear, become, feel, get, grow, look, seem, sound, taste, turn

NUMBER OF

The meaning intended determines whether *number of* takes a singular or plural verb.

The number of replies that we received is gratifying.

A number of the replies were critical of our policy.

OR

When *or* joins two subject words, the verb agrees with the nearer word.

Only one or two are needed.

No pencils or paper was furnished.

PARALLEL CONSTRUCTION

If two or more sentence parts are joined by one or more conjunctions, the parts should be of like kinds; that is, all single words of the same part of speech, all phrases, or all clauses.

The shipment was returned not only because it was late but also because two items were incorrect. (*connecting two clauses*)

not:

The shipment was returned not only for being late but also because two items were incorrect. *(connecting a phrase and a clause)*

A good secretary not only is prompt but also shows initiative. *(connecting two verb phrases)*

not:

A good secretary is both prompt and shows initiative. *(connecting an adjective and a verb phrase)*

Our plan is to decide on the type of building, to choose an architect, and to let the contracts. *(connecting infinitives)*

not:

Our plan is to decide on the type of building, choosing an architect, and letting the contracts. *(connecting an infinitive and participles)*

PARTICIPLES, DANGLING

A participial construction should modify a related, logical word except when the construction is absolute (modifying nothing).

Dangling: Leaving the office, the letter was dropped.

Logical: Leaving the office, I dropped the letter.

Absolute: The situation having developed, let's accept the changes it necessitates.

PLURALS

Since standard dictionaries give irregularly formed plurals of words, this section will provide only that information pertaining to common problems that confront writers in day-to-day business usage. Refer also to "The Apostrophe" under "Punctuation."

Abbreviations

(a) For most, add *s:* gals, yds, Drs., bbls

(b) For abbreviations in all caps, add *s:* CPSs, CPAs, R.N.s, RNs

(c) For abbreviations consisting of single lowercase letters, add *'s:* btu's, cc's

Compound Nouns

(a) The plurals of compound nouns are generally formed by adding *s* to the principal word in the compound: attorneys general, judge advocates, notaries public, trade unions, assistant postmasters general.

(b) Compound nouns that contain prepositions form the plural by adding *s* to the principal word: chambers of commerce, attorneys at law, powers of attorney, points of view, bills of lading.

(c) Hyphenated compounds form the plural by adding *s* to the noun: lookers-on, passers-by, hangers-on, runners-up, goings-on.

(d) If there is no important word in the hyphenated compound noun, add an *s* to the end of the compound to form the plural: forget-me-nots, Jack-in-the-pulpits.[4]

(e) Some compounds form their plurals by making both parts plural: manservant, menservants; woman doctor, women doctors; Knight Templar, Knights Templars or Knights Templar.

(f) Compounds ending in *ful* form their plurals by adding *s* to the end of the compound: spoonfuls, cupfuls, handfuls, bucketfuls.

Foreign Words

Given a choice between a foreign and an English plural, use the English.

English Plural	Foreign Plural
appendixes	appendices
criterions	criteria
curriculums*	curricula
indexes	indices
mediums	media*
memorandums	memoranda
ultimatums	ultimata

*Use the plural that is most familiar for the subject matter.

Numbers

See page 720.

Proper Names

(a) To form the plurals of proper names add *s* or *es*: the Smiths, the Joneses, the Foxes, the Americas, the Eskimos, the Lillys, the Murrays, the Randolphs.

4If neither word in a compound is a noun, add *s* to the last word: also-rans, come-ons, follow-ups, go-betweens, higher-ups, trade-ins.

PREFIXES, JOINED

Compounds with the following prefixes are usually written as one word.

anti	antifreeze	*over*	overanxious
bi	bimonthly	*post*	postdate
co	coplanner	*pre*	prearrange
dis	disaffect	*pro*	procreate
extra	extracurricular	*pseudo*	pseudointellectual
fore	foreknown	*re*	restyle
hydro	hydrochloride	*semi*	semicircular
hyper	hypertension	*sub*	substandard
in	incapable	*super*	superstructure
infra	infrastructure	*supra*	supranational
inter	international	*trans*	transcontinental
intra	intramural	*tri*	tricity
mis	misread	*ultra*	ultrasound
non	noncombatant	*un*	unsuitable
out	outdistance	*under*	underestimate

When the second element is capitalized or a figure, use the hyphen; for example, anti-American, pre-Raphaelite, pre-1914, post-1945. Use the hyphen to distinguish homonyms: re-cover, re-form.

PREPOSITIONS

Prepositions should end a construction only to avoid awkward phrasing or when used in a prepositional idiom.

A collective noun takes a singular verb when the *group* is thought of. He left his car to be worked on.

REDUNDANCY

Redundancy is the needless repetition of words. In each redundant phrase below, the italicized word is sufficient for clarity.

both *alike*   *depreciate* in value
close *proximity*   month of *April*
continue on   *repeat* again
customary *practice* two *twin sisters*

SPLIT INFINITIVES

See "Infinitives."

SUBJUNCTIVE MOOD

In formal writing the subjunctive mood is commonly used in contrary-to-fact clauses; clauses expressing doubt; clauses expressing wishes, regrets, demands, recommendations, and the like.

Subjunctive mood

If he were here, he would agree with me.
If time were available, I would come.
If that be true, we must act now.
I wish I were confident of the outcome.
We recommend that it be tried.

Conventional (indicative) usage

I know he was here because he left a note.
If he was (*not* were) here earlier, he didn't leave a note.
If she was planning to go, she didn't tell me.

Professor Porter G. Perrin in his book *Writer's Guide and Index to English* says that, actually, subjunctives are a trait of style rather than a matter of grammar.

SUFFIXES

The following suffixes usually are joined to the base word.

fold	threefold, multifold
hood	childhood, motherhood
like*	catlike, childlike
proof	burglarproof, fireproof
wide	nationwide, worldwide

Exceptions: compounds formed from proper names, words ending in ll, and word combinations.

Indian-like	bell-like	vacuum-bottle-like

THAT, WHICH, WHO

(a) *That* and *which* are not always interchangeable. *That* is preferred for introducing a restrictive clause.

The phrasing that you suggest is good.
The book that you recommend is excellent.

(b) *Which* is preferred for introducing a nonrestrictive clause.

Examples at top of page 741.

The new phrasing, which seems clearer, is better.
Your help, which we need badly, will save the day.

(c) *Who* refers to persons, and sometimes to animals. *Who* can introduce either restrictive or nonrestrictive clauses.

The members who favored the amendment voted yes.
Mr. Jones, who was out of town, voted by proxy.
Native Dancer, who won many important races, was a famous racehorse.

(d) In formal writing do not omit *that* as a conjunction.

Formal: We think that this proposal is fair.
Informal: We think this idea is a good one.

TRANSITIVE (ACTION) VERBS

Dictionaries designate verbs as *transitive* or *intransitive (linking)* verbs.

(a) Transitive (action) verbs take objects. Intransitive (linking) verbs do not.

Transitive: Send the letter today.

Intransitive: She arrived this morning.

(b) Some verbs are transitive *and* intransitive.

Transitive: I wrote a full report.
She left her luggage at the hotel.

Intransitive: I wrote yesterday.
She left yesterday.

VERBAL PHRASES

See "Infinitives" and "Participles, Dangling."

WHO, WHOM

Use *who* as the subject of a verb, *whom* as the object of a verb or a preposition, or as the subject of an infinitive.

Send it only to those *who asked* for it.
Who do you think *will be made* chairman?
Everyone *upon whom* I called accepted.
Whom shall I *ask* first?
Whom did they ask *to be* chairman?

WHOSE

Use *whose* as a possessive conjunction if *of which* is awkward.

The manual for systems and procedures, whose author is unknown, is excellent.

but:

A large box, the contents of which were unknown, stood on the loading dock.

WORD DIVISION

Typewriters without proportional spacing cannot and need not maintain the even right margins of typeset material. But because the reader will be distracted both by an unduly ragged margin and by excessive end-of-line word divisions the best course is to follow (judiciously) these rules:

ACCEPTED USAGE

1. Divide words

(a) After an internal one-letter syllable

criti-cism   tele-vision   sepa-rate

Except: Do not divide *able, ible, icle, ical, cial,* or *sion.*

biolog-ical   *change-able*   *deduct-ible*   *spe-cial*

radi-ator   sci-ence   cli-ents   situ-ation

(b) Between two vowels separately pronounced

(c) Preferably at a prefix or suffix

mis-spelled   driv-ing   depart-ment   exten-sion

(d) Between double consonants unless the base word ends in a double consonant

neces-sary   capil-lary   car-rier   excel-lent
will-ing   tell-ing   careless-ness   staff-ing

But: *discus-sion*   *impres-sive*   *impres-sion*

(e) To improve readability by putting as much of a word on a line as is practical, even though the word has several acceptable points of division

considera-tion (*not* consid-eration)   documenta-tion (*not* docu-mentation)

2. Divide hyphenated words only at the hyphen

self-criticism   high-sounding

3. Do not divide

(a) One-syllable words

(b) Words of five or fewer letters (preferably six or fewer)

into   after   until   proper   notice

(c) Abbreviations, numbers, dates, names of persons (Avoid separating titles, initials, and professional and scholastic degrees from a name. If necessary to divide, do so at a logical point: May 14,/1979, or Mr. James A./Hanover.)

(d) Two-letter first or last syllables

(d) Contractions

(f) The last word in over two successive lines of typing

(g) The last word in a paragraph or on a page

REFERENCE SOURCES

As a secretary you fill find three reference sources indispensable in helping you fulfill your administrative support responsibilities—a dictionary, a secretarial handbook, and a telephone directory. You will want to have these sources readily available at your work station as you perform your secretarial functions.

DICTIONARIES

The dictionary is probably the most useful secretarial reference source of all. You will find the dictionary an invaluable tool in verifying the spelling, syllabication, and proper usage of words. In addition, most dictionaries contain not only comprehensive definitions of English language terms but also the meanings of foreign terms, commonly used abbreviations, biographical and geographical names, and other essential information.

In any dictionary you will find much helpful information about a great many words, provided you know how to use the dictionary properly. When you use a dictionary, especially the first time, you should study the pages at the beginning to learn to use the dictionary. Then you will be able to use the dictionary effectively as a guide for determining definitions, correct spelling and pronunciation, lists of synonyms and antonyms, commonly used abbreviations, and foreign words and phrases.

Every secretary should have an up-to-date desk size dictionary at his or her desk. If a desk size dictionary is not available, a paperback pocket-size dictionary should be used. The following are two desk size dictionaries that should be considered for secretarial use:

Thorndike, E. L., and Clarence L. Barnhart. *Advanced Dictionary*, Glenview, Ill.: Scott Foresman and Company, 1979.

Webster's New Collegiate Dictionary. Springfield, Mass.: G. & C. Merriam Company, 1981.

HANDBOOKS

A handbook for secretarial work should be a compact, completely indexed reference. This handbook should cover such topics as the proper use of grammar, plural and possessive forms, punctuation rules, and the correct writing of numerals in reports and letters. As a guide, a handbook can be of great help in deciding, for example, where to place the dateline or the attention line of a business letter, whether to put the apostrophe before or after the letter *s* in *boss's work load*, and when to capitalize geographic locations such as *West Coast* or *western Kentucky*.

Some good general handbooks for secretarial use are:

House, Clifford R., and Kathie Sigler. *Reference Manual for Office Personnel*, 6th ed. Cincinnati: South-Western Publishing Co., 1981.

Nanassy, Louis C., William Selden, and Jo Ann Lee. *Reference Manual for Office Workers*. Beverly Hills: Glencoe Press, 1977.

Sabin, William A. *The Gregg Reference Manual*, 5th ed. New York: McGraw-Hill Book Company, 1977.

Skillin, Marjorie, and Robert M. Gay. *Words into Type*, 3d ed. Englewood Cliffs, New Jersey: Prentice-Hall, Inc., 1974.

TELEPHONE DIRECTORIES

At the beginning of every telephone directory is a user guide that is filled with information on such topics as doing business with the telephone company, directory assistance, and local and long-distance calling. Inside the directories are alphabetic listings of names, street addresses, and telephone numbers. Directories are used by secretaries to find the telephone numbers of listed business customers to verify the spelling of their names, and the accuracy of their addresses.

The Yellow Pages may serve as a buyer's guide because the names, addresses, and telephone numbers of businesses are listed under their products or services. A community street directory and ZIP Codes for the local area may also be included in the Yellow Pages. In most large localities, there are consumer and business-to-business Yellow Pages.

A small personal telephone directory can save considerable telephoning time. On alphabetically arranged pages, most personal directories provide spaces for writing the names, addresses, area codes, and telephone numbers of frequently called local and out-of-town telephones. A small booklet supplied by the telephone company can be used as your personal directory.

NUMERALS — CARDINAL (ARABIC, ROMAN), ORDINAL

Two types of numerals are used in business — cardinal and ordinal. Cardinal numerals are used in simple counting: one (1), two (2), three (3). They may be used as nouns (a count of ten), as adjectives (ten persons), or as pronouns (ten were lost). Ordinal numerals are used to show the order or succession in which such items as names, objects, and periods of time are considered (the seventh month, the fifth row of seats, the twentieth century). Arabic and Roman symbols distinguish cardinal numerals. Below is a table of numerals that shows the usual range of numbers that an executive or secretary will need in business.

TABLE OF NUMBERS

CARDINAL NUMBERS

NAME	Arabic	Roman*
zero or naught or cipher	0	
one	1	I
two	2	II
three	3	III
four	4	IV
five	5	V
six	6	VI
seven	7	VII
eight	8	VIII
nine	9	IX
ten	10	X
eleven	11	XI
twelve	12	XII
thirteen	13	XIII
fourteen	14	XIV
fifteen	15	XV
sixteen	16	XVI
seventeen	17	XVII
eighteen	18	XVIII
nineteen	19	XIX
twenty	20	XX
twenty-one	21	XXI
twenty-two	22	XXII
twenty-three	23	XXIII
twenty-four	24	XXIV
twenty-five	25	XXV
twenty-six	26	XXVI
twenty-seven	27	XXVII
twenty-eight	28	XXVIII
twenty-nine	29	XXIX
thirty	30	XXX
thirty-one	31	XXXI
thirty-two	32	XXXII
forty	40	XL
forty-one etc	41	XLI
fifty	50	L
sixty	60	LX
seventy	70	LXX
eighty	80	LXXX
ninety	90	XC
one hundred	100	C
one hundred and one or one hundred one	101	CI
one hundred and two etc	102	CII
two hundred	200	CC
three hundred	300	CCC
four hundred	400	CD
five hundred	500	D
six hundred	600	DC
seven hundred	700	DCC
eight hundred	800	DCCC
nine hundred	900	CM
one thousand or ten hundred etc	1,000	M
two thousand etc	2,000	MM
five thousand	5,000	$\bar{V}$
ten thousand	10,000	$\bar{X}$
one hundred thousand	100,000	$\bar{C}$
one million	1,000,000	$\bar{M}$

ORDINAL NUMBERS

NAME	SYMBOL
first	1st
second	2d or 2nd
third	3d or 3rd
fourth	4th
fifth	5th
sixth	6th
seventh	7th
eighth	8th
ninth	9th
tenth	10th
eleventh	11th
twelfth	12th
thirteenth	13th
fourteenth	14th
fifteenth	15th
sixteenth	16th
seventeenth	17th
eighteenth	18th
nineteenth	19th
twentieth	20th
twenty-first	21st
twenty-second	22d or 22nd
twenty-third	23d or 23rd
twenty-fourth	24th
twenty-fifth	25th
twenty-sixth	26th
twenty-seventh	27th
twenty-eighth	28th
twenty-ninth	29th
thirtieth	30th
thirty-first	31st
thirty-second etc	32d or 32nd
fortieth	40th
forty-first	41st
forty-second etc	42d or 42nd
fiftieth	50th
sixtieth	60th
seventieth	70th
eightieth	80th
ninetieth	90th
hundredth or one hundredth	100th
hundred and first or one hundred and first	101st
hundred and second etc	102d or 102nd
two hundredth	200th
three hundredth	300th
four hundredth	400th
five hundredth	500th
six hundredth	600th
seven hundredth	700th
eight hundredth	800th
nine hundredth	900th
thousandth or one thousandth	1,000th
two thousandth etc	2,000th
ten thousandth	10,000th
hundred thousandth or one hundred thousandth	100,000th
millionth or one millionth	1,000,000th

*Repeating a letter in a Roman numeral increases its value. This is done up to three times. Placing a letter of lesser value before another subtracts its value. (This is done rather than repeat the letter four times.)

XX = 20   XXX = 30
XL = 40 (L, 50 minus X, 10)
CM = 900 (M, 1,000, or ten hundred, minus C, 100)

Placing a letter of lesser value after one of greater value increases the value:

XIII = 13;   XIV = 14;   XVI = 16.

A dash over a number multiplies it by one thousand: $\bar{V}$ = 5,000; $\bar{M}$ = 100,000.

COMMUNICATIONS GUIDE

The following pages contain a condensed communications guide for reference.

1. Block style, open punctuation

ARMSTRONG & SONS
Professional Outdoor Advertisers

6858 River Road   Portland, OR 97222-9004   Telephone 503-555-1171

December 10, 19--

Mr. Edward McDaniel
Akron Chamber of Commerce
74 South Main Street
Akron, OH 44308-7417

Dear Mr. McDaniel

This letter is typed in block style with open punctuation. Every line begins at the left margin. Only essential punctuation marks are are used in the opening and closing lines.

The distinctive feature of this letter style is that the date, the letter address, the salutation, the attention line (when used), all lines in the body, the complimentary close, and all signature lines begin at the left margin. No tabulator stops are necessary.

Typing time is accordingly reduced. First, time required to set tabulator stops and to use the tabulator is saved. Second, by omitting all except the essential punctuation marks, the number of typing strokes is decreased.

The use of open punctuation is appropriate with this letter style.

Cordially yours

Janet Harvet
Janet Harvet, Consultant

ao

2. Modified block style, blocked paragraphs, open punctuation

Fairmeadows East   720 Saint Paul Place   Baltimore, MD 21202-3401   301-555-3383

December 10, 19--

Mrs. Anna James
Caswell-Higgins Associates
385 Maumee Tower
Toledo, OH 43604-3639

Dear Mrs. James

SUBJECT: The Modified Block Letter Style

This letter is typed in modified block style with blocked paragraphs. Open punctuation is used in the opening and closing lines.

Contrast this style with the block style, and you will notice that the dateline has been moved to begin at the horizontal center (although it is appropriate also to end at the right margin) and that the complimentary close and the signature lines have been blocked at the horizontal center of the letter. All other lines begin at the left margin. These modifications of the block style give the style its name--modified block.

When an attention line is used in this style of letter, it is begun at the left margin. If a subject line is used, it is begun at the left margin or centered over the body of the letter. A double space below the salutation.

Although open punctuation is used in this letter, it is equally appropriate to use mixed punctuation.

Sincerely yours

David N. Belz
David N. Belz, Director

mcn

3. Modified block style, indented paragraphs, mixed punctuation

Commercial Distributors, Inc.

78 UNIVERSITY BOULEVARD • DENVER, CO 80206-4444 • 303-555-6663

December 10, 19--

Mr. William Summers
Electromagnetic Company, Inc.
One Erieview Plaza
Cleveland, OH 44124-5629

Dear Mr. Summers:

This letter is typed in modified block style with indented paragraphs. Mixed punctuation is used in the opening and closing lines. This punctuation style calls for a colon after the salutation and a comma after the complimentary close. All other punctuation is omitted in the letter address, unless a line ends in an abbreviation that requires the usual abbreviation period.

Note that the dateline is centered (although it could have been typed to begin at the center or end at the right margin); the first line of each paragraph is indented five spaces (although 10- or 15-space indentations are also commonly used). All other lines begin at the left margin. The closing lines are blocked at the horizontal center of the letterhead.

Although mixed punctuation is used in this letter, it is equally acceptable to use open punctuation.

Sincerely yours,

George R. Sanders
George R. Sanders

ck

4. Simplified style

ECKERT Equipment Co.

41 Monte Vista Boulevard   Albuquerque, NM 87106-5792   505-555-1865

Dated Today

Office Secretary
Better Business Letters, Inc.
One Main Street
Clarkstown, NY 20969-4789

AMS SIMPLIFIED LETTER

There's a movement under way to take some of the monotony out of letters given you to type. The movement is symbolized by the simplified letter being sponsored by the American Management Society.

What is it? You're reading a sample.

Notice the left block format and the general positioning of the letter. We don't write Dear ...., nor will we write Yours truly or Sincerely yours. Are they really important? We feel that as friendly toward you without them.

Notice the following points:

1. Date location
2. The address
3. The subject
4. The name of the writer

Now take a look at the suggestions prepared for you. Talk them over with your coworkers. Form a final opinion until you have really tried the simplified letter. That's what our secretaries did. As a matter of fact, they finally wrote most of the suggestions themselves.

They say they are sold--and hope you'll have good luck with better (simplified) letters.

Arthur E. Every
ARTHUR E. EVERY, STAFF DIRECTOR
TECHNICAL DIVISION

Enclosure

ENVELOPE ADDRESS PARTS FOR OCR

wbg 3 villa dr. blue ash, ohio 45242-7747

December 10, 19--

Dear Henry,

This letter address typed at the end of a letter removes the business touch and tone from the letter and makes it more personal.

This letter form is used also for very formal letters, such as letters to public officials and honored persons. In addition, letters of appreciation or sympathy or congratulations are typed in this form.

The reference initials are omitted. If the person receiving the letter knows the writer well, it is not necessary that his name be typed as part of the signature.

Cordially,

Bill

Mr. Henry D. Ransom
302 Peachtree Street
Atlanta, GA 30308-4848

PERSONAL AND FORMAL STYLE TYPED ON PERSONAL LETTERHEAD

RMN interoffice memorandum

DATE: December 10, 19--

SUBJECT: Interoffice Correspondence

TO: New Members of the
Stenographic Pool

FROM: Judith L. Reese
Correspondence Supervisor

The interoffice or interdepartment letterhead is used, as the name implies, for correspondence between offices or departments within the company. One advantage of this form is that it can be set up quickly. For instance, this letter requires settings for only the margins and one tabulator stop. Titles (Mr., Mrs., Dr., etc), the salutation, the complimentary close, and the formal signature are usually omitted.

Triple-space between the last line of the heading and the first line of the message. Short messages of no more than five lines may be double-spaced; longer messages should be single-spaced.

Reference initials should be included. When enclosures are sent, the enclosure notation should appear below the reference initials.

sva

INTEROFFICE MEMORANDUM

NOTATIONS TO POST OFFICE

Begin at least three line spaces above the address, below the stamp. Type in all capital letters. Underline if desired. Such notations include:

SPECIAL DELIVERY REGISTERED
HAND STAMP

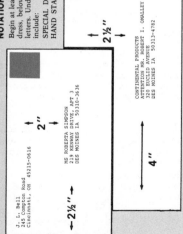

J. L. Bell
245 Compton Road
Cincinnati, OH 45215-0616

← 2½" →

↕ 2"

MS ROBERTA SIMPSON
219 KENWAY DRIVE, APT 3
DES MOINES IA 50310-3636

← 4" →

2½"

CONTINENTAL PRODUCTS
ATTENTION MR. ROBERT I. OMALLEY
320 EUCLID AVENUE
DES MOINES IA 50313-4782

FOREIGN ADDRESS

The last word in the address block should be the country name in all capitals. Where an address code is used in that country, it should be placed on the left side of the last line or on the next to the last line.

ON-RECEIPT NOTATIONS

Type (in all capitals) a triple space below the return address and 3 spaces from the left edge of the envelope. Such notations include:

HOLD FOR ARRIVAL
PLEASE FORWARD
CONFIDENTIAL

Type an *attention line* immediately below the company name.

FORM AND PLACEMENT OF ENVELOPE ADDRESS PARTS FOR OPTICAL CHARACTER READERS

REQUIREMENTS FOR OPTICAL CHARACTER READERS

Post office optical character readers are programmed to scan a specific area on all envelopes; so the address must be completely within this read-zone, *blocked in style, single-spaced*. The 2-letter state abbreviations (typed in upper case) must be used. An apartment or room number should follow the street address *on the same line*. Acceptable placements for a No. 10 and a No. 6¾ envelope are specified in the illustration above. The U.S. Postal Service prefers the use of uppercase letters and no punctuation in envelope addresses.

Letter Part	Line Position	Horizontal Placement	Points to Be Observed	Acceptable Forms
DATE	If a floating dateline is used, the date is typed from 12 to 20 lines from the top of the letterhead or plain sheet, depending on letter length. A fixed dateline is usually typed a double space below the last line of the letterhead.	*Block, Simplified Styles:* Even with left margin. *Modified Block Style:* Begun at center of the sheet; to end flush with right margin; or according to the letterhead.	1. Do not abbreviate names of months. 2. Unusual 2- and 3-line arrangements are not commonly used. 3. Do not use *d, nd, rd, st,* or *th* following the day of the month.	December 14, 19-- 2 May 19-- (Used primarily in government and military correspondence.)
ADDRESS	*With Floating Dateline:* Typed on 4th line below the date. *With Fixed Dateline:* Typed from 3 to 9 lines below the date, depending on letter length. *Government Letter:* Typed on the 14th line. *Personal Style:* Placed at the left margin 5 or 6 lines below the last closing line.	Single-spaced with all lines even at left margin. Use at least three lines for address. Place business title at end of first line or beginning of second line, whichever gives better balance. For a long company name indent the second line 2 or 3 spaces.	1. Follow addressee's letterhead style. 2. Do not abbreviate *Street* or *Avenue* unless it improves appearance. 3. For the name of a town or city, do not use *City.* 4. Use postal ZIP Codes in addresses. 5. Do not use *%* for *In Care of.* (This follows the name line.)	Miss Rose Bannaian Manager, Rupp Steel Co. 2913 Drexmore Avenue Dallas, TX 75206-8215 Mr. Russell H. Rupp 68 Devoe Avenue Dallas, TX 75206-8116 (Refer to the Reference Guide for specific comments.)
ATTENTION LINE	*Preferred:* Typed a double space below address and a double space above salutation.	Typed even with left margin, at paragraph point, or centered.	1. Do not abbreviate *Attention.* 2. Unnecessary to use *of* as in *Attention of Mr. R. H. Rupp.*	Attention Mr. R. H. Rupp Attention Purchasing Agent Attention Mr. L. Cox, Agent
SALUTATION	Typed a double space below last line of address or a double space below attention line. (Note: Omitted in the Simplified style and in interoffice correspondence.)	1. Use *Gentlemen* for a company, a committee, a numbered post office box, a collective organization made up entirely of men. 2. In addressing women substitute *Ladies* or *Mesdames* for *Gentlemen; Madam* for *Sir; Miss* or *Mrs.* for *Mr.;* use *Ms.* when the martial status of a woman is unknown. 3. Use *Ladies and Gentlemen* for a company, committee, post office box, or organization made up of men and women. 4. The salute opening is growing in popularity. This salutation uses the reader's name in the first sentence: Thank you, Mrs. Williams, for your recent order for . . .		Dear Mr. Rupp Gentlemen Dear Sir: Dear Russell: Dear Miss Mason Dear Ms. Willis Dear Mrs. Cox Ladies and Gentlemen

SUBJECT (or REFERENCE) LINE	Typed a double space below salutation. Some printed letterheads indicate position for subject or file number (usually at the top of the letterhead).	Typed even with left margin in the block and Simplified styles. (In the Simplified style, the word *Subject* is omitted and the line is typed in all capitals a triple space below last line of address.) *Modified Block Style:* Typed even with left margin, at paragraph point, or centered.	1. *Subject* may be typed in all capitals or with only first letter capitalized. *Subject* may be omitted; if it is used, it should be followed by a colon. 2. Do not abbreviate *Subject;* capitalize important words in the subject line.	Subject: Pension Plan SUBJECT: Pension Plan Pension Plan PENSION PLAN Reference: File #586 Your File 987 Re: File 586
BODY	Typed a double space below salutation or subject (reference) line.	*Simplified Style:* Typed a triple space below subject line. *Block Style:* First line of each paragraph typed even with left margin. *Modified Block Style:* First line of each paragraph typed even with left margin or indented 5 or 10 spaces.	1. Keep right margin as even as possible, avoiding hyphens at ends of lines where possible. 2. For enumerated material, indent 5 spaces from both margins and double-space after each item. (In the Simplified style, indent listed items 5 spaces except when numbered.)	Single-space lines of paragraphs; double-space between paragraphs. A short one-paragraph letter may be double-spaced with indented paragraphs.
SECOND-PAGE HEADING and BODY	*Heading:* Begin approximately 1" (6 blank lines) below the top edge of the sheet. *Body:* Begin on the 3rd line from the head, using the same margins as for the preceding page. Do not begin with the last part of a divided word. Include at least two lines of a paragraph.	Type the second and succeeding pages on plain paper. The heading is typed even with the left margin in block form or in a one-line arrangement (illustrated below). Use the one-line arrangement if a page might be crowded.		Mr. Jerry W. Robinson Page 2 (Current Date) ~~~~~~~~~~ Mr. Jerry W. Robinson 2 (Current Date) ~~~~~~~~~~
COMPLIMENTARY CLOSE	Typed a double space below the last line of letter body. Omitted in the Simplified letter style and in interoffice correspondence.	Begin at the center except in block style where the complimentary close is typed flush with the left margin.	1. Do not extend the longest of closing lines noticeably beyond right margin. 2. Capitalize first word only. 3. Avoid contractions.	Very truly yours,* Sincerely yours,* Cordially, or Cordially yours,* Respectfully yours, *Also written with *Yours* as the first word.
COMPANY NAME	If used, typed a double space below the complimentary close.	Typed flush with the beginning of the complimentary close.	1. Capitalize all letters. 2. Type name exactly as it appears on letterhead.	RAND CLOTHING, INC. JOHNSON SHOE CO.

Letter Part	Line Position	Horizontal Placement	Points to Be Observed	Acceptable Forms
SIGNATURE (Name and Title of Signer)	Typed 3 blank lines below complimentary close (or company name, if used). *Simplified Style:* All capital letters at least 4 lines below last line of body. NOTE: If both the name and title are used, they may be typed on the same line or the title may be typed on the next line below the typed name. The style giving the best balance should be used.	Typed flush with first letter of complimentary close (or company name if used.) *Simplified Style:* Flush with left margin.	1. Capitalize important words in title. 2. When dictator's name appears in letterhead, use the title only. 3. Do not use *Mr.* in typing a man's name, unless the name can be either masculine or feminine: Chris, Dana, Lynn.	Harold A. Wenchstern Director of Personnel Brenda Ryan, Manager Purchasing Department Mr. Lynn B. Carter Mrs. Beverly Compton *Simplified Style:* LOUIS K. COX-AGENT
IDENTIFICATION NOTATION	Typed a double space below or on the same line with the last of closing lines.	Typed flush with the left margin. (For a complete discussion on the use of reference initials, see page 190.)	Omit dictator's initials when his or her name is typed as part of closing lines.	jc JWR/jc jwr/jc JWR:jc JWRobinson/jc
ENCLOSURE	Typed a double space below the identification notation.	Typed flush with the left margin.	While *Enc.* and *Encl.* are not preferred forms, they are in common use because they save time.	Enclosure Enc. Enclosures 3 Encs. 2 Enclosures: Check Contract
POSTSCRIPT	Typed a double space below the identification notation or the last typed line.	Indent or block the postscript according to the style used in other paragraphs of the letter.	Initials of the writer may be typed below the postscript in place of a second signature.	P.S. Or omit the P.S. and write in the same form as a paragraph in the letter.
PHOTOCOPY or CARBON COPY NOTATION	Typed a double space below the identification notation or the last typed line. (If notation not to appear on original, type at top of carbon or photo copies.)	Typed flush with the left margin. (When typed at the top of carbon copies, may be centered or placed at the left margin.)	1. *cc* or *Copy* to are generally used to indicate *Carbon Copy to.* 2. Use *bc* for *blind copy* if notation is typed on copies only. 3. Use *pc* or *copy* for *photocopy.*	cc: pc: bc: copy: cc: Mr. H. R. King Miss K. Neilen Copy to Mr. H. R. King, bc to HRKing
MAILING NOTATION	Typed midway between date and first line of address; may be typed two lines below the last typed line.	Typed flush with the left margin.	1. Typed in all capital letters. 2. May be typed on carbon copies only.	SPECIAL DELIVERY REGISTERED MAIL CERTIFIED MAIL
SEPARATE MAIL NOTATION	Typed a double space below last typed line.	Typed flush with the left margin.	Indicates method of transportation and number of envelopes or packages.	Separate Mail-Express Separate Mail-2

PART TEN Reference Guide

CORRECT FORMS OF ADDRESS AND REFERENCE

Person and Address (Envelope and Letter)	Salutation	Complimentary Close	In Referring to the Person: Informal Introduction	In Speaking to the Person
U.S. PRESIDENT The President The White House Washington, D.C. 20500	Dear President (Surname[1]) Mr. President Dear Mr. President Dear Madam President	Respectfully yours Very truly yours	The President Mr. (Surname)	Mr. President Sir (in prolonged conversation)
WIFE, U.S. PRESIDENT Mrs. (Last name only) The White House Washington, D.C. 20500	Dear Mrs. (Last name only)	Respectfully yours	Mrs. (Last name only)	Mrs. (Last name only)
U.S. VICE-PRESIDENT The Vice-President United States Senate Washington, D.C. 20510	Dear Vice-President (Surname) Dear Mr. Vice-President Mr. Vice-President Dear Madam Vice-President	Respectfully yours Very truly yours	The Vice-President Mr. (Surname)	Mr. Vice-President Mr. (Surname)
U.S. CHIEF JUSTICE The Chief Justice The Supreme Court Washington, D.C. 20543	Mr. Chief Justice Dear Mr. Chief Justice	Respectfully yours Very truly yours	The Chief Justice	Mr. Chief Justice
U.S. ASSOCIATE JUSTICE Justice (Full Name) The Supreme Court Washington, D.C. 20543	Mr. Justice Madam Justice Dear Mr. Justice Dear Madam Justice (Surname)	Very truly yours Sincerely yours	Mr. Justice (Surname) Madam Justice (Surname)	Mr. Justice (Surname) Madam Justice (Surname)
CABINET OFFICER The Honorable (Full Name) Secretary of (Office) Washington, D.C. 20520 The Secretary of (Office) Washington, D.C. 20520	Dear Mr. Secretary Dear Secretary (Surname) Dear Madam Secretary	Very truly yours Sincerely yours	The Secretary of . . . , Mr. (Surname) The Secretary of . . . , Mrs. or Miss (Surname)	Mr. Secretary (Surname) Madam Secretary Mrs., Miss, or Ms. (Surname)
SPEAKER OF THE HOUSE OF REPRESENTATIVES The Honorable (Full Name) Speaker of the House of Representatives Washington, D.C. 20515	Dear Mr. Speaker Mr. Speaker Madam Speaker Dear Madam Speaker	Very truly yours Sincerely yours	The Speaker, Mr. (Surname) Mr. (Surname) Mrs. or Miss (Surname)	Mr. Speaker Madam Speaker (Surname) Mrs., Miss, or Ms. (Surname)

[1]Surname: a person's last name; the name borne in common by members of a family.

Person and Address (Envelope and Letter)	Salutation	Complimentary Close	In Referring to the Person; Informal Introduction	In Speaking to the Person
U.S. SENATOR, SENATOR-ELECT The Honorable (Full name) United States Senate Washington, DC 20510 _or_ The Honorable (Full name), Senator-elect	Dear Senator (Surname) Dear Senator (Surname) Dear Mrs., Miss, _or_ Ms. (Surname)	Very truly yours Sincerely yours	Senator (Surname)	Senator (Surname) Mr. (Surname) Senator (Surname) Mrs., Miss, _or_ Ms. (Surname)
U.S. REPRESENTATIVE The Honorable (Full name) House of Representatives Washington, DC 20515 Representative (Full name) House of Representatives Washington, DC 20515	Dear Representative (Surname) Dear Representative (Surname) Dear Mrs., Miss, _or_ Ms. (Surname)	Very truly yours Sincerely yours	Representative (Surname) Mr. (Surname) Representative (Surname) Mrs., Miss, _or_ Ms. (Surname)	Mr. (Surname) Mrs., Miss, _or_ Ms. (Surname)
U.S. GOVERNMENT OFFICIAL The Honorable (Full name) Director of Bureau of the Budget Washington, DC 20503 Librarian of Congress Washington, DC 20540	Dear Mr. (Surname) Dear Mrs., Miss, _or_ Ms. (Surname)	Very truly yours Sincerely yours	Mr. (Surname) Mrs., Miss, _or_ Ms. (Surname)	Mr. (Surname) Mrs., Miss, _or_ Ms. (Surname)
AMERICAN AMBASSADOR The Honorable (Full name) American Ambassador Paris, France	Dear Mr. Ambassador Dear Ambassador (Surname) Dear Madam Ambassador	Very truly yours Sincerely yours	The American Ambassador The Ambassador Mr. (Surname) Madam Ambassador Mrs. _or_ Miss (Surname)	Mr. Ambassador Mr. (Surname) Madam Ambassador Mrs., Miss, _or_ Ms. (Surname)
AMERICAN MINISTER TO ANOTHER COUNTRY The Honorable (Full name) American Minister Ottawa, Canada	Dear Mr. Minister Dear Minister (Surname) Dear Mrs., Miss, _or_ Ms. (Surname) Dear Madam Minister	Very truly yours Sincerely yours	The American Minister, Mr. (Surname)[2] The Minister; Mr. (Surname) The American Minister, Mrs., Miss, _or_ Ms. (Surname) The Minister Mrs., Miss, _or_ Ms. (Surname)	Mr. Minister Mr. (Surname) Madam Minister Mrs., Miss, _or_ Ms. (Surname)

[2]In presenting or referring to American Ambassadors and Ministers in any Latin American country, say "Ambassador of the United States" or "Minister of the United States."

Person and Address (Envelope and Letter)	Salutation	Complimentary Close	In Referring to the Person; Informal Introduction	In Speaking to the Person
U.S. REPRESENTATIVE TO THE UNITED NATIONS The Honorable (Full name) United States Representative to the United Nations New York, New York 10017	Dear Mr. (Surname) Dear Mrs., Miss, or Ms. (Surname) *With Ambassadorial Rank:* Dear Ambassador (Surname)	Very truly yours Sincerely yours	Mr. (Surname) Mrs., Miss, or Ms. (Surname) Madam Ambassador Mr. Ambassador	Mr. (Surname) Mrs., Miss, or Ms. (Surname) Madam Ambassador Mr. Ambassador
FOREIGN AMBASSADOR IN U.S. His/Her Excellency (Full name) The Ambassador of France Washington, DC 20516	Excellency Dear Mr. Ambassador Dear Madam Ambassador Dear Ambassador (Surname)	Respectfully yours Sincerely yours Very truly yours	The Ambassador of . . . , Mr. (Surname) The Ambassador Mr. (Surname) Madam Ambassador	Mr. Ambassador Mr. (Surname) Madam Ambassador Mrs., Miss, or Ms. (Surname)
FOREIGN MINISTER IN U.S. The Honorable (Full name) Minister of Italy Washington, DC 20516	Dear Mr. Minister Dear Madam Minister (Surname) Dear Minister (Surname)	Respectfully yours Sincerely yours Very truly yours	The Minister of . . . , Mr. (Surname) The Minister Mr. (Surname) Madam Minister	Mr. Minister Mr. (Surname) Madam Minister Mrs., Miss, or Ms. (Surname)
AMERICAN CONSUL (Full name), Esq. The American Consul United States Embassy (Foreign City, Country)	Dear Mr. (Surname) Dear Mrs., Miss, or Ms. (Surname)	Very truly yours Sincerely yours	Mr. (Surname) Mrs., Miss, or Ms. (Surname)	Mr. (Surname) Mrs., Miss, or Ms. (Surname)
FOREIGN CONSUL (Full name), Esq. The French Consul (American City, State)	Dear Mr. (Surname) Dear Madam (Surname)	Very truly yours Sincerely yours	Mr. (Surname) Madam (Surname)	Mr. (Surname) Madam (Surname)
GOVERNOR OF A STATE His/Her Excellency, the Governor of (State) or The Honorable (Full name), Governor of (State) (Capital City, State)	Dear Governor Dear Governor (Surname)	Respectfully yours Very truly yours Sincerely yours	Governor (Surname) The Governor The Governor of (State)	Governor (Surname) Governor
MEMBER, STATE LEGISLATURE The Honorable (Full name) The State Senate or The House of Representatives (Capital City, State)	Dear Senator or Representative (Surname) Dear Mr. (Surname) Dear Mrs., Miss, or Ms. (Surname)	Very truly yours Sincerely yours	Mr. (Surname) Senator (Surname) Representative (Surname) Mrs., Miss, or Ms. (Surname)	Mr. (Surname) Senator (Surname) Representative (Surname) Mrs., Miss, or Ms. (Surname)
MAYOR OF A CITY The Honorable (Full name) Mayor of the City of . . . . (City, State)	Dear Mayor (Surname)	Very truly yours Sincerely yours	Mayor (Surname) The Mayor	Mayor (Surname) Mr. Mayor Madam Mayor

PART TEN Reference Guide

Person and Address (Envelope and Letter)	Salutation	Complimentary Close	In Referring to the Person; Informal Introduction	In Speaking to the Person
JUDGE OF A COURT The Honorable (Full name) Judge of the . . . . Court (Local Address)	Dear Judge (Surname)	Very truly yours Sincerely yours	Judge (Surname)	Judge (Surname)
MILITARY PERSONNEL (Rank) (Full name) Post or Name of Ship City, State	Dear (Rank) (Surname)	Very truly yours Sincerely yours	(Rank) (Surname)	(Rank) (Surname)
CLERGY (PROTESTANT) The Reverend (Full name), D.D. or The Reverend (Full name) Parsonage Address City, State	Dear Mrs., Miss, or Ms. (Surname) Dear Dr. (Surname) Dear Mr. (Surname) Dear Reverend (Surname)	Respectfully yours Sincerely yours Yours faithfully	The Reverend Doctor (Surname) Doctor (Surname) The Reverend (Surname) Mr. (Surname) Mrs., Miss, or Ms. (Surname)	Dr. (Surname) Sir Mr. (Surname) Mrs., Miss, or Ms. (Surname)
RABBI (JEWISH FAITH) Rabbi (Full name) Rabbi (Full name), D.D. Local Address	Sir My dear Rabbi (Surname) My dear Rabbi	Respectfully yours Sincerely yours Yours faithfully	Dr. (Surname) Rabbi (Surname)	Dr. (Surname) Rabbi (Surname)
PRIEST (ROMAN CATHOLIC) The Reverend (Full name) followed by comma and initials of order) Local Address	Reverend Father Dear Father (Surname)	Sincerely yours Respectfully yours Yours faithfully	Dr. (Surname) Father (Surname)	Dr. (Surname) Father (Surname)
SISTER (ROMAN CATHOLIC) Sister (Full name) followed by comma and initials of order) Local Address	Dear Sister Dear Sister (Religious name)	Sincerely yours Respectfully yours Yours faithfully	Sister (Religious name) Sister	Sister (Religious name) Sister
PRESIDENT (COLLEGE OR UNIVERSITY) Dr. (Surname) or President (Surname), (Degree) Name of University City, State	Dear President (Surname) Dear Dr. (Surname)	Very truly yours Sincerely yours	Dr. (Surname)	Dr. (Surname)

STATE ABBREVIATIONS

Name	Standard Abbreviation	Two-Letter Abbreviation	Capital
Alabama	Ala.	AL	Montgomery
Alaska	Alaska	AK	Juneau
Arizona	Ariz.	AZ	Phoenix
Arkansas	Ark.	AR	Little Rock
California	Calif.	CA	Sacramento
Colorado	Colo.	CO	Denver
Connecticut	Conn.	CT	Hartford
Delaware	Del.	DE	Dover
District of Columbia	D.C.	DC	Washington (National capital)
Florida	Fla.	FL	Tallahassee
Georgia	Ga.	GA	Atlanta
Hawaii	Hawaii	HI	Honolulu
Idaho	Idaho	ID	Boise
Illinois	Ill.	IL	Springfield
Indiana	Ind.	IN	Indianapolis
Iowa	Iowa	IA	Des Moines
Kansas	Kans.	KS	Topeka
Kentucky	Ky.	KY	Frankfort
Louisiana	La.	LA	Baton Rouge
Maine	Maine	ME	Augusta
Maryland	Md.	MD	Annapolis
Massachusetts	Mass.	MA	Boston
Michigan	Mich.	MI	Lansing
Minnesota	Minn.	MN	St. Paul
Mississippi	Miss.	MS	Jackson
Missouri	Mo.	MO	Jefferson City
Montana	Mont.	MT	Helena
Nebraska	Nebr.	NE	Lincoln
Nevada	Nev.	NV	Carson City
New Hampshire	N. H.	NH	Concord
New Jersey	N. J.	NJ	Trenton
New Mexico	N. Mex.	NM	Santa Fe
New York	N. Y.	NY	Albany
North Carolina	N. C.	NC	Raleigh
North Dakota	N. Dak.	ND	Bismarck
Ohio	Ohio	OH	Columbus
Oklahoma	Okla.	OK	Oklahoma City
Oregon	Oreg.	OR	Salem
Pennsylvania	Pa.	PA	Harrisburg
Rhode Island	R. I.	RI	Providence
South Carolina	S. C.	SC	Columbia
South Dakota	S. Dak.	SD	Pierre
Tennessee	Tenn.	TN	Nashville
Texas	Tex.	TX	Austin
Utah	Utah	UT	Salt Lake City
Vermont	Vt.	VT	Montpelier
Virginia	Va.	VA	Richmond
Washington	Wash.	WA	Olympia
West Virginia	W. Va.	WV	Charleston
Wisconsin	Wis.	WI	Madison
Wyoming	Wyo.	WY	Cheyenne

FOOTNOTE AND BIBLIOGRAPHY ENTRIES

Footnote entries are illustrated below.

One author → 1David G. Heinze, Fundamentals of Managerial Statistics (Cincinnati: South-Western Publishing Co., 1980), p. 9.

Two authors → 2G. H. Trice and M. Robert Trice, Basics of Real Estate (Chicago: Business Books, Inc., 1976), p. 86.

Ibid. → 3Ibid., pp. 158-160.

Three authors → 4P. F. Ostrow, Gail Barrington, and Erwin H. Swillinger, Handbook of Graphic Processes (3d ed.; Sacramento: CP Publications, 1978), pp. 56-59.

Four or more authors → 5Dale Keiger et al., A Guide to International Trade (4th ed.; New York: Macauley Publishing Co., 1982), pp. 115-117.

Author and editor → 6Douglas S. Sherwin, "The Meaning of Control," Readings in Management, edited by Max D. Richards (6th ed.; Cincinnati: South-Western Publishing Co., 1982), p. 255.

Editor → 7Max D. Richards (ed.), Readings in Management (6th ed.; Cincinnati: South-Western Publishing Co., 1982), p. 255.

Magazine article → 8"CPA Firms Use Business Graphics," InfoSystems (November, 1981), p. 71.

Newspaper article → 9Alan L. Otten, "Japanese Firms Press European Ventures to Help Profits and Deter Protectionism," The Wall Street Journal, April 16, 1982, p. 44.

Unpublished material → 10Lou Vega, "Implementing Affirmative Action Programs" (A mimeographed report by the Diaz School of Business, Richmond, Virginia, 1978).

Government agency → 11U. S. Treasury Department, Internal Revenue Service, Audit Guide and Standards for Revenue Sharing Recipients, Publication No. 22P (Washington: U. S. Government Printing Office, 1976), p. 48.

Note: Footnote 3 above, Ibid. (ibidem, the same) is used to refer to a single work cited in the note immediately preceding. It is not italicized. Op. cit. (opere citato, in the work cited) and loc. cit. (loco citato, in the place cited) have, for convenience, been replaced by a short title form of footnote. For example:

12Heinze, Managerial Statistics, p. 15. (op. cit., different page)

13Heinze, Managerial Statistics, p. 9. (loc. cit., same page)

FOOTNOTE AND BIBLIOGRAPHY ENTRIES (Continued)

Bibliography entries are illustrated below.

8 Magazine article → "CPA Firms Use Business Graphics." Info-Systems (November, 1981), p. 71.

1 One author → Heinze, David G. Fundamentals of Managerial Statistics. Cincinnati: South-Western Publishing Co., 1980.

5 Four or more authors → Keiger, Dale, E. H. Peterson, John Cartwright, and Alan Biondi. A Guide to International Trade. 4th ed. New York: Macauley Publishing Co., 1982.

4 Three authors → Ostrow, P. F., Gail Barrington, and Erwin Swillinger. Handbook of Graphic Processes. 3d. ed. Sacramento: CP Publications, 1978.

9 Newspaper article → Otten, Alan L. "Japanese Firms Press European Ventures to Help Profits and Deter Protectionism." The Wall Street Journal, April 16, 1982, p. 44.

7 Editor → Richard, Max D. (ed.). Readings in Management. 6th ed. Cincinnati: South-Western Publishing Co., 1982.

6 Author and editor → Sherwin, Douglas S. "The Meaning of Control." Readings in Management. Edited by Max D. Richards. 6th ed. Cincinnati: South-Western Publishing Co., 1982.

2 Two authors → Trice, G. H., and M. Robert Trice. Basics of Real Estate. Chicago: Business Books, Inc., 1976.

11 Government agency → U. S. Treasury Department, Internal Revenue Service. Audit Guide and Standards for Revenue Sharing Recipients. Publication No. 22P. Washington: U. S. Government Printing Office, 1976.

10 Unpublished material → Vega, Lou. "Implementing Affirmative Action Programs." Mimeographed. Richmond, Va.: Diaz School of Business, 1978.

Note: Notice the differences between footnote construction and bibliography construction. Periods rather than commas are used between items in a bibliography. Footnotes use paragraph indentations; bibliographies use hanging indentations. Footnotes are listed by number; bibliographies are listed alphabetically. In bibliographies, facts of publication are placed in parentheses for periodicals only.

PROOFREADERS' MARKS

INSERT MARKS FOR PUNCTUATION

∨ Apostrophe

[/] Brackets

: ⊙ Colon

∧ ⋰ Comma

×××/ Ellipsis

!/ Exclamation point

-/ Hyphen

∧ ⌃ Inferior figure

.../ Leaders

(/) Parentheses

⊙ Period

?/ Question mark

⋩ ⋨ Quotation mark

; ⌣ Semicolon

∨ ⋁ Superior figure

OTHER MARKS

‖ Align type; set flush

bf Boldface type

× ⊗ Broken letter

Cap Capitalize

C+sc Capitals and small capitals

ℓ Delete

ℐ Delete and close up

∧ Insert (caret)

ital Italic, change to

ital Italic boldface

stet Let type stand ∙∙∙∙∙

ℓc Lower case type

⊔ Move down; lower

⊓ Move up; raise

⊐ Move to left

⊏ Move to right

¶ Paragraph

No ¶ No new paragraph

rom Roman, change to

⊙ Reverse; upside down

run in Run in material
(on same line)

Space, add (horizontal)

∨ Space, add (vertical)

⌒ Space, close up (horizontal)

< Space, close up (vertical)

sp Spell out

tr ∩ Transpose

wf Wrong font

(?) ⟨?⟩ Verify or supply information

out
s.c. Out; omit; see copy

#
same
B/S

All marks should be made in the margin on the line in which the error occurs; if more than one correction occurs in one line, they should appear in their order separated by a slanting line. Errors should not be blotted out.

WEIGHTS AND MEASURES WITH METRIC EQUIVALENTS

There are two commonly used methods of measurement. One, the *English*, or *imperial*, system, is used in the United States; the other is the *metric* system which is used in most parts of the world. In the English system, for example, units used for measuring lengths are inches, feet, yards, and miles. The basic unit in the metric system for these measurements is the meter. The metric system is a decimal system, which means that you change from one measurement to another by merely moving a decimal point. For example: 10 decimeters = 1 meter. By moving the decimal point one place to the left, you have converted decimeters into meters.

LENGTHS

English System

12 inches = 1 foot
3 feet = 1 yard
5,280 feet = 1 mile

Metric System

10 millimeters = 1 centimeter
10 centimeters = 1 decimeter
10 decimeters = 1 meter
10 meters = 1 decameter
10 decameters = 1 hectometer
10 hectometers = 1 kilometer

Equivalencies

1 inch = 2.540 centimeters
1 foot = 30.48 centimeters
39.37 inches = 1 meter
1 mile = 1.609 kilometers

WEIGHTS

English System

16 ounces = 1 pound
100 pounds = 1 hundredweight
2,000 pounds = 1 ton

Metric System

10 milligrams = 1 centigram
10 centigrams = 1 decigram
10 decigrams = 1 gram
10 grams = 1 decagram
10 decagrams = 1 hectogram
10 hectograms = 1 kilogram

Equivalencies

1 ounce = 28.35 grams
1 pound = 453.6 grams
1 ton = 907.2 kilograms

DRY AND LIQUID MEASURES

English System

Dry Measure:
2 pints = 1 quart
8 quarts = 1 peck
4 pecks = 1 bushel

Liquid Measure:
2 pints = 1 quart
4 quarts = 1 gallon

Metric System

Dry and Liquid Measure:
10 milliliters = 1 centiliter
10 centiliters = 1 deciliter
10 deciliters = 1 liter
10 liters = 1 decaliter
10 decaliters = 1 hectoliter
10 hectoliters = 1 kiloliter

Equivalencies

Dry Measure:
1 pint = 0.550 liters
1 quart = 1.101 liters
1 peck = 8.809 liters
1 bushel = 35.238 liters

Liquid Measure:
1 pint = 0.473 liters
1 quart = 0.946 liters
1 gallon = 3.785 liters

TEMPERATURE CONVERSION

From Celsius to Fahrenheit

F = 9/5 C + 32.

From Fahrenheit to Celsius.

C = 5/5 (F − 32)

PRACTICAL BUSINESS MATHEMATICS

Every business person uses percentages in one form or other for calculating interest, costs, commissions, discounts, taxes, and the like. The following pages provide a reference covering the principles of determining percentages and should be helpful to the executive or secretary who needs a quick memory refresher.

PERCENTAGE

Percent is an abbreviation for the Latin term *per centum* meaning for each hundred. Six percent (6%) means 6 parts of 100 or 6/100. The symbol (%) is also used to denote percent.

Since *percent* means a part of 100, any fraction whose denominator is 100 may be written as a percentage or as a common fraction. For example:

25% = ²⁵/₁₀₀ = ¼

75% = ⁷⁵/₁₀₀ = ¾

66⅔% = $\frac{66\ 2/3}{100}$ = ⅔

2½% = $\frac{2\ 1/2}{100}$ = ¹/₄₀

50% = ⁵⁰/₁₀₀ = ½

33⅓% = $\frac{33\ 1/3}{100}$ = ⅓

5% = ⁵/₁₀₀ = ¹/₂₀

12½% = $\frac{12\ 1/2}{100}$ = ⅛

EXPRESSING DECIMALS AS PERCENTAGES

Write the decimal as hundredths (two places) and the number of hundredths is the percent. For example:

.4 = .40 = ⁴⁰/₁₀₀ = 40%

.8 = .80 = ⁸⁰/₁₀₀ = 80%

.25 = ²⁵/₁₀₀ = 25%

.33⅓ = $\frac{33\ 1/3}{100}$ = 33⅓%

.50 = ⁵⁰/₁₀₀ = 50%

.87½ = $\frac{87\ 1/2}{100}$ = 87½%

If the decimal has more than two decimal places, the figures after the second one are written as a fraction of a percent. For example:

.255 = $\frac{25\ 1/2}{100}$ = 25½%

.163 = $\frac{16\ 3/10}{100}$ = 16 ³/₁₀%.

To change a common fraction to percent:

1. Change the fraction to a decimal.

2. Express the decimal as hundredths.

3. The result is the percent desired.

For example:

½ = .5 = .50 = 50%

¾ = .75 = 75%

⅔ = .66⅔ = 66⅔%

$^9/_{10}$ = .90 = 90%

$^8/_9$ = .88$^8/_9$ = 88$^8/_9$%

$^7/_8$ = .87½ = 87½%

Or they may be written this way:

¾ = ¾ of $^{100}/_{100}$ = $^{75}/_{100}$ = 75%

⅔ = ⅔ of $^{100}/_{100}$ = $\frac{66\ 2/3}{100}$ = 66⅔%

½ = ½ of $^{100}/_{100}$ = $^{50}/_{100}$ = 50%

$^9/_{10}$ = $^9/_{10}$ of $^{100}/_{100}$ = $^{90}/_{100}$ = 90%

TERMS USED IN CALCULATING PERCENTAGES

There are three major terms or quantities to consider in working with percentage: *base (principal)*, *percentage rate*, and *amount*. When any two are given, the third can be calculated.

1. Rule for *finding amount* if the base and rate are given: (base × rate = amount)

If the down payment on a car costing $5,000 is 6%, how much is the down payment?

$5,000.00 = Base
×.06 = Percentage rate expressed as a decimal
$300.00 = Amount

2. Rule for *finding base* if amount and rate are given: (amount ÷ rate = base)

Marie received interest of $16 on a savings account earning 4%. What was the base or principal on which the interest was calculated?

$16.00   Amount   = $400.00 Base
.04   Rate

Betty bought a bracelet for $186; this amount includes 4% sales tax. What was the net cost of the bracelet (the cost before the sales tax)?

Amount $186.00   = $178.85 (net cost)
1.00 plus rate   1.04

3. Rule for *finding rate* if the amount and base are given: $\dfrac{\text{Amount}}{\text{Base}} = \text{Rate}$

Andrew paid $120 interest on a loan of $1,000 for one year. What was the rate of interest paid by Andrew?

$$\dfrac{\$120}{\$1,000} = \dfrac{\text{Amount}}{\text{Base}} = \dfrac{\$120}{\$1,000} = 0.12 = 12\% \text{ Rate}$$

PROFIT AND LOSS

When an item is sold for more than it cost the seller, it is sold at a profit. If it is sold for less than the cost, it is sold at a loss. Therefore,

Profit = Selling Price − Cost Price

Loss = Cost Price − Selling Price

A profit or loss is generally figured as a percentage. It is always understood that the percentage is calculated on the cost price.

Example: You buy wheat at 60 cents and sell it for 75 cents. What is the percentage of gain?

Solution: The gain is the difference between 75 cents and 60 cents, or 15 cents; 15 cents is 25% of the cost. Therefore, you gain 25%.

That is: 75 cents − 60 cents = 15 cents

15 cents ÷ 60 cents = .25 or 25%

Example: You bought flour at $3.50 a barrel. At what price must you sell it to gain 20%?

Solution: You must sell it for 100% of the cost plus 20% of the cost, or 120% of the cost.

120% of $3.50 = $4.20

Example: You sold your camera for 80% of its cost and received $90.00 for it. What was the cost?

Solution: 1% of the cost is ⅟₈₀ of $90.00 or $1.125.

100% of the cost = 100 × $1.125 or $112.50

$$\dfrac{\$90.00}{.80} = \$112.50$$

INTEREST

When money is borrowed, interest is charged for the loan. The amount borrowed is called the *principal*. The amount paid for use of the money is called *interest*. Interest is calculated at a percentage rate per year.

Example: If you borrow $400.00 at 12% for one year, you will pay the lender $48.00 at the end of one year. One of the simplest ways of calculating interest uses 360 days as a business year. The formula is: principal × rate × time = interest.

If you borrow $1,200.00 for 96 days at 12% interest, how much interest will you pay the bank at maturity?

$1,200.00 × ¹²⁄₁₀₀ × ⁹⁶⁄₃₆₀ = $38.40

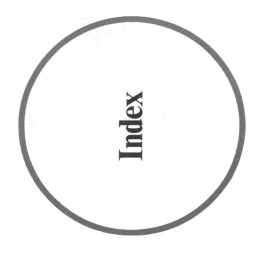

Index

763